MW01014492

Federal Income Taxation of Trusts and Estates

Carolina Academic Press
Law Casebook Series
Advisory Board

❦

Gary J. Simson, Chairman
Dean, Case Western Reserve University School of Law

Raj Bhala
University of Kansas School of Law

John C. Coffee, Jr.
Columbia University Law School

Randall Coyne
University of Oklahoma College of Law

Paul Finkelman
Albany Law School

Robert M. Jarvis
Shepard Broad Law Center
Nova Southeastern University

Vincent R. Johnson
St. Mary's University School of Law

Michael A. Olivas
University of Houston Law Center

Kenneth L. Port
William Mitchell College of Law

H. Jefferson Powell
Duke University School of Law

Michael P. Scharf
Case Western Reserve University School of Law

Peter M. Shane
Michael E. Moritz College of Law
The Ohio State University

Emily L. Sherwin
Cornell Law School

John F. Sutton, Jr.
Emeritus, University of Texas School of Law

David B. Wexler
John E. Rogers College of Law, University of Arizona
University of Puerto Rico School of Law

Federal Income Taxation of Trusts and Estates

Cases, Problems, and Materials

Third Edition

Mark L. Ascher
Joseph D. Jamail Centennial Chair in Law
University of Texas School of Law

Robert T. Danforth
Associate Dean for Academic Affairs and Professor of Law
Washington and Lee University School of Law

Carolina Academic Press
Durham, North Carolina

Copyright © 2008
Mark L. Ascher
Robert T. Danforth
All Rights Reserved

ISBN: 978-1-59460-564-2
LCCN: 2008928532

Carolina Academic Press
700 Kent Street
Durham, North Carolina 27701
Telephone (919) 489-7486
Fax (919) 493-5668
www.cap-press.com

Printed in the United States of America

To Kerry
and
Johanna and Laura

To Lee-Anne, Dinah,
Emmeline, and Robert Evan

Contents

Table of Internal Revenue Code Sections

Table of Treasury Regulations

Table of Cases

Table of Revenue Rulings

Revenue Rulings that have been reproduced are in italics.

Table of Revenue Procedures

Table of Private Letter Rulings

Private letter rulings that have been reproduced are in italics.

Preface

This book began as a set of course materials prepared by Professor Ascher when he first went into teaching in 1982. Now in its third edition, the book has a new co-author, along with new cases, problems, and other materials; the essential approach of the book, however, remains the same. Over the years the book has profited from comments and criticisms of numerous classes taught by the authors at the University of Arizona, the University of Miami, the University of Missouri, New York University, the University of Texas, and Washington and Lee University, as well as from the suggestions of our faculty colleagues at other schools. To all those who have contributed to the success of this book, we extend our warmest thanks.

But publication of this book is not solely for the relatively few instructors who presently teach classes on subchapter J. The earth-shattering changes in the federal wealth transfer taxes (particularly with respect to the unified credit) that began with the Tax Reform Act of 1976 and blossomed in the Economic Recovery Tax Act of 1981 have as a central feature a congressional intention to make those taxes applicable to fewer and fewer taxpayers. Twenty years later the Economic Growth and Tax Relief Reconciliation Act of 2001 implemented a phased-in increase of the estate tax exclusion to $3,500,000, followed by a repeal of the tax with respect to estates of decedents dying after December 31, 2009 (although, under EGTRRA, the tax is reinstated as of January 1, 2011). As of the date of publication of this edition, permanent repeal of the estate tax seems unlikely; more likely is a permanent increase of the exclusion to $3,500,000 or more. But whatever action Congress ultimately takes, it is apparent that the estate tax will continue to apply to a decreasing number of estates.

Yet the federal income tax rolls merrily along. We all know that the income tax applies to trusts and estates. Still, almost all of us—even the I.R.S.—have frequently underestimated the importance of income tax considerations in both our practices and our teaching. Section 1(e) of the Code subjects trusts and estates to an onerously compressed rate schedule; one therefore ignores at one's peril such topics as the distribution deduction and the grantor trust rules—mechanisms designed to shift tax liability from an estate or trust to individuals, who are typically taxed at lower rates. Teachers in the wealth transfer area thus face a challenge. They can continue to focus exclusively on the decreasingly relevant taxes on gratuitous transfers, or they broaden their teaching packages to include the subjects of this course.

This course is not easy to teach. However, we really do believe that this book takes student and teacher alike firmly enough in hand that any teacher reasonably well-grounded in the basics of federal income taxation can successfully survive a first run through the course. A teacher's manual is available from the publisher. For those who wish to do additional reading, we recommend the following:

B. Abbin, *Income Taxation of Fiduciaries and Beneficiaries* (2007).

J. Blattmachr, A. Michaelson & L. Boyle, *Income Taxation of Estates and Trusts* (15th ed. 2007).

M. Ferguson, J. Freeland & M. Ascher, *Federal Income Taxation of Estates, Trusts, and Beneficiaries* (3d ed. 1998, supplemented annually).

H. Zaritsky, N. Lane & R. Danforth, *Federal Income Taxation of Estates and Trusts* (3d ed. 2001, supplemented semi-annually).

J. Peschel & E. Spurgeon, *Federal Taxation of Trusts, Grantors and Beneficiaries* (3d ed. 1997, supplemented annually).

We also recommend an article that nicely attempts to summarize subchapter J: Sherman, *All You Really Need to Know About Subchapter J You Learned from This Article*, 63 Mo. L. Rev. 1 (1998).

Unless otherwise indicated, all section references are to the Internal Revenue Code. In a deliberate effort to force students to deal directly with the Code, we have deleted from the reproduced materials almost all quotations of Code provisions. Students must, therefore, possess and be willing frequently to refer to a current version of the Code. References to obsolete Code provisions are, unfortunately, unavoidable, but we have tried hard to identify such references for the reader. We have tried to indicate all omissions, except footnotes, in reproduced materials. The remaining footnotes retain their original numbering. The Uniform Principal and Income Act (1997), our standard authority for questions of state law, appears as an appendix.

Mark L. Ascher
Austin, Texas

Robert T. Danforth
Lexington, Virginia

May 2008

Introduction

This book examines federal income taxation of trusts and estates. It does not deal with federal estate and gift taxation. The federal estate and gift taxes are excise taxes on the transfer of property at death or by gift. They are imposed by chapter 11 (sections 2001 to 2210) and chapter 12 (sections 2501 to 2524) of subtitle B ("Estate and Gift Taxes") of the Internal Revenue Code. The estate and gift taxes have little to do with how the income of trusts and estates is taxed. They are taxes on gratuitous transfers of property, not on income generated by that property.

Trusts and estates pay income taxes much as the rest of us do. Each year we add up what we take in, subtract out various exclusions and deductions, and pay a percentage of the remainder to the federal government. The basic system for taxing the income of trusts and estates is the same as that for taxing the income of individuals. Section 641(b) makes this very clear: "The taxable income of an estate or trust shall be computed in the same manner as in the case of an individual, except as otherwise provided in this part." Thus, everything the student (may have) learned in the basic course on individual income taxation, which generally deals almost exclusively with chapter 1 (sections 1 to 1400T) of subtitle A ("Income Taxes") of the Internal Revenue Code, is potentially relevant.

This book is not, however, a review of the basic course on individual income taxation (although it is possible to view chapter 2 that way). More than anything else, it is an examination of the ways in which the income taxation of trusts and estates differs from that of individuals. Section 641(b) acknowledges these differences when it refers to "this part." That reference is to part I ("Estates, Trusts, and Beneficiaries"), which consists of sections 641 to 685. Part I, along with the two sections (691 and 692) of part II ("Income in Respect of Decedents"), make up subchapter J ("Estates, Trusts, Beneficiaries, and Decedents"). Thus, subchapter J is the primary focus of this book. Like it or not, an alternative title for the book would have been "Subchapter J of Chapter 1 of Subtitle A of the Internal Revenue Code."

Individuals bear the full tax consequences of their income. Thus, they are pure taxpayers. Partnerships and S corporations, on the other hand, generally pay no taxes on their income; the Code shifts their income to the partners or shareholders for taxation. Partnerships and S corporations, then, are pure conduits. Subchapter J blends these two, distinct modes of taxation into a unique system for taxing the income of trusts and estates. Such entities are, simultaneously, both taxpayers and conduits. They are taxpayers insofar as section 641(b) treats them as individuals. But part I of subchapter J allows trusts and estates a deduction for distributions to beneficiaries. This is the mechanism by which such entities also serve as conduits.

There is another major wrinkle. Subchapter J directs that some trusts, because of interests or powers retained by their grantors, are not treated as taxpayers at all. Their items of income, deductions, and credit are attributed directly to their grantors. These trusts are commonly referred to as "grantor trusts."

This book very deliberately follows the organization of subchapter J. Thus, one, fairly accurate, way of visualizing the book is:

Chapter 1 Section 641(a)
Chapter 2 Sections 641(b), 642
Chapter 3 Sections 643, 651–663
Chapter 4 Sections 671–678
Chapter 6 Section 691

Strong pedagogical and thematic concerns are, however, also present in the book's organization. Chapter 1 asks the logically first question, "Which entities are subject to income taxation under subchapter J?" Chapter 2 examines the entity as taxpayer, i.e., how the familiar principles of basic income taxation apply to entities. Chapter 3 then examines the entity as conduit, i.e., how the distribution deduction works to shift some of the income taxation of entities to their beneficiaries. Chapter 4 inquires into when the entity is to be ignored, either under assignment-of-income principles or the grantor trust rules. Chapter 5 provides the student with an opportunity to reconsider the complete picture in the context of manipulative and, arguably, abusive use of entities. Chapter 6, which deals with income and deductions in respect of decedents, mars the organization of the book, just as it does that of subchapter J, but contains obviously important material that fits better in this course than in any other.

The provisions of subchapter J are the core of this book. Its overwhelming first priority is understanding of those provisions and how they work. Likely criticisms are the book's detail and attention to mechanics. But, clearly, such is stuff tax lawyers are made of. Those who wish to pursue tax policy more thoroughly than the book at first seems to must start somewhere. This book can be that springboard. Even the most unabashed would-be technical expert ought to be willing to pause over the concept of "distributable net income" after reading *Irwin v. Gavit* alongside *Harkness* (ch. 3, sec. A). Three series of cases, far longer than the would-be technical expert needs, are not included just to acquaint students with the anguish of the common law or even with the interaction of judicial and legislative lawmaking. These series are included primarily to force the student to ask tough "why" questions. (In tax law "why" questions are especially tough for many students (and teachers) to ask because they often have only "because" for an answer.) The *Manufacturers Hanover Trust Co.-Tucker-Whittemore-Fabens* series (ch.2, sec. B(3)(b)) ought to stimulate questions about why entities are not taxed exactly as individuals are. It also ought to focus attention on why distributable net income occupies the role it does in subchapter J. The *Trust Company of Georgia-Keck-Sidles-Peterson* series (ch. 6, sec. A(2)) should force analysis of whether there is a need for a concept similar to "income in respect of a decedent" and whether the current concept either fills that need or is worth the candle. Moreover, it should prompt students to question the soundness of section 1014. *Estelle Morris* and *Stephenson* (ch. 5, sec. A) have survived the Tax Reform Act of 1984 not only to illustrate the potential operation and flaws of section 643(f), but also to necessitate analysis of whether there remains a need for section 643(f) after the Tax Reform Act of 1986. Most importantly, however, *Estelle Morris* and *Stephenson* should force each student to ask the central policy question of a course on the income taxation of trusts and estates: Should trusts and estates have separate income tax existences?

We offer the following suggestions for coming to terms with these challenging materials:

1. Your starting point should always be the words of the Internal Revenue Code.

2. Use the Treasury Regulations as your primary tool for understanding the Code.
3. Use the cases, the rulings, the Illustrative Material, and the problems strictly as tools to understand the Code and regulations.
4. Ask whether the regulations, cases, etc. fairly and accurately interpret the Code.
5. Ask whether the Code makes sense and, if not, whether there is a better alternative.

Federal Income Taxation of Trusts and Estates

Chapter 1

Entities Subject to Income Taxation under Subchapter J

Section 641(a) of the Internal Revenue Code states that "[t]he tax imposed by section 1(e) shall apply to the taxable income of estates or of any kind of property held in trust." The Code defines neither "estates" nor "trust." Though there is little doubt about what constitutes an estate for purposes of section 641(a), the materials that follow indicate that the meaning of "trust" is attended by some uncertainty. This chapter also considers circumstances under which a trust may be taxed as a corporation or partnership.

A. Is an Entity Subject to Taxation?

Internal Revenue Code:
    Sections 1(e); 641(a); 643(c); 7701(a)(6)
Regulations:
    Sections 1.641(a)-2; 301.7701-4(a), (b), -6(b)

Revenue Ruling 68-47
1968-1 C.B. 300

Advice has been requested whether a trust is created and the filing of a fiduciary income tax return is required under the circumstances described below.

A purchased a single premium life insurance contract on his life from the *Y* life insurance company. A settlement agreement was subsequently entered into between *A* and *Y* as to the manner of payments upon *A*'s death. The agreement provided that all of the insurance proceeds would be retained by *Y* as "trustee" and that *Y* would pay a fixed rate of interest to the beneficiaries of the policy. The proceeds would eventually be paid to the heirs of the beneficiaries without regard to any appreciation or depreciation. *Y* reserved the right to mingle the proceeds of the insurance policy with its general corporate funds.

Upon *A*'s death, *Y* began making the payments of interest to the beneficiaries in accordance with the settlement agreement.

Section 641(a) of the Internal Revenue Code of 1954 provides that the taxes imposed on individuals shall apply to the taxable income of any kind of property held in trust.

Where, under a settlement agreement, an insurance company instead of paying a lump-sum to the beneficiary at the maturity of the policy makes deferred payment, is obligated to pay a fixed rate of interest and not the income from investment of the proceeds, the beneficiaries have no interest in any appreciation or depreciation of the proceeds, and the company is not required to and does not segregate the proceeds but commingles such proceeds with its other funds and merely undertakes to make the payment out of its general fund, the company is not a trustee. This is true even though the insurance company agrees to pay the proceeds to itself as trustee, if it is also agreed that the proceeds shall not be segregated from the other assets of the company. A debt and not a trust is created. Sections 12 and 87, *Scott on Trusts*, Second Edition; sections 12 and 87, *Restatement of Trusts*, Second Edition.

Accordingly, under the foregoing circumstances, a trust is not created and, therefore, Y is not required to file a fiduciary income tax return under section 1.6012-3 of the Income Tax Regulations.

Illustrative Material

Transfers to Minors. Section 11(b) of the Uniform Transfers to Minors Act states that "the custodial property is indefeasibly vested in the minor." As a matter of trust law, therefore, a UTMA transfer does not create a trust. Thus, if the test is whether a trust exists under state law, income derived from UTMA property generally should be taxable directly to the minor, as full owner of the property, rather than under subchapter J. Indeed, in *Estate of Stevens v. Commissioner*, T.C. Summ. Op. 2003-163 (2003), the Tax Court so held. *See also Joseph Anastasio*, 67 T.C. 814, *aff'd mem.*, 573 F.2d 1287 (2d Cir. 1977) (involving the Uniform Gifts to Minors Act, immediate predecessor of the UTMA); Rev. Rul. 59-357, 1959-2 C.B. 212 (involving both the UGMA and the Model Gifts of Securities to Minors Act); Rev. Rul. 56-484, 1956-2 C.B. 23 (involving another forerunner of the UTMA).

Prior to the UTMA and its predecessors (and undoubtedly also today), property intended as an outright gift to a minor often was titled in the name of one or both of the minor's parents, to facilitate management of the property. Generally, courts refused to treat the income from such property as income from property held in trust and instead taxed such income directly to the minor. *E.g., Prudence Miller Trust*, 7 T.C. 1245 (1946). Eventually, the I.R.S. conceded, acquiescing in *Miller*, 1947-1 C.B. 3, and later issuing Rev. Rul. 55-469, 1955-2 C.B. 519, and Rev. Rul. 58-65, 1958-1 C.B. 13, both of which treated income from property held in an adult's name as income earned directly by the minor for whom the property was held. The difficulty of proving such a gift nonetheless strongly suggests that use of a UTMA transfer is a far preferable technique for shifting assets (and income) to minors. *Compare Minor v. Commissioner*, 60 T.C.M. (CCH) 435 (1990) (parents carried burden of proving they had made a bona fide gift to their own children), *with Gray v. United States*, 738 F. Supp. 453 (N.D. Ala. 1990) (parents taxable on capital gains on sale of securities they had registered in their children's names, as well as on interest the sales proceeds generated).

Another device sometimes used to transfer assets to minors, especially by will, is called the "power in trust." Property is devised outright to the minor, but an adult or corporation, usually either the testator's executor or the trustee of a conventional trust under the will, is given authority to hold the property for the benefit of the minor until the minor reaches the age of majority. Title technically is in the minor, but possession is denied the minor until he or she reaches the age of majority. Both theory and analogy to the UTMA transfer suggest that the minor ought to be taxable directly on the income from assets held under a power in trust. Nevertheless, in Rev. Rul. 75-61, 1975-1 C.B. 180, the I.R.S. ruled that the holder was taxable under subchapter J on the property's income:

> A "power in trust" involves a form of express fiduciary obligation similar to that of an express trust, and it therein differs from a mere agency, revocable at pleasure, which imposes no duty, but merely grants authority to act. A power in trust places on the grantee a duty to execute a trust in favor of a person or persons other than himself and involves the idea of a trust as much as does a trust estate....

> The will, in the instant case, passed legal title ... to [the minor.] However, it is manifest that complete control over the realty conveyed to [the minor] was given to the trustee. [The minor] could not collect the rental income [him]self regardless of where the bare legal title to the real estate might vest....

> Thus, the trustee of the properties of [the minor] is vested with the responsibility for the protection and conservation of property for [a] beneficiar[y] who cannot share in the discharge of the responsibility.

Compare the last sentence of the above quote with the last sentence of Treas. Reg. § 301.7701-4(a).

The Tax Reform Act of 1986 substantially decreased the attractiveness, for income tax purposes, of shifting property to minors. Section 1(g), which imposes the so-called "kiddie tax," generally taxes the unearned income of a minor or dependent child at the marginal rate of his or her parent. Section 1(g) applies to (i) a child under age 18 and (ii) a child who has reached age 18 but is under age 19 (or 24, in the case of a full-time student), but only if the age 18 or older child's earned income does not exceed one-half of the child's support. However, the first $1,000 (adjusted for inflation) of unearned income, and sometimes more, remains subject to tax at the child's own rate.

Revenue Ruling 76-486

1976-2 C.B. 192

Advice has been requested whether, under the circumstances described below, a bequest in trust for the care of a pet animal creates a valid trust for purposes of the imposition of tax under section 641 of the Internal Revenue Code of 1954.

A, a resident of State *X*, died testate in 1976. Under the terms of *A*'s will *A*'s entire property passed to designated individuals, including a residuary legatee, with the exception of a fund that was established to care for *A*'s pet animal. The income of the fund, to the extent required, is to be used for the care of the animal. Upon the death of the animal, the corpus of the fund is to be distributed to *A*'s heirs, if living, or their descendants.

Under the common law rule against perpetuities, the period during which vesting of interests in property may be postponed is limited to a life or lives in being plus twenty-one years and any period of gestation involved in the situation to which the limitation applies. It has generally been assumed that the lives that measure the period of perpetuities should be human lives. *II Scott on Trusts*, section 124.3 (3d ed. 1967); *Restatement of Property*, section 374, comment h (1944).

In the absence of statutory abrogation, the rule against perpetuities is part of the common law in most jurisdictions in the United States. State X has adopted no statute that would render the rule against perpetuities inapplicable in the circumstances set forth in the instant case. Since the life of an animal is not a proper measuring life in being under the rule against perpetuities in State X, the bequest in trust to provide for the care of the animal was void from its inception.

The law of State X provides that personal property comprising any bequest that fails, is void, or is otherwise incapable of taking effect, will be included in the residuary bequest, if any, contained in the decedent's will, unless a contrary intention appears in the will.

Accordingly, in the instant case, since the bequest in trust for the care of the pet animal was void from its inception, a valid trust never came into being for purposes of the imposition of tax under section 641 of the Code. Further, the property passed to the residuary legatee pursuant to the law of State X, because no contrary intention appears in the will, and the income earned on such property is includible in the income of the residuary legatee in the year the income is received.

A bequest in trust for the care of a pet animal is not void from its inception in all states. In those jurisdictions where a trust created by such a bequest is valid, the trust is unenforceable because there is no one who as beneficiary can compel the trustee to carry out the purpose of the testator. Such intended trusts have been characterized as "honorary trusts," the conscience of the trustee being the only compelling influence on performance. However, should the trustee fail to perform the intention of the testator, the trustee will not be allowed to keep the property; instead a resulting trust will arise in favor of the testator's residuary legatees. See *Scott on Trusts*, sections 123(2) and 124 (3d ed. 1967). The income tax consequences of an honorary trust will depend on whether it will qualify as a valid trust for purposes of section 641 of the Code.

Section 641 of the Code provides, in part, that the taxable income of a trust is computed in the same manner as in the case of an individual, except as otherwise provided. Also, a trust is generally allowed, in computing its taxable income, the deduction provided by either section 651 or section 661 and the regulations thereunder, relating to distributions to beneficiaries.

Section 651 of the Code provides for a deduction in the case of a trust that distributes current income only. The deduction is limited to the amount of the distributable net income regardless of whether the amount of income required to be distributed currently exceeds the distributable net income of the trust for the taxable year. Section 652 provides, in part, that the amount of income for the taxable year required to be distributed currently by a trust shall be included in the gross income of the beneficiaries to whom the income is required to be distributed, whether distributed or not. Such includible amount shall be an amount equal to each beneficiary's share of distributable net income of the trust.

Section 661 of the Code allows a deduction to a trust not qualifying under the provisions of section 651 in computing its taxable income, for any amount of its income for such taxable year required to be distributed currently and any other amount properly paid or credited or required to be distributed to a beneficiary for the taxable year to the extent such deduction does not exceed the distributable net income of the trust. Section 662 provides generally that the beneficiary of a trust must include in gross income all amounts that are deductible by the trust under section 661(a).

Section 301.7701-4(a) of the Income Tax Regulations provides that in general, the term "trust" as used in the Internal Revenue Code refers to an arrangement created either by a will or by an inter vivos declaration whereby trustees take title to property for the purpose of protecting or conserving it for the beneficiaries under the ordinary rules applied in chancery or probate court.

The term "beneficiary," for purposes of Part I, subchapter J, of the Code, is defined in section 643(c) to include heirs, legatees, and devisees. Heirs, legatees, and devisees are persons. See 96 C.J.S. *Wills*, section 1097 (1957). For purposes of the Code, where not otherwise distinctly expressed to the contrary or manifestly incompatible with the intent thereof, the term "person" is construed to mean and include an individual, trust, estate, partnership, association, company or corporation. Section 7701(a). Since animals do not fall within this category, they cannot be beneficiaries for purposes of section 643(c).

Since a beneficiary is lacking, a bequest in trust for a pet animal does not fit into the traditional concept of a trust, as set out in section 301.7701 of the regulations. Such an arrangement, however, should nonetheless be classified as a trust for tax purposes under section 641 of the Code in those jurisdictions where it would not be invalid. To treat this arrangement as not being a taxable trust would, in addition to ignoring its validity under local law, cause the income on the bequest to escape taxation altogether, since the distributions of income for the benefit of the pet animal would similarly not be taxed.

Accordingly, the taxable income of a fund, which is not invalid under state law, bequeathed in trust for the benefit of an animal, is subject to the imposition of the tax of section [1(e)] of the Code pursuant to section 641. See Rev. Rul. 58-190, 1958-1 C.B. 15, which holds that a trust is created for purposes of section 641 where funds are received by a cemetery company or corporation for the perpetual care of an individual lot or mausoleum crypt.

Furthermore, since the amounts of income required to be distributed under section 651 of the Code, and amounts properly paid, credited, or required to be distributed under section 661 are limited to distributions intended for beneficiaries, a deduction under those sections is not available for distributions for the benefit of a pet animal. Similarly, such distributions are not taxed to anyone under sections 652 and 662.

Illustrative Material

1. Section 2-907 of the Uniform Probate Code and section 408 of the Uniform Trust Code change the common law by providing that a trust for the benefit of an animal alive during the settlor's lifetime is both valid and enforceable. Indeed, as of this printing, more than thirty states have enacted legislation authorizing trusts for animals. *See generally* 2 *Scott and Ascher on Trusts* § 12.11.3 (5th ed. 2006).

2. *Perpetual Care of Burial Lot.* According to Rev. Rul. 58-190, 1958-1 C.B. 15, cited in Rev. Rul. 76-486, a trust subject to section 641 may exist if a cemetery corporation receives funds for the perpetual care of an individual burial lot. *See also William A. Clark Trust,* 49 T.C. 456 (1968); Rev. Rul. 59-30, 1959-1 C.B. 161. The issue seems to depend on whether there is an intention to create a "trust" and whether legal title to the trust property vests in a "trustee." Section 642(i), enacted after the dates of these precedents, recognizes the possibility of a cemetery corporation serving as trustee of perpetual care funds and provides a special distribution deduction.

3. *Passive Trusts.* In *Meeker v. Durey,* 92 F.2d 607 (2d Cir. 1937), a committee undertook to build a war memorial. The committee purchased the necessary real property but, for convenience, took title in the name of one individual. Thereafter, the project failed for lack of financial support. Pursuant to an agreement with the committee, the titleholder transferred the property to a bank, for sale and distribution of the proceeds among the

members of the committee. The Second Circuit, in an opinion by Judge Augustus N. Hand, held that the bank was not required to pay income tax on the gain realized in the sale. The bank had "no active duties" with respect to the property. It therefore held the property under a "passive trust." The bank thus was "a mere agent" of the members of the committee, each of whom was required to include his or her share of the gain in gross income directly.

In *Estate of O'Connor v. Commissioner*, 69 TC. 165 (1977), the Tax Court suggested that what appeared to be a passive trust, i.e., a trust that had no purpose other than immediately upon receipt to distribute the trust property to its beneficiary, was not a trust for purposes of subchapter J. The opinion cited Treas. Reg. § 301.7701-4(a) as support for the proposition that the subchapter J definition of "trust" required "more activity on the part of a trust than [a] simple conduit role." 69 TC. at 176.

4. *Security Deposits.* Where, under state law, a landlord entitled to security deposits from his tenants was "considered to take title to [such deposits] as a trustee for purposes of protecting and conserving them for the benefit of the tenants," the arrangement was deemed to be a trust under Treas. Reg. § 301.7701-4(a). Rev. Rul. 77-260, 1977-2 C.B. 466. The I.R.S. ruled that the landlord should therefore file Form 1041 if the requirements of Treas. Reg. § 1.6012-3 were met. Would the result differ if state law did not view the landlord as a trustee? What if state law were silent on the issue?

5. *"Trustee" or "Stakeholder"?* In *Lee McRitchie*, 27 T.C. 65 (1956), the seller of shares of a corporation later disputed the validity of the sale. Accordingly, the purchaser's title was at issue. The corporation filed an interpleader action in the federal court and deposited various dividends, declared during 1948, 1949, and 1950, into the registry of the court. At the conclusion of the litigation, in 1951, the court released the funds to the purchaser. In order to avoid payment of income tax on the entire amount in one year, the year of receipt, the purchaser argued that the court had held the funds in trust and should have paid the tax thereon each year it received income. The Tax Court rejected the purchaser's argument:

> [I]t is plain that there was no trust within the usually accepted meaning of that term. [The federal court] did not hold the shares of stock upon which the dividends were paid; it did not receive any income on property held by it in a fiduciary capacity; it was a mere stakeholder of money turned over to it without the ordinary duties which customarily devolve upon a trustee or fiduciary to administer a trust fund or other assets; it did not in fact file any return, and there is no showing of any general administrative practice whereby returns have been filed by other courts in like circumstances. Surely, it is not uncommon to deposit disputed funds into the registry of a court, and, in the absence of any clear expression of legislative intent or the existence of a practice recognizing the duty of the court to file a return, we should be slow to read such a requirement into the statute.
>
> Moreover, we think that the dividends in question were not being accumulated for "unascertained persons" within the meaning of [the predecessor of section 641(a)(1)]. The controversy between [seller] and [purchaser] raised the question as to which one of two *ascertained* persons had the superior right to the dividends.

27 T.C. at 68–69 (emphasis in original). The purchaser therefore was required to include the entire amount in his gross income for taxable year 1951. Similarly, in Rev. Rul. 71-119, 1971-1 C.B. 163, money was deposited with a federal court under a compromise

agreement. Neither the court nor the special master appointed by the court to administer the fund and supervise the settlement was required to file Form 1041, because neither "had title to the settlement fund for the purpose of protecting or conserving it for the beneficiaries under the ordinary rules applied in chancery or probate courts." The I.R.S. also held that the settlement fund was not "property held in trust" under section 641(a).

Rev. Rul. 70-567, 1970-2 C.B. 133, held that a bank that, pursuant to court order, held proceeds from a wrongful death action as "escrowee" pending judicial determination of distribution and had "none of the ordinary duties of a trustee or fiduciary" was not required to file Form 1041. On the other hand, where a court appointed a bank to act as "custodian" of shares in a land trust pending judicial determination of the ownership of such shares, the bank's "broad discretionary powers of administration and management," which included the power to vote at shareholders' meetings, approve or oppose reorganizations and refinancings, invest earnings, retain counsel, exercise or sell conversion and subscription rights, and hold property in its own name or in street name, caused the bank to be a "fiduciary." Rev. Rul. 69-300, 1969-1 C.B. 167. The bank was therefore required to file Form 1041.

This case-by-case analysis of whether the holder of funds was a "fiduciary" proved unsatisfactory and was supplanted in 1988 by section 468B, which provides in subsection (g) that "nothing in any provision of law shall be construed as providing that an escrow account, settlement fund, or similar fund is not subject to current income tax." Under section 468B, and pursuant to regulations promulgated under that section, there is now in place a detailed scheme for the taxation of "designated settlement funds," "qualified settlement funds," "disputed ownership funds," and other settlement and escrow arrangements. These arrangements are generally taxed on their modified gross income, at the highest rate applicable to trusts and estates. If a qualified settlement fund has only a single transferor, the transferor may elect to have the fund treated as a grantor trust, so that the transferor, rather than the fund, will be taxed on the income generated by the fund. Chapter 4 considers grantor trusts in detail.

6. Bankruptcy Estates. Section 1398, added to the Code by the Bankruptcy Tax Act of 1980, provides independent, non-subchapter J statutory treatment of the income of individuals' bankruptcy estates. Section 1399 states that, other than as provided in section 1398, "no separate taxable entity shall result from the commencement of a case under title 11 of the United States Code." The Act reversed the position of the IRS, which had long asserted that income earned by a bankruptcy estate was taxable under subchapter J. Rev. Rul. 72-387, 1972-2 C.B. 632; Rev. Rul. 68-48, 1968-1 C.B. 301; *see also* Rev. Rul. 73-94, 1973-1 C.B. 322 (trustee to whom a general assignment of assets for the benefit of creditors had been made under local insolvency law). The Act also resolved a long-standing split among the courts as to the proper treatment of bankruptcy estates. Many courts had agreed with the Service, *In re Joplin,* 882 F.2d 1507 (10th Cir. 1989); *Williams v. United States,* 667 F.2d 1108 (4th Cir. 1981); *In re Goff,* 86-1 U.S.T.C. ¶9104 (Bankr. W.D. Tex. 1985); *In re Steck,* 62-2 U.S.T.C. ¶9702 (S.D. Ill. 1962); *cf. Richardson v. United States,* 552 F.2d 291 (9th Cir. 1977) (per curiam) (section 642(h) excess deductions not allowable to bankrupt); *Schilder v. United States,* 71-2 U.S.T.C. ¶9595 (N.D. Cal. 1971) (individual bankrupt not entitled to deduct loss incurred by bankruptcy trustee on sale of assets); *Norris Bloomfield,* 52 T.C. 745 (1969) (same), while others had rejected the government's position, *In re Samoset Associates,* 81-2 U.S.T.C. ¶9694 (Bankr. D. Me. 1981); *In re 4100 North High Limited,* 80-1 U.S.T.C. ¶9454 (Bankr. S.D. Ohio 1980); *In re Kirby,* 62-2 U.S.T.C. ¶9752 (S.D. Tex. 1962). (The Bankruptcy Tax Act was not effective with respect to the taxable years at issue in any of these cases.)

United States v. De Bonchamps
278 F.2d 127 (9th Cir. 1960)

MERRILL, Circuit Judge.

These three cases, consolidated for our decision, present the question whether legal life tenants are taxable either as owners or as fiduciaries on capital gains realized in sales of portions of the corpus. In all three cases, gains were realized by sales of estate assets. Taxes were paid thereon by the life tenants as owners; claims for refund were made and these actions were brought to recover such refunds. In each action the United States has counterclaimed for the amount of tax payable by the taxpayer as fiduciary of a trust.[1] In each case summary judgment by the trial court was rendered in favor of the taxpayer. Appeals have been taken by the United States.

The life estates were created by will under California law and grant broad powers to the life tenants to use and consume the corpus for their needs, maintenance and comfort.

In the De Bonchamps and Cowgill cases, the taxpayers are daughters of the testator. The will granted one-half of the estate to each daughter for her use during her life. Upon her death, the remainder was to go to her children then living and the issue of any deceased child per stirpes. It provided:

> "Each of my said daughters may consume, use, invest and reinvest her share and the income therefrom for her needs, maintenance and comfort during her life without any restriction and her children and the issue of any predeceased child shall take only what remains of her share on her death."

In the King case, the taxpayer is the wife of the testator. The will granted to her the entire estate for her use during her life, the remainder upon her death to go to the daughters of the decedent and the issue of any deceased child per stirpes. It provided:

> "My said wife in her discretion may convert any of said property into cash and she shall have and enjoy the rents, issues, income and profits during her life and she also shall be free to invade and use the corpus for her own needs, maintenance and comfort as well as for those of my daughters and their issue or any of them. I declare that it is my wish and intention to have my wife enjoy the free use of said corpus and income during her natural life and that my daughters or their issue, as heretofore provided, shall have and take what is left thereof at the time of her death."

The first contention of the United States is that under these broad powers the life tenants are to be treated and taxed as the beneficial owners of the capital gains.[2]

Under California law, the estates so created are regarded as life estates with powers of consumption annexed. The power to consume does not enlarge the estate into a fee. Adams v. Prather, 1917, 176 Cal. 33, 167 P. 534; Luscomb v. Fintzelberg, 1912, 162 Cal.

---

1. The De Bonchamps case involves tax for the years 1954 ($6,622.17 as owner or $3,806.07 as fiduciary) and 1955 ($9,612.56 as owner or $6,690.31 as fiduciary). It has been stipulated that this case is representative of the Cowgill case, and no record on the latter case is before us. The King case involves tax for the year 1955 ($5,666.88 as owner or $3,027.69 as fiduciary).

2. No issue is raised as to the ownership of income other than capital gains. It is apparently conceded that, under California law, the ownership of all such income under these facts is vested in the life tenant.

433, 123 P. 247; Estate of Smythe, 1955, 132 Cal.App.2d 343, 282 P.2d 141. Capital gains accrue to the principal and, subject to the life tenant's powers of use and consumption, belong to the remainderman. California Civil Code, §730.05(2).

The United States refers to language in Corliss v. Bowers, 1930, 281 U.S. 376, 377, 50 S.Ct. 336, 74 L.Ed. 916, and Burnet v. Wells, 1933, 289 U.S. 670, 677–678, 53 S.Ct. 761, 77 L.Ed. 1439. In the former the Supreme Court stated:

> "But taxation is not so much concerned with the refinements of title as it is with actual command over the property taxed—the actual benefit for which the tax is paid."

In Burnet v. Wells, the court stated [289 U.S. 677, 53 S.Ct. 763]:

> "In these and other cases there has been a progressive endeavor by the Congress and the courts to bring about a correspondence between the legal concept of ownership and the economic realities of enjoyment of fruition. * * *
>
> "* * * Liability does not have to rest upon the enjoyment by the taxpayer of all the privileges and benefits enjoyed by the most favored owner at a given time or place. * * * Government in casting about for proper subjects of taxation is not confined by the traditional classifications of interests or estates. It may tax not only ownership, but any right or privilege that is a constituent of ownership. * * * Liability may rest upon the enjoyment by the taxpayer of privileges and benefits so substantial and important as to make it reasonable and just to deal with him as if he were the owner and to tax him on that basis."

The United States contends that the right of these taxpayers to create and consume statutory items of income renders it reasonable and just to deal with them as owners of such income items. It asserts that the power possessed by the life tenants here is similar to the power to dispose and the right to receive, which were held sufficient for attribution of income in Helvering v. Horst, 1940, 311 U.S. 112, 61 S.Ct. 144, 85 L.Ed. 75, and North American Oil Consolidated v. Burnet, 1932, 286 U.S. 417, 52 S.Ct. 613, 76 L.Ed. 1197.

Of the cases relied upon by the United States, those appearing to us as most pertinent are cases dealing with tax problems arising in the Clifford area[3] and, more specifically, under the Mallinckrodt case.[4] The rules of these cases formed the basis for ... the 1954 amendment of the Revenue Code, Subpart E of Part I of Subchapter J, dealing with estates, trusts, beneficiaries and decedents. By Section 671, the attributes of exclusiveness attach to these code provisions. They deal for the most part with situations in which the grantor, notwithstanding his having parted with ownership, is nevertheless treated as the owner for tax purposes. Section 678 deals with the situation which confronts us here. It provides in pertinent part:

> "(a) General rule.—A person other than the grantor shall be treated as the owner of any portion of a trust with respect to which:
>
> "(1) such person has a power exercisable solely by himself to vest the corpus or the income therefrom in himself * * *."

While Subpart E deals with trust situations, nevertheless we feel that Section 678 should be recognized as applicable to the instant cases. Here it is contended that, notwithstand-

---

3. Helvering v. Clifford, 1940, 309 U.S. 331, 60 S.Ct. 554, 84 L.Ed. 788, dealing with powers held by the grantor of a trust estate.

4. Mallinckrodt v. Nunan, 8 Cir., 1945, 146 F.2d 1, dealing with powers in one other than the grantor.

ing lack of ownership, a taxpayer is to be treated as owner by virtue of his beneficial interest in the capital gain. Congress, in Section 678, has spoken positively upon this subject. This Court, in 1949, recognized the [predecessors of Subpart E] to have a persuasive effect in a non-trust case. Hawaiian Trust Company v. Kanne, 9 Cir., 1949, 172 F.2d 74.

The question then is whether the powers of these taxpayers may be said to constitute a power to vest the corpus in themselves.

We have concluded that, upon the record before us, the powers of these life tenants are not the equivalent of a power to vest in themselves the corpus of the estate or the capital gains in question. A life tenant under these testamentary provisions may not in any manner control the disposition of the corpus save by consuming it for the enumerated purposes. She may not give it away nor make testamentary disposition of it. She has no power of appointment. She may not change the beneficiaries nor reapportion their shares.

Nor has any one of these life tenants the unlimited power to take the corpus of the estate to herself. Her power to consume is expressly limited to her needs, maintenance and comfort. Nor may it be said that the boundaries of such power as so expressed are so vague as to constitute no real limitation upon the power to consume. Smither v. United States, D.C.S.D.Tex.1952, 108 F.Supp. 772, adopted by reference, United States v. Smither, 5 Cir., 1953, 205 F.2d 518.[5]

The power of the life tenant which is granted here is essentially the power to determine for herself her own personal mode of living. Such control as she may have over the disposition of the corpus is necessary to such purpose. Any beneficial interest she may have in the corpus is limited to the extent to which it is required to effectuate such purpose. It is not a situation where failure of the life tenant to take to herself a portion of the corpus may be regarded as a gift of such portion to the remainderman.[6] There is no right to take which she has forborne to exercise.

Nor has it been contended that a remainder in any of these cases is in truth fictitious and that the expressed limitation upon its consumption is therefore falsely apparent rather than real. There is nothing in the record to indicate in any case that, by exercise of these limited powers, a full consumption of the corpus was reasonably to be expected. Nor is there any suggestion that these limitations have not been respected by these life tenants.

Upon the face of the record then, the bestowal of the powers of use and consumption would appear to be pursuant to legitimate and good faith estate planning: to the normal desire of a husband or father that, to the fullest measure within his control, his wife or

---

5. California's attitude with reference to these powers is indicated in King v. Hawley 1952, 113 Cal.App.2d 534, 248 P.2d 491, 496, where (quoting with approval from Corpus Juris) it is stated:
>   "A power to consume or dispose of property for the donee's 'benefit' is broader than one for his support or maintenance, and, in general, includes whatever promotes his personal prosperity and happiness, so that he may consume or sell the property as he chooses, without limitation except that of good faith. Likewise, a power of sale or disposition for the donee's 'comfort' is broader than one for his maintenance, and encroachment on the property is not restricted to the necessaries of life, but may include things which bring ease, contentment, or enjoyment to the donee, and, in general, such a power authorizes the expenditure of the property or its proceeds for any purpose, consistent with the donee's former manner of living and station in life, and taking into consideration the value of the property, which the donee thinks will give him personal comfort."

6. Compare Smith v. United States, 5 Cir., 1959, 265 F.2d 834; Spies v. United States, 8 Cir., 1950, 180 F.2d 336; Mallinckrodt v. Nunan, *supra*, footnote 4; Jergens v. Commissioner, 5 Cir., 1943, 136 F.2d 497; Irish v. Commissioner, 3 Cir., 1942, 129 F.2d 468; Richardson v. Commissioner, 2 Cir., 1941, 121 F.2d 1.

daughter may realize the needs and comforts of life. Upon the face of the record, this arrangement does not suggest a device the choice of which has been directed by motives of tax avoidance. The choice between a grant in fee or a life estate with powers of consumption, from all that appears in this record, was based upon the desire of the testator to retain control over the disposition of the remainder while assuring to his wife or daughter the highly personal right to live her life as she might choose.

We conclude that the capital gains in question may not be taxed to these taxpayers as owners.

The alternative contention of the United States (in support of its counterclaims) is that the corpus of the estate, for purposes of income taxation, should in each case be recognized to constitute property held in trust and that the life tenant should be taxable as trustee for capital gains realized by the estate.

The United States relies on 26 U.S.C. §641(a), which reads....[7]

In United States v. Cooke, 9 Cir., 1955, 228 F.2d 667, this contention was made by the United States and was rejected by this Court. The Court of Claims recently reached the opposite result. Weil v. United States, Ct.Cl., 180 F. Supp. 407. The United States now suggests that in this respect Cooke should be re-examined and overruled. Such is the course we have chosen to adopt.

Cooke rejected the contention that property subject to a life estate should be treated as property held in trust upon the ground that the life estate there under scrutiny did not square with the definition of "trust" set forth in Regulation 118, §39.3797-3 [the predecessor of Treas. Reg. §301.7701-4(a)]:

> "The term 'trust,' as used in the Internal Revenue Code, refers to an ordinary trust, namely, one created by will or by declaration of the trustees or the grantor, the trustees of which take title to the property for the purpose of protecting or conserving it as customarily required under ordinary rules applied in chancery and probate courts."

Cooke reasoned that, by this definition, application of 26 U.S.C. §641(a) had been limited to a particular kind of trust, namely, an *ordinary* trust; more specifically, one in which the duties of the trustee in protection and conservation of trust assets are those *customarily* required under *ordinary* rules of equity. It was held (228 F.2d at 668):

> "Assuming but not deciding that Mrs. Cooke took title to the property in which she is a life tenant she did not do so for the purpose of 'conserving it as *customarily* required under *ordinary* rules applied in chancery and probate courts.'"

We address ourselves first to the proposition embraced by Cooke that the definition served to exempt from taxation under 26 U.S.C. §641(a) all trusts save those in which the trustee's duties of protection and conservation were those customarily required under ordinary rules of equity.

The United States contends, and we agree, that in Cooke undue emphasis and significance were read into the regulation's reference to the customary requirements of protection and conservation. In searching for the meaning of the distinction which this regulation makes (between ordinary trusts and other types of trusts), we should be guided

---

7. Subsection (b) of §641 requires computation and payment of the tax by the fiduciary. §6012(b)(4) requires the fiduciary of a trust to make a return and [§7701(a)(6)] defines fiduciary as meaning "a guardian, trustee, executor, administrator, receiver, conservator, or any person acting in any fiduciary capacity for any person."

by the fact that this is a tax measure. The distinction intended then should be meaningful and purposeful in a tax context.

Certainly an active trust can be effectively created in which extraordinary powers or freedom from responsibility or liability are given to the trustee.[8] Absent the regulation, we have no doubt that a trust estate so created would have been held a taxable estate. Under the regulation as construed in Cooke, however, such an estate would have been held not an ordinary trust and thus not taxable. The effect of the regulation so construed is thus to exclude from taxation property which theretofore was taxable. Such could hardly have been the intent in the light of the recognized "legislative design to reach all gain constitutionally taxable unless specifically excluded." General Investors Co. v. Commissioner, 1955, 348 U.S. 434, 436, 75 S.Ct. 478, 479, 99 L.Ed. 504; see also Commissioner v. Glenshaw Glass Co., 1955, 348 U.S. 426, 429–430, 432, 75 S.Ct. 473, 99 L.Ed. 483. Nor can we find tax significance in isolating those trusts in which the duties of the trustee to conserve and protect the estate for others than himself are less strict than is customarily the case.

The United States asserts that this definition should be construed as an effort to distinguish the so-called business trust from the ordinary type of trust. Reason would seem to support this construction. The regulation in question did not appear until eighteen years after the word "trust" was first used in the code with reference to a separate taxable entity[9] and at a time when the problem of separating associations from trusts was receiving attention.[10] The proposed construction has tax significance. It does not exclude property from taxation; rather, it aids in the determination of whether a taxable entity should be taxed as a trust or as a corporation.

Under the language of Regulation 118, then, our concern for what is "customary" should not be directed to the nature and extent of the required protection and conservation (in which event, the taxable status of property could be made to depend upon the existence of an infinite number of details, all of which might be said to be "customary") but rather to the purposes of the arrangement.

Accepting such a construction, our final question is whether in these cases the corpus of the estate can be considered "property held in trust" under Section 641(a).

We may note that Cooke did not concern itself with labels. We did not there hold that, for tax purposes, a life estate as such cannot be regarded as a trust. As heretofore noted, our concern there was with the extent of the duties of that particular life tenant in comparison with those customarily imposed upon a trustee.

Nor have other courts, in construing the phrase "property held in trust," felt themselves bound to regard Section 641(a) as applying only to "technical trusts." Instead, they have remained mindful of the legislative design to reach all income constitutionally taxable and of the fact that the word "trust," in the sense of a separate taxable entity, was originally used in the context of this design. General Investors v. Commissioner, supra; Commissioner v. Glenshaw Glass Company, supra; Smietanka v. First Trust and Savings Bank, supra, footnote 9. The inquiry has been whether the relationship created is one which might be said to be "clothed with the characteristics of a trust."[11]

---

8. See, Restatement (Second), Trusts, §187, comment j; §222 (1957); 1 Scott, Trusts, §99.3 at 774 (2d Ed., 1956).

9. See, Smietanka v. First Trust & Savings Bank, 1922, 257 U.S. 602, 607, 42 S.Ct. 223, 66 L.Ed. 391.

10. Morrissey v. Commissioner, 1935, 296 U.S. 344, 56 S.Ct. 289, 80 L.Ed. 263.

11. Hart v. Commissioner, 1 Cir., 1932, 54 F.2d 848, 851; Ferguson v. Forstman, 3 Cir., 1928, 25 F.2d 47, 49; see Commissioner of Internal Revenue v. Owens, 10 Cir., 1935, 78 F.2d 768; Goforth v.

In Weil v. United States, supra, it is stated [180 F.Supp. 411]:

> " * * * we believe that the taxability of the gains involved here should depend not on whether there is a separation of the legal and equitable interests in the life estate but on the relationship between the holder of the life interest and the owners of the succeeding future interests."

The duties of a life tenant have been characterized by the California courts as "in the nature of a trust," King v. Hawley, 1952, 113 Cal.App.2d 534, 538, 248 P.2d 491, 494, and, by Bogert, as a "quasi-trust," 1 Bogert, Trusts and Trustees, §27, pp. 214–219 (1951). See also Restatement, Property, §204, comment a (1936) and 1948 Supplement; Annotation, 137 A.L.R. 1054 (1942). The Restatement of the Law of Property, §202, comment g, notes that the life tenant may be required to post security for the performance of his fiduciary duties by a court of equity. Section 202, comment d, indicates that, were the life interest alone in trust, the relationship between the trustee and the remainderman would be identical to that obtaining between an ordinary life tenant and the remainderman.

We have in the corpus of each estate an expressly created ascertainable entity. In each life tenant we have a person, notwithstanding her extensive powers of beneficial use, who occupies a fiduciary relationship with the remaindermen respecting that estate, with the duty to maintain for the remaindermen such as is not required for need, maintenance and comfort. Such a relationship, in our view, is clothed with the characteristics of a trust.

We conclude that the capital gain here involved is taxable as income of property held in trust under 26 U.S.C. §641(a).

In each case: reversed and remanded with instructions that summary judgment be set aside and for further proceedings.

JERTBERG, Circuit Judge (dissenting).

I am in complete agreement with that portion of the majority opinion which concludes by stating, "We conclude that the capital gains in question may not be taxed to these taxpayers as owners." However, I must part company with the majority opinion wherein it concludes "that the capital gain here involved is taxable as income of property held in trust under 26 U.S.C. §641(a)."

While the imposition of a tax under the circumstances reflected in the record may be a consummation devoutly to be desired, such consummation should be effected by Congress and not by the judiciary. In my view Congress has not done so, although there is recent indication that Congress intends to do so shortly. H.R. 9662 was introduced by the chairman of the House Ways and Means Committee on January 18, 1960. It is known as the "Trust and Partnership Income Tax Revision Act of 1960." On January 28, 1960, the bill was committed to the Committee of the whole House. H.R. 9662 contains a provision amending Section 641 of the Revenue Code of 1954, by adding a new sub-section, imposing upon the legal life tenant the liability to report and pay a tax on gross income not otherwise taxable. The new sub-section also provides that the legal life tenant shall be deemed to be a fiduciary. The text of the portion of the bill which contains the amendment to Section 641 of the Revenue Code is as follows:

Commissioner, 1935, 32 B.T.A. 1206, 1215–1217. But see Lee McRitchie, 1956, 27 T.C. 65. We regard as distinguishable Shea v. Commissioner, 1934, 31 B.T.A. 513, and G.C.M. 14693, 14-1 Cum.Bull. 197 (1935) holding life estates not to be taxable as trusts. These appear to be situations in which vested remaindermen had present rights to the gain in question and thus were to be regarded as present owners and individually taxable as such. See Restatement Property, §126(e) (1936); 1 Orgel, Valuation under the Law of Eminent Domain, §118 (2d Ed., 1953).

"Title I—Estates and Trusts [Bill Sec. 101]

"Sec. 101. Imposition of Tax-Amendments of Section 641. [Bill Sec. 101(a)]

"(a) Application of Tax.—Section 641 is amended by adding at the end thereof the following new subsection:

"'(c) Legal Life Estates and Other Terminable Legal Interests.—If—

"'(1) any person owns a legal interest in property which may terminate on the lapse of time on [sic] the occurrence of an event or contingency, or on the failure of an event or contingency to occur, and

"'(2) at any time during any calendar year there is gross income attributable to such property—

"'(A) which (but for this subsection) would not be currently includible in the gross income of any person because such person is not then ascertainable or for any other reason, but

"'(B) which would be currently includible in the gross income of a trust with respect to such property if such trust existed (determined without regard to subpart E),

then for purposes of this subchapter and subtitle F, a trust shall be deemed to exist for such calendar year with respect to all gross income described in paragraph (2) attributable to such property, and the person (or persons) described in paragraph (1) shall be deemed to be a fiduciary of such trust.'"

The congressional activity thus cited establishes, at the least, grave congressional doubt that under current legislation a life estate of the character here involved can be deemed to be a trust and the legal life tenant deemed to be a fiduciary. Further, the proposed amendment of Section 641 is consistent with past congressional policy to accord separate treatment to legal life tenants. Thus while Sections 1 and 641 of the Internal Revenue Code of 1954 and their predecessors which impose tax liability with respect to capital gains accruing to principal refer only to individual owners and estates and trusts, and not to life tenants, other sections of the Code deal specifically with legal life tenants. Section 62 deals with "adjusted gross income." Section 62(6) [the predecessor of Section 62(a)(5)] provides:

"(6) Certain deductions of life tenants and income beneficiaries of property.— In the case of a life tenant of property, or an income beneficiary of property held in trust, or an heir, legatee, or devisee of an estate, the deduction for depreciation allowed by section 167 and the deduction allowed by section 611.

"Nothing in this section shall permit the same item to be deducted more than once."

Section 167 deals with depreciation. Section 167(g) [the predecessor of Section 167(d)] provides:

"(g) Life tenants and beneficiaries of trusts and estates.—In the case of property held by one person for life with remainder to another person, the deduction shall be computed as if the life tenant were the absolute owner of the property and shall be allowed to the life tenant. In the case of property held in trust, the allowable deduction shall be apportioned between the income beneficiaries and the trustee in accordance with the pertinent provisions of the instrument creating the trust, or, in the absence of such provisions, on the basis of the trust income allocable to each. In the case of an estate the allowable deduction shall be apportioned between the estate and the heirs, legatees, and devisees on the basis of the income of the estate allocable to each."

Section 611 deals with depletion. Section 611(b) provides:

"(b) Special rules.—

"(1) Leases.—* * *

"(2) Life tenant and remainderman.—In the case of property held by one person for life with remainder to another person, the deduction under this section shall be computed as if the life tenant were the absolute owner of the property and shall be allowed to the life tenant.

"(3) Property held in trust.—* * *

"(4) Property held by estate.—* * * ."

[Former] Section 169 deal[t] with amortization of grain-storage facilities. Section 169(g) provide[d]:

"(g) Life tenant and remainderman.—In the case of property held by one person for life with remainder to another person, the amortization provided in subsection (a) shall be computed as if the life tenant were the absolute owner of the property and shall be allowed to the life tenant."

Congress has made provision for the special case of legal life tenants in regard to depletion, depreciation and amortization, but in my view has failed to do so in the case of capital gains or losses realized with respect to life estate principal although under existing law a trustee is made liable for collection and payment of tax on capital gains.

The portion of the majority opinion with which I am dealing expressly overrules the decision of this Court in United States v. Cooke, 9 Cir., 1955, 228 F.2d 667, on the ground that in Cooke "undue emphasis and significance were read into the regulation's reference to the customary requirements of protection and conservation." In Cooke the Court simply held that "assuming the contention of the United States that the conveyance created a trust in Mrs. Cooke, it is not an 'ordinary trust' and hence not taxable." Further in the opinion the Court stated:

"Our discussion above has been based on the government's contention that Mrs. Cooke was a trustee holding the shares for the benefit of the remaindermen. We do not think she had such a trustee title to the shares. She is not in any way the owner of the shares, and is not a trustee. Her estate is only a life estate."

It appears to me that the Court would have reached the same result absent the regulation.

The majority opinion is grounded on two propositions: First the "legislative design to reach all gain constitutionally taxable unless specifically excluded," and, second, the life estates in question are "clothed with the characteristics of the trust." The legislative design is to tax the owners of the gain, or in the case of trusts and estates to place on the fiduciary the collection and payment. The majority opinion correctly holds that the legal life tenants are not the owners of the gains in question. Admittedly Congress has not placed on legal life tenants as such the duty of collection and payment. H.R. 9662 if enacted into law would do so. In considering the legislative design one must bear in mind the admonition of the Supreme Court of the United States in Smietanka v. First Trust & Savings Bank, 257 U.S. 602, at page 605, 42 S.Ct. 223, at page 224, 66 L.Ed. 391, in which the Court stated:

"It may be that Congress had a general intention to tax all incomes whether for the benefit of persons living or unborn, but a general intention of this kind must be carried into language which can be reasonably construed to effect it. Otherwise the intention cannot be enforced by the courts. The provisions of such acts are not to be extended by implication. Treat v. White, 181 U.S. 264, 267; United States v. Field, 255 U.S. 257; Gould v. Gould, 245 U.S. 151, 153."

Attention is also called to the following quotation from Crooks v. Harrelson, 282 U.S. 55, at page 61, 51 S.Ct. 49, at page 51, 75 L.Ed. 156:

> "Finally, the fact must not be overlooked that we are here concerned with a taxing act, with regard to which the general rule requiring adherence to the letter applies with peculiar strictness. In United States v. Merriam, 263 U.S. 179, 187–188, after saying that 'in statutes levying taxes the literal meaning of the words employed is most important, for such statutes are not to be extended by implication beyond the clear import of the language used,' we quoted with approval the words of Lord Cairns in Partington v. Attorney-General, L.R. 4 H.L. 100, 122, that 'if the Crown seeking to recover the tax, cannot bring the subject within the letter of the law, the subject is free, however apparently within the spirit of the law the case might otherwise appear to be. In other words, if there be admissible in any statute, what is called an equitable construction, certainly such a construction is not admissible in a taxing statute, where you can simply adhere to the words of the statute.'"

Under the De Bonchamps and Cowgill wills the legal life tenants had the power to consume the corpus and the income therefrom for their needs, maintenance and comfort during their lives without any restriction, and the remaindermen were to take only what remains at their deaths. The will in the King case is about the same except the legal life tenant could use and consume the corpus and income not only for her own needs, maintenance and comfort but as well for the needs, maintenance and comfort of her daughters and their issue. I am unable to agree that by such language trusts were created. Clearly under California law the life tenants in these cases are not trustees. Hardy v. Mayhew, 158 Cal. 95, 110 P. 113; Skellenger v. England, 81 Cal.App. 176, 253 P. 191; California Civil Code, Section 2221 et seq. In my view they should not be made such for federal tax purpose by judicial pronouncement.

I would affirm the judgments entered below.

[The dissenting opinion of Judge Barnes is omitted.]

Illustrative Material

1. *Life Tenants Taxable as Owners.* Occasionally life tenants have been held taxable in their individual capacities on gains derived from sales of assets subject to legal life estates. Typically in such cases the life tenants have had powers of consumption so broad the courts have construed them as unrestricted. *See Hirschmann v. United States,* 309 F.2d 104 (2d Cir. 1962); *Smith v. United States,* 265 F.2d 834 (5th Cir. 1959); *Myrtle Mercer,* 7 T.C. 834 (1946). In such instances the courts have treated the life tenants as though they owned the assets.

Another case that held a life tenant taxable individually was *West v. United States,* 310 F. Supp. 1289 (N.D. Ga. 1970). *West* involved gains from sales of timber. Under Georgia law, according to the court, the sale of timber did not constitute waste, the only ground upon which a legal life tenant could be held accountable to a remainder beneficiary. Thus, the gains effectively "belonged" to the life tenant, and taxation of the gains to the life tenant seemed appropriate.

2. *Life Tenants Taxable as Fiduciaries. Weil v. United States,* 148 Ct. Cl. 681, 180 F. Supp. 407, *cert. denied,* 364 U.S. 822 (1960), cited in *De Bonchamps,* likewise involved a legal life estate created by will. It, too, required the life tenant to file fiduciary income tax returns reporting gains realized upon sales of the devised assets. The court based its decision on the fiduciary obligation of the life tenant:

> [W]e believe that the taxability of the gains involved here should depend, not on whether there is a separation of the legal and equitable interests in the life estate, but on the relationship between the holder of the life interest and the owners of the succeeding future interests.
>
> Under applicable state law the legal life tenant and the trustee of a life interest only have the same fiduciary obligation toward the owners of succeeding future interests. They cannot appropriate the principal to themselves or intentionally injure the remaindermen by the way in which they use the property. And a court of equity may require a life tenant to safeguard the remainderman's interest by giving security for property in his possession....
>
> It is in this sense that the plaintiff (as well as a technical trustee for life interest only) is the fiduciary of "property held in trust" within the meaning of [the predecessor of section 641(a)(1)].

180 F. Supp. at 411. *Security-First National Bank v. United States,* 181 F. Supp. 911 (S.D. Cal. 1960), is to the same effect. *Robinson v. United States,* 192 F. Supp. 253 (N.D. Ga. 1961), followed *De Bonchamps, Weil,* and *Security-First National,* but did so rather regretfully, sounding at times like Judge Jertberg's dissent in *De Bonchamps.* Specifically, *Robinson* rejected the notion "that under Georgia law a life tenant is in any sense a trustee for a remainderman." 192 F. Supp. at 254.

Rev. Rul. 61-102, 1961-1 C.B. 245, not surprisingly, took the position that the gain realized by a life tenant on a sale of property devised subject to a legal life estate was taxable under subchapter J in the hands of the life tenant. The I.R.S. relied not on the life tenant's fiduciary duties to the remainder beneficiaries, but on the literal fit of the words of section 641(a)(1), "income accumulated or held for future distribution under the terms of the will." Does the I.R.S. rationale suggest a different result if the legal life estate were created by deed, rather than by will?

3. *Life Tenants and Remainder Beneficiaries Taxable as Sellers. Robinson* (discussed *supra*), in dictum only, and G.C.M. 14693, XIV-1 C.B. 197 (1935), distinguished in *De Bonchamps* and Rev. Rul. 61-102 (also discussed *supra*), suggested a third rationale for taxing the gain realized by the sale of an asset subject to a legal life estate. Under that rationale, the tax on the gain would be allocated (presumably on an actuarial basis) between the life tenant and the remainder beneficiaries, as though each had sold his or her interest directly. Is a remainder beneficiary likely to be pleased by such a proposition? (Especially a contingent remainder beneficiary?) Why? Who would pay the tax if the remainder beneficiary were unascertainable? The answers to such questions perhaps explain why this rationale appears never to have caught on.

4. *Others Holding Sales Proceeds.* In *United States v. National City Bank,* 21 F. Supp. 791 (S.D.N.Y. 1937), a court-appointed trustee held the sales proceeds of real property sold pursuant to statutory authorization at the request of one who by will had received a legal life estate in the property. The court held that the trustee was liable to pay the income tax on the gain realized. The court stated that it believed the language of the predecessor of section 641(a)(1), "income accumulated in trust," applied. The court's holding, however, seems to be that the other language of the predecessor of section 641(a)(1), "in-

come accumulated or held for future distribution under the terms of the will," more clearly applied.

Rev. Rul. 59-99, 1959-1 C.B. 158, likewise held that a court-appointed trustee holding sales proceeds of real property devised subject to a legal life estate was taxable on the gain. The ruling gave no indication that the trustee was not considered a fiduciary under local law. Nonetheless, the I.R.S. stated that, "regardless of whether the local law constituted the holder of the income as a trustee or a fiduciary," the words of section 641(a)(1) taxing income "held for future distribution under the terms of a will" applied.

Had either the legal life estate in *National City Bank* or that in Rev Rul. 59-99 been created by deed, the *National City Bank* court's supposition about the applicability of the first portion of section 641(a)(1) would, of course, have been unavoidably at issue.

B. How Is an Entity Taxed?

Internal Revenue Code:
   Sections 641(a); 7701(a)(3)
Regulations:
   Sections 301.7701-2(a), -4(a), (b)

Morrissey v. Commissioner
296 U.S. 344 (1935)

MR. CHIEF JUSTICE HUGHES delivered the opinion of the Court.

Petitioners, the trustees of an express trust, contest income taxes for the years 1924 to 1926, inclusive, upon the ground that the trust has been illegally treated as an "association." The Circuit Court of Appeals affirmed the decision of the Board of Tax Appeals, which sustained the ruling of the Commissioner of Internal Revenue. 74 F. (2d) 803. We granted certiorari because of a conflict of decisions as to the distinction between an "association" and a "pure trust," the decisions being described in one of the cases as "seemingly in a hopeless state of confusion." *Coleman-Gilbert Associates v. Commissioner,* 76 F. (2d) 191, 193.

The facts were stipulated. In the year 1921 petitioners made a declaration of trust of real estate in Los Angeles. They were to be designated in "their collective capacity" as "Western Avenue Golf Club." The trustees were authorized to add to their number and to choose their successors; to purchase, encumber, sell, lease and operate the "described or other lands"; to construct and operate golf courses, club houses, etc.; to receive the rents, profits and income; to make loans and investments; to make regulations; and generally to manage the trust estate as if the trustees were its absolute owners. The trustees were declared to be without power to bind the beneficiaries personally by "any act, neglect or default," and the beneficiaries and all persons dealing with the trustees were required to look for payment or indemnity to the trust property. The beneficial interests were to be evidenced solely by transferable certificates for shares which were divided into 2,000 preferred shares of the par value of $100 each, and 2,000 common shares of no par value, and the rights of the respective shareholders in the surplus, profits, and capital assets were defined. "Share ledgers" showing the names and addresses of shareholders were to be kept.

The trustees might convene the shareholders in meeting for the purpose of making reports or considering recommendations, but the votes of the shareholders were to be advisory only. The death of a trustee or of a beneficiary was not to end the trust, which was to continue for twenty-five years unless sooner terminated by the trustees.

During the years 1921 and 1922, the trustees sold beneficial interests and paid commissions on the sales. About 42 acres (of the 155 acres described by the declaration of trust) were plotted into lots which were sold during the years 1921 to 1923, most of the sales being on the installment basis. On the remaining property a golf course and club house were constructed, and in 1923 this property with the improvements was conveyed to Western Avenue Golf Club, Inc., a California corporation, in exchange for its stock. Under a lease from the corporation petitioners continued the operation of the golf course until January 12, 1924. After that date petitioners' activities were confined to collections of installments of principal and interest on contracts of purchase, the receipt of interest on bank balances and of fees on assignments by holders of purchase contracts, the execution of conveyances to purchasers, the receipt of dividends from the incorporated club, and the distribution of monies to the holders of beneficial interests. On December 31, 1923, the total number of outstanding beneficial interests was 3016, held by 920 persons; by December 31, 1926, the number of interests had been gradually decreased to 2172, held by 275 persons. The holdings by the trustees ranged approximately from 16 to 29 per cent.

Petitioners contend that they are trustees "of property held in trust," within section 219 of the Revenue Acts of 1924 and 1926 [predecessor of section 641(a)], and are taxable accordingly and not as an "association." They urge that, to constitute an association, the applicable test requires "a quasi-corporate organization in which the beneficiaries, whether or not certificate holders, have some voice in the management and some control over the trustees and have an opportunity to exercise such control through the right to vote at meetings"; and that, in any event, the activities in which petitioners were engaged, during the tax years under consideration, did not constitute "a carrying on of business"....

The Government insists that the distinction between associations and the trusts taxed under section 219 is between "business trusts on the one side" and other trusts "which are engaged merely in collecting the income and conserving the property against the day when it is to be distributed to the beneficiaries"; that Congress intended that all "business trusts" should be taxed as associations.

1. The Revenue Acts of 1924 and 1926 provided:

"The term 'corporation' includes associations, joint-stock companies, and insurance companies." 1924, §2(a)(2); 1926, §2(a)(2) [predecessor of section 7701(a)(3)].

* * *

The text of the regulations relating to associations, so far as pertinent here, promulgated under the Act of 1924, is set forth in the margin. Regulations No. 65, Arts. 1502, 1504, as amended [predecessors of Treas. Reg. §§301.7701-2 and -4].[10] These regulations

---

10. "Art. 1502. *Association.*—Associations and joint-stock companies include associations, common law trusts, and organizations by whatever name known, which act or do business in an organized capacity, whether created under and pursuant to state laws, agreements, declarations of trust, or otherwise, the net income of which, if any, is distributed or distributable among the shareholders on the basis of the capital stock which each holds, or, where there is no capital stock, on the basis of the pro-

were continued substantially unchanged under the Revenue Acts of 1926 and 1928. No. 69, Arts. 1502, 1504; No. 74, Arts. 1312, 1314....

2. As the statute merely provided that the term "corporation" should include "associations," without further definition, the Treasury Department was authorized to supply rules for the enforcement of the Act within the permissible bounds of administrative construction....

The question is not one of the power of Congress to impose this tax upon petitioners but is simply one of statutory construction,—whether Congress has imposed it. See *Burk-Waggoner Oil Assn. v. Hopkins*, 269 U. S. 110, 114. The difficulty with the regulations as an exposition was that they themselves required explication; that they left many questions open with respect both to their application to particular enterprises and to their validity as applied.... While it is impossible in the nature of things to translate the statutory concept of "association" into a particularity of detail that would fix the status of every sort of enterprise or organization which ingenuity may create, the recurring disputes emphasize the need of a further examination of the congressional intent.

3. "Association" implies associates. It implies the entering into a joint enterprise, and, as the applicable regulation imports, an enterprise for the transaction of business. This is not the characteristic of an ordinary trust—whether created by will, deed, or declaration—by which particular property is conveyed to a trustee or is to be held by the settlor, on specified trusts, for the benefit of named or described persons. Such beneficiaries do not ordinarily, and as mere *cestuis que trustent*, plan a common effort or enter into a combination for the conduct of a business enterprise. Undoubtedly the terms of an association may make the taking or acquiring of shares or interests sufficient to constitute participation, and may leave the management, or even control of the enterprise, to designated persons. But the nature and purpose of the cooperative undertaking will differentiate it from an ordinary trust. In what are called "business trusts" the object is not to hold and conserve particular property, with incidental powers, as in the traditional type of trusts, but to provide a medium for the conduct of a business and sharing its gains. Thus a trust may be created as a convenient method by which persons become associated for dealings in real estate, the development of tracts of land, the construction of improvements, and the purchase, management and sale of properties; or for dealings in securities or other personal property; or for the production, or manufacture, and sale of commodities; or for commerce, or other sorts of business; where those who become beneficially interested, either by joining in the plan at the outset, or by later participation according

---

portionate share or capital which each has or has invested in the business or property of the organization...."

"Art. 1504. *Association distinguished from trust.*—Where trustees merely hold property for the collection of the income and its distribution among the beneficiaries of the trust, and are not engaged, either by themselves or in connection with the beneficiaries, in the carrying on of any business, and the beneficiaries have no control over the trust although their consent may be required for the filling of a vacancy among the trustees or for a modification of the terms of the trust, no association exists, and the trust and the beneficiaries thereof will be subject to tax as provided by section 219 and by articles 341–347. If, however, the beneficiaries have positive control over the trust, whether through the right periodically to elect trustees or otherwise, an association exists within the meaning of section 2. Even in the absence of any control by the beneficiaries, where the trustees are not restricted to the mere collection of funds and their payment to the beneficiaries, but are associated together with similar or greater powers than the directors in a corporation for the purpose of carrying on some business enterprise, the trust is an association within the meaning of the statute."

to the terms of the arrangement, seek to share the advantages of a union of their interests in the common enterprise.

The Government contends that such an organized community of effort for the doing of business presents the essential features of an association. Petitioners stress the significance of, and the limitations said to be implied in, the provision classifying associations with corporations.

4. The inclusion of associations with corporations implies resemblance; but it is resemblance and not identity. The resemblance points to features distinguishing associations from partnerships as well as from ordinary trusts. [T]he classification cannot be said to require organization under a statute, or with statutory privileges. The term embraces associations as they may exist at common law. [Dictionary definitions show] the ordinary meaning of the term as applicable to a body of persons united without a charter "but upon the methods and forms used by incorporated bodies for the prosecution of some common enterprise." These definitions, while helpful, are not to be pressed so far as to make mere formal procedure a controlling test. The provision itself negatives such a construction. Thus unincorporated joint-stock companies have generally been regarded as bearing the closest resemblance to corporations. But, in the revenue acts, associations are mentioned separately and are not to be treated as limited to "joint-stock companies," although belonging to the same group. While the use of corporate forms may furnish persuasive evidence of the existence of an association, the absence of particular forms, or of the usual terminology of corporations, cannot be regarded as decisive. Thus an association may not have "directors" or "officers," but the "trustees" may function "in much the same manner as the directors in a corporation" for the purpose of carrying on the enterprise. The regulatory provisions of the trust instrument may take the place of "by-laws." And as there may be ... an absence of control by beneficiaries such as is commonly exercised by stockholders in a business corporation, it cannot be considered to be essential to the existence of an association that those beneficially interested should hold meetings or elect their representatives. Again, while the faculty of transferring the interests of members without affecting the continuity of the enterprise may be deemed to be characteristic, the test of an association is not to be found in the mere formal evidence of interests or in a particular method of transfer.

What, then, are the salient features of a trust — when created and maintained as a medium for the carrying on of a business enterprise and sharing its gains — which may be regarded as making it analogous to a corporate organization? A corporation, as an entity, holds the title to the property embarked in the corporate undertaking. Trustees, as a continuing body with provision for succession, may afford a corresponding advantage during the existence of the trust. Corporate organization furnishes the opportunity for a centralized management through representatives of the members of the corporation. The designation of trustees, who are charged with the conduct of an enterprise, — who act "in much the same manner as directors" — may provide a similar scheme, with corresponding effectiveness. Whether the trustees are named in the trust instrument with power to select successors, so as to constitute a self-perpetuating body, or are selected by, or with the advice of, those beneficially interested in the undertaking, centralization of management analogous to that of corporate activities may be achieved. An enterprise carried on by means of a trust may be secure from termination or interruption by the death of owners of beneficial interests and in this respect their interests are distinguished from those of partners and are akin to the interests of members of a corporation. And the trust type of organization facilitates, as does corporate organization, the transfer of beneficial interests without affecting the continuity of the enterprise, and also the introduction of large numbers of participants. The trust method also permits the limitation of the personal liability of participants to the property embarked in the undertaking.

It is no answer to say that these advantages flow from the very nature of trusts. For the question has arisen because of the use and adaptation of the trust mechanism. The suggestion ignores the postulate that we are considering those trusts which have the distinctive feature of being created to enable the participants to carry on a business and divide the gains which accrue from their common undertaking,—trusts that thus satisfy the primary conception of association and have the attributes to which we have referred, distinguishing them from partnerships. In such a case, we think that these attributes make the trust sufficiently analogous to corporate organization to justify the conclusion that Congress intended that the income of the enterprise should be taxed in the same manner as that of corporations.

5. Applying these principles to the instant case, we are of the opinion that the trust constituted an association. The trust was created for the development of a tract of land through the construction and operation of golf courses, club houses, etc., and the conduct of incidental businesses, with broad powers for the purchase, operation and sale of properties. Provision was made for the issue of shares of beneficial interests, with described rights and priorities. There were to be preferred shares of the value of $100 each and common shares of no par value. Thus those who took beneficial interests became shareholders in the common undertaking to be conducted for their profit according to the terms of the arrangement. They were not the less associated in that undertaking because the arrangement vested the management and control in the trustees. And the contemplated development of the tract of land held at the outset, even if other properties were not acquired, involved what was essentially a business enterprise. The arrangement provided for centralized control, continuity, and limited liability, and the analogy to corporate organization was carried still further by the provision for the issue of transferable certificates.

Under the trust, a considerable portion of the property was surveyed and subdivided into lots which were sold and, to facilitate the sales, the subdivided property was improved by the construction of streets, sidewalks and curbs. The fact that these sales were made before the beginning of the tax years here in question, and that the remaining property was conveyed to a corporation in exchange for its stock, did not alter the character of the organization. Its character was determined by the terms of the trust instrument. It was not a liquidating trust; it was still an organization for profit, and the profits were still coming in. The powers conferred on the trustees continued and could be exercised for such activities as the instrument authorized.

* * *

The judgment is

Affirmed.

Illustrative Material

1. For years, former Treas. Reg. § 301.7701-2(a)(1) listed six characteristics of "associations": (1) associates; (2) an objective to carry on business and divide the gains therefrom; (3) continuity of life; (4) centralization of management; (5) liability for corporate debts limited to corporate property; and (6) free transferability of interests. Former Treas. Reg. § 301.7701-2(a)(2), however, stated that because the latter four characteristics were "generally common to trusts and corporations," the determination of whether a trust that

had such characteristics was to be treated for tax purposes as a trust or as an association depended on whether there were associates and an objective to carry on business and divide the gains therefrom. *Howard v. United States*, 5 Cl. Ct. 334, 84-1 U.S.T.C. ¶ 9494 (1984), *aff'd mem.*, 770 F.2d 178 (Fed. Cir. 1985), therefore held that an entity designated as a trust was taxable as an association after analysis of only the first two characteristics. Similarly, *Anesthesia Service Medical Group, Inc. Employee Protective Trust v. Commissioner*, 85 T.C. 1031 (1985), *aff'd*, 825 F.2d 241 (9th Cir. 1987), and *Estate of Harry M. Bedell, Sr., Trust v. Commissioner*, 86 T.C. 1207 (1986), verified that entities designated as trusts were taxable as trusts after consideration of only those two factors. *Bedell* in fact specified that *both* of the first two characteristics must be present before an entity is classifiable as an association:

> In the case of classifying an entity as an association rather than a trust, the regulations provide that the result depends merely upon the two (not six) critical criteria relating to trusts, i.e., "whether there are associates *and* an objective to carry on business and divide the gains therefrom". (Emphasis supplied.) In short, applying the regulations literally, ... the Bedell Trust cannot be classified as an association unless it satisfies both the associates and the business tests. Not only do the regulations refer to both attributes in the conjunctive, but they also specifically require that, after eliminating "all characteristics common to both types of organizations", an organization "shall not be classified as an association unless [it] * * * has *more* corporate characteristics than noncorporate characteristics". (Emphasis supplied.) [Former] Section 301.7701-2(a)(3), Proced. & Admin. Regs. Thus, in accordance with the latter requirement, since the trust must have "more" than half of the two determinative characteristics to qualify as an "association" rather than a trust, it must fail to qualify as such if it satisfies only one of the tests.

86 T.C. at 1218. *See also Water Resource Control v. Commissioner*, 61 T.C.M. (CCH) 2102, 2114–16 (1991), *aff'd mem. sub nom. Whitehouse v. Commissioner*, 972 F.2d 1328 (2d Cir. 1992), *cert. denied*, 507 U.S. 960 (1993). *Allen v. Commissioner*, 62 T.C.M. (CCH) 741 (1991), *aff'd mem.*, 993 F.2d 875 (3d Cir. 1993), did inquire into the existence of each of the six characteristics, but the court expressly noted that existence of the first two was sufficient to justify the conclusion that the entities involved were not taxable as trusts. The court examined the other four factors "to determine whether the [entities were] associations taxable as corporations as opposed to some other form of flowthrough entity." 62 T.C.M. at 751. Likewise, *Arcadia Plumbing Trust v. Commissioner*, 68 T.C.M. (CCH) 699 (1994), inquired into four of the six characteristics but stated that the first two were "determinative" of association status.

The so-called "check-the-box regulations" appeared in 1996. T.D. 8697, 1997-1 C.B. 215. Though they drastically alter the categorization of business entities, they have little effect on the definition of a "trust" for tax purposes. Treas. Reg. § 301.7701-4(a), which defines a trust as an arrangement whose beneficiaries are "not associates in a joint enterprise for the conduct of business for profit," is unamended. Thus, the explanation accompanying the new regulations states that the test for whether an entity is taxable as a trust remains the same:

> An organization that is recognized as a separate entity for federal tax purposes is either a trust or a business entity.... The regulations provide that trusts generally do not have associates or an objective to carry on business for profit. The distinctions between trusts and business entities, although restated, are not changed by these regulations.

1997-1 C.B. at 216. If, however, under the usual two-part test, an entity is *not* taxable as a trust, the new regulations generally allow classification as either a partnership or a corporation.

2. *Elm Street Realty Trust v. Commissioner*, 76 T.C. 803 (1981), *acq.*, 1981-2 C.B. 1, refused to reclassify an *inter vivos* trust as an association, due to a lack of associates. The court wrote: "Where nongrantor beneficiaries receive their beneficial interests gratuitously, without solicitation, it is doubtful that they can be considered associated together in a common enterprise in the absence of some further joint activity (or at least the potential therefor) vis-a-vis the trust." 76 T.C. at 814.

3. Estate planners generally consider testamentary trusts immune from reclassification as associations, even in instances in which such trusts own and operate full-fledged businesses. One reason is that stated in *Elm Street* (discussed *supra*). Another is that important nonbusiness motivations almost always underlie such trusts. In addition, the fact that someone has to die to create a testamentary trust serves to limit the abuse potential of such trusts. In short, testamentary trusts rarely bear any significant practical resemblance to corporations.

Nevertheless, *Bedell* (discussed *supra*), involved a testamentary trust, which the I.R.S. sought to reclassify as an association. In finding that the *Bedell* trust lacked associates, the Tax Court noted that the beneficiaries "neither created nor contributed to the trust," that their interests were not transferable, and that only "a few" of the beneficiaries participated in the trust affairs. 86 T.C. at 1221. Thus, the trust was not taxed as an association. The court, however, went out of its way to suggest that testamentary trusts were not immune from reclassification:

> A final note. We wish to emphasize that the result reached herein is based upon this record, and that the case should not be regarded as authority for the conclusion that no testamentary trust can be classified as an association.... We understand that the Government regarded this case as a test case in respect of testamentary trusts and trusts engaged in the conduct of a business, and that high levels in the IRS were active in pressing the matter. It is difficult to imagine a more unsuitable vehicle than this case for any such purpose, and we think it regrettable that extensive misguided efforts were exerted to such a fruitless end in this litigation.

Id. at 1222. The I.R.S. has acquiesced "in result" in *Bedell*. 1987-2 C.B. 1.

4. In Private Letter Ruling 9547004 (1995), six grandchildren pooled their own funds with those of two of their grandparents to create a trust that would terminate upon the death of the last to die of all eight. The I.R.S. determined that the participants were "associates who ha[d] pooled their assets with an object to carry on business and divide the gains therefrom." The I.R.S. therefore ruled that the trust was taxable as an association.

Chapter 2

The Entity as Taxpayer: Basic Principles of Income Taxation under Subchapter J

Subchapter J of chapter 1 of subtitle A of the Internal Revenue Code deals specifically with the income taxation of trusts and estates. It subjects them to a unique, hybrid form of taxation. These entities sometimes pay the tax on all their income. On such occasions they seem to be pure taxpayers. On other occasions trusts and estates pay no tax at all. They reach this enviable position by making (or being required to make) distributions that qualify for the distribution deduction under section 651 or section 661, in amounts equal to the taxable income they otherwise would have. The consequence of an entity's qualification for such a deduction is that the recipient of the distribution must include an appropriate share of the entity's income in his or her gross income. On these occasions trusts and estates seem to be pure conduits. Sometimes the entity simultaneously displays both taxpayer and conduit characteristics, paying the tax on part of its income and passing along the rest to its beneficiaries.

Chapter 2 of this book deals with the entity as taxpayer. Section 641(b) states, "The taxable income of an estate or trust shall be computed in the same manner as in the case of an individual, except as otherwise provided in this part [part I of subchapter J (sections 641 through 685)]." Thus, the structure that describes the income taxation of individuals generally controls. As a consequence, this chapter examines how the familiar principles of basic individual income taxation apply (or must be adapted to apply) to trusts and estates. In a sense, then, this chapter is but a review of what the student has already been exposed to. There are no new central principles. What is gross income? What is deductible in arriving at taxable income? These are the principal inquiries.

A. Gross Income

Internal Revenue Code:
 Sections 1(e); 61(a); 641(a), (b)
Regulations:
 Sections 1.641(a)-1; 1.641(b)-2

Under section 641(b), the rules that control includibility in an individual taxpayer's gross income also control includibility for trusts and estates. Section A of this chapter considers several specific applications of these familiar principles.

Personal Property. Title to the personal property of the decedent, even if specifically bequeathed, is generally in the executor during the course of administration. Not surprisingly, until distribution occurs, the estate is taxable on the income derived from all of the personal property of the decedent. *See, e.g., Woolley v. Malley,* 30 F.2d 73 (1st Cir.), *cert. denied,* 279 U.S. 860 (1929). Even if state law provides that title to personal property is in the decedent's heirs or beneficiaries during administration, income and deductions with respect to the property are nonetheless reportable by the estate. See *Jones v. Whittington,* 194 F.2d 812 (10th Cir. 1952), in which the Tenth Circuit explained:

> If the right to take a capital loss deduction occurring during the period of administration belongs to the heir in whom the title to [personal] property is vested under state law, then perforce he must also return in his individual income tax return income realized therefrom, because income and deductions go hand in hand. Such a holding would in states like Texas nullify the Federal statutory mandate that executors and administrators must file estate income tax returns reporting all income, taking all proper deductions and paying the tax due, as in the case of individuals, because the title to all property of the estate and in their possession as executors or administrators, whether personal or real, vests in the heirs, legatees and devisees.

> Notwithstanding the Texas law placing the title to all property immediately in those entitled to receive it, the Federal Government has power to treat the estate as a separate entity, during the period of administration, for income tax purposes, irrespective of where the legal title of the property might be and this we think is the effect of the Federal income tax law.

Id. at 816–17.

Assets Subject to Elective Share. Smith's Estate v. Commissioner, 168 F.2d 431 (6th Cir. 1948), held that income earned, prior to distribution, on a dissenting widow's share of a Tennessee estate was includible in the estate's gross income. Similarly, the I.R.S. has ruled that income received by a Florida estate on property subsequently judicially assigned to the surviving spouse as an interest in dower was includible, through the date of the decree, in the estate's gross income. Rev. Rul. 71-167, 1971-1 C.B. 163 (declared obsolete, apparently on other grounds, T.D. 8849, 2000-1 C.B. 244, 247).

Real Property. Upon the death of an owner of real property, title to such property is generally said to pass directly from the owner to the owner's heirs or devisees. Nevertheless, until estate administration is complete, under local law or the will the administrator or executor may be entitled to possess and control decedent's real property and to receive all rents and profits therefrom. Where real property is thus "subject to administration," income and deductions derived from it are includible in and deductible from the gross income of the estate under section 641(a)(3). Rev. Rul. 75-61, 1975-1 C.B. 180; Rev. Rul. 57-133, 1957-1 C.B. 200. *See also Anderson v. Wilson,* 289 U.S. 20 (1933); *Estate of B. Brasley Cohen,* 8 T.C. 784 (1947). If real property is not subject to administration, the income is instead directly includible in the gross income of the heir or devisee under section 61(a)(5) or (6). *See Abbot v. Welch,* 31 F. Supp. 369 (D. Mass. 1940); *Guaranty Trust Co. of New York,* 30 B.T.A. 314 (1934); *George L. Craig,* 7 B.T.A. 504 (1927). This is so even if the executor sells the property pursuant to a power of sale for the benefit of the heir or devisee. *See Weber v. Commissioner,* 111 F.2d 766 (2d Cir. 1940); *Arrott v. Heiner,* 92 F.2d 773 (3d Cir. 1937); *Sam S. Brown,* 20 T.C. 73 (1953), *acq.,* 1953-2 C.B. 3. In such a case, any gain or loss realized is that of the heir or devisee.

In Rev. Rul. 59-375, 1959-2 C.B. 161, the personal property of an intestate decedent was insufficient to pay the estate's debts, taxes, and administration expenses. The applicable local law (that of North Carolina) provided that decedent's real property was not subject to administration but permitted his administrator to seek judicial authorization for a sale of such property to pay the estate's obligations. Because many heirs were entitled to share the real property, partition in kind was not feasible, and they, too, sought authorization for a sale. Accordingly, the property was sold by judicially appointed commissioners who distributed to the administrator only that portion of the sales proceeds necessary to pay the estate's obligations and held the rest for the heirs. The I.R.S. ruled that the estate was required to include in its gross income that portion of the capital gains realized on the sales that was proportionate to the share of the proceeds actually received by the administrator. The remainder of the gain did not constitute an amount "received" by the estate within section 641(a)(3).

Community Property. Only one-half of the income from community property is includible in the gross income of the estate of the first spouse to die, even if the entire community is subject to administration. *E.g., Henderson's Estate v. Commissioner,* 155 F.2d 310 (5th Cir. 1946) (Louisiana) ("In whom is the real ownership ... ?"); *Bishop v. Commissioner,* 152 F.2d 389 (9th Cir. 1945) (California) ("ownership is the test of taxability"); *Estate of Bessie A. Woodward,* 24 T.C. 883 (1955) (Texas), *acq.,* 1956-1 C.B. 6, *aff'd sub nom. Barnhill v. Commissioner,* 241 F.2d 496 (5th Cir. 1957); Rev. Rul. 55-726, 1955-2 C.B. 24; *see also United States v. Merrill,* 211 F.2d 297 (9th Cir. 1954) (Washington); *Grimm v. Commissioner,* 89 T.C. 747 (1987) (opinion, dealing with Philippine "conjugal partnership" property, contains detailed analysis of precedents relevant to the American community property issue), *aff'd,* 894 F.2d 1165 (10th Cir. 1990). The other one-half of the income is directly includible in the gross income of the surviving spouse, who, even prior to the death of the first spouse to die, owned an undivided one-half interest in the property.

Sales on Behalf of Beneficiaries. In Rev. Rul. 68-666, 1968-2 C.B. 283, charities were beneficiaries of specific bequests of securities. They asked the executor, who was about to distribute the securities, to sell the securities and to distribute the sales proceeds instead. The I.R.S. ruled that the estate was not required to include in its gross income the gain it realized in complying with the charities' request. The I.R.S. reasoned that the executor's actions were "the equivalent of a distribution of the securities to the beneficiaries, accompanied by an immediate return of the securities by the beneficiaries with instructions to the executor to sell on their behalf." The gain was deemed, therefore, not to have been "received" by the estate.

Discharge of Estate Indebtedness. In *Carl T. Miller Trust v. Commissioner,* 76 T.C. 191 (1981), an estate realized income under section 61(a)(12) from the discharge of indebtedness in the year Wisconsin's nonclaim statute barred payment of debts owed by the decedent to family corporations, which had failed to file claims against the estate. The court emphasized that the Wisconsin statute provided that claims against an estate were "forever barred" unless filed within the specified time period and that the estate could not waive the bar. To the same effect is *Estate of Emelil Bankhead*, 60 T.C. 535 (1973) (Alabama). Similarly, if an estate satisfies indebtedness by the transfer of assets in kind, it realizes gain or loss to the extent of any difference between its basis in the assets transferred and the amount of the claim discharged. Rev. Rul. 74-178, 1974-1 C.B. 196. (As discussed, *infra*, ch. 3, sec. G(1)(a), the same principle leads to realization of gain or loss if an estate transfers non-cash property to a beneficiary who is entitled to a cash bequest.)

B. Deductions

Internal Revenue Code:
    Section 641(b)

Regulation:
    Section 1.641(b)-1

Under section 641(b), the allowability of deductions in computing the taxable income of an estate or a trust is generally determined under the same rules that apply to an individual taxpayer. Section B of this chapter examines the deductions most frequently available to trusts and estates.

The fact that a decedent or a grantor would have been entitled to a deduction had he or she paid a particular expense is irrelevant to the allowability of a deduction to the entity that pays the expense, except where section 691(b), discussed *infra* (ch. 6, sec. B), applies. The entity itself must be entitled to the deduction. Thus, in *Greggar P. Sletteland*, 43 T.C. 602 (1965), the court held that payment by an estate of notes endorsed by the decedent in his business did not entitle the estate to an income tax deduction under section 165(c), though the decedent might have been so entitled had he paid the notes. The court reasoned that, unlike the decedent, the estate was not involved in a "trade or business" (section 165(c)(1)). Neither had the estate entered into a transaction "for profit" (section 165(c)(2)). Obviously, the estate had also not incurred "fire, storm, shipwreck, or other casualty or ... theft" (section 165(c)(3)). The estate was, however, entitled, under sections 163 and 691(b), to deduct any interest it paid on the notes.

Similarly, an estate or trust is not entitled to a deduction for expenses paid by another. Thus, in *Sletteland* the court also held that the estate was not entitled to deduct that portion of the interest paid by the decedent's widow in her individual, as opposed to her fiduciary, capacity.

1. Interest

Internal Revenue Code:
  Sections 163(a), (d), (h); 265(a)(2)

Section 163 allows all taxpayers—including estates and trusts—to deduct interest paid on indebtedness. The indebtedness must, however, be that of the taxpayer involved. In *Jones v. Hassett*, 45 F. Supp. 195 (D. Mass. 1942), a testamentary trust paid interest on an estate tax deficiency. The court held that the trust was not entitled to an interest deduction, because the interest had accrued on indebtedness of the estate, not on that of the trust.

Sometimes local law requires an executor to pay interest on undistributed general bequests. In such a case, is the estate entitled to deduct the payments as "interest" under section 163? Rev. Rul. 73-322, 1973-2 C.B. 44, ruled that such payments were deductible under section 163. The I.R.S. also ruled that the interest would be treated as payable with regard to an indebtedness of the estate and not as part of the bequest; thus, the payee-beneficiary was required to include the payments in gross income as "interest" under section 61(a)(4). *United States v. Folckemer*, 307 F.2d 171 (5th Cir. 1962), is to the same effect. *Folckemer* held that such payments were taxable to the payee-beneficiary in the year of receipt under section 61(a)(4) (as interest), rather than in accordance with section 662(c) (as distributions by an estate to a beneficiary), notwithstanding that the applicable local law (that of California) appeared to treat the payments as "part of" the underlying bequest. The regulations on the application of the separate share rule to estates take a similar position. *See* Treas. Reg. § 1.663(c)-5, Ex. 7(ii) ("interest" payment on a surviving spouse's elective share).

The Tax Reform Act of 1986 enacted section 163(h), which disallows deduction of "personal interest" in the case of any taxpayer "other than a corporation." The definition of "personal interest" includes several important exceptions: "investment interest," defined as interest "on indebtedness properly allocable to property held for investment," IRC §§ 163(d)(3)(A), (h)(2)(B); "qualified residence interest," defined as interest on certain types of indebtedness secured by a "qualified residence" of the taxpayer, IRC §§ 163(h)(2)(D), (h)(3); interest incurred because of deferral of the federal estate tax under section 6163, IRC § 163(h)(2)(E); *but see* IRC § 163(k) (disallowing a deduction for interest on estate tax deferred under section 6166); and interest allowable as a deduction under section 221 for educational loans, IRC § 163(h)(2)(F). Nonetheless, section 163(h) clearly denies deductibility of some types of interest previously deductible by estates. For example, interest paid by an estate on unsecured indebtedness incurred by the decedent for personal reasons is now generally not deductible. In addition, section 163(h) may threaten the deductibility, under section 163, of interest on undistributed bequests, discussed *supra*. See *Schwan v. United States*, 264 F. Supp. 2d 887 (D.S.D. 2003), in which the court denied a deduction under section 163 for interest paid on deferred legacies, reasoning such payments were not "investment interest," within the meaning of section 163(d)(3)(A). After study of chapter 3, consider whether, despite authorities such as *Folckemer*, such payments ought to be deductible instead under section 661.

2. Taxes

———

Internal Revenue Code:
Sections 164(a); 265(a)(1); 275(a)(1)

———

Revenue Ruling 61-86
1961-1 C.B. 41

Advice has been requested regarding the deductibility of State income taxes paid by a fiduciary of an estate or trust which receives taxable income, tax-exempt interest income, and other exempt income.

Section 641(b) of the Internal Revenue Code of 1954 provides that the taxable income of an estate or trust shall be computed in the same manner as in the case of an individual, with certain exceptions not here material.

[The I.R.S. quotes a predecessor of section 164(a).]

Section 212 of the Code provides, in part, that in the case of an individual, there shall be allowed as a deduction all the ordinary and necessary expenses paid or incurred during the taxable year for the production or collection of income.

State income tax imposed upon net income of estates and trusts is deductible from income under the provisions of section 164 of the Code in the same manner as in the case of an individual. Since State income tax is not an expense relating to the production of income, its deductibility by an estate or trust is not controlled by section 212 of the Code.

[The I.R.S. quotes a predecessor of section 265(a)(1).]

From the foregoing, it is evident that section 265 of the Code prohibits the deduction of an item otherwise allowable as a deduction, which is attributable to tax-exempt interest income only if such item is deductible under section 212 of the Code as an expense related to the production of income. State income tax is not considered an expense for the production of income, deductible under section 212 of the Code. However, the portion of such tax allocable to exempt interest income is deductible under section 164 of the Code. State income tax attributable to the income of an estate or trust which is subject to the Federal income tax is also deductible under that section. However, any State income tax allocable to exempt income, other than exempt interest income, is nondeductible under section 265 of the Code.

Accordingly, it is held that in the case of an estate or trust only that portion of its State income taxes which is allocable to exempt income, other than exempt interest income, is nondeductible under section 265 of the Code. That portion of such taxes attributable to exempt interest income and to income subject to the Federal income tax is deductible under section 164 of the Code.

Illustrative Material

The practical import of Rev. Rul. 61-86 may be illustrated by a simple example. Consider a trust whose income is subject to Virginia income tax and that holds bonds issued by a North Carolina municipality. The municipal bond interest would be excluded from gross income for federal income tax purposes under section 103, but would be included in gross income for state income tax purposes. The state income taxes paid would be deductible under section 164(a), notwithstanding section 265(a)(1).

3. Expenses Incurred in the Production of Income

a. In General

Internal Revenue Code:
  Sections 212; 67(a), (b), (c), (e)

Regulation:
  Section 1.212-1

Proposed Regulation:
  Section 1.67-4

Trust of Bingham v. Commissioner
325 U.S. 365 (1945)

MR. CHIEF JUSTICE STONE delivered the opinion of the Court.

Petitioners are the trustees of a testamentary trust created for a term of twenty-one years under the will of Mary Lily (Flagler) Bingham. The testatrix bequeathed to the trustees the residue of her estate, including a large number of securities. The trustees were empowered in their discretion to sell any of the property held in trust (except certain securities of two companies designated as the "principal properties"), to invest and reinvest the proceeds and the income from the trust fund, and to use the proceeds and the income for the benefit of the principal properties and for the "maintenance, administration or development of the said principal or subsidiary properties." The trustees were to pay specified amounts annually to certain legatees. When the niece of the testatrix reached a certain age, she was to receive from the trust a specified amount in cash or securities. At the end of twenty-one years, the trustees were directed to pay other legacies, and to distribute the remainder of the fund in equal parts to a brother and two sisters of the testatrix.

In 1935 petitioners paid the bequest to the niece partly in securities. The Commissioner assessed a deficiency of over $365,000 for income tax upon the appreciation in value of the securities while they were in petitioners' hands. In contesting unsuccessfully this deficiency, petitioners paid out in the year 1940 approximately $16,000 in counsel fees and expenses. In that year, also, petitioners paid out about $9,000 for legal advice in connection with the payment of one of the cash legacies, and in connection with tax and other problems arising upon the expiration of the trust and relating to the final distribution of the trust fund among the three residuary legatees.

The question is whether these legal expenses, paid in 1940, are deductible from gross income in the computation of the trust's income tax, as "non-trade" or "nonbusiness" expenses within the meaning of §23(a)(2) [predecessor of section 212] of the Internal Revenue Code. That section ... authorizes the deduction of "all the ordinary and necessary expenses paid or incurred during the taxable year for the production or collection of income, or for the management, conservation, or maintenance of property held for the production of income." Section 162 [predecessor of section 641(b)] of the Code, so far as now relevant, makes §23(a)(2) applicable to the income taxation of trusts.

Petitioners, in their income tax return for 1940, took deductions for the legal expenses. The Commissioner disallowed the deductions and assessed a tax deficiency, and petitioners filed the present suit in the Tax Court to set aside the assessment. That Court, after finding the facts as we have stated them, found that the trust property was held for the production of income; that all the items in question were ordinary and necessary expenses of the management of the trust property; and that the fees and expenses for contesting the income tax deficiency assessment were also for the conservation of the trust property. It therefore concluded that all were rightly deducted in calculating the taxable net income of the trust. 2 T.C. 853.

On the Government's petition for review, the Court of Appeals for the Second Circuit reversed. 145 F.2d 568. We granted certiorari, 324 U.S. 835, on a petition which asserted as grounds for the writ that the decision of the Court of Appeals ... conflicted in principle with *Commissioner v. Heininger,* 320 U.S. 467, and *Kornhauser v. United States,* 276 U.S. 145.

The Court of Appeals left undisturbed the Tax Court's findings that the questioned items were ordinary and necessary expenses for the management or conservation of the trust property, but it held that the fees for contesting the tax deficiency were nevertheless not deductible under §23(a)(2). [Section 212(3) was enacted later.] It thought that the expenses of contesting the income tax had nothing to do with the production of income and hence were not deductible as expenses "for the production of income" within the meaning of the statute. The court also thought that these expenses were not deductible, because they were paid in connection with property held by the trustees "ready for distribution," and hence not "for the production of income." Similarly it held that the fees for professional services rendered in connection with the payment of legacies and the distribution of the trust fund, were not expenses relating to the management of property held for the production of income, since they were rendered after the trust term had expired and when the property was ready for distribution.

The Government makes like arguments here. In addition it urges that the expenses in connection with the distribution of the trust fund were not expenses of management of the trust property held for the production of income but only expenses relating to its devolution; and that the expenses are not deductible under §23(a)(2) because there was no proximate relationship between the expenses when paid and the property then held in trust.

We think that these objections to the deductions fail to take proper account of the plain language of §23(a)(2), and the purpose of the section as disclosed by its statutory setting and legislative history....

The requirement of §23(a)(2) that deductible expenses be "ordinary and necessary" implies that they must be reasonable in amount and must bear a reasonable and proximate relation to the management of property held for the production of income. See H. Rep. No. 2333, 77th Cong., 2d Sess., p. 75; Sen. Rep. No. 1631, 77th Cong., 2d Sess., p. 88....

Here the decision of the Court of Appeals was that the expenses were not deductible because they were not for the purpose of producing income or capital gain, and because the trust property, being ready for distribution, was no longer held for the production of income. The terms of the trust, the nature of the property, and the duties of the trustees with respect to it, were all found by the Tax Court and are not challenged. The questions whether, on the facts found, the expenses in question are nondeductible, either because they were not to produce income or because they were related to the management of property which was not held for the production of income, turn in this case on the meaning of the words of §23(a)(2), "property held for the production of income." ...

We turn to the first ground for reversal relied on by the Court of Appeals, that the property was held for distribution, and no longer for the production of income. The fact that the trustees, in the administration of the trust, were required to invest its corpus for the production of income and to devote the income to the purposes of the trust, establishes, as the Tax Court held, that the trust property was held for the production of income during the stated term of the trust. The decisive question is whether the property ceased to be held for the production of income because, as the trust term reached its expiry date, the trustees were under a duty to distribute the property among the remaindermen.

It is true that expiration of the trust operated to change the beneficiaries entitled to receive the income of the trust property, from those entitled to the income during the term of the trust to the remaindermen. But the duty of the trustees to hold and conserve the trust property, and until distribution, to receive income from it, continued. The property did not cease to be held for the production of income because, upon the expiration of the trust and until distribution, the trustees were under an additional duty to distribute the trust fund, or because the trustees, upon distribution, were then accountable to new and different beneficiaries, the residuary legatees, both for the principal of the fund and any income accumulating after the expiry date. To exclude from the deduction privilege, expenses which the Tax Court has held to be expenses of management of the trust, on the ground that the trust fund, upon the expiration of the trust, ceased to be "held for the production of the income" would be to disregard the Tax Court's findings of fact and the words of the statute, and would defeat its obvious purpose.

Nor is there merit in the court's conclusion that the expenses were not deductible because they were not for the production of income. Section 23(a)(2) provides for two classes of deductions, expenses "for the production ... of income" and expenses of "management, conservation, or maintenance of property held for the production of income." To read this section as requiring that expenses be paid for the production of income in order to be deductible, is to make unnecessary and to read out of the section the provision for the deduction of expenses of management of property held for the production of income.

There is no warrant for such a construction. Section 23(a)(2) is comparable and *in parti materia* with §23(a)(1) [predecessor of section 162], authorizing the deduction of business or trade expenses. Such expenses need not relate directly to the production of income for the business. It is enough that the expense, if "ordinary and necessary," is directly connected with or proximately results from the conduct of the business. *Kornhauser v. United States, supra,* 152–153; *Commissioner v. Heininger; supra,* 470–471. The effect of §23(a)(2) was to provide for a class of nonbusiness deductions coextensive with the business deductions allowed by §23(a)(1), except for the fact that, since they were not incurred in connection with a business, the section made it necessary that they be incurred for the production of income or in the management or conservation of property held for the production of income. *McDonald v. Commissioner,* [323 U.S. 57,] 61–62, 66; and see H. Rep. No. 2333, 77th Cong., 2d Sess., pp. 46, 74–76; S. Rep. No. 1631, 77th Cong., 2d Sess., pp. 87–88.

Since there is no requirement that business expenses be for the production of income, there is no reason for that requirement in the case of like expenses of managing a trust, so long as they are in connection with the management of property which is held for the production of income. Section 23(a)(2) thus treats the trust as an entity for producing income comparable to a business enterprise, and like §23(a)(1) permits deductions of management expenses of the trust, even though the particular expense was not an expense directly producing income. It follows that all of the items of expense here in question are deductible if, as the Tax Court has held, they are expenses of management or conservation of the trust fund, whether their expenditure did or did not result in the production of income.

The Government contends that the expenses incurred in connection with the distribution of the corpus of the trust to legatees are not deductible, because they are not expenses of managing income producing property, but expenses in connection with the devolution of the property. If the suggestion is correct, it would follow that expenses incurred in distributing the income of the trust to the income beneficiaries are likewise not deductible, since the distribution of income is also a devolution of trust property. But the duties of the trustees were not only to hold the property for the production of income and to collect the income, but also, in administering the trust, to distribute the income and the principal so held from time to time, and the remainder of the principal at the expiration of the trust. Performance of each of these duties is an integral part of carrying out the trust enterprise. Accordingly, as the Tax Court held, the costs of distribution here were quite as much expenses of a function of "management" of the trust property as were expenses incurred in producing the trust income; and if "ordinary and necessary," they were deductible.

* * *

What we have said applies with equal force to the expenses of contesting the tax deficiency. Section 23(a)(2) does not restrict deductions to those litigation expenses which alone produce income. On the contrary, by its terms and in analogy with the rule under §23(a)(1), the business expense section, the trust, a taxable entity like a business, may deduct litigation expenses when they are directly connected with or proximately result from the enterprise—the management of property held for production of income. *Kornhauser v. United States, supra,* 152–153; *Commissioner v. Heininger, supra,* 470–471. The Tax Court could find as a matter of fact, as it did, that the expenses of contesting the income taxes were a proximate result of the holding of the property for income. And we cannot say, as a matter of law, that such expenses are any less deductible than expenses of suits to recover income. Cf. *Commissioner v. Heininger; supra.*

* * *

We find no error of law in the judgment of the Tax Court. Its judgment will be affirmed and that of the Court of Appeals reversed.

[The concurring opinion of Mr. Justice Frankfurter is omitted.]

Illustrative Material

A trust may not deduct, under section 212, compensation paid to its trustee for services performed as executor of the estate of its grantor. *Mary E. Burrow Trust,* 39 T.C. 1080 (1963), *aff'd,* 333 F.2d 66 (10th Cir. 1964). The Tax Court reasoned that taxpayers "should not be allowed to juggle expenses between the trust and the probate estate and thereby gain a tax benefit by virtue of the fact that the [trustee] was serving both as trustee and as executor." 39 T.C. at 1085–86.

In *Schwan v. United States,* 264 F. Supp. 2d 887 (D.S.D. 2003), the court denied a deduction under section 212 for interest paid on deferred legacies. The court reasoned that, given the premature distribution to charity of the bulk of the assets that would otherwise have been available to satisfy the estate's tax obligations, such payments were neither necessarily incurred for the benefit of the estate, incurred in the conservation of estate assets, nor incurred in connection with the determination of any tax, within the meaning of the statute.

———————

Alfred I. duPont Testamentary Trust v. Commissioner
514 F.2d 917 (5th. Cir. 1975)

CLARK, Circuit Judge:

The Commissioner disallowed deductions claimed by the taxpayer, a testamentary trust created under the will of Alfred I. duPont, in the tax years 1966 and 1967 for expenses of maintaining an estate owned by the taxpayer but which was then being used as Mrs. duPont's home. The expense deductions were claimed to be ordinary and necessary expenses under Int.Rev.Code of 1954 §212 because the estate was rental property or alternatively because the estate was part of an income producing entity comprised of the estate and securities owned by taxpayer. The Tax Court upheld the Commissioner, Alfred I. duPont Testamentary Trust, 62 T.C. 36 (1974).... We affirm in part and remand.

About 1910 Alfred I. duPont built a mansion on a 300 acre tract in Brandywine Hundred, New Castle County, Delaware which he named "Nemours." Mr. duPont lived at Nemours with his wife, Jessie Ball duPont, from their marriage in 1921 until 1926. After 1926 they resided principally in Florida, but spent an average of two months a year at Nemours. By the time of his death in 1935 Nemours included formal gardens, man-made lakes, a greenhouse, large monuments built in honor of Mr. duPont's ancestors, an extensive system of roadways, bridges, walkways, stables, and various other buildings.

In 1925 Mr. duPont organized Nemours, Inc. (the corporation) and transferred to it full title to the mansion house and grounds in exchange for all of the corporation's stock. Subsequently Mr. and Mrs. duPont leased Nemours for the term of their joint lives plus the life of the survivor. The agreed rental was one dollar a year. The duPonts were required by the lease agreement to pay all taxes and the expense of the upkeep of the buildings and grounds. In January 1929 Mr. duPont transferred to the corporation 20,000 shares of preferred stock of Almour Securities, Inc. valued at 2,000,000 dollars. In exchange for this transfer, the lease agreement was amended to provide that the corporation would pay taxes and expenses of upkeep.

* * *

Mr. duPont died in 1935, survived by his wife. His will vested title to the stock of the corporation in his executors who were instructed by the will to set up a trust to continue the maintenance of the grounds. The stock of the corporation was to comprise the corpus of this testamentary trust along with large blocks of other securities. [In 1937 the corporation was dissolved.] Mrs. duPont was a trustee and the principal income beneficiary for her life. The trust was to pay her 200,000 dollars a year plus any income remaining after the payment of specified annuities. The trustees were directed to organize a charitable foundation at the death of Mrs. duPont and to transfer to it the trust assets....

From 1962 until her death in 1970, Mrs. duPont resided full time at Nemours....

During 1966 and 1967, the tax years in question, the gross income of the trust was 13,000,000 dollars. Of this sum 11,000,000 dollars was distributed to Mrs. duPont. The trust spent 255,753 dollars in 1966 and 274,451 dollars in 1967 for general maintenance of the Nemours estate. An additional 114,284 dollars was expended during 1967 for repaving existing paved roadways and walkways; paving existing unpaved roadways; rehabilitating various structures such as a classical temple, ornamental balustrades, steps, fountains, terraces, flagstones, and urns; and purchasing a jeep and a dump truck. The Commissioner disallowed all of these deductions....

Prepaid Rent

The taxpayer maintains that the deductions were proper under Int.Rev.Code of 1954 §212(1)....

Taxpayer contends that under the 1929 amendment to the 1925 lease to the duPonts, the transfer of 2,000,000 dollars worth of Almour securities constituted pre-paid rent, and therefore that, insofar as the corporation and the trust were concerned, Nemours was income producing rental property.

The attempt to characterize the transfer of the Almour securities as pre-paid rent was correctly rejected by the Tax Court both as a matter of form and of substance. No part of these assets or the dividends therefrom were ever reported as taxable rental income on the corporation's income tax returns. The 1929 agreement clearly establishes that Mr. duPont conveyed the Almour securities to the corporation which he continuously owned and controlled until the time of his death, to enable it to pay taxes and maintenance expenses he had previously borne personally. The only payment specified as rent in the initial agreement and in the 1929 amendment was a token 1 dollar a year. The record contains no other indication that the conveyance of Almour stock was intended to constitute pre-paid rent. Neither the documentation nor the conduct of the parties indicates that the securities were transferred for any purpose other than to relieve the duPonts of the day-to-day burdens of administering the estate.

No attempt was made to show what the anticipated expenses of maintaining the estate might be as compared to the income produced by or the total value of Almour securities. In short, the taxpayer trust simply failed to carry its burden of proving that Nemours was rental property in these tax years....

Property Held for the Production of Income

Alternatively, the taxpayer urges the upkeep and maintenance expense was deductible under section 212(2)....

To support this argument before us, taxpayer relies principally on Bingham's Trust v. Commissioner of Internal Revenue, 325 U.S. 365, 65 S.Ct. 1232, 89 L.Ed. 1670 (1945) in which the Court held that legal fees incurred to contest an income tax deficiency were deductible since they were funds expended for the conservation of trust property which was held for the production of income. The taxpayer asserts that *Bingham's* rationale covers the expenses incurred in maintaining Nemours even though Nemours was not strictly property held for the production of income.

The thrust of the argument is that the taxpayer trust, an entity for the production of income comparable to a business enterprise, could deduct these expenses as maintenance expenses even though Nemours did not directly produce income, because payment of the maintenance and upkeep expense was a fundamental duty of the trustees in the administration of the trust. This interpretation glosses over the fact that a threshold determination in *Bingham* was that the property which the expenditure protected was held for the production of income. Although it was the duty of the trustees to maintain Nemours, Nemours was not property held for the production of income. See Estate of Mortimer B. Fuller, 9 T.C. 1069 (1947), aff'd per curiam 171 F.2d 704 (3d Cir. 1948). In the case at bar, the question which concerned the Court in *Bingham*—whether the expense incurred was connected with, or proximately resulted from, the management of property held for production of income—is never reached.

Despite the lease agreements between the wholly-owned corporation and the duPonts and the controlling terms of Mr. duPont's testamentary trust, Nemours remained the duPonts' personal residence. It was the antithesis of income producing property. The expenses incurred in the maintenance and upkeep of this private residence never were deductible expenses relating to property held for the present or future production of income. See Eugene H. Walet, Jr., 31 T.C. 461 (1958), aff'd per curiam 272 F.2d 694 (5th. Cir. 1959).

Alternative Trust Deductions

* * *

The taxpayer makes [the] *arguendo* assertion, if the deductions are denied under section 212, that the Tax Court erred in not treating them as deductions allowable under section 651 or 661 because they were amounts expended by a trust for its beneficiary. Section 651 permits a trust to deduct current income required by the terms of the trust to be distributed currently. Its companion, section 652, provides that such required amount shall be included in the gross income of the beneficiary. Section 661 permits a deduction by a trust when accumulated income is required to be distributed, paid or credited in the current tax year, such as the year in which a trust is terminated. Its companion, section 662, requires such distribution, payment or credit to be reported as a part of the gross income of the beneficiary. The Tax Court did not mention this contention in its opinion.

The obligation to maintain Nemours was created by the 1929 amendment to the lease agreement. It was, in that year, a commitment by a wholly owned corporation to pay personal living expenses[7] of Mr. and Mrs. duPont which he funded by the conveyance of Almour stock. It primarily retained this same personal expense character in 1966 and 1967 as to Mrs. duPont, a trustee as well as the principal beneficiary of the trust. The record before us does not reveal whether Mrs. duPont reported any part of these payments as income to her in either tax year. She would have been required to do this by sections 652 and 662, if the payments had qualified for deductions by the trust as funds distributed to her pursuant to the trust agreement under section 651 or 661. *Cf.* Commissioner of Internal Revenue v. Plant, 76 F.2d 8 (2d Cir. 1935).

… We decline to determine the right of the trust to deduct these challenged amounts under section 651 or 661 until the matter has been squarely presented to and decided by the Tax Court. Except as expressly set out herein, we intimate no views on this issue.

Conclusion

Deductions are a matter of legislative grace. *See* Deputy v. DuPont, 308 U.S. 488, 60 S.Ct. 363, 84 L.Ed. 416 (1940). The deductions claimed by the taxpayer here must fit into

---

7. Section 262 prohibits deductions for personal living or family expenses.

a statutory category of deductibility, else the trustees must carry out their fiduciary duty at the expense of the trust, rather than the public fisc.

We agree with the Tax Court that the trustees were entitled to no deduction for the expenses incurred in the maintenance and upkeep of Nemours during Mrs. duPont's life under [section 212]. We reach no conclusion as to deductibility under section 651 or 661, nor as to the collateral effect the allowance of such deductions would have had on Mrs. duPont's tax liability under section 652 or 662, nor whether limitations would bar the present assessment or allocation of such amounts to her personally. The cause is remanded for such further proceedings as the Tax Court may determine are necessary to enable it to consider and decide these issues. [The Tax Court's subsequent opinion is *infra* (ch. 3, sec. C).]

Affirmed in part and remanded.

Illustrative Material

Moreell v. United States, 221 F. Supp. 864 (W.D. Pa. 1963), similarly held that a trust was not entitled to deduct, presumably under section 212, the expenses of maintaining its primary beneficiary's private residence.

Knight v. Commissioner
128 S. Ct. 782 (2008)

Chief Justice ROBERTS delivered the opinion [for a unanimous] Court.

Under the Internal Revenue Code, individuals may subtract from their taxable income certain itemized deductions, but only to the extent the deductions exceed 2% of adjusted gross income. A trust may also claim those deductions, also subject to the 2% floor, except that costs incurred in the administration of the trust, which would not have been incurred if the trust property were not held by a trust, may be deducted without regard to the floor. In the case of individuals, investment advisory fees are subject to the 2% floor; the question presented is whether such fees are also subject to the floor when incurred by a trust. We hold that they are and therefore affirm the judgment below, albeit for different reasons than those given by the Court of Appeals.

The Internal Revenue Code imposes a tax on the "taxable income" of both individuals and trusts. 26 U.S.C. § 1(a). The Code instructs that the calculation of taxable income begins with a determination of "gross income," capaciously defined as "all income from whatever source derived." § 61(a). "Adjusted gross income" is then calculated by subtracting from gross income certain "above-the-line" deductions, such as trade and business expenses and losses from the sale or exchange of property. § 62(a). Finally, taxable income is calculated by subtracting from adjusted gross income "itemized deductions"— also known as "below-the-line" deductions—defined as all allowable deductions other than the "above-the-line" deductions identified in § 62(a) and the deduction for personal exemptions allowed under § 151 (2000 ed. and Supp. V). § 63(d) (2000 ed.).

Before the passage of the Tax Reform Act of 1986, 100 Stat. 2085, below-the-line deductions were deductible in full. This system resulted in significant complexity and potential for abuse, requiring "extensive [taxpayer] recordkeeping with regard to what commonly are small expenditures," as well as "significant administrative and enforcement problems for the Internal Revenue Service." H.R.Rep. No. 99-426, p. 109 (1985).

In response, Congress enacted what is known as the "2% floor" by adding § 67 to the Code. Section 67(a) provides that "the miscellaneous itemized deductions for any taxable year shall be allowed only to the extent that the aggregate of such deductions exceeds 2 percent of adjusted gross income." The term "miscellaneous itemized deductions" is defined to include all itemized deductions other than certain ones specified in § 67(b). Investment advisory fees are deductible pursuant to 26 U.S.C. § 212. Because § 212 is not listed in § 67(b) as one of the categories of expenses that may be deducted in full, such fees are "miscellaneous itemized deductions" subject to the 2% floor. 26 CFR § 1.67-1T(a)(1)(ii) (2007).

Section 67(e) makes the 2% floor generally applicable not only to individuals but also to estates and trusts,[1] with one exception relevant here. Under this exception, "the adjusted gross income of an estate or trust shall be computed in the same manner as in the case of an individual, except that ... the deductions for costs which are paid or incurred in connection with the administration of the estate or trust and which would not have been incurred if the property were not held in such trust or estate ... shall be treated as allowable" and not subject to the 2% floor. § 67(e)(1).

Petitioner Michael J. Knight is the trustee of the William L. Rudkin Testamentary Trust, established in the State of Connecticut in 1967. In 2000, the Trustee hired Warfield Associates, Inc., to provide advice with respect to investing the Trust's assets. At the beginning of the tax year, the Trust held approximately $2.9 million in marketable securities, and it paid Warfield $22,241 in investment advisory fees for the year. On its fiduciary income tax return for 2000, the Trust reported total income of $624,816, and it deducted in full the investment advisory fees paid to Warfield. After conducting an audit, respondent Commissioner of Internal Revenue found that these investment advisory fees were miscellaneous itemized deductions subject to the 2% floor. The Commissioner therefore allowed the Trust to deduct the investment advisory fees, which were the only claimed deductions subject to the floor, only to the extent that they exceeded 2% of the Trust's adjusted gross income. The discrepancy resulted in a tax deficiency of $4,448.

The Trust filed a petition in the United States Tax Court seeking review of the assessed deficiency. It argued that the Trustee's fiduciary duty to act as a "prudent investor" under the Connecticut Uniform Prudent Investor Act, Conn. Gen. Stat. §§ 45a-541a to 45a-541 (2007),[2] required the Trustee to obtain investment advisory services, and therefore to pay investment advisory fees. The Trust argued that such fees are accordingly unique to trusts and therefore fully deductible under 26 U.S.C. § 67(e)(1). The Tax Court rejected this argument, holding that § 67(e)(1) allows full deductibility only for expenses that are not commonly incurred outside the trust setting. Because investment advisory fees are commonly incurred by individuals, the Tax Court held that they are subject to the 2% floor when incurred by a trust. *Rudkin Testamentary Trust v. Commissioner,* 124 T.C. 304, 309–311 (2005).

The Trust appealed to the United States Court of Appeals for the Second Circuit. The Court of Appeals concluded that, in determining whether costs such as investment advi-

1. Because this case is only about trusts, we generally refer to trusts throughout, but the analysis applies equally to estates.
2. Forty-four States and the District of Columbia have adopted versions of the Uniform Prudent Investor Act. See 7B U.L.A. 1–2 (2006) (listing States that have enacted the Uniform Prudent Investor Act). Five of the remaining six States have adopted their own versions of the prudent investor standard. See Del. Code Ann., Tit. 12, § 3302 (1995 ed. and 2006 Supp.); Ga. Code Ann. § 53-12-287 (1997); La. Stat. Ann. § 9:2127 (West 2005); Md. Est. & Trusts Code Ann. § 15-114 (Lexis 2001); S.D. Codified Laws § 55-5-6 (2004). Kentucky, the only remaining State, applies the prudent investor standard only in certain circumstances. See Ky. Rev. Stat. Ann. § 286.3-277 (Lexis 2007 Cum. Supp.); §§ 386.454(1), 386.502 (Supp. 2007).

sory fees are fully deductible or subject to the 2% floor, § 67(e) "directs the inquiry toward the counterfactual condition of assets held individually instead of in trust," and requires "an objective determination of whether the particular cost is one that is peculiar to trusts and one that individuals are incapable of incurring." 467 F.3d 149, 155, 156 (2006). The court held that because investment advisory fees were "costs of a type that *could* be incurred if the property were held individually rather than in trust," deduction of such fees by the Trust was subject to the 2% floor. *Id.*, at 155–156.

The Courts of Appeals are divided on the question presented. The Sixth Circuit has held that investment advisory fees are fully deductible. *O'Neill v. Commissioner,* 994 F.2d 302, 304 (1993). In contrast, both the Fourth and Federal Circuits have held that such fees are subject to the 2% floor, because they are "commonly" or "customarily" incurred outside of trusts. See *Scott v. United States,* 328 F.3d 132, 140 (C.A.4 2003); *Mellon Bank, N.A. v. United States,* 265 F.3d 1275, 1281 (C.A.Fed. 2001). The Court of Appeals below came to the same conclusion, but as noted announced a more exacting test, allowing "full deduction only for those costs that *could not* have been incurred by an individual property owner." 467 F.3d, at 156 (emphasis added). We granted the Trustee's petition for certiorari to resolve the conflict, 551 U.S. ___, 127 S.Ct. 3005, 168 L.Ed.2d 725 (2007), and now affirm.

II

"We start, as always, with the language of the statute." *Williams v. Taylor,* 529 U.S. 420, 431, 120 S.Ct. 1479, 146 L.Ed.2d 435 (2000). Section 67(e) sets forth a general rule: "[T]he adjusted gross income of [a] ... trust shall be computed in the same manner as in the case of an individual." That is, trusts can ordinarily deduct costs subject to the same 2% floor that applies to individuals' deductions. Section 67(e) provides for an exception to the 2% floor when two conditions are met. First, the relevant cost must be "paid or incurred in connection with the administration of the ... trust." § 67(e)(1). Second, the cost must be one "which would not have been incurred if the property were not held in such trust." *Ibid.*

In applying the statute, the Court of Appeals below asked whether the cost at issue *could* have been incurred by an individual.[3] This approach flies in the face of the statutory language. The provision at issue asks whether the costs "would not have been incurred if the property were not held" in trust, *ibid.*, not, as the Court of Appeals would have it, whether the costs "could not have been incurred" in such a case, 467 F.3d, at 156. The fact that an individual could not do something is one reason he would not, but not the only possible reason. If Congress had intended the Court of Appeals' reading, it easily could have replaced "would" in the statute with "could," and presumably would have.

---

3. The Solicitor General embraces this position in this Court, arguing that the Court of Appeals' approach represents the best reading of the statute and establishes an easily administrable rule. See Brief for Respondent 17–20, 22. Indeed, after the Court of Appeals' decision, the Commissioner adopted that court's reading of the statute in a proposed regulation. See Section 67 Limitations on Estates or Trusts, 72 Fed. Reg. 41243, 41245 (2007) (notice of proposed rulemaking) (a trust-related cost is exempted from the 2% floor only if "an individual *could not* have incurred that cost in connection with property not held in an estate or trust" (emphasis added)). The Government did not advance this argument before the Court of Appeals. See Brief for Appellee in No. 05-5151-AG (CA2), pp. 3–4, 22–24. In fact, the notice of proposed rulemaking appears to be the first time the Government has ever taken this position, and we are the first Court to which the argument has been made in a brief. See Brief for United States in *Mellon Bank v. United States,* No. 01-5015 (CA Fed.), p. 27 ("[I]f a trust-related administrative expense is also customarily or habitually incurred outside of trusts, then it is subject to the two-percent floor"); Brief for United States in *Scott v. United States,* No. 02-1464 (CA4), p. 27 (same).

The fact that it did not adopt this readily available and apparent alternative strongly supports rejecting the Court of Appeals' reading.[4]

Moreover, if the Court of Appeals' reading were correct, it is not clear why Congress would have included in the statute the first clause of §67(e)(1). If the only costs that are fully deductible are those that *could* not be incurred outside the trust context—that is, that could *only* be incurred by trusts—then there would be no reason to place the further condition on full deductibility that the costs be "paid or incurred in connection with the administration of the ... trust," §67(e)(1). We can think of no expense that could be incurred exclusively by a trust but would nevertheless *not* be "paid or incurred in connection with" its administration.

The Trustee argues that the exception in §67(e)(1) "establishes a straightforward causation test." Brief for Petitioner 22. The proper inquiry, the Trustee contends, is "whether a particular expense of a particular trust or estate was caused by the fact that the property was held in the trust or estate." *Ibid.* Investment advisory fees incurred by a trust, the argument goes, meet this test because these costs are caused by the trustee's obligation "to obtain advice on investing trust assets in compliance with the Trustees' particular fiduciary duties." *Ibid.* We reject this reading as well.

On the Trustee's view, the statute operates only to distinguish costs that are incurred by virtue of a trustee's fiduciary duties from those that are not. But all (or nearly all) of a trust's expenses are incurred because the trustee has a duty to incur them; otherwise, there would be no reason for the trust to incur the expense in the first place. See G. Bogert & G. Bogert, Law of Trusts and Trustees §801, p. 134 (2d rev. ed. 1981) ("[T]he payment for expenses must be reasonably necessary to facilitate administration of the trust"). As an example of a type of trust-related expense that would be subject to the 2% floor, the Trustee offers "expenses for routine maintenance of real property" held by a trust. Brief for Petitioner 23. But such costs would appear to be fully deductible under the Trustee's own reading, because a trustee is obligated to incur maintenance expenses in light of the fiduciary duty to maintain trust property. See 1 Restatement (Second) of Trusts §176, p. 381 (1957) ("The trustee is under a duty to the beneficiary to use reasonable care and skill to preserve the trust property").

Indeed, the Trustee's formulation of its argument is circular: "Trust investment advice fees are caused by the fact the property is held in trust." Brief for Petitioner 19. But "trust investment advice fees" are only aptly described as such because the property is held in trust; the statute asks whether such costs would be incurred by an individual if the property were not. Even when there is a clearly analogous category of costs that would be incurred by individuals, the Trustee's reading would exempt most or all trust costs as fully deductible merely because they derive from a trustee's fiduciary duty. Adding the modifier "trust" to costs that otherwise would be incurred by an individual surely cannot be enough to escape the 2% floor.

What is more, if the Trustee's position were correct, then only the first clause of §67(e)(1)—providing that the cost be "incurred in connection with the administration

---

4. In pressing the Court of Appeals' approach, the Solicitor General argues that "to say that a team would not have won the game if it were not for the quarterback's outstanding play is to say that the team could not have won without the quarterback." Brief for Respondent 19. But the Solicitor General simply posits the truth of a proposition—that the team would not have won the game if it were not for the quarterback's outstanding play—and then states its equivalent. The statute, in contrast, does not posit any proposition. Rather, it asks a question: whether a particular cost *would* have been incurred if the property were held by an individual instead of a trust.

of the … trust"—would be necessary. The statute's second, limiting condition—that the cost also be one "which would not have been incurred if the property were not held in such trust"—would do no work; we see no difference in saying, on the one hand, that costs are "caused by" the fact that the property is held in trust and, on the other, that costs are incurred "in connection with the administration" of the trust. Thus, accepting the Trustee's approach "would render part of the statute entirely superfluous, something we are loath to do." *Cooper Industries, Inc. v. Aviall Services, Inc.,* 543 U.S. 157, 166, 125 S.Ct. 577, 160 L.Ed.2d 548 (2004).

The Trustee's reading is further undermined by our inclination, "[i]n construing provisions … in which a general statement of policy is qualified by an exception, [to] read the exception narrowly in order to preserve the primary operation of the provision." *Commissioner v. Clark,* 489 U.S. 726, 739, 109 S.Ct. 1455, 103 L.Ed.2d 753 (1989). As we have said, § 67(e) sets forth a general rule for purposes of the 2% floor established in § 67(a): "For purposes of this section, the adjusted gross income of an estate or trust shall be computed in the same manner as in the case of an individual." Under the Trustee's reading, § 67(e)(1)'s exception would swallow the general rule; most (if not all) expenses incurred by a trust would be fully deductible. "Given that Congress has enacted a general rule…, we should not eviscerate that legislative judgment through an expansive reading of a somewhat ambiguous exception." *Ibid.*

More to the point, the statute by its terms does not "establis[h] a straightforward causation test," Brief for Petitioner 22, but rather invites a hypothetical inquiry into the treatment of the property were it held outside a trust. The statute does not ask whether a cost was incurred *because* the property is held by a trust; it asks whether a particular cost "would not have been incurred if the property were not held in such trust," § 67(e)(1). "Far from examining the nature of the cost at issue from the perspective of whether it was caused by the trustee's duties, the statute instead looks to the counterfactual question of whether *individuals* would have incurred such costs in the *absence* of a trust." Brief for Respondent 9.

This brings us to the test adopted by the Fourth and Federal Circuits: Costs incurred by trusts that escape the 2% floor are those that would not "commonly" or "customarily" be incurred by individuals. See *Scott,* 328 F.3d, at 140 ("Put simply, trust-related administrative expenses are subject to the 2% floor if they constitute expenses commonly incurred by individual taxpayers"); *Mellon Bank,* 265 F.3d, at 1281 (§ 67(e) "treats as fully deductible only those trust-related administrative expenses that are unique to the administration of a trust and not customarily incurred outside of trusts"). The Solicitor General also accepts this view as an alternative reading of the statute. See Brief for Respondent 20–21. We agree with this approach.

The question whether a trust-related expense is fully deductible turns on a prediction about what would happen if a fact were changed—specifically, if the property were held by an individual rather than by a trust. In the context of making such a prediction, when there is uncertainty about the answer, the word "would" is best read as "express[ing] concepts such as custom, habit, natural disposition, or probability." *Scott, supra,* at 139. See Webster's Third New International Dictionary 2637–2638 (1993); American Heritage Dictionary 2042, 2059 (3d ed. 1996). The Trustee objects that the statutory text "does not ask whether expenses are 'customarily' incurred outside of trusts," Reply Brief for Petitioner 15, but that is the direct import of the language in context. The text requires determining what would happen if a fact were changed; such an exercise necessarily entails a prediction; and predictions are based on what would customarily or commonly occur. Thus, in asking whether a particular type of cost "would *not* have been incurred" if the property were held by an individual, §67(e)(1) excepts from the 2% floor only those costs that it would be *un*common (or unusual, or unlikely) for such a hypothetical individual to incur.

III

Having decided on the proper reading of §67(e)(1), we come to the application of the statute to the particular question in this case: whether investment advisory fees incurred by a trust escape the 2% floor.

It is not uncommon or unusual for individuals to hire an investment adviser. Certainly the Trustee, who has the burden of establishing its entitlement to the deduction, has not demonstrated that it is. See *INDOPCO, Inc. v. Commissioner*, 503 U.S. 79, 84, 112 S.Ct. 1039, 117 L.Ed.2d 226 (1992) (noting the "'familiar rule' that 'an income tax deduction is a matter of legislative grace and that the burden of clearly showing the right to the claimed deduction is on the taxpayer'" (quoting *Interstate Transit Lines v. Commissioner*, 319 U.S. 590, 593, 63 S.Ct. 1279, 87 L.Ed. 1607 (1943))); Tax Court Rule 142(a)(1) (stating that the "burden of proof shall be upon the petitioner," with certain exceptions not relevant here). The Trustee's argument is that individuals cannot incur trust investment advisory fees, not that individuals do not commonly incur investment advisory fees.

Indeed, the essential point of the Trustee's argument is that he engaged an investment adviser because of his fiduciary duties under Connecticut's Uniform Prudent Investor Act, Conn. Gen. Stat. §45a-541a(a) (2007). The Act eponymously requires trustees to follow the "prudent investor rule." See n. 2, *supra*. To satisfy this standard, a trustee must "invest and manage trust assets *as a prudent investor would,* by considering the purposes, terms, distribution requirements and other circumstances of the trust." §45a-541b(a) (emphasis added). The prudent investor standard plainly does not refer to a prudent *trustee*; it would not be very helpful to explain that a trustee should act as a prudent trustee would. Rather, the standard looks to what a prudent investor with the same investment objectives handling his own affairs would do—*i.e.,* a prudent individual investor. See Restatement (Third) of Trusts (Prudent Investor Rule) Reporter's Notes on §227, p. 58 (1990) ("The prudent investor rule of this Section has its origins in the dictum of *Harvard College v. Amory*, 9 Pick. (26 Mass.) 446, 461 (1830), stating that trustees must 'observe how men of prudence, discretion, and intelligence manage their own affairs, not in regard to speculation, but in regard to the permanent disposition of their funds, considering the probable income, as well as the probable safety of the capital to be invested'"). See also, *e.g., In re Musser's Estate*, 341 Pa. 1, 9–10, 17 A.2d 411, 415 (1941) (noting the "general rule" that "a trustee must exercise such prudence and diligence in conducting the affairs of the trust as men of average diligence and discretion would employ in their own affairs"). And we have no reason to doubt the Trustee's claim that a hypothetical prudent investor in his position would have solicited investment advice, just as he did. Having accepted all this, it is quite difficult to say that investment advisory fees "would not have been incurred"—that is, that it would be unusual or uncommon for such fees to have been incurred—if the property were held by an individual investor with the same objectives as the Trust in handling his own affairs.

We appreciate that the inquiry into what is common may not be as easy in other cases, particularly given the absence of regulatory guidance. But once you depart in the name of ease of administration from the language chosen by Congress, there is more than one way to skin the cat: The Trustee raises administrability concerns in support of his causation test, Reply Brief for Petitioner 6, but so does the Government in explaining why it prefers the Court of Appeals' approach to the one it has successfully advanced before the Tax Court and two Federal Circuits. Congress's decision to phrase the pertinent inquiry in terms of a prediction about a hypothetical situation inevitably entails some uncertainty, but that is no excuse for judicial amendment of the statute. The Code elsewhere poses similar questions—such as whether expenses are "ordinary," see §§ 162(a), 212; see also *Deputy, Administratrix v. du Pont,* 308 U.S. 488, 495, 60 S. Ct. 363, 84 L. Ed. 416 (1940) (noting that "[o]rdinary has the connotation of normal, usual, or customary")— and the inquiry is in any event what § 67(e)(1) requires.

As the Solicitor General concedes, some trust-related investment advisory fees may be fully deductible "if an investment advisor were to impose a special, additional charge applicable only to its fiduciary accounts." Brief for Respondent 25. There is nothing in the record, however, to suggest that Warfield charged the Trustee anything extra, or treated the Trust any differently than it would have treated an individual with similar objectives, because of the Trustee's fiduciary obligations. See App. 24–27. It is conceivable, moreover, that a trust may have an unusual investment objective, or may require a specialized balancing of the interests of various parties, such that a reasonable comparison with individual investors would be improper. In such a case, the incremental cost of expert advice beyond what would normally be required for the ordinary taxpayer would not be subject to the 2% floor. Here, however, the Trust has not asserted that its investment objective or its requisite balancing of competing interests was distinctive. Accordingly, we conclude that the investment advisory fees incurred by the Trust are subject to the 2% floor.

The judgment of the Court of Appeals is affirmed.

Illustrative Material

What does it mean that a deduction "would not have been incurred if the property were not held in such trust or estate"? A trustee's commission would not have been incurred if property were not held in trust and thus may be allowable in whole. On the other hand, some of the services a trustee provides are similar to services that might have been availed of even if the trust had not been created. For example, a trustee's prudent investment of trust assets is similar to investment advice that might have been obtained if the property were not held in trust. Is a portion of a trustee's commission therefore subject to the 2% haircut? *See* Boring, *Deduction of Trust Expenses for Outside Investment Advisory Fees,* 29 ACTEC J. 98, 100 (2003) (worrying that the I.R.S. might require institutional fiduciaries to "unbundle" their fees). If so, how does one determine what portion? Some, who assume that a portion of every trustee's commission is subject to the "haircut," have suggested that Congress or the Treasury should designate a fixed percentage as subject to section 67. Allowance of the entire trustee's fee would be simpler and would do no violence to the statutory language.

Shortly after the Supreme Court granted certiorari in *Knight,* the Service announced proposed regulations dealing with the applicability of § 67 to expenses incurred by fiduciaries. REG-128224-06, 2007-36 I.R.B. 551. Not surprisingly, the proposed regulations leave no doubt that investment advisory fees are subject to the limitations of § 67. More generally, the test for determining whether an expense is subject to the limitations of § 67, according to the proposed regulations, is whether the expense in question is unique to estates and trusts. This, in turn, depends on whether an individual could incur it in connection with property not held in an estate or trust. Only those expenses that are unique to estates and trusts escape the statutory limitations. The proposed regulations also provide that all fiduciary expenses, including executor's commissions and trustees' fees, are subject to being "unbundled," to identify any included fees that are subject to the limitations of § 67. *See* Proposed Reg. § 1.67-4.

b. Disallowance of Expenses Attributable to Production of Tax-Exempt Income*

Internal Revenue Code:
> Sections 212; 263(a); 265(a)(1); 643(a), (b)

Regulations:
> Sections 1.212-1(i), (k); 1.265-1

Manufacturers Hanover Trust Co. v. United States
160 Ct. Cl. 582, 312 F.2d 785
cert. denied, 375 U.S. 880 (1963)

DAVIS, *Judge*, delivered the opinion of the court:

This is a suit brought by plaintiff, as trustee under a trust indenture executed by Henry H. Rogers on November 5, 1927, to obtain a refund of income taxes and interest in the amount of $23,008.89, which was paid by the trust for calendar year 1954. The case is before the court on plaintiff's motion and defendant's cross-motion for summary judgment, and presents three issues which call for resolution: (1) whether attorneys' fees incurred by the taxpayer in certain trust litigation are deductible as ordinary and necessary expenses for management, conservation, or maintenance of property held for the production of income, or whether the expenses were capital expenditures incurred in defending or perfecting title to property; (2) whether capital gains and other gross income allocated to trust principal are to be taken into account in determining the amount of expenses, otherwise deductible by the trust, which are rendered non-deductible because allocable to tax-exempt income; and (3) whether taxpayer, in its claim for refund, made a sufficient demand for a deduction for the amount of income which it was required to distribute currently to the beneficiaries.

Plaintiff is a corporation organized under New York law for the conduct of a banking and trust business. On November 5, 1927, Henry H. Rogers executed an indenture transferring property in trust to an individual trustee, since deceased, and to plaintiff's predecessor, in contemplation of his daughter Millicent's forthcoming marriage to Arturo Peralta Ramos. The marriage took place two days later. Under the terms of the indenture, the net income of the trust was payable to Millicent for life, and at her death the trust was to be divided into equal shares (after making provision for her husband, if he survived her and had the marriage not terminated in divorce—as it did), one share to be held in trust for and the net income paid for life to each surviving child of the marriage. Thereafter, the corpus was to be paid to that child's issue *per stirpes*; or, in default of issue, to his brothers or sisters or their issue; and in case

---

* Section B(3)(b) of this chapter focuses on the allowability of deductions under section 212 for indirect expenses partially allocable to tax-exempt income. They are difficult materials, in part because they raise inherently complex and technical issues, but also because they implicate the concept of "distributable net income," which later materials (ch. 3, sec. B) treat in greater detail. Some instructors may therefore prefer to consider these materials later. The authors offer two reasons for the suggested sequence: (1) these materials really do involve section 212 issues—not distributable net income issues—and therefore organizationally belong here; and (2) presenting these materials here serves as an introduction to (and dry run for) the difficult and crucial material in chapter 3. The student should be aware that it is not fair to expect comprehension of these materials from a casual reading.

of default of such beneficiaries, to the grantor or those entitled to take under his will. The indenture also contained reservations of reversionary interests in the event that Millicent might be survived by only one child, or by no children, but these provisions never came into effect, for at her death on January 1, 1953, she was survived by two sons of her marriage to Ramos — Arturo Henry Peralta Ramos and Paul Jaime Peralta Ramos, who were born on November 14, 1928, and February 18, 1931, respectively. The grantor, Henry H. Rogers, died testate on July 25, 1935, leaving a part of his residuary estate in trust for his widow, Pauline. She survived him, and by remarriage became Pauline V. Hoving.

After the death of Millicent, early in 1953, there was uncertainty as to the validity of the continuing trusts to Arturo Henry and Paul under Section 11 of the New York Personal Property Law, which prohibits suspension of the absolute power of alienation for more than two lives in being. On January 7, 1954, the plaintiff filed a petition in the Supreme Court of the State of New York for an order settling its account as trustee and fixing and allowing its commissions, and also construing the trust indenture and the grantor's will and instructing plaintiff as to the disposition of the trust assets. Millicent's executors, her two sons born of the marriage with Ramos, the infant son of Arturo Henry Ramos, another son of Millicent by a later marriage, and Mrs. Hoving were among those made parties to the proceeding, and they, as well as plaintiff, participated and prepared briefs on the issue of the validity of the trust. The position of Mrs. Hoving, residuary legatee of Henry Rogers, was that under New York law the continuing trusts for Arturo Henry and Paul were illegal and void, and she may also have attacked the entire inter vivos trust indenture of November 5, 1927. The other participants, opposing the interpretation advanced by Mrs. Hoving, contended that the trust indenture was wholly valid.

On November 29, 1954, before the cause was decided by the state court, the parties settled the proceeding by stipulation, after extended negotiations. Under the terms of this agreement, Mrs. Hoving withdrew her answer, consented that an order be entered construing the secondary trusts as valid, and assigned any rights of hers to the assets of these trusts to Arturo Henry and Paul in return for their paying her from their own funds the sum of $40,000. The parties also stipulated, subject to court approval, the various allowances to be paid to the different attorneys (and to the guardian *ad litem* of the infant respondent), and that all such allowances should be paid by the trust. The court entered a final order on December 6, 1954, in conformity with the stipulations, that plaintiff's accounts as trustee were approved and settled; that the trusts to commence upon the death of Millicent for the benefit of Arturo Henry and Paul were valid and enforceable; and that the trustee was to pay out of the trust corpus $49,000 in attorneys' fees and $15.25 as disbursements.

When it filed its fiduciary income tax return for 1954, plaintiff claimed a deduction of the entire $49,015.25 paid out in the trust litigation. Upon audit, the Commissioner of Internal Revenue disallowed the deduction "to the extent of $35,315.25 for the reason that to that extent the expenditures were not deductible under section 212 of the Internal Revenue Code of 1954 but should be capitalized under section 263 as an expenditure to perfect title." The $13,700 allowed by the Commissioner was attributed by him to the accounting aspect of the litigation and therefore allowable as an ordinary and necessary expense of the trust. Plaintiff paid the deficiency and then filed a refund claim asserting that the entire amount of attorneys' fees was deductible (except to the extent, if any, allocable to tax-exempt income) as an ordinary and necessary expense. Rejection of the refund claim brings the matter before us.

There is no dispute as to the allocation of these litigation fees between the accounting and the trust-construction phases. Plaintiff's position is the broader one that the sums attributable to the construction aspect of the suit must also be allowed as a deduction under Section 212 ... and more particularly by Treasury Regulation §1.212-1(i).... On the other hand, defendant relies, of course, on Treasury Regulation §1.212-1(k)....[3]

[T]hese sections of the statute and the regulations, taken together, require that, before the expenditures can be deductible, they must be (a) "ordinary and necessary"; (b) "paid or incurred during the taxable year"; (c) "for the production or collection of income," or "for the management, conservation, or maintenance of property held for the production of income"; and (d) other than capital expenditures, including expenditures incurred in "defending or perfecting title to property." ... In this case the critical question is whether the expenditures were incurred in the defense or perfection of title.[4]

The binding effect of the rule that expenditures incurred in defending or perfecting title must be capitalized has long been recognized, and often applied. See, for example, *Bowers v. Lumpkin,* 140 F. 2d 927 (C.A. 4, 1944); ... *United States v. St. Joe Paper* Co., 284 F. 2d 430 (C.A. 5, 1960); *Brown v. Commissioner,* 215 F. 2d 697 (C.A. 5, 1954); *Safety Tube Corp. v. Commissioner,* 168 F. 2d 787 (C.A. 6, 1948).... The validity of the rule is settled, but problems continue to arise in its application to the varieties of particular circumstance. See, *e.g.,* the various opinions in *Ruoff v. Commissioner,* 277 F. 2d 222 (C.A. 3, 1960), and 30 T.C. 204 (1958). When is an expenditure merely conservative, and when does it exceed this line and become an element of title perfection or defense? The subsidiary principles are not fully developed; the answer often depends, also, on a weighing of the individual facts. There is as yet "no hard and fast rule" by which deductibility can "easily be determined" (*Brown v. Commissioner, supra,* 215 F. 2d 697, 699 (C.A. 5, 1954)); but certain helpful guidelines have been fixed, even though there may still be dispute as to others.

In ascertaining the character of an expenditure for legal fees, the courts uniformly look first to the primary purpose of the litigation. "[I]f the primary purpose * * * was title, then the expenditure is capital in nature and must be capitalized; if the aspect of title is only incidental to the primary purpose of the litigation, then the expense is deductible as such and need not be capitalized." *Loyd v. United States,* 139 Ct. Cl. 626, 632, 153 F. Supp. 416, 419 (1957); *Industrial Aggregate Co. v. United States,*[284 F. 2d 639, 645 (C.A. 8, 1960)]; *Ruoff v. Commissioner, supra,* 277 F. 2d 222 (C.A. 3, 1960). It makes no difference that the expenditures were ordinary and necessary in the colloquial sense, or that they affected the possibility of obtaining income, or even that they arose from following the only feasible course open to the taxpayer. If the primary purpose of the proceeding was defense or perfection of title to property, the expenses must be capitalized. Especially in this area is it true that "not every expenditure can be claimed as a deduction and this is so whatever may be the effect of the expenditure upon the profit-seeking activities of the taxpayer." *Lewis v. Commissioner,* 253 F. 2d 821, 825 (C.A. 2, 1958). Moreover, contrary to plaintiff's assertion, section 1.212-1(i) of the Treasury Regulations ... does not "flatly

---

3. This regulation comports with Sections 261 and 263 of the Code, which together declare that "in computing taxable income no deduction shall in any case be allowed" for capital expenditures, defined to include "any amount paid out * * * for permanent improvements or betterments made to increase the value of any property or estate." Treas. Reg. §1.263(a)-2(c) defines "the cost of defending or perfecting title to property" as a capital expenditure.

4. The assets of the trust consisted almost entirely of various types of securities (see footnote 8, *infra*) as to which Treas. Reg. §1.212-1(k) can undoubtedly be invoked (if it is otherwise applicable)....

allow" all fiduciaries' expenses of litigation as deductions. Such expenses are allowed only so long as they do not fall within the proscription of subsection (k) of the same regulation (and Section 263 of the Code and its regulations), pertaining to nondeductible capital expenditures. We find nothing in the 1954 Code or regulations indicating that fiduciaries, when faced with the necessity of making capital expenditures, should be afforded treatment so radically different from that accorded other taxpayers. Neither Congress nor the Treasury has purported to authorize a fiduciary to consider *all* of its litigation expenditures as "ordinary and necessary expenses."

Attempting to show that, in any case, the trust-construction proceeding did not have as its primary goal the defense of the trust's title to its assets, the plaintiff asserts that under New York law it had acquired an unimpeachably valid title to the entire trust property upon creation of the trust in 1927, and that the litigation was simply to determine the proper disposition in 1954 of the property committed to its care, *i.e.,* whether after the death of Millicent Rogers in 1953 the trust assets should be used for the secondary trusts created for Arturo Henry and Paul Ramos or should be paid to the residuary legatees of Henry Rogers. Plaintiff says that under New York law the trust was indisputably lawful throughout the life of Millicent, and the only question which could possibly arise would be the continuing validity of the trusts for her sons after her death in 1953. The Government counters that the litigation was primarily to determine the initial validity of the trust's title to the property beginning with 1927; the brief points to certain principles of New York law holding that, if a grant violates the New York rules against perpetuities and the suspension of the power of alienation, it may be void from its inception and title, by operation of law, will remain in the grantor despite the trust agreement. Mrs. Hoving's challenge to the trust's title, the Government says, was of this fundamental character, raising the issue of whether the trustee ever had any valid title to the trust assets.

It is unnecessary, we think, to determine whether the question of New York law involved in the state litigation was the trust's right to the property *ab initio,* or solely the trust's continued legal title after the death of Millicent. A decision adverse to the plaintiff, rendered on either of these theories, would have deprived it of the title to the property, which it would certainly have claimed and retained if it were not for this or comparable litigation. There was much more to the case than a mere request by plaintiff for directions as to the future distribution of trust assets which the trustee admittedly owned. The plaintiff was, at the least, seeking to perfect (and to defend) its very title to the property from and after January 1, 1953, when Millicent died; the minimal issue in the proceeding was a possible defect which would have voided the trustee's title on that date and would have required the property to revert back to the grantor's residuary estate. There was a direct challenge to the trustee's continued title, not simply a dispute between beneficiaries of the trust. Moreover, this defect, if it existed under New York law, was already inherent in the title when the trustee acquired the assets under the trust indenture in 1927; it was a substantial pre-existing flaw in the basic indenture, not a subsequent cloud upon a once perfect and unquestioned title. Thus, it seems to us plain that, even on plaintiff's understanding of the precise issue in the construction proceeding, the perfection and defense of the trustee's claimed title to the trust property under the trust indenture was the essence of that suit. The litigation costs are therefore capital expenditures, rather than expenses deductible as ordinary and necessary under section 212....

This situation is to be distinguished from that which would arise if a fiduciary sought to deduct expenses incurred in determining which of several potential beneficiaries was entitled to receive trust property. There the fiduciary's title would not be at issue, and it would not be engaged in perfecting or defending title. In *Trust of Bingham v. Commissioner,*

325 U.S. 365 (1945), expenses were incurred in winding up the trust after its expiration; the Court held that the *costs of distribution,* if ordinary and necessary, were deductible expenses incurred in the management of the trust property. *Trust of Spero v. Commissioner,* 30 T.C. 845, 855–56 (1958), is also a case in which the court felt itself to be dealing with expenses incurred in deciding which beneficiaries were the proper recipients of assets to be distributed by a fiduciary, as opposed to determining whether the trust had itself lost title to the property. Here the facts are the reverse.

Plaintiff argues that, nevertheless, we are compelled by our decision in *Loyd v. United States,* 139 Ct. Cl. 626, 153 F. Supp. 416 (1957), to rule in its favor. That case involved the deductibility of legal fees by the executors of a daughter's estate, which were paid to counsel for litigating the validity of a charitable bequest by her mother, the amounts of which would be included in the estate of the daughter, as sole heir of the grantor, if the mother's charitable grant was invalid under state law. As a result of this litigation holding the charitable bequest partly invalid, most of the property was delivered to the executors of the daughter. While recognizing the validity of the rule requiring capitalization of the expenses of title, the court interpreted the record as indicating that "the primary purpose, or at least the motivating force, of the litigation was not the question of who had title to the property, rather it was that the proper distribution of the estate's assets could not have been had without a prior determination by the court of the validity of the gift." *Loyd v. United States, supra,* 139 Ct. Cl. at 634, 153 F. Supp. at 421. Although title to certain property was one aspect of the litigation, it was incidental to the primary purpose of settling the two estates. The daughter's executors had a disputed claim to the assets marked for the charitable gift, but the overriding concern of the litigation, the court held (139 Ct. Cl. at 633–34), was not the issue of title but the proper administration of the daughter's estate which could not have been had without "first obtaining the answer to the question of validity of the grant to the church." In the present case, unlike *Loyd,* there is no showing, and on this record no reason to believe, that the proceeding by plaintiff in the New York Supreme Court was instituted because it was absolutely essential to the further management of the trust. There was no impending marshalling and distribution of the assets held by plaintiff; the trust could well have gone on, as provided by the indenture, until challenged by a proper adverse party. In this light, the litigation voluntarily begun after Millicent's death had for its direct, if not sole, purpose a legal declaration, helpful but not mandatory, whether the indenture was effective to give the trust continued title to the property. The costs of this type of quiet-title proceeding are capital expenditures rather than deductible expenses of trust administration.[7]

The second issue relates to the allocation of the legal fees and trustee's commissions paid or incurred by the taxpayer, and otherwise allowable as "ordinary and necessary" deductions under Section 212, between taxable income and tax-exempt income (here, tax-exempt interest) received by the trust in 1954. Section 265 provides that no deduction shall be allowed for any amount allocable to a class of income wholly exempt from income tax. Treasury Regulation §1.265-1(c), promulgated under this section of the Code, sets forth, in general terms, the method by which this allocation is to be made.

Plaintiff reported the receipt of $8,370.85 during 1954 as interest wholly exempt from federal income taxes.[8] The defendant allocated the indirect expenses (legal fees and com-

---

7. The Tax Court has recently disallowed, as a deduction under Section 212, the $20,000 payment made by Arturo Henry Peralta Ramos to Mrs. Hoving, and has held it to be a capital expenditure. *Ramos v. Commissioner,* 38 T.C. 820 (1962).

8. On its tax return plaintiff reported receipt of the following types and amounts of income during the year: domestic dividends allocable to income—$26,245.95; foreign dividends allocable to income—$150.00; interest allocable to income—$468.75; taxable stock dividends allocable to principal—

missions) between tax-exempt interest, on the one hand, and dividends and taxable interest on the other, but, in so doing, excluded from the allocation base capital gains and taxable stock dividends, both of which, although elements of the trust's taxable income, were allocable to the principal of the trust under local law and the trust indenture. By the exclusion of these elements of taxable income from the base, the portion of the indirect expenses allocable to tax-exempt interest, and hence not deductible, was significantly increased. It is this refusal of the Internal Revenue Service to consider all the elements of the trust's taxable income, in making the allocation, which prompts plaintiff's complaint.

Since trust income is involved, it will help to begin with a brief outline of the special taxing system established by subchapter J of chapter 1 of the 1954 Code, the portion dealing with the income taxation of estates, trusts, beneficiaries, and decedents. "The basic principle underlying the taxation of * * * ordinary trusts is that all the taxable income is to be taxed as income only once — either to the * * * trust, or to the beneficiary, or in part to each. This is accomplished by allowing the estate or trust a deduction for certain amounts distributed or required to be distributed [whether or not actually distributed], and taxing the beneficiary on such amounts." Montgomery's Federal Taxes, 20.1 (38th ed. 1961). In general, this scheme of taxation is implemented by treating a trust as a separate taxable entity, the taxable income of which is computed in the same manner, and taxed to the same extent, as the taxable income of an individual — with certain exceptions set forth in the Code.[9] §§641, 642, 651, 1954 I.R.C. Chief among these exceptions is the authorization of a deduction for that "income"[10] of the taxable year which is required to be distributed currently. §651(a), 1954 I.R.C. This deduction is designed to avoid the double taxation that would result if the income required to be distributed were first taxed to the trust, and then taxed again when distributed to the beneficiaries. So that the income not go untaxed, the Code requires that the beneficiaries include in their gross incomes the trust income to them, whether it is actually distributed or not. §652(a), 1954 I.R.C.

The central device utilized to effectuate this "flowthrough" scheme of taxation is "distributable net income" — a crucial term in the present case. This is defined by Section 643(a) as the taxable income of the trust with certain important modifications, the most pertinent of which are:

1. Distributions to beneficiaries are *not deducted*.

$162.25; long-term capital gain allocable to principal — $71,205.24; short-term capital loss allocable against principal — $171.10; and tax-exempt interest — $8,370.85. In addition to the legal fees of $49,015.25 discussed above, plaintiff and defendant do not dispute that the following amounts were paid or incurred during the year for trustee's commissions — $3,350.68; and for N.Y. Corpus Profits Tax — $1,658.88. Defendant allowed deduction of the latter amount in its entirety without requiring allocation to tax-exempt income.

9. The Code contains separate provisions dealing with those trusts which are required to distribute income currently, do not provide that amounts are to be paid or set aside for charitable purposes, and do not distribute amounts other than current income during the taxable year, from the provisions relating to "trusts accumulating income or distributing corpus." Although the basic principle underlying the taxation of both types of trust is the same (see subparts B and C, part I, subchapter J, chapter 1, Internal Revenue Code of 1954), our discussion will not refer to subpart C, governing "trusts accumulating income or distributing corpus."

10. "Income" in this sense is defined in Section 643(b) as "the amount of income of the * * * trust for the taxable year determined under the terms of the governing instrument and applicable local law. Thus, capital gains allocable to principal are not considered as "income," for this purpose, although they are an element of taxable income, while tax-exempt interest is normally included in "income" for this purpose.

2. Capital gains allocable to corpus (as here), and not paid, credited, or required to be distributed to any beneficiary, or paid or permanently set aside for charitable purposes, are *excluded.*

3. For trusts like plaintiff's which distribute current income only, extraordinary dividends or taxable stock dividends not paid or credited to any beneficiary because allocated by the fiduciary (in good faith) to principal, are *excluded.*

4. Tax-exempt interest, "reduced by any amounts which would be deductible in respect of disbursements allocable to such interest but for the provisions of section 265 (relating to disallowance of certain deductions)," is *included.*

Around this concept of "distributable net income" the Code builds its provisions for (a) the deduction allowed the trust for its current distributions to the beneficiaries, and (b) the distributions which the beneficiaries must include in their own gross incomes.[11] "Thus, distributable net income has been termed the measuring rod or yardstick to be employed in determining, on the one hand, the maximum deduction for distributions which may be allowed to the estate or trust and for gauging, on the other hand, the extent to which beneficiaries may be taxable on the distributions." 6 Mertens "Law of Federal Income Taxation" §36.04.

"Distributable net income" first appears on our stage in plaintiff's claim that, by excluding capital gains and taxable stock dividends from the allocation base used in determining the amount of administration expenses deductible, the Commissioner of Internal Revenue followed Special Instruction 39 of the instructions to Form 1041, the fiduciary income tax return. Instruction 39 applies to the separate schedule on the form to be used for the computation of "distributable net income," and says that for this purpose tax-exempt interest is to be reduced by

> any amounts which, but for the provisions of Section 265, would be deductible in respect of disbursements, expenses, losses, etc., of the trust or estate, directly or indirectly allocable to such interest. The amount of the indirect disbursements, etc., allocable to tax-exempt interest is that amount which bears the same ratio to the total disbursements, etc., of the trust or estate not directly attributable to other items of income as the total tax-exempt interest received bears to the total of all the items of gross income (including tax-exempt interest * * *) entering into *distributable net income* (emphasis added).

By including only those items of gross income which enter into distributable net income, this instruction excludes capital gains and taxable stock dividends (both allocable to cor-

---

11. Under Section 651(b), distributable net income, as adjusted by excluding the tax-exempt income of the trust and the deductions allocable to tax-exempt income, establishes the maximum deduction to be allowed to the trust on account of distributions to beneficiaries. In this manner, the trust's maximum deduction for distributions will be roughly equivalent to the gross taxable income entering into the computation of fiduciary income (*e.g.,* tax-exempt income and capital gains, etc. allocable to corpus are excluded), reduced by the deductible expenses of the trust (including deductible expenses allocable to corpus, but excluding expenses that are non-deductible because allocable to tax-exempt income). Secondly, distributable net income — without the above-mentioned adjustment — establishes the maximum amount of the distributions which the beneficiaries must include in their gross incomes. §652(a). The Code also specifies that the amounts includible in the beneficiaries' gross incomes "shall have the same character in the hands of the beneficiary as in the hands of the trust," and for this purpose requires that the proportionate composition of distributable net income is to be used to determine the amounts of the various classes of income (*e.g.,* a distribution composed partly of tax-exempt interest, and partly of rents, etc.) includible by the beneficiaries. §652(b).

pus). The plaintiff says that the Commissioner also presumably relied on the examples in section 1.652(c)-4 of the Treasury Regulations, which similarly determine the amount of administration expenses allocable to tax-exempt interest. The argument is that the instruction and the regulation are unreasonable in arbitrarily ignoring large classes of income, and that this exclusion will result, through the years, in the over-collection of tax. Plaintiff urges that, although the "artificial concept" of distributable net income may be suited to the determination of the maximum amount of income taxable to beneficiaries, "it is peculiarly ill-adapted to answer the far more simple and truly unrelated question of what general administration expenses are allocable to tax-exempt interest."

The defendant's reply is that Instruction 39 to Form 1041, and the examples set forth in various regulations under subchapter J, are irrelevant to the question of allocation of deductions by the trust; they relate to the computation of distributable net income, and "although in such computation capital gains and losses are also excluded, this has only an indirect bearing upon the reasonableness of the allocation under Section [265(a)(1)] which is here involved." Thus abandoning the stance taken by the Commissioner, the Government proposes a new theory which in this case (it says) would reach approximately the same result as that of the Commissioner and would therefore deprive the plaintiff of its claimed refund.[12] Plaintiff, in turn, attacks the defendant's substitute theory as wholly unwarranted.

On the narrowest view of the question presented to us by this case, we would not have to resolve these controversies. Strictly, only the *trust's* taxable income is before us. And where, as here, the allowable deductions [other than the distribution deduction] are insufficient to absorb the distributable net income of the trust (excluding tax-exempt income and deductions allocable thereto) the result of the subchapter J system of taxation is that the taxable income of the trust is unchanged, whether or not income allocable to principal account is included in the base for the allocation of otherwise deductible expenses between taxable and tax-exempt income.[13] This is true because the deduction for income required to be distributed currently—which in this case equals (and can never exceed) the distributable net income reduced by tax-exempt income and the deductions allocable thereto—and the allowable operating expenses are both proper deductions, in themselves, from the trust's taxable income, but at the same time the expense deductions are also proper deductions in computing distributable net income itself. Since the expense deductions enter into the computation of taxable income, and distributable net income (which here equals the current distribution deduction) is a function of taxable income, the two types of deduction are intimately related, varying inversely with each other. If plaintiff is right and capital gains allocable to principal are included in the allocation

---

12. Defendant contends that Section 265, which disallows deductions allocable to tax-exempt interest "whether or not any amount of such interest is received or accrued," shows on its face that the allocation of deductions is not to be made solely on the basis of annual income. It asserts that, considering the mandate of Treasury Regulation §1.265-1(c), that "a reasonable proportion * * * [of expenses allocable to both exempt and non-exempt income] determined in the light of all the facts and circumstances in each case shall be allocated to each," it is "unfortunate" that the Commissioner of Internal Revenue assumed that the allocation was to be in accordance with income received in 1954, for the correct criterion for allocation of the legal expenses here involved would seem to be the proportionate values of the property held for the production of taxable and tax-exempt income. As we have indicated, defendant points out that allocation under the latter method would, in this instance, reach approximately the same result as the Commissioner's. The primary reason suggested for the proposition that capital gains are to be excluded from the allocation base is that capital gain is a "random factor" bearing no direct relationship to the claimed deductions.

13. Had plaintiff's primary contention, that the legal fees incurred in the construction proceeding were deductible under Section 212, been sustainable, the allowable deductions would have absorbed the distributable net income. The problems would then have been different.

base, the deduction for legal fees (and trustee's commissions) will be increased, but that increase will necessarily push down the taxable income (before deduction for current distributions), and therefore the current distribution deduction, by the same amount. Since the adjusted distributable net income limits the deduction available to the trust for amounts of income required to be distributed currently, the changes in the amount of expenses deductible by the trust will be offset by countervailing changes in the amount of the deduction for distributions, and the taxable income of the trust will be static. So far as the trust is concerned, we could, therefore, under the present circumstances, abstain from deciding the exact make-up of the deductions.

However, it will not do to stop so short of giving a response to the issue argued to us. While in these circumstances the inclusion of capital gains (and other amounts not includible in the computation of distributable net income) in the allocation base does not alter the taxable income of the trust, it would decrease the tax liability of the income beneficiaries. This would be the direct result of the decrease in distributable net income stemming from that inclusion, for distributable net income limits the amount required to be included in gross income by the income beneficiaries. It seems appropriate, therefore, to take the step of answering on its merits the allocation issue posed by the parties.

Returning then to the arguments on allocation, we find it necessary to consider the plaintiff's attack on the Commissioner's method of allocation because we cannot agree with the defendant's assertion that Instruction 39 and the regulations under subchapter J are irrelevant to the reasonableness of the allocation of trust expenses under Section [265(a)(1)]. Treasury Regulation §1.652(c)-4, to which taxpayer refers, furnishes an example of the application of the rules for trusts required to distribute all income currently. Subparagraph (e) of this example consists of a computation of the taxable income of a trust, and the allocation of indirect expenses to the taxable and nontaxable portions of the trust's income is made, without discussion, on a distribution base from which capital gains allocable to corpus have been excluded. This is a plain enough indication, which we cannot ignore, of the specific method the Commissioner has chosen, *by regulation,* for the allocation of the expenses of trusts. Instruction 39, which by its terms purports to operate within the boundaries of Section 265, simply follows suit. More generally, the over-all regulation on allocation of expenses between taxable and tax-exempt income (Section 1.265-1(c) ...) requires that allocation of indirect expenses should be made "in the light of all facts and circumstances in each case." When the income of a trust is involved, the concept of distributable net income, as well as the special system of taxation in subchapter J, is an important component "of all the facts and circumstances." That concept and system are, as we have said, the primary mechanisms by which the income of a trust is taxed but once, either to the trust or to its beneficiaries; ... they should not be disregarded in applying the general allocation provisions of Section 265 to the particular problems of trust income....

Since the challenged regulation and instruction are thus applicable, we are controlled by their provisions unless we can agree with plaintiff that they are unreasonable as applied to the case before us.... But in the present circumstances—where the deductible expenses fall short of absorbing the distributable net income—the regulation and the instruction do not unfairly ignore large classes of income in making the expense allocation. The income beneficiaries are taxable only to the extent of distributable net income, which excludes gains attributable to corpus. It is not out of key, therefore, to insist that the allocation of expenses between taxable and tax-exempt income should be restricted to the same type of non-corpus gains. This is all the more so since, under Section 652(b), the amounts included in the income beneficiary's gross income have the same character in his hands—*e.g.,* as taxable dividends or tax-exempt interest—as in the hands of the trust (see footnote 11, *supra*). Moreover, under the 1954 Code, as a result of the structure of distributable net income (which has as its starting point the taxable income of the trust), the tax benefit of deductions allocable to corpus is generally shifted to the income beneficiaries.... The challenged regulation and instruction allowably balance this incongruity— that the income beneficiary, not the corpus beneficiary, receives the tax benefit of expenses allocable to corpus—by providing that those indirect expenses which are usually chargeable against capital gains must be allocated by the income beneficiary to all the income (both taxable and tax-exempt) required to be distributed by him. *All* the income required to be distributed currently by the trust and "included" in gross income by the beneficiary (particularly tax-exempt income), rather than just the taxable elements, bears the burden of the expenses attributable to capital gain. The tax benefit of the portion of these expenses assigned to tax-exempt income is lost, but this is not unfair to a taxpayer who has the special advantage of deductions attributable to gains he does not receive. Perhaps there may be other trust situations in which the Commissioner's regulations on allocation are unreasonable, but they are not so in the circumstances we have here. Plaintiff cannot recover the tax computed under those regulations.

In partial answer, plaintiff relies strongly on a twenty-year old internal directive of the Revenue Service to its agents (Field Procedure Memorandum No. 232, dated October 30, 1942), which authorized capital gains to be taken into account in full for trust allocation purposes. We doubt the weight to be given at this time to such non-public internal instructions, but in any event it must be recognized that the memorandum was addressed to agents charged with the administration of a law prohibiting the tax benefit of deductions chargeable to corpus from being enjoyed by the income beneficiaries, and the system of allocation of expenses it suggested was tailored to that need.[16] The changed system of taxing fiduciaries set forth in subchapter J of the 1954 Code robs the memorandum of continued persuasiveness in this field.

Finally, we must consider, as our third issue, plaintiff's claim that it is entitled to a deduction under Section 651 for amounts of income for the taxable year which it is required to distribute to its beneficiaries. See footnote 11, *supra*. When plaintiff filed its return, the full deduction it took for attorneys' fees swallowed all distributable net income, and there was therefore no occasion to claim such a deduction. Now that we diminish the deduction for legal fees, distributable net income reappears and a deduction is warranted. The only barrier is the possibility that plaintiff may not have adequately preserved this item in its refund claim. That claim asserted that "in the taxable year, claimant was required by the trust agreement to distribute all its income currently to beneficiaries, and was entitled to deduct the amount of such income under Section 651 in computing its taxable income." This explicit reference to a deduction for distributable net income was sufficient to alert the Commissioner of Internal Revenue to the taxpayer's potential entitlement to the deduction claimed. It is reasonable to assume that, his attention being directed to the

---

16. Section 24(d) of the 1939 Code provided that amounts paid under local law as income to the holder of a life or terminable interest acquired by gift, bequest, or inheritance "shall not be reduced or diminished * * * by any deduction allowed by this chapter * * * for the purpose of computing the net income of an estate or trust but not allowed under * * * [local law] for the purpose of computing the income to which such holder is entitled."

Under this provision, if a trust was required to distribute all its income currently, and had no gains allocable to corpus against which an expense chargeable to corpus could be deducted, the tax benefit of the deduction was lost.

Subchapter J of the 1954 Code was expressly drafted to prevent the wastage of deductions chargeable to corpus for fiduciary accounting purposes, by generally shifting the tax benefit of such deductions to the income beneficiaries.

increased taxable income (before deduction for distributions) which his denial of other claimed deductions had brought about, the Commissioner would have, and should have, considered the effect upon the deduction provided by the Code for amounts of income required to be distributed currently, when plaintiff had expressly claimed that the deduction was available to it....

For these reasons, the plaintiff is entitled to recover on the third issue,[17] with interest as provided by law, and judgment will be entered to that effect.... As to the first and second issues, defendant's motion for summary judgment is granted, plaintiff's motion is denied, and the petition is dismissed.

Illustrative Material

1. The court in *Manufacturers Hanover* stated cryptically that, regardless of what portion of the indirect expenses was disallowed under section 265 as allocable to tax-exempt income, the trust's taxable income would remain "static." The following example is intended to demonstrate that proposition.

Assume that a simple trust, i.e., one described in section 651(a), has income and expenses in the following amounts: cash dividends, $20,000; taxable interest, $10,000; tax-exempt interest, $15,000; long-term capital gain, $30,000; and trustee's compensation, $4,000. Under the Uniform Principal and Income Act (1997) the trust's fiduciary accounting income, i.e., the amount distributable to the income beneficiary under state law, is computed as follows:

$20,000	cash dividends (§401(a), (b))
10,000	taxable interest (§406(a))
15,000	tax-exempt interest (§406(a))
0	long-term capital gain (§404(2))
(2,000)	trustee's commission (§501(1)) [one-half of $4,000]
$43,000	FIDUCIARY ACCOUNTING INCOME

Gross income is computed as follows:

$20,000	cash dividends (§61(a)(7))
10,000	taxable interest (§61(a)(4))
0	tax-exempt interest (§103)
30,000	long-term capital gain (§61(a)(3))
$60,000	GROSS INCOME

Before computing taxable income, one must resolve the second issue involved in *Manufacturers Hanover*, i.e., determination of the portion of indirect expenses disallowed by section 265 as allocable to tax-exempt income. Both the taxpayer and the I.R.S. (in its audit position) agreed that the determination should be made on the basis of the ratio of tax-exempt income to total income. The disagreement was with respect to whether capital gains should be included in "total" income for purposes of that allocation. Under the taxpayer's approach, the portion of indirect expenses disallowed by section 265 is calculated as follows:

---

17. The Internal Revenue Service will be able to reopen the tax returns of the income beneficiaries to take into account our holding that the trust was entitled to a deduction for income required to be distributed currently. See Section 1311, 1954 I.R.C., and following sections.

$20,000 cash dividends
 10,000 taxable interest
 15,000 tax-exempt interest
 30,000 long-term capital gains
$75,000 total income

$$\frac{\$15,000 \quad \text{(tax-exempt income)}}{\$75,000 \quad \text{(total income)}} \times \$4,000 \text{ (indirect expenses)} = \$800 \text{ disallowed by } \S265$$

Under the I.R.S. audit approach, the disallowed portion is:

$20,000 cash dividends
 10,000 taxable interest
 15,000 tax-exempt interest
$45,000 total income

$$\frac{\$15,000 \quad \text{(tax-exempt income)}}{\$45,000 \quad \text{(total income)}} \times \$4,000 \text{ (indirect expenses)} = \$1,333 \text{ disallowed by } \S265$$

The process of determining taxable income begins with gross income and proceeds, under both the taxpayer's and the I.R.S. audit approaches, as follows:

Taxpayer	*I.R.S.*	
$60,000	$60,000	gross income
(300)	(300)	exemption (§642(b))
(3,200)	(2,667)	trustee's commission (§212)
		[Taxpayer: $4,000 less $800 disallowed; I.R.S.:
		$4,000 less $1,333 disallowed]
$56,500	$57,033	TENTATIVE TAXABLE INCOME

In order to determine taxable income it is necessary to compute the distribution deduction allowable under section 651. In general, the distribution deduction, under section 651(a), equals "the amount of the income for the taxable year which is required to be distributed currently," which, under section 643(b), is fiduciary accounting income, or, in this case, $43,000. However, section 651(b) limits the distribution deduction to a modified version of "distributable net income," which, in turn, is derived, under section 643(a), from taxable income. Thus, in a sense, one must know taxable income before one can find taxable income. "Tentative taxable income," calculated above, although not statutorily defined, serves to break the definitional circle. It consists, simply, of the trust's taxable income, calculated without reference to the distribution deduction. Omission of the distribution deduction at this point introduces no error, because section 643(a)(1) requires taxable income to be increased by the distribution deduction in calculating distributable net income. Thus, the process of computing the distribution deduction begins with that of computing distributable net income, which, in turn, begins with tentative taxable income:

Taxpayer	*I.R.S.*	
$56,500	$57,033	tentative taxable income
300	300	exemption (§643(a)(2))
(30,000)	(30,000)	capital gain (§643(a)(3))
14,200	13,667	net tax-exempt interest (§643(a)(5))
		[Taxpayer: $15,000 less the allocable $800; I.R.S.:
		$15,000 less the allocable $1,333]
$41,000	$41,000	DISTRIBUTABLE NET INCOME

The modifications to distributable net income required for purposes of section 651(b) are as follows:

Taxpayer	I.R.S.	
$41,000	$41,000	distributable net income
(14,200)	(13,667)	net tax-exempt interest
$26,800	$27,333	CEILING ON DISTRIBUTION DEDUCTION

Because fiduciary accounting income ($43,000) exceeds the ceiling on the distribution deduction, the trust's distribution deduction equals the section 651(b) ceiling. Finally, calculation of taxable income becomes possible:

Taxpayer	I.R.S.	
$56,500	$57,033	tentative taxable income
26,800	27,333	distribution deduction
$29,700	$29,700	TAXABLE INCOME

As the court noted, disallowance of any portion of the trust's indirect expenses would have had no effect upon the trust's taxable income (or its tax liability), assuming that the increased distribution deduction was still available procedurally. The court nevertheless decided the issue, because its resolution directly affected the taxation of the trust's beneficiaries.

Under section 652(a), a beneficiary of a simple trust is subject to taxation on the fiduciary accounting income, limited by distributable net income. In the fact pattern assumed above, the lesser of such amounts is $41,000. However, section 652(b) states that the amounts distributed "have the same character in the hands of the beneficiary as in the hands of the trust." Under the taxpayer's allocation, only $800 of indirect expenses are charged to the $15,000 of tax-exempt interest. Therefore, $14,200 of the $41,000 subject to taxation in the beneficiary's hands is tax-exempt, leaving income taxable to him or her of $26,800. However, the I.R.S., in its audit position, allocated $1,333 of indirect expenses to the tax-exempt interest, leaving only $13,667 of tax-exempt income for the beneficiary. Of the $41,000 subject to taxation in the beneficiary's hands, $27,333 would thus be taxable.

2. In finding Treas. Reg. § 1.652(c)-4 and Instruction 39 not unreasonable, the court in *Manufacturers Hanover* stated that the regulation and instruction "allowably balance this incongruity—that the income beneficiary, not the corpus beneficiary, receives the tax benefit of expenses allocable to corpus." See, also, *infra*, footnote 2 of *Tucker v. Commissioner*. To illustrate this proposition, consider a trust, the terms of which require the payment of all income currently and which permit no distributions of principal. Assume that the trust generates $5,000 of taxable dividend income during the taxable year, all of which is allocated to income for fiduciary accounting purposes. Assume further that the trust incurs a trustee's commission of $1,000 during the year and that the commission is charged one-half to income and one-half to principal under the state's fiduciary accounting rules. To further simplify the example, assume that there is no personal exemption. Note that the income beneficiary is entitled to receive $4,500, fiduciary accounting receipts ($5,000) reduced by one-half of the trustee's commission ($500); the principal account bears the other one-half of the commission. Who benefits from the section 212 deduction for the trustee's commission? The trust is entitled to a distribution deduction under section 651. The beneficiary must correspondingly include in his or her income an amount determined under section 652 (the two amounts will be the same). The distribution deduction is limited to DNI; DNI, *in this case*, is the same as the tentative taxable income of the trust, which is $4,000, because all of the trustee's commission is fully deductible under section 212 (notwithstanding that a portion of it was actually paid by the principal account). If DNI is $4,000, then the distribution de-

duction is $4,000, which eliminates the tax liability of the trust. Under section 652, the beneficiary must include in gross income the amount of the distribution, but no more than DNI. In this case, the beneficiary has received $4,500, but DNI is only $4,000. Thus, the amount taxed to the beneficiary is limited to $4,000; the beneficiary has, in effect, received $500 tax free. Note that the income beneficiary has benefitted from the *entire* deduction, notwithstanding that the remainder beneficiaries (who will ultimately receive the principal account) have borne one-half of the cost of the deduction. Because the income beneficiary benefits from this incongruity, the court decides that it is not unreasonable to impose the section 265 disallowance disproportionately on the income beneficiary.

3. In *Stevens v. Commissioner,* 78 T.C.M. (CCH) 230 (1999), the court denied deductibility under section 212 of expenses a successor trustee incurred in defending a lawsuit against the trust. The lawsuit derived from "allegations that [the settlor] was mentally incompetent and that [the taxpayer] caused, induced, deluded, misled, forced, and/or otherwise unduly influenced [the settlor] to execute the Trust. None of the claims included allegations of mismanagement or waste of Trust assets, or diversion of Trust income." 78 T.C.M. (CCH) at 234. Thus, according to the court, the lawyer's fees involved "had their origin in a dispute over title to property. Therefore, those fees must be capitalized." *Id.* at 235; *see* Treas. Reg. § 1.263(a)-2(c).

Tucker v. Commissioner
322 F.2d 86 (2d Cir. 1963)

LEONARD P. MOORE, Circuit Judge.

This is a petition for review of a decision of the Tax Court, reported at 38 T.C. 955 (1962), determining a deficiency of $28,703.71 in the income tax of the petitioner, Marcia Brady Tucker, and her deceased husband for the calendar year 1955. Marcia Brady Tucker is the income beneficiary of a trust created under the will of her father. The entire net income from the trust, other than capital gains, is payable to her for life. The income of the trust for 1955 consisted of $380,122.21 of tax-exempt municipal bond interest, $607,497.84 of taxable dividends and interest, and $1,408,887.31 of net long term capital gains.

The trust expenditures not directly attributable to any specific class of income amounted to $148,817.36. These expenses were all chargeable to and paid out of the corpus of the trust.[2] The sole controversy between the parties is over the method of allocation of these administrative expenses between the tax-exempt and taxable income of the trust. The trustee allocated these expenses pro rata among all items of tax-exempt and taxable income, including capital gains, thereby arriving at an allocation of $23,464.09 to tax-exempt income and $125,353.27 to taxable income. The Commissioner made the allocation only among the items of tax-exempt and taxable income distributable to the income beneficiary. By excluding capital gains, he arrived at an allocation of $56,456.84 of the expenses to tax-exempt income and $92,360.52 to taxable income, thus increasing the amount of the expenses allocated to tax-exempt income by $32,992.77. The Commissioner's alloca-

---

2. Under the 1954 Code, the income beneficiary receives the benefit of all the deductions of the trust not attributable to tax-exempt interest, including those deductions, if any, properly allocable to capital gains. This change from the practice under the Internal Revenue Code of 1939 was made to avoid the wasting of deductions that was possible under that Code. See generally, H.Rep. No. 1337, 83rd Cong., 2d Sess., A196-198 (1954); S.Rep. No. 1622, 83rd Cong., 2d Sess., 345–47 (1954)....

tion has no effect on the amount of income which is taxable to the trust,[3] but it does increase by $32,992.77 the amount of the distribution which must be included in the gross income of the taxpayer. This increase produced the deficiency of $28,703.71. The Tax Court upheld the Commissioner's determination on the ground that Section 652(b) of the Internal Revenue Code of 1954 mandated the allocation as made by the Commissioner. We affirm.

Section 652(b) ... provides....

Section 643 defines the term "distributable net income" to mean the taxable income of the estate or trust computed with certain modifications. One of the modifications enumerated is the exclusion of capital gains to the extent that these gains are allocated to corpus and are not paid, credited, or required to be distributed to any beneficiary during the taxable year. Section 643(a)(3). As noted earlier, the capital gains of the trust in question are not distributed to the beneficiary but are required to be retained in the trust corpus. Thus, the capital gains of the trust are not part of the distributable net income of the trust as defined in section 643 and are, therefore, not an "item of distributable net income" for purposes of allocation under section 652(b). According to the terms of the statute itself, then, the allocation of the Commissioner is the proper one.[5]

Taxpayer seeks to avoid the mandate of section 652(b) and the regulations promulgated thereunder by arguing that section 265, and not section 652(b), controls the allocation in question. She argues that trust disbursements (expenses) are to be allocated to tax-exempt interest according to the principles of section 265,[6] and that the amount of the expenses held to be nondeductible, because allocated to tax-exempt interest under section 265, is not an item of deduction entering into the computation of distributable net income for purposes of section 652(b). According to the taxpayer, section 652 is concerned only with the allocation of deductions, for the purpose of determining the income character in the hands of the beneficiary, after the amount of the deduction has been determined under section 265.

Taxpayer's analysis would leave no operative significance for section 652(b). Carrying the analysis to its logical conclusion and still giving effect to section 652(b) would produce strange results. For example, section 652(b) requires that deductions entering into the computation of distributable net income be allocated among the items of distributable net income. One of the items of distributable net income is tax-exempt income. Section 643(a)(5). Allocating a portion of the deduction (defined by taxpayer to exclude the amount allocated to tax-exempt income under section 265) to tax-exempt income would mean that expenses clearly attributable to taxable income would be lost to the taxpayer. The only way to avoid that result would be to exclude tax-exempt interest from the base for the purpose of the section 652(b) allocation. This would do violence to the clear requirement of that section.

---

3. This method of allocation does not change the total amount of the deductions available to the trust. When the trust's deductible expenses are decreased, the deduction allowed for the amount of the income required to be distributed to beneficiaries is increased by an equal amount. See Section 651 of the Internal Revenue Code of 1954.

5. The Regulations to section 652(b) also call for the allocation made by the Commissioner. See Treas. Reg. § 1.652(b)-3(b).

6. Treas. Reg. § 1.265-1(c) provides that if an expense is allocable to both exempt and nonexempt income, a "reasonable proportion thereof * * * shall be allocated to each."

Taxpayer argues that the trustee's allocation of the expenses among all classes of income is the only reasonable one under this section. The Court of Claims, however, has held that the Commissioner's allocation is reasonable under section 265. Manufacturers Hanover Trust Co. v. United States, 312 F.2d 785 (Ct.Cl. 1963).

The basic fallacy in taxpayer's argument is that it contemplates two allocations, one to determine the trust's deductions and the other to allocate those deductions among the items of distributable net income. The statutory pattern calls for one allocation and that allocation is governed by section 652. To hold otherwise would be to deny any effect to the language of that section.

Affirmed.

Illustrative Material

Obviously, the Second Circuit in *Tucker* reaches the same result as the Court of Claims reached in *Manufacturers Hanover*. The Second Circuit, however, offers a very different, and far more persuasive, rationale, which relies on two independent propositions. The first of the *Tucker* propositions is that, in the second sentence of section 652(b), Congress itself tells us how to calculate the disallowance ratio, at least for purposes of determining the impact on the beneficiaries' taxable incomes. Under section 652(b), only those items of income that enter into DNI count. Under section 643(a)(3), capital gains rarely enter into DNI. Thus, capital gains are rarely relevant in calculating the disallowance ratio, at least for purposes of determining the impact on the beneficiaries' taxable incomes. The second of the *Tucker* propositions is that the disallowance ratio mandated by section 652(b) on the beneficiaries' side of the equation must also control for purposes of calculating the distribution deduction on the section 651 side of the equation, or the trust's distribution deduction will not equal the total increase in the beneficiaries' taxable incomes. The fundamental purpose of sections 651 and 652 is to allocate a trust's actual income between the trust and its beneficiaries — not to increase or decrease that income. If it were permissible to use one disallowance ratio to compute the distribution deduction under section 651 and another to compute the increase in the beneficiaries' taxable incomes under 652, the total amount of income on which the trust and its beneficiaries would pay tax would differ from the trust's actual income — and that would constitute a fundamental breakdown in the operation of subchapter J.

Revenue Ruling 77-355
1977-2 C.B. 82

Advice has been requested whether, under the circumstances described below, a simple trust that does not distribute capital gains, because they are allocable to corpus under the trust instrument or applicable local law, may include, for purposes of computing its distributable net income under section 643(a) of the Internal Revenue Code of 1954, capital gains in the formula for allocating indirect expenses to tax-exempt income.

In 1975 *A* created a simple trust for the benefit of *A*'s child, *B*. The trust instrument provides that the trustee shall distribute, currently, the entire net income of the trust to *B*. The trust instrument does not authorize distributions of corpus during *B's* lifetime. Capital gains are allocable to corpus under state law.

For the taxable year 1976 the trust's income consisted of taxable interest, tax-exempt interest, and capital gains. In the trust's U.S. Fiduciary Income Tax Return (Form 1041) for 1976, the trustee in computing distributable net income allocated its compensation between taxable and tax-exempt income on the basis of a formula that included the trust's capital gains.

Section 641(b) of the Code provides that the taxable income of an estate or trust will be computed in the same manner as in the case of an individual, except as otherwise provided.

Section 643(a)(3) of the Code provides, in part, that in computing distributable net income, capital gains are excluded to the extent they are allocable to corpus and are not (A) paid, credited, or required to be distributed to any beneficiary during the taxable year, or (B) paid, permanently set aside, or to be used for the purpose specified in section 642(c).

Section 652(a) of the Code provides for the amount of income for the taxable year required to be distributed currently by a trust described in section 651 to be included in the gross income of the beneficiaries to whom the income is required to be distributed to the extent of their respective shares of distributable net income.

Section 652(b) of the Code provides, in part, that the items of deduction entering into the computation of distributable net income shall be allocated among the items of distributable net income in accordance with regulations prescribed by the Secretary or the Secretary's delegate.

Section 1.652(b)-3(b) of the Income Tax Regulations provides, in part, that deductions that are not directly attributable to a specific class of income may be allocated to any item of income (including capital gains) included in computing distributable net income, but a portion must be allocated to nontaxable income ... pursuant to section 265 and the regulations thereunder.

Section 1.652(b)-3(b) of the regulations further indicates that deductions that are not directly attributable to a specific class of income are not to be allocated to capital gains of the trust allocable to corpus since the capital gains are not taken into account in the computation of distributable net income.

With regard to a trust required to distribute all its income currently, section 1.652(c)-4 of the regulations sets forth a comprehensive example showing the application of the allocation rule for deductions not directly allocable to a specific class of income for a trust that has tax-exempt income and capital gains allocable to corpus.

Section [265(a)(1)] of the Code provides, in part, that no deduction shall be allowed for any amount otherwise allowable as a deduction that is allocable to one or more classes of income other than interest wholly exempt from tax, or any amount otherwise allowable under section 212 that is allocable to interest wholly exempt from tax.

Section 1.265-1(c) of the regulations provides, in part, that if an expense or amount otherwise allowable is indirectly allocable to both a class of nonexempt income and a class of exempt income, a reasonable proportion thereof determined in light of all the facts and circumstances in each case shall be allocated to each.

Section 265 of the Code governs the allocation of expenses between taxable and tax-exempt income. Section 1.265-1(c) of the regulations requires that allocation of indirect expenses be made "in light of all facts and circumstances in each case." The distributable net income concept is the primary mechanism by which the income of a trust is taxed only once, either to the trust or to its beneficiaries, and should not be disregarded in applying the general allocation provisions of section 265 to the particular problems of trust income. See *Manufacturers Hanover Trust Co. v. United States,* 312 F.2d 785 (Ct. Cl. 1963); and *Tucker v. Commissioner,* 322 F.2d 86 (2d Cir. 1963).

Rev. Rul. 73-565, 1973-2 C.B. 90, holds that for purposes of the allocation required under section 265 of the Code, an individual taxpayer whose income included capital gains and losses, tax-exempt and taxable interest, and gross rents, properly determined the deductible portion of office expenses not directly allocable to a particular item of income or loss by use of a fraction that included the capital gains but disregarded capital losses in both the numerator and denominator.

Rev. Rul. 73-565 is distinguishable from the instant case. Rev. Rul. 73-565 deals with the allocation of expenses to the tax-exempt income of an individual taxpayer and does not apply to the allocation of indirect expenses to tax-exempt income in computing the distributable net income of a simple trust when the distributable net income of the trust does not include capital gains.

In the case of an individual taxpayer there is no division of the taxable income between two or more parties. Therefore, it is proper to allocate expenses under section 212 of the Code to all of the taxable income (including capital gains) of the individual. However, in the case of a simple trust, there may be a division of the taxable income earned by the trust between the trust and its beneficiaries. Therefore, in computing the distributable net income of such trusts, which will determine the amount to be included by the beneficiaries in their gross income, the allocation of indirect expenses must be made only with respect to the income (taxable and tax-exempt) that is to be distributed currently to the beneficiaries by the trust.

In the instant case, the trust's capital gains are not included in the computation of distributable net income under the provisions of section 643(a)(3) of the Code. Therefore, the capital gains may not be included in the formula for allocating indirect expenses to tax-exempt income, and the trustee's allocation was improper.

Rev. Rul. 73-565 is distinguished.

Illustrative Material

In Rev. Rul. 80-165, 1980-1 C.B. 134, the I.R.S. ruled that a corporate distribution described in section 301(c)(2) should not be included in the formula for allocating indirect trust expenses to tax-exempt income. Such a distribution is excluded from gross income, as a return of capital. Though section 643(a) does include in distributable net income some items of tax-exempt income (such as interest described in section 103), distributable net income does not include distributions described in section 301(c)(2).

Whittemore v. United States
383 F.2d 824 (8th Cir. 1967)

HEANEY, Circuit Judge.

This case presents the question: Are fiduciary fees for the management, conservation or maintenance of that part of a trust or estate consisting of municipal bonds (the interest income which [sic] is tax-free) deductible under 26 U.S.C. §212 (1964)? We reverse the decision of the District Court and hold that to the extent that the municipals produced taxable income or were held for that purpose, the fees, whether measured by the income or the value of the municipals, are deductible and that a reasonable basis for determining the deductible portion is the ratio of taxable to nontaxable income.

In particular, we are concerned with two trusts and one estate. The grantor of the trusts established an intervivos trust in 1910 and a testamentary trust in 1919. After his death, both trusts paid the net annual income to his widow and daughters for their lives. The last surviving daughter died in 1958. The assets of the trusts and daughter's estate were distributed in 1959 and 1960 to the children and grandchildren of the last surviving daughter.

The intervivos trust contained assets at termination valued at $2,307,493, of which $705,400, or 30.5%, was invested in municipals. The testamentary trust contained $4,269,239, of which $1,688,870, or 39.5%, was invested in municipals. From 1950 to 1959, the investment in municipals varied from a high of 47.8% to a low of 37.8% in the testamentary trust, and from 40.2% to 30.7% in the intervivos trust. The estate consisted of assets totaling $1,365,345, of which $29,213, or 2.985%, were in municipals.[2]

The St. Louis Union Trust Company was the common corporate fiduciary for both trusts and the estate. Upon termination of the testamentary trust, a child of the last surviving daughter was co-trustee; and, until his death, he was a co-executor of his mother's estate. He received one-half of the corporate trustee's fees, both annual and termination, for the testamentary trust during the thirteen months he served as co-trustee.

The fee paid by the intervivos trust, established by agreement, was 2.5% of the yearly income of the trust, and 2.5% of the value of the corpus at termination. The fee paid by the testamentary trust, based on the customary charge of the corporate trustee at the inception of the trust, was 5% of yearly income, and 5% of value of corpus at termination. The executor's fee was determined in accordance with Missouri statutory law. Mo.Rev.Stat. §473.153 (1955). In addition, the estate incurred legal expenses totaling $17,500.

Total fiduciary fees of $585,730 were paid as follows:

	INTERVIVOS TRUST	TESTAMENTARY TRUST	ESTATE	TOTAL
Annual fees measured by income from time to time collected	$64,561.05	$198,307.74	$262,868.79	
Termination fees measured by the value of the corpus	$57,263.35	$230,046.30	$35,552.27	$322,861.92
TOTALS	$121,824.40	$428,354.04	$35,552.27	$585,730.71

Interest income from the municipals was included in total income for the purpose of determining the trustee's annual compensation but consistent with 26 U.S.C. §103 (1964) was excluded from gross income for income tax purposes. That portion of the annual fee deemed allocable to interest on the municipals was not deducted in computing the annual income tax. The basis of the allocation was the ratio of tax-exempt income to total income. The entire termination fees were taken as deductions from gross income in the years in which each trust terminated. As the fees exceeded taxable income, the beneficiary took the excess deduction against his own income in accordance with the provisions of 26 U.S.C. §[642(h)(2)].

In auditing the fiduciary and individual returns, the District Director of the Internal Revenue Service refused to permit the taxpayer to deduct any part of the termination fees paid for services of the trustee in administering that part of the corpus invested in municipals. The Director used the ratio of the value of the municipals to the value of the

---

2. This discussion will concern itself with the major trusts—as the lower court and the parties agree that the same principles are applicable to the estate.

total assets to determine what portion of the fees represented the efforts of the trustee in administering the municipals. In explaining the disallowance, it was stated:

> "Since the municipal bonds' income is tax exempt, the commission charged on these assets would not be deductible under Section 1.265-1(a)(2) of the Regulations which does not allow a deduction for expenses pertaining to exempt income."

A deficiency was assessed and paid. The taxpayer, as a beneficiary entitled to the benefit of any excess deduction allowed, filed a timely claim for a refund. Upon disallowance of his claim, an action was commenced in U.S. District Court.

The District Court sustained the position of the Commissioner of Internal Revenue and held that the Commissioner had properly refused to permit the taxpayer to deduct any part of the termination fee paid for services relating to the municipals....

The court also stated that even if that portion of the termination fees (based on the value of the municipals) which relate to the preservation of the corpus was deductible, it would not be allowed here because the taxpayer had failed to establish the extent to which the trustee's services related to preservation of the corpus.

The taxpayer contends: that the termination fees were expenses solely for the management, conservation or maintenance of property held for the production of income, and were fully deductible under the provisions of §212(2) of the Internal Revenue Code without regard to the type of income produced; and that expenses under §212(2) are not subject to disallowance under §[265(a)(1)].

He argues, in the alternative, that if the termination fees were not entirely deductible, they were at least partially deductible. In the event that his alternative position is accepted, he urges that the allocation should be based on the ratio of tax-exempt income to total income rather than the ratio of the value of municipals to the value of total assets.

In our judgment, a proper construction of §§212 and 265 requires that we reject the taxpayer's principal contention that the entire termination fee is deductible, and the District Court's holding that no part of it is deductible.

(1) *Section 212 permits expenses for the production of income, or the management, conservation or maintenance of property held for the production of income to be deducted.*

[The court quotes section 212(1) and (2) and discusses and quotes from *Trust of Bingham v. Commissioner,* 325 U.S. 365 (1945), *supra* (ch 2., sec. B(3)(a)).]

(2) *Section [265(a)(1)] limits the deductibility of expenses otherwise allowable under §212(2) to those incurred in whole or in part for the production of taxable income.*

The *Bingham* case did not, as urged by the taxpayer, answer the question—are all expenses incurred for the management, conservation or maintenance of property held for the production of income deductible or may such expenses be nondeductible in whole or part by operation of 26 U.S.C. §[265(a)(1)]? It provides....

Since expenses deductible under §§212(1) and (2) are either directly or indirectly related to income, the problem becomes apparent—does the language of §[265(a)(1)] disallowing expenses "allocable" to tax-exempt interest refer only to expenses *directly* relating to income, or does it also encompass expenses *indirectly* relating to income?

The current regulation, Treas.Reg. §1.212-1 (1954), appears to require that expenses deductible under both subsections of §212 be apportioned between taxable and nontaxable income. [The court quotes Treas.Reg. §1.212-1(e).] However, the taxpayer argues that subsection (i) of the same regulation permits §212(2) expenses to be deducted in their entirety.... We consider subsection (e) to be controlling since it was there that the Treasury specifically addressed itself to the question of which §212 expenses were to be disallowed by §265. This subsection is also consistent with subsection (a)(1) of the same regulation which clearly states that an expense may be deducted under §212 only if it has been incurred "(i) for the production or collection of *income which, if and when realized, will be required to be included in income for Federal income tax purposes* or (ii) for the management, conservation, or maintenance of property held for the production of *such income* * * *."* (Emphasis added.)

The Tax Court has faced the issue presented by §§212(2) and [265(a)(1)] in the context of legal expenses incurred by the estates of living persons and has concluded that expenses under §212(2) must be apportioned between taxable and nontaxable income....

Initially, it should be noted that the second clause of §[265(a)(1)] disallows expenses allocable to tax-exempt interest which are "otherwise allowable under §212." Since §212 is referred to as a whole, it seems clear that the plain meaning of §265 is to disallow expenses otherwise allowable under either §§212(1) or (2).

Although §212 is referred to as a whole in §265, arguably that reference is immediately qualified by a parenthetical suggesting a different result. Including the parenthetical, the section provides:

"No deduction shall be allowed for—

" * * * any amount otherwise allowable under section 212 (*relating to expenses for production of income*) which is allocable to interest (whether or not any amount of such interest is received or accrued) wholly exempt from the taxes imposed by this subtitle." [Emphasis added.]

Thus, it could be argued that "(* * * expenses for production of income)" parallels §212(1) which generally allows "expenses * * * for the production or collection of income" and does not parallel §212(2) which generally allows "expenses * * * for the management, conservation, or maintenance of property held for the production of income." However, the argument is without merit when considered in the light of the statutory evolution of §§212 and 265.

* * *

In 1954, §23(a)(2) [of the 1939 Code] was reenacted in §§212(1) and (2). The 1954 Code also, for the first time, provided for a deduction of expenses relating to the payment of taxes. This provision was enacted in §212(3).... At the same time §24(a)(5) became §265[. I]t was also at that time that the parenthetical—"(relating to expenses for the production of income)"—first appeared in that section. Since the legislative history indicates that no substantive change in §265 was intended,[17] the inclusion of the parenthetical, in the reenacted section, only makes it clear that expenses relating to the determination, collection, or refund of taxes would not be disallowed because the expense involved issues related to tax-exempt interest. For example, the litigation expenses incurred by the taxpayers in this appeal would presumably be deductible even though issues are presented in this case relating to the interest income from municipals.[18]

---

17. H.R.Rep.No. 1337, U.S.CODE CONG. & ADM.NEWS, pp. 4025, 4196 (1954); Sen.Rep.No. 1622, U.S.CODE CONG. & ADM.NEWS, pp. 4621, 4855 (1954).

18. Cf. Kaufmann v. United States, D.C., 227 F.Supp. 807 (1963) (legal expenses incurred in obtaining a ruling that a proposed stock exchange was tax free held to be deductible under §212(3)). Compare, TREA.REG. §1.212-1(a)(1)(i) & (ii), with TREA.REG. §1.212-1(a)(1)(iii).

Not only does the language of the statute suggest that both §§212(1) and (2) expenses must be apportioned between taxable and nontaxable income; the policy underlying the statute also suggests the same result. [I]n 1941 the Supreme Court held that investment counseling expenses were not deductible because the then applicable section of the Code only allowed deductions for "trade or business expenses." However, since nonbusiness income was included in gross income, Congress enacted what is now §§212(1) and (2) which provides that certain nonbusiness expenses are deductible. Thus, by providing for nonbusiness expenses, Congress furthered the underlying philosophy of a tax on net income rather than on gross income. This is evidenced by the statement of Representative Disney:

> "The Internal Revenue Code provides that expenses incurred in the trade or business of the taxpayer may be deducted in arriving at *net income*. The law also provides that personal living or family expenses may not be deducted. There is left a great borderland of doubt. Trade or business has received such a narrow interpretation that many meritorious deductions are denied. The Supreme Court, in the case of Higgins v. Commissioner of Internal Revenue (312 U.S. 212, 61 S.Ct. 475, 85 L.Ed. 783 (1941)), held that expenses in connection with a taxpayer's investments in income-producing properties were not deductible, on the ground that making casual investments was not a trade or business. *Since the income from such investments is clearly taxable it is inequitable to deny the deduction of expenses attributable to such investments.*"[19] [Emphasis added.]

The enactment of §§212(1) and (2) matched up nonbusiness expenses with the current or future nonbusiness income.

Since the section matches nonbusiness expenses to taxable nonbusiness income, it follows that to the extent that the nonbusiness income need not be included in the gross taxable income, the corresponding expense should not be allowed. If it were otherwise, the taxpayer would receive a double advantage—he could take a deduction against other taxable income and yet receive tax free the income to which the expense related. The purpose of §[265(a)(1)] is to eliminate this double advantage. Cf. C.I.R. v. McDonald, 320 F.2d 109 (5th Cir. 1963); Lewis v. Commissioner of Internal Revenue, 47 F.2d 32 (3d Cir. 1931)....

In this case, the taxpayer argues that no double advantage will accrue to him since the capital gains income from the municipals is taxable.[20] However, the argument ignores the fact that the municipals are currently held for the production of two types of income—nontaxable coupon interest and taxable capital gains income. Furthermore, §212 provides a deduction for nonbusiness expenses because the nonbusiness income is taxable. Thus, to the extent that the trust holds the municipals for the production of nontaxable income, that portion of the §212(2) expenses must be disallowed. Conversely, to the extent that municipals are held for the production of taxable income, a portion of the expense must be allowed.

(3) *A reasonable basis for determining the deductible portion of the fiduciary's termination fee as it relates to the municipals in trust is the ratio of taxable to nontaxable income over the life of the trust.*

---

19. 88th Cong.Rec., Part 5, p. 6376....

20. In general, capital gains on the sale of municipal bonds are taxable. Willcuts v. Bunn, 282 U.S. 216, 51 S.Ct. 125, 75 L.Ed. 304 (1931)....

The government's allocation (based on the ratio of municipals to other securities) would deny the taxpayer the right to deduct any portion of the termination fee computed on the value of the municipals. The taxpayer's allocation would permit the deduction of the entire fee. Neither approach is proper for neither recognizes that a fiduciary invests in municipals to produce taxable and nontaxable income, and manages them for the same purposes.

While we accept the trial court's finding that the fiduciary here invested in municipals for the *primary* purpose of producing tax-exempt income, it does not follow that the primary purpose was the only one. Other factors, notably appreciation and safety, enter into an investment decision.

The ratio of taxable to nontaxable income was used as a basis for determining the extent to which the trustee's annual fees were deductible. CASNER, ESTATE PLANNING, Vol. II, 1161 n. 17 (1961). Cf. William H. Jamison, 8 T.C. 173, 182 (1947); George N. Meissner, 8 T.C. 780 (1947); Edward Mallinckrodt, Jr., 2 T.C. 1128 (1943); Cynthia K. Herbst, 2 CCH Tax Court Memorandum Decisions 361, 364–65 (1943). Contra, Estate of Elsie Weil, [13 CCH Tax Court Memorandum Decisions 653 (1954)]. But cf. Manufacturers Hanover Trust Co. v. United States, 160 Ct.Cl. 582, 312 F.2d 785, 794, n. 12 (1963); Valerie Norrie Pozzo di Borgo, [23 T.C. 76 (1954)]; Kilborn, Deductible Expenses; Transactions Entered Into for Profit; Income-Producing Property, 21 N.Y.U.FED.TAX INST. We see no sound reason why the same ratio cannot be used to determine the extent to which the termination fees are deductible. Indeed, support for such a position is contained in the trial court's findings that the annual and termination fees should be considered as "one" and as having been rendered for "past services."

While no formula can measure with exactness the value of a fiduciary's fees as they relate to taxable and nontaxable income, a ratio based on the earnings from each serves as a reasonably accurate measuring stick, particularly when the life of the trust extends, as here, over an extended period of years.

We believe the income ratio to be a reasonable one for allocating the expenses for the production of taxable income and for the production of nontaxable income. It is simple and is supported not only by precedent but also by the manner in which the annual fiduciary's fees were handled. Clearly, the asset ratio used by the government is inappropriate because, as was already noted, that method disallows the total portion of the fees allocable to municipals. Thus, since the municipals produce both taxable and nontaxable income, a second allocation would be necessary if it were used. If the second allocation were on an income basis, the result achieved would be similar to that under the formula we suggest. If some other rule of thumb were used, it would have to be supported by reasons justifying its use. No other logical allocation formula has been suggested here.

To summarize, we hold a fiduciary's fee (annual or termination) for the production of *taxable* income or for the management, conservation or maintenance of property held for the production of *taxable* income is deductible under §212(1) and (2) and is not disallowed by §265. Thus, to the extent that municipals in a trust or an estate produce *taxable* income or are held for the purpose, the fee of the fiduciary, whether measured by the income or value of the municipals in the trust, is deductible.

Under the facts of this case, a reasonable basis for determining the extent to which the fiduciary's fee was related to taxable income and thus deductible is the ratio of taxable income to nontaxable income over the life of the trust.

This matter is reversed and remanded to the District Court for action consistent with this opinion.

Illustrative Material

In *Estate of O'Connor v. Commissioner,* 69 T.C. 165 (1977), the Tax Court allocated to tax-exempt income a portion of executors' commissions paid pursuant to a judicial accounting, despite the fact that the estate had had no tax-exempt income during the tax year in which the commissions were paid. The nondeductible portion was determined by multiplying the commissions by a fraction, the numerator of which was tax-exempt income earned during the entire accounting period and the denominator of which was total income earned during the same period. The court noted, however, that it viewed the issue as "abandoned" because of the taxpayers' failure to address it in their briefs.

Fabens v. Commissioner

519 F.2d 1310 (1st Cir. 1975)

McENTEE, Circuit Judge.

The parties stipulated that from 1953 to 1969 taxpayer Fabens maintained in a trust account municipal bonds, the income from which was tax-exempt, and other securities the income from which was taxable. The trust also realized capital gains and losses from transactions involving its holdings. Upon termination the fair market value of the trust assets included a considerable amount of unrealized capital appreciation[1] which was reflected in the fiduciary fees paid on termination and computed under local law as a percentage of current market value. Taxpayer deducted the full amount of these commissions as expenses for the production of income under Int.Rev.Code §212.[2] The Commissioner

---

1. The stipulation as to these amounts is summarized in the following table:

	Applicable to municipal bond holdings	Applicable to non-municipal bond holdings	Total
Income due to dividends and interest realized over the life of the trust, 4/9/53–6/16/69	$211,443	$503,641	$715,084
Capital gain income realized over the life of the trust as a result of sales, liquidations, distributions or uncollectibility of principal, 4/9/53–6/19/69	($127,340)	$152,349	$25,009
Unrealized appreciation during period 4/9/53–6/16/69	–0–	$1,476,023	$1,476,023
Ordinary income realized by the trust for the calendar year 1969	$9,028	$15,715	$24,743

2. Upon termination of the trust on June 16, 1969, taxpayer paid trustee the following fiduciary commissions:

A.   Receiving and Paying Commissions:
   (a)   Receiving Commissions:
        (i)   Receiving commissions based on capital appreciation of assets sold, redeemed and collected $717.31
        (ii)   Receiving commission based on capital increase of assets distributed   <u>18,401.12</u>
                            $19,118.43
   (b)   Paying Commissions:
        (i)   Paying commission based on market value at date of distribution, administrative expenses and assets remaining on hand   <u>31,576.30</u>
           TOTAL Receiving and Paying Commissions: $50,694.73

disallowed a portion of this deduction pursuant to Int.Rev.Code §[265(a)(1)] prohibiting the deduction of expenses directly or indirectly allocable to the production of tax-exempt income. The fees were disallowed in the ratio of tax-exempt income over the life of the trust to total income (including net capital gains) realized during that period.[3] In the Tax Court taxpayer argued that this formula was not reasonable in the light of all the facts and circumstances, Treas.Reg. §1.265-1(c), because it did not reflect the unrealized appreciation of the trust assets. The court upheld the Commissioner's allocation and taxpayer appeals.

The Commissioner argues there was no evidence that the trust assets were actually managed for capital appreciation; and that to the extent they were so managed, the Commissioner's inclusion in his allocation formula of net capital gains realized over the life of the trust reasonably reflect this fact. We disagree on both counts. As an initial matter even if achieving appreciation were not a prime goal of the trustee's management, it would remain unclear how fees created solely because of a rise in the value of taxable investments could be considered "allocable" within the statute to the production of tax exempt income. At any rate, while there is no specific evidence as to the trustee's investment objectives, that appreciation was such an objective is inferable from the facts that the trustee apparently insisted on compensation for appreciation when the trust was established, and that appreciation under the trustee's management comprised more than half of the corpus value at termination. As to the second point, since the trustee's decision to sell securities (thereby realizing capital appreciation) is dictated by considerations other than that of the trust's termination date, there is no necessary reason to suppose that the net capital gains realized over the life of the trust and included in the Commissioner's formula will fairly reflect the trustee's division of labor between exempt and taxable income-production activities in administering the trust.[4] Since the value of the property comprising

---

B. Trustee's annual principal commission (based on the then current
    market value of the fund)   1,279.42
C. Trustee's annual income commission (based on income collected
    for period 5/3/68–6/1/69   1,920.52
TOTAL fiduciary commissions due and paid Bankers Trust Company
upon termination of Trust Agreement in June 1969 $53,894.67

3. In allocating a portion of these expenses to the tax-exempt income, the Commissioner first determined the total amount of tax-exempt income earned by the trust between 1953 and 1969 ($211,443), and then computed the total income of the trust for this period ($740,093) [$715,084 plus $25,009], which included taxable interest and dividends and capital gains [and losses], plus the tax-exempt income. Tax-exempt income was then expressed as a percentage of total income

$\left(\frac{\$740,093}{\$211,443} = 28.57 \text{ percent}\right)$ [sic], and this percentage was applied to the total amount of receiving and paying commissions incurred upon termination of the trust ($50,695) to determine the amount of the termination commissions ($14,484) allocable to tax-exempt income. The Commissioner made a separate allocation with respect to the annual commissions (income and principal commissions) for 1969 in the total amount of $3,241. The Commissioner allocated this commission by computing the total income (taxable and tax exempt) of the trust for 1969 ($24,743), and computing tax-exempt income for 1969 ($9,028) as a percentage of total income

$\left(\frac{\$9,028}{\$24,843} = 36.49 \text{ percent}\right)$. The percentage was applied to the total annual commissions ($3,241) for 1969 to determine the amount ($1,183) allocable to tax-exempt income for that year. The total amount ($15,667) allocable to tax-exempt income ($14,484 of the termination charges, plus $1,183 of the annual commissions) was disallowed as a deduction pursuant to the provisions of Section 265 of the Code. The Commissioner allowed the remaining amounts ($38,269) as deductions for 1969.

4. Here the unrealized appreciation exceeded the net capital gain included in the Commissioner's ratio by a factor of 60. It is not wholly unrealistic to conceive of a trust owning common stock, which experiences enormous appreciation during the trust's existence while paying little or nothing in div-

corpus generates the fee, an allocation measure like taxpayer's which somehow reflects that value will seemingly result in a fairer apportionment.[5] See M. Ferguson, J. Freeland & R. Stephens, Federal Income Taxation of Estates and Beneficiaries 492–93, 644 n. 115 (1970). The Tax Court characterized the appreciation as "ephemeral," but the commissions it produced represented an outlay very tangible indeed.

It is clear as a general matter that expenditures aimed at the production of future capital gains are deductible under Treas.Reg. §1.212-1(b). It is also clear as a general matter that in the application of §265, an allocation based on realized income is not mandatory, Rev. Rul. 63-27, and this was true as regards trustee's fees too, at least under the 1939 Code. *Edward Mallinckrodt, Jr.,* 2 T.C. 1128, 1148 (1943). The Commissioner argues, however, that where a trust is involved, the concept of distributable net income, see Int.Rev.Code §643(a), and the special system of taxation in subchapter J (dealing with trusts and estates) are important components of "all the facts and circumstances" mentioned in Treas.Reg. §1.265-1(c). *Manufacturers Hanover Trust Co. v. United States,* 312 F.2d 785, 795, 160 Ct.Cl. 582 (1963). Trusts are taxable entities which compute their deductions basically as do individuals, though in order to effectuate the "flow-through" scheme of taxation of subchapter J they are allowed a special deduction for distributions to beneficiaries. Int.Rev.Code §641(b); Treas.Reg. §1.641(b). This distribution deduction is limited by distributable net income, Int.Rev.Code §661(a). The statute contemplates that items of deduction like fiduciary fees be allocated exclusively among items of distributable net income. Int.Rev.Code §661(b); Treas.Reg. §1.652(b)-3(b). Thus, in *Manufacturers Hanover Trust v. United States, supra,* and *Tucker v. Commissioner,* 322 F.2d 86 (2d Cir. 1963), the courts upheld the Commissioner's excluding from the allocation base realized capital gains allocable to corpus not required to be distributed in the current year, hence excluded from distributable net income. Int.Rev.Code §643(a)(3). Since capital appreciation is never included in distributable net income, the Commissioner contends, it may never be included in the base for allocating commissions between exempt and taxable income.

The Commissioner himself acknowledges that the allocation of termination fees like those involved here may not be subject to the strictures of the distributable net income concept, conceding that the deductions may instead pass to beneficiaries under the general allocation provisions and the excess deduction provisions of §642(h)(2). We think this is in fact the case. Distributable net income is an annual concept. Int.Rev.Code §643(a). *Manufacturers Hanover Trust* and *Tucker* involved annual commissions and income beneficiaries.[6] Since income beneficiaries would not be taxed for capital gains (which were allocated to corpus under the trust instrument), the Court of Claims saw no reason to give them the added advantage of a deduction for expenses which would be inflated if it included fees based on such gains—gains which would eventually be a tax burden to another (the remainderman). 312 F.2d at 796. In the present case taxpayer will receive the benefit of the appreciation if anyone does. There is no authority in the Code for computing,

---

idends as growth stocks often do, along with a single municipal bond paying a steady coupon interest. In such a situation the Commissioner's formula would obviously result in a distorted apportionment of termination fees paid for the whole job of administering the trust. See *In re Gildersleeve's Estate,* 75 Misc.2d 207, 347 N.Y.S.2d 96 (Sur.Ct.1973).

5. This may be a special "fact and circumstance" to be considered in making the allocation under Treas.Reg. §1.265-1(c). M. Ferguson, J. Freeland & R. Stephens, Federal Income Taxation of Estates and Beneficiaries 493 (1970).

6. The Court in *Manufacturers Hanover Trust* twice noted, 312 F.2d at 794, 796 & nn. 13, 15, that the case would "present different problems" if the allowable deductions exceeded distributable net income as the Tax Court found was the case here.

as the Commissioner in effect wishes, a second, analogous distributable net income based on figures from the entire duration of the trust. Thus the court in *Whittemore v. United States*, 383 F.2d 824 (8th Cir. 1967), facing the identical issue as we are, seemingly did not feel constrained by Treas.Reg. §1.652(b)-3 in applying §642(h)(2).[7]

In sum, we agree that the Commissioner's allocation was proper as to the annual fees but conclude it was not reasonable in light of all the facts and circumstances, including taxpayer's proposed allocation, insofar as the termination fees were concerned.

Affirmed in part and reversed in part. Remanded for further proceedings consistent with this opinion.

Illustrative Material

Rev. Rul. 63-27, 1963-1 C.B. 57, cited in *Fabens,* admitted that allocation of indirect expenses to taxable and tax-exempt income in the proportion that each bore to total income was not mandatory. The ruling, which involved an estate, instead referred to the rule of Treas. Reg. §1.265-1(c) requiring a "reasonable" allocation "in the light of all the facts and circumstances." The I.R.S. elaborated on Rev. Rul. 63-27 in Rev. Rul. 77-466, 1977-2 C.B. 84. Though a trust had earned tax-exempt income, it earned only taxable income in its year of termination. As a result, the taxpayer allocated none of the termination commissions to tax-exempt income. The I.R.S. found the taxpayer's method unreasonable and ruled that, in the instant case, a reasonable and appropriate method of allocation would be one based on the ratio of tax-exempt income realized by the trust during its existence to the total of ordinary income (including tax-exempt income) realized by the trust during its existence plus the excess of capital gains realized over capital losses sustained over the life of the trust plus any net unrealized capital appreciation of the assets distributed.

Problem

2-1. A trust, which is required to distribute all of its income currently, has the following receipts:

	Year 1	Year 2	Year 3
Dividends	$10,000	$10,000	$10,000
Tax-exempt interest	0	10,000	10,000
Realized capital gains	0	0	80,000

At the end of each year, the value of the trust's assets is as follows:

	Year 1	Year 2	Year 3
Stock	$100,000	$150,000	$200,000
Tax-exempt bonds	150,000	150,000	150,000
All others	100,000	130,000	180,000

No appreciation occurs during Year 1.

a. In Year 1 the trustee's annual fee is $4,000. How much is deductible under section 212?

---

7. Though the allocation fashioned by the court in that case was the one adopted by the Commissioner here, the possibility of considering capital appreciation was not before the court there. The problem it perceived in allocating on the basis of corpus value—that part of the value of the exempt securities represented appreciation which would be taxable when realized even though the income from these securities was not—is absent here where the exempt securities actually depreciated.

b. In Year 2 the trustee's annual fee is $5,000. How much is deductible under section 212?

c. In Year 3 the trustee's annual fee is $6,000. How much is deductible under section 212?

d. At the end of Year 3 the trust terminates. The trustee's termination fee is $6,000. How much is deductible under section 212?

e. Assume instead that at the end of Year 2 the trustee had made a discretionary distribution of one-half of the trust principal to one of its beneficiaries. On account of that distribution the trustee earned a fee of $2,000. How much of this paying-out fee is deductible under section 212?

4. Deduction for Personal Exemption

Internal Revenue Code:
    Section 642(b)

Regulation:
    Section 1.642(b)-1

In lieu of the personal exemption under section 151, estates and trusts are entitled to smaller exemptions under section 642(b). Note carefully that the test for determining whether a trust is entitled to the $300 exemption (as opposed to the $100 exemption) is whether it is "required to distribute all of its income currently"—not whether it qualifies as a "simple" trust under section 651.

In the Taxpayer Relief Act of 1997, Congress enacted a new section 645, which provides an election to treat the decedent's revocable trust as part of the decedent's estate, rather than as a separate trust, for most income tax purposes. If no estate tax return is due, this consolidation is effective for only two years after the decedent's death. If an estate tax return is due, the consolidation generally remains effective until six months after the final determination of the estate tax liability. Such a trust qualifies for neither the $300 nor the $100 exemption; instead, it "shares" the estate's $600 exemption. *See* Treas. Reg. §1.645-1(e)(2)(ii)(A).

In the Victims of Terrorism Tax Relief Act of 2001, Congress amended section 642(b), to allow a "qualified disability trust" a larger exemption, calculated under section 151, as though the trust were a unmarried individual. For the definition of such a trust, see section 642(b)(2)(C)(ii).

5. Income for Charity

Internal Revenue Code:
    Section 642(c)(1), (2)

Regulations:
    Sections 1.642(c)-1, -2(a), -3(a), (b)

Under section 642(c) estates and trusts can qualify for charitable deductions. Section 642(c)(1) expressly states that its deduction is "in lieu" of that allowed by section 170(a).

Thus, estates and trusts are not subject to the percentage limitations imposed by section 170(b). *See* Rev. Rul. 66-259, 1966-2 C.B. 214 (trust required to expend all of its income for charitable purposes entitled to deduction equal to its entire income). But under section 642(c) they are subject to other limitations.

Gross Income Limitation. Section 642(c)(1) allows as a deduction in computing the taxable income of an estate or a trust "any amount of gross income, without limitation" that is "paid for a purpose specified in section 170(c)." Thus, in general, estates and trusts can obtain charitable deductions only on account of amounts of "gross income" paid for charitable purposes.

As a general rule, distributions of corpus are not deductible under section 642(c). *Crestar Bank v. Internal Revenue Service,* 47 F. Supp. 2d 670 (E.D. Va. 1999); Rev. Rul. 2003-123, 2003-2 C.B. 1200; Rev. Rul. 68-667, 1968-2 C.B. 289. *See also W. K. Frank Trust v. Commissioner,* 145 F.2d 411 (3d Cir. 1944). In Rev. Rul. 68-667, decedent's will provided for a pecuniary bequest to charity but failed to specify who was entitled to the estate's income during administration. As a result, under local law, the residuary, non-charitable beneficiary was entitled to all of the estate's income. The I.R.S. ruled that no deduction was allowable on account of amounts paid to the charity, because such amounts were necessarily principal. On the other hand, where a trust agreement failed to specify whether a charitable annuity was to be paid out of principal or income, but local law required such payments to be made first out of income, the annuity payments, to the extent of trust income, qualified for the charitable deduction. Rev. Rul. 71-285, 1971-2 C.B. 248.

In Rev. Rul. 78-24, 1978-1 C.B. 196, a terminating trust sold property to permit distribution of a specific sum to a noncharitable beneficiary and distributed the remainder of its property to charity. The I.R.S. ruled that the trust was entitled, under section 642(c)(1), to deduct the capital gains realized, up to the amount of property distributed to the charity, because the charity was entitled to the benefit of any gain realized by the trust and had been "paid" all of the trust property in excess of the specific sum.

Payments to charity need not be "actually paid out of receipts during a particular tax year." *Old Colony Trust Co. v. Commissioner,* 301 U.S. 379, 384 (1937). In *Old Colony Trust,* the Supreme Court allowed a charitable deduction that exceeded the year's otherwise undistributed income. The trustee proved that, in the year of the charitable payment, sufficient accumulated income was available to fund the charitable distribution. *See also* Treas. Reg. §1.642(c)-1(a)(1).

Charitable Set-Asides. Section 642(c)(2) allows estates and certain venerable trusts deductions for gross income "permanently set aside for a purpose specified in section 170(c)" or "to be used exclusively for" various charitable purposes. (Trusts whose governing instruments were executed after October 9, 1969, cannot qualify for the so-called set-aside deduction.)

Certain revocable trusts also qualify for the set-aside deduction. Under section 645, if both the trustee of a decedent's revocable trust and the decedent's executor so elect, a revocable trust may be treated as part of the decedent's estate for most income tax purposes. If no estate tax return is due, this consolidation is effective for only two years after the decedent's death. If an estate tax return is due, the consolidation generally remains effective until six months after the final determination of the estate tax liability. During the election period, such a trust can qualify for the set-aside charitable deduction. *See* Treas. Reg. §§ 1.645-1(e)(2)(i), 1.645-1(e)(3)(i).

An executor need not take any particular action, such as crediting income to charity's account, to qualify for a set-aside deduction. All that is necessary is that the governing document entitle charity to the income. *Bowers v. Slocum,* 20 F.2d 350 (2d Cir. 1927). On the other hand, estates do not continue indefinitely for tax purposes. If an estate continues after the I.R.S. has determined that it should have terminated, the I.R.S. may treat the continuing entity as a post-1969 trust, which cannot qualify for a set-aside deduction. *See Estate of Berger v. Commissioner,* 60 T.C.M. (CCH) 1079 (1990) (gains in question occurred less than six years after the decedent's death).

Frequently estates are entitled to set-aside deductions for charitable residuary beneficiaries. Income earned during administration generally falls, pursuant to state law, into the residuary estate. *See* Uniform Principal and Income Act §§ 201(4), 202 (1997). Thus, a charity entitled to part or all of the residuary estate may be entitled to part or all of the estate's income. Similarly, if an executor sells property to pay estate obligations, that portion of any capital gain realized attributable to the share of the sales proceeds remaining for charity often qualifies for a set-aside charitable deduction under section 642(c)(2). *Compare* Rev. Rul. 68-440, 1968-2 C.B. 289, Rev. Rul. 66-367, 1966-2 C.B. 241, and Rev. Rul. 64-253, 1964-2 C.B. 166, in which capital gains realized by pre-1969 trusts qualified for set-aside charitable deductions, *with* Rev. Rul. 74-410, 1974-2 C.B. 187, and Rev. Rul. 73-95, 1973-1 C.B. 322, in which capital gains realized by such trusts did not. If the fiduciary has discretion to allocate gains between income and principal, however, gains that ordinarily would have been allocable to principal under either state law or the governing instrument, and that thus would have been set aside for charity, may not generate a set-aside deduction, even if the trustee allocates them to principal, because of the possibility that the fiduciary might have chosen not to do so. *Samuel P. Hunt Trust v. United States,* 93 A.F.T.R.2d 351 (D.N.H. 2003) (involving pre-1969 trusts).

Estates can be entitled to set-aside deductions for other reasons. Income earned during administration on a particular asset that is the subject of a specific devise or bequest generally belongs, under state law, to the specific devisee or legatee. *See* Uniform Principal and Income Act § 201(1) (1997). Thus, an estate that is required to include in its gross income rents derived from real estate specifically devised to a charitable trust is allowed a charitable deduction for the amount of the rents. Rev. Rul. 57-133, 1957-1 C.B. 200.

On the other hand, a charity entitled to only a pecuniary (or general) bequest is generally not entitled to any of the estate's income. *See* Uniform Principal and Income Act §§ 201(3) (1997) (recipient of pecuniary bequest not in trust receives interest on the pecuniary amount, but only to the extent required by the instrument or state law). As a result, an estate generally cannot deduct income as set aside for a charitable pecuniary beneficiary, even if the amounts it designates for the charity actually consist of items of income. *See Wellman v. Welch,* 99 F.2d 75 (1st Cir. 1938).

If the governing document does entitle charity to the income, it may not matter that the income in question is actually used for noncharitable purposes, such as paying the debts or the administration expenses of the estate. *See, e.g., Rockland Oil Co.,* 22 T.C. 1307 (1954), *acq.,* 1955-1 C.B. 6; *Estate of John E. Myra,* 4 T.C.M. (CCH) 958 (1945). This can be true, for example, if charity is the estate's residuary beneficiary. Charity's status as residuary beneficiary means that the estate's income is set aside for charity. Debts and administration expenses must nonetheless be paid and, theoretically, should be paid out of residuary principal. Whether the executor pays them out of principal or income does not affect the charity, which is entitled to the remainder of both. Assuming that residuary principal is sufficient to meet the expenses, there seems to be no sound reason to deny the deduction solely because of the executor's choice of source of payment. But if the governing document requires payment of such expenses out of income, the charitable deduction is reduced to the extent income is so used. *Bank of America Nat'l Trust & Savings Ass'n v. Commissioner,* 126 F.2d 48 (9th Cir. 1942).

Hartwick College v. United States
801 F.2d 608 (2d Cir. 1986)

PIERCE, Circuit Judge:

This is an appeal from an order of the United States District Court for the Northern District of New York, Neal P. McCurn, *Judge,* granting the plaintiffs a refund of taxes paid on income earned by the estate of Jessie Smith Dewar during the period from May 28, 1976 through April 30, 1977. After the income tax was paid, appellees filed this tax refund suit on behalf of the estate subsequent to the executors of the estate having been duly discharged in the Surrogate's Court of Ostego County, New York, for all purposes except the filing of amendments to the estate's state and federal fiduciary income tax return and the subsequent filing with the Surrogate's Court of a supplemental accounting with respect to these amended tax filings. Appellees are charitable organizations under the Internal Revenue Code of 1954 ("IRC"), 26 U.S.C. §170(c) and residuary legatees of the estate. Appellees have claimed that the estate was due a refund, under IRC §642(c), for amounts "permanently set aside" for them as charitable organizations.

After the district court issued decisions holding that the appellees had properly filed for the refund, 588 F.Supp. 926, and that the estate could take a deduction under IRC §642(c), the parties were still unable to agree as to the amount of the deduction available to the estate. The gravamen of this remaining dispute was whether the income tax deduction allowed the estate under IRC §642(c) was required to equal the amount to be received by the charities once income taxes were paid or the amount "permanently set aside," pre-tax, under the terms of the will. The district court ruled that the pre-tax amount provided the appropriate basis for the deduction. 611 F.Supp. 400. The government appeals this ruling and, in addition, challenges the subject matter jurisdiction of the district court to hear this case on the ground that the appellees had not exhausted their administrative remedy before the Internal Revenue Service ("IRS"). We reject both of the government's challenges and affirm the rulings of the district court.

BACKGROUND

On May 28, 1976, Jessie Smith Dewar died testate leaving an estate of approximately $49 million. Her will established the following priorities for distribution of the estate. First in priority were "all ... debts and funeral and administrative expenses." Further, "all inheritance, estate, transfer, succession and death taxes" were specifically directed to be paid out of the "general estate as expenses of the administration thereof." Following in priority were several specific individual bequests. Finally, the will directed that the residuary estate be apportioned among the appellees and two additional charitable organizations.

On June 8, 1976, the last will and testament of the decedent and a codicil thereto were admitted to probate in the Surrogate's Court of Ostego County, New York. Rutson R. Henderson, Wendell F. Couse and Charles H. Bissell were designated to serve as co-executors of the estate.

On August 19, 1977, the co-executors filed a Fiduciary Federal Income Tax Return (Form 1041) with the IRS for the period May 28, 1976 through April 30, 1977. The return reported a total income of $3,583,840 and various deductions and exemptions totaling $1,752,775 [sic, probably should be $1,152,775] resulting in a taxable income of $2,431,065. The executors took no deduction for amounts permanently set aside for charitable purposes. The income tax liability, which was paid with the return, totaled $1,728,879.

In November 1978, the co-executors filed a final accounting and petition for judicial settlement of the account with the Surrogate's Court. The appellees filed objections to this accounting claiming that the co-executors had failed to claim a charitable income tax deduction to which the estate was entitled under IRC §642(c) and had thereby overpaid the income taxes of the estate. On December 29, 1978, Surrogate Robert A. Harlem ruled that, since the possibility was more than negligible that income taxes would consume the remainder of the estate and eliminate the charitable gift, "the court [was] not constrained to direct the fiduciaries to file amended income tax returns with respect to income earned during the course of administration to claim a charitable deduction."

In the same ruling the surrogate granted appellee Hartwick College's motion to compel the executors to take a deduction on the fiduciary income tax return for estate taxes paid during the administrative period. In all other respects, however, the surrogate accepted the accounting of the co-executors, subject to revision by a subsequent accounting to reflect submission of amended fiduciary income tax returns to claim the deduction for estate taxes paid. At this point, the co-executors were discharged for all purposes except the filing of the revised return and the submission of this additional accounting. The co-executors filed the amended federal tax return, and included $330,208 in additional deductions and $35,774 in additional income, on July 17, 1979. On February 16, 1981, the IRS issued a refund of $189,557 to the estate, representing the allowance on the additional deductions claimed.

On March 5, 1980, after the co-executors had filed the amended return but before the IRS had issued the refund, the IRS received another amended return on behalf of the estate, signed by Philip S. Wilder, Jr., the president of appellee Hartwick College. This return claimed an additional charitable deduction under IRC §642(c) in the amount of $2,431,765 [sic, probably should be $2,431,065] which reduced the taxable income of the estate to zero and supported a refund of the $1,728,879 in income taxes previously paid by the estate.

On August 11, 1980, an attorney for the estate informed the IRS that the amended return signed by Wilder was not filed at the direction or with the authorization of the representatives of the estate and that the estate was not seeking a refund based upon a claimed charitable deduction. Thereafter, the IRS took no action to allow or deny the purported claim for refund filed by Wilder.

Six months later, appellees filed this tax refund suit in the United States District Court for the Northern District of New York. Appellees claimed that each of them was a residuary legatee of the estate, that as such they were qualified to file a suit for refund because the accounts of the co-executors of the estate had been judicially settled and the co-executors discharged as to the issues raised in the complaint. Appellees also alleged that the tax returns filed by the co-executors on behalf of the estate for the period of administration were incorrect and that the estate was entitled to a charitable deduction in an amount equal to the entire income of the estate. Since they claimed the entire income of the estate as a deduction, the resulting tax liability alleged in the complaint was reduced to zero. Therefore, appellees sought a refund of the entire amount of income taxes paid.

In December 1981, the government filed a motion to dismiss the complaint pursuant to Rule 12(b)(1) of the Fed.R.Civ.P. challenging the court's jurisdiction to hear the case.

The government claimed that the appellees were not the proper parties to file the claim for a refund under IRC §7422. The district court found that [Revenue Ruling 73-366, 1973-2 C.B. 408] allowed residuary legatees to file tax returns on behalf of the estate where the executors have been discharged and the final accounting has been rendered. The district court ruled against the government holding that, since the co-executors had been discharged as to the issues raised by appellees, the circumstances of this case met the basic requirements of IRS policy as expressed in the Revenue Ruling.

On May 15, 1984, Judge McCurn granted the appellees' motion for partial summary judgment on the issue of whether the estate could claim the charitable deduction under IRC §642(c). The government moved to have the judge reconsider his disposition of the motion for partial summary judgment on the ground that the issue had been precluded or collaterally estopped by the surrogate's previous determination of the same issue. On May 31, 1984, the district court issued its decision denying the government's motion for reconsideration on the ground that the Surrogate's Court was without jurisdiction to decide the matter. 588 F.Supp. 926. In addition, the district judge indicated that he intended to refer the matter of the exact calculation of the deduction to be allowed under §642(c) to a special master, after finding that "the amount of the estate income which was 'permanently set aside' for charitable purposes was not the entire $2.4 million reported as 'taxable income' on the fiduciary return, but only the amount that the residuary beneficiaries would have received but for the income tax." Subsequently, the parties requested the court to withhold (or defer) appointment of a master to afford them an opportunity to reach a mutually agreeable calculation on their own. This effort resulted in a disagreement over whether an "interrelated computation"[2] or a "straight deduction"[3] method should be used to calculate the charitable deduction allowable under IRC §642(c). On February 25, 1985, Judge McCurn resolved this dispute in favor of a "straight deduction" method. The government now appeals this ruling as well as the district court's denial of its motion to dismiss the complaint under Rule 12(b)(1) of the Fed.R.Civ.P.

DISCUSSION

I. *Jurisdiction of the District Court.*

We reject the government's claim that the district court lacked subject matter jurisdiction over this case. The jurisdiction of a federal district court in a tax refund suit is governed by 28 U.S.C. §1346 and IRC §7422(a). Section 1346 grants jurisdiction to federal district courts with respect to actions against the United States "for the recovery of any internal-revenue tax alleged to have been erroneously or illegally assessed or collected." However, §7422(a) of the IRC conditions the jurisdiction of the court in such cases upon "a claim for refund or credit [having been] duly filed with the Secretary."(emphasis added). The government claims that appellees did not duly file their tax return for two reasons: (1) because the appellees were not authorized to file a tax return on behalf of the estate, and (2) because the appellees did not submit documentary proof of their authority to

---

2. The "interrelated computation" which was proposed by the government is so described because it provides a mathematical solution to problems involving two unknown but related variables. A more intuitive approach to such problems utilizes an iterative calculation which approximates the result of the "interrelated computation" through successive calculations. *See* n. 5, *infra.*

3. The so called "straight deduction" allows the estate to take a deduction under §642(c) for the entire amount which has been "permanently set aside" for charitable purposes without considering income taxes to be extracted from the estate. Therefore, under the "straight deduction" method a portion of the residue would actually reach the charities while a portion would be used to pay the estate's income taxes, but the deduction would not reflect any such diversion.

act on behalf of the estate with their claim as the government contends is required by Revenue Ruling 73-366, 1973-2 C.B. 408.

As a general rule, the claim for refund required by §7422(a) must be filed by the taxpayer claiming such refund. *See* 26 C.F.R. §301.6402-2(a)(1). However, where the taxpayer has died, a tax return or a refund claim may be filed on his behalf by his legal representative. *See* 26 C.F.R. §301.6402-2(e). As the district court noted Revenue Ruling 73-366 identifies circumstances under which the proper party to file a claim for credit or a refund may be someone other than the taxpayer's legal representative. The revenue ruling discusses some hypothetical situations where others might appropriately file, stating in pertinent part:

> Situation 2. Subsequent to the distribution of an estate's assets, rendering of the final accounting, and discharge of the executor, it was discovered that the executor had overpaid the estate's Federal income tax. Under the terms of the decedent's will, the estate's Federal income tax liability was required to be paid from the residuary estate. However, the residuary estate was not sufficient to satisfy the estate's Federal income tax liability and, under state law, specific legacies to other beneficiaries had to be reduced either in whole or in part.

> Situation 3. The facts are the same as in situation 2, except that the residuary estate was sufficient to satisfy the estate's Federal income tax liability.

Revenue Ruling 73-366, 1973-2 C.B. 408. The present case falls within the purview of "Situation 3." But for the fact that the co-executors herein were retained for the limited purpose of filing an amended tax return and to submit an accounting as to the outcome of the new tax return, the situations would be identical. In our view, these differences do not provide a sufficient basis for distinguishing the instant case from "Situation 3."[4]

The agency's position with respect to the revenue ruling is that "the residuary legatee is the proper party to file a claim for credit or refund." It also directs that "the claim for refund or credit *should* show the decedent's date of death and be accompanied by a certified copy of the court order granting the discharge of the executor and a certified copy of the order of distribution." *Id.* (emphasis added). We interpret this ruling as reflecting an agency policy under which the appellees would be the proper parties to file for the refund but should have submitted some documentation of their status. The use of the permissive term "should" suggests that the agency's policy does not mandate such proof and would not support the dismissal of this case absent such proof. For these reasons, we affirm the district court's assertion of jurisdiction herein.

II. *Method for Calculating Deduction.*

As to the dispute over the appropriate method for calculating the deduction due the estate, the gravamen of the dispute is whether a deduction for a residuary donation permanently set aside for charitable purposes must be reduced to reflect an anticipated tax

---

4. The agency's contention that appellees could not rely upon Revenue Ruling 73-366, 1973-2 C.B. 408, because the executors of the estate had not rendered a "final accounting" or been "discharged" within the meaning of that Ruling must be rejected. Under New York law, ... the Surrogate Court's decree is the "final" resolution of the accounts embraced by the decree, *In re Grace's Estate,* 62 Misc. 2d 51, 308 N.Y.S.2d 33, 40 (Sur.Ct.1970), *aff'd mem.,* 35 A.D.2d 783, 315 N.Y.S.2d 816 (1971), and is no less "final" simply because other aspects of the estate remain unsettled. *Id.; In re Jones' Will,* 13 Misc. 2d 678, 177 N.Y.S.2d 307 (Sur.Ct.1958), *aff'd,* 8 A.D.2d 829, 190 N.Y.S.2d 166 (1959); *In re Crawford's Will,* 207 Misc. 145, 136 N.Y.S.2d 716, 720 (Sur.Ct.1955); *In re Blake's Will,* 46 N.Y.S.2d 549 (Sur.Ct.1943).... There was therefore no danger that the IRS would have to deal with different beneficiaries simultaneously taking conflicting positions with respect to requests for refunds.

liability. The appellees assert, and the district court agreed, that the deduction should be equal to the amount of money remaining in the estate prior to the payment of taxes and that the amount actually received by the charities should be reduced to cover the tax liability. We agree.

Specifically, the estate had roughly $2.4 million of taxable income during the year in question. One million dollars of this income had been used for administrative expenses and deducted on the estate tax return and, therefore, was not deductible for purposes of income tax. [IRC §642(g).] As a result, $1.4 million in cash remained in the estate. The appellees contend that this entire amount should be reflected on the income tax return as the charitable donation deduction. Since there was $1 million of non-deductible expenses and the applicable tax rate was 70%, if the $1.4 million were allowed as a deduction there would remain a tax liability of $700,000 for the year in question.

Under the appellees' suggested approach, we need go no further: the deduction should be for $1.4 million, the government should receive $700,000 in taxes and the appellees should receive the remaining $700,000. The government's claim is that as a basic principle of taxation no deduction for charitable donations can include money used to pay taxes, and, therefore, since only $700,000 would be available as a charitable donation after payment of the known $700,000 tax liability on the $1 million in income that went to administrative expenses, only $700,000 may be deducted. Further, the government argues that as the deduction is reduced, more taxable income is exposed and more tax must be diverted from the residuary legatees. The government contends that, since the deduction may not include money used or to be used to pay taxes, the appropriate deduction may be no more than money to be actually donated. By recalculating the deduction in this iterative fashion it becomes clear that the only point at which the deduction would include no taxes is where the deduction is equal to zero.[5]

Therefore, two alternatives are apparent, a deduction of $1.4 million or no deduction at all. The determinative issue is whether the deduction under IRC §642(c) is required to reflect only the amount actually donated to a charitable organization excluding money that ultimately will be used to pay taxes.

[The court quotes section 642(c)(2).] Although this language clearly allows a deduction of "any amount of the *gross income, without limitation* ... pursuant to the *terms of the governing instrument*"(emphasis added), the government argues that an overriding principle of taxation precludes the inclusion within a deduction category of any amount eventually paid as taxes of the estate.

The issue of the appropriate regard to be given such espoused "principles" in the interpretation of tax provisions which grant deductions for charitable bequests was addressed by the Supreme Court in the context of the Revenue Act of 1918, 40 Stat. c. 18,

---

5. Since at least $700,000 must be used to pay the tax on the non-deductible administrative expenses and by applying the principle that the deduction must not include money used or to be used to pay taxes, the resulting deduction could not exceed the $700,000 remaining in the estate after taxes are paid. However, under the government's theory, since the deductions must be reduced from $1.4 million to $700,000 an addition of $700,000 of taxable income would be exposed. This results in $490,000 additional tax to be paid, 70% of the newly exposed income. Therefore, since the deduction cannot include money needed to pay this additional tax liability, the resulting deduction could not exceed $310,000 [sic, probably should be $210,000]. Finally, this deduction in the actual charitable donation would expose another $490,000 of income to taxation and result in the total elimination of any charitable deduction.

Title IV, which established an estate tax deduction for such bequests. *Edwards v. Slocum,* 264 U.S. 61, 44 S.Ct. 293, 68 L.Ed. 564 (1924). In *Edwards,* the Court closely examined the language of the applicable estate tax statute to determine whether the deduction for a residuary charitable gift had to be reduced by the amount to be diverted for the payment of taxes. The Court concluded that the specific language of the statute compelled the conclusion that no such reduction was required and noted that:

> The Government offers an algebraic formula by which it would solve the problems raised by two mutually dependent indeterminates. It fairly might be answered ... that "algebraic formulae are not lightly to be imputed to legislators," but it appears to us that the structure of [this] statute is sufficient to exclude the imputation.

Id. at 63, 44 S.Ct. at 293.

The government addresses this precedent by noting that shortly after the *Edwards* decision Congress demonstrated its displeasure with the result by modifying the language of the estate tax charitable deduction statute. Congress modified the estate tax code to require any such deduction to be reduced to reflect the portion of the fund actually used to pay estate taxes, although initially set aside for charitable purposes under the governing instrument. *See* Revenue Act of 1924, ch. 234, 43 Stat. 253, §303(a)(3). The government relies upon this subsequent legislative action in urging its position herein.

However, as the government's own citation suggests, the Congressional intent in this regard has not been so broad and unfaltering as to support the conclusion that the interpretation of the legislative intent embodied in the Revenue Act of 1918 was incorrect in *Edwards:*

> The 1924 provision overruling *Edwards v. Slocum* was eliminated in 1926, but was restored in the Revenue Act of 1932, ch. 209, Sec. 807, 47 Stat. 69, as an amendment to the Revenue Act of 1926. See S.Rep. No. 665, 72d Cong., 1st Sess. at 52 (1939-1 Cum.Bull. (Pt. 2) 496, 537). An equivalent provision has been part of the estate tax ever since. See Sec. 812(d) of the 1939 Code and Sec. 2055(c) of the 1954 Code.

Government's Brief at p. 29 n. 11.

More importantly, the government provides little authority for its "basic principle of taxation" except citation to cases which principally address post-*Edwards* estate tax law. *See, e.g., Commissioner v. Estate of Sternberger,* 348 U.S. 187, 197–98, 75 S.Ct. 229, 234–35, 99 L.Ed. 246 (1955) (disallowing estate tax deduction for bequest which was conditional under the terms of the will); *Harrison v. Northern Trust Co.,* 317 U.S. 476, 480, 63 S.Ct. 361, 363, 87 L.Ed. 407 (1943) (limiting the amount of the federal estate tax deduction for charitable residuary bequest to amounts actually passing to the charitable beneficiaries after provision for taxes under §303(a) of the Revenue Act of 1926); *Irving Trust Co. v. United States,* 221 F.2d 303, 306 (2d Cir. 1955) (estate tax deduction only available for amounts actually received by the charity); *Estate of Thompson v. Commissioner,* 123 F.2d 816, 818 (2d Cir. 1941) (estate tax charitable deduction initially paid to charities reduced by amount subsequently paid to decedent's next of kin in settlement of objections to probate); *Ahmanson Foundation v. United States,* 674 F.2d 761, 762 (9th Cir.1981) (reversing in part an estate tax refund). The other cases cited by the government concern income tax law in situations where the funds were found not to have been permanently set aside under the terms of the governing instrument. *See, e.g., Estate of Wright v. United States,* 677 F.2d 53 (9th Cir.1982) (income not "permanently set aside" where contest ultimately resulted in partial distribution to noncharitable beneficiary and deduction under §642(c) reduced by that amount); *Estate of Freund v. Commissioner,* 303 F.2d 30, 32 (2d Cir.1962) (income not actually received by the estate found not to have been "permanently set aside" under §642(c)); *Estate of Luehrmann v. Commissioner*, 287 F.2d 10, 13–15 (8th Cir.1961) (denying income tax deduction where it appeared that amounts claimed as charitable deductions were in fact expended for purposes of administration). Rather than providing evidence of some broad principle of taxation, these cases simply give application to the text of the applicable legislation.

We conclude that Congress knew that the algebraic formula for calculations would not be used unless expressly provided for by the statute and that by limiting its amendment to §2055 it did not contemplate that the formula would be applied under other statutes such as §642(c). Moreover, its limited authorization of the formula is in keeping with the countervailing policy in favor of a liberal construction of statutes authorizing deductions for charitable contributions, *Helvering v. Bliss*, 293 U.S. 144, 150–51, 55 S.Ct. 17, 20–21, 79 L.Ed. 246 (1934), so that people will be encouraged to make such contributions. *Commissioner v. Estate of Sternberger*, 348 U.S. 187, 198–99, 75 S.Ct. 229, 235, 99 L.Ed.2d 246 (1955); *United States v. Benedict*, 338 U.S. 692, 696–97, 70 S.Ct. 472, 475–76, 94 L.Ed.2d 478 (1950).

Even if the government is correct in its view of Congress' intent regarding the calculation of the charitable deduction for estate tax purposes, such does not logically require the further conclusion that Congress devised the same formula for estate income tax purposes. We can discern two reasons that support a principled distinction between the tax calculation for estate taxes and estate income taxes. First, the size of the estate in all but the rarest instances ordinarily exceeds that of the income it receives. The facts of the present case bear this out. Ms. Dewar left an estate worth approximately $49 million. In contrast, her estate received approximately $3.5 million in income following her death. Thus, the income tax lost to the collector by the use of the "straight-line" formula will usually be small compared to the amount that would be lost were the straight-line method applied in calculating the charitable deduction for the estate tax. The facts in *Edwards* illustrate this proposition. There the decedent's estate was worth $49 million, and the executors claimed a charitable deduction of $35 million.... By way of contrast, here the charitable deduction claimed is $1.4 million.

Of course, it is possible that by our holding the deduction received for the same amount of a bequest might differ depending on whether the money or property was drawn from an estate or the estate's income. Although not confined to this situation, the second reason for distinguishing the treatment of the charitable deduction directly addresses it. Most testators carefully plan their dispositions either to eliminate or minimize the burden of the estate tax. The testator, with the aid of experienced counsel, is usually aware of the value of his or her assets, their intended dispositions, and the tax consequences of those dispositions. Such careful planning is not possible with respect to an attempt to minimize the tax burden on the estate's income. All that a testator knows is the intended disposition of that income; the amount available is unknown, especially in light of the various uncertainties attendant upon the administration of an estate. *See* 2 W. Bowe & D. Parker, Page on Wills §18.19, at 20–21 (4th ed. 1960). Such uncertainties may generate substantial administrative expenses, further depleting the amount earmarked for the charity. Indeed, the facts of the present case attest to this—estate administration consumed nearly one third of the income generated by the corpus.

Recognition of these difficulties may reasonably justify the difference in the calculation of the charitable deduction. This case itself suggests why Congress has not changed the estate income tax provision to parallel its estate tax counterpart. If we were to adopt the government's suggested formula, the charities that Ms. Dewar intended to benefit would receive nothing. As noted, after paying administrative expenses, the estate had $1.4 million in cash to meet its tax liability and to make the charitable donations. Adopting the government's position would set the estate's income tax liability at approximately $1.7 million, completely adeeming the charitable bequests.

Therefore, based upon what appears to us to be the clear language of the statute and in light of the dearth of authority supporting any contrary principle of taxation, we affirm the judgment of the district court.

Illustrative Material

1. For an example of a legislative attempt at sidestepping the *Hartwick College* problem, see N.Y. Est. Powers & Trusts Law § 11-2.1(d)(2)(B)(ii), which states that "any amount allowed as a tax deduction to the estate for income payable to a charitable organization shall be paid, without diminution for taxes, to the charitable organization entitled to receive such income."

2. The courts have found the availability of set-aside charitable deductions particularly difficult to resolve in cases involving settlements of will contests. Consider a fact pattern faced by several courts: the will leaves the entire residue to charity, but the settlement of a will contest divides the residue equally between charity and noncharitable beneficiaries. As a result, only one-half of the income earned by the estate during administration ends up in the hands of charity. At least one, early case held that the estate was nonetheless entitled to deduct all its income as set-aside for charity. *Hu L. McClung,* 13 B.T.A. 335 (1928), *nonacq.,* VII-2 C.B. 49. The theory was that the will left the entire residue (and all the estate's income) to charity. All the income was thus "set aside" for charity. The fact that the charity, for its own reasons, agreed to take less than the will gave it was irrelevant to the estate's entitlement to a charitable deduction. More recently, on such facts, the Ninth Circuit allowed a set-aside charitable deduction for only one-half of the estate's income earned during the period prior to the settlement. *Estate of Wright v. United States,* 677 F.2d 53 (9th Cir.), *cert. denied,* 459 U.S. 909 (1982). In dictum, however, the court implied that the executor had acted properly in claiming the full deduction pending resolution of the will contest and filing an amended return after the settlement. *Genesee Merchants Bank & Trust Co. v. United States,* 76-1 U.S.T.C. ¶ 9212 (E.D. Mich. 1976), allowed no set-aside deduction for income earned by the estate prior to the year in which the settlement occurred. There, the testator, shortly before her death, had revoked the will that set forth the bequest to charity. The court found it impossible to view any of the estate's income as set aside for charity prior to the settlement. *Emanuelson v. United States,* 159 F. Supp. 34 (D. Conn. 1958), however, on similar facts, treated the settlement as retroactively applicable and allowed the set-aside deduction for income earned prior to the settlement, to the extent of charity's entitlement under the settlement. Rev. Rul. 59-15, 1959-1 C.B. 164, cited *Emanuelson* and reached the same result. Where charity's entitlement to income was similarly uncertain during administration, but only because of ambiguities in the will, which named both charitable and noncharitable beneficiaries, *Middleton v. United States,* 99 F. Supp. 801 (E.D. Pa. 1951), also allowed the set-aside deduction for income earned prior to settlement, to the extent of charity's entitlement under the settlement.

3. Both section 642(c)(1) and section 642(c)(2) impose the additional requirement that amounts be paid to or set aside for charity "pursuant to the terms of the governing instrument." *See Goldsby v. Commissioner,* 92 T.C.M. (CCH) 529, 532 n.6 (2006). In *Marquis v. United States,* 146 Ct. Cl. 243, 173 F. Supp. 616 (1959), a wife's will left the bulk of her estate to her husband. However, he died prior to distribution of her estate. His will left his entire estate, which included his interest in her estate, to charity. Thus, the

income earned by the wife's estate appeared set aside for charity. Nevertheless, the Court of Claims denied the wife's estate a deduction under section 642(c) because the income was not set aside "pursuant to the terms of" her will:

> As to the income here in question, or the property which produced that income, [the wife's] will expressed no intimation whatever in the direction of charity. She gave the property, outright, to her husband.... He could have spent it, given it *inter vivos* to any person he chose, or devised it to individuals or to noncharitable or charitable entities as he chose. Whatever he did with it was not "pursuant to the terms of" [the wife's] will.

173 F. Supp. at 618. *Williams v. United States,* 158 F. Supp. 227 (N.D. Cal. 1957), *aff'd per curiam,* 251 F.2d 847 (9th Cir. 1958), also denied a set-aside deduction to the estate of the first spouse to die. There, the husband died first, leaving his entire estate to his widow. She died shortly thereafter, leaving her residuary estate to charity. The wills were reciprocal, so that, had the wife died first, husband's estate would have gone to charity directly. Nonetheless, the court held that the income of the husband's estate, even after the wife's death, did not go to charity pursuant to the terms of his will. Similarly, where a widow, promptly after her husband's death, assigned to charity her entire interest in a marital deduction trust in which she had an unrestricted lifetime right of withdrawal, the husband's estate was not entitled to a section 642(c) deduction for estate income paid to charity pursuant to the assignment, because the husband's will did not contain a "manifestation of charitable intent." *Estate of O'Connor v. Commissioner,* 69 T.C. 165 (1977). *See also Brownstone v. United States,* 465 F.3d 525 (2d Cir. 2006) (beneficiary exercised power of appointment in favor of charity; trust not entitled to section 642(c) deduction); *Ernest and Mary Hayward Weir Foundation v. United States,* 362 F. Supp. 928 (S.D.N.Y. 1973), *aff'd per curiam,* 508 F.2d 894 (2d Cir. 1974) (same); *Trust of John Walker,* 30 T.C. 278 (1958) (same).

In contrast, it appears that both estates and trusts can deduct, under section 642(c), their distributive shares of charitable contributions made by partnerships in which they hold interests, even if the instrument governing the estate or trust neither requires nor authorizes payments to charity. *See Estate of Bluestein,* 15 T.C. 770 (1950), *acq.,* 1951-1 C.B. 1; *Estate of Lowenstein,* 12 T.C. 694 (1949), *acq.,* 1949-2 C.B. 2., *aff'd sub nom. First Nat'l Bank of Mobile v. Commissioner,* 183 F.2d 172 (5th Cir. 1950), *cert. denied,* 340 U.S. 911 (1951); Rev. Rul. 2004-5, 2004-1 C.B. 295 (as to both simple and complex trusts).

If the governing instrument confers upon the trustee discretion to make payments to charity, payments made pursuant to that discretion are *"pursuant to* the terms of the governing instrument." *Old Colony Trust Co. v. Commissioner,* 301 U.S. 379 (1937). On the other hand, if a trustee who is authorized to make payments to charity only upon termination of the trust makes them prior to termination, they are not "pursuant to the terms of the governing instrument." Rev. Rul. 55-92, 1955-1 C.B. 390. Similarly, if a trustee pays income to charity following judicial approval of the settlement of a will contest, but neither the terms of the trust nor those of the settlement require payment of the disputed amounts, they are not paid "pursuant to the terms of the governing instrument." *John Allan Love Charitable Foundation v. United States,* 710 F.2d 1316 (8th Cir. 1983). Likewise, if the governing instrument authorizes the trustee to make payments to charity only after complying with certain procedural requirements, payments that occur prior to compliance with those requirements are not "pursuant to the terms of the governing instrument" and do not qualify for the deduction under section 642(c). *Rebecca K. Crown Income Charitable Fund v. Commissioner,* 98 T.C. 327 (1992), *aff'd,* 8 F.3d 571 (7th Cir. 1993).

4. Treas. Reg. §1.642(c)-2(d) requires that "under the terms of the governing instrument and the circumstances of the particular case the possibility that the amount set aside, or to be used [for a charitable purpose], will not be devoted to such purpose or use [must be] so remote as to be negligible." The regulation then provides an example involving a distribution by an estate to a charitable remainder trust. Because of the possibility of invasion of trust principal to make the required annuity or unitrust amount, according to the regulation, no charitable deduction is available to the estate. Technical Advice Memorandum 8810006 (1987) reached the same conclusion, even as to capital gains, which, under local law, became part of the principal of the trust. The taxpayer had argued that the high prevailing interest rates and the advanced age of the annuitant made the possibility of invasion "so remote as to be negligible." (Charitable remainder trusts are described in section 664.) The I.R.S. no longer issues private letter rulings on the allowability of deductions for amounts set aside for charitable purposes when there is a possibility that the corpus may be invaded. Rev. Proc. 2008-3, 2008-1 I.R.B. 110, 114. In Private Letter Ruling 200142011 (2001), however, the I.R.S. ruled that a pre-1969 trust would not continue to qualify for the set-aside charitable deduction after judicial modification creating a unitrust interest in the noncharitable beneficiary, because the possibility that amounts thereafter set aside for charity would not be so used was not so remote as to be negligible.

5. It does not matter that, at the time of decedent's death, the charitable beneficiary does not exist, if, under the will, it is certain that the charitable beneficiary will come into existence in due course. *See Estate of J.B. Whitehead,* 3 T.C. 40 (1944), *nonacq.,* 1944 C.B. 51, *aff'd sub nom. Commissioner v. Citizens & Southern Nat'l Bank,* 147 F.2d 977 (5th. Cir. 1945); *Potter v. Bowers,* 89 F.2d 687 (2d Cir. 1937); Private Letter Ruling 9840025 (1998) (estate may deduct income paid to or set aside for private foundation not in existence at decedent's death, once estate notifies I.R.S. of foundation's existence and application for tax-exempt status).

6. Depreciation and Depletion

Internal Revenue Code:
    Sections 167(d); 611(b); 642(e)
Regulations:
    Sections 1.167(h)-1; 1.611-1(c)(4), (5); 1.642(e)-1

Section 642(e) allows an estate or a trust a deduction for depreciation or depletion only to the extent not allowable to the beneficiaries under section 167 or section 611. Section 167(d) establishes two different rules, one for allocating the depreciation deduction between a trust and its income beneficiaries, and the other for allocating the deduction between an estate and its "heirs, legatees, and devisees." The rules under section 611 for depletion deductions are identical; thus, the precedents under one section should be equally relevant under the other.

With respect to an estate, the deduction is apportioned between the estate and its "heirs, legatees, and devisees" on the basis of the income of the estate allocable to each. The materials at the end of section B(6) of this chapter consider the meaning of the terms "heirs, legatees, and devisees" for purposes of this rule.

With respect to property held in a trust, section 167(d) provides alternative methods of allocating the depreciation deduction. Reading the statute and Treas. Reg. §1.167(h)-

1(b) together creates basically the following rules: (1) to the extent that the terms of the trust or local law require the trustee to (*or to the extent a trustee is permitted to and does*) maintain a depreciation reserve out of income, the deduction is allocated to the trust; and (2) to the extent that the deduction exceeds the amount set aside for the reserve, the deduction is apportioned between the income beneficiaries and the trust on the basis of trust income (*other than* the income set aside for the reserve). Comparing the regulation with the statute, one notes that the regulation both expands and limits the circumstances in which the deduction will be allocated on other than an income basis—it expands the section 167(d) rule by referring to "local law" (the issue addressed in *Hay*); it limits the rule by referring to the creation of depreciation reserves (the issue addressed in *Dusek*).

Hay v. United States

263 F. Supp. 813 (N.D. Tex. 1967)

SUTTLE, District Judge.

Edward L. and Elise W. Hay brought this action to recover an alleged overpayment of income taxes plus the interest thereon for the calendar year 1962....

The ... issue is whether the trustees of a discretionary trust who retain as an increment to trust corpus [i.e., as a depletion reserve] 27½% of the annual oil and gas income are entitled to deduct an amount of the depletion allowable for tax purposes identical to the 27½% of the trust income so set aside; or, are the beneficiaries entitled to have the depletion allowance apportioned to them on the basis of the trust income distributed to them?

* * *

The plaintiffs ... contend that the depletion deduction of $300,499.73 allowed by Section 611 of the 1954 Code for the oil and gas income realized by the trust during its 1962 fiscal year, was improperly allocated $293,996.04 to the trustees and $6,503.69 to the beneficiaries, and that the depletion deduction should have been allocated among the trustees and the beneficiaries on the basis of the trust income allocable to each of the beneficiaries. The plaintiffs rely on Section 611(b)(3).... The government contends that the allocation as made was proper and in accordance with the provisions of Section 1.611-1(c)(4) of the Federal Tax Regulations....

The court ... holds that the trustees are entitled to deduct an amount of the depletion allowed for tax purposes that is identical to the 27½% of the trust's income set aside as an increment to corpus.

* * *

Since the year 1952, the ... trust ha[s] received oil and gas income. Such receipts have been allocated 27½%, but not to exceed 50% of the net after deducting the expense and carrying charges on such property, to corpus and the balance to income. This method has been followed because there is no provision in the trust instrument which specifies how the income is to be allocated, and therefore Section 33 of the Texas Trust Act has been applied by the trustees to provide the method of allocation described. Vernon's Ann.Tex.Rev.Civ.Stat. art. 7425b-33 (1945).

During its fiscal year ended November 30, 1962, the [trust] realized gross income from oil and gas operations in the amount of $1,153,581.13. On that amount there was allowable for federal income tax purposes a depletion deduction, comprised partly of percentage depletion and partly of cost depletion, in the amount of $300,499.73.

On the Trust's fiduciary income tax return filed for the fiscal year ended November 30, 1962, the trustees claimed a depletion deduction of $293,996.04, a figure corresponding to the amount of oil and gas income treated as trust corpus under Section 33 of the Texas Trust Act. The remaining portion of the depletion deduction allowable, $6,503.69, representing the amount by which cost depletion exceeded percentage depletion on certain of the trust properties, was allocated to the beneficiaries of the trust. Of the $6,503.69 allocated to the beneficiaries, the amount of $1,726.28 was allocated to the plaintiff, Elise W. Hay.

The trust created under the will of Guy L. Waggoner, Deceased, does not apportion the depletion deduction on oil income between the income beneficiaries and trustees. The plaintiffs contend that since the trust does not contain any such provisions, the depletion deduction on oil income must be allocated among the beneficiaries and the trustees proportionately on the basis of the trust income allocable to each, which would entitle them to a depletion deduction of $17,854.46, or such other greater amounts as might be refundable by law should the income received from the trust be determined to be an amount exceeding $65,000.00. The defendant contends that the depletion deduction on the oil and gas income of the trust was properly allocated among the trustees and beneficiaries.

Section 611 of the Internal Revenue Code of 1954 provides....

The plaintiffs contend that the language of Code Section 611(b)(3) controls this case. They allege that there are no "pertinent provisions of the instrument creating the trust," (the will of Guy L. Waggoner) which apportion between them and the trustees the depletion deduction, and that, in the absence of express provisions allocating the depletion allowances, the depletion deduction must be allocated on the basis of the trust income distributed to them.

The plaintiffs further contend that Section 33 of the Texas Trust Act, Tex.Rev.Civ.Stat. art. 7425b-33 (1945), is inapplicable for trust depletion purposes. They contend that Section 33 is intended merely to provide a means of accounting for the mineral receipts and to create a depletion reserve for the trust. They distinguish that procedure from the depletion deduction established for tax purposes in Section 611(b)(3) of the Code.

Section 33 of the Texas Trust Act provides:

> "Where any part of the principal consists of any interest in lands, including royalties, overriding royalties, and working interest, from which may be taken timber, minerals, oil, gas or other natural resources, and the trustee or tenant is authorized by law or by the terms of the transaction by which the principal or trust was established to sell, lease, or otherwise develop such natural resources, and no provision is made for the disposition of the proceeds thereof, such proceeds, if received as delay rentals on a lease shall be deemed income, but if received as consideration, whether as bonus or consideration for the execution of the lease or as royalties, overriding or limited royalties, oil payments or other similar payments, received in connection with the physical severance of such natural resources, shall be apportioned to principal and income as follows: 27½% of the gross proceeds (but not to exceed 50% of the net, after deducting the expense and carrying charges on such property) shall be treated as principal and invested or held for the use and benefit of the remainderman, and the balance shall be treated as income subject to be disbursed to the tenant or person entitled thereto. Such disposition of proceeds shall apply whether the property is producing or nonproducing at the time the trust becomes effective."

As an alternative, the plaintiffs contend that should Section 33 of the Texas Trust Act be held to apply to the Guy L. Waggoner Trust, then Section 1.611-1(c)(4) of the Federal Tax Regulations is an unlawful extension of Code Section 611(b)(3) because it recognizes depletion reserves created for trusts by local law to be as effective for tax depletion deduction purposes as provisions in the trust instrument which specifically allocate the tax deduction for depletion.

Section 1.611-1(c)(4) of the Federal Tax Regulations provides....

The issues thus framed call for the Court to decide first, whether the terms of the trust instrument, within the meaning of Section 611(b)(3) of the Code, apportion the depletion deduction between the beneficiaries and the trustees; second, whether Section 33 of the Texas Trust Act applies to the trust; and third, whether Section 1.611-1(c)(4) of the Federal Tax Regulations is invalid. For the reasons which follow, the court concludes the trust instrument does apportion the depletion deduction within the meaning of Section 611(b)(3), Section 33 of the Texas Trust Act does apply to the trust, and Section 1.611-1(c)(4) of the Regulations is valid.

While Section 611(b)(3) of the Code provides that the depletion deduction allowed to trusts "shall be apportioned between the income beneficiaries and the trustees in accordance with the pertinent provisions of the instrument creating the trust," it does not require the deduction to be allocated in specific terms or express words.

Where the settlor fails to specifically allocate the depletion deduction in the trust instrument, as he did in this case, it is the duty of the court to ascertain, if possible, from the words used in the trust instrument the settlor's intent with regard to such allocation. "* * * As in the case of any other term or condition of a trust instrument, if the intention of the trustor can be determined from an examination of the pertinent provisions of the instrument that intention will be given effect whether or not stated in express terms." Upton v. Commissioner, 283 F.2d 716, 721 (9th Cir. 1960),[9] cert. denied 366 U.S. 911, 81 S.Ct. 1086, 6 L.Ed.2d 236; Commissioner v. Netcher, 143 F.2d 484, 488 (7th Cir. 1944), cert. denied 323 U.S. 759, 65 S.Ct. 92, 89 L.Ed. 607.

There are provisions in the will of Guy L. Waggoner which indicate that it was his intent to preserve the corpus of the trust which he created. He directed that the trust principal should remain intact until distributed to his great-grandchildren, and that no part of the corpus should ever be distributed to his son.[10] He empowered the trustees with

---

9. The instant case is similar to Upton v. Commissioner, … : "* * * [t]here is no provision in that will which in express terms grants all depletion allowances to the trustees or apportions them between the income beneficiaries and the trustees. The will does not use the word 'depletion' and does not expressly provide for the apportionment or allocation of anything for income tax purposes."

"There is nothing in section 23(m) [identical to §611(b)(3)], however, to indicate that an apportionment of depletion allowances as therein referred to must be stated in express terms. As in the case of any other term or condition of a trust instrument, if the intention of the trustor can be determined from an examination of the pertinent provisions of the instrument that intention will be given effect whether or not stated in express terms. * * *"

10. "The principal of my estate shall remain intact and subject to the terms of this trust during the lives of my son, W. T. Waggoner, Jr., and my son's children above named and those hereafter born to him prior to my death, and twenty one years after the death of the last survivor of my said son and his said children living at my death, and, at that time I direct the trustees to terminate the trust and pay over and deliver the balance of my estate, both principal and income, to the bodily heirs of my son's children * * *."

* * *

"Provided that the trustees shall never pay out to or use for any beneficiary more than such beneficiary's accumulated or undistributed income, unless the trustees in their sole discretion and judg-

uncontrolled discretion[11] to continue his ranching and oil and gas operations, and to use such principal and income of the trust as in their judgment was necessary to perform those operations.[12] Only "income" was allowed to be distributed to the beneficiaries.

Once it is established that it was the settlor's intent to preserve the corpus and keep it intact, it is presumed that the testator intended to create a depletion reserve, and the trustees are entitled to the depletion deduction to the extent provided by law.[14] There is some authority that the mere vesting of complete discretion in the trustees with regard to the income and principal is of itself sufficient to entitle the trustees to the deduction.[15]

If, however, the intent of the testator regarding the apportionment of depletion allowances between the trust and its beneficiaries cannot be determined from the provisions of the trust instrument, or if the court takes the view that depletion must be allocated in specific terms in the instrument (See Estate of Little v. Commissioner of Internal Revenue, 274 F.2d 718 (9th Cir. 1960)), the Court must determine whether any local law exists which affects the trust transaction. 26 C.F.R. §1.611-1(c)(4), and cases, note 18, infra.

---

ment may determine that the net income of my estate allocable to such beneficiary or beneficiaries is insufficient or inadequate for the upkeep, maintenance, education and general welfare of such beneficiary or beneficiaries, in which event I authorize and hereby empower the trustees to resort to the corpus for such purposes to the extent necessary, provided further that in no event shall any part of the corpus ever be paid over to my son, William Thomas Waggoner, Jr."

The intent to preserve and keep the trust corpus intact has been held to warrant the trustee's taking the deduction. Upton v. Commissioner, 283 F.2d 716 (9th Cir. 1960), cert. denied 366 U.S. 911, 81 S.Ct. 1086, 6 L.Ed.2d 236; Commissioner v. Netcher, 143 F.2d 484 (7th Cir. 1944), cert. denied 323 U.S. 759, 65 S.Ct. 92, 89 L.Ed. 607; Newbury v. United States, 102 Ct.Cl. 192, 57 F.Supp. 168 (1944), cert. denied 323 U.S. 802, 65 S.Ct. 559, 89 L.Ed. 640.

11. "The trustee may make division or distribution of my estate in kind or in cash, or partly in kind and partly in cash, and the determination of the trustees as to the fairness and equitableness of any such devision [sic] or distribution shall be conclusive upon all persons now or hereafter interested in my estate whether for life or in remainder."

* * *

"It is my will and direction that the foregoing powers and authorities given to my trustees shall not be exclusive of any other powers and authorities necessary or advisable for the proper administration of my estate, but all other powers and authorities I do confer upon my trustees and executors whether or not named, to the same extent as if I were still living, it being my intention that the sole and absolute control of any and all of my estate shall be and is hereby vested in my trustees and executors."

* * *

Section 1.611-1(c)(4) appears to contemplate that this power of discretion alone may be sufficient to entitle the trustee to the deduction. See example (ii). This view is supported in Commissioner v. Saltonstall, 124 F.2d 110 (1st Cir. 1941). However, Fleming v. Commissioner, 43 B.T.A. 229, affirmed 5th Cir., 121 F.2d 7(1941), holds that discretion vested in the trustees is not an "allocation" within the meaning of the statute.

12. "(1) To continue the operation of any property or properties or businesses or oil or gas lease or leases or ranches that I may own or be operating at the time of my death, and to make all purchases, sales or exchanges in connection with their operation, so long as, in the judgment of my executors and trustees, it is to the best interest of my estate to do so, *and to use the principal and or income of my estate in their operations.*"

In Commissioner v. Netcher, 143 F.2d 484 (7th Cir. 1944), cert. denied 323 U.S. 759, 65 S.Ct. 92, 89 L.Ed. 607; and in Newbury v. United States, 102 Ct.Cl. 192, 57 F.Supp. 168, 174 (1944), cert. denied 323 U.S. 802, 65 S.Ct. 559, 89 L.Ed. 640, language in the trust instrument showing the testator's intent to keep the corpus intact, and powers delegated to the trustees, authorizing him to incur a large indebtedness in expanding the capital assets of the corpus, were emphasized by the courts in determining that it was the testator's intent to provide for a depreciation reserve.

14. See note 10, supra.

15. [See note 11, supra.]

Turning then to Texas law, one finds that any person establishing a trust in Texas consisting of "timber, minerals, oil, gas or other natural resources" has the right to determine how the income, expenses and principal are to be apportioned between the tenants and remaindermen. Tex.Rev.Civ.Stat. art. 7425b-26 (1945). When he fails to do so, Section 33 of the Texas Trust Act governs the ascertainment of income and principal and the apportionment of income, expenses and principal among the tenants and remaindermen. Tex.Rev.Civ.Stat. art. 7425b-33 (1945), St. Marks Episcopal Church v. Lowry, 271 S.W.2d 681, 684 (Tex.Civ. App. Fort Worth 1954, err. ref'd n. r. e.)

Section 33 is a statutory enactment of a duty which the Court of Appeals for the Fifth Circuit recognizes is imposed upon all trustees to preserve a trust, the corpus of which contains wasting assets.[16]

The trust created in the will of Guy L. Waggoner contains no provisions for the disposition of proceeds received from the oil and gas producing interests owned by the trust and all distributions are within the sole discretion of the trustees. It follows that Section 33 of the Texas Trust Act applies to the trust.

Section 33 of the Texas Trust Act is not intended to be merely a procedure for accounting for the income receipts of the trust as the plaintiff contends. That the percentages set out in Section 33 were enacted with the federal income tax depletion allowances in mind is clear from the historical note following the statute which quotes Section 33 as it existed prior to amendment in 1945. It stated in part that the proceeds were to be apportioned to principal and income as follows:

> "Such percentage thereof as is permitted to be deducted for depletion under the then existing laws of the United States of America for federal income tax purposes shall be treated as principal and invested or held for the use and benefit of the remainderman, and the balance shall be treated as income subject to be disbursed to the tenant or person entitled thereto, * * *."

It appears, therefore, that Section 33 was enacted not only for the purpose of providing a reserve for trusts with wasting natural resources as part of their assets, but also for the purpose of obtaining the maximum advantage through tax depletion allowances for the trusts.

The plaintiffs insist that by allowing local law, which creates a reserve for depletion, and thereby entitling the trustee to a deduction to the extent of the income so reserved, the Regulations unreasonably extend the language of the Code and are therefore invalid. The Supreme Court "has many times declared that Treasury regulations must be sustained unless unreasonable and plainly inconsistent with the revenue statutes and that they constitute contemporaneous constructions by those charged with administration of these statutes which should not be overruled except for weighty reasons." See e. g., Commissioner v. South Texas Lumber Co., 333 U.S. 496, 501, 68 S.Ct. 695, 698, 92 L.Ed. 831 (1948); Fawcus Machine Co. v. United States, 282 U.S. 375, 378, 51 S.Ct. 144, 75 L.Ed. 397 (1931).

Congress, with regard to Section 611 of the Code, made it clear that it invited regulations supplementing this phase of the Code: "* * *, such reasonable allowance in all cases

---

16. "It is basic trust law that the trustee has a duty to preserve the principal of the trust if it is a wasting asset, unless provided otherwise in the trust instrument. This duty entails the setting aside as part of corpus so much of the trust income as is necessary to replace the depreciation and depletion of the property comprising the trust corpus." Levin v. Commissioner, 355 F.2d 987, 989 (5th Cir. 1966).

to be made under regulations prescribed by the Secretary or his delegate." 26 U.S.C.A. §611(a). This delegation of authority is a result of the complex nature of the depletion problem with relation to income taxes, and the Supreme Court has held that because of the highly technical and involved factors entering into a practical solution of the problem of depletion in administration of tax laws, the administrative powers to deal with it equitably and reasonably should be interpreted so as to strengthen rather than to weaken them. Helvering v. Wilshire Oil Co., 308 U.S. 90, 102–103, 60 S.Ct. 18, 84 L.Ed. 101 (1939).

The provisions of Section 1.611-1(c)(4), recognizing depletion reserves created by local law to be as effective for tax deduction purposes as allocating provisions in the trust instrument, are reasonable. Identical provisions in the companion area of depreciation have been held not to conflict with the Code. Dusek v. Commissioner, 45 T.C. 355 (1966). Other cases have recognized local law as controlling of the tax consequences when it requires the creation of a depletion or depreciation reserve.[18]

The treatment of the problem by the Regulations is equitable as well as reasonable. When trustees are required by the trust instrument or local law to set aside a certain portion of the income from the trust's oil and gas operations in order to replace the value of the corpus assets which have been converted, a tax-free restoration of the converted capital is accomplished. This permits a preservation of the corpus for the remainderman. The vested owners of the trust assets, the trust and the remaindermen, receive the benefit of the deduction to replace their capital which has been converted; no tax is paid by them on their return of capital. The beneficiary on the other hand receives the benefit of any depletion deduction, which is in excess of the replaced capital of the trust.

... Judgment will be entered in accordance [herewith].

Dusek v. Commissioner
376 F.2d 410 (10th Cir. 1967)

BREITENSTEIN, Circuit Judge.

Petitioners seek review of a Tax Court decision[1] disallowing deductions claimed on account of depreciation of property held in trust for the benefit of petitioner Velma Dusek.

Raymond Dusek created a trust in favor of Velma, his wife. Raymond was both the grantor of the trust and the trustee. The term of the trust was 10 years and one month. The trust agreement provided that the net income "may be distributed" to Velma when, in the discretion of the trustee, her needs required. Net income was all income from the trust property after payment of "all the necessary costs and expenses incident to the management, maintenance and conservation of this Trust," the compensation of the trustee, and "such adjustments thereto as are permitted and provided for hereinafter in Item (f) of Article V."

---

18. Grey v. Commissioner, 118 F.2d 153 (7th Cir. 1941), 141 A.L.R. 1113; Laflin v. Commissioner, 69 F.2d 460 (7th Cir. 1934); Dixon v. Commissioner, 69 F.2d 461 (7th Cir. 1934), cert. denied 293 U.S. 560, 55 S.Ct. 72, 79 L.Ed. 661; Newbury v. United States, 57 F.Supp. 168, 102 Ct.Cl. 192 (1944), concur. opin., cert. denied 323 U.S. 802, 65 S.Ct. 559, 89 L.Ed. 640; Freuler v. Lelvering [sic], 291 U.S. 35, 54 S.Ct. 308, 78 L.Ed. 634 (1934), decree of State (Cal.) court; Upton v. Commissioner, 283 F.2d 716 (9th Cir. 1960), cert. denied 366 U.S. 911, 81 S.Ct. 1086, 6 L.Ed.2d 236, decree of state (Cal.) court.

1. See 45 T.C. 355.

The latter item relates to the determination of net income and provides, among other things, that "depreciation and depletion shall be reserved out of income." Article V, Item (m), reads:

> "The Trustee is authorized to apportion and allocate between the Trust and the Primary Beneficiary [Velma] all appropriate tax deductions for depletion and depreciation and any other apportionable tax deductions in such manner as he may see fit."

Raymond contributed over $100,000 to the trust. These funds were used for the purchase of rental property. During the three tax years in question, 1959, 1960, and 1961, the net income of the trust before depreciation ranged from $5,100 to $15,800, and in the same period the depreciation ranged from $4,500 to $11,000. In each year, the trustee distributed only $100 to Velma and, at the same time, allocated to her all of the federal income tax deductions for depreciation. In their joint federal income tax returns for each year the taxpayers claimed as a deduction from their gross income the depreciation on the trust property. Although he made no point of the propriety or accuracy of the depreciation computations made by the trustee, the Commissioner disallowed the deductions and assessed deficiencies.

The controlling provisions of the applicable statute, §[167(d)] are....

The question is what are the "pertinent provisions" of the trust agreement. The Commissioner says they are those of Article V, Item (f), requiring that depreciation be reserved out of income. The taxpayers say they are those of Article V, Item (m), relating to the allocation of tax deductions for depreciation. The Tax Court adopted the theory of the Commissioner and upheld the deficiency determination.

Section [167(d)] is a carry-over from §23(k) of the Revenue Act of 1928.... Before the enactment of §23(k) the rule was that the trust as the entity with legal title to the depreciable assets was the only taxpayer entitled to any portion of the depreciation deduction regardless of whether it would derive any tax benefit therefrom.[2] This situation had caused "uncertainty and considerable hardship."[3] An example of the operation of the provisions that became §23(k) is given thus in the House Conference Report:[4]

> "* * * if the trust instrument provides that the income of the trust computed without regard to depreciation shall be distributed to a named beneficiary, such beneficiary will be entitled to the depreciation allowance to the exclusion of the trustee, while if the instrument provides that the trustee in determining the distributable income shall first make due allowance for keeping the trust corpus intact by retaining a reasonable amount of the current income for that purpose, the allowable deduction will be granted in full to the trustee."

The taxpayers say that this legislative history is not pertinent because the statute is not ambiguous. The answer is that the statute does not define "pertinent provisions" and the example given in the House Conference Report is significant to show what Congress considered a pertinent provision.

From 1928 until amended in 1956, the applicable regulations stated the substance of the statute and gave the same example as that contained in the House Conference Report. As amended, the pertinent provisions of [Treas. Reg. §1.167(h)-1(b)] are....

The taxpayers argue that the amended regulation rewrites the statute because its effect is to say that the only pertinent provision in a trust instrument is one permitting a

2. Lambert Tree Trust Estate v. Commissioner of Internal Revenue, 38 T.C. 392, 403.
3. See S.Rep. No. 960, 70th Cong., 1st Sess., 1939-1 Cum.Bull. (Part 2) 409, 423.
4. H.Conf.Rep. No. 1882, 70th Cong., 1st Sess., 1939-1 Cum.Bull. (Part 2) 444, 445.

trustee to set aside from trust income a reserve for depreciation. The argument over-looks what we believe to be the intent of Congress in enacting §23(k). The purpose was to recognize that the equitable interest of a trust beneficiary, as reflected in the trust in-come allocable to him, is sufficient to entitle him to claim the depreciation deduction to the extent of the income so allocable. Income set aside in a depreciation reserve is not so allocable.

The treatment of depreciation in the cases of life estates with remainder over and of beneficiaries of estates is covered by the same section as that applying to beneficiaries of trusts. For life tenants, heirs, legatees, and devisees, Congress required that the deduction for depreciation follow the income on the depreciable property. It would be strange in-deed to construe the section so as to permit, in the case of a trust beneficiary, a complete separation of the income and the deduction. In Calvin v. United States, 10 Cir., 354 F.2d 202, 204, we held that an income tax deduction may be taken only by the taxpayer who incurs it. The same principle applies here. The depreciation here was incurred by the trustee—not by the beneficiary.

The taxpayers' contention that Article V, Item (m), controls and permits the trustee to apportion tax deductions for depreciation is unconvincing. We are not presently con-cerned with the effect such provision might have if the trust instrument did not require that depreciation shall be reserved out of income. The fact that under the trust instrument the income was allocable to the beneficiary makes no difference. The allocation was to be made only out of net income and that is what remains after various adjustments includ-ing those "permitted and provided" in Item (f) of Article V. The depreciation claimed by the taxpayers is that appearing on a schedule attached to the trustee's return. The ques-tion of whether the trustee actually set up a reserve account is immaterial.

Our conclusion is in accord with that reached by other courts. Commissioner of In-ternal Revenue v. Netcher, 7 Cir., 143 F.2d 484, cert. denied 323 U.S. 759, 65 S.Ct. 92, 89 L.Ed. 607, and Newbury v. United States, 57 F.Supp. 168, 102 Ct.Cl. 192, cert. denied 323 U.S. 802, 65 S.Ct. 559, 89 L.Ed. 640, each involved the same trust which contained a provision that the property shall be "held together for the benefit of my entire Estate and the beneficiaries thereunder," a provision much less explicit than that with which we are here concerned. In Upton v. Commissioner of Internal Revenue, 9 Cir., 283 F.2d 716, cert. denied 366 U.S. 911, 81 S.Ct. 1086, 6 L.Ed.2d 236, a state court decision required the trust to set up a reserve for depletion. In all three of these cases the reserve require-ment was treated as the pertinent provision. None of the cases cited by the taxpayers re-late to trust instruments which contain a specific statement that depreciation shall be reserved out of income.

Affirmed.

Revenue Ruling 90-82

1990-2 C.B. 44

ISSUE

If a trust holds mortgaged property, and if the trustee, in accordance with the terms of the trust's governing instrument, charges the payments of principal on the mortgage note against the trust's income in determining the amounts to be distributed to the trust's beneficiaries, then should the depreciation deduction attributable to the mortgaged prop-erty be allocated, in part, to the trust?

FACTS

G, a grantor, established an irrevocable trust, *TR*, by executing a trust instrument and by conveying property to *T* as trustee. The trust instrument provides that *T* is to pay trust income to *B* for *B*'s life, and after *B*'s death, *T* is to distribute the entire trust principal to *C*. *G* did not retain any power over or interest in *TR* that would cause *G* to be treated as an owner of *TR* under the grantor trust provisions of the Internal Revenue Code (sections 671 through 679).

The trust instrument of *TR* directs *T*, as trustee, to distribute at least annually to *B* all income realized by *TR* during the taxable year. For this purpose, the trust instrument defines income to include all income (other than capital gains) minus certain specified expenses, including both interest and principal on any mortgage indebtedness.

The Revised Uniform Principal and Income Act provides that, unless the governing instrument provides otherwise, a trustee is to charge against trust principal the payments of principal on an indebtedness. Rev. Unif. Principal and Income Act section 13(c)(2), 78 U.L.A. 177 (1962). *TR* is subject to the laws of a state that has adopted the Revised Uniform Principal and Income Act.

In accordance with discretion granted to it under the terms of the trust instrument, *T* purchased on behalf of *TR* income-producing real estate. The purchase price of the real estate was $1,100*x*. *T* paid $100*x* cash to the seller, and gave a mortgage to the seller for the $1,000*x* balance. The mortgage required equal quarterly payments of principal and interest for a period of 15 years.

For its first full taxable year, *TR* realized $140*x* of rental income. During that year, *T*, as trustee, paid $130*x* on the mortgage, and of that amount, $100*x* represented interest and $30*x* represented principal. In accordance with the terms of *TR*'s governing instrument, *T* charged the entire $130*x* of mortgage payments against *TR*'s income, and distributed $10*x* to *B*.

For *TR*'s first full taxable year, the allowable depreciation deduction attributable to the mortgaged real estate was $40*x*. *TR* had no other items of income or deduction. *T* did not establish a reserve for depreciation.

LAW AND ANALYSIS

Section 642(e) of the Code provides that a trust shall be allowed the deduction for depreciation only to the extent that it is not allowable to the beneficiaries under section [167(d)].

Section [167(d)] of the Code and the related regulations provide that, if the trustee does not maintain a reserve for depreciation, deductions for depreciation are apportioned between the income beneficiaries of the trust and the trustee in the same proportion that trust income is allocable to each. Section 1.167(h)-1(b)(2) of the Income Tax Regulations specifically states that no effect is to be given to any allocation of the depreciation deduction that gives any beneficiary or the trustee a share of such deduction greater than that person's prorata share of trust income, irrespective of any provision in the trust instrument other than a provision that requires or allows the trustee to establish a reserve for depreciation.

Section 643(b) of the Code and the related regulations provide that the term "income," when not preceded by the words "distributable net," "undistributed net," or "gross," means the amount of income of the trust for the taxable year determined under the terms of its governing instrument and applicable local law. Section 1.643(b)-1 of the regulations states, however, that trust provisions that depart fundamentally from concepts of local law in determining trust income are not recognized for federal income tax purposes. [Compare the regulation's slightly different current wording.] The example set out in section 1.643(b)-1 indicates that if a trust instrument directs a trustee to distribute all income currently, but allocates ordinary dividends and interest to principal, the trust would not be considered one that is required to distribute all its income currently. In other words, the trust provision defining income and principal is ignored, and, for federal income tax purposes, the crediting of dividends and interest to principal is considered an accumulation of income for the benefit of the remainderman.

Generally, payment of the principal portion of an outstanding mortgage is charged against trust principal and is not, therefore, taken into account in determining "trust income" as that term is defined in section 643(b) of the Code. See Rev. Unif. Principal and Income Act section 13(c)(2), 7B U.L.A. 177 (1962); Unif. Principal and Income Act section 12, 7B U.L.A. 191 (1931); G. Bogert, *The Law of Trusts and Trustees*, sections 603, 808 (rev. 2d ed., 1981); *Restatement (Second) of Trusts* section 233; Annot., 68 A.L.R.3d 811 (1976). The rationale for this general rule is that the reduction of the principal balance on an outstanding mortgage increases the equity held by the trust in the encumbered real estate, and therefore the remainder beneficiary suffers no loss through application of trust principal to such payments. *See* G. Bogert, *supra*, section 808; Annot., 68 A.L.R.3d at 813. Rather, by charging mortgage principal payments against trust principal, the trustee merely decreases the trust's investment in one asset (e.g., principal cash), and increases the trust's investment in the encumbered real estate. If, however, a trustee charges mortgage principal payments against income, the amount available for distribution to the income beneficiary is diminished, and the amount available for the remainder beneficiary is increased because the value of trust principal is enhanced by the amount of the payment. *See* G. Bogert, *supra*, section 808; Annot., 68 A.L.R.3d at 814.

Charging mortgage principal payments against trust income produces the same result that occurs if items normally considered to be trust income, such as interest and dividends, are allocated to trust principal. In both situations, amounts that would be included in trust income, but for provisions of the governing instrument that depart from general concepts of local law, are added to trust principal for the benefit of the remainderman. In this case, therefore, consistent with the example set out in section 1.643(b)-1 of the regulations, the provision in the trust instrument directing the trustee to charge mortgage principal payments against income is ignored for federal income tax purposes.

Accordingly, for its first full taxable year, *TR* is to compute trust income for purposes of section 643(b) of the Code as follows:

Rental Income	$140x
Minus interest on mortgage	$100x
Income computed under section 643(b)	$40x

Because the provision in the trust instrument directing the trustee to charge mortgage principal payments against trust income is disregarded for federal income tax purposes, that amount is not deducted in determining trust income under section 643(b).

Although the provision of the trust instrument directing the trustee to charge mortgage principal payments against income is disregarded for federal income tax purposes, the trustee must follow that direction in determining the amount of income to be distributed to B. Consequently, T could distribute only $10x of income to B ($140x rental income—$130x interest and principal on the mortgage). Because that amount represents one-fourth of total trust income computed under section 643(b) of the

Code, *B* may deduct one-fourth of the $40*x* depreciation attributable to the mortgaged real estate, or $10*x*. The balance of the depreciation deduction, $30*x*, is allocated to *TR* because it retained three-fourths of total trust income computed under section 643(b).

HOLDING

If a trust holds mortgaged property, and if the trustee, in accordance with the terms of the trust instrument, charges payments of mortgage principal against trust income in determining the amount to be distributed to the trust's beneficiaries, a portion of the depreciation deduction attributable to the mortgaged property must be allocated to the trust. By charging mortgage principal payments against income, the trustee, in effect, accumulates income for the benefit of the remainderman, and, under section [167(d)] of the Code, depreciation is to be allocated between the trust and the beneficiaries based on the amount of income allocable to each. The portion of the depreciation allocated to the trust, therefore, is determined by multiplying the total allowable depreciation by a fraction, the numerator of which is the amount of income accumulated, and the denominator of which is the total trust income computed under section 643(b).

Lamkin v. United States

533 F.2d 303 (5th. Cir. 1976)

RONEY, Circuit Judge:

This appeal involves an issue of tax law which has, apparently, reached the courts on only one previous occasion. We are called upon to decide whether 26 U.S.C.A. §[167(d)] permits an estate in administration to take a depreciation deduction on real property when the estate distributed the income generated by that property to income beneficiaries of the trust that will eventually hold the property. The Government allocated a pro rata share of the depreciation deduction to the distributees of the income and assessed a deficiency against the estate. The taxpayer estate paid the deficiency and brought this suit for refund, in which the district court granted the Government's motion for summary judgment. We affirm.

Under the second sentence of §[167(d)], the depreciation deduction may be taken by the *trust* only when the trustee is "directed" by local law or by the trust instrument to retain income in a depreciation reserve for the purpose of preserving corpus. Treas.Reg. §1.167(h)-1(b)(2) (1960). *See Sue Carol,* 30 BTA 433 (1943). Had the distributees received the real property income from the incipient trust rather than from the estate, the depreciation deduction would be allocated pro rata to the income distributees, there being no indication in the record of a required depreciation reserve.

The present dispute arises in the interpretation of the third sentence of §[167(d)], which controls the disposition of this case.... This provision does not in specific terms cover distributions, made during the administration of an estate, to the income beneficiaries of a testamentary trust which is not yet operative. The question before this Court, therefore, is whether the income beneficiary of the yet-to-be-established trust may be considered either an heir, legatee or devisee of the estate for the purposes of §[167(d)]. The taxpayer contends that the income beneficiary does not fall within any of these three categories, and therefore, a pro rata portion of the depreciation deduction is not to be allocated to the beneficiary, but may be taken by the estate.

The estate relies, in support of its position, on a Fourth Circuit case which is similar to ours, yet distinguishable in one critical respect. *In re Nissen*, 345 F.2d 230 (4th Cir. 1965). That action was brought to determine whether an estate could properly take a property depreciation deduction during its administration, the court ruling that the deduction was available to the estate. The property giving rise to the deduction would, upon closing of the estate, be distributed to testamentary trusts which would distribute all income to life beneficiaries. Acting under authorization in the will, the executor made discretionary income distributions to the future life beneficiaries, but the estate took the depreciation deduction. The executor acted in accordance with the following provision in the will:

> ... I authorize my Executor to pay to or apply from the net income of my estate such sums and at such intervals and in such manner as my Executor in its sole discretion shall from time to time deem requisite or desirable in providing for the reasonable support, maintenance and education of my granddaughter ... [and] my son....

See Estate of Nissen, 41 T.C. 522, 525 (1964). Because these discretionary distributees, the son and granddaughter of the testatrix, were also the future life income beneficiaries, it is easy to misunderstand the holding of *In re Nissen, supra*, 345 F.2d 230. Since the son and granddaughter received income distributions from the estate in accordance with their status under the will as income distributees at the discretion of the executor, and not in accordance with their status as future trust beneficiaries, we understand the Fourth Circuit's holding to be that those who so receive income under the will during estate administration are not heirs, devisees or legatees of specific real property, entitled to the depreciation deduction accruing to that property. Indeed, it is entirely possible that the *Nissen* distributees received income generated by assets other than the real property.

By contrast, in the case before us the will did not provide for the distribution of income during the period of administration. Therefore we can only conclude that the distribution to the future life income beneficiary was based on her status vis-a-vis the trust. Our case is in this critical respect distinct from *Nissen*.

As a generally accepted matter, an executor can legally distribute income only to a legatee, or heir if the will is silent. *See, e. g.*, Vernon's Tex.Civ.Stat.Ann., Probate Code, §239. To be legal the income distributions here in question must be viewed in either of two ways. First, treating the real property as constructively being in the trust, the distribution could have constructively been made from the trust to the estate and then from the estate to the income beneficiaries. By this view the depreciation deduction would be allocated under the second sentence of §[167(d)], there being no local law or trust instrument provision directing a depreciation reserve. Alternatively, the will might be construed to permit direct distribution to the trust beneficiaries as if they were, during administration, legatees of the real property. Under this concept, depreciation allocation is mandated by the third sentence of §[167(d)]. According to either view, the distributee clearly takes according to her status vis-a-vis the real property under the trust. It is equally clear that the income she receives is income generated by the real property which gives rise to the depreciation deduction.

The statute appears to follow a general policy that the depreciation deduction travels with the income from the property. Thus, the first sentence of §[167(d)] directs that in every instance life tenants will receive the depreciation deduction, and the third sentence mandates allocation of the deduction pro rata, on the basis of the receipt of income. The second sentence is consistent, even though it allows the settlor of a trust to preserve corpus by setting aside a depreciation reserve, because under the statute and longstanding regulations, the trust may take the depreciation deduction, but only to the extent that it withholds *income* in its reserve. In view of the policy of this statute, it would be anomalous to permit an estate to distribute income which can be identified as coming from the real property, but retain the depreciation deduction as an offset against income from unrelated sources.

AFFIRMED.

Illustrative Material

1. Note that, in *Hay*, the taxpayers are the beneficiaries (not the trustees), who claim that a greater portion of the depletion deduction should have been allocated to them. Normally, if the tentative taxable income of a trust is reduced, that in turn reduces DNI, which ultimately reduces the amount on which the beneficiaries are subject to taxation. In other words, allocating the depreciation deduction to the trust normally benefits the beneficiaries *indirectly*, even though not directly. Why then do the taxpayers in *Hay* care? Why might the beneficiaries be better off having the deduction allocated *directly* to them on the basis of income? The most likely reason is that allocating the depletion deduction based on income paid to the reserve disproportionately benefitted the trust remainder beneficiaries, the income allocated to the reserve being fully offset by a deduction. Necessarily, then, a smaller portion of the income distributed to the income beneficiaries would be offset by a deduction.

A simple example illustrates the point. Assume a wholly discretionary trust for the benefit of A for life, remainder to B. The trust receives $40,000 in oil and gas income and no other income during the year. Assume asset values remain constant, except as augmented by income. Assume further that applicable local law requires the trustee to retain 25% of the income as a depletion reserve. Assume that the section 611 depletion deduction is $12,000. The trustee determines in its discretion to distribute $15,000 to A. Assume that both A and the trust are subject to income tax at a single rate of 20%.

Allocation pursuant to Section 1.611-1(c)(4). Under the approach mandated by section 1.611-1(c)(4), the first $10,000 of the depletion deduction (25% of $40,000) is allocated to the trust; the remaining $2,000 is allocated $1,000 to the trustee and $1,000 to A. Disregarding other deductions (including the personal exemption), the tentative taxable income of the trust is $29,000 ($40,000 less $11,000); the trust is entitled to a distribution deduction of $15,000, leaving trust taxable income of $14,000. The $2,800 tax on trust income will be paid from either principal or undistributed fiduciary accounting income, or both, depending on state law. The net increase in trust assets during the year is $22,200 ($40,000 less $15,000 less $2,800). Note that the income allocated to the reserve is fully offset by a deduction. The amount subject to taxation in the hands of A is $15,000; A is also entitled to a $1,000 section 611 deduction; thus, the net amount subject to taxation for A with respect to trust oil and gas revenues is $14,000, on which A pays a tax of $2,800. The net benefit to A during the year is $12,200 ($15,000 less $2,800).

Allocation on the basis of income. Under the approach advocated by the taxpayers in *Hay*, $7,500 of the depletion deduction (25/40 of $40,000) is allocated to the trustee, and $4,500 (15/40 of $40,000) is allocated to A. Disregarding other deductions (including the personal exemption), the tentative taxable income of the trust is $32,500 ($40,000 less $7,500); the trust is entitled to a distribution deduction of $15,000, leaving taxable income of $17,500. The $3,500 tax on trust income will be paid from either principal or undistributed fiduciary accounting income, or both. The net increase in trust assets during the year is $21,500 ($40,000 less $15,000 less $3,500). Irrespective of the account from which the tax is paid, the increased tax burden under this approach diminishes the value of the trust and thus the assets available for eventual distribution to B. The amount subject to taxation in the hands of A is $15,000; A is also entitled to a $4,500 section 611 deduction; thus, the net amount subject to taxation for A with respect to the trust oil and gas revenues is $10,500, on which A will pay a tax of $2,100. The net benefit to A during the year is $12,900 ($15,000 less $2,100). Thus, under the approach advocated by the taxpayers in *Hay*, A is $700 better off, and the trust (and therefore, indirectly, B) are $700 worse off.

2. *Lamkin* distinguished *In re Estate of Nissen v. Commissioner*, 345 F.2d 230 (4th Cir. 1965), primarily on the basis that *Nissen* involved estate distributions that were not necessarily directly traceable to the depreciating property. *Nissen*, however, appears not to turn on that fact. Instead, *Nissen* appears to stand squarely for the proposition that an estate need not allocate the depreciation deduction among trust beneficiaries to which it makes distributions, because trust beneficiaries are not "heirs, legatees, [or] devisees" under section 167(d).

3. Rev. Rul. 74-530, 1974-2 C.B. 188, points out that, although apportionment of depreciation and depletion deductions between fiduciary and beneficiary depends upon the amount of income allocated to each, it is possible for a beneficiary to be entitled to a deduction in excess of his, her, or its allocable share of income:

> [I]t is possible under section [167(d)] and section 611(b) of the Code to allocate depreciation and depletion deductions between an estate and its heirs, legatees, and devisees or between a trust and its beneficiaries in amounts that are greater than their pro rata shares of the income of the estate or income of the trust. This is so because although the depreciation and depletion deductions are apportioned on the basis of the income of the estate or income of the trust allocable to each of the parties (without regard to any depreciation or depletion allocable to them), they are not limited by the amount of such income.

4. The fraction used in computing the depreciation or depletion deduction to which a particular beneficiary is entitled must include, as a part of its denominator, any income paid to or set aside for the benefit of charity. *See Lambert Tree Trust Estate,* 38 T.C. 392 (1962), *acq.*, 1964-2 C.B. 7. Otherwise, the beneficiary would receive a disproportionate share of the total deduction.

5. If a trust or an estate is itself a beneficiary of a trust or an estate entitled to a deduction for depreciation or depletion, the beneficiary trust or estate may, in turn, apportion any depreciation or depletion apportioned to it between itself and its own beneficiaries in accordance with the provisions of section 642(e). Rev. Rul. 61-211, 1961-2 C.B. 124, *clarified,* Rev. Rul. 66-278, 1966-2 C.B. 243.

7. Expenses Deducted for Estate Tax Purposes

Internal Revenue Code:
Sections 642(g); 2053(a); 2054

Regulations:
Sections 1.642(g)-1, -2

Estate of Orville F. Yetter
35 T.C. 737 (1961)

TIETJENS, *Judge*:

* * *

The only question to be decided is whether funeral and burial expenses are properly deductible on the estate's fiduciary income tax return.

* * *

Orville F. Yetter died on April 29, 1955.

* * *

The funeral and burial expenses in the amount of $2,197.50 were paid by the estate of Orville F. Yetter prior to April 16, 1956, and the expenses were claimed as a deduction on the estate's fiduciary income tax return for the taxable period April 30, 1955, to December 31, 1955.

Attached to and made a part of the fiduciary income tax return for the estate of Orville F. Yetter for the taxable period April 30, 1955, to December 31, 1955, is a statement waiving the right to have funeral and burial expenses allowed at any time as a deduction in computing the taxable estate of the decedent.

* * *

As a general proposition the income of an estate is computed and taxable in the same manner as that of an individual, with certain differences under the Code which are not here applicable. This general principle is set out in section 641....

Deductions, of course, are a matter of legislative grace and the person claiming a deduction must bring himself within the clear intendment of the taxing statutes. We have found no provision of the statute which would allow funeral expenses to be deducted in computing the taxable income of an estate.

Petitioner relies on section 642(g) as providing for the claimed deduction if the waiver required by that section is filed. Such a waiver was filed in this case. Section 642(g) reads as follows....

To complete the statutory scheme we quote section [2053(a)] which is referred to in section 642(g)....

If we follow petitioner's argument, it is that the deductions provided for in section 2053 for the purpose of computing the taxable estate may be used as income tax deductions if the statement and waiver required by section 642(g) are filed. We do not think any such result was intended. The purpose of 642(g) is clearly to avoid the possibility of a double deduction of items of a character which would properly be deductible for both estate tax and income tax purposes, e.g., certain administrative expenses. See sec. 1.642(g)-1.... Certainly funeral expenses are not deductions of such a character. They have nothing to do with the determination of taxable income. Followed to its logical conclusion, petitioner's argument would permit the shifting of all of the items enumerated in section 2053, such as "funeral expenses," "claims against the estate," and "unpaid mortgages" from estate tax to income tax by the simple expedient of filing the statutory notice and waiver required by 642(g). Such a result is not implicit in the sections relied on and is not warranted by any other statutory provision. It was not provided for under section 162(e) or 812(b), I.R.C. 1939, the antecedents of the sections here involved or the regulations adopted thereunder, which were in effect at the time the petition was filed in this case. Though there have been some changes in language between the related sections of the 1939 and 1954 Codes, we find nothing in these changes which would allow the deduction here claimed. The Commissioner has specifically said in Rev. Rul. 56-449, 1956-2 C.B. 180, in holding that certain administrative expenses of an estate allowable under section 2053(a)(2) may be deducted under the conditions prescribed in section 642(g) by the estate on its income tax return, that funeral expenses were only allowable as a deduction to the estate under section 2053.

The Commissioner's determination is upheld.

Illustrative Material

1. In general, section 642(g) disallows deduction for income tax purposes of items deducted for estate tax purposes under section 2053 or section 2054. Thus, for example, an executor's commission may not be deducted both under section 212 as an expense incurred for the management of income-producing property and under section 2053 as an administration expense. However, deduction under section 2053 of administration expenses paid during one tax year does not prevent the estate from deducting under section 212 such expenses paid during a later tax year. Rev. Rul. 70-361, 1970-2 C.B. 133. The I.R.S. reasons that dividing a particular type of expense involves "no duplication of a deduction."

2. Section 642(g) requires the filing of an estate tax waiver in order for administration expenses to be deductible for income tax purposes. But section 642(g) does not require an income tax waiver in order for such expenses to be deductible for estate tax purposes. *See Estate of Keitel v. Commissioner*, 60 T.C.M. (CCH) 425 (1990). Thus, if no waiver is filed, administration expenses are deductible for estate tax purposes under section 2053(a)(2) even if the expenses have already been deducted for income tax purposes. *See Estate of Street v. Commissioner*, 68 T.C.M. (CCH) 1213 (1994) (where estate never filed waiver and statute of limitations was still open for income tax purposes, estate could deduct, for estate tax purposes, post-death interest it had already deducted for income tax purposes, notwithstanding estate's failure to claim the interest for estate tax purposes in prior Tax Court litigation). If the statute of limitations is still open with respect to the income tax return, the I.R.S. will disallow the expenses as income tax deductions. If the statute of limitations bars assessment of an income tax deficiency, the I.R.S. will resort to the doctrine of equitable recoupment and offset the theoretical income tax deficiency against any estate tax refund otherwise due. Rev. Rul. 81-287, 1981-2 C.B. 183. *See generally* Andrews, *Modern-Day Equitable Recoupment and the "Two Tax Effect:" Avoidance of the Statutes of Limitation in Federal Tax Controversies*, 28 Ariz. L. Rev 595 (1986).

3. In Rev. Rul. 59-32, 1959-1 C.B. 245, the I.R.S. ruled that the portion of an estate's administration expenses attributable to the production of tax-exempt income, and therefore not deductible for income tax purposes, was deductible for estate tax purposes under section 2053(a)(2). This was so even though the estate had filed the section 642(g) waiver: "To hold that the filing of the statement of waiver under section 642(g) of the Code constitutes a relinquishment of the right to deduct, for estate tax purposes, the balance of [the] administration expenses would not give proper effect to the intent of Congress in enacting the statute."

4. Treas. Reg. § 1.642(g)-2 states that section 642(g) is inapplicable to amounts deductible under section 2053(a)(3) as *claims* against an estate. Thus, an estate that was entitled under section 2053(a)(3) to deduct the commuted value of alimony payments payable to the decedent's ex-spouse was also entitled to deduct the payments themselves under section 661, notwithstanding section 642(g). Rev. Rul. 67-304, 1967-2 C.B. 224. In general, however, double deductions are available only with respect to "deductions in respect of a decedent," considered *infra* (ch. 6, sec. B).

Problem

2-2. A trust that is required to distribute all its income annually has the following receipts: cash dividends from shares of I.B.M., $50,000; interest on Chrysler debentures, $30,000; interest on obligations of the City of New York, $40,000; and rent received from Old MacDonald for the use of Blackacre, $20,000. The trust has the following expenses: an annual trustee's fee of $2,000, of which $1,000 is based on principal and $1,000 is based on income; and local property taxes on Blackacre in the amount of $15,000.

a. Calculate the trust's gross income.

b. Calculate the trust's tentative taxable income. (Tentative taxable income refers to taxable income prior to the distribution deduction.)

8. Passive Activity Rules

Internal Revenue Code:
   Section 469(a), (c)(1), (h)(1)

Temporary Regulation:
   Section 1.469-1T(b)

Mattie K. Carter Trust v. United States

256 F. Supp. 2d 536 (N.D. Tex. 2003)

MCBRYDE, District Judge.

Before the court for consideration are a motion for partial summary judgment filed by defendant, United States of America (Internal Revenue Service ["IRS"]), and a motion for summary judgment filed by plaintiff, the Mattie Carter Trust ("Carter Trust"), by Benjamin J. Fortson, Jr. ("Fortson"), Trustee. The court ... concludes that IRS' motion should be denied, and that Carter Trust's motion should be granted.

I.
Undisputed Facts

Carter Trust is a testamentary trust established in 1956 under the Last Will and Testament of Mattie K. Carter, deceased. Fortson has been the trustee of Carter Trust since 1984, and manages its assets, including the Carter Ranch ("ranch"), which has been operated by Carter Trust since 1956.[1]

The ranch covers some 15,000 acres, and is used for a cattle ranching operations and for oil and gas interests.... In 1994, there were approximately 4,700 head of cattle on the ranch; there were approximately 3,300 head of cattle on the ranch in 1995.... At the relevant times, Carter Trust employed a full-time ranch manager and other full- and part-time employees who performed essentially all of the activities for the ranch....

Fortson, as trustee of Carter Trust, dedicated a substantial amount of time and attention to ranch activities:

> ... My duties include reviewing and approving all financial and operating proposals for the Ranch and the Trust, budget and budgeting for the Ranch, all investment decisions for the Trust, asset acquisition and sales, supervising all employees and agents of the Trust and the Trust's Service providers, reviewing all financial information, and responsibility for all banking relationships of the Trust. My duties and responsibilities as Trustee routinely require a significant percentage of my time and attention, and I maintain regular office hours during which I am consulted regarding any Trust matter that arises.

> * * *

> I have delegated certain aspects of the operation and management of the Ranch. [T]he Trust employs a full-time ranch manager, who is responsible for the day-to-day operations of the Ranch, subject to my approval....

> I routinely discuss management issues pertaining to the Ranch with the ranch manager....

> I have also delegated oversight responsibility for the Ranch to Benjamin J. Fortson III. Mr. Fortson III is a beneficiary of the Trust and takes a very active, hands-on role in supervising the Ranch manager and general Ranch operations. He spent well in excess of 500 hours engaged in Ranch operations and management at the Ranch in both tax years 1994 and 1995.

...In this way, Fortson, Rohn [the ranch manager], and other employees operated the ranch on behalf of Carter Trust.

Carter Trust claimed deductions in the 1994 and 1995 tax years for losses of $856,518.00 and $796,687.00, respectively, incurred in connection with the ranch operations. On April 8, 1999, IRS issued a notice of deficiency to Carter Trust related to these deductions. The trust paid the disputed tax for each year in full on September 27, 1999 ... It made timely refund claims, which IRS denied on December 3, 2001, and timely filed this suit, seeking a refund....

---

1. The parties agree that Carter Trust is a "complex trust." *See generally Hay v. United States*, 263 F.Supp. 813, 818–19 (N.D.Tex.1967).

II.
Legal Issues Presented in the Motions

The parties' cross-motions for summary judgment present an issue of first impression related to "passive activity," as defined in section 469.... IRS argues that the "material participation" of a trust in a trade or business, within the meaning of section 469(h)(1) ... should be determined by evaluating only the activities of the trustee in his capacity as such. In contrast, Carter Trust urges that, because the trust (not the trustee) is the taxpayer, "material participation" in the ranch operations should be determined by assessing the activities of Carter Trust, through its fiduciaries, employees, and agents.

III.
Analysis

IRS issued a "Notice of Deficiency" on April 8, 1999, which stated that Carter Trust owed additional taxes for 1994 and 1995:

> It is determined that the Schedule F losses claimed in connection with your ranching and cattle activities for expenses in excess of income are not allowable because it has been established that this activity is a passive activity within the meaning of Section 469....

... In response to Carter Trust's refund claim, IRS proposed "full disallowance," giving the following explanation:

> The loss from the Schedule F is being disallowed for 1994 and 1995 because the Trustee, Ben J. Forton, failed to meet the material participation requirements of IRC Section 469(h) and Temporary Treas. Reg. Section 1.469-5T....[2]

* * *

IRS could disallow the losses only if they represented a "passive activity loss" within the meaning of I.R.C. §469(a).... A "passive activity" is an activity "(A) which involves the conduct of any trade or business, and (B) in which the taxpayer does not materially participate." *Id.* §469(c)(1). IRS acknowledges that the ranch operations constitute a business. The statute defines "taxpayer" as:

> (2) Persons described.—The following are described in this paragraph:
>
> (A) any individual, estate, or trust,
>
> (B) any closely held C corporation, and
>
> (C) any personal Service corporation.

Id. §469(a)(2). Thus, Carter Trust fits within the definition of taxpayer in section 469(a)(2)(A).

In pertinent part, section 469(h) defines "material participation" by a taxpayer in a business activity as follows:

> (1) In general.—A taxpayer shall be treated as materially participating in an activity only if the taxpayer is involved in the operations of the activity on a basis which is—

---

2. IRS, through its counsel, conceded in a telephone hearing conducted on April 3, 2003, that temporary treasury regulation section 1.469-5T had no applicability to this case because that section concerns material participation for individual taxpayers. Counsel for IRS also disclosed that IRS contends that a fact issue exists in this case as to whether Fortson satisfied the material participation standard of I.R.C. §469.

(A) regular,

(B) continuous, and

(C) substantial.

I.R.C. §469(h)(1).

The question arises as to how to determine whether Carter Trust materially participated in the ranch operations. IRS takes the position that the material participation of a
trust in a business should be made by reference only to the trustee's activities.... Carter
Trust counters that, as a legal entity, it can "participate in an activity only through the
actions of its fiduciaries, employees, and agents," and that through such collective efforts,
its cattle ranching operations during 1994 and 1995 were regular, continuous, and substantial....

As discussed above, section 469 says that a trust is a taxpayer, I.R.C. §469(a)(2)(A),
and that a taxpayer is treated as materially participating in a business if its activities in pursuit of that business are regular, continuous, and substantial, *id.* §469(h)(1). It is undisputed that Carter Trust, not Fortson, is the taxpayer. Common sense dictates that the
participation of Carter Trust in the ranch operations should be scrutinized by reference
to the trust itself, which necessarily entails an assessment of the activities of those who
labor on the ranch, or otherwise in furtherance of the ranch business, on behalf of Carter
Trust. *Cf. Fojtik v. First Nat'l Bank,* 752 S.W.2d 669, 673 (Tex.App.—Corpus Christi 1988)
(explaining that "the acts of a corporation's agents are deemed to be acts of the corporation itself"), *writ denied per curiam,* 775 S.W.2d 632 (Tex.1989).[3]

IRS' contention that Carter Trust's participation in the ranch operations should be
measured by reference to Fortson finds no support within the plain meaning of the statute.
Such a contention is arbitrary, subverts common sense, and attempts to create ambigu-
ity where there is none. The court recognizes that IRS has not issued regulations that address a trust's participation in a business ... and that no case law bears on the issue.
However, the absence of regulations and case law does not manufacture statutory ambi-
guity. The court has studied the snippet of legislative history IRS supplied that purports
to lend insight on how Congress intended section 469 to apply to a trust's participation
in a business.[4] Nevertheless, the court only resorts to legislative history where the statutory language is unclear ... which ... is not the case here.

The court concludes that the material participation of Carter Trust in the ranch operations should be determined by reference to the persons who conducted the business
of the ranch on Carter Trust's behalf, including Fortson. The summary judgment evidence makes clear that the collective activities of those persons with relation to the ranch
operations during relevant times were regular, continuous, and substantial so as to constitute material participation.

Alternatively, the court concludes that, based on the undisputed summary judgment
evidence, Fortson's activities with regard to the ranch operations, standing alone, were reg-

---

3. Carter Trust likens itself to a closely held C corporation, an analogy that the court finds potentially
appropriate here.... IRS, through counsel, acknowledged that Fortson's relationship to Carter Trust
is similar to that of a chief executive officer to a corporation. However, the court did not need to resort to the statute and regulations applicable to corporations to be satisfied of the merit of Carter
Trust's position in this action.

4. *See* S. REP. NO. 99-313, 1986-3 C.B. 735.... Moreover, the court on its own located potentially relevant secondary authority, *see, e.g.,* STAFF OF J. COMM. ON TAX'N, General Explanation
of the Tax Reform Act of 1986, at 242 n. 33 (1987)....

ular, continuous, and substantial so as to constitute material participation by him, as trustee, during relevant times. Consequently, even if the court were to accept the legal standard articulated by IRS, through counsel, during the April 3, 2003, telephone hearing, Carter Trust would prevail under the summary judgment record.

The losses Carter Trust sustained in 1994 and 1995 due to the ranch operations were not passive activity losses within the meaning of section 469. IRS improperly disallowed these losses, with the consequence that Carter Trust is entitled to a refund of the overpaid taxes for the 1994 and 1995 tax years. . . .

Illustrative Material

1. Four years after its defeat in *Carter Trust*, the Service, in Technical Advice Memorandum 200733023 (2007), continued to assert that "the sole means" for a trust to establish material participation in an activity for purposes of §469 is to prove that its trustees are themselves involved in the operations of the business on a regular, continuous, and substantial basis. In the facts at hand, a testamentary trust owned an interest in a business. In accordance with the terms of the will, the trustees appointed a number of "special trustees" to perform a variety of services for the business. The combined activities of the trustees and these "special trustees," so the taxpayer argued, constituted material participation; thus, the company's losses were not passive. The Service, disregarding the activities of the "special trustees," and finding that the activities of the trustees themselves were insubstantial, ruled otherwise. According to the Service, the "special trustees" were not fiduciaries, because they could not bind the trust. And even if they were fiduciaries, many of their duties had only a "a questionable nexus" to the operations of the business.

The Service discussed *Carter Trust* at length and expressly rejected its analysis:

> The focus on a trustee's activities … accords with the general policy rationale underlying the passive loss regime. As a general matter, the owner of a business may not look to the activities of the owner's employees to satisfy the material participation requirement. … Indeed, because an owner's trade or business will generally involve employees or agents, a contrary approach would result in an owner invariably being treated as materially participating. … A trustee performs its duties on behalf of the beneficial owners. Consistent with the treatment of other business owners, therefore, it is appropriate in the trust context to look only to the activities of the trustee.

2. In Private Letter Ruling 9031022 (1990), the Service disregarded the existence of a revocable trust for purposes of applying section 469 to its grantor. Similarly, in Field Service Advice 200035006 (2000), the Service ruled that the grantor of a wholly owned grantor trust was the appropriate focus of the material participation determination. These rulings are consistent with the approach of the temporary regulations, under which section 469 does not apply to trusts (or portions of trust) described in section 671. Treas. Reg. §1.469-1T(b)(2).

3. For an exhaustive treatment of the intersection of subchapter J and section 469, see Schmolka, *Passive Activity Losses, Trusts, and Estates: The Regulations (If I Were King)*, 58 Tax L. Rev. 191 (2005).

Chapter 3

The Entity as Conduit: Allocating the Tax between the Entity and Its Beneficiaries

A. "Income" or "Bequest"?

1. The Problem

Section 102(a) of the Code excludes from gross income "the value of property acquired by gift, bequest, devise, or inheritance." On the other hand, section 102(b) excepts from this rule "the income from any property referred to in subsection (a)." With respect to property transmitted by a gift or bequest *in trust*, how do we distinguish between principal (which should be non-taxable) and income (which should be taxable) and thus preserve the integrity of section 102? This is the problem posed by *Irwin v. Gavit*.

Internal Revenue Code:
    Sections 61(a); 102(a), (b)

Irwin v. Gavit

268 U.S. 161 (1925)

MR. JUSTICE HOLMES delivered the opinion of the Court.

This is a suit to recover taxes and penalties exacted by the Collector.... The Collector demurred to the complaint. The demurrer was overruled and judgment given for the plaintiff by the District Court, 275 Fed. 643, and the Circuit Court of Appeals, 295 Fed. 84....

The question is whether the sums received by the plaintiff under the will of Anthony M. Brady in 1913, 1914 and 1915, were income and taxed. The will, admitted to probate August 12, 1913, left the residue of the estate in trust to be divided into six equal parts, the income of one part to be applied so far as deemed proper by the trustees to the education and support of the testator's granddaughter, Marcia Ann Gavit, the balance to be divided into two equal parts and one of them to be paid to the testator's son-in-law, the plaintiff, in equal quarter-yearly payments during his life. But on the granddaughter's reaching the age of twenty-one or dying the fund went over, so that, the granddaughter then being six years old, it is said, the plaintiff's interest could not exceed fifteen years. The Courts below held that the payments received were property acquired by bequest, were not income and were not subject to tax.

The [predecessor of section 61] provides that there shall be levied a tax "upon the entire net income arising or accruing from all sources in the preceding calendar year to every citizen of the United States." If these payments properly may be called income by the common understanding of that word and the statute has failed to hit them it has missed so much of the general purpose that it expresses at the start. Congress intended to use its power to the full extent. *Eisner v. Macomber*, 252 U. S. 189, 203. By [the predecessor of section 102, which at the time did not include a counterpart to subsection (b)(2)] the net income is to include 'gains or profits and income derived from any source whatever, including the income from but not the value of property acquired by gift, bequest, devise or descent.' By [the predecessor of section 641] trustees are to make 'return of the net income of the person for whom they act, subject to this tax,' and by [another portion of the statute] trustees and others having the control or payment of fixed or determinable gains, &c., of another person who are required to render a return on behalf of another are 'authorized to withhold enough to pay the normal tax.' The language quoted leaves no doubt in our minds that if a fund were given to trustees for A for life with remainder over, the income received by the trustees and paid over to A would be income of A under the statute. It seems to us hardly less clear that even if there were a specific provision that A should have no interest in the corpus, the payments would be income none the less, within the meaning of the statute and the Constitution, and by popular speech. In the first case it is true that the bequest might be said to be of the corpus for life, in the second it might be said to be of the income. But we think that the provision of the act that exempts bequests assumes the gift of a corpus and contrasts it with the income arising from it, but was not intended to exempt income properly so-called simply because of a severance between it and the principal fund. No such conclusion can be drawn from *Eisner v. Macomber*, 252 U. S. 189, 206, 207. The money was income in the hands of the trustees and we know of nothing in the law that prevented its being paid and received as income by the donee.

The Courts below went on the ground that the gift to the plaintiff was a bequest and carried no interest in the corpus of the fund. We do not regard those considerations as conclusive, as we have said, but if it were material a gift of the income of a fund ordinarily is treated by equity as creating an interest in the fund. Apart from technicalities we can perceive no distinction relevant to the question before us between a gift of the fund for life and a gift of the income from it. The fund is appropriated to the production of the same result whichever form the gift takes. Neither are we troubled by the question where to draw the line. That is the question in pretty much everything worth arguing in the law. *Hudson County Water Company v. McCarter*, 209 U. S. 349, 355. Day and night, youth and age are only types. But the distinction between the cases put of a gift from the corpus of the estate payable in installments and the present seems to us not hard to draw, assuming that the gift supposed would not be income. This is a gift from the income of a very large fund as income. It seems to us immaterial that the same amounts might receive a different color from their source. We are of opinion that quarterly payments, which it was hoped would last for fifteen years, from the income of an estate intended for the plaintiff's child, must be regarded as income within the meaning of the Constitution and the law. It is said that the tax laws should be construed favorably for the taxpayers. But that is not a reason for creating a doubt or for exaggerating one when it is no greater than we can bring ourselves to feel in this case.

Judgment reversed.

MR. JUSTICE SUTHERLAND, dissenting.

By the plain terms of the Revenue Act of 1913, the value of property acquired by gift, bequest, devise, or descent is not to be included in net income. Only the income derived from such property is subject to the tax. The question, as it seems to me, is really a very simple one. Money, of course, is property. The money here sought to be taxed as income was paid to respondent under the express provisions of a will. It was a gift by will,—a bequest.... It, therefore, fell within the precise letter of the statute; and, under well settled principles, judicial inquiry may go no further. The taxpayer is entitled to the rigor of the law. There is no latitude in a taxing statute,—you must adhere to the very words....

The property which respondent acquired being a bequest, there is no occasion to ask whether, before being handed over to him, it had been carved from the original corpus of, or from subsequent additions to, the estate. The corpus of the estate was not the legacy which respondent received, but merely the source which gave rise to it. The money here sought to be taxed is not the fruits of a legacy; it was the legacy itself....

2. The Solution

Internal Revenue Code:
  Sections 102(a), (b); 661–663
Regulation:
  Section 1.102-1

Harkness v. United States
199 Ct. Cl. 721, 469 F.2d 310 (1972)
cert. denied, 414 U.S. 820 (1973)

PER CURIAM: In her 1955 federal income tax return, plaintiff included in her gross income $413,379.04 as income received during that year from her husband's estate. In 1961, the District Director of Internal Revenue for the Manhattan District, New York, took the position that, instead of such sum, plaintiff should have included the amount of $630,740.04, *i.e.*, an additional $217,361. The inclusion of such larger amount in plaintiff's gross income resulted (after the making of various adjustments) in plaintiff's allegedly owing an additional $188,153.35 in income tax for such year, and the Director at that time assessed plaintiff in such amount, plus interest thereon in the amount of $60,103.40, or a total of $248,256.75. Plaintiff paid the additional tax and interest so assessed, and then filed a timely claim for refund therefor. Having received neither a notice of disallowance nor any refund, plaintiff instituted the instant suit to recover such assessed amount, plus interest.

Plaintiff's husband died on August 12, 1954. By his will, he gave plaintiff one-half of his residuary estate. The remaining half was, after the deduction therefrom of any "legacy, succession, transfer, estate or inheritance taxes payable by [the] estate with respect to any property disposed of by [the] Will or payable by any recipient of any such property," given, in equal shares, to the trustees of four testamentary trusts for the children of plaintiff and the decedent (*i.e.*, the issue of their or prior marriages). The will provided that such taxes "shall be paid by [the] Executors out of [the] estate as part of the expenses of administration thereof," with the proviso that "no part of such taxes shall be deducted from or payable out of the one-half (½) of [the] residuary estate" which the decedent bequeathed to plaintiff.

During 1955, and prior to the ultimate distribution of the residuary estate, the executors made distributions to the five beneficiaries thereof in the total sum of $36,004,082.23. Of this amount plaintiff, by eleven payments, received $27,467,768.51. The four trusts, by ten payments to each, received the balance of $8,436,295.75 (in equal shares of approximately $2,134,000). All the distributions were in the form of cash, stocks and bonds. None of the distributions were required by the will to be made prior to the ultimate distribution of the residuary estate.

The federal fiduciary income tax return filed by the executors on behalf of the estate showed distributable net income for 1955 in the amount of $1,005,682.94. A deduction of $826,758.68 was shown on the return for distributions of such income to the five residuary estate beneficiaries, the difference of $178,924.26 between such two figures consisting of tax-exempt income (and expenses allocable thereto).

Section 662(a)(2)(B) ... provides that, where the amounts distributed to all beneficiaries of an estate accumulating income or distributing corpus exceed the distributable net income of the estate, each beneficiary shall include in his gross income an amount which bears the same ratio to distributable net income as the total amount distributed to him bears to the total of the amounts distributed to all the beneficiaries.

The amount of $27,467,768.51 which plaintiff received in 1955 from the residuary estate equaled 76.2907 percent of the total amount of $36,004,082.23 distributed to all beneficiaries during such taxable year. Since such total amount distributed exceeded the distributable net income, the District Director concluded that the provisions of Section 662(a)(2)(B) were applicable and accordingly applied the same percentage to the taxable distributable net income of the estate, the resulting figure being regarded as the amount which plaintiff should have included in her gross income. Application of such 76.2907 percent to the taxable distributable net income figure of $826,758.68 produces the aforementioned figure of $630,740.04 as the amount the District Director concluded plaintiff was required by the statute to have included in her gross income. The inclusion of such amount in plaintiff's gross income produced the additional income tax which is the subject of this suit.

Plaintiff contends that, pursuant to accurate accounting by the executors in calculating the amount of the estate corpus and income which they distributed to the five beneficiaries in 1955, she in fact actually received during the year only the taxable amount of $413,379.34, which amount was but one-half of the taxable distributable net income, and not 76.2907 percent thereof, the figure that the statutory formula produces. Such accounting in the administration of the estate was, plaintiff says, in no way tax motivated, but was in accordance with common practices followed at that time by executors in New York in the administration of estates, and was permitted by the terms of the will and applicable local law. Furthermore, she points out, the accounts of the executors for the year 1955, which set forth the income distributions to plaintiff and the four trusts on a basis of one-half to plaintiff and the other half to the trusts, were judicially settled and allowed by the Surrogate Court of New York County, New York.[3]

---

3. Three of the four children were minors and a special guardian appointed by the court to represent them reported that, insofar as their interests were concerned, the executors' accounts were correct.

Although the approximately $27,500,000 paid to plaintiff during the year greatly exceeded the aggregate amount of approximately $8,500,000 paid to the four trusts, each of such total payments concededly consisting of both corpus and income, plaintiff says that such unequal amounts nevertheless included the equal amounts of $413,379.34 of taxable net income. For this result, plaintiff relies upon the manner in which the executors made their distributions of what they designated as "corpus." The executors, in accordance with a common New York practice, made simultaneous distributions of "principal" and "income" among all the residuary legatees on a basis proportionate to their respective interests in the residuary estate. Further, since here the will directed that all legacy, succession, transfer, estate, or inheritance taxes (sometimes collectively referred to as "death taxes") were to be paid as administration expenses of the estate, but with plaintiff's share of the residuary estate to be undiminished thereby, whenever the executors made any such tax payments (which were, according to their accounting, entirely out of corpus), they also made, again following a common New York practice where wills provided for payment of death taxes out of one or more shares of the residue but not out of one or more other shares, "corpus" distributions to the plaintiff with and in the same amounts as such tax payments. Thus, these simultaneous distributions to plaintiff always served, says plaintiff, to keep the remaining corpus interests of the plaintiff and the four trusts in the residuary estate in equal balance, with such equal corpus shares therefore always generating equal amounts of income. The result of adopting these simultaneous distribution practices was the avoidance of complicated calculations of shares of income earned, over varying periods of time, by unequal shares of principal (or by undistributed income). (In this case the decedent's will specifically provided that the income should be distributed proportionately to the residuary legatees, and that if distribution of the residuary estate was not made simultaneously, "an adjustment of the income shall be made by my Executors.") To illustrate, when, on January 1, 1955, the executors distributed $1,125,000 to each of the trusts—amounts which the executors designated as coming entirely from corpus[4]— they simultaneously paid plaintiff $4,500,000, also designated as a corpus distribution. And when, on February 8, 1955, they paid $4,310,000 on account of the New York estate tax, they distributed the identical amount (again designated as principal on their accounts) to plaintiff. Similarly, when, on November 14, 1955, they paid $14,621,454.81 on account of the federal estate tax, plus an amount aggregating $3,524,558.49 to the four trusts, such sums totaling $18,146,013.29, they distributed the identical total sum to plaintiff (all amounts again being designated as coming entirely out of principal). In accordance with the will, the New York and federal estate tax payments were deducted from the trusts' aggregate one-half interest in the residuary estate. The several 1955 distributions to plaintiff and the four trusts which the executors designated as distributions of estate income were so calculated by the executors that the amount of such income distributed to plaintiff on any date equaled the aggregate amount distributed to the trusts on the same date.

It is on the above basis that plaintiff argues she actually received only one-half of the distributable net income of the estate in 1955, and not 76 percent.

In a situation such as the instant one, plaintiff contends, Section 662(a)(2)(B) was not intended to be applicable for the formula there prescribed would attribute to plaintiff income which she in fact did not receive. She should not, she argues, have attributed to her more than her actual share of estate income simply because the executors, in their authorized discretion, made principal distributions to her in order to balance the death tax payments and other principal distributions to the trusts. The purpose of the statutory

4. As of that date, the executors' accounts showed $1,155.42 of undistributed 1954 estate income.

provision here involved was, she contends, to prevent fiduciaries, where the estate had principal, current income, and accumulated income, from controlling tax consequences by manipulating distributions, as, for instance, making distributions designated as coming from "income" to beneficiaries in low income tax brackets, while distributions designated as coming from "principal" are made to beneficiaries in high brackets, and therefore not taxable at all.[5] There was no intent here on the part of the executors, she argues, to gain any kind of income tax advantage for plaintiff.

These contentions cannot be accepted as justifying recovery. There can be no doubt but that plaintiff's situation falls squarely within the literal provisions of Section 662(a)(2)(B), and plaintiff is not understood to contend otherwise. The nub of her contention is that the payments here involved should not be treated as being covered by the statute because the executors' actions were not tax motivated. Even so, the section applies. Clear statutory coverage of this kind, based upon a presumption that any distribution is deemed to be a distribution of the estate's income to the extent of its income for the year, does not and cannot be made to depend on such intangible factors as the subjective intent of executors.

Section 662(a)(2)(B) was specifically intended, for the purposes of that section, "to avoid the necessity for tracing of income."[6] Such tracing was required by the 1939 Code, which provided that distributions by an estate or trust to its beneficiaries were taxed to the beneficiaries for the taxable year in which they received the distributions only if the distributions were made from the current income of the estate or trust.[7] As shown, this lent itself to various kinds of manipulations by executors in the labeling of estate moneys as "income" or "principal." To eliminate such manipulations and tax consequences based upon such estate tax accounting designations of what was "principal" and "income" and from which source a distribution had been made, the "tracing" requirement was, for such distribution purposes, eliminated. Instead, "[t]he beneficiary's proportionate share of the distributable net income * * * is determined by taking the same fractional part of [the] distributable net income as the * * * amounts * * * distributed to him * * * bear to the total of [the] amounts * * * distributed to all beneficiaries."[8] In short, Congress wished

---

5. Under 26 U.S.C. §102 (1970), the value of property acquired by bequest is not taxable income to the distributee. However, income from bequeathed property, as well as a gift composed of income from property, must be included in the legatee's gross income. The section goes on to provide, however, in subsection (b), that amounts included in the gross income of a beneficiary under Subchapter J, pertaining to "Estates, Trusts, Beneficiaries, and Decedents," and which contains Section 662, shall be treated as a bequest of income from property. Section 663(a)(1) of Subchapter J excludes from amounts falling within Section 662(a) any amount which, under the terms of the governing instrument, is paid as a gift or bequest of a specific sum of money or of specific property, provided it is paid all at once or in not more than three installments. It further provides, however, that "an amount which can be paid * * * only from the income of the estate shall not be considered as a gift or bequest of a specific sum of money."

6. H.R. Rep. No. 1337, 83d Cong., 2d Sess. A199, 3 U.S.C. Cong. & Adm. News 4017, 4339 (1954); S. Rep. No. 1622, 83d Cong., 2d Sess. 349, 3 U.S.C. Cong. & Adm. News 4621, 4990 (1954).

7. For instance, under Section 162(d) of the 1939 Code, as amended, a distribution, in the first 65 days of a taxable year, of income of the preceding taxable year, was treated as having been made in such preceding year. In addition, if there also was current year income, tracing was necessary to determine which year's income had been distributed. And, in addition to the current-accumulated interest problem, tracing would, of course, be required to determine whether the distribution contained corpus. 26 U.S.C. §162(d) (1946).

8. 3 U.S.C. Cong. & Adm. News, *supra* n. 6, at pp. 4340, 4990. The portions of the House and Senate Reports here involved are identical. *Id.*, at pp. 4339–40, 4989–90. In pertinent part, they stated:

>   Subsection (a) provides that the beneficiary of an estate or trust * * * must include in
>   gross income any amounts paid, credited, or required to be distributed to him for the tax-

to establish an easily useable formula, and to avoid both the necessity of "tracing" and an inquiry into the subjective intention of executors or trustees. As was pointed out in *Manufacturers Hanover Trust Co. v. United States,* 160 Ct. Cl. 582, 596, 312 F. 2d 785, 793, *cert. denied,* 375 U.S. 880 (1963):

> * * * Around this concept of "distributable net income" the Code builds its provisions for (a) the deduction allowed the trust for its current distributions to the beneficiaries, and (b) the distributions which the beneficiaries must include in their own gross incomes. "Thus, distributable net income has been termed the measuring rod or yardstick to be employed in determining, on the one hand, the maximum deduction for distributions which may be allowed to the estate or trust and for gauging, on the other hand, the extent to which beneficiaries may be taxable on the distributions." 6 Mertens "Law of Federal Income Taxation" §36.04.

We accept plaintiff's contention that there were no tax motivations on the part of the executors in making the distributions at the times and in the amounts they did, and that they made the "balancing" corpus distributions to plaintiff only to avoid complicated calculations of estate income due to the beneficiaries which would result from their having disproportionate interests in the residuary estate.[9] The fact nevertheless remains that, by making the discretionary "balancing" distributions as they did — required neither by the will nor state law — plaintiff received, under their estate accounting, less of the distributable net income than she probably otherwise would have. There is no showing that — either by not making distributions until the estate was wound up finally, or otherwise — the residuary estate could not have been so managed as to produce the same result as the statutory formula. Thus, in that sense (and not in the sense of tax avoidance), the distributions were "manipulated" so that plaintiff, who received over 75 percent of the 1955 payments, is nevertheless said to have received in that year only 50 percent of the taxable distributable net income. On its face and as its purpose is shown by its development and leg-

---

able year of the estate or trust; however, the amount so includible may not exceed the beneficiary's proportionate share of the distributable net income. The effect of limiting the taxation of a beneficiary to his proportionate share of the distributable net income is to preserve the conduit principle by providing that all distributions * * * from an estate or trust will be taxable but not to an extent in excess of the taxable income of the estate or trust * * *. It is thus possible largely to avoid the necessity of tracing income which exists generally under existing law. Instead of determining whether a particular distribution represents amounts of current or accumulated trust income, this revision, broadly speaking, provides that any distribution is considered a distribution of the trust or estate's current income to the extent of its taxable income for the year. This principle is similar to the determination of whether a dividend has been distributed, i.e., that every distribution made by a corporation is deemed to be out of earnings and profits to the extent thereof and from the most recently accumulated earnings and profits.

* * *

If the estate or trust pays * * * to beneficiaries amounts other than income which is required to be distributed currently, paragraph (2) provides that these other amounts * * * are includible in the gross income of the recipient beneficiaries but only to the extent of each beneficiary's proportionate share of the distributable net income * * *. * * * The beneficiary's proportionate share of the distributable net income * * * is determined by taking the same fractional part of such distributable net income * * * as the other amounts paid * * * bear to the total of other amounts paid * * * to all beneficiaries. * * *

9. Such as would occur after the death taxes were paid and deducted from the shares of the trusts, thereby diminishing the interests of the trusts in the residuary estate from the dates of such payments, with proportionate diminutions in the income which would be produced after such dates from such diminished shares.

islative history, the statute was designed to prevent such a result for tax purposes. Indeed, the statutory formula could be considered as providing the more natural and logical result—income earned during the administration of the residuary estate is allocated to the beneficiaries in the same ratio as their interests in the corpus of such estate. Generally, of course, various percentages of corpus will produce like percentages of income. It is thus plain that plaintiff's situation is, by the unambiguous provisions thereof, covered by the statute[11] and although recognizing, of course, the difficulties involved in envisaging every specific situation that could arise under general statutory language, it would nevertheless appear to constitute the type of situation that Congress intended should be covered.[12]

Plaintiff further contends that, even if Section 662(a) is applicable, its formula was erroneously applied because the death taxes should be included in the "amounts properly paid, credited, or required to be distributed to * * * beneficiaries." Crediting the trusts with such taxes as if they constituted distributions to the trusts would result in plaintiff and the trusts receiving equal total amounts. Accordingly, they would, under the statutory formula, be considered as having received equal amounts of the taxable distributable net income.

Plaintiff's basis for treating the payment of the death taxes as distributions to the trusts is based upon the provisions of Regulations §1.662(a)-4 (26 C.F.R.) that "[a]ny amount which, pursuant to the terms of a will * * * is used in full or partial discharge or satisfaction of a legal obligation of any person is included in the gross income of such person under section 662(a) * * * (2) * * * as though directly distributed to him as a beneficiary, * * *." Since the taxes were not deductible from or payable out of plaintiff's one-half of the residuary estate, they therefore were, argues plaintiff, a charge upon, or obligation of, the remaining one-half passing to the trusts. As such an obligation, they should, plaintiff says, be considered, under the Regulations, as expenditures made on behalf of the trusts.

This contention too cannot be sustained. The death tax moneys never constituted a part of, nor were they ever incorporated in, the trusts. The will bequeathed one-half of the residuary estate to the trusts "*after* the deduction therefrom of all the [death] taxes * * *." (Emphasis supplied.) There is, therefore, no warrant for adding to the amounts paid to the trusts the amount of the death taxes, an amount which was never paid or payable to the trusts and which the trusts were, under the will, never to receive. Furthermore, these

---

11. In their fiduciary income tax return for 1955, in which they took a deduction of $826,758.68 for distributions to the five estate beneficiaries, the executors attached an explanatory statement setting forth the "allocation of shares of income and credits" to such beneficiaries which "may result" from the "[a]pplication of the formula for determining inclusions in gross income of beneficiaries prescribed in Section 662(b) of the Internal Revenue Code, if proper in this case * * *."

12. It is felt by some that the present Section 662(a) provisions lead to inequitable results in certain situations, and proposals have been made which would reinstitute, at least to a limited extent, the prior "tracing" concepts and practices. See, *Final Report of the Advisory Group on Subchapter J of the Internal Revenue Code of 1954,* dated December 30, 1958, in *Hearings on Advisory Group Recommendations on Subchapters C, J and K of the Internal Revenue Code before the House Committee on Ways and Means,* 86th Cong., 1st Sess. 257, 286–92. Among the proposals of the Advisory Group was the exclusion from Section 662(a) of amounts properly paid, during the first three years of the estate, out of the corpus of the estate in full or partial satisfaction of a bequest. Effect would be given to a fiduciary's identification of the source of a distribution, as was permitted under the 1939 Code. During the hearings held in the course of consideration of proposed amendatory legislation, various examples were cited of alleged inequities under the 1954 Code provisions, including one which, on the facts, was substantially identical with the instant case. *3 Hearings on Topics Pertaining to the General Revision of the Internal Revenue Code Before the House Committee on Ways and Means,* 85th Cong., 2d Sess. 2801–2802. (The same factual situation is also discussed in Fillman, Selections From Subchapter J, 10 Tax Law Rev. 453, 471 (1955).) However, no such legislation has been enacted.

taxes were the legal obligations of the estate, and not of the trusts, the will specifically so recognizing and providing that such taxes, "payable by my estate * * * shall be paid * * * out of my estate as part of the expenses of administration thereof * * *." The taxes were a "charge" upon, or an "obligation" of, the trusts only in the loose sense that, in calculating the net amount of the residuary estate which the trusts were to receive, the amount of the taxes was to be deducted from the share left to the trusts. They were not a "legal obligation" of the trusts in the sense used by the regulation upon which plaintiff relies.

The trusts received $8,536,313.72 from the estate in 1955. It is such amount that is properly to be considered as the amount "properly paid, credited, or required to be distributed to" them under the statute. The $18,931,454.81 in death taxes paid during the year by the executors, described by the will as part of the administration expenses of the estate, were not "amounts properly paid, credited, or required to be distributed to * * * beneficiaries" within the meaning of the statute or the regulation.

Finally, plaintiff contends that if Section 662(a), properly construed, does cover the instant situation, it is unconstitutional as applied to her because it would impose an unapportioned direct tax on principal or capital in violation of Article I of the Constitution. Section 2, clause 3 of the Article provides that direct taxes shall be apportioned among the several states according to their respective numbers, and section 9, clause 4 provides that no direct tax shall be laid unless in proportion to the census or enumeration directed by the Constitution to be taken. Plaintiff relies on the cases of *Pollock v. Farmers' Loan & Trust Co.,* 158 U.S. 601 (1895), *Eisner v. Macomber,* 252 U.S. 189 (1920), and *Taft v. Bowers,* 278 U.S. 470 (1929), among others, for the proposition that a tax on principal or capital is a direct tax which must be apportioned among the states in proportion to the census.

Although Section 662(a)(2)(B) purports to be an income tax, nevertheless, plaintiff contends, the section, as here applied, actually imposes a tax on the principal or capital distributions received by plaintiff from the estate of her deceased husband. The Sixteenth Amendment, plaintiff points out, empowers only the levying of taxes "on *incomes* * * * without apportionment among the several States, and without regard to any census or enumeration." (Emphasis supplied.)[13]

Additionally, plaintiff argues that Section 662(a)(2)(B) deprives her of property without due process of law because, although she actually received only 50 percent of the taxable income which the estate distributed to the beneficiaries in 1955, she has been taxed on an additional 26.2907 percent of such income. That part of the income, she says, was in fact received by the trusts and not by her, and to attempt to measure her tax by reference to the income of others, *i.e.,* the four trusts, would, she argues, conflict with the due process clause of the Fifth Amendment.

In upholding constitutionality, defendant argues the broad proposition that, even though the disputed amount ($217,361) which taxpayer received in 1955 may have constituted corpus, still the challenged sections (as applied here) are valid on two alternative grounds, first, that the receipt of a bequest, devise or inheritance (whether or not it be from corpus) properly falls within the Sixteenth Amendment as "income" to the recipi-

---

13. In addition to Section 662(a)(2)(B), plaintiff also attacks, for the same reasons, the constitutionality of that part of Section 102(b) which provides that any amount included in the gross income of a beneficiary under Subchapter J shall be treated as a gift, bequest, or inheritance of income from property, such gifts, bequests, or inheritances being, as hereinabove set forth, excluded from the provision of Section 102(a) that "Gross income does not include the value of property acquired by gift, bequest, devise, or inheritance." See n. 5.

ent, and, second, that in any event the sections impose an indirect tax upon the receipt of property which under the Constitution need not be apportioned. On either of these views, plaintiff's invocation of the Fifth Amendment would also fail because the taxpayer would clearly not be taxed on the income or property of others.

We do not have to delve into the difficult issues of large scope which the Government presents because, as we see it, there is a much narrower ground upon which to sustain the statute as applied to plaintiff's case. That more limited approach stresses the factor (which plaintiff underplays) that the executors did have a choice in 1955 whether to make the distributions in the form they did or, instead, so to manage distributions, to the extent governed by Section 662(a), that the several beneficiaries would not be taxable under Section 662(a) on more than their share of the estate's income. Plaintiff has failed to show that this could not be done. There was no legal compulsion, in the will or in New York law, to make the "balancing" distributions of corpus and income which were made. That course was selected because the other would have been much more burdensome, requiring over the years complicated calculations of shares of income, earned either by principal or by undistributed income, which were due to the various residuary legatees. But the choice was not a forced one, and the other route could have been picked (though at the cost of more work and trouble). If the application of section 662(a)(2)(B) was deemed unfair to plaintiff taxwise, when such "balancing" distributions were made, the presumed inequity could be avoided by not making "balancing" distributions but employing the other methods of distribution which were available.

That these other methods would have occasioned more trouble (and possibly some more expense) does not invalidate the statutory formula. As we have already indicated, Congress could properly assume, as it did, that in the generality of instances the formula would correspond to reality and not be unfair to any beneficiary. At least where an option is open to avoid an unfair and unrealistic result, use of the formula is not prohibited in the minority of instances in which it may be thought harsh or inequitable. In view of the broad Congressional power in taxation (*cf. Fernandez v. Wiener*, 326 U.S. 340, 351–53 (1945); *A. Magnano Co. v. Hamilton*, 292 U.S. 40, 44 (1934)), Congress is not required by the Constitution to assure that the way of the option be just as easy as the way of the formula; added work and some added expense, if the option is selected, are permissible accompaniments of that choice. Taxation is not a field in which Congress must use a watchmaker's refinement and instruments, or a jeweler's balance, to achieve precise equality in treatment.

The use of formulas which can be avoided if the taxpayer considers them unfair or not to reflect reality in his particular case is, of course, no stranger to the federal income tax system. The best-known is the standard formula for deductions on the individual income tax form; if the standard deduction is thought to be unfair or inadequate, the deductions can be itemized—sometimes at the cost of considerable extra work and some expense. Although the parallel is not exact (particularly since the standard deduction involves deductions, not income), the option available in plaintiff's case is roughly comparable to this common choice open each year to millions of individual taxpayers. We cite this example to show that formula solutions are not uncommon, and are invulnerable to attack where an escape-hatch is available if the formula proves unjust in a particular instance.

It may be said that Mrs. Harkness, the taxpayer, did not have or make the choice here—the executors did. Technically that is the situation, but there is no hint that plaintiff objected in any way to the estate's course of action, or suggested the other course, or was compelled to accept the large distributions of principal in 1955. It is unrealistic to suppose that, if she had objected on the ground that the estate's mode of distribution increased her own taxes, the executors would nevertheless have forced her to accept those large payments. Indeed, there is no reason to believe that under the will the executors could lawfully compel her to accept the large corpus distributions in 1955, if she was unwilling to do so because of the tax consequences to her. Plaintiff's reply brief to the court makes it clear that plaintiff was not so compelled, and suggests that a deliberate chance was taken as to how the law would be applied. The brief indicates that the executors (and probably plaintiff's own counsel) believed that §662(a)(2)(B) should not be interpreted (in this type of case) as the Internal Revenue Service and we have construed it—and they acted accordingly.[17]

Without intimating in any way that the statute would be invalid if applied where there was no such option as in this case, we hold that the existence of the choice removes whatever defect there might otherwise be. At least where the option is present, Congress can reasonably and validly forbid "tracing" and presume that its formula in §662(a)(2)(B) gives an accurate reflection of the division of the estate's "distributable net income" among the beneficiaries. *Cf. Smith v. Westover*, 191 F. 2d 1003 (9th Cir. 1951), *aff'g* 89 F. Supp. 432 (S.D. Cal. 1950). Normally, use of the formula would be fair and accurate enough. If discretionary "balancing" payments which include large amounts of corpus are made and accepted, as here, the necessary consequence is to invoke the formula nonetheless, and the taxpayer will not be allowed to "trace" in order to show that the source of part of his receipts was in fact not "distributable net income" but corpus. If the tax consequences of this approach are deemed sufficiently undesirable, there is the other route which can and should be taken. In these circumstances, there is no compulsion to accept an unfair or unrealistic division of "distributable net income."

For these reasons, we hold that the tax was lawfully imposed and that plaintiff is not entitled to recover.

SKELTON, *Judge*, dissenting:

I respectfully dissent. In my opinion, the majority opinion by failing to hold that Section 662(a)(2)(B) ... and the related Treasury Regulations 1.662(a)-3 are unconstitutional and invalid, has placed a stamp of approval upon the acts of the Internal Revenue Service in collecting income taxes from the plaintiff that she did not owe and in exempting the trusts from income taxes that they owed. This has caused an unconscionable result to be reached in this case.

* * *

[T]he statute and related regulations, as well as the acts of the Internal Revenue Service, were unconstitutional and invalid, which is the main thrust of plaintiff's appeal. The majority chose to sidestep this question and refused to decide it. Instead, they decided the case on the narrow basis that the executors of the estate had an option to distribute the corpus and income as they did which resulted in the tax on plaintiff, or to effect distribution a different way without such resulting tax on plaintiff. There is no showing that plaintiff had any control over the executors or that she had anything whatever to do with what they did. It seems unjust to me to place a beneficiary of an estate in a position of

---

17. The 1954 Internal Revenue Code, which first contained §662(a)(2)(B), became law on August 16, 1954, and the first full calendar year of its effectiveness was 1955, the year involved here.

owing or not owing an income tax according to the whim and actions of the executors of the estate....

In my opinion, the court should have decided the constitutional question instead of avoiding it....

The defendant argues that Congress enacted Section 662(a)(2)(B) in order to eliminate the necessity of "tracing" the source of distributed property and to facilitate bookkeeping and auditing by executors and the IRS. Even though this may be a laudable intent, such purpose does not allow the Congress to circumvent or override the provisions of the Constitution....

The majority opinion states:

> * * * [T]he taxpayer will not be allowed to "trace" in order to show that the source of part of his receipts was in fact not "distributable net income" but corpus.

This is directly contrary to the decision of the Supreme Court in *Heiner v. Donnan,* [285 U.S. 312 (1932)], when the court said in commenting upon the statute, involved in *Schlesinger v. Wisconsin,* 270 U.S. 230 (1926):

> * * * a statute which imposes a tax upon an assumption of fact *which the taxpayer is forbidden to controvert, is so arbitrary and unreasonable that it cannot stand under the Fourteenth Amendment.* [Emphasis supplied.] [*Id.* at 325.]

The court stated further in that case:

> Nor is it material that the Fourteenth Amendment was involved in the *Schlesinger* case instead of the Fifth Amendment, as here. The restraint imposed upon legislation by the due process clauses of the two amendments is the same. *Coolidge v. Long,* 282 U.S. 582, 596. That a federal statute passed under the taxing power may be so arbitrary and capricious as to cause it to fall before the due process of law clause of the Fifth Amendment is settled.... [*Id.* at 326.]

It appears that the majority opinion, contrary to the above decision of the Supreme Court, is upholding a statute which "assumes as a fact which the taxpayer is forbidden to controvert" that the $217,361 was "income" and not "corpus." The statute, given this meaning, clearly violates the due process clause of the Fifth Amendment to the Constitution.[3]

The majority opinion holds, in effect, that Section 662(a)(2)(B) creates a *conclusive* presumption that distributions subject to the operation of that section are distributions of *income,* and, consequently cannot be rebutted by the taxpayer....

Since the majority refuses to face the constitutional issue, an equitable solution of the whole problem would be to interpret the statute in such a way as to hold that it creates a rebuttable presumption that such distributions as we have here are from income, which

---

3. See George Craven, *Taxation of Estate and Trust Income Under the 1954 Code,* 103 Univ. of Pa. L. Rev., 602, 614 (1954–1955), where it is stated: " * * * There is a serious question about the constitutionality of an income tax statute which taxes to a beneficiary receiving principal an amount of income in excess of an amount which may inure to his benefit. This provision requires prompt remedial action by Congress in order to eliminate any requirement that amounts of principal distributed by an estate in process of administration shall be treated as distributions of income."

may be overcome by evidence of the taxpayer. On that basis, the plaintiff would prevail in this case because it is admitted by the government that the distribution of $217,361 to the plaintiff on which she was taxed was to that extent corpus and not income of the estate received by plaintiff during the taxable year in question. Such an interpretation of the statute would remove the constitutional question from the case.

A solution to this whole problem would be for Congress to amend Section 663(c) of the Internal Revenue Code so as to make it apply to estates. As now written, it only applies to trusts and is known as the "separate share" rule. In other words, where a trust has more than one beneficiary, the separate shares of the beneficiaries are treated as separate trusts. This prevents a beneficiary who receives corpus from being taxed on an amount in excess of the distributable net income of the trust of his share. If the separate share rule were extended to estates, the problem we have in the present case would not arise.[5] There is no logical reason why Section 663(c) should not apply to estates as well as to trusts. This was no doubt an oversight when the statute was drafted.

When the facts and the arguments of the parties are carefully considered and one arrives at the moment of decision in this case, it is clear that the IRS either taxed the plaintiff on the $217,361 of the income of the estate that she did not receive, or it levied and collected such tax on the corpus of the estate which she did receive under the guise of an income tax. In either case, the tax was unconstitutional and invalid.

For all of the foregoing reasons, I would hold that Section 662(a)(2)(B) and Section 1.662(a)-3 of the Treasury Regulations as applied to plaintiff in this case are unconstitutional and the collection of the tax from the plaintiff was invalid. Alternatively, I would hold that the statute and the regulations create a rebuttable presumption that distributions such as we have here are from income which might be overcome by the taxpayer by credible evidence, and that the taxpayer has overcome such presumption in this case....

Illustrative Material

1. What, then, is the "solution" to the problem posed on page 109? In simple terms, subchapter J establishes a conclusive presumption that all distributions are income, to the extent that the trust or estate has income available. The reason for this presumption is explained in *Harkness*, in the paragraph beginning at the bottom of page 114. An unfortunate side effect of this statutory scheme is that distributions of principal may end up being subject to taxation, as happened to the beneficiary in *Harkness*.

2. *Constitutionality. Lemle v. United States,* 77-2 U.S.T.C. ¶ 9653 (S.D.N.Y. 1977), *aff'd,* 579 F.2d 185 (2d Cir. 1978), similarly upheld subchapter J in the face of taxpayer arguments that it unconstitutionally taxed principal distributed by an estate to its beneficiary.

3. As Judge Skelton suggested in his dissent, a solution to the unfairness of section 662(a) would be to apply the section 663(c) "separate share" rule to estates. A quarter

---

5. For a discussion of the separate share rule, see George Craven, *Taxation of Estate and Trust Income Under the 1954 Code, supra,* at 616; and Kamin, Surrey & Warren, *The Internal Revenue Code of 1954, Trusts, Estates and Beneficiaries,* 54 Colum. L. Rev. 1237, 1257–59 (1954).

century later, Congress obliged, amending section 663(c) to so provide. Thus, under current law, the outcome in *Harkness* would be different.

4. *Section 102(b)*. Not all amounts described in section 102(a) are excluded from gross income, because section 102(b) takes back much of what section 102(a) seems to give. As a result, many amounts that, for other purposes, unquestionably are gifts, bequests, devises, and inheritances are subject to income taxation. Thus, confirming the result in *Irwin v. Gavit*, section 102(b)(2) denies the exclusion to a gift, bequest, devise, or inheritance of *income* from property. This exception was at the heart of the fascinating case, *Getty v. Commissioner*, 91 T.C. 160 (1988), *rev'd*, 913 F.2d 1486 (9th Cir. 1990). One of the sons of J. Paul Getty sued the Getty Museum, the primary beneficiary under Getty's will. This son sought to impose a constructive trust on the assets the museum had received from Getty's estate. The son's theory was that Getty had promised — but failed — to "equalize," by will, his position (under an *inter vivos* trust created by Getty and Getty's mother) with those of his siblings. The museum settled the litigation for $10,000,000. The issue that faced the Tax Court was whether the settlement proceeds were gross income to the son or excluded under section 102(a). The Tax Court admitted that, had Getty kept his promise, he "probably" would have equalized the son's position by a bequest of property. But, since the son's claim against the museum sought equalization based on an income interest, and since the son had not proven that Getty "necessarily" would have equalized his position by a bequest of property, the Tax Court concluded that what he took the proceeds "in lieu of" was an income interest in trust. Thus, according to the Tax Court, the proceeds were an inheritance of "income from property" under section 102(b)(2). As a result, the entire $10,000,000 was includible in the son's gross income. The Ninth Circuit reversed. Acknowledging that taxpayer (the son) bore the burden of proof, it nonetheless held that he had carried that burden by proving that Getty, in the Tax Court's own words, "probably" would have chosen a bequest of property to equalize his position. According to the Ninth Circuit, the Tax Court, by requiring the son to prove that Getty "necessarily" would have chosen a bequest of property, had erroneously imposed on the taxpayer a burden of proof greater than the "preponderance of the evidence" standard.

In addition, the second-last sentence of section 102(b) provides that if a gift, bequest, devise, or inheritance is to be paid "at intervals," it is subject to section 102(b)(2) to the extent it is to be paid out of income. In *Harte v. United States*, 252 F.2d 259 (2d Cir. 1958), a largely disinherited heir settled her claims in exchange for a monthly lifetime stipend to be funded primarily from estate income. The court denied the exclusion because the payments were derived from income. For a similar case interpreting the predecessor of section 102, see *James F. Edwards*, 37 T.C. 1107 (1962), *acq.*, 1963-1 C.B. 4.

Moreover, the last sentence of section 102(b) treats any amount included in the gross income of a beneficiary under subchapter J as a gift, bequest, devise, or inheritance of *income* from property. Thus, in *Mahler v. Commissioner*, 52 T.C.M. (CCH) 1552 (1987), a trust beneficiary entitled to $500 per month failed to qualify for the exclusion because subchapter J provided otherwise. *United States v. James*, 333 F.2d 748 (9th Cir.), *cert. denied*, 379 U.S. 932 (1964), denied the exclusion for an Arizona widow's allowance that was subject to taxation according to subchapter J. Similarly, payments made by an estate to a widow pending resolution of a dispute concerning her right to elect against her husband's will were subject to income taxation in the widow's hands, as specified in subchapter J, notwithstanding that a compromise agreement, which had been judicially approved, characterized such payments as principal. *Lemle v. United States,* 419 F. Supp. 68 (S.D.N.Y. 1976); *Lemle v. United States,* 77-2 U.S.T.C. ¶ 9653 (S.D.N.Y. 1977), *aff'd,* 579 F.2d 185 (2d Cir. 1978).

B. Distributable Net Income

Internal Revenue Code:
  Section 643(a), (b)
Regulations:
  Sections 1.643(a)-0, -1, -2, -3(a), (b), (e), -4, -5; 1.643(b)-1, -2; 1.643(d)-2

Baker v. Commissioner
59 T.C.M. (CCH) 10 (1990)

WHITAKER, Judge:

* * *

The remaining [issue is] whether petitioner is entitled to a deduction for certain partnership losses "allocated" to him by the trust of which he is the sole beneficiary....

Petitioner is the sole beneficiary of the Charles Stewart Baker Trust (Trust). Basil S. Baker and Lois M. Baker, petitioner's parents, established the Trust as an irrevocable, complex trust....

Articles 2.3 and 2.11 of the governing trust instrument provide that the Trustee has the power to determine what is income and what is principal. There is no provision in the trust instrument granting authority to the Trustee to determine that distributions to petitioner may consist solely of one particular class of income.

During the year in issue, the Trust was a limited partner in several partnerships, including Allen Parkway Investors, Ltd. (Allen Parkway). For its fiscal year 1982, the Trust reported the following:

Items of Income		Loss and Expense Deductions	
Interest	$36,410.32	Partnership losses	$43,690.96
Dividends	1,031.60	Interest expense	52.24
Capital gains	80,043.05	Trustee fees	832.33

The partnership losses which the Trust deducted from income included the Trust's distributive share of partnership loss from Allen Parkway's investment in Sentinel Government Securities (Sentinel). The loss attributable to Sentinel amounted to $5,424.82.

During 1982, the Trust made a discretionary distribution of $50,000 to petitioner, all of which the Trustee characterized as long-term capital gain. The Trustee determined that the remainder of the Trust's realized capital gains constituted trust principal. In addition, the Trust "allocated" $7,142.61 in purported partnership losses to petitioner in that year. Schedule K-1 of the Trust's fiscal 1982 return reflected the $50,000 distribution and the $7,142.61 "allocation" of losses to petitioner, but did not indicate from which sources the losses "allocated" to petitioner stemmed. For tax accounting purposes, when it "allocated" partnership losses to petitioner, the Trust acted as though it was a pass-through entity, such as a partnership or Subchapter S corporation.

On his 1982 return, petitioner included $50,000 as a distribution of trust income, all of which he characterized as long-term capital gain. In addition, petitioner claimed a deduction for $7,142.61 in partnership losses "allocated" to him by the Trust. As a result of these transactions, petitioner's 1982 gross income reflected a net amount of $42,857.39 from the Trust, i.e., $50,000 – $7,142.61. This amount exactly equaled the Trust's reported distributable net income (DNI).

* * *

Subsequently, we held that Sentinel was created solely for the purpose of generating tax losses. See *Maring v. Commissioner*, T.C. Memo. 1988-469. Respondent treated the losses "allocated" to petitioner as including the Trust's entire Sentinel loss, and disallowed $5,424.82 of the $7,142.61 in "allocated" partnership losses for which petitioner claimed a deduction in 1982. In the statutory notice of deficiency, respondent stated that the excess, $1,717.79, was petitioner's proper "distributive share of loss" from the Trust. Respondent did not disallow petitioner's deduction of that amount of "allocated" partnership losses.

The parties agree that a deduction for losses attributable to the Trust's distributable share of Allen Parkway's investment in Sentinel ($5,424.82) is not allowable. However, the parties disagree on whether the Sentinel loss was included in the "allocated" losses for which petitioner claimed a deduction.

Respondent argues that petitioner is liable for the entire deficiency unless he can prove that the Sentinel loss was not included in the "allocated" partnership losses for which he claimed a deduction. In the alternative, respondent urges that the Trust must adjust its net income and DNI to reflect the disallowed Sentinel loss. Thus, the Trust's allowable partnership losses must decrease by $5,424.82, and net income and DNI must increase by the same amount. Respondent further maintains that petitioner may claim a deduction for only his proper "distributive share" of the Trust's losses. This proper "distributive share" would purportedly decrease, by reason of the adjustment to the Trust's income and DNI, by the same amount to $1,717.79 ($7,142.61 – $5,424.82). We agree that the Trust should adjust its income and DNI to reflect the disallowed Sentinel loss. The Trust, however, is not a party to the present action. Further, respondent cites no authority for his position that a beneficiary may deduct a "distributive share" of losses sustained by a trust.

Petitioner maintains that the provisions of Subchapter J authorize apportioning the disallowance between the Trust and petitioner. Thus, petitioner contends that he is liable for only a portion of the deficiency resulting from disallowance of the Sentinel loss. According to petitioner, the Trust should be liable for the remainder of the deficiency.

Petitioner's argument is without merit. The authority which petitioner cites in his trial memorandum and brief does not support his position. We find no other authority in Subchapter J for apportioning the disallowance and resulting deficiency between petitioner and the Trust.

Further, we agree that petitioner is liable for the entire deficiency. Respondent's determination of deficiency is presumed correct…. Deductions are a matter of legislative grace and petitioner bears the burden of proving entitlement to any claimed deductions. *New Colonial Ice Co. v. Helvering*, 292 U.S. 435 (1934).

Petitioner offered no evidence that the disallowed Sentinel loss was not one of the partnership losses "allocated" to him by the Trust. Moreover, petitioner offered no evidence that the partnership losses for which he claimed a deduction did not include the disallowed Sentinel loss. Therefore, we find that petitioner deducted the disallowed Sentinel loss in 1982. *Wichita Terminal Elevator Co.*, 6 T.C. 1158 (1946), affd. 162 F.2d 513 (10th Cir. 1947). On the basis of that finding, and because we find no authority for apportioning the deficiency between petitioner and the Trust, we hold that petitioner failed to satisfy his burden of proof and is liable for the deficiency as determined by respondent.

However, we cannot decide this case solely on burden of proof without risking that the parties would infer an implied authorization for beneficiaries to claim deductions for losses which have been "allocated" or "distributed" to them by ongoing trusts after deduction from trust gross income. This premise underlies petitioner's arguments. Respondent acceded to the theory by characterizing the "allocated" partnership losses which exceeded the amount of the disallowed Sentinel loss as petitioner's deductible "distributive share" of the Trust's partnership losses. Both parties are mistaken in their assumptions.

Our opinion in this case in no way reflects approval of beneficiaries deducting losses "allocated," "distributed," or otherwise passed through from a trust, after the trust deducted those same losses from gross income, without express statutory authority. Indeed, there is no reference in the statutes and regulations governing taxation of trusts and beneficiaries to "allocations" or "distributive shares." A discussion of the proper application of the statutory provisions governing the tax consequences of transactions between trusts and their beneficiaries to the facts in this case is therefore appropriate.

The statutory provisions of Subchapter J govern the manner in which petitioner should have determined his 1982 trust income. Subchapter J also sets forth the manner in which the Trust should have computed its income and tax liability. A trust is a separate taxable entity which generally computes income in the same manner as individuals. Sec. 641(b). Therefore, a trust is not a pass-through entity which may "allocate" a "distributive share," or otherwise pass losses through to beneficiaries in the manner of a partnership or Subchapter S corporation.

The general rule of Subchapter J is that trust income is taxed only once, either to the trust or to the beneficiaries, or partly to both. *O'Bryan v. Commissioner*, 75 T.C. 304, 308 (1980) (discussing taxation of an estate and its beneficiary, governed by the same provisions of Subchapter J as apply to the taxation of trusts and their beneficiaries); J. Mertens, Law of Federal Income Taxation, sec. 36.04 (1989). The concept of DNI is the key to determining who bears the tax liability for trust income. DNI is essentially a trust's gross income, excluding capital gains allocated to principal, minus allowable deductions and losses. Sec. 643(a).

As opposed to a pass-through entity such as a partnership, trust income is taxed at the trust level to the extent that the income is not distributed and taxed to trust beneficiaries. Secs. 641, 643, and 661–663. Trusts are either simple or complex. In general, simple trusts must distribute all income currently while complex trusts may distribute as well as accumulate income or pay or set aside income for charitable purposes. Secs. 651 and 661.

Beneficiaries of complex trusts must include trust distributions in gross income to the extent of DNI. Sec. 662(a). The regulatory scheme of section 662(a) generally treats distributions in excess of DNI as nontaxable distributions of trust principal. Sec. 1.662(a)-1 through (a)-4, Income Tax Regs. Thus, trusts make distributions out of trust income which are taxable to the beneficiaries or distributions out of principal which are nontaxable to beneficiaries. *O'Bryan v. Commissioner, supra* at 309.

Trusts generally compute their deductions in the same manner as individuals, except that trusts are allowed a special deduction for income distributions to beneficiaries. *Fabens v. Commissioner*, 519 F.2d 1310, 1313 (1975), affg. in part and revg. in part 62 T.C. 775 (1974). Complex trusts may take a deduction for distributions to beneficiaries, whether the distributions are mandatory or discretionary under the controlling trust instrument, in an amount not exceeding DNI. Sec. 661(a).[3]

Taxation of complex trusts and their beneficiaries is designed so that there is no duplication of taxation, no wasting of deductions on termination of trusts, and no duplication of deductions by trusts and their beneficiaries. Secs. 661, 662 and 642(h); *O'Bryan v. Commissioner, supra* at 308–311. In general, trusts are entitled to a deduction for losses sustained during the taxable year under the same conditions applicable to individual taxpayers. J. Rabkin & M. Johnson, Federal Income, Gift and Estate Taxation, par. 54.02(13) (1989). Therefore, as is the case in determining entitlement to any deduction, absent express statutory authority to the contrary, only the trust sustaining a loss is entitled to take a loss deduction. See, e.g., *New Colonial Ice Co. v. Helvering*, 292 U.S. 435 (1934); *Calvin v. United States*, 354 F.2d 202, 204 (10th Cir. 1965); *Moore v. Commissioner*, 70 T.C. 1024, 1032 (1978).

Thus, the first step in ascertaining the proper tax treatment of the transactions between petitioner and the Trust is to determine if express statutory authority exists entitling petitioner to claim a deduction for partnership losses sustained by the Trust. We find no such authority.

Except for depreciation and depletion,[4] income beneficiaries may claim deductions for losses sustained by the corresponding trust only upon termination of the trust. Sec. 642(h)(1) and (2); J. Rabkin & M. Johnson, Federal Income, Gift and Estate Taxation, *supra* at par. 54.03(12). Further, such deductions are limited to deductions for the trust's unused net operating loss or capital loss carryovers and for the excess of trust deductions over gross income in the year of termination. Sec. 642(h)(1) and (2). However, the provisions of section 642(h) are not applicable to the facts of this case.

Beneficiaries indirectly obtain the benefits of other losses and expenses, for which only the trust may take a deduction, when a trust deducts losses or expenses in calculating DNI. Had Congress intended to allow a beneficiary of an ongoing trust to deduct partnership losses sustained by the trust, it would specifically have provided for such deductions as it did for the deductions allowed beneficiaries pursuant to section 642(h).

The Trust deducted the partnership losses at issue from gross income prior to attempting to "allocate" those same losses to petitioner. Further, the Trust utilized those losses in computing DNI. Accordingly, petitioner obtained all allowable benefit when the Trust deducted the losses in calculating net income and DNI. Because trusts are not passthrough entities which may allocate distributive shares of loss, the Trust improperly "allocated," or passed through, $7,142.61 in partnership losses to petitioner. Normally, to allow a claim such as petitioner's would be to allow a double deduction.

---

3. However, trusts may not take deductions for those portions of income distributions which correspond to items which the trust does not include in gross income. Sec. 661(c). For taxable year 1982, certain dividends were excluded from trust gross income. Sec. 116. Section 116 was repealed by the Tax Reform Act of 1986, Pub. L. 99-514, sec. 612(a), 100 Stat. 2250. However, this repeal does not affect the tax year in issue. Therefore, in the year in issue a trust could take no income distribution deduction for dividends excluded pursuant to section 116, even though such dividends are included in the computation of DNI. Sec. 1.661(c)-1 and (c)-2, Income Tax Regs.

4. Section 611(b)(3) provides that depletion deductions must be apportioned between income beneficiaries and trustees. Section [167(d)] mandates the same apportionment of depreciation deductions.

However, the statutory notice of deficiency did not disallow petitioner's claim of those partnership losses attributable to the Trust's investment in Sentinel on the basis that such deductions were double deductions. Further, respondent did not request to amend his answer to assert such grounds for disallowing those partnership losses claimed by petitioner which exceeded the disallowed Sentinel losses, i.e., the $1,717.79 excess, until the filing of his post-trial brief. Thus, we will not at this time increase the amount of petitioner's deficiency because of the improperly claimed partnership losses which exceeded the amount of the disallowed Sentinel loss. Sec. 6214(a); Rule 41(a).

We next consider the portion of the $50,000 distribution which petitioner should have included in income. In order to determine the amount petitioner must include, we must first calculate the Trust's DNI, as adjusted to reflect the disallowed Sentinel loss. When respondent disallowed the Sentinel partnership loss of $5,424.82, the Trust's distributive share of partnership losses decreased from $43,690.96 to $38,266.14. The Trust's taxable income thus increased by $5,424.82 to $78,325.36, and DNI increased by the same amount to $48,282.21.[6] Because the Trust is not a party before us, we note once again that these figures merely reflect the proper adjustments which should have occurred upon disallowance of the Sentinel loss.

The Trust made a discretionary distribution to petitioner of $50,000, all of which the Trustee characterized as long-term capital gain. Petitioner, as sole beneficiary of the Trust, should have included in income all distributions required to be made or properly paid or credited to him by the Trust up to an amount equal to DNI, as adjusted to reflect the disallowed Sentinel loss. Sec. 662(a); *Scheft v. Commissioner*, 59 T.C. 428, 429–430 (1972). The Trust's $50,000 discretionary distribution was an amount properly paid to petitioner within the meaning of section 662(a). Sec. 1.662(a)-3(b), Income Tax Regs.

The amount of the distribution to petitioner which exceeds DNI, as adjusted to reflect the disallowed loss, is considered a nontaxable distribution of trust principal. Sec. 1.662(a)-3, Income Tax Regs.; *O'Bryan v. Commissioner*, *supra* at 309. Therefore, petitioner was required to include only $48,282.21, an amount equal to the Trust's DNI as adjusted for the disallowed loss, in his income for 1982.[7] The $1,717.79 excess ($50,000 – $48,282.21) should have been treated as a nontaxable distribution of Trust principal. Petitioner, however, did include the $1,717.79 excess as long-term capital gain. Correspondingly, the Trust's deduction for income distributions to petitioner may not exceed DNI, as adjusted for the disallowed loss. Section 661(a).

Even after disallowance of the Sentinel loss, and assuming proper adjustment to the Trust's DNI, the peculiar "allocation" and corresponding deduction of partnership losses resulted in petitioner including a net amount from the Trust equal to DNI. Thus, petitioner, in effect, did not include more than he was required to include by section 661(a). Nor did petitioner receive the prohibited benefit of a double deduction.

---

6. Arts. 2.3 and 2.11 of the governing trust instrument gave the Trustee authority to allocate capital gain receipts to either income or principal. The Texas Property Code provides that trust receipts should be allocated to income or principal according to the terms of the trust instrument. Tex. Prop. Code Ann. sec. 113.101(a) (Vernon 1989). Therefore, in distributing capital gains to petitioner, the Trustee treated such gains as income rather than principal. Sec. 1.643(a)-3, Income Tax Regs. Distributed income in the nature of capital gains is included in the computation of DNI. Sec. 643(a)(3).

7. Under the facts of this case, we do not decide the amount includable in gross income had there been multiple beneficiaries of the Trust or had the Trust been required to currently distribute income to petitioner. In either case, the two-tier treatment of income recognition to beneficiaries set forth in the regulatory scheme of section 662 would come into play.

However, we emphasize that in terms of both the net amount included in income and the existence of a prohibited double deduction, petitioner reached the desired end using improper means. It is not a foregone conclusion that this happy coincidence would ever again occur. We do not imply that petitioner received no benefit by virtue of the manner in which he computed his income. However, under the circumstances of this case and as discussed below, such benefit is limited to that occurring because of characterization of the entire $50,000 distribution as long-term capital gain.

Finally, we consider the character of classes of income composing the Trust's distribution to petitioner, and the amount of each class of income so distributed. Schedule K-1 of the Trust's return characterized the entire amount distributed to petitioner, and petitioner included the entire distribution, as long-term capital gain. However, the Trust also had interest and dividend income which entered into the computation of DNI.

Distributions have the same character in the hands of beneficiaries as in the hands of the distributing trust. Sec. 662(b). Furthermore, unless otherwise provided, distributions are deemed to consist of the same proportion of each class of income entering into the computation of DNI as the total of each class bears to total DNI. Sec. 1.662(b)-1, Income Tax Regs. When trusts have receipts comprised of more than one class of income, distributions consisting only of one class of income are not allowed unless specifically provided for under the terms of the governing instrument, or unless local law requires such an allocation. Sec. 1.662(b)-1, Income Tax Regs.

The Trust was created in Texas. Texas law, as the local law governing administration of the Trust, does not require the Trustee to make distributions consisting only of one class of income (in this case, capital gains). Under the terms of the Trust's governing instrument the Trustee does not have the specific authority to distribute only one class of income to petitioner. Further, characterization of the entire $50,000 distribution as capital gains has no economic consequence other than tax-related ones. *Van Buren v. Commissioner*, 89 T.C. 1101, 1109 (1987). Therefore, the distribution to petitioner is deemed to have consisted of long-term capital gains, interest, and dividend income, rather than to have been composed entirely of long-term capital gains. Sec. 1.662(b)-1, Income Tax Regs.

The amount of long-term capital gains, interest, and dividend income comprising the distribution to petitioner is calculated in accordance with the regulations under section 662(b). However, simply determining the ratio of the total of each class of income included in DNI to total DNI, as described in section 1.662(b)-1, Income Tax Regs., is not adequate to determine the amount of each class of income distributed. Deductions of the Trust which enter into the computation of DNI must be allocated between income classes comprising the distribution, as petitioner reaps the benefits of such deductions only indirectly through DNI computation.

We have not previously discussed the allocation of deductions when determining the amount of each class of income included in distributions from a complex trust. The regulations under section 662(b) do not specifically address the allocation of such deductions. However, section 1.662(b)-1, Income Tax Regs., states that the principles set forth in section 1.652(b)-1, Income Tax Regs., determining the character of distributions from simple trusts, shall apply in determining the amount of each class of income included in a distribution from a complex trust. Section 1.652(b)-3, Income Tax Regs., describes the manner of allocating deductions for purposes of determining the amount of each class of income includable under section 1.652(b)-1, Income Tax Regs. Further, examples illustrating the provisions of section 662, contained in section 1.662(c)-4, Income Tax

Regs., comport with the treatment of deductions detailed in section 1.652(b)-3, Income Tax Regs. Therefore, we turn to section 1.652(b)-3, Income Tax Regs., for guidance.

Section 1.652(b)-3, Income Tax Regs., states that items of deduction of trusts which enter into the computation of DNI are allocated among the various items of income. All deductible items directly attributable to one class of income (except dividends excludable in 1982 under section 116) are allocated to that class. Sec. 1.652(b)-3(a), Income Tax Regs. The deductions not directly attributable to a specific class of income comprising DNI may be allocated to any item of income, including capital gains, with certain exceptions where a trust has nontaxable income. Sec. 1.652(b)-3(b), Income Tax Regs., *supra*.

We considered the application of section 1.652(b)-3, Income Tax Regs., in *Van Buren v. Commissioner, supra.* We stated in that case that:

> The purpose of the 1954 Code, expressed in section 652(b), was to give to the income beneficiary the benefit of all deductions attributable to taxable income which was distributed to her, excluding those deductions attributable to tax-exempt income. *Tucker v. Commissioner*, 322 F.2d 86 (2d Cir. 1963), affg. 38 T.C. 955 (1962). Respondent's regulations carry out this intention, providing that after allocating a proportionate part of the expenses to tax-exempt income, and after excluding capital gains [included in principal] (there were none here) from the allocation computation, the remaining deductions not directly attributable to a specific class of income "may be allocated to the [taxable income] in such proportions as the trustee may elect." Sec. 1.652(b)-3, Income Tax Regs. We think it clear, both from the way the income was reported, as well as from petitioner's computation herein, that it was the trustee's intention that petitioner should have the benefit of all available deductions. * * *

Van Buren v. Commissioner, supra at 1110–1111. We find our rule in *Van Buren* equally applicable to the present case. Beneficiaries of complex trusts, as well as simple trusts, should be given all allowable benefit of deductions when determining the amount of each class of income comprising a distribution. This conclusion is supported by the fact that the examples set forth in section 1.662(c)-4, Income Tax Regs., comport with both section 1.652(b)-3, Income Tax Regs., and our rule in *Van Buren*.

As was the case in *Van Buren*, we presume that the Trustee intended that petitioner should have all possible indirect benefits of the Trust's deductions. Thus, in determining the character of the net amount of each class of income comprising that portion of the distribution taxable to petitioner ($48,282.21), losses used in computing DNI may be allocated first to ordinary income and then to capital gain income used in the DNI calculation.

We emphasize that deductible losses are allocated to the various items of trust income solely to determine character of the net amounts of each class of income comprising the distribution. Such allocation does not have the effect of offsetting ordinary loss against long-term capital gain or vice versa. Therefore, after adjusting Trust income for the disallowed Sentinel loss, petitioner should have included $100 as ordinary income from dividends and $48,182.21 as long-term capital gain.[8] As previously noted, the remainder of

---

8. The amount of each class of income distributable to petitioner is computed by allocating deductions included in computing DNI as follows:

	Interest	Dividends	Excluded Dividends	Capital Gain	Total
Items of Income included in DNI Computation:	$36,401.32	$931.60	$100.00	$50,000.00	$87,432.92

the $50,000 distribution should have been treated as a nontaxable distribution out of principal.

To the extent that petitioner included $100 as long-term capital gains rather than as ordinary income, he received a benefit in the form of the lower rate of taxation of capital gain income.... Since respondent did not place petitioner's compliance with section 662(b) in issue, the difference in tax due because of the improper characterization is a windfall to petitioner.

* * *

Schaefer v. Commissioner
46 T.C.M. (CCH) 986 (1983)

PARKER, Judge:

* * *

Finally, petitioner seems to argue that respondent erred in computing the estate's DNI during the years in issue. A large part of the estate's gross income during these years was from a partnership. The decedent and his brother, Arthur Schaefer, had been partners in various real estate investments, and the partnership had not yet wound up its affairs by the end of 1976, the last year in issue. See *Matter of Trust Estate of Schaefer,* 91 Wis. 2d 360, 283 N. W. 2d 410 (Ct. App. 1979). Citing Wisconsin law, petitioner seems to argue that the partnership income is not a part of the estate's DNI. We disagree.

DNI is an estate's taxable income, with certain adjustments. Sections 642, 643(a). Except for the adjustments provided in sections 642 and 643(a), an estate's taxable income is "computed in the same manner as in the case of an individual." Section 641(b). None of these adjustments involve an estate's income from a decedent's interest in a partnership. Gross income includes a taxpayer's distributive share of partnership income. Section 61(a)(13). Thus, an estate's share of partnership income properly goes into the calculation of the estate's taxable income and its DNI. Even if petitioner's argument under state law is correct, it is irrelevant. State law creates legal interests and rights, but the Federal revenue law designates what legal interest or rights, so created, will be taxed. *Morgan v. Commissioner,* 309 U. S. 78, 80 (1940). DNI and taxable income of an estate are questions of Federal tax law that must be determined under a uniform Federal standard, and not be subject to the vicissitudes of state law. See *Lyeth v. Hoey,* 305 U. S. 188 (1938).

Moreover, we believe petitioner's argument is incorrect under state law....

Less DNI deductions:					
Interest expense	52.24				52.24
Trustee expense	832.33				832.33
Partnership loss	35,516.75	931.60		1,817.79	38,266.14
Amount distributable to petitioner	–0–	–0–	$100.00	$48,182.21	$48,282.21

The proper amount of each class of income comprising the distribution is calculated as follows:

Interest $0 ÷ $48,282.21 × $48,282.21 = $0
Dividend $100.00 ÷ $48,282.21 × $48,282.21 = $100
Capital gain $48,182.21 ÷ $48,282.21 × $48,282.21 = $48,282.21
[sic; the last number in the third equation should be $48,182.21]

See examples, sec. 1.662(c)-4(e) and (g), Income Tax Regs.; S. Rept. 1622, 83d Cong., 2d Sess., at 351–353 (1954).

Crisp v. United States

34 Fed. Cl. 112, 95-2 U.S.T.C. ¶ 50,493 (1995)

ANDEWELT, Judge.

I.

In this tax refund action, plaintiff, Don W. Crisp, trustee of the Caroline Hunt Trust Estate (the Trust or Trust Estate), seeks a refund of $2,993,572.81 for income taxes the Trust allegedly overpaid for the tax year ending June 30, 1987, and the shortened tax period ending December 31, 1987.[2]

In 1935, Caroline Hunt's parents, H.L. and Lyda Hunt, established the Trust Estate through an "Articles of Agreement and Declaration of Trust" (the Trust Agreement). The Trust Agreement provides that the trustee may, at his or her discretion, make periodic payments to Caroline Hunt during her lifetime and then, for the next 21 years after her death, make periodic payments to Caroline Hunt's heirs. At the end of the 21-year period following Caroline Hunt's death, the Trust Agreement obliges the trustee to dissolve the Trust and disburse the assets to Caroline Hunt's heirs.

I.R.C. §641 obliges trusts to pay taxes on trust income. When calculating taxable trust income for any given tax year, I.R.C. §661 permits a deduction from trust income of all distributions made to trust beneficiaries during that tax year up to the amount of the trust's distributable net income (DNI). I.R.C. §643(a) sets forth the method for calculating a trust's DNI.

For the two tax periods in issue here, the Trust distributed to Caroline Hunt $4.5 million and $1.6 million, respectively. Pursuant to I.R.C. §661, the Trust deducted from its income the full amounts distributed to Caroline Hunt because the Trust's DNI for these periods, as calculated by the trustee, exceeded the amounts distributed. In calculating the Trust's DNI for these two periods, the trustee included within the DNI all capital gains credited to the Trust's capital account by ZH Associates (ZH), a limited partnership in which the Trust is a limited partner.

After conducting an audit, the Internal Revenue Service (IRS) concluded that the trustee had improperly included the ZH capital gains in the Trust's DNI. When the IRS recalculated the Trust's DNI to exclude these capital gains, the DNI for the respective tax periods fell to $2,665,300 and $600,252. Because the Trust's distributions to Caroline Hunt exceeded the recalculated DNI, and because I.R.C. §661 provides that any deduction from trust income "shall not exceed the [DNI]," the IRS recalculated the Trust's tax burden to include, as taxable income, the amount of the Trust's distributions to Caroline Hunt that exceeded the reduced DNI. As a result, the Trust owed taxes, penalties, and interest in the amounts of $2,895,496 and $98,076, respectively.

Plaintiff paid the taxes, penalties, and interest calculated by the IRS, and thereafter filed the instant suit to secure a refund. This action is presently before the court on the parties' cross-motions for summary judgment on the issue of whether the trustee prop-

---

2. Plaintiff shortened the fiscal tax year beginning July 1, 1987, to December 31, 1987, in compliance with the Tax Reform Act of 1986, Pub. L. No. 99-514, Title XIV, §1403, 100 Stat. 2713 (codified at I.R.C. §645(a) [now section 644(a)]), which required all trusts to conform their tax years to the calendar year beginning after December 31, 1986.

erly included in the Trust's DNI the ZH capital gains credited to the Trust. There are no material issues of fact in dispute. For the reasons set forth below, plaintiff's motion for summary judgment is granted and defendant's cross-motion is denied.

II.

The Trust Estate and Robert E. Zoellner (Zoellner) formed ZH pursuant to the New Jersey Uniform Limited Partnership Act and through a January 1, 1982, "Agreement of Limited Partnership" (the Partnership Agreement). The Partnership Agreement designated the Trust as the sole limited partner and Zoellner as the general partner....

The Partnership Agreement describes ZH's business as follows:

> The purposes of the Partnership are to engage in trading for its own account, including to deal in arbitrage, hedge arbitrage, option arbitrage, international securities arbitrage (but not currency or commodities arbitrage) and hedge trading and securities trading in connection therewith and otherwise to deal in securities being traded in connection therewith....

ZH engaged primarily in "deal arbitrage" which involves the purchase of securities sought in cash tender offers, exchange offers, or mergers and then the tendering of those securities for cash or new securities.[4] ZH also engaged in option arbitrage and hedge trading. Option arbitrage seeks, *inter alia,* to capture profits derived from the disparity between the open-market share price of a particular stock and the market price for options to purchase or sell that some stock. Hedge trading involves, *inter alia,* establishing securities positions in one industry and offsetting those positions by taking long or short positions in securities of another industry. ZH received some cash dividends as a consequence of owning securities, but ZH's primary focus was to buy and sell securities in an attempt to profit from the sudden swings in market value that resulted from the numerous mergers and acquisitions which were prevalent in the 1980s.

* * *

III.

Congress created DNI specifically to deal with the taxation of estates and trusts and their beneficiaries. See Treas. Reg. §1.643(a)-0. I.R.C. §661(a) employs DNI to determine the proportions of the income tax burden borne by the trust or estate and by its beneficiaries. I.R.C. §643(a) defines DNI as [a modified version of taxable income.] The listed modifications include deductions for distributions, personal exemption, capital gains and losses, extraordinary dividends and taxable stock dividends, tax-exempt interest, and income of a foreign trust. With respect to capital gains and losses, I.R.C. §643(a)(3) requires a trustee, when calculating DNI, to exclude capital gains from trust income under [specified circumstances].

The legislative history of the Internal Revenue Code explains Congress' rationale for including capital gains in DNI except when the gains are allocated to corpus and not paid, credited, or required to be distributed. The pertinent House Report states:

> Subsection (a) defines the term "distributable net income" to mean the taxable income of the estate or trust with certain modifications. This concept of

---

4. Shares of a company subject to a tender offer typically sell at a discount to the amount of the tender offer. This discount, *inter alia,* reflects the uncertainty that the deal will consummate and the offeror will actually purchase the shares at the tender price. Deal arbitrage attempts to capture, as profit, the value of that discount by purchasing securities subject to a tender offer, and if the deal consummates, tendering the shares at the full price offered.

[DNI] serves the general purposes of limiting the additional deductions allowed to estates and trusts (under sections 651 and 661) for amounts paid, credited, or required to be distributed to beneficiaries and also of determining how much of an amount distributed or required to be distributed to a beneficiary will be taxed to him. In effect, the concept of [DNI] gives statutory expression to the principle underlying the taxation of estates and trusts, that is, that these separate taxable entities are only conduits through which income flows to the beneficiaries except where income is accumulated by the estate or trust for future distribution.

* * *

To the extent that gains from the sale or exchange of capital assets must be allocated to corpus and are not (A) paid or credited to any beneficiary during the taxable year or (B) paid, permanently set aside or to be used for the purposes specified in section 642(c) (charitable deduction), they are excluded from the computation of [DNI]. The effect of this modification is to tax capital gains to the estate or trust where the gains must be added to principal. However, where the gains, though allocable to corpus, are actually distributed to beneficiaries during the taxable year—for example, in the year of termination of the trust—then the gains are included in the computation of [DNI].

H.R. Rep. No. 1337, 83rd Cong., 2d Sess., at 194–95 (1954), *reprinted in* 1954 U.S.C.C.A.N. 4025, 4333. Thus, unlike a corporate structure which can be subject to double taxation, with the corporation first paying tax on its income and then the shareholder paying a second tax when it receives a cash dividend distribution from the corporation, Congress anticipated that when a trust is involved, capital gains distributed to trust beneficiaries in the year earned would be taxed only once, as income to the beneficiaries. The definition of DNI in I.R.C. §643(a) and its use in I.R.C. §661 as a ceiling on the deductibility of distributions permit a trust to function as a conduit in that the statutes allow the trust to deduct from trust income capital gains distributed to its beneficiaries during the tax period in which the gains were earned.

Treas. Reg. §1.643(a) implements I.R.C. §643(a) and defines DNI.... Regarding capital gains, Treas. Reg. §1.643(a)-3 provides.... The two alternative allocations to which the regulation refers—income and corpus (alternatively referred to as principal)—are the two possible allocations of funds within a trust. The term "income" as used in Treas. Reg. §1.643(a) refers to "the amount of income of an estate or trust for the taxable year determined under the terms of its governing instrument and applicable local law." Treas. Reg. §1.643(b)-1. Hence, under [former] Treas. Reg. §1.643(a)-3, capital gains are includable in DNI if they are either (1) allocated to income or (2) allocated to corpus and actually distributed to the beneficiary during the tax year.

In the instant case, plaintiff contends that he properly applied Treas. Reg. §1.643(a) when he included in the Trust's DNI the ZH capital gains because the Trust's auditor had allocated these gains to income rather than to corpus. In response, defendant acknowledges that plaintiff's auditor allocated the ZH capital gains to income, but contends that this allocation was erroneous, *i.e.*, that the Trust Agreement (the trust instrument) and the applicable local law (Texas state law) required instead that the trustee allocate the capital gains to corpus. Defendant appreciates that under [former] Treas. Reg. §1.643(a)-3 corpus that is properly distributed to the beneficiary in the tax year is includable in DNI. Defendant argues correctly, however, that because the instant trust instrument specifically precludes any distribution of corpus to the beneficiary, the ZH capital gains cannot be classified as distributed corpus includable in DNI under [former] Treas. Reg. §1.643(a)-

3. Thus, the crucial issue on summary judgment under the controlling statute and regulation is whether the trustee had authority to distribute to Caroline Hunt the capital gains earned by ZH and credited to the Trust. If the trustee had such authority, then the ZH capital gains were not corpus and the trustee properly allocated the gains to income and properly included the gains in the Trust's DNI.

[The court quotes former Treas. Reg. §1.643(a)-3(a)(1).] In the instant case, Texas state law is the applicable local law, and the Texas Trust Code provides that, to the extent a trust dictates such an allocation, a trustee shall allocate receipts between income and principal according to the provisions of the trust instrument. Therefore, both [former] Treas. Reg. §1.643(a)-3(a)(1) and the applicable local law point this court initially to the Trust Agreement. If the Trust Agreement dictates the allocation of the ZH capital gains to income, or alternatively to corpus, then that allocation would be determinative. If the Trust Agreement fails to allocate the gains to either income or corpus, then the court must consult the other applicable provisions of Texas state law.

IV.

The Trust Agreement contains a series of introductory clauses, a series of articles that establish the powers and rights of the trustee (Article I), the advisory board (Article II), and the beneficiary (Article III), and then an article that contains miscellaneous provisions (Article IV). Article I, Section 4(b), expressly precludes distribution of corpus. ("[T]he corpus of [the] Trust Estate shall never be diminished through a distribution to the Beneficiary.")[7] Although the trustee may not distribute corpus, the trustee may, at his or her discretion, distribute "net profits" or "net earnings," two terms the Trust Agreement appears to use synonymously. Article IV, Section 4, referring to the trustee's distribution of net profits, provides:

> The Beneficiary may receive from time to time during the life of this trust, such portions of the net profits accruing from time to time to this Trust Estate, as the Trustee, acting with the advice and consent of the Advisory Board, may see fit to pay over and deliver to the Beneficiary. Net profits shall be determined by the annual audits as provided for herein, and the Trustee shall never in any event pay to the Beneficiary, during any one calendar year, any sum in excess of the Net Profits for the preceding calendar year. No duty is imposed upon the Trustee to make such distribution of net profits, but the power is conferred upon him, acting with the advice and consent of the Advisory Board, so to do, and in exercising this discretion said Trustee and Advisory Board shall give full consideration to the interest of both the Beneficiary and this Trust Estate.

Article III, Section 1, referring to the trustee's distribution of net earnings, provides: "The beneficiary shall have no right to the corpus of the Trust property ... and the Beneficiary shall have no right with respect to [the] Trust other than to receive distribution of net earnings awarded her by the Trustee with consent of the Advisory Board, as is elsewhere herein provided...."

Because the trustee may never distribute corpus but may distribute net profits and net earnings, the Trust Agreement necessarily treats net profits and net earnings as distinct from corpus. [Former] Treas. Reg. §1.643(a)-3, however, employs only two classifica-

---

7. Article III, Section 1, when defining the rights of the beneficiary, reiterates the settlors' intent to preclude distribution of corpus during the life of the beneficiary as follows: "The beneficiary shall have no right to the corpus of the Trust property...."

tions—trust corpus and trust income. Therefore, to the extent that the Trust Agreement allocates the ZH capital gains to net profits or net earnings, in applying the regulation, the allocation will be treated as an allocation to income. Hence, the court must determine whether the Trust Agreement dictates the allocation of ZH capital gains to either net profits or net earnings or rather to corpus. As explained above, if the Trust Agreement dictates a particular allocation, then that allocation would control.

V.

The Trust Agreement does not define the terms "net profits" and "net earnings." In the absence of such definitions, the settlors' intent in 1935 would seem best unveiled by consulting contemporaneous law dictionaries....

Although the dictionary definitions do not specifically refer to partnerships or, more specifically, to the treatment of partnership profits credited to a limited partner, the definitions are broad enough to encompass such profits.... Although the Internal Revenue Code's classification of such profits as capital gains rather than ordinary income may affect the ultimate rate of taxation of these profits, such a classification does not affect the allocation of these profits to either net profits or net earnings or alternatively to corpus. Instead, the Trust Agreement and Texas state law control that allocation.

Hence, the terms "net profits" and "net earnings," as employed by the Trust Agreement and as defined in the contemporaneous law dictionaries, encompass the profits earned by ZH and credited to the Trust, regardless of whether the Internal Revenue Code classifies these profits as ordinary income or as capital gains.

VI.

Defendant argues that the ZH profits credited to the Trust could not properly be classified as net profits or net earnings because these profits fit squarely within the definition of corpus provided in the Trust Agreement. Upon review, however, the Trust Agreement contains no provision that directs the trustee to treat as corpus profits such as those credited to the Trust from the ZH limited partnership.

* * *

The ZH profits credited to the Trust resulted from ZH's acquisition and sale of stocks and stock options (hereinafter securities or stocks). These securities do not themselves qualify as corpus under the ... Trust Agreement definition because the Trust did not "acquire" the securities, but rather ZH, a distinct legal entity, acquired the securities.[10] ... Thus, although the Trust "acquired" its limited partnership interest in ZH, the Trust did not "acquire" the securities owned by the partnership and, hence, those securities are not classified as corpus. Because the securities themselves are not corpus, it would follow that the ZH profits credited to the Trust based on the sale of those securities likewise would not be classifiable as corpus....

For the foregoing reasons, the ZH capital gains credited to the Trust fit squarely within the applicable definitions of distributable net profits and net earnings and do not fit

---

10. Defendant argues that a partnership is not a separate taxpayer under I.R.C. §§701 and 702 and, therefore, a partnership is no more than a conduit through which tax items flow to its partners. There is no dispute, however, that ZH functions as a conduit for tax purposes. Rather, the crucial issue is whether the profits credited by ZH, a distinct legal entity, to the Trust's capital account are allocable by the Trust to income or to principal. I.R.C. §§701 and 702 offer no instruction as to allocation between income and principal.

squarely within the Trust Agreement's definition of undistributable corpus. Because the Trust Agreement authorized the trustee to distribute the ZH capital gains to Caroline Hunt, for the reasons explained above and on the facts of the instant case, the profits are properly allocable to income and thus includable in DNI under I.R.C. §643(a)(3) and [former] Treas. Reg. §1.643(a)-3(a)(1).

VII.

If the Trust had directly acquired the securities that produced the profits in issue, rather than purchasing an interest in a partnership which in turn acquired the securities, then the securities would constitute corpus, and apparently so too would any profits that resulted from the sale of those securities. Defendant argues that given this result, this court's interpretation of net profits and net earnings as encompassing the capital gains in issue would unreasonably give the trustee the power to convert undistributable corpus into distributable net profits simply by interposing a partnership between the trustee and the underlying securities. Rather than this result being unreasonable, however, it would appear that the settlors of the Trust intended to grant the trustee such power.

First, as described above, the court's interpretation flows directly from the ordinary meaning of the words chosen by the settlors in drafting the Trust Agreement. Unless the Trust Agreement demonstrates a contrary intent, the best way to give effect to the settlors' intent is to interpret the settlors' words consistent with their ordinary meaning....

Second, at the time the settlors created the Trust, the common law permitted a trustee to choose among various business structures to direct receipts from an investment either to income beneficiaries or to remaindermen. For example, if the trustee invested corpus directly in securities, any increase in the market value of the securities would also constitute corpus. On the other hand, if the trustee invested in securities indirectly by purchasing shares of a corporation that purchased the securities, distributions of profits from the corporation in the form of cash dividends ordinarily would be classifiable as income rather than corpus. *Restatement of Trusts* §236 (1935); *see also,* Tex. Trust Code §§113.102(a)(3) and 113.104(a)(1). Given this result, it is not apparent why, assuming the trustee chose to invest a portion of the Trust assets in a business such as ZH so as to produce distributable income, the settlors would have restricted the trustee to the use of a corporate structure, which would result in double taxation, rather than authorizing the use of a limited partnership structure, which would allow for single taxation. In addition, in 1935, case law supported a trustee using a limited partnership structure in order to have receipts from an investment, in the form of capital gains, classifiable as income distributable to income beneficiaries. *Appeal of Merchants' Funds Ass'n,* 20 A. 527, 528–29 (Pa. 1890), involved facts similar to those involved in the instant case. In *Merchants,* a trust owned a limited partnership interest in a business that bought and sold land. The issue presented therein was whether capital gains earned by the partnership and credited to the trust could be distributed to the income beneficiary. The court concluded that they could. Thus, in 1935, the settlors of the Trust should have recognized that by choosing different business structures, the trustee, in effect, could vary the allocation of receipts from an investment between distributable income and corpus. Given this state of the law, had the settlors intended to preclude the trustee from investing in a business that would result in capital gains being treated as distributable income, the settlors reasonably would be expected to have demonstrated such an intent in the wording of the Trust Agreement.

Third, and related to the second point, perhaps the most convincing evidence in the Trust Agreement that the settlors did not intend to force the trustee to treat as corpus all profits classified as capital gains is the very broad degree of discretion the settlors allowed the trustee and advisory board. In theory, a trustee can direct individual investments of trust assets either toward growing corpus, income, or some combination of the two. Article I, Section 4(c), of the Trust Agreement essentially permits the trustee, with the advisory board's approval, to invest Trust assets in any way the trustee and advisory board deem appropriate so long as the investments are in the interest of the Trust Estate. Thus, the Trust Agreement does not require the trustee to invest a specified minimum portion of Trust assets in investments that would tend to grow corpus or alternatively in investments that would tend to grow net profits. In addition, even when investments produce distributable net profits, the trustee has the discretion as to whether to distribute those profits. Given this very broad discretion granted to the trustee and advisory board with respect to investing and distributing trust assets, it would seem incongruous for the settlors to have restricted the trustee and advisory board from taking advantage of the benefits of a limited partnership arrangement for Trust investments directed at producing net profits. In other words, given the broad discretion granted the trustee and advisory board, if the trustee and advisory board decided to invest $5 million so as to produce net profits for possible distribution to Caroline Hunt, and also determined that the most efficient way to maximize these net profits was to invest in a limited partnership such as ZH, then it is not apparent why the settlors would have precluded such an option.

VIII.

Defendant contends that the settlors' primary intent was to accumulate property, particularly capital gains, for the eventual benefit of the remaindermen and that allowing distribution of capital gains to Caroline Hunt would frustrate this intent. The absence of a mandate in the Trust Agreement requiring the trustee and advisory board to invest a minimum proportion of the Trust assets in investments that would tend to grow corpus, however, belies any such intent. Indeed, on balance, the wording of the Trust Agreement and the surrounding facts support the conclusion that the settlors' primary concern was to accumulate net profits for possible distribution to Caroline Hunt rather than to accumulate corpus for the remaindermen. On the first page of the Trust Agreement, H.L. and Lyda Hunt state that they are the parents of Caroline Hunt and that "it is [their] desire and purpose ... to create an irrevocable trust, known as the Caroline Hunt Trust Estate, for the use and benefit of Caroline Hunt." Caroline Hunt was 12 years old when her parents created the Trust and her parents could not have possibly known at that time who would succeed Caroline Hunt. The Trust Agreement does not mention successors to Caroline Hunt until Article III, Section 3, positioned on the second to last page of the 10-page Trust Agreement, which states:

> At the time of the death of the Beneficiary, her equitable interest in said Trust Estate, unless disposed of otherwise by said Beneficiary, shall pass to and vest in her heirs in accordance with the laws of descent and distribution then in force, applicable to the equitable interest of such Beneficiary in said Trust Estate. (The term "Beneficiary" applies not only to Caroline Hunt but to all her successors to beneficial interests under this trust.)

The court appreciates that a prohibition on the distribution of corpus tends to ensure that assets will remain in the Trust upon Caroline Hunt's death. In light of Caroline Hunt's youth at the time the settlors created the Trust, however, this prohibition seems at least as likely to promote Caroline Hunt's interests. A prohibition on the distribution of corpus would help to ensure that the corpus of the Trust Estate would be preserved over many years so that Caroline Hunt could receive profits earned on remaining corpus throughout her lifetime, *i.e.,* that distributions would not completely dissipate the Trust Estate prior to Caroline Hunt's death.

IX.

[T]he court concludes that the Trust's auditor correctly classified the ZH capital gains credited to the Trust as net profits potentially distributable to Caroline Hunt. Because these gains constitute net profits ... the trustee properly allocated the profits to income and included the profits in the calculation of the Trust's DNI. Thus, plaintiff is entitled to summary judgment.

Even if the court had concluded that the Trust Agreement was ambiguous with respect to the allocation of the ZH profits between corpus and income, plaintiff still would be entitled to summary judgment on an alternative ground. If the terms of a trust instrument do not direct the allocation of a receipt to either income or principal, Subchapter D of the Texas Trust Code controls. Thereunder, if the provisions of the Texas Trust Code defining income and principal, Tex. Trust Code §113.102, fail to provide direction, then the trustee must make the allocation "in accordance with what is reasonable and equitable in view of the interests of those entitled to income and to principal." Tex. Trust Code §113.101(a).[16]

In the instant case, the Texas Trust Code definitions of income and principal do not direct the allocation of the ZH capital gains either to income or to corpus. The Texas Trust Code defines income as "the return derived from the use of principal including...," and then provides eight examples. Tex. Trust Code §113.102(a). None of the examples addresses profits credited to a trust from a limited partnership. The Texas Trust Code lacks a similar generic definition of principal and relies exclusively upon ten examples ("Principal includes ..."). Tex. Trust Code §113.102(b). Again, none of the examples addresses profits of a limited partnership credited to a trust. Example eight of Section 113.102(b) broadly defines principal as "profit resulting from any change in the form of principal." As explained generally above, however, the ZH profits credited to the Trust did not result from any change in the form of principal. The Trust's limited partnership interest in ZH was part of the principal of the Trust but the Trust's interest in ZH did not change in form during the tax periods in issue. The securities purchased and sold by ZH were not Trust investments and thus cannot be classified as principal of the Trust Estate.

Assuming that the Trust Agreement and the Texas Trust Code definitions of income and principal do not dictate the allocation of ZH capital gains to either corpus or income, the court must then determine whether the trustee's allocation of ZH profits to income

---

16. Tex. Trust Code §113.101(a) directs a trustee to allocate between principal and income as follows:

> [B]y crediting a receipt or charging an expenditure to income or principal or partly to each:
> (1) in accordance with the terms of the trust instrument;
> (2) in the absence of any contrary terms of the trust instrument, in accordance with this subtitle; or
> (3) if neither of the preceding rules of administration is applicable, in accordance with what is reasonable and equitable in view of the interests of those entitled to income and to principal.

was "reasonable and equitable in view of the interests of those entitled to income and to principal." Tex. Trust Code §113.101(a)(3). Upon review, the court concludes that the trustee's allocation satisfies this standard.

First, the process by which the trustee made the allocation to income supports the trustee's action. The Trust Agreement provides that net profits are to "be determined by the annual audits as provided for [in the Trust Agreement]." Consistent with this mandate, the trustee hired a nationally known certified public accounting firm which, based on its expertise, concluded that "in accordance with the Trust Instrument and the Texas Trust Code," the ZH profits should be allocated to earnings available for distribution. Hence, in allocating the ZH profits, the trustee merely relied upon the advice of an expert. Such reliance would seem both equitable and reasonable. Second, the small proportion of Trust assets invested in ZH and the broad discretion allowed the trustee and advisory board in making trust investments also support the trustee's action. The $5 million investment in ZH constituted less than one percent of the value of the Trust at that time. The trustee's determination to allocate to income capital gains resulting from an investment of less than one percent of the Trust assets would not seem to pose any substantial risk to the interests of the remaindermen. Moreover, given the broad discretion allowed the trustee and advisory board in allocating investments, the determination to invest a minor proportion of the assets of the Trust Estate toward producing distributable net profits would be well within that discretion. Indeed, to the extent that the allocation to income of the ZH profits potentially tipped the balance too far in favor of Caroline Hunt's interests as opposed to the interests of the remaindermen, the trustee could either determine not to distribute all the income to Caroline Hunt or, with the advisory board's approval, shift other Trust assets toward increasing the growth of corpus. In this factual setting, the trustee's allocation does not unreasonably or inequitably affect the interests of the remaindermen.

X.

One last point warrants mention. This suit does not raise an issue of whether profits resulting from a purchase of securities are subject to federal income taxation. The profits in issue here are indisputably subject to taxation. The only issue is to which entity the ZH profits constitute income and hence, which entity is responsible for paying tax on those profits. As described above, Congress envisioned trusts being used as conduits through which income can flow to its beneficiaries and anticipated that either the trust or the income beneficiaries, but not both, would pay tax on trust income in the year the income was earned. Congress left it up to the settlors of a trust when drafting the trust instrument to determine whether the trust or the income beneficiaries would bear the tax burden on income earned by the trust. Hence, the central question in the instant case is not whether tax will be paid on the ZH capital gains credited to the Trust, but rather whether the settlors, in effect, determined that the Trust or the beneficiary should pay that tax. For the reasons set forth above, the court finds the trustee's conclusion to be correct that the settlors determined that the beneficiary should bear the tax burden for the ZH capital gains at issue here.

Conclusion

For the reasons set forth above, plaintiff's motion for summary judgment is granted and defendant's cross-motion is denied....

Revenue Ruling 68-392

1968-2 C.B. 284

Advice has been requested whether capital gains are excludable from distributable net income of a trust under the circumstances described below.

Under the will of A, assets with a fair market value of $268x$ dollars were transferred to a trust for the benefit of his daughter, B. The testator directed that $24x$ dollars be paid annually to B for her lifetime, first out of income of the trust and if necessary, out of corpus.

For its first taxable year, the trust had income of $10x$ dollars all of which was distributed by the trustee to B. In satisfaction of her right to receive an additional $14x$ dollars, B agreed to accept securities that were part of trust corpus. The securities had a fair market value of $14x$ dollars at the time of distribution and a basis of $12x$ dollars in the hands of the trust.

The governing instrument is silent on the treatment of capital gains. However, in the absence of a provision in the trust instrument, local law requires that such gains be allocated to corpus.

The transaction whereby the trustee distributed securities to B in partial satisfaction of the annuity payments, to the extent of their fair market value, is treated as though the trustee sold the securities to B for cash, and immediately thereafter the trustee distributed the entire proceeds from the sale to her. Since the securities distributed had a fair market value in excess of their basis at the time of distribution, this excess must be included in the gross income of the trust as capital gain. [*See infra* (ch. 3, sec. G(1)(a)).]

Under the provisions of section 1014 of the Internal Revenue Code of 1954 as implemented by section 1.1014-4(a)(3) of the Income Tax Regulations, when property is transferred by a trustee to a beneficiary under such circumstances that the transfer is considered a sale or exchange, the beneficiary acquires a basis equal to the fair market value of the property on the date of the transfer.

Section 643(a)(3) of the Code provides, in part, that gains from the sale or exchange of capital assets shall be excluded from distributable net income to the extent that such gains are allocated to corpus and are not (A) paid, credited, or required to be distributed to any beneficiary during the taxable year, or (B) paid, permanently set aside, or to be used for the purposes specified in section 642(c) of the Code.

[Former section] 1.643(a)-3(a) of the regulations provides that gains from sale or exchange of capital assets are ordinarily excluded from distributable net income, and are not ordinarily considered as paid, credited, or required to be distributed to any beneficiary unless they are:

(1) Allocated to income under the terms of the governing instrument or local law by the fiduciary on its books or by notice to the beneficiary,

(2) Allocated to corpus and actually distributed to beneficiaries during the taxable year, or

(3) Utilized (pursuant to the terms of the governing instrument or the practice followed by the fiduciary) in determining the amount which is distributed or required to be distributed.

The first instance under the regulations for inclusion in distributable net income requires that capital gains be allocated to income under the terms of the governing instrument or local law by the fiduciary on its books or by notice to the beneficiary. This requisite is not met in the instant case since the governing instrument is silent as to allocation of capital gains and, in the absence of a provision therein, local law requires that capital gains be allocated to corpus.

The second instance under the regulations for inclusion in distributable net income requires that capital gains be allocated to corpus and actually distributed to beneficiaries during the taxable year. As illustrated by Examples (3), (4) and (5) of [former] section 1.643(a)-3(d) of the regulations, this provision regarding the inclusion of capital gains in distributable net income applies only where there is a distribution required by the terms of the governing instrument upon the happening of a specified event. In the instant case, such a condition for inclusion of capital gains in distributable net income is not present.

The third instance under the regulations for inclusion in distributable net income requires that capital gains be utilized (pursuant to the terms of the governing instrument or the practice followed by the fiduciary) in determining the amount that is distributed or required to be distributed. In the instant case, capital gains are not being utilized pursuant to the terms of the governing instrument in determining the amount that is distributed or required to be distributed. Furthermore, since this is the first taxable year of the trust, capital gains are not utilized pursuant to the practice followed by the fiduciary in determining the amount that is distributed or required to be distributed.

Accordingly, under the facts set forth above, where income of the trust for its first taxable year is insufficient to make the annuity payment to B and in accordance with the agreement with her, the trustee distributes securities to her in partial satisfaction of the annuity payment, capital gain of $2x$ dollars resulting from the transaction is includible in gross income of the trust but is excludable from its distributable net income.

B is required to include $10x$ dollars (the trust's distributable net income as determined under section 643 of the Code) in gross income as ordinary income. Also B is treated as having $14x$ dollars (such amount being in excess of the trust's distributable net income) as a distribution of corpus.

The basis of the securities in the hands of B is $14x$ dollars representing fair market value on the date of transfer.

Illustrative Material

1. Both *Crisp* and Revenue Ruling 68-392 concern an earlier version of section 1.643(a)-3, which was substantially rewritten in late 2003; thus, several of the references in these authorities are no longer current. The prior version of section 1.643(a)-3 provided as follows:

[G]ains from the sale or exchange of capital assets are ordinarily excluded from distributable net income, and are not ordinarily considered as paid, credited, or required to be distributed to any beneficiary unless they are:

(1) Allocated to income under the terms of the governing instrument or local law by the fiduciary on its books or by notice to the beneficiary,

(2) Allocated to corpus and actually distributed to beneficiaries during the taxable year, or

(3) Utilized (pursuant to the terms of the governing instrument or the practice followed by the fiduciary) in determining the amount which is distributed or required to be distributed.

Crisp seems consistent with the current regulations, *see* Treas. Reg. § 1.643(a)-3(b)(1) (capital gains are included in DNI "to the extent they are, pursuant to the terms of the governing instrument and applicable local law, … [a]llocated to income"), and, under the current regulations, the result in Revenue Ruling 68-392 would likely be the same, *see* M. Ferguson, J. Freeland & M. Ascher, Federal Income Taxation of Estates, Trusts & Beneficiaries § 5.03[C] (3d ed. 1998 & Supp. 2008). On the other hand, the assertion in Revenue Ruling 68-392 that, "since this is the first taxable year of the trust, capital gains are not utilized [in determining the amount distributed or required to be distributed] pursuant to the *practice* followed by the fiduciary" (emphasis added) clearly fails to reflect current law; the 2003 regulations no longer include the term "practice," and they include examples suggesting that utilizing gains to determine the distributable amount could affect DNI even in the first year of a trust's existence.

2. Under section 643(a)(3), capital losses, too, are generally disregarded in computing DNI. *See Sylvan Agatstein,* 23 T.C.M. (CCH) 62 (1964). Under the 2003 regulations, losses apparently are excluded from DNI unless they are utilized by the fiduciary in determining the amount to be distributed or required to be distributed to the beneficiary. Treas. Reg. § 1.643(a)-3(d).

3. In Private Letter Ruling 9811037 (1997) and Private Letter Ruling 9811036 (1997), the Service ruled that short-term capital gains designated as "ordinary dividends" on a trust's Form 1099-DIV from a mutual fund were includible in DNI, even though they were properly allocable to principal under state law. The Service explained that section 852, pertaining to mutual funds, provides for only two types of income — capital gain dividends, which the recipient treats as gains from the sale or exchange of capital assets held for more than a year, and ordinary dividends, which include short-term capital gains. According to the Service, the latter are includible, in their entirety, in DNI.

Technical Advice Memorandum 8728001 (1986)

ISSUES

(1) Whether capital gains are included in the computation of distributable net income when a trustee exercises his discretionary power under the trust instrument to allocate receipts from the sale of trust principal to income.

* * *

FACTS

In 1981, G established an *inter vivos* trust for the benefit of his grandchildren. G transferred c shares of stock in X, a closely held corporation, to the Trust. The Trust agreement provides that the trustees shall divide and administer the principal of the Trust estate into seven equal shares, one share for each of G's grandchildren.

Paragraph 2(A) of the Trust agreement states that while any such beneficiary is under the age of twenty-five years, the trustees shall pay or apply $b annually out of income and/or principal of his or her share, in such installments as the trustees deem advisable for his or her support, comfort and education. After such beneficiary attains that age, the trustees shall pay all the current net income of his or her fund to such beneficiary. However, if any beneficiary discontinues his or her education before attending at least three years of college, then the annual payment shall not be made for the three years follow-ing the termination of his or her schooling, except the trustees have the power to waive this provision in any case where the education has been terminated for reasons the trustees deem to be good and reasonable.

Paragraph 2(C) of the Trust agreement states that when any such beneficiary shall have attained the age of twenty-five years, the trustees shall distribute to him or her one-third of the principal of his or her fund as constituted at the time of distribution. When such beneficiary shall have attained the age of thirty years, the trustees shall further distribute to him or her one-half of the remaining principal of his or her fund as constituted at the time of distribution. When such beneficiary shall have attained the age of thirty-five years, the trustees shall further distribute to him or her the balance of his or her fund.

* * *

Paragraph 4(H) of the Trust agreement provides that the trustees have the power to de-termine the manner of ascertainment of income and principal, and the apportionment of income and principal, and the apportionment between income and principal of all re-ceipts and disbursements, and to select an annual accounting period.

* * *

The entire corpus of Trust, consisting of shares of X stock, was sold in the taxable year ending July 31, 1983. Trust realized a gain of $f on the sale. Of this amount, the trustees allocated $g to income pursuant to the exercise of their discretionary authority. Trust re-ceived additional income of $h in the year. Each beneficiary received a distribution of $j in the succeeding taxable year representing his or her pro rata share of Trust's income, in-cluding the gain from the sale of stock, for the taxable year ending July 31, 1983. Trustees made an election to have section 663(b)(1) of the Code apply to the distributions made in the succeeding year.

In the taxable year ending July 31, 1983, all the beneficiaries of Trust were under the age of 25.

LAW AND RATIONALE

Section 643(a) of the Code provides, in part, that the term "distributable net income" means, with respect to any taxable year, the taxable income of the estate or trust com-puted with certain modifications. Section 643(a)(3) provides, in part, that when com-puting distributable net income, gains from the sale or exchange of capital assets shall be excluded to the extent that such gains are allocated to corpus and are not (A) paid, credited, or required to be distributed to any beneficiary during the taxable year, or (B) paid, permanently set aside, or to be used for purposes specified in section 642(c)....

[Former section] 1.643(a)-3(a) of the Income Tax Regulations provides, in part, that except as provided in section 1.643(a)-6, gains from the sale or exchange of capital assets are ordinarily excluded from distributable net income, and are not ordinarily considered as paid, credited, or required to be distributed to any beneficiary unless they are: (1) al-located to income under the terms of the governing instrument or local law by the fidu-ciary on its books or by notice to the beneficiary, (2) allocated to corpus and actually distributed to beneficiaries during the taxable year, or (3) utilized (pursuant to the terms of the governing instrument or the practice followed by the fiduciary) in determining the amount which is distributed or required to be distributed.

Section 641(b) of the Code provides that the taxable income of an estate or trust shall be computed in the same manner as in the case of an individual, except as otherwise provided in this part. The tax shall be computed on such taxable income and shall be paid by the fiduciary.

Section 661(a) of the Code provides that in any taxable year there shall be allowed as a deduction in computing the taxable income of an estate or trust (other than a trust to which subpart B applies), the sum of (1) any amount of income for such taxable year required to be distributed currently (including any amount required to be distributed which may be paid out of income or corpus to the extent such amount is paid out of income for such taxable year); and (2) any other amounts properly paid or credited or required to be distributed for such taxable year; but such deduction shall not exceed the distributable net income of the estate or trust.

Section 663(b)(1) of the Code provides that if within the first 65 days of any taxable year of a trust, an amount is properly paid or credited, such amount shall be considered paid or credited on the last day of the preceding taxable year. Paragraph (1) shall apply with respect to any taxable year of a trust only if the fiduciary of such trust elects, in such manner and at such time as the Secretary prescribes by regulations, to have paragraph (1) apply for such taxable year.

The issue of whether capital gains are includable in distributable net income was considered in Rev. Rul. 68-392, 1968-2 C.B. 284. In that case, a testamentary trust had insufficient income in its first taxable year to pay the beneficiary the specified annuity amount for that year. The trustee paid, from corpus, the balance of the annuity due the beneficiary by distributing securities that had a fair market value in excess of basis in the hands of the trust. The testator's will directed the annuity be paid first out of income of the trust and if necessary, out of corpus. The governing instrument was silent on the treatment of capital gains. However, in the absence of a provision in the trust instrument, local law required that such gains be allocated to corpus. The ruling held that the distribution of securities to the beneficiary should be treated as a sale, followed by a distribution of the entire proceeds. Since the distributed securities had a fair market value in excess of their basis, this excess must be included in the gross income of the trust as a capital gain.

Rev. Rul. 68-392 also discussed the application of the various provisions of [former] section 1.643(a)-3(a) of the regulations in determining whether the capital gain resulting from the distribution should be excluded from distributable net income. The gain was not included in distributable net income pursuant to the first instance under the regulations because the governing instrument was silent as to the allocation of capital gains and, in the absence of a provision therein, local law required that capital gains be allocated to corpus. The facts in the revenue ruling failed to meet the test set forth in the second instance under the regulations for inclusion in distributable net income. The second test requires that capital gains be allocated to corpus and actually distributed to beneficiaries during the taxable year. Rev. Rul. 68-392 provides that this provision regarding inclusion of capital gains in distributable net income applies only where there is a distribution required by the terms of the governing instrument upon the happening of a specified event. In the revenue ruling, such a condition was not present. Further, the test set forth in the third instance under the regulations was not met because the capital gains were not utilized (pursuant to the terms of the governing instrument or the practice followed by the fiduciary) in determining the amount that is distributed or required to be distributed.

In this case, the trustee was granted discretionary authority under paragraph 4(H) of the Trust agreement to allocate all receipts between income and principal. Accordingly, the trustee allocated $g of the gain from the sale of Trust corpus to income. This grant of discretionary authority to the trustee under paragraph 4(H) of the Trust agreement is permissible under the law of State [New York] (EPTL Article 11, section 2.1).

The law of State provides that a trust is administered with respect to the allocation of receipts and expenditures if a receipt is credited or an expense is charged to income or to principal or partly to each in accordance with the terms of the trust instrument, notwithstanding any contrary provisions within such section of the law. Further, a trust is administered with respect to such allocations if made in accordance with the provisions of such section of the law, in the absence of any contrary terms in the trust instrument.

Therefore, we conclude that the $g of gain from the sale of Trust corpus that was allocated to income by the trustee, pursuant to paragraph 4(H) of the trust agreement, is included in the computation of distributable net income under section 643(a)(3) of the Code. This conclusion is consistent with the first instance under [former] section 1.643(a)-3(a) of the regulations for inclusion in distributable net income which requires that capital gains be allocated to income under the terms of the governing instrument or local law by the fiduciary on its books or by notice to the beneficiary. Because we find that this transaction satisfies the requirements under the first instance listed in [former] section 1.643(a)-3(a) of the regulations, it is unnecessary to consider whether the transaction satisfies the requirements of the other alternatives listed in the regulations. Therefore, it is immaterial that the transaction fails to satisfy the requirements of the second instance under [former] section 1.643(a)-3(a) of the regulations because distribution of the gain was not required by the terms of the governing instrument upon the occurrence of a specified event as provided in Rev. Rul. 68-392.

* * *

CONCLUSIONS

(1) Capital gains allocated to income pursuant to the exercise of a trustee's discretionary authority that was granted under the trust agreement to allocate all receipts between income and principal are included in the computation of distributable net income under section 643(a)(3) of the Code.

* * *

Private Letter Ruling 8429005 (1984)

ISSUE

Whether under section 643(a)(3) of the Internal Revenue Code, the distributable net income of an estate, X, includes capital gains recognized by X when the governing instrument contains no provision specifically addressing the distribution of capital gains.

FACTS

A, a resident of S, died on March 23, 1981, leaving a gross estate of $4,500x, as returned for federal estate tax purposes. An installment note, with a balance payable to X of $2,521x and a remaining basis of $1x, was includible in X. The executors of X, B and C, elected a fiscal year ending on September 30 of each year.

X had no capital gains in its first taxable year ending September 30, 1981. In October of 1981, the installment note was paid in full, resulting in a capital gain of $2,520x. In the same fiscal year, X had a capital loss of $19.5x and a capital loss carryover of $.5x. Thus, the net capital gain for X's second fiscal year is $2,500x.

There is no provision in A's will concerning the distribution or allocation of capital gains realized by X during the administration of X. The law of S provides that when the governing instrument is silent with respect to capital gains, as in the present case, such gains are allocable to corpus.

Before the end of the fiscal year in which the note was satisfied, the executors made a discretionary distribution of most of the assets of X. The executors retained $250x to cover final estate taxes, attorneys' fees, executors' commissions and a bequest of $2x to a charitable beneficiary.

On X's return for the fiscal year ending September 30, 1982, the entire net capital gain was included in distributable net income and treated as having been actually distributed in the same year. The agent maintains that none of the net capital gain is includible in distributable net income because its distribution was not required by the terms of A's will and because X is not considered terminated in that year.

APPLICABLE LAW

Paragraphs (1) and (4) of section 691(a) of the Code provide, in part, that when an installment obligation, reportable by the decedent under section 453, is (1) acquired by the decedent's estate from the decedent, (2) satisfied by the obligor at its face value and (3) not properly includible in respect of a taxable period of the decedent, then an amount equal to the excess of the face amount of the obligation over the decedent's basis in the obligation shall be included in the gross income of the estate in the taxable year when received.

Section 641(a) of the Code applies the tax imposed by section 1(e) to the taxable income of estates. Section 641(b) provides that the taxable income of an estate shall be computed in the same manner as in the case of an individual, except as otherwise provided in Part l of Subchapter J.

Section 661(a) of the Code provides, in part, that a deduction shall be allowed in computing the taxable income of an estate for amounts properly paid or credited or required to be distributed for such taxable year, provided such deduction does not exceed the distributable net income of the estate.

Section 643(a) of the Code provides, in part, that for purposes of Part I of Subchapter J, the term "distributable net income" means, with respect to any taxable year, the taxable income of the estate computed with certain modifications. Section 643(a)(3) provides that gains from the sale or exchange of capital assets shall be excluded from distributable net income to the extent such gains are allocated to corpus and are not (A) paid, credited, or required to be distributed to any beneficiary during the taxable year, or (B) paid, permanently set aside, or to be used for the purposes specified in section 642(c).

[Former section] 1.643(a)-3(a) of the Income Tax Regulations provides, in part, that gains from the sale or exchange of capital assets are ordinarily excluded from distributable net income, and are not ordinarily considered as paid, credited, or required to be distributed to any beneficiary unless they are (1) allocated to income under the terms of the governing instrument or local law by the fiduciary on its books or by notice to the beneficiary, (2) allocated to corpus and actually distributed to beneficiaries during the taxable year, or (3) utilized (pursuant to the terms of the governing instrument or the practice followed by the fiduciary) in determining the amount which is distributed or required to be distributed.

* * *

RATIONALE

The net capital gain realized by X in its second fiscal year is includible in X's gross income for that year. Section 691(a) of the Code. However, in computing its taxable income, X is allowed a deduction for amounts properly paid, credited or required to be distributed in the taxable year. Such deduction cannot exceed X's distributable net income. Section 661(a)(2) of the Code. Thus, in order to compute X's taxable income, it is necessary to determine how much, if any, of the net capital gain is includible in X's distributable net income.

[Former section] 1.643(a)-3(a)(1) of the regulations provides that capital gains are includible in distributable net income if, under the terms of the governing instrument or local law, they are allocated to income by the fiduciary on its books or by notice to the beneficiary. This requirement is not met in the present case since the governing instrument is silent as to capital gains and the law of S allocates such gains to corpus.

[Former section] 1.643(a)-3(a)(3) of the regulations provides that capital gains are includible in distributable net income if they are utilized (pursuant to the terms of the governing instrument or the practice followed by the fiduciary) in determining the amount which is distributed or required to be distributed. Because the terms of the instrument are silent on this point and the fiduciary had no established practice of utilizing capital gains in making distributions, this requirement is also not met.

[Former section] 1.643(a)-3(a)(2) of the regulations provides that capital gains are includible in distributable net income if they are allocated to corpus and actually distributed. In the present case, under the law of S, the capital gains of X are allocated to corpus. Thus, to the extent the capital gains are actually distributed, they will be includible in the distributable net income of X.

Examples (3), (4) and (5) of [former] section 1.643(a)-3(d) of the regulations illustrate that capital gains will be considered actually distributed when the distribution is required by the terms of the governing instrument upon the happening of a specified event. Rev. Rul. 68-392, 1968-2 C.B. 284, states that capital gains realized by a trust will not be considered actually distributed under [former] section 1.643(a)-3(a)(2) of the regulations unless they are required to be distributed by the terms of the governing instrument upon the happening of a specified event. However, in Rev. Rul. 68-392, the assets remaining in the trust after the distribution exceeded the amount of capital gains realized by the trust.

The governing instrument in this case is silent with respect to the distribution of capital gains. However, in contrast to the situation in Rev. Rul. 68-392, the assets remaining in X after the distribution were less than the capital gain recognized by X. Therefore, a portion of the gain was necessarily distributed. The amount so distributed is $2,250x, which is equal to the total net capital gain ($2,500x) less the assets remaining in X after the distribution ($250x). Thus, $2,250x of the net capital gain recognized by X in its second fiscal year will be includible in the distributable net income of X, since this amount was allocated to corpus and actually distributed in that year. [Former section] 1.643(a)-3(a)(2) of the regulations. The balance of the gain ($250x) is not considered actually distributed and is excludable from X's distributable net income, since its distribution was not required by the terms of the governing instrument upon the happening of a specified event. See Rev. Rul. 68-392.

CONCLUSION

X's net capital gain of $2,500x is includible in its gross income for its second taxable year. A portion of that amount, equal to $2,250x, is includible in X's distributable net income. X will also be entitled to a deduction, but not in excess of its distributable net income, for amounts which were properly paid, credited or required to be distributed in the same taxable year. Section 661(a)(2) of the Code.

Illustrative Material

Technical Advice Memorandum 8728001 and Private Letter Ruling 8429005 both also arose under the previous version of section 1.643(a)-3, though they seem entirely consistent with the current version. With respect to Technical Advice Memorandum 8728001, see Treas. Reg. § 1.643(a)-3(b)(1). Note, however, the regulation's insistence that the exercise of discretion be "reasonable and impartial." Regarding Private Letter Ruling 8429005, see Treas Reg. § 1.643(a)-3(e), Ex. 7.

Revenue Ruling 61-20
1961-1 C.B. 248

Advice has been requested whether the net operating loss carryback allowed to an estate under section 642(d) of the Internal Revenue Code of 1954 reduces the distributable net income of the estate, thereby permitting a beneficiary to recompute his Federal income tax liability for the year to which the net operating loss is carried....

In 1955, the taxpayer received a distribution from an estate which he properly included in gross income to the extent of his part of the distributable net income of the estate for such year. In 1957, the estate sustained a net operating loss. The estate carried the net operating loss back to 1955 which resulted in a decrease of its distributable net income for that year. The beneficiary recomputed his tax liability for 1955 based upon his portion of the distributable net income of the estate for such year as revised and filed a claim for refund based upon his taxable income as revised.

[The I.R.S. reproduces section 642(d).]

Section 172 of the Code provides, in effect, that there shall be allowed as a deduction for the taxable year an amount equal to the aggregate of the net operating loss carryovers to such year plus the net operating loss carrybacks to such year.

Under the provisions of section 662(a) of the Code, the income from an estate for a taxable year, which is to be included in the gross income of the beneficiary, is limited by the amount of the distributable net income of the estate as finally determined for such year.

Section 643(a) of the Code provides, in part, that distributable net income means, with respect to any taxable year, the taxable income of the estate computed with certain modifications. None of the modifications is concerned with the net operating loss deduction.

Section 641(b) of the Code provides, in part, that the taxable income of an estate or trust shall be computed in the same manner as in the case of an individual, except as otherwise provided in Part 1 of Subchapter [J], relating to estates, trusts, beneficiaries and decedents.

Thus, it is evident that, in the case of an estate or trust, a net operating loss deduction is taken into account in determining taxable income of the estate or trust which, when further modified to the extent provided in section 643(a) of the Code, results in distributable net income.

In *Amy C. Mellott, et al. v. United States,* 257 Fed. (2d) 798, certiorari denied, 358 U.S. 864, the beneficiaries of an estate sought to offset income received from the estate in 1949 with a carryback of a net operating loss of the estate for its taxable year ended in 1950. The court held that, since net operating losses may be carried back only by the taxpayer who sustained such losses, the beneficiaries of the estate could not utilize a net operating loss sustained by the estate for the purpose of reducing their otherwise taxable income.

In *Agness Sargent v. United States,* 48 American Federal Tax Reports 1695, 55-1 U.S. Tax Cases 9424, a trust sustained a net operating loss in the year 1947 which it carried back to 1945. The income beneficiary of the trust filed a claim for refund for taxes paid on the difference between the amount originally reported as income from the trust and the amount reported as income of the trust after the net operating loss was carried back. The United States District Court for the Southern District of California held that the net operating loss carryback of the trust had no effect on the amount distributable to the beneficiary in such prior year under the terms of the governing instrument or the applicable laws of the State and, therefore, had no effect on the amount taxable to the beneficiary.

Although a taxpayer who qualifies under the provisions of section 642(h) of the Code may receive a direct benefit with respect to the net operating loss carryover of an estate or trust upon its termination, no provision of the Code allows the taxpayer to receive a direct benefit with respect to a net operating loss carryback of an estate or trust. However, section 643(a) of the Code does not require that the taxable income of an estate or trust be modified by the elimination of the net operating loss deduction in arriving at the distributable net income of the estate or trust. Thus, the estate or trust income taxable to the beneficiary is limited by the amount of the distributable net income determined by taking into account the net operating loss deduction. Therefore, a net operating loss carryback of an estate or trust may result in an indirect benefit to the beneficiary by reducing the distributable net income of the estate or trust.

The instant case is not inconsistent with the *Mellot* [sic] and *Sargent* cases. In each of those cases, the years involved were governed by the Internal Revenue Code of 1939. Under the 1939 Code, the beneficiaries of the estate, in each case, were not permitted to utilize the net operating loss sustained by the estate for the purpose of otherwise reducing taxable income. However, the 1954 Code first introduced the concept of "distributable net income" into the law. Since the 1954 Code is applicable in the instant case, the estate income which is taxable to the beneficiary is limited by the amount of the distributable net income of the estate even though the amount distributable to the beneficiary under the terms of the governing instrument or the applicable local law was not decreased by the net operating loss. There was no such limitation under the 1939 Code.

* * *

Accordingly, it is held that the net operating loss carryback allowable to an estate under section 642 of the Code has the effect of reducing the distributable net income of the estate for the prior taxable year to which the net operating loss is carried, thereby permitting the estate beneficiary to recompute his tax liability for such prior year based upon the revised distributable net income of the estate after allowance of the net operating loss deduction....

Problems

3-1. Calculate the distributable net income of the trust in Problem 2-2.

3-2. Assume that the trust in Problem 2-2 also realized a $200,000 long-term capital gain. Assume further that the gain is allocable to principal under state law or the governing instrument.

a. Calculate the trust's distributable net income if the trustee distributes only fiduciary accounting income to the beneficiaries.

b. Calculate the trust's distributable net income if the trustee distributes not only fiduciary accounting income, but also $200,000 of principal, to the beneficiaries.

c. Calculate the trust's distributable net income if the trustee distributes not only fiduciary accounting income, but also $200,000 of principal, to the beneficiaries, and, thereafter, only $50,000 of principal remains in the trust.

References

Holland, Kennedy, Surrey & Warren, *A Proposed Revision of the Federal Income Tax Treatment of Trusts and Estates—American Law Institute Draft,* 53 Colum. L. Rev. 316 (1953), is a clear overview of subchapter J written prior to its enactment by persons deeply involved in its formulation. Kamin, Surrey & Warren, *The Internal Revenue Code of 1954: Trusts, Estates and Beneficiaries,* 54 Colum. L. Rev. 1237 (1954), is a similar effort written immediately after enactment. Both are excellent and are especially helpful in understanding distributable net income. *See also* Bryant, *Final Regulations Under Section 643 Revise the Definition of "Income" and Determine Its Tax Impact on Trusts and Estates,* 22 J. Tax'n of Invs. 283 (2005); Danforth, *Allocation of Capital Gains to DNI under Section 643,* 30 Est., Gifts & Tr. J. 242 (2005); Blattmachr & Gans, *The Final "Income" Regulations: Their Meaning and Importance,* 103 Tax Notes 891 (2004).

C. Distributions to Beneficiaries

Internal Revenue Code:
    Sections 643(c); 651(a); 661(a)
Regulation:
    Section 1.643(c)-1

Brigham v. United States
160 F.3d 759 (1st Cir. 1998)

ALDRICH, Senior Circuit Judge.

This is an action to recover income tax payments that, allegedly, were not due. On cross motions for summary judgment the court ruled for the United States. We affirm.

In 1988 Kendal Ham died leaving a will with several provisions for his wife. Seasonably she chose, instead, to waive her rights under the will and elect the share of his estate permitted by the New Hampshire statute, N.H.Rev.Stat. Ann. § 560:10, in her case a one-third "portion of the estate remaining after the payment of debts and expenses of administration." In 1990 and 1991 Mr. Ham's executor made payments to Mrs. Ham on account of the principal of her elected share. These payments included amounts equivalent to the total income received by Mr. Ham's estate during those two years. His executor classified these inclusions as "distributable net income" (DNI) pursuant to 26 U.S.C. §643(a) and claimed a deduction from the estate's gross income pursuant to 26 U.S.C. §661, which the government allowed. Mrs. Ham, in turn, reported and paid an income tax on the received DNI pursuant to 26 U.S.C. §662.

Mrs. Ham's executor, plaintiff Paul Brigham, Jr., Esq., now claims it was inappropriate to apply the tax transfer [sic] of §§661 and 662 to payments in satisfaction of a widow's elective share and that the income tax on Mr. Ham's estate's 1990 and 1991 earnings should not have been passed on. No income tax was required of Mrs. Ham on the portion of the payments that exceeded Mr. Ham's estate's income, *see* 26 U.S.C. §662(a), but, obviously, to the extent that payments to her were taxable, Mrs. Ham was paid her elected share in funds subject to depreciation through taxes.

Unreasonable and unfair as this might seem, plaintiff has an impossible row to hoe here.[1] If a payee within the 26 U.S.C. §643(c) definition of "beneficiary" receives DNI pursuant to §661 that is an "other amount properly paid, credited, or required to be distributed to such beneficiary for the taxable year," §662(a)(2), then she is bound to pay an income tax even if the payment was in satisfaction of a principal obligation.

Sections 661 and 662 are lengthy.... We believe these statutes sufficiently clear as to need no history, but we remark that they are the product of the difficulty ... of tracing the source of distributions from estates with many beneficiaries. *See* S.Rep. No. 83-1622, at 83 (1954), *reprinted in* 1954 U.S.C.C.A.N. 4621, 4715 ("The approach adopted by the bill eliminates the necessity, in determining the taxability of distributions, of tracing such distributions to the income of the estate or trust for the current taxable year."). While the solution may over-simplify, it has never been found beyond the federal taxing power. Obviously the taxpayer must adjust to the government, not the government adjust to accommodate him.

Plaintiff, accordingly, claims that Mrs. Ham, as the receiver of a one-third portion of Mr. Ham's estate, was not a "beneficiary" within the meaning of §662. This contention, however, fails. For definition, 26 U.S.C. §643(c) provides that "the term 'beneficiary' includes heir, legatee, devisee." The word "elector" (of a spouse's share) does not appear, but "includes" is not limiting. Rather, "the terms 'includes' and 'including'... shall not be deemed to exclude other things otherwise within the meaning of the term defined." 26 U.S.C. §7701(c). In light of this we apply the principle that a list of terms should be construed to include by implication those additional terms of like kind and class as the expressly included terms. Surely the widow has elected to be within the group. In common parlance, is not any person who gratuitously receives estate assets a beneficiary? If there is no will, the widow is an heir, and she receives a portion of the estate as determined by the legislature. If there is a will, she may be a legatee, or she may waive her rights under it and receive a different portion. But, in all cases, on its face, the §§661–662 tracing purpose applies precisely.

Plaintiff's remaining argument is that the payments in satisfaction of Mrs. Ham's elective share were not §662(a)(2) distributions because the elective share is a state law interest not subject to the estate income distribution provisions in §§661 and 662. He has found in his favor the case of *Deutsch v. Commissioner of Internal Revenue*, 74 T.C.M. (CCH) 935, 1997 WL 633208 (1997) (holding that the Florida elective share is not subject to the entire Subchapter J, 26 U.S.C. §§641–692). We disagree fully.

The *Deutsch* court would draw comparisons between elective shares and the Florida dower. Assuming that Florida dower may be exempt, which we may doubt, this would be

---

1. He can, of course, negotiate with the other estate.

because it is directly involved with real estate title which, like jointly owned property may, in a technical sense, not pass through the estate, a claim that plaintiff here cannot make. By definition, Mrs. Ham received "a portion of the estate." Next, standing with one foot on the dower concept, *Deutsch* reasons that in enacting a provision for elective shares the state was protecting the interests of its widows. Passing the fact that $800,000 is a good deal of protection, the proposition that, simply by fiat, a state may preserve its citizens from federal taxes is absurd. The list of exclusions in 26 U.S.C. §663 clearly does not exclude an elective share, and we note that the Treasury Regulations expressly deny exclusion even to a widow's temporary allowance.[3]

Plaintiff's appeal is without merit.

Illustrative Material

In the Taxpayer Relief Act of 1997 Congress amended section 663(c), to extend the separate share rule to estates, as well as trusts. In 1999 the Treasury promulgated regulations clarifying that a surviving spouse's elective share is, in fact, a separate share. *See* Treas. Reg. §§1.663(c)-4(a), 1.663(c)-5, Ex. (7)(ii). Thus, the outcome in *Brigham* would differ under current law.

Alfred I. duPont Testamentary Trust
66 T.C. 761 (1976)
aff'd per curiam, 574 F.2d 1332 (5th. Cir. 1978)

RAUM, *Judge*: This case is now before us on remand from the Fifth Circuit Court of Appeals. Our original opinion, 62 T.C. 36, was accompanied by detailed findings of fact which are incorporated herein by this reference. We set forth below only those facts necessary to an understanding of the issue which we have been directed by the Court of Appeals to resolve.

In 1925, Alfred I. duPont organized Nemours, Inc., a corporation. In exchange for all of the corporation's stock he transferred to it full title to his elaborate Delaware residential estate known as "Nemours" (consisting of a mansion and some 300 acres of surrounding grounds on which were located various other buildings and structures). Mr. duPont and his wife, Jessie Ball duPont, thereafter leased Nemours from the corporation, for the term of their joint lives plus the life of the survivor, for an annual rental of $1. Subsequently, Mr. duPont transferred securities valued at $2 million to the corporation in return for its further agreement to pay all taxes assessed against Nemours as well as the expenses of maintaining the grounds (including the mansion's exterior). The expenses incurred inside the mansion house and the salaries of the duPonts' personal employees remained the responsibility of the lessees.

Mr. duPont and his wife resided at Nemours until 1926 when they acquired a second home, Epping Forest, in Jacksonville, Fla., which became their principal residence. They used Nemours about 2 months a year until 1935 when Mr. duPont died; thereafter Mrs. duPont continued to use it also about 2 months a year until 1962. In that latter year, while in Delaware, Mrs. duPont broke a leg and remained at Nemours until her death in 1970 when she was 86 years old. As the result of a second accident in 1966, she was confined

---
3. *See* Treas. Reg. §1.662(a)-3(b)(6)....

almost entirely to a wheelchair. She was an invalid, and made very little use of the elaborate facilities at Nemours, although they were available to her.

Mr. duPont's will made certain specific bequests (including the contents of the Nemours mansion to his wife) and then established a testamentary trust, the petitioner herein, to which he gave the remainder of his estate, which included all of the stock of Nemours, Inc. The trustees were directed to pay out of income the first $200,000 a year to Mrs. duPont, then to pay certain enumerated annuities, after which any remaining income was to be paid to Mrs. duPont. (During each of the tax years the total income of the trust was in excess of $13 million and the amount payable to Mrs. duPont was in excess of $11 million.) ...

Upon Mr. duPont's death, in 1935, title to the stock of Nemours, Inc., passed, according to the directions of his will, to the executors of his estate. The stock was held by Mr. duPont's executors from the time of his death in 1935 until 1937, when they liquidated the corporation and transferred its assets (consisting of Nemours and certain securities) to the testamentary trust, subject to the continuing obligation to maintain the grounds and pay the taxes during Mrs. duPont's life tenancy. Prior to its liquidation the corporation had paid the maintenance expenses and taxes; thereafter the charges of both categories were paid by the testamentary trustees.

As indicated above, Mrs. duPont resided at Nemours from 1962 until her death in 1970. The trust spent $255,753 in 1966 and $274,451 in 1967 for general maintenance of the Nemours estate; it expended an additional $114,284 during 1967 for improvements thereon, including the paving of certain roadways, the restoration of ornamental stonework, and the purchase of certain vehicles for use in connection with the estate. On the Federal fiduciary income tax returns for 1966 and 1967 the trustees claimed deductions in respect of these amounts. The Commissioner disallowed these deductions in their entirety.

In our earlier opinion we held that the trust could not deduct, under section 212, the expenses of maintaining Nemours either as expenses proximately related to property held for the production of income or as expenses incurred in the management of trust property....

The Court of Appeals affirmed.... 514 F.2d 917 [*supra* (ch. 2, sec. B(3)(a))]. However, it also considered petitioner's additional contention (raised for the first time in the appellate proceeding) that the trust should be allowed to deduct these amounts under section 651 or 661, which define the tax consequences to a trust of certain transactions between the trust and its beneficiaries. [The Court of Appeals therefore remanded the case for consideration of the newly claimed deductions under section 651 or 661.]

Sections 661 and 662, I.R.C. 1954, together apply the conduit principle as the basic pattern of income taxation of "complex" trusts.[4] Apart from these provisions, a trust com-

---

4. Likewise secs. 651 and 652 apply the conduit principle to the income taxation of "simple" trusts. In general, a simple trust is one that is required to distribute all of its income currency, whose terms do not provide for any amounts to be paid or permanently set aside for charitable purposes, and which does not make any distribution other than of current income. Sec. 1.651(a)-1, Income Tax Regs. All other trusts and all decedents' estates are treated as complex trusts. Sec. 1.661(a)-1, Income Tax Regs. It appears from petitioner's Federal fiduciary income tax returns that in both 1966 and 1967 it realized capital gains, allocable to corpus, in respect of which it claimed a charitable deduction under sec. 642(c). Therefore, although the parties have expressed considerable uncertainty on this matter, we shall treat petitioner as a complex trust whose liability is governed, inter alia, by secs. 661 and 662. However, insofar as we can determine, our resolution of the central issue before us would be unchanged, if we applied, instead, secs. 651 and 652. Similar underlying principles guide the taxation of transactions between trusts and their beneficiaries, whichever pair of Code provisions by their terms applies.

putes its taxable income and pays the tax thereon according to rules generally similar to those applicable to individuals. Sec. 641–643, I.R.C. 1954. However, because of sections 661 and 662, a beneficiary—and not the trust—is taxed, to the extent of the trust's "distributable net income" as defined in section 643(a), on any amounts which are actually distributed to, or which by the trust instrument are required to be distributed to, that beneficiary. Section 661 allows the trust a deduction for these amounts while section 662 requires their inclusion in the gross income of the beneficiary.… We hold that the amounts paid by the trustee for the maintenance and improvement of Nemours may not be deducted as distributions to Mrs. duPont as the residuary beneficiary of the testamentary trust.

(1) In the first place, it must be remembered that the obligation to make these expenditures had for many years been that of Nemours, Inc., the corporation to which Mr. duPont had transferred Nemours in 1925. That obligation arose when in 1929 he transferred $2 million of securities to the corporation in a transaction that we previously regarded as in effect a contribution to capital. When Mr. duPont died, his stock in Nemours, Inc., passed to his executors, who dissolved the corporation and thereby received its assets while they at the same time assumed its obligations and liabilities. Thereafter, when the executors transferred Nemours (which they had received upon liquidation of the corporation) to the testamentary trust, the trust, petitioner herein, took the property subject to the same obligations and liabilities formerly incurred by the corporation and subsequently assumed by the executors. Of those obligations and liabilities the one which concerns us here was the duty to maintain Nemours throughout the remainder of Mrs. duPont's life.

Accordingly, even if the payments here in issue be regarded as having been made primarily for Mrs. duPont's benefit, she received the benefit thereof *not* as a beneficiary of the testamentary trust but rather as a result of contractual arrangements with Nemours, Inc., made long prior to Mr. duPont's death. The burden of these contractual arrangements (i.e., the duty to maintain Nemours) passed to each successive owner of Nemours: from the corporation as the original obligor, first to the executors when the corporation was dissolved, and then to the testamentary trustees when Nemours was transferred to the testamentary trust.

To be deductible by the trust under section 661 (or section 651), a distribution must be made to a beneficiary in his status as a beneficiary, not as a creditor or in some other capacity. *Thomas Lonergan Trust*, 6 T.C. 715, 718; Rev. Rul. 68-48, 1968-1 C.B. 301, 303; cf. *Mott v. United States*, 462 F.2d 512, 517–518 (Ct. Cl.), certiorari denied 409 U.S. 1108. For this reason alone, petitioner is not entitled to prevail. As explained in detail above, Mrs. duPont's rights to the maintenance of Nemours depended not upon her status as the beneficiary of a testamentary trust, but rather upon her status as a lessee whose tenancy was created and defined by a 1925 lease agreement and a 1929 amendment thereto. To the extent that she received benefits from the trustees' expenditures, the benefits had their ultimate source in these contractual arrangements.[6] Thus, such payments cannot be regarded as distributions to a beneficiary, deductible by the trustees and taxable to the beneficiary under sections 661 and 662, or comparable provisions of the revenue laws.

---

6. The conclusion that Mrs. duPont's rights stemmed from these contractual obligations is in no way inconsistent with our previous determination that the expenses incurred by the petitioner were not deductible under sec. 212. That determination rested on our view that the lease and its amendment were not profit-seeking transactions. And this view was affirmed by the Court of Appeals. 514 F.2d at 920–921. However, notwithstanding the fact that the leasing arrangement was not a transaction entered into for profit, it did create bona fide rights and obligations between the lessee and the lessors. It was because of these obligations that the trust was required to make the payments here in controversy.

(2) Relying upon *Commissioner v. Plant,* 76 F.2d 8 (2d Cir.), affirming 30 B.T.A. 133, the Government urges another, and perhaps less clear, reason for the inapplicability of sections 661 and 662. Under the theory of *Plant,* the maintenance and improvement expenditures in the unusual circumstances before us would not be regarded as distributions to Mrs. duPont within the meaning of sections 661 and 662.

To be sure, expenditures may be deductible as distributions to a beneficiary, even though the amounts are not paid directly to the beneficiary. *Bergan v. Commissioner,* 80 F.2d 89, 91 (2d Cir.); *Rodman Wanamaker Trust,* 11 T.C. 365, 373–374, affirmed per curiam on another issue sub nom. *Commissioner v. Trustees Common Stock John Wanamaker, Philadelphia,* 178 F.2d 10 (3d Cir.); cf. *Chandler v. Commissioner,* 119 F.2d 623, 628 (3d Cir.). But *Plant* raises a serious question whether payments of the character here involved may be regarded within provisions like section 661 as having been made for the benefit of the beneficiary. A detailed examination of the *Plant* case is required for an understanding of this point.

The decedent in *Plant* created a residuary testamentary trust to pay over the net income in specified shares to his widow, his son Henry, and his adopted son Philip during their respective lives. In addition he made further provision for Henry, directing his trustees to continue to maintain his elaborate estate at Eastern Point, Conn., so long as Henry "may wish to occupy the same as a permanent or summer residence and to charge the expense of such maintenance proportionately against the income of the trusts hereby created for the benefit of my wife and sons, before ascertaining the net income from such trusts." 76 F.2d at 9. During 1924 and 1925 the trustees expended (exclusive of taxes) $14,754.47 and $37,221.98, respectively, in the maintenance of the Eastern Point residence, and charged the amounts proportionately against the income of the "three trusts" in the residuary estate. The trustees treated the amounts as undistributable income, and paid income taxes thereon. The Commissioner determined that the trustees' expenditures constituted taxable income to Henry. At issue was the application of section 219(b)(2) of the Revenue Act of 1924, which in its basic operation was comparable to sections 661 and 662 of the Code to the extent of the present problem. The court, in an opinion by Judge Augustus N. Hand, addressed the question whether the income used in maintaining the property was "distributable income" within the meaning of section 219(b)(2). It held that (76 F.2d at 9):

> In spite of the fact that the taxpayer received some benefit from the expenditures at Eastern Point which he might have avoided by abandoning his right to occupy the premises, we do not regard the income thus expended as "distributed" to him as that word is used in the Revenue Act.

The instant case, with its unusual facts, is comparable. From 1926 to 1962 Nemours was not Mrs. duPont's principal residence, although she did spend about 2 months a year there. As the result of an accident in 1962 while in Delaware, she remained at Nemours for the rest of her life. During the tax years she was an invalid, and the record shows that she made but scant use of its elaborate facilities. And, insofar as the record reveals, none of the expenses here in controversy were incurred in connection with the inside of the mansion house or with Mrs. duPont's personal employees.

* * *

[T]he facts of the two cases are virtually indistinguishable. If anything, the expenditures in *Plant* were, according to the terms of the will, somewhat more directly connected to Henry's use of the Eastern Point property than were the expenditures here in controversy connected to Mrs. duPont's occupancy of Nemours. See *Hayward v. Hayward,* 95

Conn. 122, 111 A. 53. In both cases, the person who had the right to take full advantage
of the property for life could have avoided the enjoyment of the expenditures in whole
or in part by abandoning the right to occupy the premises or by utilizing them only to a
limited extent. And in the present case, no less than in *Plant,* the expenditures could be
regarded as "employed in maintaining a capital asset of the trust estate," for the record herein
also shows that Mr. duPont had been concerned about maintaining Nemours as an ever-
lasting memorial to his ancestors as well as a place where his widow could pass her remaining
years. The parallel between the two cases is striking.... We think that the cases are in fact
so close that if *Plant* is regarded as good law it must govern. However, although *Plant* is
an old case, it has only rarely been cited over the years (cf. *Estate of Mortimer B. Fuller,*
9 T.C. 1069, 1073, affirmed per curiam 171 F.2d 704 (3d Cir.), certiorari denied 336 U.S.
961), and we do not feel completely comfortable with that decision. In any event, we
need not rest our result here on *Plant,* since as has been spelled out above.... there is an
entirely independent basis for the conclusion that we reach.

Illustrative Material

1. *"Beneficiary" or "Creditor"?*

a. *Contract obligations. Thomas Lonergan Trust,* 6 T.C. 715 (1946), cited in *duPont,* involved monthly distributions of $300 out of trust income. The Tax Court denied the trust
distribution deductions because the distributions were made, pursuant to local court
order, in discharge of a contract obligation of the decedent. The recipients of the distributions thus received them as creditors—not as beneficiaries—though the recipients
were also beneficiaries of other amounts under decedent's will.

b. *Maintenance of gravesites.* In Rev. Rul. 87-97, 1987-2 C.B. 155, the I.R.S. ruled that
a cemetery corporation did not receive payments for maintenance of gravesites as a beneficiary of the payor-trust. Even though the trust met the requirements of section 642(i),
and thus qualified for a special distribution deduction, the cemetery corporation received
the payments as "compensation for services." Thus, the tax-exempt character of the payments did not pass through, under either section 652(b) or section 662(b), to the cemetery corporation. For the same result under pre-1954 law, see *Metairie Cemetery Association
v. United States,* 282 F.2d 225, 230–31 (5th Cir. 1960) (Wisdom, J.) ("If Metairie Cemetery did not receive the money for services rendered, it had no right to it at all. We hold
therefore that this compensation ... is taxable income....").

c. *Interest on unpaid general bequests.* The I.R.S. has ruled that the distribution deduction is not allowable if, pursuant to the terms of local law, an executor pays interest
on account of unpaid general bequests. The I.R.S. reasons that "the relationship between
the parties is that of debtor and creditor rather than that of estate and income beneficiary." Rev. Rul. 73-322, 1973-2 C.B. 44. However, Rev. Rul. 73-322 also ruled that the
payments were deductible by the estate as interest under section 163. Similarly, in *United
States v. Folckemer,* 307 F.2d 171 (5th Cir. 1962), the court held that such payments were
includible, as interest, in the recipient's gross income in the year of receipt, rather than,
in accordance with section 662(c), as distributions in the year in which the taxable year
of the estate ended. The court noted that the recipient was not "an income beneficiary of
the estate." *Davidson v. United States,* 137 Ct. Cl. 416, 149 F. Supp. 208 (1957), is directly
contrary to Rev. Rul. 73-322 and *Folckemer.* It refused to treat such payments as interest
and instead treated them as distributions to beneficiaries under the predecessor of section
662. As suggested *supra* (ch. 2, sec. B(1)), the new restrictions on deductibility of interest under section 163 may force reexamination of the availability of distribution deduc-

tions for such payments. *See also Schwan v. United States,* 264 F. Supp. 2d 887, 896 (D.S.D. 2003) ("It would be absurd" to conclude that interest paid on deferred legacies might generate an interest deduction, because "legacies are not properly characterized as 'indebtedness.'"). Nonetheless, Treas. Reg. § 1.663(c)-5, Ex. (7)(ii), takes the position that an "interest" payment on a surviving spouse's elective share is taxable to the surviving spouse, as interest, under section 61, rather than in accordance with sections 661 and 662.

d. *Continuing payments to ex-spouse.* An estate may deduct, as distributions under section 661, payments it makes to the decedent's ex-spouse pursuant to a divorce property settlement agreement. Rev. Rul. 67-304, 1967-2 C.B. 224. Section 682(b) seems to confer beneficiary status on the recipient ex-spouse. At least that is what *Laughlin's Estate v. Commissioner,* 167 F.2d 828 (9th Cir. 1948), and *Estate of Daniel G. Reid,* 15 T.C. 573 (1950), *aff'd sub nom. Izrastzoff v. Commissioner,* 193 F.2d 625 (2d Cir. 1952), construing a predecessor of section 682(b), held. In contrast, in *Kitch v. Commissioner,* 104 T.C. 1 (1995), the Tax Court held that, when an estate satisfied its decedent's overdue alimony obligations to the estate of an ex-spouse, the payments were subject to taxation, as alimony, in the hands of the payee estate, as income in respect of a decedent. (Pre-1985 versions of sections 71 and 682(b) applied.) Thus, the payee estate was subject to taxation on the entire amount of the payments as ordinary income, rather than as limited and characterized under section 662 by the distributable net income of the payor estate. Though not directly at issue, a clear implication is that payments of alimony to an ex-spouse's estate are *not* distributions that entitle the payor estate to a deduction under section 661. The court reached this result by interpreting the pre-1985 version of section 682(b) narrowly: "Section 682(b) applies as a timing provision and does not invoke the conduit rules of Subchapter J." Thus, the court apparently rejected (though it did not cite) Rev. Rul. 67-304. The court emphasized that it was applying section 682(b) as it was prior to the Deficit Reduction Act of 1984—not section 682(b) in its current form.

The Tenth Circuit affirmed but used an entirely different analysis. *Kitch v. Commissioner,* 103 F.3d 104 (10th Cir. 1996). The court expressly rejected the notion "that § 682(b) is merely a timing provision." 103 F.3d at 107. Instead, the court held that, because section 682(a) applies literally only when the payor is a trust—not when the payor is an estate, section 682(b) did not apply. Thus, the payor estate's distributable net income neither limited nor characterized the amount on which the payee was subject to taxation. Instead, the amounts the payee estate received were exclusively income in respect of its own decedent, taxable in full as ordinary income. In dictum, the Tenth Circuit continued: "We have no doubt that § 682 applies to the extent it permits a decedent's estate to claim a deduction on its [income] tax return for alimony payments made to a spouse, even for arrearages." 103 F.3d at 108. In short, it may be that an alimony payee can be an estate beneficiary for purposes of entitling the payor estate to a distribution deduction, but not for purposes of limiting or recharacterizing income in respect of its own decedent. The Tenth Circuit clearly considered and seems to have applied post-1984 versions of all relevant statutes.

e. *Family allowances.* In *United States v. James,* 333 F.2d 748 (9th Cir.), *cert. denied,* 379 U.S. 932 (1964), the court held that an Arizona widow's allowance was subject to taxation in her hands under section 662. Responding to the widow's argument that she did not take the allowance as a "beneficiary," the court stated:

> We think that the widow's position is much closer to that of a "beneficiary" of the estate than to that, for example, of a creditor. She gets the allowance only by reason of her husband's death; she is entitled to it because of her status as widow; she receives it from his estate.

333 F.2d at 750. In *Estate of Lawrence R. McCoy,* 50 T.C. 562 (1968), *acq.,* 1973-2 C.B. 2, the Tax Court allowed a distribution deduction for an estate's payment of a Vermont widow's allowance. In reaching its holding, the court invalidated former Treas. Reg. §1.661(a)-2(e), which allowed a distribution deduction for payment of a family allowance only if the allowance was payable out of income. *Cummings v. United States,* 69-1 U.S.T.C. ¶9359 (C.D. Cal. 1969), followed suit. T.D. 7287, 1973-2 C.B. 210, amended Treas. Reg. §1.661(a)-2(e) to conform to *McCoy.* Treas. Reg. §§1.662(a)-2(c) and 1.662(a)-3(b) were also amended to subject recipients of family allowances to taxation. Thereafter, Rev. Rul. 75-124, 1975-1 C.B. 183, held that amounts paid by an executor as an allowance for the support of the decedent's surviving spouse and dependents qualified for the distribution deduction under section 661 and were subject to taxation in the recipients' hands under section 662, "even though such amounts [were] considered to be debts of the estate rather than payments to beneficiaries under the probate law of the state." *Cameron v. Commissioner,* 68 T.C. 744 (1977), holding that minors were subject to taxation on amounts received as California family allowances, upheld the amendments to the regulations. The Tax Court expressly held that the minors were "beneficiaries as defined in section 643(c)." *Schaefer v. Commissioner,* 46 T.C.M. (CCH) 986 (1983), upheld and applied the amended regulations to a Wisconsin widow's allowance.

f. *Dower.* Mesne profits received by a Florida estate on property subsequently judicially assigned to the surviving spouse as an interest in dower were deductible by the estate under section 661 and subject to taxation in the hands of the surviving spouse under section 662 when paid by the estate to the surviving spouse pursuant to the terms of the dower decree. Rev. Rul. 71-167, 1971-1 C.B. 163, *modifying* Rev. Rul. 64-101, 1964-1 C.B. 77, which took the opposite position. In contrast, in *Deutsch v. Commissioner,* 74 T.C.M. (CCH) 935 (1997), the court held that satisfaction of a Florida surviving spouse's elective share did not constitute a distribution for purposes of Subchapter J. The court relied on Revenue Ruling 64-101, which involved Florida dower, the predecessor of Florida's elective share. But the court also emphasized that under Florida law the elective share could not participate in estate income. Of course, the Code does not rely on participation in the estate's income. For exactly the opposite conclusion, with respect to the New Hampshire elective share, see *Brigham, supra. See generally* Hart, *Electing Against the Will—The DNI Problem for Spousal Shares,* J. Tax'n, March 1998, at 164 (written by taxpayer's lawyer in *Deutsch*). Both Revenue Ruling 64-101 and Revenue Ruling 71-167 are now, in part at least, obsolete. *See* T.D. 8849, 2000-1 C.B. 244, 247 (promulgating regulations on the application of the separate share rule to estates).

g. *Loans.* A trust is not entitled to a distribution deduction on account of loans made to a beneficiary. *Fear v. Commissioner,* 57 T.C.M. (CCH) 306 (1989). Similarly, when an estate borrows from a testamentary trust, the amounts the estate thereafter pays to the trust are not necessarily beneficiary distributions within the scope of the subchapter J conduit rules. Instead, they may be interest taxable directly to the trust in its capacity as creditor. *See Geftman v. Commissioner,* 72 T.C.M. (CCH) 816 (1996), *rev'd,* 154 F.3d 61 (3d Cir. 1998) (holding that no bona fide loan existed between trust and estate).

2. *Testamentary Trusts.* A testamentary trust is a "beneficiary" of its estate. Treas. Reg. §1.643(c)-1; Rev. Rul. 64-314, 1964-2 C.B. 167.

3. *Residential Maintenance Expenses as Distributions. Carson v. United States,* 161 Ct. Cl. 548, 317 F.2d 370 (1963), refused to treat estate expenditures for maintenance of a home owned by the estate as distributions taxable to the estate's beneficiaries. Similarly, Private Letter Ruling 8341005 (1983) ruled that trust expenditures for maintenance of a summer home owned by the trust were not taxable to the trust's mandatory income benefi-

ciary, who occupied the home. On the other hand, *Moreell v. United States,* 221 F. Supp. 864 (W.D. Pa. 1963), seems to have treated expenditures by a trust for maintenance of the personal residence of its primary beneficiary as distributions taxable to her.

The I.R.S. belatedly acquiesced in *H.B. Plant,* 30 B.T.A. 133 (1934), discussed in *duPont.* 1976-2 C.B. 2.

D. Simple Trusts

Internal Revenue Code:
  Sections 643(b); 651; 652

All Regulations under Sections 651 and 652; and Section 1.643(b)-1

Seligson v. Commissioner
63 T.C.M. (CCH) 3101 (1992)
aff'd mem., 15 F.3d 1089 (9th Cir. 1994)

GOLDBERG, Special Trial Judge:

* * *

Respondent determined a deficiency in petitioner's Federal income tax for the year 1986 in the amount of $4,550....

[T]he issues for our decision are: (1) Whether petitioner is required to recognize as taxable income the amounts of $9,453 in interest and $1,542 in dividends distributable to him from a trust created for his benefit by his father, Charles Seligson....

* * *

Petitioner is the sole income beneficiary of a testamentary trust (the Trust) created by his father, Charles Seligson, who died on September 10, 1975. Petitioner was estranged from his father and for personal reasons does not wish to receive the income from the Trust. The Trust, which is administered by a law firm in New York City, has a fiscal year ending October 31.

The terms of the will which create the Trust are as follows:

ARTICLE NINTH: The following are the terms of the separate trust for the benefit of my son, STUART ALAN SELIGSON:

(A) During the lifetime of my son, my Trustees shall pay to him, or apply for his benefit, the entire net income in quarter annual or more frequent installments as may be convenient to my Trustees.

(B) In addition, my Trustees may at any one time or from time to time, and without regard to my son's assets or resources apart from this trust, pay to my son, or apply for his benefit, so much or all of the principal of this trust as my Trustees shall deem advisable for his support, maintenance and health, and to enable him to maintain his accustomed standard of living, even though any such distribution of principal may terminate this separate trust.

(C) Upon the death of my son, the then remaining principal of the trust, together with all accrued and undistributed income, shall be disposed of pursuant to paragraph "(A)" of Article EIGHTH of this Will on the basis of the facts then prevailing as though I had died immediately after my son.

Article EIGHTH is the residuary clause of the will, providing for Charles Seligson's daughter, her descendants, and other family members.

Petitioner received copies of the fiduciary income tax return of the Trust for the fiscal year ending October 31, 1986, an annual accounting, and a Schedule K-1, Beneficiary's Share of Income, Deductions, Credits, etc. According to these documents, as of the end of fiscal 1986, the Trust had undistributed income which was distributable to petitioner in the amount of $111,504.63.

Petitioner's Schedule K-1 and the Trust's annual accounting for fiscal 1986 reported the following amounts as distributable income to petitioner:

Dividends	$1,542
Interest	9,453
Total	$10,995

Accompanying these documents, petitioner received a letter dated March 2, 1987, from Samuel H. Laitman, acting on behalf of the Trust, informing petitioner that the Trust had on hand income of $111,504.63 which was distributable to him. The letter requested of petitioner: "Please advise me if you will accept distribution of this amount at this time and it will be remitted to you."

Petitioner has made no such requests for distributions. Petitioner received no distributions of income or principal from the Trust in 1986. Petitioner has not disclaimed, renounced, or assigned his rights in the Trust.

Respondent determined that petitioner is taxable on the income of the Trust. Her rationale was that the Trust is a simple trust, all of whose income is required to be distributed to petitioner. Petitioner's position is that the income is not taxable to him, as the Trust is a complex trust which accumulates income for unascertained beneficiaries. The determination of respondent is presumed to be correct, and petitioner bears the burden of proving respondent's determination to be erroneous. Rule 142(a); *Welch v. Helvering*, 290 U.S. 111 (1933).

Respondent's position is that, pursuant to the provisions of section 651(a), the Trust is a simple trust.... A trust to which section 651 applies, i.e., a trust which is required to distribute all of its income currently, which has no provisions for charitable contributions, and which makes no distributions which are not out of current income, is referred to as a "simple trust". Sec. 1.651(a)-1, Income Tax Regs.

[Sec. 1.651(a)-2(a), Income Tax Regs., explains] the meaning of section 651(a).... The regulations also state that a trust may be a simple trust for 1 year and a complex trust for another year. Sec. 1.651(a)-1, Income Tax Regs.

As a correlate of the provisions of section 651(a), providing a deduction to a trust for amounts required to be distributed currently, section 652(a) requires the beneficiary to include such amounts in his or her income.... Thus, a simple trust acts as a conduit: the income which is required to be distributed flows through the trust and is taxed to the beneficiary.

The terms of the Trust require that all income be distributed currently to petitioner. The will of Charles Seligson provides: "During the lifetime of my son, my Trustees *shall* pay to him, or apply for his benefit, the entire net income in quarter annual or more frequent installments." (Emphasis supplied.) The terms of the Trust also permit the trustees to make distributions of principal, but in 1986, no such distributions were made. The Trust makes no provision for charitable contributions. Hence, the Trust is a simple trust for tax year 1986. (The fiduciary income tax return of the Trust for fiscal year 1986 erroneously classified it as a complex trust; this error has no bearing upon our determination of the Trust's classification.)

Petitioner points to three cases in which income was held to be taxable to an entity (trust or estate) because the income was required to be accumulated and distributed in a later year. *Graham v. Miller*, 137 F.2d 507 (3d Cir. 1943); *Commissioner v. Dean*, 102 F.2d 699 (10th Cir. 1939), affg. 35 B.T.A. 839 (1937); *Eustis v. Commissioner*, 30 B.T.A. 820 (1934). These cases can be distinguished because all dealt with entities whose terms differed from those of the Trust in that they were required to accumulate some or all of their income and distribute it in a later year. Hence, these entities would now be classified as complex trusts under the second-to-last sentence of section 1.651(a)-2(a), Income Tax Regs.... We also note that the cases upon which petitioner relies were decided before the enactment of the Internal Revenue Code of 1939, and well before the adoption of the current regulations.

In two of the cases cited by petitioner, the beneficiaries for whom income was accumulated were found to be unascertained at the date on which the amount of distributable income was determined. *Graham v. Miller, supra; Eustis v. Commissioner, supra*. Petitioner argues that at the time of his death the undistributed income of the Trust is not payable to his estate, but is to be distributed under the residuary clause of his father's will to beneficiaries who are not currently ascertainable. Hence, petitioner argues, the Trust is a complex trust.

Petitioner ignores [the fourth sentence of] section 1.651(a)-1, Income Tax Regs.... The Trust may indeed become a complex trust in the year of petitioner's death or under other circumstances about which the Court may only speculate. This possibility is provided for in section 1.651(a)-2(c), Income Tax Regs....

For the year in question, the trustees of the Trust were required to distribute all income currently, and they made no principal distributions or charitable distributions. Hence, we find that, for that year, the Trust was a simple trust and petitioner was required to include in his gross income the income currently distributable to him from the Trust. Sec. 652(a).

* * *

Decision will be entered for respondent.

Illustrative Material

1. The distribution deduction, allowed by either section 651 or section 661, and the allocation of entity income to beneficiaries, required by either section 652 or section 662, are the centerpieces of subchapter J. They determine the extent to which entities are conduits, rather than full-fledged taxpayers. Sections 651 and 652 apply to "simple trusts," and sections 661 and 662 apply to "complex trusts" (and estates). Neither term appears in the Code, but both appear in the regulations. *See, e.g.,* Treas. Reg. §1.651(a)-1.

2. A "simple trust" is one that meets the specifications of section 651(a). First, the trust instrument must require that all of the trust income be distributed currently. Second, the trust must not pay, permanently set aside, or use any amount for charitable purposes.

Third, the trust must distribute current income only. All trusts that are not "simple trusts" are "complex trusts" and are subject to sections 661 and 662.

3. Section 651(a) allows a deduction for income "required to be distributed currently." Section 652(a) subjects a beneficiary to taxation on amounts "required to be distributed, whether distributed or not." Thus, a beneficiary entitled to receive trust income is subject to taxation on that income even if it is erroneously distributed to someone else. *Estate of James Max Harrison*, 62 T.C. 524 (1974), *acq.*, 1974-2 C.B. 2. Since the beneficiary is entitled to the income, the beneficiary can force the trustee to pay him or her the income in question, notwithstanding the prior erroneous distribution.

Rev. Rul. 75-68, 1975-1 C.B. 184, illustrates the apparent inevitability of the operation of sections 651 and 652 if income is required to be distributed currently. A trust was required to pay all of its income to a beneficiary, who was the owner of property on which the trust held mortgage notes. The trustee agreed with the owner that the owner would pay no interest on the notes and that, because there would therefore be no trust income, the trustee would pay the owner-beneficiary no income. Nevertheless, the I.R.S. ruled that the trust was required to include in its gross income the interest due on the notes, and the beneficiary was subject to taxation on the amount of income that, in the absence of the agreement, would have been distributed to him. The trust was presumably entitled to an offsetting distribution deduction under section 651, and the owner of the mortgaged property was presumably entitled to an offsetting interest deduction under the version of section 163 then in effect.

A literal reading of sections 651 and 652 suggests that they apply even if a trustee withholds distribution of a beneficiary's income because of doubts concerning the beneficiary's entitlement to it. In fact, according to several courts, if a trustee withholds distribution of a beneficiary's income pending termination of litigation concerning the beneficiary's entitlement to that income, the trust is nevertheless entitled to a distribution deduction, and the beneficiary is subject to taxation on the trust's income. This is true, for example, if the dispute concerns the allocation of certain receipts between principal and income. *DeBrabant v. Commissioner*, 90 F.2d 433 (2d Cir. 1937). It is also true if the dispute concerns validity of the trust under the rule against perpetuities. *United States v. Higginson*, 238 F.2d 439 (1st Cir. 1956). In Rev. Rul. 62-147, 1962-2 C.B. 151, the I.R.S. announced it would follow *DeBrabant* and *Higginson*, both of which construed pre-1954 law, in dealing with sections 651 and 652. The I.R.S. explained: "[T]he determination of whether trust income … is required to be distributed currently depends upon the terms of the trust instrument and the applicable local law.… The fact that the trustee does not comply with such terms, therefore, is not decisive of the question whether trust income is distributable currently."

On the other hand, if the outcome of litigation concerning a beneficiary's entitlement to trust income results in entitlement to less than the amount he or she appeared entitled to at the time the income tax returns were filed, the beneficiary is required to include in income only the lesser amount. *Freuler v. Helvering*, 291 U.S. 35 (1934). (An amended return reporting only the lesser amount would be in order.) Presumably, the trust's distribution deduction similarly would decrease. Though the language of the Supreme Court in *Freuler* construed pre-1954 law, it seems equally appropriate under sections 651 and 652:

> [T]he fiduciary may be required to accumulate [income]; or, on the other hand, he may be under a duty currently to distribute it. If the latter, then the scheme of the Act is to treat the amount so distributable, not as the trust's income, but as the beneficiary's. But as the tax on the entire net income of the trust is to be

paid by the fiduciary or the beneficiaries, or partly by each, the beneficiary's share of the income is considered his property from the moment of its receipt by the [trust]. This treatment of the beneficiary's income is necessary to prevent the possibility of postponement of the tax to a year subsequent to that in which the income was received by the trustee. If it were not for this provision the trustee might pay on part of the income in one year and the beneficiary on the remainder in a later year. For the purpose of imposing the tax, the Act regards ownership, the right of property in the beneficiary, as equivalent to physical possession. The test of taxability to the beneficiary is not receipt of income, but the present right to receive it. Clearly, an overpayment to a beneficiary by mistake of law or fact, would render him liable for the taxable year under consideration, not on the amount paid, but on that payable. If the trustee should have deducted a sum for depreciation from the year's gross income before ascertaining the amount distributable to [the beneficiary], but failed to do so, he paid [the beneficiary] more than was properly distributable for the taxable year. Both the language used and its aptness to effect the obvious scheme for the division of tax between the [trust] and the beneficiary seem so plain as not to require construction.

291 U.S. at 41–42.

Estate of Mildred Bruchmann
53 T.C. 403 (1969)

TIETJENS, *Judge*: We must decide whether [Mildred Bruchmann] was taxable in the years 1949 through 1955 on certain trust income which was not distributed until 1962, after a judicial determination that she was an income beneficiary of the trust....

Mildred Bruchmann, nee Ann Mildred Anderson, was legally adopted by Phillip Bruchmann and his wife Elizabeth on October 9, 1912. In 1949, Mildred Bruchmann was adjudicated an incompetent. In 1952, the petitioner was appointed conservator of her estate and acted in such capacity until her death on April 11, 1959. On or about May 5, 1959, the petitioner was granted a letter of administration as administrator of the Estate of Mildred Bruchmann and is the duly qualified and presently acting administrator of the estate.

On July 21, 1922, John Brockman, hereinafter referred to as the settlor, an uncle of Phillip Bruchmann, established a trust with the Security Trust & Savings Bank of Los Angeles, Calif., the successor of which is hereinafter referred to as the trustee. The settler reserved a life estate in the trust property and the right to revoke the trust during his lifetime. The settlor died on March 29, 1925.

Under the terms of the trust, after the settlor's death, the trust property was to be disposed of in various ways. Since we are only concerned with the disposition in trust of a portion of the trust property, we will hereinafter refer to such disposition in trust as the trust and the property subject to such trust as the trust property.

Upon the settlor's death, the trust property was to be held for 24 nieces and nephews of the settlor. Phillip Bruchmann was one of the nephew beneficiaries of the trust. The trustee was to pay the net income of the trust in equal shares to the nieces and nephews quarterly each year. Upon the death of a nephew, his share of the trust income was to be paid to his widow for as long as such widow remained alive and unmarried. Upon the death or remarriage of the widow, the nephew's share of the trust income was to be paid to his "issue." Upon the death of all of the nieces and nephews, the trust was to terminate and the corpus and all undistributed net income were to be distributed to the surviving "lawful issue of the bodies" of the nieces and nephews.

Phillip Bruchmann died on September 19, 1940, and was survived by his widow, Elizabeth Bruchmann, and his daughter, Mildred Bruchmann. Elizabeth Bruchmann died, not having remarried, on July 6, 1949, survived by Mildred Bruchmann. Except for one child who died in infancy, Phillip Bruchmann had no other children, either natural or adopted, except for Mildred Bruchmann.

In 1952, the trustee instituted suit in the Superior Court of the State of California, County of Los Angeles, for declaratory and other relief respecting the trust. One of the questions raised by the trustee was whether adopted children were to be considered as "issue" and "lawful issue of the body" for purposes of the trust. The petitioner, as conservator of the Estate of Mildred Bruchmann, filed an answer requesting the court to find in the affirmative with respect to the above question. The effect of such a finding would have been that Mildred Bruchmann was an income beneficiary of the trust and was capable of becoming a residuary beneficiary when all the nieces and nephews had died.

On July 13, 1956, the court entered its findings of fact and conclusions of law determining that, for purposes of the trust, adopted children should be considered as "issue" but not as "lawful issue of the body." The effect of these holdings was to make Mildred Bruchmann an income beneficiary of the trust but to deny her any chance of becoming a residuary beneficiary.

During the years 1949 through 1955, the trustee impounded Mildred Bruchmann's distributive share of the trust income.... In 1962, after the time for appeal in the California litigation expired, the trustee distributed $23,573.92 to the Estate of Mildred Bruchmann. This amount represented the income that accrued to Mildred Bruchmann from 1949 through 1955....

The ... issue for decision is whether Mildred Bruchmann was taxable in the years 1949 through 1955 on her share of the income earned by the trust in those years, even though it was not distributed by the trust until 1962.

* * *

Section 641 makes clear that all the income of the trust is subject to taxation, including that which is accumulated and that which is currently distributable. Without doubt, the income of the trust which was set aside for Miss Bruchmann was includable in the trust's income under section 641. The real issue in the case is whether the tax burden on such income is to be borne by the trust or whether it can be shifted to the beneficiary, and the answer to that question depends upon whether the trust is entitled to a deduction for such income. The language of section 641 has no relevancy in answering that question. Rather, the answer depends upon whether such income is "required to be distributed currently" within the meaning of section 651. Manifestly the terms of the trust provide that all of its income is required to be distributed currently. There is no suggestion in this case that resort to local law for construction of the trust terms could result in any determination other than a finding that the income was required to be distributed currently, either to Mildred Bruchmann or to the other income beneficiaries. On the other hand, the trustee during the taxable years in question was uncertain as to whether Mildred Bruchmann was entitled to receive a share in the income or whether the other income beneficiaries were entitled to receive such share. Accordingly, under State law, until he could secure an interpretation of the trust instrument, the trustee could not be compelled to distribute the income either to Mildred Bruchmann or to the other income beneficiaries. Bogert,

Trust and Trustees, sec. 814 (2d ed. 1962); 2 Scott, Trusts, sec. 182 (3d ed. 1967). See also *Feldmeier v. Superior Court,* 12 Cal. 2d 302, 83 P. 2d 929 (1938). Instead he impounded the income awaiting determination of Mildred Bruchmann's claim to it.

We hold the trust income was, nevertheless, "required to be distributed currently" within the meaning of section 651, entitling the trust to a deduction therefor, and within the meaning of section 652(a), causing the income to be taxable to the beneficiary (Mildred Bruchmann) to whom the income was required to be distributed. The statutory scheme we are dealing with is one for the allocation of the tax burden as between the trust on the one hand and its income beneficiaries on the other. It distinguishes between income which is to be distributed currently (whether distributed or not), on the one hand, and income which may be accumulated in trust on the other. This allocation may safely be made and the trust be shown entitled to the deduction provided by section 651 when the terms of the trust provide that all of its income is to be distributed currently and there is no provision for accumulation. That is the case we have before us. In fact the income in this case was impounded, awaiting actual distribution to the income beneficiaries entitled to receive it. The income was "out of the trust," and it seems reasonable that the trust should be allowed the deduction. At the same time, the statutory scheme clearly contemplates that the income is to be taxable to somebody in the years it is received. Section 652 taxes such income to the beneficiaries to whom it is required to be distributed, whether distributed or not. The subsequent determination of her claim established that Mildred Bruchmann was such a beneficiary. We hold the income was taxable to her in the years it was required to be distributed to her.

We think this conclusion is dictated by the holdings of *Mary Clark DeBrabant,* 34 B.T.A. 951 (1936), affd. 90 F. 2d 433 (C.A. 2, 1937); *Estate of Robert A. Dula,* 23 T.C. 646 (1955), affirmed sub nom. *Polt v. Commissioner,* 233 F. 2d 893 (C.A. 2, 1956); and *United States v. Higginson,* 238 F. 2d 439 [(C.A. 1, 1956)], which we follow. The reasoning of those cases is clear and can be gained from the reading. It need not be repeated here....

RAUM, *J.*, dissenting: I agree with the conclusions in Judge Simpson's opinion ... which are underscored by the dilemma with which the beneficiary would be faced annually at the time of filing her return during the long period of years when the matter of her right to trust income was in litigation. It seems highly unlikely to me that she was required by statute to guess at the future outcome of that litigation, and to report annually the income which was not in fact distributed to her at that time, and where her right thereto was open to serious doubt in the pending litigation....

SIMPSON, *J.*, dissenting: ...

I am aware that the majority's conclusion ... is supported by prior decisions of this and other courts. *United States v. Higginson,* 238 F. 2d 439 (C.A. 1, 1956); *Estate of Robert L. Dula,* 23 T.C. 646 (1955), affirmed sub nom. *Polt v. Commissioner,* 233 F. 2d 893 (C.A. 2, 1956); *Robert F. Chapman,* 3 T.C. 708 (1944); *F. T. Bedford,* 2 T.C. 1189 (1943), affd. 150 F. 2d 341 (C.A. 2, 1945); *Thalia W. Malcom,* 36 B.T.A. 358 (1937), affd. 97 F. 2d 381 (C.A. 2, 1938). Although no judge should lightly cast aside the accumulated wisdom of precedent, it is also true, as stated by Justice Brandeis, that "*Stare decisis* is not, like the rule of *res judicata,* a universal, inexorable command." *Burnet v. Coronado Oil & Gas Co.,* 285 U.S. 393, 405 (1932). In my judgment, this case presents one of those situations in which the rule of stare decisis should not be applied.

In *Mary Clark DeBrabant,* 34 B.T.A. 951 (1936), affd. 90 F. 2d 433 (C.A. 2, 1937), Mrs. DeBrabant was the beneficiary of a trust and, under the trust instrument, was entitled to have trust income distributed to her currently. However, in 1930, the trustee withheld from her certain distributions which it received on corporate stock because it believed that such distributions constituted principal and not income. In 1933, Mrs. De-Brabant obtained an adjudication by the New Jersey courts that all of the distributions were income, and such income was thereupon distributed to her. Both the Board of Tax Appeals and the Court of Appeals for the Second Circuit held that all the income was taxable to Mrs. DeBrabant in 1930. The Second Circuit said at 90 F. 2d 435:

> The question before us is whether the income received by the trustee in 1930, which the New Jersey Court of Chancery held to belong to the taxpayer, was: "Income accumulated in trust for the benefit of * * * unascertained persons, * * * and income held for future distributions under the terms of the * * * trust," in which case it was taxable against the trustee, or whether it was "income * * * to be distributed currently by the fiduciary to the beneficiaries," in which case it was deductible by the trustee in its return but to be "included in computing the net income" of the beneficiary and taxable against her.

> It seems evident that the income of any trust which under the terms of the trust instrument is made payable to a life beneficiary is "to be distributed currently by the fiduciary," but that it was to be thus distributed here is especially plain because of the direction in the trust deed that "all payments of income hereunder shall be made on the second days of January and July in each and every year." We are satisfied that the instrument specifically provides for current distributions of income and can nowhere find in it even a suggestion of an accumulation of income "for the benefit of * * * unascertained persons." The clause of section 161(a)(1) of the Revenue Act of 1928 (26 U.S.C.A. §161 and note) which refers to accumulations of income for "unascertained persons" indicates the sort of persons contemplated when it uses the words "unborn" and "with contingent interests" to describe the class it has in mind. Thus under the rule of "ejusdem generis," as well as by reason of the almost inevitable meaning of the words "unascertained persons," reference is made to those whose identification depends on future contingencies rather than on a correct understanding of the application of the law to existing facts.

A careful examination of the reasoning in this case convinces me that there are several objections to the Court's conclusion.

The principal objection to the *DeBrabant* rule is that it is based upon an untenable interpretation of the statute. In *DeBrabant,* the trust instrument apparently made no express provision for the trustee to withhold income when he was in doubt as to whether a beneficiary was entitled to it, and the court appears to have based its decision on the lack of such a provision in the trust instrument. However, section 1.651(a)-2, Income Tax Regs., provides in part: "The determination of whether trust income is required to be distributed currently depends upon the terms of the trust instrument and the applicable local law." Almost identical language appears in the committee reports accompanying the enactment of section 651, and those reports indicate that such rule is merely the continuation of the rule previously established. H. Rept. No. 1337, to accompany H.R. 8300 (Pub. L. 591), 83d Cong., 2d Sess., p. 61, A196 (1954); S. Rept. No. 1622, to accompany H.R. 8300 (Pub. L. 591), 83d Cong., 2d Sess., p. 84, 345 (1954); *Smith's Estate v. Commissioner,* 168 F. 2d 431 (C.A. 6, 1948); *Hale v. Anglim,* 140 F. 2d 235 (C.A. 9, 1944); *Letts v. Commissioner,* 84 F. 2d 760 (C.A. 9, 1936); *Horace Greeley Hill, Jr.,* 24 T.C. 1133 (1955).

Under local law, when a trustee, acting in good faith, is uncertain as to whether a beneficiary is entitled to income, he may seek an interpretation of the governing trust instrument, and until he secures such an interpretation, he is not required to distribute the income. Such actions on his part are consistent with his fiduciary responsibility, and no penalty will be imposed upon him for his failure to distribute the income in controversy. Bogert, Trust and Trustees, sec. 814 (2d ed. 1962); 2 Scott, Trusts, sec. 182 (3d ed. 1967). See also *Feldmeier v. Superior Court*, 12 Cal. 2d 302, 83 P. 2d 929 (1938). Thus, although the Brockman trust instrument included no express authorization for the trustee to withhold income, it was, as a matter of local law, not required to distribute the income to Miss Bruchmann during the years 1949 through 1955. Her right to the income during those years was no greater than what it would have been had the trust instrument expressly authorized the trustee to accumulate the income under these circumstances. In my opinion, the *DeBrabant* holding is inconsistent with the statute in failing to inquire into local law and in failing to recognize that the trustee was not required to distribute the income.

In *Horace Greeley Hill, Jr., supra*, this Court did consider the effect of local law. We said at page 1138:

> In order that income be currently distributable within the meaning of section 162(b), the person or persons to whom such income is so distributable must have a present, enforceable, vested right to such income. * * * This right must be clear, and not subject to any condition as to its enforceability. The mere right to apply to a court of competent jurisdiction to compel distribution, where it is possible, but not clear, that such application would be granted, is not equivalent to a present enforceable right. * * *

Clearly, Miss Bruchmann had no such enforceable right. During the years 1949 through 1955, she had merely a hope that the trust instrument would be construed so as to include her as an income beneficiary. However, there existed the possibility that the term "issue" might be construed to exclude adopted children, and in that event, she would receive none of the trust income. Hence, it is anomalous to say that the trust income was required to be distributed to her in the years in issue.

Another criticism of the *DeBrabant* holding is that it rests in part upon an unsound application of language contained in *Freuler v. Helvering*, 291 U.S. 35, 42 (1934). In *Freuler*, the Supreme Court said that "The test of taxability to the beneficiary is not receipt of income, but the present right to receive it," and this statement was relied upon by *DeBrabant* to tax the beneficiary on income which she had not received. However, in *Freuler*, the beneficiaries had received more than they were entitled to, and the question was whether they were taxable on the entire amount that they had in hand, or only on the amount to which they were entitled. The Court held that the tax was limited to the amount to which they were entitled.

Although the language quoted from *Freuler* appears to apply to the *DeBrabant* problem, the issues are significantly different. The language was used to justify taxing beneficiaries on only that income received by them to which they had a right; it is not at all clear that the Supreme Court would have applied the same test to a beneficiary who claimed a right but who possessed nothing.

For the beneficiary, the *DeBrabant* rule results in tax consequences that are inconsistent with general principles of taxation. Under *DeBrabant*, a beneficiary is taxed because he has a so-called right, although in fact all that he has is a mere claim to income. His claim is quite different than the fixed right which is taxable to a taxpayer using the accrual method of accounting. See secs. 1.446-1(c)(1)(ii), 1.451-1(a), Income Tax Regs.; *Boston Elevated Railway Co.*, 16 T.C. 1084, 1104–1105 (1951), affd. 196 F. 2d 923 (C.A. 1, 1952); *Cold Metal Process Co.*, 17 T.C. 916, 932 (1951). Nor is the beneficiary like a taxpayer who has received a corporate distribution which may be a taxable dividend or a nontaxable return of capital. See *Lou Levy,* 30 T.C. 1315, 1328 (1958). Such a taxpayer has something in hand which may be taxable in some manner, but the beneficiary has received nothing.

Nor can the *DeBrabant* rule be justified as the most workable interpretation of the statute; on the contrary, it results in administrative problems for the beneficiary, the trustee, and the Government. While the right to the income is being adjudicated, the taxable years of the beneficiary and the trust may be kept open so that appropriate adjustments may be made when the litigation is concluded, but that course may postpone for a number of years the final accounting for the years to which the income is attributable and subject to [sic] the beneficiary and the trust to liability for interest on underpayments of tax. On the other hand, the trustee and the beneficiary must act at their peril, if they act without awaiting the final settlement of the controversy. In addition, this case illustrates well the plight of a beneficiary who seeks to follow *DeBrabant.* If Miss Bruchmann's share of the income had been reported each year, with what was the tax to be paid? During the years 1949 through 1955, all that she had was a hope that the court would eventually determine that she was entitled to a share of the trust income, but it is doubtful that the respondent would accept that hope as currency for the payment of the tax.

Although this Court has followed *DeBrabant,* it has narrowly restricted its applicability. Prior to *DeBrabant,* it was held that a claimant was not taxable on income which was withheld from him pending an adjudication of his right to it. *Ferguson v. Forstmann,* 25 F. 2d 47 (C.A. 3, 1928); *Commissioner v. Owens,* 78 F. 2d 768 (C.A. 10, 1935). *DeBrabant* distinguished such cases on the basis that they did not involve express trusts. Cases arising after *DeBrabant* have not applied its holding when the years in which the income was earned were closed by the statute of limitations, when an estate rather than a trust was involved, and when the beneficiary was unaware of his claim to the income. *Mary DeF. Harrison Geary,* 9 T.C. 8 (1947); *Horace Greeley Hill, Jr., supra; Ralph E. Hedges,* 18 T.C. 681 (1952), affirmed per curiam 212 F. 2d 593 (C.A. 9, 1954). See also Surrey & Warren, Federal Income Taxation 901–902 (1962); Moore & Sorlien, "Homeless Income," 8 Tax. L. Rev. 425 (1953). There are no sound reasons for distinguishing these cases from *DeBrabant.* It is difficult to see how the existence, or nonexistence, of an express trust should affect the taxability of a claimant to income which is withheld from him because of a dispute over his right to it. Nor is there any reason for applying a different rule when the statute of limitations has run, or when an estate is involved (since the same statutory provisions are applicable to estates and trusts), or when the claimant is unaware of his rights to the income. The reluctance to apply the *DeBrabant* rule more broadly must reflect an inherent dissatisfaction with the consequences of such rule.

Although I am reluctant to disagree with the earlier decisions of this and other courts, I am convinced that on this occasion, we should decline to follow those decisions. For us to apply such rule once more would merely breathe additional life into a rule that lacks justification and would compound the difficulty of bringing about its demise. The objections to the *DeBrabant* rule lead me to conclude that it is clearly wrong. In addition, the impracticability of the rule has frequently led to its challenge by both taxpayers and the respondent; the courts, for their part, have drawn questionable distinctions in order to avoid having to apply the rule. See, e.g., *United States v. Higginson, supra; Estate of Robert L. Dula, supra; Mary DeF. Harrison Geary, supra;* Rev. Rul. 62-147, 1962-2 C.B. 151; I.T. 1733, II-2 C.B. 169 (1923). Thus, the *DeBrabant* holding, despite the time that has passed, has not succeeded in settling the controversy. In these circumstances, I believe that we should recognize *DeBrabant* to be a mistake made by the courts, which can and should be corrected by the courts. See Final Report on Estates, Trusts, Beneficiaries, and Decedents from the Advisory Group on Subchapter J of the Internal Revenue Code of 1954, p. 41 (1958).

* * *

Revenue Ruling 85-116
1985-2 C.B. 174

ISSUE

Under the circumstances below, is any portion of a capital gain realized by a trust that is allocated to trust income under state law deductible by the trust and includible by the income beneficiary of the trust in the taxable year the gain is realized?

FACTS

T is a trust established in 1977 under A's will for the benefit of A's family. The terms of the trust instrument require that all trust income be paid out currently to A's child B for life. A's grandchildren are the remaindermen. T was funded exclusively with all the shares of X, a closely held corporation that A founded. In 1979, X adopted a plan of liquidation and sold all of its assets. In 1980, the proceeds of the sale in the amount of $390x$ dollars were distributed to T in complete liquidation of X.

Under the law of state V which is applicable to T, a portion of the proceeds of any transaction with respect to underproductive property, that is, trust property that has not produced for more than a year an average net annual income of one percent of its cost or value when acquired by the trust, is treated as "delayed income" which, in the absence of trust provisions to the contrary, is allocated to trust income rather than principal. The portion of the proceeds that is treated as delayed income is the difference between the proceeds and the amount which, had it been invested at five percent annually during the time the property was underproductive, would have produced the proceeds, less any income received by the beneficiary during that time. The balance is treated as principal. The trust instrument is silent concerning the allocation of the sale proceeds to trust income or principal.

The trustee of T allocated the liquidating distribution from X to principal and petitioned the state surrogate's court for approval of that action. T made no distribution to any beneficiary in 1980. In 1981, the court ordered that a portion of the liquidating distribution should be allocated to T's income account as delayed income because the X stock was underproductive property. In that year, after appropriately adjusting the books of T to reflect the allocation, the trustee made a distribution to B in the amount of $91x$ dollars, which was the amount of delayed income ordered by the court to be allocated to T's income account.

Both T and B file income tax returns on the calendar year basis. On its 1980 fiduciary income tax return, T reported a capital gain of $30x$ dollars as a result of the liquidation of X. B did not include any of the capital gain on B's individual income tax return for 1980 or for 1981.

LAW AND ANALYSIS

Section 651 of the Internal Revenue Code provides that, in the case of any trust the terms of which (1) provide that all of its income is required to be distributed currently, and (2) do not provide that any amounts are to be paid, permanently set aside, or used for the purposes specified in section 642(c) (relating to the deduction for charitable, etc., purposes), there shall be allowed as a deduction in computing the taxable income of the trust the amount of the income for the taxable year which is required to be distributed currently. If the amount of the income required to be distributed currently exceeds the distributable net income of the trust for the taxable year, the deduction shall be limited to the amount of the distributable net income.

Section 652 of the Code provides that the amount of income for the taxable year required to be distributed currently by a trust described in section 651 shall be included in the gross income of the beneficiaries to whom the income is required to be distributed, whether distributed or not. If that amount exceeds the distributable net income of the trust, there shall be included in the gross income of each beneficiary an amount which bears the same ratio to distributable net income as the amount of income required to be distributed to that beneficiary bears to the amount of income required to be distributed to all beneficiaries. The amount which the beneficiary is required to include in gross income is based upon the amount of income of the trust for any taxable year or years of the trust ending within or with the beneficiary's taxable year.

Income received by a trust that is required to be distributed currently to a beneficiary is taxable to the beneficiary in the taxable year of the beneficiary ending within or with the taxable year of the trust in which the income is received, even though the beneficiary receives the income at a later time due to the trustee's erroneous belief that the receipt constituted corpus and not income. *DeBrabant v. Commissioner,* 90 F. 2d 433 (2d Cir. 1937). *See, Polt v. Commissioner,* 233 F. 2d 893 (2d Cir. 1956); *United States v. Higginson,* 238 F. 2d 439 (1st Cir. 1956); Rev. Rul. 62-147, 1962-2 C.B. 151.

Section 643(a) of the Code defines distributable net income to mean the taxable income of the trust computed with the modifications set forth in section 643(a)(1) through [(7)]. Section 643(a)(3) provides that gains from the sale or exchange of capital assets are excluded to the extent that such gains are allocated to corpus and are not (A) paid, credited, or required to be distributed to any beneficiary during the taxable year, or (B) paid, permanently set aside, or to be used for the purposes specified in section 642(c).

[Former section] 1.643(a)-3(a)(1) of the Income Tax Regulations provides that gains from the sale or exchange of capital assets are not ordinarily considered as paid, credited or required to be distributed to a beneficiary unless they are (1) allocated to income under the terms of the governing instrument or local law by the fiduciary on its books or by notice to the beneficiary, (2) allocated to corpus and actually distributed to beneficiaries during the taxable year, or (3) utilized (pursuant to the terms of the governing instrument or the practice followed by the fiduciary) in determining the amount which is distributed or required to be distributed.

Section 643(b) of the Code provides that for purposes of subparts A through D of subchapter J of the Code (sections 641 through 668 of the Code), the term "income," when not preceded by the words "taxable," "distributable net," "undistributed net," or "gross," means the amount of income of the trust for the taxable year determined under the terms of the governing instrument and applicable local law.

In the present case, the trust realized a capital gain in 1980 on the liquidation of X corporation. Under applicable local law, the law of state V, $91x$ dollars of the amount received by T in 1980 was treated as income and, therefore, was "income" within the meaning of section 643(b) of the Code. Under the terms of the trust instrument, all trust income was required to be distributed currently to B. Accordingly, under section 651, T is allowed a deduction in computing its taxable income for 1980 for the amount of income required to be distributed currently to *B*, limited to the distributable net income of *T*. Under section 652, *B* is required to include in gross income for 1980 an amount equal to the amount deductible by the trust under section 651. This is so despite the fact that the 91*x* dollars was not distributed to *B* until 1981. *DeBrabant v. Commissioner.*

To the extent that capital gains are allocated to income, they are included in computing distributable net income for purposes of section 651 of the Code. [Former section] 1.643(a)-3(a)(1) of the regulations. In this case, 91/390 of the proceeds received by *T* is allocated to income under the law of state *V*. Therefore, a proportionate part of the capital gain realized by *T*, 7*x* dollars (91/390 x 30*x* dollars), is considered allocated to income and hence includible in the computation of distributable net income. *See,* example 5 of [former] section 1.643(a)-3(d), showing that where half the proceeds of the sale of stock by a trustee was distributed to a beneficiary, half the capital gain is considered allocable to the beneficiary.

HOLDING

The 91*x* dollars of delayed income constitutes trust income required to be distributed to *B* in 1980. The total amount of trust income required to be distributed to *B* in 1980 is included in *B*'s gross income for that year, and is allowed as a deduction to *T*, to the extent this amount does not exceed *T*'s distributable net income for 1980. *T*'s distributable net income for that year includes 7*x* dollars of the capital gain *T* realized on the liquidation of *X*.

Illustrative Material

1. As discussed *supra,* in section B of this chapter, Treas. Reg. § 1.643(a)-3 was substantially revised in 2003. The result in Revenue Ruling 85-116, however, seems consistent with the current regulations. *See* Treas. Reg. § 1.643(a)-3(b)(1).

2. In *Plunkett v. Commissioner,* 118 F.2d 644 (1st Cir. 1941), a trustee, in the course of surcharge litigation, reimbursed its trust in the amount of $500,000 on account of improper nonincome-producing investments. Later, in 1934, a state court held that $70,000 of the $500,000 was income payable to the trust's income beneficiary on account of income lost as a result of the trustee's improper investments during the period 1930–1934. The income beneficiary did not, however, receive the entire $70,000 until 1935. The First Circuit nevertheless held that the entire $70,000 was includible in the income beneficiary's gross income in 1934 under a predecessor of section 652(a). Similarly, in *Polt v. Commissioner,* 233 F.2d 893 (2d Cir. 1956), a trustee allocated an undivided interest in certain bonds and mortgages to the income beneficiary pursuant to the requirement of local law that principal reimburse income when nonincome-producing assets were disposed of. The allocations occurred in 1945 on account of years 1933–1944. However, the income beneficiary received no property on account of the allocation until a local court approved the allocations in 1947. The Second Circuit held that the entire amount of the allocations was includible in the income beneficiary's gross income in 1945, the year they were made (but not paid) by the trustee. The court wrote:

> [T]ax consequences to the beneficiaries cannot be determined by the timing of payment over by the trustee, even though he may be guided by an honest ... interpretation of the state law. ... Income of a trust distributable to a beneficiary is taxable to the beneficiary, even though the trustee refuses to distribute it pending court approval of his action.

Id. at 896–97.

In *Myers v. Commissioner*, T.C. Summ. Op. 2005–15 (2005), the Tax Court held that the beneficiary of a simple trust was required to report all of the trust's income, notwith-standing the fact that the corporate trustee, which was in the process of winding up the trust, had not yet distributed all of the income.

3. On the other hand, only amounts of "income … required to be distributed currently" are includible in the gross income of the beneficiary. Such amounts are deter-mined under the trust instrument and local law. Thus, if a beneficiary entitled to receive all of a trust's income is required to return to the trustee amounts already distributed, only the net amount to which the beneficiary is entitled is includible in his or her gross income. *Commissioner v. Pearson*, 154 F.2d 256 (3d Cir. 1946); *Saltonstall v. Hassett*, 32 F. Supp. 583 (D. Mass. 1940). Dividends declared on corporate shares owned by a trust but paid, pursuant to judicial decree, to a creditor of the trust's grantor are not taxable to the beneficiaries of the trust. *Harry Makransky*, 36 T.C. 446 (1961), *acq.*, 1966-2 C.B. 6, *aff'd*, 321 F.2d 598 (3d Cir. 1963). Similarly, income derived from es-tate assets that have been used to pay debts, taxes, administration expenses, and gen-eral bequests is not income "required to be distributed" to the beneficiaries of simple trusts receiving residuary distributions from the estate if, as is usually the case, the gov-erning instrument or local law permits or requires such income to be added to corpus. *Baldwin v. United States*, 214 F. Supp. 16 (E.D. Mo. 1962). And, of course, if a state court has ordered the trustee to accumulate all of the trust income, none of the trust bene-ficiaries are subject to taxation, regardless of what the governing instrument says. *Stein-gold v. Commissioner*, 80 T.C.M. (CCH) 95 (2000), *aff'd per curiam*, 13 Fed. Appx. 209 (4th Cir. 2001).

4. *Mismatched Taxable Years.*

a. *In general.* Section 652(c) states that the amount of income the beneficiary of a sim-ple trust is required to include in gross income "shall be based upon the amount of in-come of the trust for any taxable year or years of the trust ending within or with his taxable year." Thus, prior to enactment of section 644, if a trust was on a January 31 fis-cal year, for example, a calendar-year beneficiary did not report income that, for the most part, was earned by the trust during Calendar Year #1 until the beneficiary filed an indi-vidual return for Calendar Year #2—on April 15th of Calendar Year #3. Conversely, a calendar-year beneficiary calculated his or her tax for Calendar Year #2 by reference to the trust's income for all of its fiscal year ending on January 31st (of Calendar Year #2), regardless of the fact that the beneficiary may actually have received a much smaller amount from the trust during Calendar Year #2. *See Dunbaugh v. Commissioner*, 48 T.C.M. (CCH) 485 (1984).

The possibilities for tax deferral under section 652(c) resulted, prior to enactment of section 644, in the selection by most trusts of fiscal years ending shortly after the taxable years of their calendar-year beneficiaries ended. Thus, many trusts had fiscal years end-ing January 31. Section 644, enacted by the Tax Reform Act of 1986, now requires almost all trusts to be calendar-year taxpayers. As a result, section 652(c) is much less frequently applicable. One of its continuing applications is with respect to fiscal-year beneficiaries, a rather rare commodity. Given the current unavailability of mismatching through cre-ation of fiscal-year trusts, should estate planners seek to achieve the benefits of mis-matching through creation of fiscal-year beneficiaries? In particular, should estate planners advise that children who are likely to be beneficiaries of substantial trusts begin their tax-paying lives as fiscal-year taxpayers with years ending, for example, on November 30? In any event, the possibility of mismatching is very much alive and well with respect to estates, to which section 644 does not apply. Estates are not subject to section 652(c); they are governed by the virtually identical section 662(c) instead.

In the Taxpayer Relief Act of 1997, Congress enacted section 645, which provides an election to treat the decedent's revocable trust as part of the decedent's estate, rather than as a separate trust, for most income tax purposes. If no estate tax return is due, this consolidation is effective for only two years after the decedent's death. If an estate tax return is due, the consolidation generally remains effective until six months after the final determination of the estate tax liability. During the election period, such a trust can utilize a fiscal year. *See* Treas. Reg. §§ 1.645-1(e)(2)(i) & (ii), 1.645-1(e)(3)(i).

b. *Death of beneficiary.* Rev. Rul. 59-346, 1959-2 C.B. 165, held that all income earned by a simple trust prior to the death of its accrual-method beneficiary was reportable on the beneficiary's final income tax return. With respect to cash-method beneficiaries, Treas. Reg. §1.652(c)-2 provides a very different rule. If the trust's taxable year does not end at the death of the beneficiary, the only trust income reportable on the beneficiary's final return with respect to that year is the amount of "income actually distributed to the beneficiary before his death." (The rest of the trust income earned prior to the beneficiary's death is reportable by the beneficiary's estate.) Prior to enactment of section 644, this rule sometimes resulted in serious bunching of income on decedents' final returns. For example, a trust could have a taxable year ending January 31. If the beneficiary died on November 29, the income reportable on her final return included not only the trust's income for its taxable year ending January 31 (pursuant to section 652(c)), but also all trust income received by her during the period January 31 through November 29. On just such facts, *Schimberg v. United States,* 245 F. Supp. 616 (N.D. Ill. 1965), *aff'd,* 365 F.2d 70 (7th Cir. 1966), upheld the regulation.

c. *Loss of citizenship.* In *Estate of Petschek v. Commissioner,* 81 T.C. 260 (1983), *aff'd,* 738 F.2d 67 (2d Cir. 1984), the Tax Court held that section 652(c) did not apply to a fact pattern involving a beneficiary's change of citizenship. For many years Mr. Petschek, beneficiary of a calendar-year, cash-basis simple trust, was an American citizen living in France and, as such, was fully subject to the United States income tax. *See generally* Treas. Reg. §1.1-1(b). On November 24, 1975, Mr. Petschek became a French citizen and thus, on December 31, 1975, the end of his tax year, was no longer subject to United States income taxation on the income of the trust in question. *See generally* I.R.C. §872(a). Mr. Petschek died sometime thereafter. Rejecting Mr. Petschek's executor's argument that section 652(c) barred inclusion of any trust income in Mr. Petschek's 1975 gross income because the trust's tax year ended within a tax year for which Mr. Petschek was not subject to United States income taxation, the Tax Court reasoned:

> [P]etitioner argues that section 652(c) implies an end-of-year inclusion rule for the trust income. That subsection provides that when the taxable year of a beneficiary differs from that of the trust, the beneficiary must include in his income the amount of trust income for the taxable year or years of the trust ending within or with the beneficiary's taxable year. The case before us does not involve such different taxable years. Unquestionably, however, there is inherent in section 652(c) the implicit assumption that the respective statuses of the trust and the beneficiary will not have changed from year to year, and the section simply does not deal with atypical situations such as, for example, the situation where no trust year ends with or within the taxable year of a beneficiary who dies. Admittedly section 652(c) is conceptually at odds with the "moment of receipt" concept articulated in *Freuler v. Helvering,* [291 U.S. 35 (1934)], but we view provisions such

as section 652(c)[14] as legislative rules of convenience limited to different taxable year situations which should not be expanded to cover other cases, such as the one before us, where an analogy would be inexact at best.

In any event, whether or not in a change-of-status case a beneficiary who employs a different taxable year from his trust would be required to include the trust income daily as realized by the trust is an issue we need not deal with here.

81 T.C. at 270–71. Instead, the court held that the trust's income

should be taxed to Petschek, on the same basis as it would have been had he owned the trust assets directly.[15] Thus, Petschek's share of the income is to be considered his property from the moment of its receipt by the trust ... regardless of whether it might have been distributed to him, and thus "received" by him after the date upon which he surrendered his U.S. citizenship.

Id. at 271. Responding to Mr. Petschek's executor's argument that Mr. Petschek's taxability was determinable only by reference to distributable net income and that DNI was determinable only at the end of the trust's tax year, the court wrote:

[I]t does not logically follow that simply because DNI is usually calculated at the end of a trust's taxable year, it is only included in the gross income of the beneficiary on the last day of the trust's taxable year. We see no reason why interim calculations of both DNI and income distributable under state law cannot be made daily during the trust's taxable year. Indeed, such an interim calculation of distributable income was in fact made in *Grant v. Commissioner,* [11 T.C. 178 (1948), *aff'd,* 174 F.2d 891 (5th. Cir. 1949)], and would, in effect, be required under section 1.652(c)-3, Income Tax Regs., in a case where the existence of a beneficiary which is not an individual terminates prior to the end of a simple trust's taxable year.

In addition, the fact that interim distributable income or DNI may exceed distributable income or DNI measured at the end of the trust's taxable year does not mean that there is no distributable income or DNI until the last day of the trust's taxable year. (In such a case, a downward adjustment of interim distributable income or DNI may be necessary so as not to overtax the beneficiary; but we express no opinion on whether such an adjustment would be necessary since in the instant case [the trust's] distributable income and DNI on December 31, 1975, clearly exceeded distributable income and DNI measured on an interim basis on November 23, 1975.)

81 T.C. at 269–70.

5. An income beneficiary who is willing irrevocably to give up his or her interest may be able to avoid liability for future income taxes by disclaiming the interest. The disclaimer must, however, be valid under local law. *See, e.g., Robert E. Cleary,* 34 T.C. 728 (1960). (Section 2518, by its own terms, does not apply to questions involving the income tax.) If the disclaimer is valid, the disclaimant is not required to include in his or her gross income the trust income that accrues after the date of the disclaimer. But even

---

14. See also section 662(c) (estates and complex trusts); 706(a) (partnerships); ... and 951(a) (controlled foreign corporations).

15. As already noted, the trust is a simple trust under section 1.651(a)-1, Income Tax Regs., and both the trust and Petschek are cash basis taxpayers. We need nor decide how, if at all, income from a complex trust would be taxed, or the tax results if either Perschek or the trust were accrual basis taxpayers. [For a discussion of the complex trust issue, see *infra* (ch. 3, sec. E(1)).]

if the disclaimer is valid, the disclaimant remains subject to taxation under section 652(a) on all of the trust income to which he or she was entitled prior to the disclaimer. Rev. Rul. 64-62, 1964-1 C.B. 221. *See also Grant v. Commissioner,* 174 F.2d 891 (5th Cir. 1949). It is irrelevant that the income is distributed not to the disclaimant but to his or her children, and that the disclaimant is not the trust's income beneficiary at the end of his or her tax year.

6. It is irrelevant to the beneficiary's tax picture that, at the time of a distribution, the trust has no income, if, at the end of the trust's taxable year, it does. *See Letts v. Commissioner,* 84 F.2d 760 (9th Cir. 1936).

7. If the beneficiary of a simple trust assigns a fractional share of her interest to charity, the trust remains a simple trust. Technical Advice Memorandum 8738007 (1987).

Revenue Ruling 74-257
1974-1 C.B. 153

Advice has been requested whether a trust may be allowed a deduction for State income taxes it paid as a result of capital gains retained by the trust in accordance with the terms of its governing instrument for the benefit of noncharitable remaindermen under the circumstances described below.

The governing instrument of an irrevocable inter vivos trust provides that all of its net income is to be distributed currently in equal amounts to four beneficiaries. During the taxable year 1972 the trust collected $60x$ dollars of qualifying dividends and $1x$ dollars of interest on United States Government obligations. It also realized capital gains of $200x$ dollars on the sale of securities and paid $25x$ dollars of fiduciary income tax attributable solely to such capital gains to the department of revenue of the State in which the trust was created.

As of December 31, 1972, the trustee remitted an amount equal to the dividend income and the interest income, less a trustee's fee of $1x$ dollars, to the beneficiaries of the trust. The proceeds of the sale of the securities were retained by the trustee as principal and were reinvested, after deducting therefrom the amount of the fiduciary income taxes paid. The retention of the proceeds of the sale was in accordance with applicable local law.

Section 641 of the Internal Revenue Code of 1954 provides, in part, that the taxable income of a trust is computed in the same manner as in the case of an individual, except as otherwise provided in this part. Also, a trust is allowed to deduct, in computing its taxable income, the deductions provided by section 651 and the regulations thereunder, relating to distributions to beneficiaries.

Section 651 of the Code provides for a deduction in the case of a trust that distributes current income only. The deduction is limited to the amount of the distributable net income regardless of whether the amount of income required to be distributed currently exceeds the distributable net income of the trust for the taxable year.

Under section 1.643(a)-0 of the Income Tax Regulations "distributable net income" means for any taxable year, the taxable income of the trust computed with the modifications set forth in section 1.643(a)-1 through 1.643(a)-7. The deduction allowable to a trust under section 651 of the Code for amounts paid to beneficiaries, and the deduction for personal exemption under section 642(b) are not allowed in the computation of distributable net income. The gains or losses from the sale or exchange of capital assets, with certain exceptions not here pertinent, are ordinarily excluded from distributable net income.

Section 652 of the Code provides, in part, that the amount of income for the taxable year required to be distributed currently by a trust shall be included in the gross income of the beneficiaries to whom the income is required to be distributed, whether distributed or not. Such includible amount shall be an amount equal to each beneficiary's share of the distributable net income of the trust.

Items of deduction of a trust that enter into the computation of distributable net income are to be allocated among the items of income. Section 1.652(b)-3(a) of the regulations provides that deductions that are directly attributable to a specific class of income must be allocated to that class of income. Section 1.652(b)-3(c) provides that State income tax is an item of expense that is not directly attributable to a specific class of income. Section 1.652(b)-3(b) provides that deductions that are not directly attributable to a specific class of income may be allocated to the items of income included in computing distributable net income. Under this section of the regulations no part of any deduction may be allocable to capital gains retained by a trust if under the terms of the trust instrument the capital gains are allocable to corpus and thus excluded from the computation of distributable net income. See *Marcia Brady Tucker,* 38 T.C. 955 (1962), *aff'd.* 322 F. 2d 86 (2d Cir. 1963) and *Manufacturers Hanover Trust Co. v. United States,* 312 F. 2d 785 (Ct. Cl. 1963). In the instant case, under the terms of the trust instrument the capital gains are allocable to corpus.

Accordingly, in this case, the State income tax paid as a result of capital gains retained by the trust is allowable as a deduction in arriving at the taxable income of the trust under section 641 of the Code. Further, the State income tax paid is deducted in arriving at distributable net income as provided in section 1.652(b)-3 of the regulations. The deduction for the distribution to the beneficiaries, as provided in section 651, is limited to the distributable net income regardless of the fact that the actual distribution exceeded the distributable net income of the trust for the taxable year.

Illustrative Material

If the I.R.S. denies a trust a deduction under section 212, the mandatory income beneficiary of the trust is likely to have more taxable income under section 652. *See Mary E. Burrow Trust,* 39 T.C. 1080 (1963), *aff'd,* 333 F.2d 66 (10th Cir. 1964). Do you understand why?

Problems

3-3. A trust that is required to distribute all of its income currently to the grantor's brother nevertheless fails to distribute anything. No amounts are payable to charity. Is the trust taxable under subpart B as a "simple" trust?

3-4. A trust that is required to distribute all of its income currently to the grantor's brother is also authorized to distribute principal to him. No amounts are payable to charity. Is the trust taxable as a simple trust in a year in which no principal is distributed?

3-5. A trust is required to distribute all of its income currently to one or more of three named individuals. No amounts are payable to charity. Is the trust taxable as a simple trust?

3-6. A trust is required to distribute all of its income currently to the grantor's brother for life. The remainder is payable to charity. Is the trust taxable as a simple trust in a year in which the trust realizes a gain that is allocable, under state law or the governing instrument, to charity?

3-7. A trust that is required to distribute all of its income currently to the grantor's sister receives a single item of ordinary income, subject to taxation, in the amount of $20,000. This item is entirely allocable, under state law or the governing instrument, to principal, and the trustee has no discretion to distribute principal. The trust has no expenses.

a. What is the trust's tentative taxable income?

b. What is the trust's fiduciary accounting income?

c. What is the trust's taxable income? Apply section 651(a).

d. What amount is subject to taxation in the hands of the grantor's sister? Apply section 652(a).

3-8. A trust that is required to distribute all of its income currently to the grantor's sister receives a single item of income amounting to $10,000. This item consists entirely of tax-exempt interest. The trust has no expenses.

a. What is the trust's gross income?

b. What is the trust's tentative taxable income?

c. What is the trust's distributable net income?

d. What is the trust's fiduciary accounting income?

e. What is the trust's taxable income? Remember section 651(b).

f. What amount is subject to taxation in the hands of the grantor's sister?

g. What is the tax character of the amount on which the grantor's sister is subject to taxation? Remember the first and second sentences of section 652(b).

3-9. A trust that is required to distribute all of its income currently to the grantor's sister receives two items of income: (1) a $20,000 capital gain, entirely allocable, under state law or the governing instrument, to principal; and (2) $10,000 of tax-exempt interest. The trustee has no discretion to distribute principal. The trust has no expenses.

a. What is the trust's gross income?

b. What is the trust's tentative taxable income?

c. What is the trust's distributable net income?

d. What is the trust's fiduciary accounting income?

e. What is the trust's taxable income?

f. What amount is subject to taxation in the hands of the grantor's sister?

g. What is the tax character of the amounts on which the grantor's sister is subject to taxation?

3-10. A trust that is required to distribute all of its income currently to the grantor's sister receives two items of income: (1) $20,000 of ordinary income that is subject to taxation but entirely allocable, under state law or the governing instrument, to principal; and (2) $10,000 of tax-exempt interest. The trustee has no discretion to distribute principal. The trust has no expenses.

a. What is the trust's gross income?

b. What is the trust's tentative taxable income?

c. What is the trust's distributable net income?

d. What is the trust's fiduciary accounting income?

e. What is the trust's taxable income? Be certain to account for the third sentence of Treas. Reg. §1.651(b)-1.

f. What amount is subject to taxation in the hands of the grantor's sister?

g. What is the tax character of the amounts on which the grantor's sister is subject to taxation?

3-11. Calculate the fiduciary accounting income of the trust described in Problem 2-2.

3-12. Calculate the taxable income of the trust described in Problem 2-2.

3-13. Calculate the amount subject to taxation in the hands of the beneficiary of the trust described in Problem 2-2.

3-14. What is the tax character of the amount calculated in Problem 3-13? See Treas. Reg. §1.652(c)-4(f).

3-15. Would the answer to Problem 3-13 differ if the trustee had failed to distribute to the beneficiary any of the trust's fiduciary accounting income?

E. Complex Trusts

1. In General

———————

Internal Revenue Code:
   Sections 661; 662; 663(a), (b)
Regulations:
   Sections 1.661(a)-1, -2(a), (b), (c), (d), (e); 1.661(b)-1; 1.661(c)-1; 1.662(a)-1, -2, -3; 1.662(b)-1; 1.662(c)-1, -2, -3, -4

———————

Trusts that are not "simple trusts" are "complex trusts" and are subject to taxation under sections 661 and 662. For example, any trust not required to distribute all of its income currently is a complex trust. Thus, any trust authorized to accumulate income is subject to taxation under sections 661 and 662. Similarly, any trust that distributes principal or accumulated income is a complex trust for the year in which the distribution occurs. In addition, any trust entitled, for the year in question, to a charitable deduction under section 642(c), and all estates, are subject to taxation under sections 661 and 662.

The primary difference between sections 661 and 662, on the one hand, and sections 651 and 652, on the other, is the "tier system." Under sections 661 and 662 there are two tiers of beneficiaries. "First-tier" beneficiaries are those, if any, to whom income is required to be distributed currently. The entity's distributable net income is allocated among them first. "Second-tier" beneficiaries are all others to whom the entity properly pays, credits, or distributes any amount. In essence, all beneficiaries other than mandatory income beneficiaries are second-tier beneficiaries. Only if the entity has distributable net income in excess of the current income required to be distributed (to its first-tier beneficiaries) is any of the entity's income allocated among its second-tier beneficiaries. Even then, second-tier beneficiaries are allocated entity income only to the extent distributable net income exceeds current income required to be distributed. Of course, if there are no first-tier beneficiaries, as under a trust authorized to accumulate income, each beneficiary who receives a distribution bears a share of the entity's income, even though each is only a second-tier beneficiary.

First-tier distributions qualify for the distribution deduction under section 661(a)(1) and subject their beneficiaries to taxation under section 662(a)(1). These provisions work in precisely the same fashion as sections 651 and 652.

Second-tier distributions are described in sections 661(a)(2) and 662(a)(2). Under section 661(a)(2) a trustee is allowed to deduct amounts, other than income required to be distributed currently, that are "properly paid." Section 662(a)(2) subjects the beneficiary of any such amount to taxation. Thus, if an amount is improperly paid, as when a trustee required to accumulate income distributes it, the trust is not entitled to a distribution deduction, and the beneficiary is not required to make an inclusion in gross income on account of the distribution. *DeVilbiss v. United States,* 41-2 U.S.T.C. ¶9552 (N.D. Ohio 1941).

Revenue Ruling 67-117
1967-1 C.B. 161

Advice has been requested whether an amount distributed by a trustee to the income beneficiary of the trust, equal to the value of a nontaxable stock dividend received by the trust, is includible in the beneficiary's gross income.

A corporation distributed to a trust a nontaxable stock dividend. Under the particular State law the dividend is income for trust accounting purposes, and the trustee in his discretion can either distribute in kind the stock received, sell the stock and distribute the proceeds, or distribute cash equal to the fair market value of the stock, to the income beneficiary of the trust.

Under the terms of the trust instrument, the income of the trust may, in the discretion of the trustee, be distributed to the income beneficiary or accumulated. The trustee, upon receipt of the stock dividend, elected to distribute to the beneficiary an amount in cash equivalent to the then current fair market value of the stock.

While under local law a nontaxable stock dividend may be income for trust accounting purposes, under the provisions of section 643(a) of the Internal Revenue Code of 1954, nontaxable stock dividends do not enter into the computation of distributable net income.

Under the rules of subchapter J, chapter 1, of the Code, and the regulations thereunder, the deduction by the trust for amounts distributed to the beneficiary may not exceed its distributable net income for the taxable year. Likewise, distributions from the trust shall be included in gross income of the beneficiary only to the extent that they do not exceed the distributable net income of the trust. Amounts includible in the gross income of the beneficiary will have the same character, proportionately, as the classes of items which enter into the computation of distributable net income.

Application of the foregoing may be illustrated by the following examples:

Example (1). — A trust is created to pay the income currently to *H* for life. In the taxable year, a nontaxable stock dividend worth $1,000, which is income distributable to the income beneficiary under State law, is received by the trust, but it had no other income. The trustee elects to distribute to the beneficiary cash equal to the fair market value of the stock dividend, in lieu of distributing that stock. The trust has no deductible expenses.

Since the trust has no distributable net income, the beneficiary is not required to include in his gross income any amount of the cash distributed to him.

Example (2).—Assume the same facts as above except that the trust also receives taxable interest of $3,000.

The "income required to be distributed currently" to the beneficiary is $4,000. The distributable net income of the trust, as computed under section 643(a) of the Code, however, is only $3,000, since the stock dividend is nontaxable and does not enter into the computation of distributable net income. Therefore, the amount deductible by the trust and includible in the gross income of the beneficiary is limited to $3,000. Consequently, the $1,000 in cash distributed in lieu of the stock dividend is not includible in the gross income of the beneficiary.

Similarly where the trustee has the discretion to distribute corpus and to accumulate or distribute income of the trust, and he properly distributes to the beneficiary only an amount of cash equal to the value of the stock dividend received at a time when the trust has distributable net income, the beneficiary is required to include the amount of cash received in his gross income, under section 662(a) of the Code, to the extent that such amount does not exceed the distributable net income of the trust. The character of the items contained in distributable net income determines the character of the amount taxable to the beneficiary, as provided by section 662(b) of the Code.

Application of the foregoing may be illustrated by the following examples:

Example (3).—Under the terms of the trust instrument, the trustee may distribute income, or accumulate it for future distribution in his discretion. In the taxable year a nontaxable stock dividend having a fair market value of $1,000 is received by the trust. The trust has no other income or deductible expenses for this year. The trustee distributes $1,000 in cash to the beneficiary and retains the stock.

Since the trust has no distributable net income, the beneficiary is not required to include in his gross income any of the cash distributed to him.

Example (4).—Under the terms of the trust instrument, $1,000 is required to be paid annually out of income of the trust to beneficiary *A*. The balance of the trust income may, in the trustee's discretion, be accumulated or distributed to beneficiary *B*. The trust has the following items of income and no expenses for the taxable year:

Taxable interest	$2,000
Nontaxable stock dividend worth	1,000
Total income under state law	$3,000

During the taxable year, the trustee distributes $1,000 in cash to *A*, and $500 in cash to *B*.

The distributable net income of the trust, as computed under section 643(a) of the Code, is $2,000.

Under section 661(a)(1) and (2) of the Code, $1,500 is deductible by the trust. Under section 662(a)(1) of the Code, $1,000 is includible in the gross income of *A*. Under section 662(a)(2) of the Code, $500 is includible in the gross income of *B*. The trust's taxable income after deducting $100 for personal exemption, is $400.

Illustrative Material

1. Under section 661(a)(2) a trustee is entitled to deduct discretionary amounts it "pays" to beneficiaries. But the payment must be real. Thus, if a trustee distributes amounts

to minor beneficiaries who, by prearrangement, return them for reinvestment as part of the trust, a court may find that no payment has actually occurred. *See Cecelia K. Frank Trust,* 8 T.C. 368 (1947), *aff'd per curiam,* 165 F.2d 992 (3d Cir. 1948).

2. Alternatively, under section 661(a)(2) a trustee may deduct discretionary amounts properly "credited" to beneficiaries. In the normal case, a trustee with authority to accumulate income (as in a trust for several minor beneficiaries) is not entitled to deduct amounts accumulated, because no amounts are "credited" to beneficiaries. Instead, the trustee periodically adds the accumulated income to trust principal. In *Mary E. Fennerty Testamentary Trust,* 13 T.C.M. (CCH) 831 (1954), however, the trustee had discretion, during the minority of the beneficiaries, to accumulate, *in equal shares,* the trust income. During the years in question, the trustee made almost no distributions. Nonetheless, the Tax Court held that the main trust was not taxable on any of its income. Apparently, the court found the trust entitled to distribution deductions for the income, which the court believed should have been credited each year to *separate trusts* for the minor beneficiaries. Not discussed by the court is the logical corollary that each of the separate trusts should have included its share of the amount in question in its own gross income. In *Lynchburg Trust & Savings Bank v. Commissioner,* 68 F.2d 356 (4th Cir.), *cert. denied,* 292 U.S. 640 (1934), the court reached the same conclusion on much easier facts. There the trustees had always credited the minors' income to separate trust accounts and had filed multiple income tax returns accordingly. *A fortiori,* if a local court, construing the governing document, has directed the trustee to set up separate trust accounts for minor beneficiaries' shares of income, the main trust is entitled to distribution deductions for income credited to those accounts. *See Lindley v. United States,* 57-2 U.S.T.C. ¶ 9893 (D. Minn. 1957). Of course, if a court construes the governing document as not requiring creation of separate trust accounts for accumulation of minor beneficiaries' shares of the trust's income, no distribution deduction is allowable on account of accumulated income, even if the trustees have set up multiple trust accounts and have filed multiple tax returns, because the trustees have not done so "properly." *William L. Mellon, Jr.,* 11 T.C. 135 (1948), *aff'd per curiam,* 174 F.2d 828 (3d Cir. 1949).

3. If a trust is required to make a distribution of a specific sum of money, section 663(a)(1), discussed *infra* (ch. 3, sec. F(2)), may apply. Rev. Rul. 78-24, 1978-1 C.B. 196. If so, the distribution neither entitles the trust to a deduction under section 661 nor subjects the beneficiary to taxation under section 662.

4. Section 662(c), like section 652(c), discussed *supra* (ch. 3, sec. D), applies if a trust and its beneficiaries have different taxable years. *Hay v. United States,* 263 F. Supp. 813 (N.D. Tex. 1967), construed section 662(c) in the context of a complex trust. The trust's fiscal year ended November 30, 1962. On December 1, 1962, and February 1, 1963, the trust made discretionary distributions, admittedly on account of pre-November 30, 1962 income, to its beneficiaries. Under a prior version of section 663(b)(2), the sixty-five day rule was unavailable to treat the distributions as made on the last day of the trust's fiscal year. Though the court stated that under section 661(a)(2) the trust properly deducted the distributions as paid "for" its fiscal year ending November 30, 1962, the court held that under section 662(c) the beneficiaries properly included amounts in their gross incomes for their calendar years 1963—not their calendar years 1962. The court understood that its holding resulted in a discontinuity in the structure of sections 661 and 662 but insisted on a literal application of the words of section 662(c) referring to amounts paid to a beneficiary "during" the taxable year of the trust ending within the beneficiary's taxable year. In short, the court, rejecting Treas. Reg. §1.662(c)-1, held that "during" in section 662(c) overrode "for," which also appears in the context of beneficiary inclusions in the first sentence of section 662(a)(2).

Recall that section 644 now requires most trusts (but not estates) to be calendar-year taxpayers.

5. In *Furstenberg v. Commissioner,* 83 T.C. 755 (1984), the Tax Court faced one of the situations it said, in footnote 15 of *Petschek,* discussed *supra* (ch. 3, sec. D), had not yet been dealt with. In *Furstenberg* a complex trust made a taxable distribution of principal to a former U.S. citizen after the date (but in the same taxable year) she became a non-resident alien. The sole issue decided was that the beneficiary did not constructively receive the distribution while she was still an American citizen. Nonetheless, the resulting holding, that the beneficiary was taxable on the distribution exclusively as a nonresident alien, provides some support for the proposition that *Petschek,* which involved a simple trust, does not require proration of a complex trust's distributable net income over the entire taxable year of a second-tier beneficiary who becomes a nonresident alien during that year.

6. In *Geftman v. Commissioner,* 72 T.C.M. (CCH) 816 (1996), *rev'd on other grounds,* 154 F.3d 61 (3d Cir. 1998), the issue was whether the sole beneficiary of a discretionary trust was taxable on any portion of the amounts he received from the trust. The Tax Court explained:

> [T]o determine whether petitioner is subject to income tax on his receipt of the $46,936 distribution, we must first determine whether [the trust] had DNI equal to or greater than $46,936 for its taxable year ended February 28, 1985. If [the trust] had DNI equal to or greater than $46,936 for its taxable year ended February 28, 1985, then petitioner must include a percentage of the $46,936 distribution in his 1985 gross income, equal to the proportion of [the trust's] DNI that consists of taxable items.

Id. at 819. This appears to be a truncated, but nonetheless accurate, explanation of the workings of section 662, as applied to a particular fact pattern. Do you understand it?

2. The Separate Share Rule

———

Internal Revenue Code:
    Section 663(c)
Regulations:
    Sections 1.663(c)-1, -2, -3, -4, -5

———

Revenue Ruling 74-299
1974-1 C.B. 154

Advice has been requested concerning the treatment, for Federal income tax purposes, of an amount distributed by a nonexempt employees' trust under the circumstances described below.

In 1963 a corporation created a trust as part of a deferred compensation plan for the benefit of its employees. The trust is not qualified under the provisions of section 401(a) of the Internal Revenue Code of 1954 and therefore it is not exempt from taxation under section 501(a) of the Code. Separate accounts are maintained for each participating employee that reflect his share of the net trust assets and income. Annual employer contributions and forfeitures by disqualified employees are allocated to each participating employee's account based on his proportionate share of the total compensation of all participating employees for the year.

Employees covered under the plan, or their estates, are entitled to receive their prior years' vested interest in the net assets of the trust when they retire, terminate their employment, become disabled, or in event of death. No amount may vest in any participating employee before he has completed at least three years of continuous service for the employer. Only one of the employees covered under the plan retired in 1972. During the calendar year 1972, under the terms of the plan, the trust made distributions to the retired employee totaling $12x$ dollars. For the calendar year 1972 the trust had "distributable net income", as that term is described in section 643(a) of the Code, in the amount of $75x$ dollars. However, the distributable net income allocable to the retired employee's separately computed share was $1x$ dollars.

Section 1.661(a)-2(a) of the Income Tax Regulations provides, in part, that in computing the taxable income of an estate or trust a deduction is allowed for distributions to beneficiaries equal to the sum of the amount of income for the taxable year that is required to be distributed currently and any other amounts properly paid or credited or required to be distributed for such taxable year. However, the total amount deductible under section 661(a) of the Code cannot exceed the distributable net income as computed under the provisions of section 643(a).

Section 662(a) of the Code provides, in general, the rules for determining the amount and character of amounts to be included in the gross income of a beneficiary receiving an amount specified in section 661.

Section 402(b) of the Code provides, in part, that the amount actually distributed or made available by a nonexempt trust to any distributee shall be taxable to such distributee under rules contained in section 72 in the year in which the amount is so distributed or made available.

For the purpose of determining the taxability of beneficiaries of employees' trusts that are not exempt from tax under section 501(a) of the Code, the specific provisions of section 402(b) apply, rather than the general provisions of section 662(a). In the instant case, the fact that the provisions of section 662(a) do not apply to the employee, as beneficiary of the trust, does not preclude the application of the provisions of section 661(a) to the trust itself.

Section 663(c) of the Code provides, in part, that for the sole purpose of determining the amount of distributable net income in the application of sections 661 and 662, in the case of a single trust having more than one beneficiary, substantially separate and independent shares of different beneficiaries in the trust shall be treated as separate trusts.

Section 1.663(c)-1(a) of the regulations provides, in part, that if a single trust has more than one beneficiary, and if different beneficiaries have substantially separate and independent shares, their shares are treated as separate trusts for the sole purpose of determining the amount of distributable net income allocable to the respective beneficiaries under sections 661 and 662 of the Code.

Thus, even though for the calendar year 1972 the trust had "distributable net income," as that term is described in section 643(a) of the Code, in the amount of $75x$ dollars, the distributable net income allocable to the retired employee's separate share, under section 663, was only 1x dollars.

Accordingly, in the instant case, the deduction allowable to the trust for 1972, under section 661(a) of the Code, is limited to the retired employee's separate share of distributable net income (1x dollars) as determined under section 663(c) and the regulations thereunder.

However, as provided by section 402(b) of the Code, the taxability of the distribution of 12x dollars to the retired employee is determined in accordance with the rules contained in section 72. It is not governed by the provisions of section 662(a)

Illustrative Material

Revenue Ruling 74-299, and the tax treatment of deferred compensation plans under the separate share rule, were amplified and confirmed in Rev. Rul. 2007-48, 2007-30 I.R.B. 129.

Private Letter Ruling 200618003 (2006)

This is in response to your ... letter and other correspondence requesting a ruling concerning the income ... tax consequences of the settlement agreement as it relates to the trust.

You have requested the following rulings:

* * *

2. The execution of the Construction Agreement, the Court's approval of the Construction Agreement, the Trustee's creation of the Daughters' Trust pursuant to the authority provided in the Trust, and the Trustee's subsequent distribution of assets to the Daughters' Trust in accordance with the Construction Agreement do not cause the Daughters' Trust to receive more than its pro-rata share of the distributable net income of the Trust through the date of funding; ...

* * *

The facts submitted are as follows:

On Date 1, Grantor created Trust. Article II provides that Trust is irrevocable.

Article 3.01.A defines "Trustor's Children" as Son 1 and Son 2. Article 3.01.B provides that the trustee may distribute to Trustor's Children and their descendants so much net income and principal as will provide for the beneficiaries' health, education, maintenance, and support. Additionally, the trustee is to have the power to distribute to "Trustor's children" so much net income and principal as the trustee may determine to be appropriate to assist in any business or investment venture. Article 3.01.C provides that Trust will terminate on the first to occur of (1) the second anniversary of Grantor's death, or (2) the death of the last survivor of Trustor's Children and their descendants. Upon termination, the Trust assets will be administered in accordance with Articles 3.02 and 3.03.

Article 3.02 provides, in relevant part, that the trustee is to divide Trust into separate equal shares, one share for each then living Child and one share for the then living descendants, collectively, of each deceased Child.

Grantor's two daughters, Daughter 1 and Daughter 2, alleged that the term "Trustor's children" included them, and thus, they were eligible for distributions to assist them with business and investment ventures. Questions also arose as to whether children born or adopted by Grantor after the Trust's creation would be eligible for distributions. On Date 2, the trustee petitioned County Court to construe and interpret several provisions of the Trust. The County Court determined that any children born after the Trust's creation were not beneficiaries of the Trust. In order to settle the remaining disputes, the children entered into a Construction Agreement. The trustee represents that the Construction Agreement's interpretation of the ambiguities are consistent with the County Court's earlier order on children born after Trust's creation.

The terms of the Construction Agreement call for the daughters as well as the sons to be eligible for Trust distributions to assist in any business or investment venture. The Construction Agreement also stipulates that the maximum distribution to the daughters under the Trust would be 50 percent of the value of Trust on the date of the distribution. In order to prevent any future disagreements over distributions, the Construction Agreement calls for the trustee to distribute 50 percent of the assets, on an in-kind pro rata basis, to a new trust for the benefit of the daughters. The new trust will have provisions substantially similar to the original Trust. Once the new trust for the benefit of the daughters has been created, no further distributions will be made from the original Trust for their benefit, except in the event of the death of one of the Sons (or a descendant of one of the Sons) where that person is not survived by a descendant. Likewise, no distributions from the Daughters' Trust would be made to the Sons or any descendants of a Son except in the event of the death of one of the Daughters (or a descendant of one of the Daughters) where that person is not survived by a descendant. On Date 3, County Court approved the Construction Agreement.

LAW AND ANALYSIS

* * *

Section 643(a) provides that the term "distributable net income" means, with respect to any taxable year, the taxable income of the estate or trust computed with certain modifications.

Section 661(a) provides that in any taxable year there shall be allowed as a deduction in computing the taxable income of an estate or trust (other than a trust to which subpart B applies), the sum of (1) any amount of income for such taxable year required to be distributed currently (including any amount required to be distributed which may be paid out of income or corpus to the extent such amount is paid out of income for such taxable year); and (2) any other amounts properly paid or credited or required to be distributed for such taxable year, but such deduction is not to exceed the distributable net income of the estate or trust.

Section 662(a) provides generally that there is to be included in the gross income of a beneficiary to whom an amount specified in section 661(a) is paid, credited, or required to be distributed the sum of the following amounts: (1) the amount of income for the taxable year required to be distributed currently to such beneficiary, whether distributed or not; and (2) all other amounts properly paid, credited, or required to be distributed to such beneficiary for the taxable year. Section 662(a), however, limits the amount of trust distributions included in the gross income of a beneficiary to the distributable net income of the trust.

Section 663(c) provides for the sole purpose of determining the amount of distributable net income in the application of sections 661 and 662, in the case of a single trust

186

3 · THE ENTITY AS CONDUIT

having more than one beneficiary, substantially separate and independent shares of different beneficiaries in the trust are to be treated as separate trusts.

Section 1.663(c)-2(a) provides that a separate share comes into existence upon the earliest moment that a fiduciary may reasonably determine, based upon the known facts, that a separate economic interest exists.

Section 1.663(c)-2(b)(1) provides that the amount of distributable net income for any share under section 663(c) is computed as if each share constituted a separate trust or estate. Accordingly, each separate share is to calculate its distributable net income based upon its portion of gross income that is includible in distributable net income and its portion of any applicable deductions or losses.

Section 1.663(c)-2(c) provides that for purposes of calculating distributable net income for each separate share, the fiduciary must use a reasonable and equitable method to make the allocations, calculations, and valuations required by section 1.663(c)-2(b).

In this case, the Trustee will distribute 50 percent of the assets to Daughters' Trust on a pro rata basis. Therefore, based on the facts presented and the representations made, we conclude that the distribution will not cause the Daughters' Trust to receive more than its allocable share of the distributable net income of the Trust through the date of funding.

* * *

Illustrative Material

The Taxpayer Relief Act of 1997 amended section 663(c) to extend the separate share rule to estates, as well as trusts. Recall the discussion of this issue under prior law in the third-last paragraph of Judge Skelton's dissent in *Harkness v. United States* (*supra*, ch. 3, sec. A(2)). In 1999 the Treasury promulgated regulations on the application of the separate share rule to estates. T.D. 8849, 2000-1 C.B. 244. *See generally* Yu, *A Proposed Allocation of Distributable Net Income to the Separate Shares of a Trust or Estate*, 3 Pittsburgh Tax Rev. 121 (2006).

Problems

3-16. A testamentary trust is required to distribute all of its income currently to the testator's wife; however, the trustee is authorized to pay principal to one or both of the testator's wife and son. In a year in which both the distributable net income and the fiduciary accounting income of the trust equal $50,000, the trustee distributes $50,000 to the testator's wife and $25,000 to the testator's son. None of the trust's income is tax-exempt. What are the tax consequences to the trust, the wife, and the son?

3-17. Assume the facts of Problem 3-16, except that the trust's distributable net income is $65,000.

3-18. Assume the facts of Problem 3-16, except that the trust's distributable net income is $35,000.

3-19. A trustee is authorized to sprinkle income and principal among the testator's wife and children. In a year in which both the distributable net income and the fiduciary accounting income of the trust are $50,000, the trustee distributes $30,000 to the testator's wife and $20,000 to the testator's son. None of the trust's income is tax-exempt. What are the tax consequences to the trust, the wife, and the son?

3-20. Assume the facts of Problem 3-19, except that the trust's distributable net income is $30,000.

3-21. A trustee is authorized to distribute one-half of the trust's income and one-half of the trust's principal to the grantor's daughter and the other one-half of both to the grantor's son. Upon the death of either child, one-half of the principal is to pass to his or her issue. In a year in which distributable net income is $10,000, the trustee distributes $10,000 to the grantor's daughter but nothing to the grantor's son. None of the trust's income is tax-exempt. What are the tax consequences to the trust, the daughter, and the son? Prepare alternative answers, first assuming that the separate share rule applies, and then assuming that it does not.

3-22. A testamentary trust has the following receipts: cash dividends from shares of Sears, $10,000; interest on obligations of the City of New York, $10,000; and capital gain on the sale of Blackacre, $80,000. The trust is required to distribute all of its income to the testator's sister annually for her life. The remainder is payable to the testator's brother; however, the trustee is authorized to distribute principal to the testator's brother during the sister's lifetime. The trustee distributes $20,000 of principal to the testator's brother. Calculate the trust's fiduciary accounting income, gross income, tentative taxable income, distributable net income, section 661(a)(1) deduction, section 661(a)(2) deduction, and taxable income. Also calculate the income subject to taxation in the hands of both the brother and the sister of the testator, as well as the tax character of such amounts.

3-23. A trustee is authorized to sprinkle income and principal among the testator's children; however, the trustee is directed to distribute $30,000 to each child on his or her thirtieth birthday. During the year in which testator's daughter turns thirty, the trust has $45,000 of distributable net income. $30,000 is distributed to each of the testator's daughter and the testator's son. What are the tax consequences to the trust, the daughter, and the son?

3-24. Assume that the terms of a trust require the trustee to distribute $10,000 annually to Sister for life. The terms of the trust also authorize (but do not require) the trustee to distribute principal to Brother during Sister's lifetime. In the year in question, the trustee distributes $10,000 to Sister and $7,000 to Brother. Assume that both DNI and fiduciary accounting income are $12,000 and that none of the income is tax-exempt. What are the tax consequences to Sister, Brother, and the trust?

3-25. Assume that the terms of a trust require the trustee to distribute $10,000 annually to Sister for life. The terms of the trust also authorize (but do not require) the trustee to distribute principal to Brother and Sister during Sister's lifetime. In the year in question, the trustee distributes $25,000 to Sister and $10,000 to Brother. Assume that both DNI and fiduciary accounting income are $12,000 and that none of the income is tax-exempt. What are the tax consequences to Sister, Brother, and the trust?

3-26. Assume that the terms of a trust require the trustee to distribute one-half of all income annually to A. The terms of the trust also require the trustee to distribute $30,000 annually to B (payable from income or principal, in the trustee's discretion). The terms of the trust authorize (but do not require) the trustee to distribute any remaining income or to distribute principal to C or D or both. In the year in question, both DNI and fiduciary accounting income are $80,000, none of which is tax-exempt. The trustee distributes $40,000 to A, $30,000 to B, and $30,000 to C. The latter two distributions are charged to principal. What are the tax consequences to A, B, C, and the trust? How would your answer change if the distribution to C were charged to income?

F. Estates

1. In General

Internal Revenue Code:
Sections 661–662

Bohan v. United States
456 F.2d 851 (8th Cir. 1972)

GIBSON, Circuit Judge.

The United States appeals from the decision in the United States District Court for the Western District of Missouri in this tax refund case, Bohan v. United States, 326 F.Supp. 1356 (W.D.Mo.1971). Plaintiff taxpayer, Mrs. Ruth Bohan is the widow of Dr. Peter T. Bohan, who died in 1955, leaving an estate valued in excess of $900,000. Mrs. Bohan (hereinafter "taxpayer") was named executrix and sole residuary legatee in Dr. Bohan's will.

... During the tax year 1957, the estate had distributable net income in the amount of $29,076.15. Distributions in kind, that same year, consisting of corporate stock, rights to a declared dividend and certain rights to purchase additional stock were made to taxpayer. It is conceded that these distributions were from corpus. The value of the property so distributed was $162,076. These distributions were partial distributions made by the probate court to taxpayer, as residuary legatee, in advance of final settlement, under the authority of Mo.Rev.Stat. §473.613 (1949).[1]

For 1957 the estate reported income in the amount of the distributable net income and paid income taxes on that amount, and taxpayer did not report as income any part of the distributions made to her. The Commissioner determined that taxpayer had realized income in the amount of the distributable net income of the estate on account of the in-kind beneficiary distributions and assessed a deficiency against her calculated on that amount. A deduction in the amount of distributable net income was allowed the estate. The tax was paid and this suit for refund followed.

The Government contends that 26 U.S.C.A. §§661(a)(2) and 662(a)(2) require this distribution to be included as income by taxpayer and deducted by the estate. The receipt by taxpayer of possession of the property causes it to be an amount "properly paid" within the meaning of these two sections.

The trial court held, in an exhaustive and well-reasoned opinion by Chief Judge Becker, that the partial distributions in this case were not "properly paid or credited" within the meaning of the statute because at the time of distribution they were subject to recall under Missouri law until the decree of final distribution. This holding that the distributions were conditional is obviously a correct interpretation of Missouri law, and the Government does not challenge it on this appeal.

---

1. On approval of the probate court, specific personal property may be distributed to a distributee prior to a decree of final distribution subject to recall by that court.

Nevertheless, the Government still contends on appeal that the distributions were "properly paid" under the federal income tax statute and therefore includible in the taxpayer's return because they were received under a "claim of right", relying on North American Oil v. Burnet, 286 U.S. 417 (1932), and subsequent cases interpreting that doctrine.

The difficulty with this argument is that it is wholly inapplicable to the facts of this case; it is merely a bootstrap argument by which the Government assumes the conclusion which is at issue here — namely, whether the distributions to the taxpayer were taxable to her as income. The net income of the estate was concededly not distributed to the taxpayer and the distributions to her were admittedly made out of corpus. Whether they are nevertheless taxable to her as income depends upon whether the conditions specified in §662(a)(2) are met. Where those conditions are not met, the distributions are not taxable as income; and the "claim of right" doctrine does not convert that which is not income into income.

The "claim of right" doctrine is designed to further the federal income tax policy that income is to be returned and taxes paid thereon on the basis of an annual accounting period. "The 'claim of right' interpretation of the tax laws has long been used to give finality to that period, and is now deeply rooted in the federal tax system." United States v. Lewis, 340 U.S. 590, 592 (1961). It is used to determine when income is taxable rather than whether a receipt is taxable income, and if so, to whom it is taxable. 2 Mertens, Law of Federal Income Tax §12.103, p. 409.[4]

Moreover, it seems clear there was no "claim of right" here as that term is used in the income tax law — i. e., a claim of ownership superior to the rights of all others.

> "The phrase 'claim of right' is a term known of old to lawyers. Its typical use has been in real property law in dealing with title by adverse possession, where the rule has been that title can be acquired by adverse possession only if the occupant claims that he has a right to be in possession as owner. The use of the term in the field of income taxation is analogous." Healy v. Commissioner, 345 U.S. 278, 282 (1953).

There is no evidence in the record that taxpayer ever asserted a claim to these partial distributions to the exclusion of the rights of the probate court to recall them prior to the decree of final distribution. No doubt Mrs. Bohan had certain rights to this distribution but they were at all times subject to the superior rights of the probate court to reclaim the property for the estate. This is inconsistent with the definition of claim of right set out in Healy v. Commissioner, *supra*. The conditional nature of the distribution properly led the District Court to hold that the distributions were not "properly paid or credited."

Finally, while not necessary to the disposition of this case, we note that the position of the Government in this case seems contrary to the recent ruling of the Treasury Department relative to §661(a) that "in the absence of a testamentary provision to the contrary, the state law is determinative of the disposition of income from property during the period of administration." Revenue Ruling 71-335. Here, there was no testamentary provision to the contrary, and state law required that income from the estate be used first to pay the taxes and other expenses of the estate. The income was in fact so used. Therefore, under the above ruling the estate would not appear entitled to a deduction for its dispo-

---

4. In this connection, we think it appropriate to point out that there is no attempt in this case to avoid payment of taxes on income actually received by the estate. The estate returned its income and paid tax thereon for the year in dispute. The sole question is whether it should have deducted the distribution in question, thus making the income taxable to the distributee-taxpayer.

sition, and as a corollary, there was no income from the estate distributed to and therefore taxable to the distributee-taxpayer under §662(a).

The judgment of the District Court is affirmed.

Illustrative Material

1. In Rev. Rul. 72-396, 1972-2 C.B. 312, the I.R.S. announced it would not follow *Bohan.* Can you see why? Under *Bohan,* sections 661 and 662 would never apply to an estate, except in the year of termination, because no distribution prior to termination is final. Even a casual reading of sections 661 through 663 indicates Congress intended that estate distributions generally would draw distributable net income out of an estate to its beneficiaries. There is not a hint that the distribution rules are to apply only in the year an estate terminates. In fact, *Bohan* makes section 663(a)(3) incomprehensible.

2. In Rev. Rul. 71-335, 1971-2 C.B. 250, mentioned in *Bohan,* the I.R.S. ruled that gains realized and income received by an executor who distributed such gains and income to the residuary beneficiary pursuant to the provisions of local law were "properly" paid and therefore deductible in computing the taxable income of the estate under section 661(a). The I.R.S. stated that, in the absence of testamentary provisions to the contrary, local law was "determinative of the disposition of income from property during the period of administration." Still, the I.R.S. argued, and the court held, in *American National Bank & Trust Co. v. United States,* 81-2 U.S.T.C. ¶9780 (6th Cir. 1981), that amounts found by a local court to have been properly paid were not properly paid for purposes of section 661(a)(2). *American National* is not, however, a departure from the concept that state law controls. Both the I.R.S. and the court purported to construe the governing instrument. Thus, *American National* appears to be no more than a holding that federal courts deciding tax controversies are not bound by lower local court judgments they believe to be incorrect. *See generally Commissioner v. Estate of Bosch,* 387 U.S. 456 (1967).

3. In *Buckmaster v. United States,* 984 F.2d 379 (10th Cir. 1993), the Tenth Circuit dealt with concerns similar to those in *Bohan* but resolved them quite differently. In *Buckmaster,* an executor made distributions prior to obtaining judicial authorization, which local law (that of Oklahoma) apparently required. Though the executor subsequently obtained judicial approval of the distributions, the I.R.S. denied the estate's distribution deductions on the theory that the distributions were improper. The Tenth Circuit disagreed, holding that, even though the executor may have "act[ed] on his own at some peril," subsequent judicial approval of the distributions rendered them "properly paid" for purposes of section 661.

4. The last full paragraph of *Bohan is* very confusing and appears to reflect a serious misunderstanding of sections 661 and 662. Certainly if state law requires use of all estate income (fiduciary accounting income) for payment of administration expenses, no amount of income is required to be distributed currently under sections 661(a)(1) and 662(a)(1). This, however, is to say nothing more than that the estate would have no first-tier beneficiary. *See infra* (note 5). If the estate properly pays or credits "any other amount," sections 661(a)(2) and 662(a)(2) apply, regardless of what happens to the estate's fiduciary accounting income. They provide a completely independent method for allocating the estate's tax liability between it and its beneficiaries.

5. Estates generally have no first-tier beneficiaries, because they generally are not required to distribute their income "currently." *See Commissioner v. Stearns,* 65 F.2d 371 (2d

Cir.), *cert. denied,* 290 U.S. 670 (1933); *Martin Raymond Bowen,* 34 T.C. 222 (1960), *aff'd per curiam,* 295 F.2d 816 (2d Cir. 1961); *Estate of Andrew J. Igoe,* 6 T.C. 639 (1946), *acq.,* 1946-2 C.B. 3.

This is likely to be true even if the residuary beneficiary is a trust that is required, from the date of decedent's death, to pay out income. *See Smith's Estate v. Commissioner,* 168 F.2d 431 (6th Cir. 1948); *Woolley v. Malley,* 30 F.2d 73 (1st Cir.), *cert. denied,* 279 U.S. 860 (1929); *Lane v. United States,* 233 F. Supp. 856 (M.D. Ala. 1964); *Estate of Peter Anthony Bruner,* 3 T.C. 1051 (1944). In each of these cases the trusts had not been set up during the years in question. Yet the courts' rationale seems not to depend on that fact. Instead, the courts found that the trust beneficiaries lacked present rights to receive the income *during the years in question. Smith* explained:

> The will did not expressly provide that the income was to be currently distributed to the beneficiaries immediately following the decedent's death. The executor was entitled to temporarily accumulate the income during the necessary period of administration, even though ultimately after the administration was completed the beneficiaries would be entitled to the unused income accruing subsequent to the date of the death of the testator. Usually a careful executor will not make distribution until after the period for the filing of claims has expired, and a legatee or beneficiary can not require it. In cases where there is practical assurance that the assets of the estate are more than ample to take care of all claims and expenses, an executor may as a practical matter and for the convenience of the legatees make partial distribution before the period has expired, but he is not required to do so. In such cases the income so distributed "is properly paid or credited" during the year to the legatee and will be a deduction under [the predecessor of section 661(a)(2)], but it is not income "which is to be distributed currently by the fiduciary" under the provisions of [the predecessor of section 661(a)(1)].

168 F.2d at 434.

On the other hand, contrary to popular belief, estates do not last forever. If an executor delays too long in funding a testamentary trust, the I.R.S. may argue that the estate has, in effect, become the trust and that the "estate" and its beneficiaries ought to be taxed accordingly. *See Chick v. Commissioner,* 166 F.2d 337 (1st Cir.), *cert. denied,* 334 U.S. 845 (1948); *Alabama-Georgia Syrup Co.,* 36 T.C. 747 (1961), *rev'd on other issues sub nom. Whitfield v. Commissioner,* 311 F.2d 640 (5th. Cir. 1962). In both of these cases, the estates had gone on for more than a decade, the executors and trustees were the same persons, and all the normal duties of estate administration had been fulfilled. The courts therefore held that the beneficiaries of mandatory income testamentary trusts were taxable on the estates' incomes as first-tier beneficiaries, even in the absence of distributions. The estates were presumably entitled to distribution deductions on account of that income. For an instance in which the Commissioner's argument was rejected, see *Carson v. United States,* 161 Ct. Cl. 548, 317 F.2d 370 (1963).

Cummings v. United States, 69-1 U.S.T.C. ¶ 9359 (C.D. Cal. 1969), suggested, in dictum, that the required distribution by an estate of its income as a family allowance might fall within the first tier.

6. Sometimes an executor sees fit to make a distribution to the beneficiary of a testamentary trust. This is especially likely to happen if the executor is also named as the testamentary trustee. What are the tax consequences of such a distribution? Is such a distribution an amount "properly paid or credited or required to be distributed" for pur-

poses of either entitling the estate to a distribution deduction under section 661(a)(2) or subjecting the beneficiary to taxation under section 662(a)(2)? On a literal basis, such an estate distribution appears not to be "properly paid or credited or required to be distributed," not only because the trustee—not the executor—is supposed to make the distribution, but also because the trust beneficiary's payments theoretically must await funding of the trust, which has not yet occurred. *Hopper v. Government of the Virgin Islands,* 550 F.2d 844 (3d Cir. 1977), supports that view. In *Hopper,* the court required an estate beneficiary to compute her gross income derived from estate distributions without consideration of distributions made by the estate to a trust beneficiary, because the latter distributions were not "properly paid" by the estate. (The Virgin Islands uses the Internal Revenue Code as its tax law.) To the contrary, however, is *Estate of O'Connor v. Commissioner,* 69 T.C. 165 (1977), which, pursuant to the stipulation of the parties, concluded that trust beneficiaries who received distributions from an estate "should be treated as beneficiaries of the estate for purposes of determining the allocation of the estate's distributable net income." *Id.* at 182. Likewise, *Proctor v. White,* 28 F. Supp. 161 (D. Mass. 1939), dealing with a predecessor of section 661, allowed an estate to deduct distributions made directly to a trust beneficiary. Recall that the courts have similarly split over whether trust beneficiaries receiving estate distributions are entitled to share in the estate's depreciation deduction. *See supra* (ch. 2, sec. B(6)).

Private Letter Ruling 8506005 (1984) took a different, but apparently sound, approach. The I.R.S. refused to regard trust beneficiaries, to whom the estate had made direct distributions, as beneficiaries of the estate. The I.R.S. nevertheless required the trust beneficiaries to include the estate distributions in their gross income in accordance with the taxable years of the trusts from which the distributions should have come. Though the ruling did not expressly so state, the estate apparently was allowed distribution deductions on account of the direct distributions. Moreover, the by-passed trusts apparently were required to include the direct distributions in their gross income, offset by their own distribution deductions on account of the direct distributions. Of course, had the trusts not yet been in existence, such an approach would have required nonexistent entities to file returns. Technical Advice Memorandum 8810006 (1987) took the same tack. The I.R.S. treated distributions made by an estate directly to the annuitant of a qualified charitable remainder trust as though made *through* the trust. The I.R.S. expressly ruled that the estate was entitled to a distribution deduction under section 661(a). Both the trust and its annuitant were taxed in accordance with the trust's own status, under section 664.

7. The importance of careful timing of estate distributions is apparent from *Manufacturers Hanover Trust Co. v. United States,* 187 Ct. Cl. 686, 410 F.2d 767 (1969). Wife died first, leaving her entire residuary estate to husband. Her estate contained securities valued at $66,000. Husband died before the securities were distributed to him. At his death, the securities were worth $160,000. Shortly thereafter, the executor of wife's estate sold the securities for $161,000 and reported a gain of $95,000. Later, the executor of wife's estate filed an amended return, claiming that the gain was only $1,000 because of a step-up in basis, under section 1014, at husband's death. The court held that the basis step-up at husband's death was irrelevant, because the sale was by wife's estate. The I.R.S. conceded that the smaller amount of gain would have occurred had wife's estate distributed the securities to husband's estate prior to the sale. The bank served as executor of both estates.

Connecticut National Bank v. United States, 937 F.2d 90 (2d Cir. 1991), seems completely contrary to *Manufacturers Hanover.* In *Connecticut National,* husband's estate sold assets destined for the marital deduction trust, over which wife had a general power of appointment, after the subsequent death of wife. In computing husband's estate's gain on the sale of the assets, husband's executor claimed a basis equal to their value on the date of *wife's* death, even though husband's estate had never distributed them to the marital trust. The Second Circuit, which viewed husband's estate "as holding and managing the property for the benefit of [wife's] appointee," agreed with husband's executor and allowed the higher basis.

Estate of Johnson v. Commissioner
88 T.C. 225
aff'd mem., 838 F.2d 1202 (2d Cir. 1987)

WILLIAMS, *Judge*:

* * *

There are five residuary beneficiaries of decedent's estate: Willard T.C. Johnson (Willard), Elizabeth R. Johnson, Robert W. Johnson IV, Christopher Johnson, and Sheila Johnson Brutsch. Willard survived decedent but died soon after him, and Willard's estate was entitled to his distributive share of decedent's estate. The estates of decedent and Willard have the same executors and accountants.

* * *

The accounting firm of Main Hurdman or its predecessor has at all times served as accountant for both estates. Richard Stone, C.P.A., has been the partner charged with reviewing the estates' tax compliance. In this capacity he worked with Miles Rosenberg, C.P.A., a senior partner in Main Hurdman, and Samuel Klein, an executor of the two estates. Rosenberg is now deceased.

In the early part of 1976, Klein met with Rosenberg to discuss tax matters relating to petitioner, and particularly how to make annual distributions of income from petitioner to Willard's estate. On Rosenberg's advice, Klein instructed the accountants to transfer funds by making book entries on the records of each estate each year crediting a 20 percent share of petitioner's income to Willard's estate. The entries were characterized as deemed distributions from petitioner to Willard's estate. In the course of preparing fiduciary income tax returns for petitioner and for Willard's estate for each year, accountants at Main Hurdman prepared work papers annually for each estate showing transfers of income from decedent's estate to Willard's estate. The work papers are the only documentary evidence of income allocation from petitioner to Willard's estate.

Petitioner elected to credit Willard's account through entries on the work papers rather than actually transferring funds because of the significant contingent liabilities and other contingencies that prevented it from settling the estate. Klein testified that the executors would not make any cash distributions until they had collected all of petitioner's assets and settled its liabilities. There had been no cash transferred between the estates as of the end of 1981.... As of the close of 1981 petitioner had not made distributions of income to any of its other beneficiaries.

For each of the years 1976 through 1981 petitioner deducted as a distribution the amount of book entry credited to Willard's estate. Willard's estate included the distributions in gross income but because all of its income was irrevocably vested in a charitable foundation, it had no income tax liability.

The work paper showing petitioner's transfer of income to Willard's estate for 1981 was prepared in March 1982. The practice of the accounting firm was to prepare tax work papers after the close of the taxable year.

There is no date on the work paper for 1980 and no indication of who prepared it, but Stone testified that work papers were prepared by his staff members in the ordinary course of business. The work paper for petitioner for 1980 was prepared on a copy of the work paper in 1979. The year 1979 and the name of the preparer were crossed out, and the year 1980 and new information were inserted. The entries on the work paper were made in pencil and, in some places, numbers had been erased. Stone did not know who had made the erasures or what had been erased but stated that entries on work papers were always made in pencil. The work paper was found in petitioner's file with other 1980 work papers.

At the time of his death, decedent had amassed significant contingent assets and liabilities. Numerous disputes arose concerning decedent's liabilities and, as a result, petitioner had not been able to make principal distributions to any of its beneficiaries by the end of 1981. The many outstanding contingent liabilities and other contingencies made it reasonable for decedent's estate to be kept open through 1981.

The executors also kept Willard's estate open through 1981. There were no unsettled claims to which Willard's estate was subject in 1980 or 1981, and 100 percent of the income and corpus of the estate was irrevocably vested in the Foundation. The executors, however, had yet to collect the interest of Willard's estate in petitioner, which was a substantial asset of perhaps two million dollars. The executors determined that they could not close Willard's estate and make a final accounting until decedent's estate had settled all of the disputes concerning its liabilities and was prepared to distribute its assets.

In his notice of deficiency dated March 21, 1985, respondent disallowed petitioner's income distribution deductions for 1980 and 1981.

* * *

The … issue for decision is whether petitioner was entitled to deductions pursuant to section 661(a)(2) for income it claims to have distributed to the estate of Willard T.C. Johnson in 1980 and 1981.…

The Second Circuit has interpreted the requirement [of section 661(a)(2)] that amounts be "properly credited" as follows:

> *The income must be so definitively allocated to the legatee as to be beyond recall;* "credit" for practical purposes is the equivalent of "payment." Therefore, a mere entry on the books of the fiduciary will not serve unless made in such circumstances that it cannot be recalled. If the fiduciary's account be stated inter partes, that would probably be enough * * * But the unilateral act of entering items in the account is not conclusive. * * * [*Commissioner v. Stearns*, 65 F.2d 371, 372 (2d Cir. 1933), cert. denied sub nom. *Stearns v. Burnet*, 290 U.S. 670 (1933). Emphasis added.[7]]

Harris v. United States, 370 F.2d 887, 892 (4th Cir. 1966); see *Igoe v. Commissioner*, 19 T.C. 913, 923–924 (1953).

Petitioner and Willard's estate have the same executors and accountants. In 1976 Klein, one of the executors, met with Rosenberg, a senior partner of Main Hurdman, and in-

---

7. In *Commissioner v. Stearns*, the Second Circuit interpreted section 162(c) of the Revenue Act of 1928, which provided a deduction for an estate for amounts "properly paid or credited during such year to any legatee, heir, or beneficiary." 65 F.2d at 373. The Internal Revenue Code of 1954 did not materially change the relevant language.

structed him to make the appropriate entries each year to credit 20 percent of petitioner's income to Willard's estate. Since 1976, under the direction of Richard Stone, who was the accountant charged with reviewing tax compliance for both estates, staff members of Main Hurdman have prepared annual work papers for both estates showing the distributions. The work papers were prepared in the ordinary course of business. The entries on the work papers do not reflect any actual exchange of money, but Willard's estate treated the amounts credited as income on its 1980 and 1981 income tax returns pursuant to section 662(a), and petitioner claimed distributions deductions for the same amounts on its 1980 and 1981 returns. See sec. 661(a)(2).

Petitioner contends that because of the identity of executors and accountants, neither formal bookkeeping entries nor actual separation of funds was necessary to credit income from petitioner to Willard's estate within the meaning of section 661(a)(2). In petitioner's view the informal work papers, prepared in the ordinary course of business, were sufficient to evidence a commitment to set aside funds beyond the recall of petitioner, its creditors, and its other beneficiaries. Petitioner also argues that the consistent reporting of the transfers on the income tax returns for both estates is further evidence of its intent to permanently set aside the funds for Willard's estate. Respondent contends that the work papers did not place the amounts transferred beyond petitioner's recall and that the amounts were, therefore, not properly credited within the meaning of section 661(a)(2).

We agree with respondent. The work papers, which were informal documents prepared in pencil, are the only records showing the transfers of funds between the estates. Stone testified that work papers were prepared in the ordinary course of business after the close of each taxable year, always in pencil, and kept in the files for each estate. We nonetheless cannot find that the work papers were sufficiently permanent documents to function as the books of the estate. We are convinced that, were petitioner to make a bad investment or incur unexpected indebtedness on its large contingent liabilities, the funds credited on the work papers to Willard's estate would not be insulated from the claims of petitioner's creditors or other beneficiaries.

Petitioner chose to credit Willard's account through entries on the work papers rather than actually transferring cash specifically because of the numerous contingent liabilities and other contingencies preventing it from settling the estate. Although the consistent income tax reporting of the transfers by both estates is evidence that the amounts were intended to be permanently set aside for Willard's estate (cf. *In re Estate of O'Neil,* 68 Misc. 2d 634, 327 N.Y.S.2d 725, 732 (Surr.Ct. 1972)), it is not enough to meet petitioner's burden of proof. Willard's estate, as a residuary beneficiary, can receive only the residue of petitioner's assets. Thus, it was prudent for the executors not to make cash distributions until they had collected all of petitioner's assets and settled its liabilities. As one of the executors testified, "we did not make any distributions to any of the beneficiaries * * * we felt it would be prejudicial to them to divide the thing in five places, we felt it was our duty to stay there and settle all claims, negotiate the claims, pay our taxes, collect all the assets and dispose of the liabilities."

We do not hold that, where the representatives or accountants for estate and beneficiary are the same, funds must be physically segregated to satisfy the "properly credited" standard of section 661(a)(2). Entries on the books of the estate may be sufficient in such cases, but we do not believe that work papers such as those prepared in this case can achieve an allocation beyond the recall of the executors, and petitioner has not shown us that New York law is otherwise. The amounts credited to Willard's estate in 1980 and 1981 were not, for Federal income tax purposes, distributions within the meaning of section 661, and petitioner is not entitled to deductions for them.

* * *

Illustrative Material

1. In *Estate of Andrew J. Igoe,* 6 T.C. 639 (1946), *acq.*, 1946-2 C.B. 3, the Tax Court allowed an estate distribution deductions for amounts credited to the accounts of beneficiaries but still held by the executor. The court explained that the executors were always in a position to pay the amounts credited, that the amounts "were readily available to [the beneficiaries] at all times," and that the beneficiaries actually drew on their accounts during the years in question. In addition, the credits "were consummated with full knowledge and consent of the beneficiaries, who were notified of their respective distributive shares of the estate and who reported the amounts so distributed on their income tax returns." 6 T.C. at 647. *Alma Igoe,* 19 T.C. 913 (1953), cited in *Johnson,* held that such amounts were in fact subject to taxation in the hands of the beneficiaries.

2. In *Dominion Trust Company v. United States,* 786 F. Supp. 1321 (M.D. Tenn. 1991), *aff'd mem.*, 7 F.3d 233 (6th Cir. 1993), the court held that a trustee did not "credit" an amount to the account of its beneficiary when it filed an interpleader action against that beneficiary and deposited the amount in question with the court. Private Letter Ruling 9147022 (1991) is, however, to the contrary.

2. Exclusion of Particular Distributions

Internal Revenue Code:
   Section 663(a)

Regulations:
   Sections 1.661(a)-2(e); 1.663(a)-1, -2, -3

Revenue Ruling 57-214
1957-1 C.B. 203

Advice has been requested regarding the tax consequences for Federal income tax purposes of the funding of a testamentary trust created under the facts set forth below.

The will of the decedent provides that, from the residue of his estate, *x* dollars be placed in trust for the benefit of his son, who is to be paid the income therefrom quarterly or as he may direct during his lifetime. In order to provide immediate income to the beneficiary of the trust, the executor plans to fund the trust as soon as possible. The current distributable net income of the estate, is in excess of the amount needed to fund the trust. The possibility that the value of the estate would decrease to the extent that it would not be sufficient to fund the trust is remote.

The issue for consideration is whether the funding of the trust constitutes a payment under the terms of the will of a bequest of a specific sum of money within the meaning of section 663 of the Internal Revenue Code of 1954 and, as such, is not includible as amounts falling within the purview of sections 661(a) and 662(a) of the Code.

Section 661(a) of the Code relates to deductions for estates and trusts accumulating income or distributing corpus while in process of administration....

Section 662 of the Code relates to the amounts includable in gross income of the beneficiaries of trusts and estates accumulating income or distributing corpus....

Section 663 of the Code provides, in part, that gifts or bequests of specific sums of money or specific property paid under the terms of the governing instrument, which are paid or credited all at once or in not more than three installments, are not allowable as additional deduction [sic] to a trust accumulating income or distributing corpus or to an estate under section 661 and are not includible in the taxable income of the beneficiary under section 662. For this purpose, an amount which can be paid or credited only from the income of the estate or trust shall not be considered as a gift or bequest of a specific sum of money.

It is the well established rule that a testamentary trust may be a legatee or beneficiary. G. C. M. 24749, C. B. 1945, 237, and court decisions cited therein.

In the instant case, giving due consideration to the remoteness of the possibility that the value of the estate would decrease to the extent that the residue thereof would not be sufficient to fund the trust, it is concluded that funding of the trust would constitute a payment, under the terms of the will, of a bequest of a specific sum of money within the meaning of section 663(a)(1) of the Code and as such is neither taxable to the trustee nor deductible by the executor.

Revenue Ruling 68-49
1968-1 C.B. 304

Advice has been requested whether distribution by the executor of real property, which comprises part of a residuary estate, is deductible by the estate under section 661 of the Internal Revenue Code of 1954 and includible in the distributee's gross income under section 662 of the Code.

Under the terms of the decedent's will, after providing for certain specific bequests, all of the rest, residue, and remainder of his real property was devised to a specific devisee. Included as part of the residuary estate was a building which was not needed for the payment of claims, expenses of administration, taxes, or legacies. Pursuant to a court order the executor relinquished possession and control of the building to the devisee. Under local law title to the real property passed directly from the decedent to his heirs or devisees even though possession remained in the administrator or executor.

Sections 661 and 662, under subchapter J of chapter 1, subtitle A, of the Code provide for the deductions allowable to an estate for distributions properly made and the inclusion of such distributions in the income of the beneficiaries.

Section 1.661(a)-2(e) of the Income Tax Regulations provides, in pertinent part, that there shall be excluded from the term "any other amounts properly paid or credited or required to be distributed" the value of any interest in real estate owned by a decedent, title to which under local law passes directly from the decedent to his heirs or devisees. This provision of the regulations applies even though the real property is in the possession of the executor or administrator during the period of administration. The exclusion also is not affected by section 663 of the Code, which provides for certain exceptions to insure that gifts and legacies of specific property will not be treated as distributions for purposes of section 661 and 662 of the Code.

Accordingly, the distribution of the real property, which comprised part of the residuary estate, is not deductible by the estate under section 661 of the Code, nor is it includible in the devisee's gross income under section 662 of the Code since under local law title to such property passed directly from the decedent to his heirs or devisees. Such distribution is subject to the general provisions of section 102 of the Code relating to gifts and inheritances.

Illustrative Material

1. In Serv. Ctr. Adv. 1998-012 (Apr. 7, 1998), however, the Service ventured thoughtful analysis of the changing status of real property in estate administration and concluded that "only specifically devised real property, in New York and New Jersey, continues to enjoy the special treatment traditionally accorded real property."

2. In *Edward D. Rollert Residuary Trust v. Commissioner*, 80 T.C. 619 (1983), *aff'd*, 752 F.2d 1128 (6th Cir. 1985), the Tax Court, purporting to hold only "that sec. 691 takes precedence over secs. 661 and 662," appears to have held that no section 661 deduction was allowable for distribution of an item of income in respect of a decedent. (Income in respect of a decedent is examined *infra* (ch. 6).) *Estate of Dean v. Commissioner*, 46 T.C.M. (CCH) 184 (1983), so interpreted *Rollert* and clearly denied the distribution deduction. The theory of both cases is that the specific rules section 691 provides for the taxation of income in respect of a decedent are inconsistent with the more general principles of sections 661 and 662. Thus, distributions of items of income in respect of a decedent are not subject to sections 661 and 662. But once an estate has realized income in respect of a decedent, distribution of the proceeds can generate distribution deductions, in accordance with the usual rules. See Chief Couns. Adv. 200644016 (July 13, 2006); Priv. Ltr. Rul. 200004030 (1999).

Rev. Rul. 68-195, 1968-1 C.B. 305, ruled, without explanation, that a distribution of a right to share in a partnership's future earnings was "not within the term 'any other amounts properly paid or credited or required to be distributed' for purposes of section 661(a)" and thus did not entitle the estate to a distribution deduction. Because the share of partnership earnings was income in respect of a decedent, the ruling squares with *Rollert* and *Dean*.

In 1984 Congress codified the typical result, if not the rationale, of *Rollert* and *Dean*. Under section 643(e), in the absence of an election, a distribution occurs only to the extent of the entity's basis in property distributed. Income in respect of a decedent receives no basis "step-up" under section 1014(c) and therefore usually has a basis of zero. Thus, even if sections 661 and 662 applied to distribution of an item of income in respect of a decedent, the amount of the distribution would usually be zero.

Mott v. United States
199 Ct. Cl. 127, 462 F.2d 512 (1972)
cert. denied, 409 U.S. 1108 (1973)

COWEN, *Chief Judge*, delivered the opinion of the court:

This tax case, apparently one of first impression, comes before the court on the parties' cross-motions for summary judgment. The issue is whether an estate is entitled to a deduction from its gross income, pursuant to Section 661(a)(2) of the Internal Revenue

Code of 1954, when it makes a distribution of corpus of an estate to a qualified charitable beneficiary pursuant to a general pecuniary bequest. We have concluded that the claimed deduction is not available.

The pertinent facts ... are as follows: Walter C. Teagle died on January 9, 1962, leaving a gross estate in excess of $36,000,000. Under the terms of his will, two-thirds of the estate, after payment of debts, expenses, and specific bequests, was left to the Teagle Foundation, a tax-exempt charitable corporation. The residue of the estate, including all income earned during its administration, was left in trust for the benefit of Jane W. Teagle, an alternate life beneficiary, with specified remainders over.

The years involved in this suit are the estate's taxable years ending July 31, 1963, 1964, and 1965. During this period, the executors of the estate made the following payments out of the corpus of the estate in partial satisfaction of the bequest to the Teagle Foundation:

1963	$13,165,575.75
1964	405,379.02
1965	375,000.00

The executors also made several distributions of income to Jane during the administration period before the trust came into operation, including during the years involved here, a $100,000 payment in 1963.

In computing Mr. Teagle's taxable estate, the executors were allowed an estate tax deduction of $14,107,420.90 for the charitable bequest to the Teagle Foundation. They now assert that they are also entitled to a deduction, in computing the estate's taxable income for the years involved here, for the payments described above which they made in satisfaction of the charitable bequest. Briefly stated, they contend that such a deduction is permitted by the plain terms of Section 661(a)(2).... The Government, while conceding that a literal reading of Section 661(a)(2) would permit plaintiffs to prevail, maintains that that section cannot properly be interpreted without reference to its purpose, and that when the provision is read in the context of the entire statutory scheme of Subchapter J of Chapter 1 of the Code, it is clear that the distribution to the charitable organization in this case cannot qualify for the deduction permitted by Section 661(a)(2).

Before reaching the merits of this case, we think it is important to summarize briefly some of the basic principles of Subchapter J which relate to distributions by estates. Since the enactment of the Revenue Act of 1913, the value of "property acquired by gift, bequest, devise or inheritance"[3] has been excluded from gross income. The exclusion is not absolute, however, since income from such property, including income realized by an estate during its administration,[4] is subject to tax.[5] Similarly, a bequest of income from property is not within the statutory exclusion.[6] It has therefore become necessary to develop a system of rules which would determine the proper amounts of estate income subject to tax and, more importantly for purposes of this case, a system which would determine who should bear the burden of that tax. In making this latter determination, Congress has adopted the "conduit principle" of taxing estates (and trusts as well), through which an estate is treated as a taxable entity and is taxed, in general, on income which it realizes but which it does not distribute, or is not deemed to have distributed, to its beneficiaries. Where income is distributed to a beneficiary, or is deemed to be so distributed, that income would not be taxable to the estate but instead would be taxable to the ben-

---

3. INT. REV. CODE OF 1954, §102(a).

4. *See id.,* §641(a).

5. *Id.,* §102(b)(1)....

6. INT. REV. CODE OF 1954, §102(b)(2); *cf.,* Irwin v. Gavit, 268 U.S. 161 (1925).

eficiary, a result which is accomplished by permitting the estate a deduction for the amount of the distribution and by requiring the beneficiary to include that amount in his gross income. In this manner, the conduit principle serves to effectuate a Congressional policy to tax estate income once, and only once, by allocating the tax between estate and beneficiary.[7]

Under the present rules of Subchapter J, the allocation described above is accomplished through the combined operation of the concept of "distributable net income," or "D.N.I.," and the statutory distribution rules applicable to estates and complex trusts, which are set out in Sections 661–63. With regard to distributable net income, we limit our discussion here to only a few salient aspects of that concept, since we previously examined it in detail in *Manufacturers Hanover Trust Co. v. United States,* 160 Ct. Cl. 582, 312 F. 2d 785, *cert. denied,* 375 U.S. 880 (1963). What is important to note here is that D.N.I., which is essentially the estate's taxable income (with some modifications), serves generally as a ceiling on the combined tax liability of the estate and beneficiary, and limits the amount taxable to the beneficiary and deductible by the estate.

In addition, we should also note that D.N.I. is expressed in terms of *taxable* income, and that in computing taxable income Section 642(c), in general, allows an estate (or trust) an unlimited charitable deduction for amounts of "gross income" which, pursuant to the governing instrument, is paid, permanently set aside, or to be used for charitable purposes. Thus, a charitable distribution which is deductible under Section 642(c) has the effect of reducing the maximum aggregate amount taxable to the estate and beneficiary because it reduces D.N.I.[8]

The distribution rules of Sections 661–63 provide the mechanism for allocating D.N.I. between estate and beneficiary. Since frequently an estate makes distributions to more than one beneficiary during a particular taxable year, and since some beneficiaries have greater rights to income than do others, the distribution rules provide for priorities of taxability by establishing what is known as the "tier system." Through this system, D.N.I. is allocated under Section 662(a)(1) first to beneficiaries who have rights to current income, based upon a conclusive presumption that "any distribution is considered a distribution of the trust or estate's current income to the extent of its taxable income for the year."[9] By presuming that such distributions are income, Subchapter J eliminates the need for "tracing" the source of distributions, as was necessary under prior law, to determine what portion, if any, constitutes amounts of current income.[10]

After allocating D.N.I. among the "first-tier" beneficiaries described above, any D.N.I. remaining would be allocated among "second-tier" beneficiaries according to Section 662(a)(2). Theoretically, all distributions except first-tier distributions fall within the second tier, which is defined as "all other amounts properly paid, credited, or required to be distributed to such beneficiary for the taxable year." The term "amounts," which is central to the controversy here, is broad enough to encompass non-first-tier distributions from either principal or income, whether of money or specific property. Again, this elim-

---

7. *See generally* Holland, Kennedy, Surrey & Warren, *A Proposed Revision of the Federal Income Tax Treatment of Trusts and Estates—American Law Institute Draft,* 53 COLUM. L. REV. 316, 318 (1953); 6 MERTENS, LAW OF FEDERAL INCOME TAXATION §36.01 (rev. ed. 1968); FERGUSON, FREELAND & STEPHENS, FEDERAL INCOME TAXATION OF ESTATES AND BENEFICIARIES 382 *et seq.*(1970).

8. However, first-tier beneficiaries are taxed under Section 662(a)(1) up to the estate's D.N.I. undiminished by the deduction provided in Section 642(c).

9. S. REP. NO. 1622, 83d Cong., 2d Sess. 349 (1954).

10. *Id., see* INT. REV. CODE OF 1939, §162(b).

inates the necessity for tracing, since the statute assumes that second-tier distributions diminish whatever D.N.I. remains after allocations to first-tier distributees.

By defining second-tier distributions as any "amounts," the sweep of Section 662(a)(2) is so broad that, if left unqualified, bequests excluded under Section 102(a) could become taxable to beneficiaries under Section 662. To preserve the exemption for bequests, Section 663(a)(1) excludes from the operation of the distribution rules any amount which is not payable solely out of income and "which, under the terms of the governing instrument, is properly paid or credited as a gift or bequest of a specific sum of money or of specific property and which is paid or credited all at once or in not more than three installments." If a distribution meets these requirements, it will be considered a bequest excluded under Section 102(a). If it fails to meet them, it will be considered a bequest of income from property under Section 102(b)(2),[11] and will be taxed according to the distribution rules. Of course, the amount taxable under the distribution rules is circumscribed by the estate's D.N.I., so that amounts distributed in excess of D.N.I. would still be considered as a bequest excluded under Section 102(a), whether or not the distribution meets the specific requirements of Section 663(a)(1).[12]

A second modification to the distribution rules which is pertinent to this case is contained in Section 663(a)(2). It provides that "amounts" do not include "[a]ny amount paid or permanently set aside or otherwise qualifying for the [charitable] deduction provided in Section 642(c) * * *." The purpose of this provision, as explained by the committee reports, is that "since the estate or trust is allowed a deduction under Section 642(c) for amounts paid, permanently set aside, or otherwise qualifying for the deduction provided in that section, such amounts are not allowed as an additional deduction for distributions, nor are they treated as amounts distributed for purposes of Section 662 in determining the amounts includible in gross income of the beneficiaries."[13]

As mentioned above, amounts distributed which are includible in the gross income of a beneficiary would, in general, not be taxable to the estate. This is accomplished by Section 661, which provides for a deduction, up to the estate's distributable net income, for amounts distributed to its beneficiaries. The language and framework of this section corresponds to that of Section 662. An estate can deduct amounts "required to be distributed currently" (first-tier distributions) under Section 661(a)(1), as well as "any other amounts properly paid or credited or required to be distributed" (second-tier distributions) under Section 661(a)(2).

The foregoing discussion of the distribution scheme of Subchapter J, although considerably simplified, provides an adequate framework within which to decide whether, as plaintiffs contend, the estate is entitled to a deduction under Section 661(a)(2) for the amounts paid to the Teagle Foundation. Both parties agree that the amount of the payments, although made to a charitable organization, are not deductible under Section 642(c) in computing the estate's taxable income. Mr. Teagle's will did not provide, as Section 642(c) requires, that the payments be made out of the estate's gross income. In fact, the payments here were made out of the corpus of the estate.

In addition, the parties seem to agree that none of the provisions of Section 663(a) expressly excludes the payments here from the operation of Section 661. The excep-

11. See INT. REV CODE OF 1954, §102 (last sentence); Treas. Reg. §1.102-1(d) (1956).
12. It should be noted that the "throwback rules" of Section 665-69 do not apply to estates. Thus, current D.N.I. is the maximum taxable amount.
13. S. REP. NO. 1622, 83d Cong., 2d Sess. 354 (1954). See also H.R. REP. NO. 1337, 83d Cong., 2d Sess. A205 (1954).

tion of Section 663(a)(1), for gifts or bequests of a specific sum or of specific property which is paid or credited all at once or in not more than three installments, is not applicable here because the bequest has not been satisfied in three installments or less. Moreover, it is not a bequest of a specific sum of money since its amount, expressed as a percentage of the estate after payment of administrative expenses and other charges, was not ascertainable at the time of Mr. Teagle's death. *See* Treas. Reg. §1.663(a)-1(b)(1) (1956). Section 663(a)(2), which provides that an estate may not deduct under Section 661 any amount paid, permanently set aside, or otherwise qualifying for the charitable deduction permitted by Section 642(c), would also seem to be inapplicable because the amounts here, as noted above, do not qualify under Section 642(c) for the charitable deduction.[14]

Plaintiffs contend that since none of the express exceptions to Section 661 applies here, the amounts paid to the Teagle Foundation are properly deductible under that section because they constitute "amounts properly paid * * * for such taxable year * * *." The Government contends that "amounts" cannot be read literally and that Section 661(a)(2) does not apply to these charitable distributions. It relies principally on Section 1.663(a)-2 of the Regulations....[15] From our reading of this regulation, two things seem clear. First, [it] is dispositive of the issue in this case, since it prevents an estate from claiming as a deduction under Section 661(a)(2) any amounts distributed to a charitable beneficiary except as permitted by Section 642(c). Second, however, there is nothing in Section 663(a)(2), the statutory provision under which this regulation was promulgated, which expressly supports the rule announced in the regulation. Section 663(a)(2) provides only that an estate or trust may not deduct under Section 661 any amounts which are also deductible under Section 642(c); it does not specifically cover situations like the one here, where amounts paid to a charitable organization do not qualify for the charitable deduction.

The validity of this regulation must be sustained unless it is "unreasonable and plainly inconsistent with the revenue statutes * * *." *Commissioner v. South Texas Lumber Co.,* 333 U.S. 496, 501 (1948).... After carefully considering the parties' contentions in this case, as well as the entire distribution scheme of Subchapter J, we think that the regulation is valid and also that any other rule would be an unreasonable interpretation of the statute.

We do not adopt plaintiff's argument that Section 661(a)(2) must be read according to its literal terms. If an estate were entitled to a distribution deduction for "*any* other amounts properly paid," as that section provides, then all payments made by an estate, whether or not to a beneficiary, would be deductible. For example, contrary to *Thomas Lonergan Trust,* 6 T.C. 715 (1946), an estate would be allowed a distribution deduction when it makes payments to a creditor in satisfaction of a judgment against the estate. Moreover, under a literal interpretation of Section 661(a)(2), in many instances an estate would be entitled to a double deduction. Thus, expenses which are deductible under Section 212 would be deductible again under Section 661.

Obviously, the phrase "any other amounts paid" should not be read as broadly as its literal terms suggest. It must be interpreted in its own particular context, with reference to its relationship with the other provisions of Subchapter J, and in accordance with the consequences which Congress sought to achieve when it enacted Section 661 in 1954.

---

14. Section 663(a)(3), which precludes a double distribution deduction where an amount required to be distributed is accumulated and distributed in a later year, is by its terms inapplicable to this case.

15. ... *See also* Rev. Rul. 68-667, 1968-2 CUM. BULL. 289.

The most logical reference point in attempting to delineate the scope of Section 661 is the corollary provision of Section 662. That the two sections should be read together is not only implicit from the fact that they are similarly structured and in some instances identically worded, but also explicit from Section 662's express reference to Section 661. Thus, Section 662(a), in imposing its tax on distributees, states that "there shall be included in the gross income of a beneficiary to whom an amount specified in Section 661(a) is paid, credited, or required to be distributed * * * the sum of the following amounts * * *." By this reference, we think it is proper to confine Section 661 to distributions to *beneficiaries* of the estate, even though Section 661(a) does not specifically so provide.[16] Such a construction, implied in Section 662(a), prevents the absurd results mentioned above which would occur if the phrase "any other amounts properly paid" in Section 661(a)(2) were applied literally.

Of course, an interpretation which limits Section 661 to distributions to beneficiaries does not put an end to the matter here, since the Teagle Foundation is a beneficiary of the estate. Therefore, the Government also asks us to interpret Section 661(a) as permitting a deduction only for distributions to *taxable* beneficiaries, based upon its argument that Section 661 must be read as interdependent with Section 662. That is, as we understand the Government's argument, the incidence of the tax on the income of an estate must be allocated between estate and beneficiary, and to the extent that the beneficiary is exempt from the tax imposed by Section 662, any distributions to that beneficiary would not be deductible by the estate under Section 661.

The Government's position seems to be correct in the context of this case, but we do not hold that it is a general rule which may be applied in every conceivable situation that may arise under the provisions of the Code here considered. We think it is sufficient to say that, under the facts of this case, the Government's position accords with the general intent of Congress in enacting the distribution rules[17] and, as we discuss below, is in accord with what we believe to be an implied Congressional intent to prevent all charitable distributions, whether or not deductible under Section 642(c), from entering into the operation of the distribution rules.

As we noted above, when Congress enacted the present distribution rules its primary purpose was to eliminate the necessity for tracing the source of distributions. Under prior law, in general, beneficiaries were taxed only on amounts of current income distributed by an estate or trust. Such a simple rule led to manipulation,[18] and in 1942 Congress attempted to tighten up the statute by enacting the 65-day rules of Section 162(d) of the 1939 Code [predecessor of section 663(b)]. The end result was that the distribution rules became so difficult to apply, and so entrenched in the tracing requirements, that Congress abandoned the old system in favor of the present scheme.[19] Tracing was eliminated by

---

16. This construction is confirmed by the legislative history of Section 661. See H.R. REP. NO. 1337, 83d Cong., 2d Sess. A198 (1954); S. REP. NO. 1622, 83d Cong., 2d Sess. 347 (1954):

    "*Section 661. Deductions for estates and trusts accumulating income or distributing corpus.*

    "This section (subject to the limitation discussed below) allows an additional deduction to estates or trusts for amounts paid, credited, or required to be distributed *to beneficiaries.* * * * [Emphasis added]"

17. See H.R. REP. NO. 1337, 83d Cong., 2d Sess. 60 (1954); S. REP. NO. 1622, 83d Cong., 2d Sess. 82 (1954):

    "The bill adopts the general principle that to the extent of the trust's current income all distributions are deducible by the estate or trust and taxable to the beneficiaries."

18. *See, e.g.,* Commissioner v. Dean, 102 F. 2d 699 (10th Cir. 1939).

19. *See* Kamin, Surrey, & Warren, *The Internal Revenue Code of 1954: Trusts, Estates and Beneficiaries,* 54 COLUM. L. REV. 1237, 1246–48 (1954).

providing in Section 662 that all amounts distributed to beneficiaries would be considered to be distributions of income, subject to the modifications of Section 663 and the quantitative limitation of D.N.I. Consistent with the conduit principle, an estate or trust making such distributions would be entitled to a deduction under Section 661.

As we read Sections 661(a) and 662(a), Congress intended to do nothing more than combine the conduit principle with a conclusive presumption that distributions subject to the operation of those sections are distributions of income. Such a presumption is, we think, inapplicable to charitable distributions. As Section 642(c) provides, a charitable deduction is available only if the source of the distribution is gross income. Tracing of charitable distributions is still required under Section 642(c),[20] and to the extent that a charitable distribution is not paid out of gross income in accordance with the requirements of Section 642(c), then we think that Congress intended that no deduction is allowable.

Without the distinction between charitable and noncharitable distributions, Congress' general intent in enacting the present provisions—to prevent manipulative distributions—would be seriously thwarted. The facts of this case are a good illustration. Both the Teagle Foundation and Jane, the sole income distributee, would be second-tier beneficiaries. If the estate could deduct under Section 661(a)(2) the payments made out of the corpus of the estate in satisfaction of the charitable bequest, then the following will result: the estate will pay no tax on the income which it accumulates, because that income will be offset by deductions for its distributions of corpus to the Teagle Foundation. Later on, the estate can distribute the accumulated income to Jane tax-free. With regard to current payments to Jane, concededly out of estate income, her tax would be greatly reduced. Thus, in 1963, she received $100,000 while the Teagle Foundation received approximately $13,200,000. If both amounts were considered distributions to beneficiaries within the meaning of Section 662, then Jane would be taxable on only 1/133 of the estate's D.N.I. for 1963, up to the amount of her distribution.

Based upon our reading of the distribution sections of Subchapter J and their legislative history, we conclude that Section 1.663(a)-2 of the Regulations, which provides that amounts distributed by an estate or trust to a charitable organization are deductible only under Section 642(c), is consistent with the statutory scheme and a reasonable interpretation thereof. It necessarily follows that plaintiffs are not entitled to a deduction pursuant to Section 661(a)(2) for the amounts of corpus distributed in satisfaction of the charitable bequest. Accordingly, defendant's motion for summary judgment is granted, plaintiff's motion for summary judgment is denied, and the petition is dismissed.

Illustrative Material

To the same effect are *Rebecca K. Crown Income Charitable Fund v. Commissioner*, 98 T.C. 327 (1992), *aff'd*, 8 F.3d 571 (7th Cir. 1993); *United States Trust Co. v. Internal Revenue Service*, 803 F.2d 1363 (5th Cir. 1986); *Pullen v. United States*, 80-1 U.S.T.C. ¶ 9105 (D. Neb. 1979), *aff'd mem.*, 634 F.2d 632 (8th Cir. 1980); *Estate of O'Connor v. Commissioner*, 69 T.C. 165 (1977); Rev. Rul. 2003-123, 2003-2 C.B. 1200; Rev. Rul. 68-667, 1968-2 C.B. 289; and Technical Advice Memorandum 8738007 (1987). *But cf.* Technical Advice Memorandum 8810006 (1987) (distribution deduction allowed on account of amounts distributed to charitable remainder annuity trust). Denial of the distribution deduction for amounts not deductible under section 642(c) has, however, been criticized. *See* M.

---

20. Riggs National Bank v. United States, 173 Ct. Cl. 479, 352 F. 2d 812 (1965).

Ferguson, J. Freeland & M. Ascher, *Federal Income Taxation of Estates, Trusts, and Beneficiaries* § 6.10 (3d ed. 1998 & Supp. 2008).

3. Trapping Distributions

A "trapping distribution" was once a standard method of reducing an entity's income taxes. It was particularly effective if the entity's individual beneficiaries were in high brackets, because it deliberately exploited an artificial, low-bracket taxpayer, usually a testamentary trust.

United States v. Bank of America National Trust & Savings Association, 326 F.2d 51 (9th Cir. 1963), illustrates the technique. An estate that had distributable net income made distributions to a testamentary trust. The estate therefore was entitled to a distribution deduction, and the trust was subject to taxation on the distributions, though they constituted principal in the trustee's hands under local law. The trust was required to distribute income currently but was neither required nor permitted to distribute principal. The court therefore held that the distributions were not "required to be distributed currently" by the trust. Neither could they be "properly" paid out by the trust. Accordingly, the trust's income beneficiaries were not subject to taxation on the distributions. Because the trust was not entitled to a distribution deduction, the distributions were "trapped" there. As a result, the trust paid the income tax on a portion of the estate's income. For similar holdings, see *Casco Bank & Trust Co. v. United States,* 406 F. Supp. 247 (D. Me. 1975), and Technical Advice Memorandum 7809057 (1977).

Van Buren v. Commissioner
89 T.C. 1101 (1987)

KÖRNER, *Judge*: ... The issue for our determination is whether the character (as between taxable and tax-exempt income) of amounts reportable by the beneficiary of a simple trust is determined solely by the trust's internally generated income, or whether the character of amounts received by the trust in a distribution from an estate also enters into the determination.

* * *

Petitioner is the beneficiary of a testamentary trust created by the will of her late husband, Maurice P. van Buren, who died a resident of New York on May 8, 1979.[2] The terms of the trust require the trustee to distribute all net income to or for the benefit of petitioner at least annually during her life. The trust instrument also authorizes distribution of principal to petitioner, as might be needed for her support, although no such principal distributions were made during the taxable year at issue. The trust contains no provision authorizing amounts to be paid or permanently set aside for charitable purposes. The trust therefore qualifies as a "simple" trust during the taxable year at issue. Sec. 651; sec. 1.651(a)-1, Income Tax Regs. Upon petitioner's death, one-half of the remaining

---

2. Maurice van Buren's will was admitted to probate by the Surrogate's Court of New York County on May 22, 1979. Testamentary trusts are generally governed by the law of the state where the testator was domiciled. See *Schaffner v. Chemical Bank,* 339 F. Supp. 329 (S.D.N.Y. 1972). Therefore, as pertinent here, the law of the state of New York will control. See further discussion, *infra.*

trust principal is to be distributed in accordance with petitioner's testamentary general power of appointment. The remaining one-half is to be distributed to certain specified beneficiaries. The trust has a taxable year ending May 31.

For its taxable year ended June 30, 1980, the estate of Maurice van Buren generated $110,491 of distributable net income (hereinafter DNI) consisting of dividends, taxable and tax-exempt interest, and other income.[4] Apparently without distributing these funds (at least to petitioner), the estate made a distribution of principal to the testamentary trust, which consisted partly of common stocks and partly of tax-exempt municipal bonds. Pursuant to section 662, this distribution caused a portion of the estate's DNI to be carried out and taxed to the trust[5] resulting in the inclusion of $26,253 of dividends and $40,523 of other taxable income in the income of the trust for its taxable year ended May 31, 1981.[6] Although the estate principal distribution constituted income to the trust for tax purposes, it retained its character as principal in the hands of the trust for fiduciary accounting purposes.[7] The parties are not in disagreement as to any of this.

In addition to income attributable to the trapping distribution of principal from the estate, the instant trust also generated $7,648 of taxable dividends and $41,450 of tax-exempt interest from its own investments, for total income of $49,098, for its fiscal year 1981. This is the trust income as determined for fiduciary accounting purposes which was required, per the trust instrument, to be distributed to petitioner. The trust also paid $3,977 of trustee's commissions and $333 of New York state income tax with respect to this income.

For calendar year 1981, petitioner calculated that she had realized $44,788 of income consisting of $6,696 of taxable income and $38,092 of tax-exempt income attributable to her interest in the $49,098 of income internally generated by the trust in its taxable year

4. Basically, the DNI of an estate or trust consists of its taxable income (calculated in much the same manner as that of an individual) increased by the amount of its personal exemption, any tax-exempt income and any distribution deductions taken pursuant to sec. 651 or 661. Taxable income is reduced by any capital gains of the estate or trust which are allocable to principal. Sec. 643(a).

5. A distribution from an estate results in income to the recipient to the extent of the estate's DNI, regardless of its designation as income or principal for accounting purposes. Sec. 662; sec. 1.662(c)-3, Income Tax Regs. The estate is entitled to a concomitant distribution deduction equal to the beneficiary's required income inclusion under sec. 662. Sec. 661. This avoids "double taxation" of the estate's income to both the estate and the beneficiary and is basic to an understanding of the estate as a conduit. H. Rept. No. 1337, 83rd Cong., 2d Sess. A194 (1954); S. Rept. No. 1022, 83d Cong., 2d Sess. 343 (1954). The same principles apply to distributions from a trust. Sec. 651, 652.

6. The income inclusion consists of the same proportion of each class of income entering into the DNI of the estate as the total of that class of income bears to the total DNI of the estate. See 662(b), sec. 1.662(b)-1, Income Tax Regs.

The estate form K-1 also shows $941 of tax-exempt income carried out to the trust by the principal distribution. This amount was ignored by petitioner and omitted from respondent's deficiency notice.

7. Under New York law, a distribution from an estate to a trust is not "income" of the trust unless the items distributed were "income" of the estate. See generally New York Estates, Powers & Trusts Law section 11-2.1 (McKinney 1967). Thus the amount of the distribution was not income required to be distributed to petitioner.

The distribution of principal from an estate to a simple trust is commonly called a trapping distribution. The purpose of an estate distribution of principal to a trust is to take advantage of the trust's status as a separate taxpayer to ameliorate the effect of the graduated tax brackets on the estate's income. The distribution causes a portion of the estate's income to be "carried out" and taxed to the trust. When the principal distributed by the estate also constitutes trust principal, it is not taxed to the income beneficiaries of a simple trust. Secs. 651, 652. The taxable income is thus "trapped" at the trust level. See generally Cohan & Frimmer, "Trapping Distributions—The Trap that Pays," 112 Trusts & Estates 766 (1973).

ended May 31, 1981.[8] In determining the character of the income, petitioner ignored the trust DNI attributable to the "trapping" distribution from the estate. Her calculations are summarized as follows:

	Tax-Exempt	Taxable Dividends	Total
Internally Generated Trust Accounting Income	$41,450	$7,648	$49,098
Less:			
Trustee's Commissions			
Allocable to Tax-Exempt Income (41,450/49,098) × 3,977	(3,358)		(3,358)
Allocable to Taxable Income (7,648/49,098) × 3,977		(619)	(619)
Taxes		(333)	(333)
Petitioner's Income From Trust	$38,092	$6,696	$44,788[9]

In a notice of deficiency dated September 7, 1984, respondent determined a deficiency in petitioner's income tax for taxable year 1981 of $15,316.07. He attributed the deficiency to petitioner's failure to take into consideration the trust DNI attributable to the trapping distribution in determining the amount and character of her income attributable to her interest in the trust. Respondent determined that petitioner had $49,098 of income from the trust consisting of $13,649 of dividends, $17,834 of other taxable income and $17,615 of tax-exempt income. His calculations are summarized below:

	Tax-Exempt	Dividends	Other Taxable	Total
Internally Generated Trust Accounting Income	$41,450	$7,648		$49,098
Income Attributable to Trapping Distribution		26,253	$40,523	66,776
	$41,450	$33,901	$40,523	$115,874
Less:				
Trustee's Commissions:				
Allocable to Tax-Exempt Income (41,450/115,874) × 3,977	(1,423)			(1,423)
Allocable to Taxable Income ((33,901+40,523)/115,874) × 3,977		(2,554)		(2,554)
Taxes		(333)		(333)
Trust Distributable Net Income (DNI)	$40,027	$31,014	$40,523	$111,564
Petitioner's Allocable Share of Each Item Constituting Trust DNI (49,098/111,564)	44.01%	44.01%	44.01%	44.01%
Petitioner's Income From Trust	$17,615	$13,649	$17,834	$49,098

---

8. The gross income inclusion of a trust beneficiary pursuant to sec. 652, is based on the trust's income for the taxable year of the trust which ends with or within the beneficiary's taxable year. Sec. 652(c).

9. Petitioner's calculations indicate that she also excluded consideration of the trust DNI attributable to the trapping distribution from her determination of the *amount* of the distribution which constitutes income to her as well as its *character*. Petitioner calculated the DNI of the trust attributable to its accounting income as being $44,788. The $44,788 thus formed the upper limit (she claimed) on her income inclusion by reason of the $49,098 of accounting income required to be distributed to her. Sec. 651(b). However, on brief, petitioner acknowledges that since the $49,098 is less than the DNI of the trust as a whole, the sec. 651(b) ceiling rule does not apply.

Petitioner also seems to have conceded that trust expenses should have been allocated between tax-exempt and taxable income based on the income of the trust as a whole, rather than upon only that portion which constitutes trust accounting income. See sec. 1.652(b)-3, Income Tax Regs.

Each of these adjustments would affect both the amount and character of petitioner's income from the trust.

* * *

Subchapter J of Subtitle A of the Internal Revenue Code governs the tax treatment of trust distributions. A "simple" trust is a trust which is required to distribute all of its accounting income[10] currently, does not make any distributions of other than current income, and does not provide that any amounts be paid or permanently set aside for charitable purposes. Sec. 651(a); sec. 1.651(a)-1, Income Tax Regs. The record establishes that the trust herein was a simple trust during the taxable year at issue.

The beneficiary of a simple trust is required to include in her income the trust accounting income which is required to be distributed to her currently, whether distributed or not. Sec. 652(a); sec. 1.652(a)-1, Income Tax Regs. However, the accounting income of the trust is not taxed to the beneficiaries to the extent it exceeds the trust's distributable net income (DNI), as defined in section 643(a). Sec. 1.652(a)-2, Income Tax Regs.

The DNI concept not only places an upper limit on the amount of the distribution includable in the beneficiary's income, but determines its character as well. The amounts included in the beneficiary's income are treated as consisting of the same proportion of each class of income entering into trust DNI as the total of each class bears to such DNI, unless the terms of the trust specifically allocate different classes of income to different beneficiaries, or unless local law requires such an allocation. Sec. 652(b); secs. 1.652(b)-1, 1.652(b)-2, Income Tax Regs.

The distribution of assets by the estate to the trust is taxable to the trust to the extent of the estate's DNI, even though under local law such distribution may be principal in the hands of the trust. Sec. 662(a)(2); *Harkness v. United States,* 469 F.2d 310 (Ct. Cl. 1972), cert. denied 414 U.S. 820 (1973); *Casco B & T Co. v. United States,* 406 F.Supp. 247 (D. Me. 1975). The parties are not in disagreement on this, and have stipulated as to the amount and character of the taxable income received by the trust, as we have found.

The income of the trust—both that received from the estate as well as the trust's internally generated income is then computed under sections 641 and 642, and both the above elements go into the computation of the trust's DNI under section 643. Here, an apparent paradox arises in that the distribution from the estate to the trust—the trapping distribution—although part of the trust's DNI under section 643, is nevertheless not distributable to the income beneficiary, but remains in the hands of the trust as corpus under local law.[11] The oxymoron of "undistributable distributable net income" is explained by the fact that although the trust's DNI is computed under section 643, that which is required to be distributed to the beneficiary, taxable to her under section 652, with corresponding deduction to the trust under section 651, is governed by the standards of the trust instrument, which specifies that only the net accounting income of the trust is to be distributed.

* * *

---

10. As used in Subchapter J, the term "income," when not preceded by the words "taxable," "distributable net," "undistributed net," or "gross," means the income of the trust as determined under the trust instrument and applicable local law. Sec. 643(b). For clarity, we refer to this concept as "accounting income."

11. The treatment of trapping distributions, similar to the instant case—that such distributions, while includable in the taxable income of the trust to the extent of the DNI of the estate, are nevertheless to be considered as distributed to the beneficiary only if authorized by the trust instrument or local law—was clearly recognized in *United States v. Bank of America NT&S Assn.,* 326 F.2d 51, 53–55 (9th Cir. 1963)....

Petitioner contends that she falls within the exception to proportionate allocation which applies when specific allocations of different classes of income to different beneficiaries are contained in the trust instrument or required by local law. Sec. 1.652(b)-2, Income Tax Regs. She argues that the various classes of income constituting DNI must be allocated in the same manner as the same dollars are allocated between principal and income for fiduciary accounting purposes by the trust instrument. Petitioner argues that her method is consistent with the economic substance of the arrangement and accords with the general conduit approach of Subchapter J.

Petitioner correctly states that the trust instrument bestows the income of the trust upon one beneficiary and the trust principal to others. However, petitioner's assertion that the particular classes of income which constitute trust DNI must therefore be allocated to the persons entitled to receive the principal or income of the trust which gives rise to those particular classes of income is wholly without support in either the language of the trust instrument itself, or in applicable provisions of New York law.

To the extent petitioner equates the terms "principal" and "income" as used in the trust instrument with the "different classes of income" referred to in section 652 and the regulations thereunder, she is mistaken. The different classes of income referred to in the statute and regulations are dividends, tax-exempt interest, capital gains, etc., whose designation as such will have tax significance to the recipient. See Kamin, Surrey & Warren, "The Internal Revenue Code of 1954: Trusts, Estates and Beneficiaries," 54 Colum. L. Rev. 1237, 1246 (1954). The allocations under the trust instrument are not in terms of different classes of tax income, but rather in terms of state law definitions differentiating trust income from corpus. As to allocation of different classes of income constituting DNI, both the trust instrument and local law are silent. Since neither the trust instrument nor state law provides for an allocation of different classes of income to different beneficiaries, the exception relied upon by petitioner does not apply and the different classes of income comprising trust DNI must be allocated between petitioner and the trust proportionately. Sec. 1.652(b)-2, Income Tax Regs.

The objectives of the reforms in the area of estate and trust income taxation embodied in Subchapter J weigh against petitioner. Prior to the adoption of the 1954 Code, the beneficiary of a trust was taxed on a trust distribution only to the extent it was made from the current income of the trust as determined under local trust law. Sec. 162(b), I.R.C. 1939; H. Rept. No. 1337, 83d Cong., 2d Sess. 60 (1954). Thus, a tracing of amounts distributed to their source was necessary in order to determine the distribution's taxability to the beneficiary. The concept of DNI was introduced in Subchapter J precisely to avoid the often onerous task of tracing the source of trust distributions. S. Rept. No. 1622, 83d Cong., 2d Sess. 82, 349 (1954); H. Rept. No. 1337, 83d Cong., 2d Sess. 60, A199 (1954). The DNI concept eliminates the tracing requirement by presuming that a distribution is made out of the trust's DNI to the extent thereof, regardless of whether the distribution was actually made from income or principal. In this respect DNI serves much the same function as does earnings and profits in the area of corporate distributions. To eliminate the tracing requirement for determining the *amount* of the required distribution constituting income to the beneficiary yet retain it for *characterizing* the income would negate one of the major simplifications over prior law accomplished by Subchapter J. Tracing is only permitted in the limited cases where the trust instrument or local law *specifically* requires a nonproportionate allocation of classes of income among beneficiaries. This is not such a case.

Petitioner's reliance on cases which have found a tracing requirement pursuant to the availability of a charitable deduction to the trust is misplaced. Section 642(c)(1) allows a trust a charitable deduction for any amount of its gross income which, pursuant to the trust instrument, is paid for charitable purposes. Sec. 642(c)(1). Tracing is required since the statute specifically requires that the source of the contribution be gross income. See *Riggs National Bank v. United States*, 352 F.2d 812, 814 (Ct. Cl. 1965). This specific reference forms the basis of a limited exception to the general removal of the tracing requirement accomplished by Subchapter J. The exception is limited to the area of charitable deductions and provides no support to petitioner. See *Mott v. United States*, 462 F.2d 512, 518–519 (Ct. Cl. 1972).

Finally, we note that a specific allocation of different classes of income is only given effect if it has economic consequences aside from the income tax effect. Sec. 1.652(b)-2(b), Income Tax Regs. Even had petitioner been successful in persuading us that the trust instrument required the allocation of different classes of income to different beneficiaries, the allocation would not be effective since its only economic consequences would be tax related. The trust entitles the petitioner to the net accounting income generated by the trust. In taxable year 1981 this amount was $49,098, less commissions and local taxes totaling $4,310. Petitioner is entitled to $44,788 no matter how it is characterized. A specific non-proportionate allocation of items of trust income to petitioner would affect her tax liability, but would neither increase nor decrease the dollar amount to which she is entitled under the instrument.

To summarize, we conclude that neither the trust instrument nor local law specifically allocates different classes of income to petitioner. Petitioner's income from the trust thus consists of the same proportion of each class of income constituting the DNI of the trust as the total of each class of income bears to the total DNI of the trust. To this extent, therefore, we approve respondent's computation of the trust's DNI, his determination of the various classes of income, and his allocation of deductions among the various classes, as contained in his computation which we have reproduced above herein.

As to two further matters, however, we consider that respondent's computation was in error:

First. In his computation of petitioner's allocable share of each item constituting trust DNI, respondent constructed a fraction, in which the numerator was the *gross* internally generated trust income, and the denominator was the trust distributable *net* income. The fraction was 44.01 percent. This was clearly erroneous; the proper fraction or percentage of petitioner's allocable share was the *gross* internal income ($49,098) divided by the *gross* trust income ($115,874), or 42.37 percent.[12]

Second. Respondent then applied his erroneous percentage to each item or class of the trust's distributable *net* income, with the result that the amount of each class of income which was allocated to petitioner was in *gross*, depriving petitioner of the benefit of any deductions which pertained to that class of income.

The purpose of the 1954 Code, expressed in section 652(b), was to give to the income beneficiary the benefit of all deductions attributable to taxable income which was distributed to her, excluding those deductions attributable to tax-exempt income. *Tucker v. Commissioner*, 322 F.2d 86 (2d Cir. 1963).... Respondent's regulations carry out this intention, providing that after allocating a proportionate part of the expenses to tax-exempt income, and after excluding capital gains (there were none here) from the allocation

---

12. The proof of this proposition is that if respondent had used his same method to compute the *trust's* allocable share of trust DNI, he would have gotten a percentage of 59.85 (66,776 ÷ 11,156) which, when added to petitioner's percentage of 44.01, would have totaled 103.86 percent—more than the entire trust DNI.

computation, the remaining deductions not directly attributable to a specific class of income "may be allocated to the [taxable income] in such proportions as the trustee may elect." Sec. 1.652(b)-3, Income Tax Regs. We think it is clear, both from the way the income was reported as well as from petitioner's computation herein, that it was the trustee's intention that petitioner should have the benefit of all available deductions. This position is also in conformity with the trust instrument, which gave petitioner the right to the net income of the trust.

We conclude, then, that the proper computation of petitioner's income from the trust for 1981, under section 652, is as follows:

	Tax-Exempt	Taxable Dividends	Other Taxable	Total
Petitioner's Allocable Share of Each Item (Gross) Forming Part of Trust DNI (49,098 ÷ 115,874)	42.37%	42.37%	42.37%	42.37%
Petitioner's Share (Gross)	$17,562	$14,364	$17,170	$49,096
Less Allocable Deductions	(1,423)	(2,554)		(3,977)
		(333)		(333)
Petitioner's Reportable Income from Trust	$16,139	$11,477	$17,170	$44,786

Technical Advice Memorandum 8501011 (1984)

ISSUE

Whether an amount equal to the so-called "*Holloway* adjustment" is includible in a simple trust's income that must be distributed currently.

FACTS

The deed of T-I, a trust, provided that upon its grantor's death 40 percent of T-I's corpus would form the corpus of a trust, T-II, for the benefit of B, an individual. Under the deed of T-II, C, the trustee, must pay all of T-II's income to B not less often than annually. A majority of trustees other than C have full discretion to invade corpus either for the support, maintenance, and care of B, to meet any emergency of B, or to provide the comfort and luxuries to which B is accustomed, including recreation and travel, but the invasion may not exceed a certain amount each year. The trust terminates at B's death and any remaining principal is to be divided equally between several remaindermen.

T-I had distributable net income for the taxable year of its first distribution to T-II. During that year the trustee of T-I distributed to T-II an amount in excess of T-I's distributable net income. The excess amount constituted a portion of T-II's corpus. For federal income tax purposes, the trustee of T-I deducted an amount equal to distributable net income under section 661(a) of the Internal Revenue Code from the gross income of T-I and C included such amount under section 662(a) of the Code in the gross income of T-II. Because the entire amount distributed to T-II was under its deed allocable to corpus, C distributed nothing to B and took no distribution deduction for T-II's taxable year ending March 31, 1981, its year in which the amount was received.

For T-II's taxable year ending March 31, 1981, T-II sustained a federal income tax liability of approximately 43x dollars because of its inclusion in gross income under section 661(a) of the Code on its receipt of the distribution from T-I.

For its taxable year ending March 31, 1982, T-II had receipts considerably in excess of 43x dollars. C determined that an amount of the receipts equal to the federal tax liability for T-II's preceding taxable year was for fiduciary accounting purposes allocable to T-II's corpus. Accordingly, C did not include the amount on the Schedule K-1 to T-II's Form 1041 for T-II's year ending March 31, 1982, that C provided B. T-II's deed contains no provision expressly requiring the trustee to allocate any fiduciary accounting income to fiduciary accounting corpus to reimburse such corpus for income taxes paid out of corpus.

The administration of both T-I and T-II is subject to the law of New York.

LAW AND RATIONALE

Under section 641(b) of the Code, the taxable income of a trust is computed generally in the same manner as that of an individual.

Under section 643(b) of the Code, for purposes of the taxation of trusts and their beneficiaries, the term "income", when not preceded by the word "taxable", "distributable net", "undistributed", or "gross", means the amount of income of the trust for the taxable year determined under applicable local law.

Under section 1.643(a)-0 of the Income Tax Regulations, the term "distributable net income" has no application except in the taxation of estates or trusts and their beneficiaries. It limits the deductions allowable to estates and trusts for amounts paid, credited, or required to be distributed to beneficiaries and is used to determine how much of such amounts will be includible in the beneficiary's gross income. It also determines the character of distributions to the beneficiary.

Under section 651(a) of the Code, a trust that must distribute currently all its income for a taxable year is allowed a deduction for the amount of the income. Under section 1.652(a)-1 of the regulations, such trust is called a "simple" trust for such taxable year.

Under section 651(b) of the Code, if a simple trust's income exceeds the trust's distributable net income for the taxable year, the trust's deduction is limited to the amount of distributable net income. For this purpose, the computation of distributable net income does not include items of income that are not included in the gross income of the trust and the deductions allocable thereto.

Under section 1.651(a)-2 of the regulations, whether trust income must be distributed currently depends upon the terms of the trust instrument and applicable local law.

In *In re Holloway's Estate*, 327 N.Y.S. 2d 865 (1972), the court considered whether a trustee acted properly in not allocating to principal trust receipts of one year equal in amount to federal income taxes for the immediately preceding year that were paid on and out of receipts for the preceding year that were properly allocated to trust principal. In the preceding year the trust had received a distribution from an estate. Because the estate had distributable net income for its year in which it distributed an amount to the trust, the trust was required to include a portion of the distribution in its gross income under section 662(a) of the Code, and the trust paid federal income tax on the amount. The court held that the adjustment should be made, and directed the trustee to make it.

The *Holloway* opinion does not state whether anything in the trust deed indicated that the grantor was aware of the possibility of making the adjustment or providing the trustee with discretion or a direction with respect to it. However, in a previous opinion, concerning the same issue and parties (*In re Will of Holloway*, 323 N.Y.S. 2d 534 (1972), the court declined to require the trustee to make the adjustment. In that previous opinion the court wrote that "[t]his is not to infer (so in the original), however, that the trustees would necessarily have been found imprudent had they made the [adjustment] ... provided they were authorized ... to make such discretionary [adjustments]...." This language suggests that the court might judge the propriety of a trustee's decision on the adjustment by the terms of the trust, and would require such adjustment only if the trust deed is silent on the point.

The same court again addressed the issue of the adjustment in *Holloway* in *In re Will of Coe*, 363 N.Y.S. 2d 265 (1975). In *Coe*, the operative events occurred before the later decision in *Holloway*, which held that a trustee not granted discretion to make the adjustment was required to make it. The court held in *Coe* that the fiduciary was not required to make the adjustment.

In *Coe*, the court wrote that the fiduciary "should not be surcharged *for exercising its discretion* in not having the principal reimbursed for the taxes paid in view of the fact that *Matter of Holloway* was not decided when the taxes were paid." (Emphasis supplied.)

This language suggests that in situations occurring after the second *Holloway* decision a court would require the adjustment if the trust deed was either silent on the point or granted the trustee general discretion in making adjustments.

Nothing in either *Holloway* opinion or the *Coe* opinion suggests what a court would require of the trustee if the trustee were specifically directed not to make the adjustment.

Because T-II's deed does not direct its trustee not to make the adjustment, and the authority in New York appears to require the adjustment absent such direction, the trustee's reimbursement of fiduciary principal out of receipts for income taxes paid out of principal is excluded from the trust's income, as the term "income" is used in section 643(b) and section 652(a) of the Code.

CONCLUSION

Income of a trust that is required to be distributed currently does not include an amount equal to the so-called *Holloway* adjustment, in a state in which judicial authority generally recognizes the propriety of the adjustment, if the governing instrument does not prohibit the adjustment, and the question of the validity of such prohibition is without authority under principles of the state's law.

Illustrative Material

1. In the second *Holloway* decision, discussed in Technical Advice Memorandum 8501011, a state court modified the usual rules relating to principal and income in order to avoid what it considered an injustice caused by federal tax law, as illustrated in note 2, *infra*. In contrast, in *Hill v. Estate of Richards*, 142 N.J. 639, 667 A.2d 695 (1995), the Supreme Court of New Jersey declined to require adjustments for supposed unfairnesses resulting from application of subchapter J to disproportionate distributions pursuant to a beneficiary agreement drafted by the beneficiary requesting the adjustments. For more on these so-called equitable adjustments, see Carrico & Bondurant, *Equitable Adjustments: A Survey and Analysis of Precedents and Practice*, 36 Tax Law. 545 (1983); Dobris, *Limits on the Doctrine of Equitable Adjustment in Sophisticated Postmortem Tax Planning*, 66 Iowa L. Rev. 273 (1981); Dobris, *Equitable Adjustments in Postmortem Income Tax Planning: An Unremitting Diet of* Warms, 65 Iowa L. Rev. 103 (1979).

2. Equitable adjustments are reallocations of funds between principal and income to remedy, among other things, unfair results produced by the lack of integration of fidu-

ciary accounting rules and the rules under subchapter J. These adjustments can arise in a number of contexts; the so-called *Holloway* adjustment considered in Technical Advice Memorandum 8501011 is one of the more common ones. *See* Uniform Principal and Income Act § 506(a)(2) (1997).

Consider the following example. D dies in Year 1, leaving his entire estate to a trust that pays income to his son, S, for life (with no principal distributions), remainder to S's descendants. To simplify the example, assume that both the estate and the trust are calendar year taxpayers. In Year 1, the estate earns $20,000 of taxable interest income, all of which is distributable net income and fiduciary accounting income. The executor distributes $150,000 of principal to the trustee on December 31, Year 1. This is a trapping distribution — the $20,000 of DNI is trapped in the trust, because the entire distribution is treated as principal, none of which is distributable to S. *See* Uniform Principal and Income Act § 402 (1997). Assume that the trust pays income taxes at a flat rate of 25%. On April 15, Year 2, the trustee pays income taxes of $5,000 and charges the payment to principal. *See* Uniform Principal and Income Act § 505(b) (1997). Assume that, by the end of Year 2, the trust has collected (through investment of what remains of the $150,000 of corpus) $15,000 of fiduciary accounting income and DNI. Assuming that either the trust instrument or local law permitted such an adjustment, the second *Holloway* decision would require the income account to reimburse the principal account for the $5,000 in taxes paid by the trustee in April. (Why? See the paragraph immediately following.) As a result, the trustee has only $10,000 of fiduciary accounting income to distribute to S during Year 2. Technical Advice Memorandum 8501011 says that the *Holloway* adjustment reduces the distribution deduction available to the trust during Year 2.

The $20,000 of fiduciary accounting income earned by the estate in Year 1 will eventually flow through to S as the income beneficiary of the trust. *See* Uniform Principal and Income Act § 402 (1997). When S receives this distribution, it will likely be income tax free. To demonstrate this point, suppose that sometime in Year 3 the estate distributes all of its remaining assets to the trust. The $20,000 of income from Year 1 will be immediately distributable to the son (due to its earlier categorization as fiduciary accounting income), but will likely not be taxable to the son, because the DNI associated with the $20,000 already triggered income taxes in a prior year. According to *Holloway*, the trust income account is therefore required to reimburse the trust principal account for the income taxes that were earlier paid on these earnings.

3. Bracket compression under section 1(e) has substantially reduced the attractiveness of trapping distributions, because trusts are now almost always in the highest marginal tax bracket. Trapping distributions therefore rarely make sense if the objective is to minimize overall income taxes. *See generally* Oliver & Zawaski, *Some Tips on "Trapping" After the Tax Reform Act*, Tr. & Est., Sept. 1988, at 52.

4. Termination

a. How Long Do Estates Last?

———

Regulation:
   Section 1.641(b)-3

———

Peter J. Maresca Trust v. Commissioner
46 T.C.M. (CCH) 1147 (1983)

WHITAKER, Judge: … The only issue presented in this case is whether petitioner or the Estate of Peter J. Maresca (the Estate) was the owner and seller of 17 blocks of stock sold in February and April of 1977.[2]

… Petitioner is a testamentary trust (the Trust) established by the will of Peter J. Maresca, the decedent.…

On December 5, 1974, decedent died testate. His will, which had been executed on January 14, 1974, contained several specific bequests of stock, money and other personal property to various individuals. The residue of the estate was bequeathed to the Trust, which was directed to distribute income annually to five organizations until January 1, 2000, on which date the Trust's assets are to be divided and distributed to the five organizations.

Bruce G. Murphy was nominated in decedent's Last Will and Testament as both the trustee of the Trust and executor of the Estate. On December 13, 1974, Mr. Murphy qualified as executor, and on July 14, 1975, he filed a Federal Estate Tax Return (Form 706) on behalf of the Estate. The estate tax return was under audit by respondent from November 25, 1975, until September 21, 1976, at which time a closing letter was sent to Mr. Murphy. On January 3, 1977, Mr. Murphy was qualified as trustee of the Trust. On January 18, 1977, Mr. Murphy as executor filed with the Clerk of the Circuit Court of the City of Virginia Beach, a final accounting of the Estate. As required by Virginia probate law, the accounting was mentioned in a list of fiduciaries, whose accounts were before the Commissioner of Accounts. The list was posted at the front door of the courthouse on the first Monday in February 1977 and the accounting was not completed until 10 days or more thereafter. The accounting was approved by the Commissioner of Accounts on February 24, 1977, and confirmed by the Clerk of the Court and recorded on March 14, 1977. This accounting included the following entry: "Balance of estate to Bruce G. Murphy, Trustee, to be held, administered and disposed of as set forth in the last Will and Testament of Peter J. Maresca." It listed thereafter 21 specific blocks of securities, eight savings certificates, and cash in a checking account, and stated the values of each.

The securities listed on the final accounting as constituting the residue were sold on February 2 or 3, 1977 (except for 10 shares of Dreyfus Corporation sold on April 18, 1977), by Fahnestock & Co. as brokers for the executor. These securities had been registered in the name of the decedent and had never been formally transferred on the issuer's books either to the Estate or the Trust. In endorsing these stock certificates, Mr. Murphy signed "Bruce G. Murphy, Executor of the Estate of Peter J. Maresca." All the proceeds from the sale of the securities were paid in the form of checks drawn to "Bruce G. Murphy, Executor of the Estate of Peter J. Maresca."

On February 4, 1977, Mr. Murphy opened a checking account in the name of "Bruce G. Murphy, Trustee under the Will of Peter J. Maresca, Deceased," and the checks received from the sales of securities were deposited in this checking account after being endorsed "Bruce G. Murphy, Executor of the Estate of Peter J. Maresca."

---

2. The parties have stipulated that no income tax return was filed by the Estate for the 1977 taxable year and that if the sales were held to have been made by the Estate, it would have had an income tax liability for 1977 of $2,873.67. However, the Estate's income tax liability, if any, is not before us.

On April 24, 1978, Mr. Murphy as trustee filed a U. S. Fiduciary Income Tax Return (Form 1041) for the 1977 calendar year. This return was filed late, since the due date for filing was April 15, 1978, and no extensions had been obtained. Among the items of income reported on this return was $60,606.48 of capital gain income from the sales of the securities in February and April of 1977. A schedule attached to the return listed the specific blocks of shares and the gain (or loss) attributable to the sale of each block. On the return a deduction in the amount of $73,793.09 was claimed for amounts permanently set aside for five charitable organizations. This plus other deductions reduced the Trust's taxable income to zero.

On June 16, 1978, Mr. Murphy as trustee filed an accounting for the Trust for the period from January 3, 1977, through January 2, 1978, with the Commissioner of Accounts for the Circuit Court for the City of Virginia Beach, Virginia. The accounting was approved. It listed as Trust assets the 17 blocks of securities that were sold in February and April 1977, and reported the gains from the sales of these securities as attributable to the Trust. No returns or accountings showing the Estate as having been the seller of the shares in question have been filed.

On audit respondent determined that the Trust was liable for additional income tax because section 642(c) does not allow a trust established by a will executed after October 9, 1969, to deduct from income amounts permanently set aside for a charitable purpose. In its petition, petitioner has abandoned the claim that it was entitled to a section 642(c) deduction. Instead, petitioner claims that the Trust is not liable for additional tax because the Estate not the Trust was the seller of the securities in question. It claims that the Estate never distributed the securities to the Trust. Rather, according to petitioner, the Estate sold the securities and then distributed the sales proceeds to the Trust. Therefore, the question which we must resolve is whether the securities were sold by the Estate or by the Trust.

* * *

Generally, if a residuary trust is created by a will, the determination for Federal tax purposes of when the trust begins and receives its corpus almost invariably depends upon a determination of when the administration of the estate from which the residue is obtained comes to an end. *Chick v. Commissioner,* 7 T.C. 1414 (1946), affd. 166 F. 2d 337 (1st Cir. 1948). When the same person acts as executor and trustee, as in the present case, it may be difficult to determine the precise date when the administration of the estate comes to an end and the trust receives the residue. Guidance is provided by section 1.641(b)-3(a).... This regulation and its predecessors have been upheld as valid. *Old Virginia Brick Company v. Commissioner,* 44 T. C. 724, 729 (1965), affd. 367 F. 2d 276 (4th Cir. 1966); *Caratan v. Commissioner,* 14 T. C. 934, 938 (1950).

This regulation and the case law applying it indicate that the determination of when the process of administration of an estate terminates is a factual inquiry and that the estate will be seen as terminated for Federal income tax purposes and the residuary trust created if the administrator has performed the ordinary duties involved in winding up the estate, such as the collection of assets and the payment of debts and legacies. *Farrier v. Commissioner,* 15 T. C. 277, 282 (1950); *Alston v. Commissioner,* 8 T. C. 525, 529–530 (1947). In making this determination, we must not give controlling weight to whether State law recognizes the estate as terminated because the determination of the existence of an estate or a trust under the Federal tax statutes is a question of Federal, not State law. *Estate of Armstrong v. Commissioner,* 2 T. C. 731, 734 (1943). Thus, the Court has on several occasions found an estate to have been terminated and a residuary trust deemed to be created for Federal tax purposes even though the estate had never been formally closed and the assets distributed from the estate to the trust. E.g., *Old Virginia Brick Company v. Commissioner, supra; Pierce Estates, Inc. v. Commissioner,* 3 T. C. 875, 888 (1944); *Estate of Armstrong v. Commissioner, supra.* However, we have reached this result only where we have determined that estate administration has been unduly prolonged, that is, where the executors have long prior to the time period involved fully completed their duties of estate administration. Respondent does not argue that theory here and with good reason. The facts do not support such a contention.

The record in this case shows that the administration of the Estate was in the process of completion but clearly was not completed prior to the sale of the securities on February 2 and 3, 1977. In January 1977, Mr. Murphy qualified as trustee. The assets of the Estate had been collected and its debts and taxes paid by that time. On January 18, 1977, he started the final act of estate administration, the payment of legacies and bequests, by filing with the local court a final accounting for the Estate.

Respondent argues that prior to this date Mr. Murphy had distributed all assets including distribution to himself as trustee of the securities that were sold in February and April 1977. This final accounting contains language which might be so interpreted but the record as a whole is to the contrary. Respondent also placed much emphasis on the facts that the income tax return of the Trust for the year 1977 and the first accounting for the Trust submitted on June 16, 1978, both showed the Trust as having been the seller of the securities. There is no explanation of these facts but in any event such subsequent events cannot alter what actually occurred in the period January through April 1977.

We note first that the accounting should not be interpreted in this case as reflecting the distribution of all of the estate assets. For example, there is included in the residue set aside for the testamentary trust the sum of $1,045.97 in a "Checking Account." But the stipulation states that the Trust checking account was not opened until February 4, 1977, substantially after the accounting was filed. Thus, on the date of filing of the accounting, the cash must have been in the Estate's checking account. Of even greater significance, the securities in question were on the dates of sale still registered in the name of the decedent. At the time of delivery to the broker, they were endorsed by Mr. Murphy as executor. The checks representing the proceeds of the sales showed the executor as drawee and were endorsed by Mr. Murphy in that capacity and then deposited in the Trust checking account. These facts are consistent with a sale by the executor, not a sale by the trustee. We find that the final accounting itself did not constitute and was not intended to reflect an actual distribution of the Estate assets.

Respondent maintains that under applicable Virginia statutory and case law, registration in the name of the executor or trustee was unnecessary for the trustee to effect sale of the securities. Technically, this may be correct in that the securities could perhaps have been transferred by Mr. Murphy as executor to himself as trustee and then sold by him as trustee without the intervening steps of registration and reissuance in his name as executor and then as trustee, but in that circumstance we believe the law would require some evidence of action by the executor amounting to an act of distribution. The cases relied upon by respondent, *Looman v. Rockingham National Bank,* 220 Va. 954, 265 S. E.2d 711 (1980), and *Wrenn v. Daniels,* 200 Va. 419, 106 S. E.2d 126 (1958), simply do not address that point. Both cases focus on intent. In each, it was held that a completed gift had not been made since the original owner had not relinquished dominion and control in a property sense. By contrast, that court found a completed gift based in part on the fact that physical possession of the stock certificates had been transferred. *First National Bank of Richmond v. Holland,* 99 Va. 495, 39 S. E. 126 (1901).

Where the executor and the trustee is the same person, we must look to objective facts to ascertain whether a distribution has occurred. Here, all of the facts pertinent to the time period point to sale by Mr. Murphy as executor, not as trustee. The rule in Virginia is that—

> If an executor is also appointed as a trustee under a will, he cannot be considered as holding any part of the assets in his capacity as trustee until he has closed his accounts as executor with reference to [the particular assets] and has been charged with [the assets] as trustee. [*Rixey's Ex'rs v. Commonwealth*, 125 Va. 337, 99 S.E. 573, 575 (Va. 1919).]

Under probate practice the accounting cannot be completed until it has been posted and a period of at least 10 days has expired. Lamb, Virginia Probate Practice, p. 212 (1957). Here, the posting occurred on the first Monday in February 1977. Ten days thereafter would of necessity be subsequent to February 3, 1977. There being no basis to conclude that the administration was unduly prolonged and hence deemed terminated for Federal tax purposes, we are guided by Virginia law and we hold accordingly that the securities were held by Mr. Murphy as executor until after their sale. This is the result required by section 1.641(b)-3(a), Income Tax Regs., since Mr. Murphy had not prior to February 3, 1977, performed an essential act of estate administration, the distribution of the residue.

Illustrative Material

1. When *Maresca* was decided, it was somewhat atypical. Usually the issue was not who had sold property that had once belonged to the decedent. Usually the issue was whether the administration of an estate had been unduly prolonged, which was merely another way of asking whether the estate would be permitted to continue as a separate taxpayer. Bracket compression under section 1(e), however, has substantially reduced the temptation to prolong estate administration as a way of minimizing the family's overall income tax liability, because estates are now almost always in the highest marginal tax bracket.

2. In *Brown v. United States*, 890 F.2d 1329 (5th Cir. 1989), the Fifth Circuit, in an exhaustive opinion, upheld the validity of Treas. Reg. § 1.641(b)-3(a) and acknowledged I.R.S. authority to determine when an estate had terminated. Factually, the taxpayers' position in *Brown* bordered on the frivolous. Their strongest argument that the estate had not terminated seems to have been that it had not yet distributed all its assets (nine years after the decedent's death). For obvious reasons, failure to distribute cannot, alone, justify indefinite continuation of an estate. Legally, the taxpayers' position was slightly more interesting. An old Fifth Circuit case, *Frederich v. Commissioner*, 145 F.2d 796 (5th Cir. 1944), was, indeed, hostile to I.R.S. authority to determine when estates terminate. In *Brown*, the Fifth Circuit reexamined *Frederich* and concluded that "the legal propositions stated in *Frederich* no longer represent the law of this circuit." 890 F.2d at 1339.

In contrast, when the administration of an entity has not been unduly prolonged, failure to distribute assets does generally mean that the entity has not terminated. *See* Treas. Reg. § 1.641(b)-3(b) (first sentence); *Dominion Trust Company v. United States*, 786 F. Supp. 1321 (M.D. Tenn. 1991), *aff'd mem.*, 7 F.3d 233 (6th Cir. 1993) (trust not terminated four years after beneficiaries' shares became payable, because of ongoing litigation).

3. Whether the administration of an estate has been unduly prolonged is almost always a question of fact. For that reason, the I.R.S. generally does not issue private letter rul-

ings on the issue. Rev. Proc. 2008-3, 2008-1 I.R.B. 110, 114. *But see* Priv. Ltr. Rul. 200226031 (2002) (ruling that administration of trust would not be unduly prolonged during period necessary to pay deferred estate taxes in accordance with section 6166).

Courts have found the following excuses sufficient to justify holding administration of an estate open: (1) that claims against the estate remained unresolved, *Brown v. Commissioner*, 215 F.2d 697 (5th. Cir. 1954); *Wylie v. United States*, 281 F. Supp. 180 (N.D. Tex. 1968); *Estate of Mary Z. Bryan*, 22 T.C.M. (CCH) 864 (1963), *aff'd in part and remanded in part*, 364 F.2d 751 (4th Cir. 1966); *Edwin M. Peterson*, 35 T.C. 962 (1961), *acq.*, 1962-1 C.B. 4; (2) that claims against the estate remained unpaid, *Carson v. United States*, 161 Ct. Cl. 548, 317 F.2d 370 (1963); *Simon S. Neuman*, 28 T.C.M. (CCH) 724 (1969) (interest payments); (3) that the estate's claim for a refund of income taxes remained pending, *McCauley v. United States*, 193 F. Supp. 938 (E.D. Ark. 1961); (4) that another estate, of which the taxpayer-estate was a residuary beneficiary, had not yet completed making distributions, *Estate of Johnson v. Commissioner*, 88 T.C. 225, *aff'd mem.*, 838 F.2d 1202 (2d Cir. 1987); (5) that estate taxes deferred under section 6166 remained outstanding, Rev. Rul. 76-23, 1976-1 C.B. 264; (6) continuance of litigation over title to a parcel of real estate, *Patton v. United States*, 59-1 U.S.T.C. 9459 (N.D. Tex. 1959); (7) the need for orderly liquidation of a family corporation formerly managed by the decedent, *Stella Porter Russell*, 21 T.C.M. (CCH) 1178 (1962); and (8) continuance of litigation over whether the trust or its beneficiary was liable for the tax on capital gains resulting from sales that occurred after the trust supposedly terminated but prior to distribution, *Dominion Trust Company v. United States*, 786 F. Supp. 1321 (M.D. Tenn. 1991), *aff'd mem.*, 7 F.3d 233 (6th Cir. 1993). In addition, Treas. Reg. § 1.641(b)-3(a) provides that an estate that has made an election under section 645 generally does not terminate prior to the end of the election period.

Courts have found the following excuses insufficient to justify holding administration of an estate open: (1) continuance of an ancillary administration, *A.T. Miller*, 39 T.C. 940 (1963), *aff'd*, 333 F.2d 400 (8th Cir. 1964); *Estate of J.F. Hargis*, 19 T.C. 842 (1953), *nonacq.*, 1953-2 C.B. 8; (2) continuance of a partnership in which the estate owned an interest, *Stewart v. Commissioner*, 196 F.2d 397 (5th Cir. 1952); *A.T. Miller*, 39 T.C. 940 (1963), *aff'd*, 333 F.2d 400 (8th Cir. 1964); (3) continuance of a legal life estate created by the will, *Koffman v. United States*, 300 F.2d 176 (6th Cir. 1962) (per curiam) (nine years was "more than ample time to perform the ordinary duties of administration"); *Estate of J.P. Armstrong*, 2 T.C. 731 (1943); *Estate of Berger v. Commissioner*, 60 T.C.M. (CCH) 1079 (1990); and (4) continued operation of a business until it could be disposed of advantageously, *Chick v. Commissioner*, 166 F.2d 337 (1st Cir.), *cert. denied*, 334 U.S. 845 (1948).

4. In *Ralph E. Hedges*, 18 T.C. 681 (1952), *nonacq.*, 1952-2 C.B. 4, *aff'd per curiam*, 212 F.2d 593 (9th Cir. 1954), an executor, following his discharge as executor by the local probate court, continued to hold, improperly and for his own benefit, estate property he had concealed from both the court and the estate's beneficiaries. Several years later, upon recovery by the beneficiaries of the property and the income that had accumulated thereon, the issue arose whether the beneficiaries were required to include in gross income, in the year of recovery, all of the income accumulated during the intervening years. The Tax Court held that, even though the local probate court had discharged the executor, the administration of the estate continued as to the undisclosed assets. As a result, since no distributions occurred during the intervening years, the estate, not the beneficiaries, was liable for the income taxes on the income earned during that period. The beneficiaries were required to include amounts in gross income only on account of the income earned by the estate in the year of recovery.

5. The laws of most states provide for simplified (sometimes called "informal") estate administration procedures under certain circumstances, such as when the executors and the residuary beneficiaries are the same, when the residuary beneficiaries consent, when the value of the estate is less than a certain dollar amount, etc. In general, these simplified procedures relieve the executor from the obligation to file estate accountings. If there is no obligation to account, at what point does estate administration end? In Rev. Rul. 73-397, 1973-2 C.B. 211, the I.R.S. ruled that an estate had terminated for income tax purposes when the executor, who was also the sole beneficiary, gave a special bond relieving him of the obligation to account, even though he had not yet paid all estate debts. On the other hand, the ruling also stated that the estate had not terminated for income tax purposes when, upon giving the special bond, the executor was not the sole beneficiary; rather, the estate would terminate upon final distribution to the beneficiaries.

The Tax Court has held that an estate that was administered informally terminated when the executor obtained a release from the estate's sole beneficiary. *Charlotte Leviton Herbert*, 25 T.C. 807 (1956), *acq.*, 1956-2 C.B. 6.

6. In *Craig v. United States*, 89 F. Supp. 2d 858 (S.D. Tex. 1999), the Service issued a levy on an estate bank account, to collect taxes the executor owed in his individual capacity. The estate was subject to independent administration under Texas law. The executor had sole authority over the account and was also one the estate's two beneficiaries. Shortly after the levy, the executor became entitled, individually, to the entire account. The court held, however, that the levy was wrongful, because premature. At the time of the levy, the executor had not yet settled a claim by the other beneficiary; in addition, various estate expenses remained unpaid.

7. Section 644 requires trusts, but not estates, to adopt calendar years. Thus, the deferral possibilities under section 662(c) will continue to cause many executors to select fiscal years ending shortly after the end of the taxable year of a primary beneficiary. *See generally supra* (ch. 3, secs. D and E(1)). Because almost all trusts and individual beneficiaries are now calendar-year taxpayers, January 31 will continue to be a typical fiscal year for estates.

Section 645 provides an election to treat the decedent's revocable trust as part of the decedent's estate, rather than as a separate trust, for most income purposes. If no estate tax return is due, this consolidation is effective only for two years after the decedent's death. If an estate tax return is due, the consolidation generally remains effective until six months after the final determination of the estate tax liability. During the election period, such a trust can utilize a fiscal year. *See* Treas. Reg. §§ 1.645-1(e)(2)(i) & (ii), 1.645-1(e)(3)(i).

In the year an estate terminates the mismatching of taxable years may have adverse consequences. In Rev. Rul. 71-180, 1971-1 C.B. 204, an estate with a fiscal year ending January 31 made its final distribution on August 31, 1970. The estate's beneficiary, as usual, was a calendar-year taxpayer. Under section 662(c) the beneficiary's 1970 tax return was required to reflect the estate's distributions with respect to both of the estate's taxable years ending in 1970.

8. Trusts, too, terminate, often upon the death of an income beneficiary. Typically, a remainder person then becomes entitled to outright ownership of the trust property, though local law inevitably allows the trustee time to wind up the trust's affairs. Does the trust immediately cease to exist as a separate taxable entity? Or does the trust continue on, for tax purposes, until final distribution actually occurs? *Edith M. Bryant*, 14 T.C. 127, *acq.*, 1950-2 C.B. 1, *aff'd*, 185 F.2d 517 (4th Cir. 1950), held that the trust continued, as a separate taxpayer, for a reasonable time. The court wrote: "We do not think ... that the period from October 17, 1943, the date of the death of the primary beneficiary,

until April 3, 1944, when the corpus of the trust was finally distributed to petitioner, was an unreasonable time." 14 T.C. at 132. *See also Swoboda v. United States,* 258 F.2d 848 (3d Cir. 1958). *Leonard Marx,* 47 B.T.A. 204 (1942), however, held that three years was too long, absent proof that such a period was reasonable.

b. Excess Deductions

––––––––––

Internal Revenue Code:
   Section 642(d), (h)

Regulations:
   Sections 1.642(d)-1; 1.642(h)-2, -3, -4

––––––––––

Alan Nemser

66 T.C. 780 (1976)
aff'd mem., 556 F.2d 558 (2d Cir.)
cert. denied, 434 U.S. 855 (1977)

FEATHERSTON, *Judge*: Respondent determined a deficiency of $6,782.32 in petitioners' 1968 Federal income tax. The parties have stipulated that the issue for decision is whether petitioner Alan Nemser is a beneficiary succeeding to the property of a trust within the meaning of section 642(h)(2) so as to entitle him to take as a deduction against his personal income his pro rata share of the unused deductions in the terminal year of the trust.

* * *

During 1968 petitioner Alan Nemser (hereinafter petitioner) was a practicing, self-employed attorney. The present controversy stems from his purchase of an interest in a testamentary trust created by Silas J. Llewellyn, who died a resident of Illinois on September 3, 1925.

Under the terms of the trust created by the will of Silas J. Llewellyn, Mary Isabelle Llewellyn, a granddaughter of the testator, received a remainder interest. The extent of her interest was contingent upon her father's (Paul Llewellyn's) dying without surviving issue other than herself, and her aunt's (Gertrude Stone's) dying without issue.

On March 29, 1946, Mary Isabelle Llewellyn sold, assigned, and transferred to the Fidelity Philadelphia Trust Co., as nominee for Richard Kadish, Irving Poretz, and Aaron Miller (hereinafter the Richard Kadish group), all of her interest in a fractional portion of her interest in the Gertrude Stone portion of the trust. The consideration for the transfer was $31,500, of which $14,000 was paid by Richard Kadish, $14,000 by Irving Poretz, and $3,500 by Aaron Miller. On April 11, 1946, the Fidelity Philadelphia Trust Co. acknowledged that it held the assigned portion of the trust in its name for their benefit, in the following proportions:

   Richard Kadish   4/9
   Irving Poretz   4/9
   Aaron Miller   1/9

Neither petitioner nor any one of the Richard Kadish group was named as a beneficiary in the will of Silas J. Llewellyn.

On April 17, 1946, Richard Kadish sold and transferred to petitioner 3/14 of his 4/9 interest in Silas J. Llewellyn's trust estate for the sum of $3,000. Petitioner's purchase of the 3/14 interest in the Kadish 4/9 interest was made for investment purposes.

In 1956 both Paul Llewellyn and Gertrude Stone died. He left no issue other than Mary Isabelle Llewellyn, and Gertrude Stone died without issue. Shortly after their deaths the City National Bank & Trust Co., trustee under the will of Silas J. Llewellyn, filed an action in the Superior Court, Cook County, Ill., asking for instructions concerning the disposition of that portion of the estate which was distributable upon the death of Gertrude Stone. The court was also requested to pass upon the validity of the assignments made by Mary Isabelle Llewellyn of portions of her remainder interest. Petitioner was named as one of the defendants and was described as a person claiming distribution as an assignee of Richard Kadish.

The Appellate Court of the State of Illinois rendered its decision on June 6, 1966, holding that the March 29, 1946, assignment by Mary Isabelle Llewellyn to the Richard Kadish group was valid and enforceable and that, pursuant to the assignment, petitioner, as an assignee of Richard Kadish, was entitled to distribution of his pro rata portion of the trust estate's assets. The fund available for distribution to the Richard Kadish group and their assignees was $725,046.29. During 1968 the Richard Kadish group's share was distributed to the individuals named in the court decree, after first deducting trustee's fees, attorneys' fees, and expenses as allowed by the court for the final year of the trust. Petitioner received as his share stocks having a fair market value of $55,788.16.

The trustee reported that for 1968, the year of the termination of the trust, deductible expenses exceeded income by $134,346.15 for the Richard Kadish group's portion of the trust estate. Of this excess amount petitioner claimed $14,394.12 as a deduction on his 1968 joint Federal income tax return, representing his 10.7142 percent share of the Richard Kadish group's portion of the trust estate. Respondent disallowed the deduction on the ground that petitioner was not a beneficiary of the trust within the meaning of section 642(h)(2).

Petitioner maintains that the term "beneficiaries," as used in section 642(h)(2), should be construed broadly so as to include any person to whom property is distributed from an estate or trust, whether or not that person was designated as a beneficiary under the terms of the testator's will. In support of his position, petitioner relies on section 1.642(h)-3(a), Income Tax Regs., which provides.... Petitioner argues that the regulation establishes that if, in the year of termination of a trust, the expenses of the trust exceed the trust's income, section 642(h)(2) allows the excess expenses as deductions to any distributee whose share is diminished by those expenses. We disagree.

The regulation relied upon by petitioner provides no real help in ascertaining the meaning of the term "beneficiaries," as used in section 642(h)(2). In reality this definition begs the question we must decide. It defines "beneficiaries succeeding to the property of the estate or trust" as those beneficiaries who bear the burden of any loss or any excess of deductions over gross income. It does not give any clue as to whether purchasers of interests in an estate or trust are beneficiaries within the meaning of section 642(h)(2).

Section 642(h) was enacted by Congress to allow beneficiaries succeeding to the property of an estate or trust to deduct in the terminal year of the estate or trust unused loss carryovers and expenses in excess of the estate's or trust's income; otherwise, those deductions would be forever lost. H. Rept. No. 1337, to accompany H.R. 8300 (Pub. L. No. 591), 83d Cong., 2d Sess. 62, A201 (1954); S. Rept. No. 1622, to accompany H.R. 8300 (Pub. L. No. 591), 83d Cong., 2d Sess. 83, 343 (1954); see *Charles F. Neave*, 27 T.C. 1237, 1240–1243 (1952), for a discussion of the prior law. The use of the phrase "beneficiaries *succeeding* to the property" (emphasis added) indicates that the section was intended to refer only to recipients of property by gift, bequest, devise, or inheritance under State succession laws. The amount of the property so received by will or inheritance under State law is not includable in gross income by virtue of section 102 but is reduced by losses and expenses incurred by the estate. Thus, without section 642(h)(2), the distribution to the beneficiaries succeeding to the property would be decreased, but they would receive no deduction for the amount of such decrease.

By entering the transaction with Mary Isabelle Llewellyn, however, the Richard Kadish group acquired nothing by bequest, devise, or inheritance. Whatever that group acquired was by purchase, and what they purchased was a fractional portion of the trust principal remaining after the losses and administration expenses of the trust had been taken into account. They acquired no income rights. It is stipulated that Mary Isabelle Llewellyn "sold, assigned and transferred" to the nominee of the Richard Kadish group (of which petitioner was an assignee) "her right, title and interest in and to ¾ of the share, right, title and interest in and to the *corpus* of the estate of Silas J. Llewellyn, *which would become payable to her* in the event that her aunt, Gertrude Stone, should die without issue surviving." (Emphasis added.) None of the corpus of the trust would "become payable" to Mary Isabelle Llewellyn until after the expenses of its administration and liquidation had been paid. Petitioner, therefore, did not bear the burden of any of those expenses. As a purchaser of a portion of the trust estate remaining after the expenses were paid, he was in no sense a beneficiary succeeding to the property of the trust.

In *Greggar v. Sletteland,* 43 T.C. 602 (1965), this Court rejected the notion that the term "beneficiaries," as used in section 642(h), includes purchasers of interests in estates or trusts. In that case a taxpayer acquired an interest in an estate in consideration of legal services rendered to a client. This Court concluded (pp. 609–610) that the taxpayer "acquired the claims property, not in the capacity of a beneficiary of an estate, but rather as an attorney for services rendered to a client" and was not entitled to a deduction for the estate's expenses over gross income in the estate's terminal year. We also said at page 610:

> it seems evident that the underlying purpose of section 642(h) was to afford some measure of relief to heirs and those designated as takers under a decedent's will, who take diminished interests in a decedent's property as the result of the incurrence of expenses and losses by the estate.* * *

We adhere to the *Sletteland* opinion.

Revenue Ruling 57-31
1957-1 C.B. 201

Advice has been requested whether excess deductions allowable to a residuary testamentary trust on the termination of an estate, which trust distributes all of its current income, will be available to the income beneficiary of the trust should such deductions exceed the gross income of the trust for its taxable year.

Section 642(h)(2) of the Internal Revenue Code of 1954 provides that any deductions (other than deductions for personal exemption and charitable contributions) in excess of the gross income of an estate or trust for its year of termination may be allowed as a deduction to the beneficiaries succeeding to the property of the estate or trust. A testamentary trust may be a legatee or beneficiary of an estate for purposes of section 642(h). See G.C.M. 24749, C.B. 1945, 237.

In the instant case, the decedent provided in his will that the rest and residue of his estate be placed in trust and that the income therefrom be distributed currently to his surviving spouse. Deductions of the estate for the year in which it was terminated exceeded gross income and resulted in the allowance of the excess thereof to the residuary trust. The excess deductions exceeded the gross income of the trust for its taxable year.

Since the amount of trust income taxable to a beneficiary of a trust is limited to that beneficiary's proportionate share of the distributable net income of the trust, excess deductions from an estate which become available through operation of section 642(h)(2) to a testamentary trust having the status of a beneficiary under section 642(h) would in turn reduce the amount of income taxable to the beneficiary of the trust.

If a testamentary trust has deductions in excess of its gross income after the allowance of deductions from an estate made available to it through section 642(h)(2), the amount in excess of the gross income would not be deductible by the income beneficiary of the trust. However, if the trust also terminates during the taxable year in which it is allowed the section 642(h)(2) deductions, the deductions in excess of its gross income will be available under section 642(h)(2) to the remaindermen succeeding to the property.

In view of the foregoing, it is held that where a residuary testamentary trust, which has the status of a beneficiary succeeding to the property of the estate within the meaning of section 642(h) of the Internal Revenue Code of 1954, has deductions from an estate as authorized by section 642(h)(2), the amount in excess of the gross income of the trust would not be deductible by the income beneficiaries of the trust; but, if the trust terminated in the year in which it was allowed the section 642(h)(2) deductions, they would be available to the remaindermen.

O'Bryan v. Commissioner

75 T.C. 304 (1980)

NIMS, *Judge*: [T]he sole issue remaining for the Court's determination is the proper method of calculating under section 642(h)(2) an estate's "excess deductions" when the estate has made charitable contributions in its year of termination which are deductible under section 642(c).

I

* * *

The estate in question is that of petitioner's husband, Leslie L. O'Bryan, who died on November 21, 1970. Mr. O'Bryan's will contained various specific bequests to petitioner, and it also left property to a marital trust sufficient for the estate to obtain the maximum marital deduction. The residue of the estate was left to a residuary trust, which required that all the trust income be distributed currently to the petitioner.

The final return for the estate representing the period from August 1, 1973, to June 30, 1974, inclusive, reflected a gross income of $879,446.55 and the following deductions:

Interest	$10,599.71
Taxes	1,176.79
Charitable deduction	776,500.00
Miscellaneous expense	593.46

Executor's commissions	65,000.00
Attorney's fee	85,000.00
Accounting fees	2,980.00
	$941,849.96

The charitable deduction was claimed pursuant to section 642(c)(2)(B). Claimed deductions exceeded reported income by $62,403.41.

The residuary trust established pursuant to the terms of the will, the Leslie L. O'Bryan Trust, received gross income during 1974 of $72,739.59. Relying on section 642(h)(2), the trust claimed an excess deduction from the estate in the amount of $62,403.41. The parties stipulated that under the rules of subchapter J the excess deduction claimed by the trust had no effect on the trust's taxable income. The deduction did, however, reduce the income beneficiary's (i.e., the petitioner's) taxable income by the aforesaid $62,403.41.[2]

In the notice of deficiency the Commissioner determined that the estate's deductions under section 642(h)(2) had been calculated incorrectly and that petitioner's taxable income for 1974 was to be increased by $62,403.41.

II

This is a case of first impression. At issue is the interpretation and construction of section 642(h)(2), which provides.... The focal point of the dispute before us is the application of the parenthetical clause "(other than the deductions allowed under subsections (b) or (c))." Section 642(b) permits a $600 personal exemption deduction and section 642(c) permits a deduction for amounts paid or permanently set aside for a charitable purpose.

Like many simple rules, the rule contained in section 642(h)(2), when applied to a concrete set of facts, creates an enigma. We are told that no part of the charitable deduction may be included in "excess deductions," but we are not told how to determine whether, on facts such as ours, the excess of deductions over income actually includes any charitable deduction.

Respondent contends that section 642(h)(2) invokes a simple one-step procedure in which all deductions are totaled, except for the personal exemption and charitable contribution, and that figure is given first priority in reducing gross income to determine whether there are any excess deductions.[3]

Petitioner reads the section 642(h)(2) parenthetical clause as excluding the section 642(c) deduction, not from total deductions calculated under section 642(h)(2), but only from the amount determined to be the excess. Arithmetically, this translates into a two-step calculation: the first step is to determine the amount by which total deductions ex-

---

2. Petitioner was the sole income beneficiary of the trust.
3. Respondent's computation is as follows:

a. Gross income of estate		$879,446.55
Less deductions:		
b. Interest, taxes, fees, and miscellaneous expenses	($165,349.96)	
c. Sec. 642(c) charitable deductions	0	
d. Total deductions		(165,349.96)
e. Excess of deductions over gross income (0 if line a exceeds line d)		0

ceeds gross income, and the second step is to determine what amount of this excess consists of deductions other than the section 642(b) and (c) deductions. In essence, says petitioner, the amount by which total estate deductions exceed gross income is an excess deduction under section 642(h)(2) to the extent that the estate has deductions other than a section 642(c) deduction.[4]

From the above it is apparent that, regardless of the arguments made to support the respective positions, each party is simply asking us to afford priority to a preferred type of deduction in reducing estate gross income. If, under petitioner's theory, gross income is first to be reduced (but not below zero) by the charitable deduction, the excess deductions allowable to the trust, and ultimately in fact to petitioner, must perforce consist of allowable deductions. Under respondent's theory, the reverse would be true.

There can be little argument that respondent's construction follows more comfortably the literal dictates of a statute. Petitioner asks the Court to look beyond a literal construction of the statute and to read section 642(h) in the context of the entire statutory scheme of subchapter J. Petitioner argues that her interpretation preserves the integrity of the section 642(c) charitable deduction and also balances the goal of section 642(h) to ameliorate wastage of deductions with what she perceives as the purpose of the parenthetical in section 642(h)(2) to prevent any charitable deduction from being passed from an estate or trust to a noncharitable beneficiary.

Section 642(h) is only one part of a tightly woven and intricate statutory scheme. Before turning to the specifics of this case, we need to review the basic provisions and underlying principles of subchapter J of the Code, which deals with the taxation of estates, trusts, beneficiaries, and decedents, generally. We have couched this overview in terms of the tax treatment of estates; but the rules of subchapter J apply with equal force, with appropriate modifications, to trusts as well.

Subchapter J sets forth the rules for determining the proper amount of estate income subject to tax as well as the rules for determining whether the beneficiary or estate should bear the burden of this tax.[5] Simply stated, subchapter J is built on the "conduit principle" of taxation; i.e., estate income is taxed only once, either to the estate or to the beneficiaries, or partly to each. The estate is treated as a taxable entity and is taxed, in general, on income which it realizes but does not distribute to its beneficiaries. Income distributed to a beneficiary is not taxable to the estate but instead is taxable to the beneficiary. This result is accomplished by permitting the estate a deduction for the amount of the distribution.

---

4. The following computation results from petitioner's approach:

a. Gross income of estate		$879,446.55
Less deductions:		
b. Interest, taxes, fees, and miscellaneous expenses	($165,349.96)	
c. Sec. 642(c) deduction	(776,500.00)	
d. Total deductions		(941,849.96)
e. Excess of deductions over income		(62,403.41)
f. Amount attributable to deductions other than sec. 642(c) deductions		(165,349.96)
g. Deduction allowable to beneficiary (lower of e or f)		(62,403.41)

5. Subch. J was the product of an extensive 1954 revision of the income tax of trusts and estates. See generally H. Holland, L. Kennedy, S. Surrey & W. Warren, "A Proposed Revision of the Federal Income Tax Treatment of Trusts and Estates—American Law Institute Draft," 53 Colum. L. Rev. 316, 318 (1953); S. Kamin, S. Surrey & W. Warren, "The Internal Revenue Code of 1954: Trusts, Estates and beneficiaries," 54 Colum. L. Rev. 1237 (1954); A.L.I. Federal Income Tax Statute, February 1954 Draft, Vol. II, secs. X800–X885 (1954); Report of Committee on Taxation of Income of Estates and Trusts, Section of Taxation, A.B.A. (June 1, 1953).

The device that serves as the linchpin for this statutory scheme is the concept of distributable net income (D.N.I.). D.N.I., which is defined in section 643 and is essentially the estate's taxable income (with some modifications), serves generally as a ceiling on the combined tax liability of the estate and beneficiary. D.N.I. is allocated between the estate and beneficiaries in accord with the distribution rules of sections 661–663.

When distributions to beneficiaries exceed D.N.I., the tier structure of section 662 determines who among the beneficiaries are deemed to have received taxable distributions out of income and who have received nontaxable distributions out of corpus. D.N.I. is allocated under section 662(a)(1) first to the beneficiaries who have a right to income that is "required to be distributed currently to such beneficiary," and the distribution to those beneficiaries is taxable to that extent. Sec. 1.662(a)-2(a), Income Tax Regs. All distributions within that tier are treated ratably should D.N.I. be less than total first-tier distributions. Any remaining D.N.I. is allocated pursuant to section 662(a)(2) among all other taxable beneficiaries, so called second-tier beneficiaries, and distributions to those beneficiaries are taxable to that extent. Sec. 1.662(a)-3(a), Income Tax Regs.

Section 661 complements section 662 by providing the estate a deduction up to the estate's D.N.I. for amounts distributed to its beneficiaries.

The rules of subchapter J become more complex when charitable beneficiaries are involved. In lieu of the charitable deduction allowed under section 170, section 642(c) in general allows an estate an unlimited charitable deduction for amounts of "gross income" which, pursuant to the governing instrument, are paid, permanently set aside, or to be used for charitable purposes.

On the estate side of the equation, the charitable contribution authorized by section 642(c) is simply one of numerous deductions that may be claimed in computing the estate's taxable income. To avoid duplicating deductions, section 663(a)(2) provides that distributions qualifying for the charitable deduction under section 642(c) are not included for purposes of calculating the estate's section 661 distribution deduction.

On the beneficiary side, however, the effect of the section 642(c) charitable distribution depends upon whether the beneficiary is a first- or a second-tier beneficiary. Section 662(a) is structured so that first-tier beneficiaries do not benefit from the charitable deduction.[6] Conceptually, section 662 accomplishes this by factoring charitable distributions into the tier system of priorities in such a way that the pool of income that can potentially be taxed to the beneficiaries (potentially taxable income)[7] is deemed to flow first to first-tier beneficiaries. It is only if the pool of potentially taxable income exceeds first-tier distributions that the distribution to charitable beneficiaries is deemed to come out of that pool. In effect, the section 642(c) charitable distribution is an "intermediate tier"[8] between tier-one and tier-two beneficiaries. We say intermediate tier because section 662(a)(2) is designed so that tier-two beneficiaries[9] benefit from the section 642(c) charitable distribution deduction: the pool of potentially taxable income for determining the

---

6. We have drawn much of our analysis of the effect of the charitable deduction on first- and second-tier beneficiaries from the discussion on these points contained in M. Ferguson, J. Freeland & R. Stephens, Federal Income Taxation of Estates and Beneficiaries 426–432, 466–468 (1970). For an excellent recent article on termination problems in general, see S. Ross, "Income Tax Planning for Estate Termination," 51 Taxes 660 (Nov. 1973).

7. The pool of income that can potentially be taxed to the beneficiaries is D.N.I. without the sec. 642(c) deduction.

8. A. Michaelson, Income Taxation of Trusts and Estates 12 (P.L.I. 1963), is cited as the source of this concept in M. Ferguson, J. Freeland & R. Stephens, *supra* note 6, at 458.

9. Tier two does not include the charitable distributees. See sec. 662(b).

amount of a distribution that is taxable to tier-two beneficiaries is reduced by the section 642(c) charitable distributions (as well as the tier-one distributions). Section 662(a) and (b).

Finally, we reach section 642(h)(2), which allows estate beneficiaries to take a deduction on their individual return for certain excess deductions of the estate in the year of termination. Section 642(h) had no counterpart in the 1939 Internal Revenue Code. Prior to 1954 excess deductions of an estate could not be passed onto beneficiaries. The problem was particularly acute in the estate's final year when the windup expenses of estate administration are generally heaviest and the deductions for those expenses often are greater than income. Congress, as part of a general effort to prevent wastage of deductions,[10] ameliorated this problem through the enactment of section 642(h)(2).[11]

Petitioner has drawn on two themes present in subchapter J in an attempt to show her construction of section 642(h)(2) best implements policy considerations underlying subchapter J. One is the familiar axiom that Congress seeks to encourage charitable contributions and foster charitable organizations and that this policy is manifested in section 642(c). The second is that unused deductions for expenses incurred in the year of termination should be passed on to beneficiaries.

While these themes are present in subchapter J, countervailing considerations surface in section 642(h)(2). Charitable deductions are allowed "without limitation" on the estate side only for purposes of calculating the *estate's* taxable income. On the beneficiary side, the section 662(a) tier system imposes a substantial limitation by barring first-tier beneficiaries from gaining any tax benefit from the presence of a section 642(c) charitable distribution deduction. The structure of section 662 reflects a distinct lack of concern on the part of Congress for "wastage" of charitable deductions insofar as determining the tax liability of income beneficiaries.

---

10. H. Rept. 1337, 83d Cong., 2d Sess. 201 (1954); S. Rept. 1622, 83d Cong., 2d Sess. 343 (1954).
11. The Senate Finance Committee report states:
    "In the computation of such excess [deductions over gross income], the deduction allowed under subsection (b) for personal exemption and the deduction allowed under subsection (c) for amounts paid or permanently set aside for charitable purposes are not taken into account. [S. Rept. 1622, 83d Cong., 2d Sess. 343 (1954).]"
    This legislative history of sec. 642(h)(2) does not precisely explain the policy reason for or the operation of the statute. We do know that much of the impetus for revising the income taxation of trusts and estates came from the American Law Institute and the American Bar Association, each of which exhaustively studied the problems at length over a number of years. One of the key areas of concern to both organizations was the problem of wasted deductions. The American Law Institute proposal (see note 5) relied simply on the concept of D.N.I. to ameliorate the problem of wasted deductions. Since termination expenses are deductible in determining D.N.I., and D.N.I. serves as a ceiling on the amount of income that must be recognized by a beneficiary, the effect of D.N.I. is to pass on to the beneficiaries deductions for these expenses up to the point of gross income.
    The concept of D.N.I. did not solve the problem in cases where terminating expenses exceeded gross income for that period. The American Bar Association proposal (see note 5) met this problem in part through a provision (sec. 162.4) which is markedly similar to sec. 642(h)(2) except it made no reference to sec. 642(b) and 642(c) charitable deductions. This provision was adopted as sec. 662(d) in H.R. 8300 (83d Cong., 2d Sess.) as reported out of the Ways and Means Committee and passed by the House of Representatives on Mar. 9, 1954. The Senate renumbered this section to sec. 642(h)(2) and added the references to secs. 642(b) and 642(c). Other than noting the change, the Senate Committee report did not dwell on the significance of the section 642(c) reference. S. Rept. 1622, 83d Cong., 2d Sess. 343 (1954).

In the instant case all the deductions, other than the section 642(b) personal exemption and the section 642(c) charitable deduction, have already been taken into account in determining the pool of income potentially taxable to beneficiaries. The only deduction that has been wasted here, i.e., that does not operate to reduce the income beneficiary's tax liability, is the section 642(c) deduction for charitable distributions. Given the lack of concern evinced by Congress in section 662 for wasted charitable deductions, we are not troubled by a reading of section 642(h)(2) which allows these deductions to go unused. Mathematically, this result is accomplished by excluding altogether the section 642(c) charitable deduction from the section 642(h)(2) computation, which is the construction of the statute called for by respondent.

Under the circumstances, we reject petitioner's argument that the policy considerations underlying subchapter J are best implemented by her reading of section 642(h)(2). In summary, we hold that to determine whether there are excess deductions available to beneficiaries under section 642(h)(2), deductions exclusive of the personal exemption under section 642(b) and the charitable deduction under section 642(c) are to be totaled and matched against the gross income of the terminating estate or trust. If the deductions so computed in fact exceed such gross income, then, and only then, will there be excess deductions as contemplated by section 642(h)(2).

Illustrative Material

1. Of course, for deductions to be available under section 642(h), the estate or trust must have terminated. *Mary C. Westphal,* 37 T.C. 340 (1961), held that, as of the date of an "Order Allowing Final Account" and a "Decree of Distribution" entered by the local probate court, an estate had not yet terminated for section 642(h) purposes. It was stipulated that, on such date, the estate's assets had remained undistributed and that the executors had not been discharged.

2. According to Treas. Reg. §1.642(h)-2(a), excess deductions allowable to beneficiaries under section 642(h)(2) are itemized deductions in the beneficiaries' hands. Are these deductions also subject to the 2% "haircut" under section 67? What, if any, impact will section 67(e) have at the beneficiary level?

3. In *Kitch v. Commissioner,* 104 T.C. 1 (1995), an ex-wife, whose ex-husband owed her large arrearages of alimony, died. He died shortly thereafter, and her estate filed a claim for the arrearages against his estate. In settlement of the claim, his estate transferred substantial amounts of cash and property to her estate, which, in turn, distributed both to her beneficiaries. Thereupon, both estates terminated. His estate had an excess capital loss deduction, which her estate claimed. The Tax Court held that her estate was not a beneficiary of his estate. Thus, her estate could not deduct his estate's excess capital losses under §642(h). The Tenth Circuit affirmed. *Kitch v. Commissioner,* 103 F.3d 104 (10th Cir. 1996).

G. Realization of Gain upon Distribution of Property in Kind

1. By the Entity

a. Mandatory

Internal Revenue Code:
 Sections 1022, 1040 (both applicable only to estates of decedents dying after December 31, 2009)
Regulations:
 Sections 1.651(a)-2(d), 1.661(a)-2(f), 1.663(a)-1(b)(1)

Kenan v. Commissioner
114 F.2d 217 (2d Cir. 1940)

AUGUSTUS N. HAND, Circuit Judge.

The testatrix, Mrs. Bingham, died on July 27, 1917, leaving a will under which she placed her residuary estate in trust and provided in item "Seventh" that her trustees should pay a certain amount annually to her niece, Louise Clisby Wise, until the latter reached the age of forty, "at which time or as soon thereafter as compatible with the interests of my estate they shall pay to her the sum of Five Million ($5,000,000.00) Dollars." The will provided in item "Eleventh" that the trustees, in the case of certain payments including that of the $5,000,000 under item "Seventh", should have the right "to substitute for the payment in money, payment in marketable securities of a value equal to the sum to be paid, the selection of the securities to be substituted in any instance, and the valuation of such securities to be done by the Trustees and their selection and valuation to be final."

Louise Clisby Wise became forty years of age on July 28, 1935. The trustees decided to pay her the $5,000,000 partly in cash and partly in securities. The greater part of the securities had been owned by the testator and transferred as part of her estate to the trustees; others had been purchased by the trustees. All had appreciated in value during the period for which they were held by the trustees, and the Commissioner determined that the distribution of the securities to the niece resulted in capital gains which were taxable to the trustees under the rates specified in Section 117 of the Revenue Act of 1934 [loosely, the predecessor of sections 1(h), 1221, and 1222], which limits the percentage of gain to be treated as taxable income on the "sale or exchange" of capital assets. On this basis, the Commissioner determined a deficiency of $367,687.12 in the income tax for the year 1935.

The Board overruled the objections of the trustees to the imposition of any tax and denied a motion of the Commissioner to amend his answer in order to claim the full amount of the appreciation in value as ordinary income rather than a percentage of it as a capital gain, and confirmed the original deficiency determination. The taxpayers contend that the decision of the Board was erroneous because they realized neither gain from the sale or exchange of capital assets nor income of any character by delivering the securities to the legatee pursuant to the permissive terms of the will. The Commissioner contends that gain was realized by the delivery of the securities but that such gain was ordinary income not derived from a sale or exchange and therefore taxable in its entirety. The trustees have filed a petition to review the order of the Board determining the deficiency of $365,687.12 and the Commissioner has filed a cross-petition claiming a deficiency of $1,238,841.99, based on his contention that the gain was not governed by Section 117, and therefore not limited by the percentages therein specified.

The amount of gain is to be determined under Section 111 of the Revenue Act of 1934 [the predecessor of section 1001], which provides:

"(a) Computation of Gain or Loss. The gain from the sale or other disposition of property shall be the excess of the amount realized therefrom over the adjusted basis * * *.

"(b) Amount Realized. The amount realized from the sale or other disposition of property shall be the sum of money received plus the fair market value of the property (other than money) received."

Section 113 [the predecessor of sections 1012 and 1014] is claimed by the taxpayers to be relevant and provides:

"(a) The basis of property shall be the cost of such property; except that—

* * *

"(5) Property transmitted at death. If the property was acquired by bequest, devise, or inheritance, or by the decedent's estate from the decedent, the basis shall be the fair market value of such property at the time of such acquisition."

The Taxpayer's Appeal.

In support of their petition the taxpayers contend that the delivery of the securities of the trust estate to the legatee was a donative disposition of property pursuant to the terms of the will, and that no gain was thereby realized. They argue that when they determined that the legacy should be one of securities, it became for all purposes a bequest of property, just as if the cash alternative had not been provided, and not taxable for the reason that no gain is realized on the transfer by a testamentary trustee of specific securities or other property bequeathed by will to a legatee. We do not think that the situation here is the same as that of a legacy of specific property. The legatee was never in the position occupied by the recipient of specific securities under a will. She had a claim against the estate for $5,000,000, payable either in cash or securities of that value, but had no title or right to the securities, legal or equitable, until they were delivered to her by the trustees after the exercise of their option. She took none of the chances of a legatee of specific securities or of a share of a residue that the securities might appreciate or decline in value between the time of the death of the testator and the transfer to her by the trustees, but instead had at all times a claim for an unvarying amount in money or its equivalent.

If there had merely been a bequest to the legatee of $5,000,000 and she had agreed with the trustees to take securities of that value, the transaction would have been a "sale or other disposition" of the securities under Suisman v. Eaton, 15 F.Supp. 113, affirmed, 2 Cir., 83 F.2d 1019, certiorari denied 299 U.S. 573, 57 S.Ct. 37, 81 L.Ed. 422. There, a will creating a trust provided that each of the testator's children was to receive $50,000 on attaining the age of twenty-five. The trustee transferred stock of the value of $50,000 to one of the children, Minerva, in satisfaction of her legacy. Judge Hincks said in the district court (15 F.Supp. at page 115), that the "property which the trust estate received from the 'sale or other disposition' of said stocks was the discharge of the corpus from Minerva's equitable right to receive $50,000 therefrom; the amount realized, i.e., the 'fair market value of the property (other than money) received,' * * * was $50,000; and the excess of the amount realized over the basis was properly computed by the Commissioner, legally assessed as part of the taxable income of the trust estate, and the tax thereon was legally collected."

In the present case, the legatee had a claim which was a charge against the trust estate for $5,000,000 in cash or securities and the trustees had the power to determine whether the claim should be satisfied in one form or the other. The claim, though enforceable only in the alternative, was, like the claim in Suisman v. Eaton, supra, a charge against the entire trust estate. If it were satisfied by a cash payment securities might have to be sold on which (if those actually delivered in specie were selected) a taxable gain would necessarily have been realized. Instead of making such a sale the trustees delivered the securities and exchanged them pro tanto for the general claim of the legatee, which was thereby satisfied.

It is said that this transaction was not such a "sale or other disposition" as is intended by Section 111(a) or was dealt with in Suisman v. Eaton, because it was effectuated only by the will of the trustees and not, as in Suisman v. Eaton, through a mutual agreement between trustee and legatee. The Board made no such distinction, and we are not inclined to limit thus the meaning of the words "other disposition" used in Section 111(a), or of "exchange" used in Section 117. The word "exchange" does not necessarily have the connotation of a bilateral agreement which may be said to attach to the word "sale." Thus, should a person set up a trust and reserve to himself the power to substitute for the securities placed in trust other securities of equal value, there would seem no doubt that the exercise of this reserved power would be an "exchange" within the common meaning of the word, even though the settler consulted no will other than his own, although, of course, we do not here advert to the problems of taxability in such a situation.

The Board alluded to the fact that both here and in Suisman v. Eaton the bequest was fixed at a definite amount in money, that in both cases there was no bequest of specific securities (nor of a share in the residue which might vary in value), that the rights of the legatee, like those in the Suisman case, were a charge upon the corpus of the trust, and that the trustees had to part either with $5,000,000 in cash or with securities worth that amount at the time of the transfer. It added that the increase in value of the securities was realized by the trust and benefited it to the full extent, since, except for the increase, it would have had to part with other property, and it cited in further support of its position United States v. Kirby Lumber Co., 284 U.S. 1, 52 S.Ct. 4, 76 L.Ed. 131. Under circumstances like those here, where the legatee did not take securities designated by the will or an interest in the corpus which might be more or less at the time of the transfer than at the time of decedent's death, it seems to us that the trustees realized a gain by using these securities to settle a claim worth $5,000,000, just as the trustee in Suisman v. Eaton realized one.

It seems reasonably clear that the property was not "transmitted at death" or "acquired by bequest * * * from the decedent." Section 113(a)(5). It follows that the fears of the taxpayers that double taxation of this appreciation will result because the legatee will take the basis of the decedent under Brewster v. Gage, 280 U.S. 327, 50 S.Ct. 115, 74 L.Ed. 457, are groundless. It is true that under Section 113(a)(5) the basis for property "acquired by bequest, devise, or inheritance" is "the fair market value of such property at the time of such acquisition" and that under Brewster v. Gage, supra, the date of acquisition has been defined as the date of death of the testator. But the holding of the present case is necessarily a determination that the property here acquired is acquired in an exchange and not "by bequest, devise, or inheritance," since Sections 117 and 113(a)(5) seem to be mutually exclusive. The legatee's basis would seem to be the value of the claim surrendered in exchange for the securities; and the Board of Tax Appeals has so held. Sherman Ewing v. Commissioner of Internal Revenue, 40 B.T.A. 911.

The Commissioner's Appeal.

We have already held that a taxable gain was realized by the delivery of the securities. It follows from the reasons that support that conclusion that the appreciation was a capital gain, taxable at the rates specified in Section 117. Therefore, neither under Section 111(a) nor under Section 22(a) [the predecessor of section 61] can the gain realized be taxed as ordinary income.

There can be no doubt that from an accounting standpoint the trustees realized a gain in the capital of their trust when they disposed of securities worth far more at the time of disposition than at the time of acquisition in order to settle (pro tanto) a claim of $5,000,000. It would seem to us a strange anomaly if a disposition of securities which were in fact a "capital asset" should not be taxed at the rates afforded by Section 117 to individuals who have sold or exchanged property which they had held for the specified periods. It is not without significance that the appeal of the Commissioner was plainly an afterthought. The original deficiency was determined on the theory that the capital gains rates were applicable and the Commissioner sought to amend his answer so as to claim that ordinary rates should be applied only after the case had been orally argued before the Board. The Board denied his motion to reopen the case for the consideration of this contention. Since we find that the Commissioner's cross-petition is unfounded on the merits, we have no reason to consider the technical question whether the denial of the motion to amend the answer was otherwise an abuse of discretion.

The purpose of the capital gains provisions of the Revenue Act of 1934 is so to treat an appreciation in value, arising over a period of years but realized in one year, that the tax thereon will roughly approximate what it would have been had a tax been paid each year upon the appreciation in value for that year. Cf. Burnet v. Harmel, 287 U.S. 103, 106, 53 S.Ct. 74, 77 L.Ed. 199. The appreciation in value in the present case took place between 1917 and 1935, whereas the Commissioner's theory would tax it as though it had all taken place in 1935. If the trustees had sold the securities, they would be taxed at capital gain rates. Both the trustees and the Commissioner, in their arguments as respondent and cross-respondents, draw the analogy between the transaction here and a sale, and no injustice is done to either by taxing the gain at the rates which would apply had a sale actually been made and the proceeds delivered to the legatee. It seems to us extraordinary that the exercise by the trustees of the option to deliver to the legatee securities, rather than cash, should be thought to result in an increased deficiency of enormous proportions.

Orders affirmed.

Illustrative Material

1. The litigation expenses generated in *Kenan* were at issue in *Trust of Bingham v. Commissioner,* 325 U.S. 365 (1945), *supra* (ch. 2, sec. B(3)(a)).

2. In Rev. Rul. 55-117, 1955-1 C.B. 233, a beneficiary was entitled to receive one-fourth of the trust corpus prior to termination of the trust. The trustee proposed to dis-

tribute to the beneficiary appreciated securities equal in value to one-fourth of the trust corpus. The I.R.S. ruled that the estate would not realize *Kenan* gain. The transfer was "a partial distribution of a share of the trust principal" rather than a "sale or exchange," because it was "not in satisfaction of an obligation of the trust for a definite amount of cash or equivalent value in securities."

In Private Letter Rulings 200405001, 200405002, 200405003, and 200405004 (all dated 2003), the Service ruled that a proposed distribution was not "a distribution in satisfaction of a right to receive a distribution in a specific dollar amount or in specific property other than that distributed, nor [was] it a distribution in satisfaction of a general claim for an ascertainable value." Thus, the trust that proposed to make the distribution would realize neither gain nor loss upon doing so.

Revenue Ruling 67-74
1967-1 C.B. 194

Under the terms of the instrument which created a trust, the trustee is required to distribute currently to the beneficiary all of the income of the trust for each year. For the taxable year under consideration, the trustee had sufficient cash on hand to enable him to distribute in cash all of the trust income for that year which he was required to distribute to the beneficiary. However, in accordance with an agreement with the beneficiary, the trustee distributed, in lieu of cash, stock which was a part of the trust corpus and which had a fair market value equal to the amount of trust income for that year required to be distributed to the beneficiary. The value of the stock so distributed exceeded the basis of the stock in the hands of the trust.

Held, for Federal income tax purposes, the transaction is treated as though the trustee had actually distributed to the beneficiary cash in an amount equal to the trust income required to be distributed currently, and the beneficiary had purchased the stock from the trustee with cash. The trust is allowed a deduction under section 651(a) of the Internal Revenue Code of 1954, limited by the distributable net income of the trust, for the amount of income required to be distributed currently, and the beneficiary must report a like amount in gross income under section 652(a) of the Code. The instant transfer, involving stock having a fair market value equal to the trust income for the year in question which the trustee was required to distribute to the beneficiary, resulted in a capital gain to the trust equal to the difference between the basis of the stock in the hands of the trustee and the amount of the obligation satisfied by the transfer.... Further, the basis of the stock in the hands of the beneficiary is his cost, that is, the price he is deemed to have paid for it. See section 1012 of the Code.

Illustrative Material

Similarly, in Rev. Rul. 83-75, 1983-1 C.B. 114, the I.R.S. ruled that a charitable lead trust that did not have enough income to pay its charitable annuity, and therefore funded the annuity in part by distributing to charity appreciated assets, realized gain on the difference between the amount of the shortfall and the trust's basis in the appreciated assets distributed. (A charitable lead trust is one described in section 2055(e)(2)(B).)

Revenue Ruling 66-207

1966-2 C.B. 243

Advice has been requested whether a decedent's estate will realize taxable gain when a final distribution of appreciated property is made to satisfy a pecuniary legacy, but is of an insufficient amount to completely satisfy such a bequest.

By the terms of the decedent's will he made a bequest of a specific sum of money in the amount of 250x dollars to be used to create a trust for the benefit of a designated beneficiary. After payment of all debts, costs of administration, claims, and specific bequests, other than the sum of 250x dollars, the executor finds that all he has left in the estate are assets now having a fair market value of 200x dollars and an aggregate basis to the estate of 150x dollars. Included among these assets is cash in the amount of 10x dollars. All of these assets will be transferred in trust to the designated trustee in accordance with the terms of the will.

Section 663 of the Internal Revenue Code of 1954 provides that there shall not be included as amounts falling within section 661(a) or 662(a) of the Code any amount which, under the terms of the governing instrument, is properly paid or credited as a gift or bequest of a specific sum of money or of specific property and which is paid or credited all at once or in not more than three installments.

Under section 1.663(a)-1(b)(1) of the Income Tax Regulations, in order to qualify as a bequest of a specific sum of money, the amount of money must be ascertainable under the terms of the testator's will as of the date of his death. The bequest of 250x dollars is a "bequest of a specific sum of money" as that term is defined in section 1.663(a)-1(b)(1) of the regulations. The fact that the fair market value of the property remaining in the estate is not equal in amount to the bequest of the specific sum of money does not transform that bequest into a bequest of the residue of the estate. That circumstance merely means that the bequest of a specific sum has been abated in the amount of 50x dollars and thereby reduced from 250x dollars to 200x dollars.

[Former section] 1.661(a)-2(f) of the regulations provides, in part, that no gain or loss is realized by the trust or estate by reason of the distribution of property in kind unless the distribution is in satisfaction of a right to receive a distribution in a specific dollar amount. [But see section 643(e)(3), enacted by the Tax Reform Act of 1984.] Under this provision of the regulations whenever property other than money is distributed by an estate to any beneficiary, including a trust, in satisfaction of a cash bequest the estate realizes gain or loss measured by the difference between the amount of the bequest satisfied and the basis to the estate of the property so distributed. See *William R. Kenan, Jr., et al. v. Commissioner,* 114 F. 2d 217 (1940); and *Sarah P. Suisman v. Eaton,* 15 F. Supp. 113 (1935), affirmed per curiam, 83 F. 2d 1019, certiorari denied, 299 U.S. 573.

When the executor of this estate distributes the property remaining in the estate to the designated trustee in creation of the trust the estate will realize a gain of 50x dollars. This is the difference between the amount of the bequest satisfied by distribution of property other than cash (200x dollars less 10x dollars cash, or 190x dollars) and the basis (150x dollars less 10x dollars cash, or 140x dollars) to the estate of the assets other than cash distributed in satisfaction of the bequest of a specific sum of money. The effect of the distribution will be the same as if the executor sold the remaining assets of the estate and distributed the proceeds to the trustee in trust.

No amount is deductible by the estate under section 661 of the Code or includible in gross income of the trust under section 662 of the Code since the distribution will be in satisfaction of a bequest of a specific sum of money, as defined by section 1.663(a)-1(b) of the regulations.

Accordingly, a final distribution by the executor of an estate of appreciated property, in order to satisfy a pecuniary legacy, will result in a gain to the estate, although such distribution is of an insufficient amount to completely satisfy such bequest.

Illustrative Material

1. Due to amendments to the regulations in 2003, the reference in Rev. Rul. 66-207 to section 1.661(a)-2(f) is no longer current. The ruling itself, however, seems consistent with the new version of the regulation.

2. To similar effect is Rev. Rul. 86-105, 1986-2 C.B. 82. There the I.R.S. ruled that a bequest of "assets, in cash or in kind or partly in each … with a fair market value at the date of distribution equal to 2,000x dollars" was a bequest of a "specific sum of money" under section 663(a)(1). The estate was therefore denied a distribution deduction on account of the distribution, and the beneficiary was not required to include in income any amount on account of receipt of the distribution. The I.R.S. also ruled that the bequest created "a right to receive a distribution in a specific dollar amount." Thus, when the estate satisfied that right with appreciated assets, it realized gain.

3. In Rev. Rul. 72-295, 1972-1 C.B. 197, the decedent's will required distribution to a beneficiary of x dollars' worth of the shares of a particular corporation, to be valued at date of distribution. In no event, however, was the beneficiary to receive more than all the shares the decedent owned at his death. At his death the decedent owned more shares than were required to satisfy the bequest. The I.R.S. ruled that, because the amount of the bequest was not ascertainable at the decedent's death, as required by Treas. Reg. §1.663(a)-1(b)(1), the bequest was not described in section 663(a)(1). As a result, distribution of the bequest drew out a portion of the estate's distributable net income. Similarly, since the bequest was not of a specific dollar amount, the estate realized no gain when the bequest was funded with appreciated shares. Is there any important difference between the bequest involved in this ruling and that involved in Rev. Rul. 66-207?

Revenue Ruling 82-4
1982-1 C.B. 99

ISSUE

Under the circumstances described below, does an estate realize gain for federal income tax purposes when an executor distributes property to one of two heirs to equalize their respective shares?

FACTS

In 1980 A gratuitously transferred to B, A's adult child, 100,000 shares of X company stock. A died in 1981. A's will provides that after the payment of debts, expenses, taxes, and the satisfaction of certain specific bequests, the residue of the estate is to be divided equally between the decedent's adult children, B and C. However, the will further provides that the executor, in determining the allocation of the residue to B and C, is to take into account the date of death value of the 100,000 shares of stock transferred to *B*. This provision was intended to equalize, to the extent possible, the value of the property transferred to *B* and *C*, taking into consideration the lifetime transfer to *B*. The will also provides that any assets distributed in kind are to be valued at the date of distribution.

At the time of final distribution, the residuary estate consisted solely of 60,000 shares of *X* company stock with a value of $3 per share. The value of the stock at the date of death was $2 per share. Because the value of the residue at the date of distribution ($180,000) was less than the value at the date of death of the stock previously transferred by the decedent to *B* ($200,000), the executor, in accordance with the terms of the decedent's will, distributed the entire residuary estate to *C*.

LAW AND ANALYSIS

Section 661(a) of the Internal Revenue Code provides that in any tax year there shall be allowed as a deduction in computing the taxable income of an estate the sum of (1) any amount of income for the tax year required to be distributed currently (including any amount required to be distributed that may be paid out of income or corpus to the extent the amount is paid out of income for the tax year); and (2) any other amounts properly paid or credited or required to be distributed for the tax year. However, the deduction cannot exceed the distributable net income of the estate.

[Former section] 1.661(a)-2(f)(1) of the Income Tax Regulations provides that an estate does not realize a gain or loss from the distribution of property in kind unless the distribution is in satisfaction of a right to receive a distribution in a specific dollar amount. [Compare section 643(e)(3).] Under this provision of the regulations, whenever an estate distributes property other than money to any beneficiary in satisfaction of a specific dollar amount, the estate realizes gain or loss measured by the difference between the amount of the bequest satisfied and the basis to the estate of the distributed property. See *Kenan v. Commissioner*, 114 F.2d 217 (2d Cir. 1940); and *Suisman v. Eaton*, 15 F. Supp. 113 (D. Conn. 1935), *aff'd per curiam*, 83 F. 2d 1019 (2d Cir. 1936), *cert. denied*, 299 U.S. 573 (1936).

Section 663(a) of the Code excludes from amounts falling within section 661(a) any amount that, under the terms of the governing instrument, is properly paid or credited as a gift or bequest of a specific sum of money or of specific property.

Section 1.663(a)-1(b)(1) of the regulations provides that in order to qualify as a gift or bequest of a specific sum of money or of specific property under section 663(a) of the Code, the amount of money or the identity of the specific property must be ascertainable under the terms of a decedent's will as of the date of the decedent's death.

[The I.R.S. summarizes Rev. Rul. 66-207, *supra*.]

In the present situation, the decedent's will provides that the residue of the estate is to be divided equally between *B* and *C*. However, in order to equalize to the extent possible the respective shares of *B* and *C*, the executor must take into account the value at the date of death of the stock previously transferred to *B*.

In this case, as in Rev. Rul. 66-207, the residue equal to the value of 100,000 shares of *X* company stock as of date of death bequeathed to *C* is a "bequest of a specific sum of money," as that term is defined in section 1.663(a)-1(b)(1) of the regulations, because the amount is ascertainable under the terms of *A*'s will as of the date of *A*'s death. Thus, no amount is deductible by the estate under section 661 of the Code or includible in the gross income of *B* under section 662. Also, under [former] section 1.661(a)-2(f)(1), the estate realizes a gain on the distribution in kind of appreciated property in satisfaction of *C*'s right to receive a distribution in a specific dollar amount.

HOLDING

The estate realizes gain of $60,000 (date of distribution value ($180,000) less the basis of the property in the estate ($120,000)) for federal income tax purposes when the executor distributes the entire residuary estate to C to equalize to the extent possible the respective shares of total transfers received from the decedent.

If in this case the value of the residuary estate had been, for example, $250,000, the property remaining after satisfaction of the $200,000 bequest to C ($50,000) would pass to B and C in equal shares. The estate would realize no gain or loss under [former] section 1.661(a)-2(f)(1) of the regulations upon distribution of this portion of the $50,000 residue because the distribution would not be in satisfaction of the right to receive a distribution in a specific dollar amount.

Illustrative Material

1. As a result of amendments to the regulations in 2003, the references in Rev. Rul. 82-4 to Treas. Reg. § 1.661(a)-2(f) are no longer current. The ruling itself, however, appears to be consistent with the new version of the regulation.

2. Funding of a trust pursuant to a formula pecuniary marital deduction clause, which, according to the I.R.S., designated a "fixed and definite 'dollar amount,'" caused the estate to realize capital gains to the extent that the fair-market value of the property transferred to the trust exceeded the estate's basis in such property. Rev. Rul. 56-270, 1956-1 C.B. 325. Gains thus realized could be offset by losses similarly realized.

Revenue Ruling 60-87
1960-1 C.B. 286

Advice has been requested whether gain or loss is recognized upon the distribution of securities by the executor of an estate to a marital deduction testamentary trust under the circumstances described below.

The decedent was a resident of a community property state. The estate consisted almost entirely of community property. The decedent's will provided that, after certain distributions of his personal property, a part of the residue and remainder of the estate be placed in trust for the benefit of his wife. The trust was to include the wife's share of certain community property, plus an amount of the decedent's separate property which, when added to the value of certain other property included in the decedent's gross estate, would equal one-half of his adjusted gross estate as finally determined for Federal estate tax purposes. On the date the will was executed, the decedent's wife executed a statement to the effect that her election to accept its provisions would be effective upon demise of her husband upon condition that his will be admitted to probate. The will has been admitted to probate and she elected to take under it. The testamentary trust is to continue during the lifetime of the decedent's wife and during such period of time she is to receive the income therefrom, with a general testamentary power of appointment, but in default of appointment with remainder over to named persons.

After the final determination of the value of the decedent's adjusted gross estate for Federal estate tax purposes, the executor of the estate transferred to the testamentary marital deduction trust securities sufficient in value, together with the other items to be included therein, to bring the value of the trust to the required one-half of the adjusted gross estate. In determining the value of the property to be transferred to the trust, the executor of the estate used the fair market value of the property at the date of the distribution. However, since the fair market value of the property transferred, at the date of the transfer to the trust, was greater than the value used for Federal estate tax purposes, the specific question arises whether gain is realized by the estate because of such transfer. A corollary question is whether such marital deduction trust may be considered as being provided for in a fixed and definite "dollar amount."

Revenue Ruling 56-270, C.B. 1956-1, 325, stands for the proposition that, if a marital deduction trust comprises a fraction or percentage of the "adjusted gross estate" of a decedent, the marital trust fund is considered to have been provided for in a fixed and definite "dollar amount." Therefore, capital gain or loss is recognized upon the distribution of property to a trust.

Insofar as is here pertinent, section 663(a) of the Internal Revenue Code of 1954 provides, in general, that a gift or bequest of a specific sum of money shall neither be allowed as a deduction to an estate or trust under section 661 of the Code nor included in the gross income of the beneficiary under section 662(a) of the Code. To qualify for this exclusion, the amount of money bequeathed must be ascertainable as of the date of death. The effect of the regulations is that a bequest under a marital deduction trust formula clause does not qualify for exclusion since the amount of the trust fund is not ascertainable at the date of the decedent's death.

Section 1.663(a)-1(b)(1) of the Income Tax Regulations provides....

Unlike section 1.663(a)-1(b)(1) of the regulations, Revenue Ruling 56-270, supra, is not concerned with the ascertainability of a specific amount at the date of death but rather whether the marital trust fund is provided for in a fixed and definite amount at the time of the distribution. Thus, to qualify for the exclusion provided for in section 663(a) of the Code, [section 1.663(a)-1(b)(1)] prescribes an entirely different test from that prescribed in Revenue Ruling 56-270, which has application only for capital gain purposes. Further, the last sentence of [section 1.663(a)-1(b)(1)] recognizes the fact that a different rule applies for capital gain purposes and clearly implies that the regulations are not to be considered inconsistent with that rule.

In the instant case, the marital deduction trust comprises a portion of the residue of the decedent's estate. However, instead of using a residuary formula clause, which leaves a percentage or fraction of the value of the residuary estate to the surviving spouse or trust, the will uses a pecuniary formula clause, as a [sic] Revenue Ruling 56-270, supra, which leaves a percentage of the "adjusted gross estate" to the surviving spouse or trust. There is a significant distinction between a marital deduction trust of the pecuniary formula type and one of the residuary formula type.

The rationale of Revenue Ruling 56-270, supra, is that a marital deduction trust of the pecuniary formula type provides for a trust fund in a fixed and definite amount, once the value of the adjusted gross estate is finally determined, which amount is unaffected by any appreciation or depreciation in value of the assets comprising the estate.

The difference is that under a pecuniary formula clause the trust will receive assets of a fixed and definite amount at the time of distribution, whereas under the residuary formula clause the percentage or fraction will be applied for the purpose of making distribution of the residuary estate as constituted at the time of distribution. Therefore, under a residuary formula clause, the trust will share in appreciation and depreciation of the value of the estate, which is not the case under a pecuniary formula clause. Thus, Revenue Ruling 56-270, supra, is not inconsistent with section 1.663(a)-1(b)(1) of the regulations.

The facts in the instant case show that the marital deduction trust comprising a portion of the residue of the estate is measured by a percentage of the value of the adjusted gross estate. Under such circumstances, the marital trust fund is considered as being provided for in a fixed and definite "dollar amount." Accordingly, gain or loss is realized by the estate measured by the difference between the fair market value of the property at the date of distribution and the value of the property determined for Federal estate tax purposes.

Revenue Ruling 56-270, C.B. 1956-1, 325, is clarified.

Reference

For more on the income tax consequences of funding bequests pursuant to formula clauses, see Barnett, *Unexpected (and Often Irrational) Income Tax Consequences of Funding the New Marital Deduction and Credit Shelter Bequests,* 16 U. Miami Inst. on Est. Plan. ¶1900 (1982). The author describes the distinction offered by Rev. Rul. 60–87 as "unconvincing" and argues that Treas. Reg. $1.663(a)-1(b)(1) is wrong. *See also* Danforth, *The Interplay of* Kenan v. Commissioner *and Section 663(a)(1),* 30 Est., Gifts & Tr. J. 139 (2005).

b. Elective

———

Internal Revenue Code:
   Section 643(e)

———

General Explanation of the Revenue Provisions of the Deficit Reduction Act of 1984
Prepared by the Staff of the Joint Committee on Taxation 253–54 (1984)

Prior Law

Under prior law, beneficiaries were taxed on amounts distributed from a trust or estate to the extent of the trust's or estate's distributable net income. The trust or estate was allowed a deduction for amounts taxed to its beneficiaries. Prior Treasury Department regulations provided that distributions of property were deemed to carry out distributable net income to the extent of the property's value at the time of distribution. In such a case, no gain or loss was realized on the distribution by the trust or estate, and the basis of the property in the hands of the beneficiary was its value to the extent it carried out distributable net income. [Former] Treas. Reg. sec. 1.661(a)-2(f).

Reasons for Change

Where a trust or estate had distributable net income and distributed property, the effect of the prior Treasury Department regulations was to exempt the gain or loss entirely from tax. Congress believed that the gain or loss should be taxed to either the beneficiary or the trust (or estate).

Explanation of Provision

The Act provides that distributions of property from a trust or estate are treated as carrying out distributable net income only to the extent of the lesser of the property's basis or its fair market value at the time of distribution. Under this rule, the basis of the property in the hands of the beneficiary will be the same as the trust's or estate's basis in the property. Alternatively, the Act permits the trustee or executor to elect to treat distributions of property as taxable events resulting in recognition of gain or loss on the distribution as if the property had been sold to the beneficiary.

The Act does not change prior law in those cases where a distribution of property to a beneficiary results in the recognition of gain or loss to the trust or estate (e.g., the rule providing a basis adjustment for property received in satisfaction of a pecuniary bequest continues to apply).[3]

Illustrative Material

1. Rev. Rul. 86-105, 1986-2 C.B. 82, states that section 643(e) "does not apply in those cases where a distribution of property results in recognition of gain or loss to the estate without regard to the enactment of section 643(e)." In other words, *Kenan* gain is independent of, and not avoidable by, the election under section 643(e).

2. Prior to enactment of section 643(e), distributions of property generally carried distributable net income out to the beneficiaries to the extent of the property's fair market value at the time of distribution. Under Treas. Reg. §1.661(a)-2(f)(3) before its amendment in 2003, the basis of such property in the hands of the beneficiaries was equal to its fair market value at the time of distribution, to the extent of distributable net income. Rev. Rul. 64-314, 1964-2 C.B. 167, illustrated the complex allocation of basis "step-up" that was required when property other than cash was distributed.

But if the estate's basis equalled the property's value at time of distribution, the old rules arrived at the same result section 643(e) now mandates. In Rev. Rul. 69-432, 1969-2 C.B. 144, an executor purchased and distributed, to a beneficiary who was entitled to receive monthly payments of a certain amount during his lifetime, a nonrefundable annuity guaranteed to pay such amount each month for the beneficiary's life. The I.R.S. ruled that the estate was entitled to deduct under section 661(a) the cost of the annuity, limited by the estate's distributable net income. Similarly, the beneficiary was required to include the cost of the annuity, also limited by distributable net income, in his gross income under section 662. The I.R.S. further ruled that the beneficiary's basis in the annuity was its cost. The I.R.S. reasoned that the transaction should be treated "as though the executor had distributed an amount of cash equal to the cost of the annuity, and the beneficiary had purchased the annuity for cash."

The 2003 amendments to section 1.661(a)-2(f) conformed that provision to the enactment of section 643(e).

3. *See generally* Freeland, Maxfield & Sawyer, *Estate and Trust Distribution of Property in Kind After the Tax Reform Act of 1984*, 40 Tax L. Rev. 449 (1985); Danforth, *Planning for the Section 643(e)(3) Election*, 29 Est., Gifts & Tr. J. 165 (2004).

---

3. In the case of a distribution by a trust of property whose value is less than its basis, section 267 would deny a loss deduction to the trust. However, section 267 does not apply to deny a deduction to an estate in such a case. [Section 267 now applies to transactions between an executor and the beneficiaries of an estate, except for sales or exchanges in satisfaction of pecuniary bequests. I.R.C. §267(b)(13).]

Problems

3-27. In a year in which an estate has distributable net income (none of which is tax-exempt) of $20,000, it distributes $5,000 in cash to a beneficiary who received a $5,000 general bequest under the decedent's will and $5,000 in cash, securities then worth $10,000, and real estate then worth $15,000 to the residuary beneficiary. Under local law, title to the real estate passed directly from the decedent to the residuary beneficiary; however, the executor is entitled to possession of such property during administration. The estate's basis in the securities is $4,000, and its basis in the real estate is $12,000.

a. Calculate the amount subject to taxation under section 662 in the hands of each beneficiary.

b. Calculate the bases of both the securities and the real estate in the hands of the residuary beneficiary.

3-28. Assume the facts of Problem 3-27, except that the residuary beneficiary receives a car instead of the real estate. The car is worth $15,000, and the estate's basis in it is $12,000.

a. Calculate the amount subject to taxation under section 662 in the hands of each beneficiary.

b. Calculate the bases of both the securities and the car in the hands of the residuary beneficiary.

3-29. Would it matter if the residuary beneficiary in Problem 3-28 had been entitled to the car under a specific rather than a residuary bequest?

3-30. Assume the facts of Problem 3-28, except that $10,000 of the estate's distributable net income is tax-exempt.

3-31. Assume the facts of Problem 3-27, except that the executor, pursuant to authority granted in the decedent's will, funds the $5,000 general bequest with securities worth $5,000 instead of cash. The estate's basis in the securities is $4,000.

a. What are the tax consequences?

b. Is the answer to either of the questions in Problem 3-27 different?

3-32. Suggest situations in which a fiduciary might elect to recognize gain under section 643(e).

2. By the Beneficiary

Revenue Ruling 69-486
1969-2 C.B. 159

Advice has been requested as to the Federal income tax treatment of a final distribution of property in kind by a trustee to the two beneficiaries of a trust under the circumstances described below.

Under terms of the trust instrument, the trustee is required to distribute currently all trust income to B for her life and upon her death distribute one-half of the trust corpus to C, an individual, and one-half to X, a charitable organization exempt from tax under section 501(c)(3) of the Internal Revenue Code of 1954.

B died on July 1, 1967. At the time of her death, the trust had ordinary income of 20*x* dollars to be reported in its current calendar year period. Subsequent to *B*'s death the trust received no income up to its termination on August 1, 1967. The distributable net income of the trust for 1967 as defined by section 643(a) of the Code was 20*x* dollars. The trustee properly distributed currently 20*x* dollars to *B*'s successor in interest.

At the time of *B*'s death, the trust corpus to be distributed to *C* and *X* consisted in part of notes that had been purchased by the trust and that had a total adjusted basis of 300*x* dollars and a total fair market value of an equal amount. The balance of the trust corpus consisted of common stock acquired by purchase with a total adjusted basis of 100*x* dollars and a total fair market value of 300*x* dollars.

The trust instrument as well as local law was silent as to the authority of the trustee to make a non-pro rata distribution of property in kind.

By mutual agreement, the two beneficiaries requested that the trustee distribute all of the notes to *C* and all of the common stock to *X*. The trustee complied with this request on August 1, 1967.

The ... issue to be decided is how the non-pro rata distribution by the trustee to *C* and *X* will be treated for Federal income tax purposes.

Since the trustee was not authorized to make a non-pro rata distribution of property in kind but did so as a result of the mutual agreement between *C* and *X*, the non pro rata distribution by the trustee to *C* and *X* is equivalent to a distribution to *C* and *X* of the notes and common stock pro rata by the trustee, followed by an exchange between *C* and *X* of *C*'s pro rata share of common stock for *X*'s pro rata share of notes.

* * *

Furthermore, *C* in substance exchanged his pro rata share of common stock with *X* for *X*'s pro rata share of notes. The amount of recognized gain to *C* is determined under sections 1001 and 1002 of the Code. Since *X* is a charitable organization exempt from tax under section 501(c)(3) of the Code, it has no tax consequence as a result of the exchange.

Illustrative Material

Even the Service, however, does not follow Revenue Ruling 69-486 when either the governing instrument or local law authorizes non-pro rata distributions. *See, e.g.,* Private Letter Ruling 200334030 (2003); Private Letter Ruling 9625020 (1996). *See generally* Randolph & Gurevitz, *Opportunities and Pitfalls with Non-Pro Rata Distributions to Residuary Beneficiaries*, Prob.& Prop., July/Aug. 2005, at 60.

Chapter 4

The Entity Ignored

A. Assignment of Income

Internal Revenue Code:
  Sections 61(a); 671

Regulation:
  Section 1.671-1(c)

Lucas v. Earl

281 U.S. 111 (1930)

MR. JUSTICE HOLMES delivered the opinion of the Court.

This case presents the question whether the respondent, Earl, could be taxed for the whole of the salary and attorney's fees earned by him in the years 1920 and 1921, or should be taxed for only a half of them in view of a contract with his wife which we shall mention. The Commissioner of Internal Revenue and the Board of Tax Appeals imposed a tax upon the whole, but their decision was reversed by the Circuit Court of Appeals, 30 F. (2d) 898. A writ of certiorari was granted by this Court.

By the contract, made in 1901, Earl and his wife agreed "that any property either of us now has or may hereafter acquire ... in any way, either by earnings (including salaries, fees, etc.), or any rights by contract or otherwise, during the existence of our marriage, or which we or either of us may receive by gift, bequest, devise, or inheritance, and all the proceeds, issues, and profits of any and all such property shall be treated and considered and hereby is declared to be received, held, taken, and owned by us as joint tenants, and not otherwise, with the right of survivorship." The validity of the contract is not questioned, and we assume it to be unquestionable under the law of the State of California, in which the parties lived. Nevertheless we are of opinion that the Commissioner and Board of Tax Appeals were right.

The [predecessor of section 61] imposes a tax upon the net income of every individual including "income derived from salaries, wages, or compensation for personal service ... of whatever kind and in whatever form paid".... A very forcible argument is presented to the effect that the statute seeks to tax only income beneficially received, and that taking the question more technically the salary and fees became the joint property of Earl and his wife on the very first instant on which they were received. We well might hesitate upon the latter proposition, because however the matter might stand between husband and wife he was the only party to the contracts by which the salary and fees were earned, and it is somewhat hard to say that the last step in the performance of those contracts could be taken by anyone but himself alone. But this case is not to be decided by attenuated subtleties. It turns on the import and reasonable construction of the taxing act. There is no doubt that the statute could tax salaries to those who earned them and provide that the tax could not be escaped by anticipatory arrangements and contracts however skillfully devised to prevent the salary when paid from vesting even for a second in the man who earned it. That seems to us the import of the statute before us and we think that no distinction can be taken according to the motives leading to the arrangement by which the fruits are attributed to a different tree from that on which they grew.

Judgment reversed.

Illustrative Material

1. In *Poe v. Seaborn,* 282 U.S. 101 (1930), the Supreme Court held that a wife correctly reported one-half of her husband's salary on her separate income tax return, because, under the community property laws of the State of Washington, "the entire property and income of the community [could] no more be said to be that of the husband, than it could rightly be termed that of the wife." *Id.* at 113.

Mr. Earl lived in California, also a community property state. Why did Mr. Earl feel compelled to rearrange his affairs as outlined in the case? In short, how could *Lucas v. Earl* have arisen in a community property state?

Lucas v. Earl involved income for 1920 and 1921. Prior to changes made in 1927, California law gave husbands powers of dominion and control over community property so extensive that the Supreme Court, in *United States v. Robbins,* 269 U.S. 315 (1926), had required a California husband to report all of the community income on his separate income tax return. Justice Holmes, writing for the Court, had described the community property interest of a California wife as "a mere expectancy while living with her husband." *Id.* at 327. As a result, Mr. Earl's effort appears to have been directed at achieving for him and his wife the income tax savings that the community property laws of other states offered.

In *United States v. Malcolm,* 282 U.S. 792 (1931) (per curiam), the Supreme Court held that a California wife properly reported one-half of her husband's 1928 salary on her separate income tax return. California thereby rejoined the ranks of the community property states for income tax purposes.

2. Mr. Earl's lack of success in achieving for himself and his wife the tax benefits generally available in community property states led Hawaii, Michigan, Nebraska, Oklahoma, Oregon, and Pennsylvania to enact community property laws for their residents. But after the Revenue Act of 1948 created the joint return, which duplicated community property income tax benefits for married residents of common law property jurisdictions, all of the new community property jurisdictions repealed their community property laws, except for Pennsylvania, whose highest court had already declared its community property act unconstitutional. *Willcox v. Penn Mutual Life Insurance Co.,* 357 Pa. 581, 55 A.2d 521 (1947).

3. In *Commissioner v. Culbertson,* 337 U.S. 733 (1949), the Court referred to "the first principle of income taxation": "income must be taxed to him who earns it." *Id.* at 739–40.

United States v. Basye, 410 U.S. 441 (1973), reiterating that language, applied the assignment-of-income doctrine to a fact pattern in which the taxpayer who earned the income clearly had never had any right to receive it. In *Basye,* a partnership of physicians contracted to provide group medical services for the employees of a corporation. In addition to direct payments, the corporation agreed to make periodic contributions to the partnership's nonqualified retirement trust. The Court held that the corporation's retirement contributions were immediately taxable to the partnership, despite the fact that neither the partnership nor the physicians were then entitled to any benefits under the retirement plan. The argument that the assignment-of-income doctrine should not apply because there was no evidence that, in lieu of the retirement contributions, the corporation would have increased its direct payments to the partnership, was expressly rejected: "The Government need not prove that the taxpayer had complete and unrestricted power to designate the manner and form in which his income is received." *Id.* at 452.

4. In *Temple v. Commissioner,* 62 Fed. Appx. 605, 2003-1 U.S.T.C. ¶ 50,411 (6th Cir. 2003) (per curiam), the taxpayer claimed that he had assigned the income from his practice as a veterinarian and from his sales of exotic animals to a series of off-shore trusts. The Sixth Circuit affirmed the Tax Court's holding that, under the assignment-of-income doctrine, the taxpayer remained subject to taxation on the income in question. The court also upheld the imposition of a variety of penalties for fraud and for making frivolous arguments.

Blair v. Commissioner
300 U.S. 5 (1937)

MR. CHIEF JUSTICE HUGHES delivered the opinion of the Court.

This case presents the question of the liability of a beneficiary of a testamentary trust for a tax upon the income which he had assigned to his children prior to the tax years and which the trustees had paid to them accordingly.

The trust was created by will of William Blair, a resident of Illinois who died in 1899, and was of property located in that State. One-half of the net income was to be paid to the donor's widow during her life. His son, the petitioner Edward Tyler Blair, was to receive the other one-half and, after the death of the widow, the whole of the net income during his life. In 1923, after the widow's death, petitioner assigned to his daughter, Lucy Blair Linn, an interest amounting to $6,000 for the remainder of that calendar year, and to $9,000 in each calendar year thereafter, in the net income which the petitioner was then or might thereafter be entitled to receive during his life. At about the same time, he made like assignments of interests, amounting to $9,000 in each calendar year, in the net income of the trust to his daughter Edith Blair and to his son, Edward Seymour Blair, respectively. In later years, by similar instruments, he assigned to these children additional interests, and to his son William McCormick Blair other specified interests in the net income. The trustees accepted the assignments and distributed the income directly to the assignees.

The question first arose with respect to the tax year 1923 and the Commissioner of Internal Revenue ruled that the income was taxable to the petitioner. The Board of Tax Appeals held the contrary. 18 B. T. A. 69. The Circuit Court of Appeals reversed the Board, holding that under the law of Illinois the trust was a spendthrift trust and the assignments were invalid. *Commissioner v. Blair,* 60 F. (2d) 340. We denied certiorari. 288 U. S. 602.

Thereupon the trustees brought suit in the Superior Court of Cook County, Illinois, to obtain a construction of the will with respect to the power of the beneficiary of the trust to assign a part of his equitable interest and to determine the validity of the assignments he had made. The petitioner and the assignees were made defendants. The Appellate Court of Illinois, First District, after a review of the Illinois decisions, decided that the trust was not a spendthrift trust and upheld the assignments. *Blair v. Linn,* 274 Ill. App. 23. Under the mandate of the appellate court, the Superior Court of Cook County entered its decree which found the assignments to be "voluntary assignments of a part of the interest of said Edward Tyler Blair in said trust estate" and as such adjudged them to be valid.

At the time there were pending before the Board of Tax Appeals proceedings involving the income of the trust for the years 1924, 1925, 1926 and 1929. The Board received in evidence the record in the suit in the state court and, applying the decision of that court, the Board overruled the Commissioner's determination as to the petitioner's liability. 31 B. T. A. 1192. The Circuit Court of Appeals again reversed the Board. That court ... decided that the income was ... taxable to the petitioner upon the ground that his interest was not attached to the corpus of the estate and that the income was not subject to his disposition until he received it. *Commissioner v. Blair,* 83 F. (2d) 655, 662.

* * *

The question remains whether, treating the assignments as valid, the assignor was still taxable upon the income under the federal income tax act. That is a federal question.

Our decisions in *Lucas v. Earl,* 281 U. S. 111, and *Burnet v. Leininger,* 285 U. S. 136, are cited. In the *Lucas* case the question was whether an attorney was taxable for the whole of his salary and fees earned by him in the tax years or only upon one-half by reason of an agreement with his wife by which his earnings were to be received and owned by them jointly. We were of the opinion that the case turned upon the construction of the taxing act. We said that "the statute could tax salaries to those who earned them and provide that the tax could not be escaped by anticipatory arrangements and contracts however skillfully devised to prevent the salary when paid from vesting even for a second in the man who earned it." That was deemed to be the meaning of the statute as to compensation for personal service, and the one who earned the income was held to be subject to the tax. In *Burnet v. Leininger, supra,* a husband, a member of a firm, assigned future partnership income to his wife. We found that the revenue act dealt explicitly with the liability of partners as such. The wife did not become a member of the firm; the act specifically taxed the distributive share of each partner in the net income of the firm; and the husband by the fair import of the act remained taxable upon his distributive share. These cases are not in point. The tax here is not upon earnings which are taxed to the one who earns them. Nor is it a case of income attributable to a taxpayer by reason of the application of the income to the discharge of his obligation. *Old Colony Trust Co. v. Commissioner,* 279 U. S. 716; *Douglas v. Willcuts,* 296 U. S. 1, 9; *Helvering v. Stokes,* 296 U. S. 551; *Helvering v. Schweitzer,* 296 U. S. 551; *Helvering v. Coxey,* 297 U. S. 694. See, also, *Burnet v. Wells,* 289 U. S. 670, 677. There is here no question of evasion or of giving effect to statutory provisions designed to forestall evasion; or of the taxpayer's retention of control. *Corliss v. Bowers,* 281 U. S. 376; *Burnet v. Guggenheim,* 288 U. S. 280.

In the instant case, the tax is upon income as to which, in the general application of the revenue acts, the tax liability attaches to ownership. See *Poe v. Seaborn,* [282 U. S.101]; *Hoeper v. Tax Commission,* 284 U. S. 206.

The Government points to the provisions of the revenue acts imposing upon the beneficiary of a trust the liability for the tax upon the income distributable to the beneficiary. But the term is merely descriptive of the one entitled to the beneficial interest. These provisions cannot be taken to preclude valid assignments of the beneficial interest, or to affect the duty of the trustee to distribute income to the owner of the beneficial interest, whether he was such initially or becomes such by valid assignment. The one who is to receive the income as the owner of the beneficial interest is to pay the tax. If under the law governing the trust the beneficial interest is assignable, and if it has been assigned without reservation, the assignee thus becomes the beneficiary and is entitled to rights and remedies accordingly. We find nothing in the revenue acts which denies him that status.

The decision of the Circuit Court of Appeals turned upon the effect to be ascribed to the assignments. The court held that the petitioner had no interest in the corpus of the estate and could not dispose of the income until he received it. Hence it was said that "the income was *his*" and his assignment was merely a direction to pay over to others what was due to himself. The question was considered to involve "the date when the income became transferable." 83 F. (2d), p. 662. The Government refers to the terms of the assignment,—that it was of the interest in the income "which the said party of the first part now is, or may hereafter be, entitled to receive during his life from the trustees." From this it is urged that the assignments "dealt only with a right to receive the income" and that "no attempt was made to assign any equitable right, title or interest in the trust itself." This construction seems to us to be a strained one. We think it apparent that the conveyancer was not seeking to limit the assignment so as to make it anything less than a complete transfer of the specified interest of the petitioner as the life beneficiary of the trust, but that with ample caution he was using words to effect such a transfer. That the state court so construed the assignments appears from the final decree which described them as voluntary assignments of interests of the petitioner "in said trust estate," and it was in that aspect that petitioner's right to make the assignments was sustained.

The will creating the trust entitled the petitioner during his life to the net income of the property held in trust. He thus became the owner of an equitable interest in the corpus of the property. *Brown v. Fletcher,* 235 U. S. 589, 598, 599; *Irwin v. Gavit,* 268 U. S. 161, 167, 168; *Senior v. Braden,* 295 U. S. 422, 432, 433; *Merchants' Loan & Trust Co. v. Patterson,* 308 Ill. 519, 530, 139 N. E. 912. By virtue of that interest he was entitled to enforce the trust, to have a breach of trust enjoined and to obtain redress in case of breach. The interest was present property alienable like any other, in the absence of a valid restraint upon alienation. *Commissioner v. Field,* 42 F. (2d) 820, 822; *Shanley v. Bowers,* 81 F. (2d) 13, 15. The beneficiary may thus transfer a part of his interest as well as the whole. See Restatement of the Law of Trusts, §§130, 132 *et seq.* The assignment of the beneficial interest is not the assignment of a chose in action but of the "right, title and estate in and to property." *Brown v. Fletcher, supra; Senior v. Braden, supra.* See Bogert, "Trusts and Trustees," vol. 1, §183, pp. 516, 517; 17 Columbia Law Review, 269, 273, 289, 290.

We conclude that the assignments were valid, that the assignees thereby became the owners of the specified beneficial interests in the income, and that as to these interests they and not the petitioner were taxable for the tax years in question. The judgment of the Circuit Court of Appeals is reversed and the cause is remanded with direction to affirm the decision of the Board of Tax Appeals.

Reversed.

Helvering v. Horst
311 U.S. 112 (1940)

MR. JUSTICE STONE delivered the opinion of the Court.

The sole question for decision is whether the gift, during the donor's taxable year, of interest coupons detached from the bonds, delivered to the donee and later in the year paid at maturity, is the realization of income taxable to the donor.

In 1934 and 1935 respondent, the owner of negotiable bonds, detached from them negotiable interest coupons shortly before their due date and delivered them as a gift to his son who in the same year collected them at maturity. The Commissioner ruled that ... the interest payments were taxable, in the years when paid, to the respondent donor who reported his income on the cash receipts basis. The Circuit Court of Appeals reversed the order of the Board of Tax Appeals sustaining the tax. 107 F. 2d 906; 39 B. T. A. 757. We granted certiorari, 309 U. S. 650, because of the importance of the question in the administration of the revenue laws and because of an asserted conflict in principle of the decision below with that of *Lucas v. Earl*, 281 U. S. 111, and with that of decisions by other circuit courts of appeals....

The court below thought that as the consideration for the coupons had passed to the obligor, the donor had, by the gift, parted with all control over them and their payment, and for that reason the case was distinguishable from *Lucas v. Earl, supra,* and *Burnet v. Leininger,* 285 U. S. 136, where the assignment of compensation for services had preceded the rendition of the services, and where the income was held taxable to the donor.

The holder of a coupon bond is the owner of two independent and separable kinds of right. One is the right to demand and receive at maturity the principal amount of the bond representing capital investment. The other is the right to demand and receive interim payments of interest on the investment in the amounts and on the dates specified by the coupons. Together they are an obligation to pay principal and interest given in exchange for money or property which was presumably the consideration for the obligation of the bond. Here respondent, as owner of the bond, had acquired the legal right to demand payment at maturity of the interest specified by the coupons and the power to command its payment to others, which constituted an economic gain to him.

Admittedly not all economic gain of the taxpayer is taxable income. From the beginning the revenue laws have been interpreted as defining "realization" of income as the taxable event rather than the acquisition of the right to receive it. And "realization" is not deemed to occur until the income is paid. But the decisions and regulations have consistently recognized that receipt in cash or property is not the only characteristic of realization of income to a taxpayer on the cash receipts basis. Where the taxpayer does not receive payment of income in money or property realization may occur when the last step is taken by which he obtains the fruition of the economic gain which has already accrued to him. *Old Colony Trust Co. v. Commissioner,* 279 U. S. 716; *Corliss v. Bowers,* 281 U. S. 376, 378. Cf. *Burnet v. Wells,* 289 U. S. 670.

In the ordinary case the taxpayer who acquires the right to receive income is taxed when he receives it, regardless of the time when his right to receive payment accrued. But the rule that income is not taxable until realized has never been taken to mean that the taxpayer, even on the cash receipts basis, who has fully enjoyed the benefit of the economic gain represented by his right to receive income, can escape taxation because he has not himself received payment of it from his obligor. The rule, founded on administrative convenience, is only one of postponement of the tax to the final event of enjoyment of the income, usually the receipt of it by the taxpayer, and not one of exemption from taxation where the enjoyment is consummated by some event other than the taxpayer's personal receipt of money or property. Cf. *Aluminum Castings Co. v. Routzahn*, 282 U. S. 92, 98. This may occur when he has made such use or disposition of his power to receive or control the income as to procure in its place other satisfactions which are of economic worth. The question here is, whether because one who in fact receives payment for services or interest payments is taxable only on his receipt of the payments, he can escape all tax by giving away his right to income in advance of payment. If the taxpayer procures payment directly to his creditors of the items of interest or earnings due him, see *Old Colony Trust Co. v. Commissioner, supra; Bowers v. Kerbaugh-Empire Co.*, 271 U. S. 170; *United States v. Kirby Lumber Co.*, 284 U. S. 1, or if he sets up a revocable trust with income payable to the objects of his bounty, §§166, 167, Revenue Act of 1934 [predecessors of sections 676 and 677], *Corliss v. Bowers, supra;* ... he does not escape taxation because he did not actually receive the money. Cf. *Douglas v. Willcuts*, 296 U. S. 1; *Helvering v. Clifford*, 309 U. S. 331.

Underlying the reasoning in these cases is the thought that income is "realized" by the assignor because he, who owns or controls the source of the income, also controls the disposition of that which he could have received himself and diverts the payment from himself to others as the means of procuring the satisfaction of his wants. The taxpayer has equally enjoyed the fruits of his labor or investment and obtained the satisfaction of his desires whether he collects and uses the income to procure those satisfactions, or whether he disposes of his right to collect it as the means of procuring them. Cf. *Burnet v. Wells, supra.*

Although the donor here, by the transfer of the coupons, has precluded any possibility of his collecting them himself, he has nevertheless, by his act, procured payment of the interest as a valuable gift to a member of his family. Such a use of his economic gain, the right to receive income, to procure a satisfaction which can be obtained only by the expenditure of money or property, would seem to be the enjoyment of the income whether the satisfaction is the purchase of goods at the corner grocery, the payment of his debt there, or such non-material satisfactions as may result from the payment of a campaign or community chest contribution, or a gift to his favorite son. Even though he never receives the money, he derives money's worth from the disposition of the coupons which he has used as money or money's worth in the procuring of a satisfaction which is procurable only by the expenditure of money or money's worth. The enjoyment of the economic benefit accruing to him by virtue of his acquisition of the coupons is realized as completely as it would have been if he had collected the interest in dollars and expended them for any of the purposes named. *Burnet v. Wells, supra.*

In a real sense he has enjoyed compensation for money loaned or services rendered and not any the less so because it is his only reward for them. To say that one who has made a gift thus derived from interest or earnings paid to his donee has never enjoyed or realized the fruits of his investment or labor because he has assigned them instead of collecting them himself and then paying them over to the donee, is to affront common understanding and to deny the facts of common experience. Common understanding and experience are the touchstones for the interpretation of the revenue laws.

The power to dispose of income is the equivalent of ownership of it. The exercise of that power to procure the payment of income to another is the enjoyment and hence the realization of the income by him who exercises it. We have had no difficulty in applying that proposition where the assignment preceded the rendition of the services, *Lucas v. Earl, supra; Burnet v. Leininger, supra,* for it was recognized in the *Leininger* case that in such a case the rendition of the service by the assignor was the means by which the income was controlled by the donor and of making his assignment effective. But it is the assignment by which the disposition of income is controlled when the service precedes the assignment, and in both cases it is the exercise of the power of disposition of the interest or compensation, with the resulting payment to the donee, which is the enjoyment by the donor of income derived from them.

This was emphasized in *Blair v. Commissioner,* 300 U. S. 5, on which respondent relies, where the distinction was taken between a gift of income derived from an obligation to pay compensation and a gift of income-producing property. In the circumstances of that case the right to income from the trust property was thought to be so identified with the equitable ownership of the property from which alone the beneficiary derived his right to receive the income and his power to command disposition of it, that a gift of the income by the beneficiary became effective only as a gift of his ownership of the property producing it. Since the gift was deemed to be a gift of the property, the income from it was held to be the income of the owner of the property, who was the donee, not the donor—a refinement which was unnecessary if respondent's contention here is right, but one clearly inapplicable to gifts of interest or wages. Unlike income thus derived from an obligation to pay interest or compensation, the income of the trust was regarded as no more the income of the donor than would be the rent from a lease or a crop raised on a farm after the leasehold or the farm had been given away.... We have held without deviation that where the donor retains control of the trust property the income is taxable to him although paid to the donee. *Corliss v. Bowers, supra.* Cf. *Helvering v. Clifford, supra.*

The dominant purpose of the revenue laws is the taxation of income to those who earn or otherwise create the right to receive it and enjoy the benefit of it when paid. See, *Corliss v. Bowers, supra,* 378; *Burnet v. Guggenheim,* 288 U. S. 280, 283. The tax laid by the 1934 Revenue Act upon income "derived from ... wages, or compensation for personal service, of whatever kind and in whatever form paid, ... ; also from interest ..." therefore cannot fairly be interpreted as not applying to income derived from interest or compensation when he who is entitled to receive it makes use of his power to dispose of it in procuring satisfactions which he would otherwise procure only by the use of the money when received.

It is the statute which taxes the income to the donor although paid to his donee. *Lucas v. Earl, supra; Burnet v. Leininger, supra.* True, in those cases the service which created the right to income followed the assignment, and it was arguable that in point of legal theory the right to the compensation vested instantaneously in the assignor when paid, although he never received it; while here the right of the assignor to receive the income antedated the assignment which transferred the right and thus precluded such an instantaneous vesting. But the statute affords no basis for such "attenuated subtleties." The distinction was explicitly rejected as the basis of decision in *Lucas v. Earl.* It should be rejected here; for no more than in the *Earl* case can the purpose of the statute to tax the income to him who earns, or creates and enjoys it be escaped by "anticipatory arrangements however skillfully devised" to prevent the income from vesting even for a second in the donor.

Nor is it perceived that there is any adequate basis for distinguishing between the gift of interest coupons here and a gift of salary or commissions. The owner of a negotiable bond and of the investment which it represents, if not the lender, stands in the place of the lender. When, by the gift of the coupons, he has separated his right to interest payments from his investment and procured the payment of the interest to his donee, he has enjoyed the economic benefits of the income in the same manner and to the same extent as though the transfer were of earnings, and in both cases the import of the statute is that the fruit is not to be attributed to a different tree from that on which it grew. See *Lucas v. Earl, supra,* 115.

Reversed.

The separate opinion of MR. JUSTICE McREYNOLDS.

* * *

The unmatured coupons given to the son were independent negotiable instruments, complete in themselves. Through the gift they became at once the absolute property of the donee, free from the donor's control and in no way dependent upon ownership of the bonds....

Illustrative Material

1. In Rev. Rul. 81-98, 1981-1 C.B. 40, the grantor-obligee transferred an installment obligation to a trust. Under the terms of the trust agreement, the trustee was entitled to the interest component of each installment payment but was required to return to the grantor the deferred profit and principal portions of each payment. In a sense, therefore, the grantor retained the "tree" on which the "fruit" grew. The I.R.S., relying on *Horst,* ruled that the grantor remained taxable on the interest component of each payment. In *Flacco v. Commissioner,* 50 T.C.M. (CCH) 632 (1985), the Tax Court expressly followed Rev. Rul. 81-98.

2. In *Helvering v. Eubank,* 311 U.S. 122 (1940), a companion case to *Horst,* the Supreme Court held that renewal commissions assigned to a trustee by a former insurance agent "were taxable as income of the assignor in the year when paid." The short opinion, written by Justice Stone, found the issues presented "not distinguishable" from those in *Horst.*

Consider the following excerpt from Justice McReynolds' dissent:

> The assignment in question denuded the assignor of all right to commissions thereafter to accrue under the contract with the insurance company. He could do nothing further in respect of them; they were entirely beyond his control. In no proper sense were they something either earned or received by him during the taxable year. The right to collect became the absolute property of the assignee without relation to future action by the assignor.
>
> A mere right to collect future payments, for services already performed, is not presently taxable as "income derived" from such services. It is property which may be assigned. Whatever the assignor receives as consideration may be his income; but the statute does not undertake to impose liability upon him because of payments to another under a contract which he had transferred in good faith, under circumstances like those here disclosed.

311 U.S. at 127.

3. In Rev. Rul. 55-2, 1955-1 C.B. 211, a surgeon assigned, to a trust for a minor child, "selected accounts receivable" from his practice. The I.R.S. ruled that he was subject to income taxation when the trust collected on the accounts assigned.

4. In Rev. Rul. 58-337, 1958-2 C.B. 13, husband and wife leased real estate to a corporation for a period of years. They then assigned the lease to a trust for their children. The I.R.S. ruled that the couple remained taxable on the rent:

Prior to the creation of the trust in the instant case, the fee owners had carved out of their ownership two separate estates, a leasehold and a reversion. The leasehold was then made the subject of the trust here involved. When a fee owner/lessor assigns a lease without assigning the reversion, only the right to the rents passes to the assignee. Accordingly, the assignment of the lease in trust without an attendant assignment of the reversion constitutes an assignment of income for which the grantor remains taxable, since he may not escape the tax on his income by giving it away or assigning the right to receive it in advance of payment.

McGinnis v. Commissioner, 65 T.C.M. (CCH) 1870 (1993), relied on Revenue Ruling 58-337 in reaching the same conclusion on similar facts.

Harrison v. Schaffner

312 U.S. 579 (1941)

MR. JUSTICE STONE delivered the opinion of the Court.

In December 1929, respondent, the life beneficiary of a testamentary trust, "assigned" to certain of her children specified amounts in dollars from the income of the trust for the year following the assignment. She made a like assignment to her children and a son-in-law in November, 1930. The question for decision is whether ... the assigned income, which was paid by the trustees to the several assignees, is taxable as such to the assignor or to the assignees.

The Commissioner ruled that the income was that of the life beneficiary and assessed a deficiency against her for the calendar years 1930 and 1931, which she paid. In the present suit to recover the tax paid as illegally exacted the district court below gave judgment for the taxpayer, which the Court of Appeals affirmed. 113 F. 2d 449. We granted certiorari, 311 U. S. 638, to resolve an alleged conflict in principle of the decision below with those in *Lucas v. Earl*, 281 U. S. 111; *Burnet v. Leininger*, 285 U. S. 136, and *Helvering v. Clifford*, 309 U. S. 331.

Since granting certiorari we have held, following the reasoning of *Lucas v. Earl, supra*, that one who is entitled to receive at a future date, interest or compensation for services and who makes a gift of it by an anticipatory assignment, realizes taxable income quite as much as if he had collected the income and paid it over to the object of his bounty. *Helvering v. Horst*, 311 U. S. 112; *Helvering v. Eubank*, 311 U. S. 122. Decision in these cases was rested on the principle that the power to dispose of income is the equivalent of ownership of it and that the exercise of the power to procure its payment to another, whether to pay a debt or to make a gift, is within the reach of the statute taxing income "derived from any source whatever." In the light of our opinions in these cases the narrow question presented by this record is whether it makes any difference in the application of the taxing statute that the gift is accomplished by the anticipatory assignment of trust income rather than of interest, dividends, rents and the like which are payable to the donor.

Respondent, recognizing that the practical consequences of a gift by assignment, in advance, of a year's income from the trust, are, so far as the use and enjoyment of the income are concerned, no different from those of the gift by assignment of interest or wages, rests his case on technical distinctions affecting the conveyancing of equitable interests. It is said that since by the assignment of trust income the assignee acquires an equitable right to an accounting by the trustee which, for many purposes, is treated by courts of equity as a present equitable estate in the trust property, it follows that each assignee in the present case is a donee of an interest in the trust property for the term of a year and is thus the recipient of income from his own property which is taxable to him rather than to the donor. See *Blair v. Commissioner*, 300 U. S. 5.

We lay to one side the argument which the Government could have made that the assignments were no more than an attempt to charge the specified payments upon the whole income which could pass no present interest in the trust property. See Scott on Trusts, §10.1, 10.6, 29, 30. For we think that the operation of the statutes taxing income is not dependent upon such "attenuated subtleties," but rather on the import and reasonable construction of the taxing act. *Lucas v. Earl, supra*, 114.

[The predecessor of section 61] provides, "'Gross income' includes gains, profits, and income derived from … interest, rent, dividends, securities or the transactions of any business carried on for gain or profit, or gains or profits, and income derived from any source whatever." By [predecessors of sections 641, 651 and 652] the tax is laid upon the income "of any kind of property held in trust," and income of a trust for the taxable year which is to be distributed to the beneficiaries is to be taxed to them "whether distributed to them or not." In construing these and like provisions in other revenue acts we have uniformly held that they are not so much concerned with the refinements of title as with the actual command over the income which is taxed and the actual benefit for which the tax is paid. See *Corliss v. Bowers*, 281 U. S. 376; *Lucas v. Earl, supra; Helvering v. Horst, supra; Helvering v. Eubank, supra; Helvering v. Clifford, supra*. It was for that reason that in each of those cases it was held that one vested with the right to receive income did not escape the tax by any kind of anticipatory arrangement, however skillfully devised, by which he procures payment of it to another, since, by the exercise of his power to command the income, he enjoys the benefit of the income on which the tax is laid.

Those decisions are controlling here. Taxation is a practical matter and those practical considerations which support the treatment of the disposition of one's income by way of gift as a realization of the income to the donor are the same whether the income be from a trust or from shares of stock or bonds which he owns. It is true, as respondent argues, that where the beneficiary of a trust had assigned a share of the income to another for life without retaining any form of control over the interest assigned, this Court construed the assignment as a transfer *in praesenti* to the donee, of a life interest in the corpus of the trust property, and held in consequence that the income thereafter paid to the donee was taxable to him and not the donor. *Blair v. Commissioner, supra*. But we think it quite another matter to say that the beneficiary of a trust who makes a single gift of a sum of money payable out of the income of the trust does not realize income when the gift is effectuated by payment, or that he escapes the tax by attempting to clothe the transaction in the guise of a transfer of trust property rather than the transfer of income where that is its obvious purpose and effect. We think that the gift by a beneficiary of a trust of some part of the income derived from the trust property for the period of a day, a month or a year involves no such substantial disposition of the trust property as to camouflage the reality that he is enjoying the benefit of the income from the trust of which he continues to be the beneficiary, quite as much as he enjoys the benefits of interest or wages which he gives away as in the *Horst* and *Eubank* cases. Even though the gift of income be in form accomplished by the temporary disposition of the donor's property which produces the income, the donor retaining every other substantial interest in it, we have not allowed the form to obscure the reality. Income which the donor gives away through the medium of a short term trust created for the benefit of the donee is nevertheless income taxable to the donor. *Helvering v. Clifford, supra; Hormel v. Helvering*, [312 U. S. 552]. We perceive no difference, so far as the construction and application of the Revenue Act is concerned, between a gift of income in a specified amount by the creation of a trust for a year, see *Hormel v. Helvering, supra,* and the assignment by the beneficiary of a trust already created of a like amount from its income for a year.

Nor are we troubled by the logical difficulties of drawing the line between a gift of an equitable interest in property for life effected by a gift for life of a share of the income of the trust and the gift of the income or a part of it for the period of a year as in this case. "Drawing the line" is a recurrent difficulty in those fields of the law where differences in degree produce ultimate differences in kind. See *Irwin v. Gavit,* 268 U. S. 161, 168. It is enough that we find in the present case that the taxpayer, in point of substance, has parted with no substantial interest in property other than the specified payments of income which, like other gifts of income, are taxable to the donor. Unless in the meantime the difficulty be resolved by statute or treasury regulation, we leave it to future judicial decisions to determine precisely where the line shall be drawn between gifts of income-producing property and gifts of income from property of which the donor remains the owner, for all substantial and practical purposes. Cf. *Helvering v. Clifford, supra.*

Reversed.

Illustrative Material

1. *Hawaiian Trust Co. v. Kanne,* 172 F.2d 74 (9th Cir. 1949), carefully considered *Harrison v. Schaffner* but nevertheless held that assignment by a life income beneficiary of her income interest for periods in excess of ten years did not trigger the assignment-of-income doctrine. The court particularly relied on the portions of the "Clifford Regulations" that were the forerunners of section 673 (prior to amendment by the Tax Reform Act of 1986). *Farkas v. Commissioner,* 170 F.2d 201 (5th Cir. 1948), and Rev. Rul. 55-38, 1955-1 C.B. 389, which also dealt with pre-1954 law, are to the same effect. What remains of these precedents after TRA 1986? Does elimination of the ten-year reversionary trust as an independent taxpayer strip these precedents of their only logic? Or is it possible to distinguish assignment of an income interest for more than ten years from the one-year assignment in *Harrison v. Schaffner* on the basis of the substantiality of the interest involved?

2. In Rev. Rul. 60-370, 1960-2 C.B. 203, a donor transferred appreciated securities to a university pursuant to an agreement that the university would sell the securities and invest the proceeds in tax-exempt securities to be held in trust for the benefit of the donor during his lifetime. The I.R.S. ruled that the donor realized the gain involved when, in accordance with the agreement, the university exchanged the securities. The I.R.S. reasoned that, even though gains from the sale were to be added to principal, in light of the agreement, "in substance, the transferor did not give the trustee appreciated property to hold in trust, but, rather, gave the trustee the proceeds of the sale or exchange of the property which the trustee was required to consummate." The I.R.S. stated that the same result would occur even if the exchange of securities occurred in connection with only an implied obligation.

3. In *Ferguson v. Commissioner,* 174 F.3d 997 (9th Cir. 1999), the taxpayers donated corporate shares to charity while a tender offer and merger were pending. The court held that, when the gifts became final, the tender offer and merger were so likely to succeed that the shares had already ripened into rights to receive cash. Thus, the donors were subject to taxation on the gain inherent in the donated shares, under the assignment-of-income doctrine.

B. Grantor Trusts:
Income Taxation under Subpart E

1. Grantor as Owner

a. Judicial Origins

Helvering v. Clifford
309 U.S. 331 (1940)

MR. JUSTICE DOUGLAS delivered the opinion of the Court.

In 1934 respondent declared himself trustee of certain securities which he owned. All net income from the trust was to be held for the "exclusive benefit" of respondent's wife. The trust was for a term of five years, except that it would terminate earlier on the death of either respondent or his wife. On termination of the trust the entire corpus was to go to respondent, while all "accrued or undistributed net income" and "any proceeds from the investment of such net income" was to be treated as property owned absolutely by the wife. During the continuance of the trust respondent was to pay over to his wife the whole or such part of the net income as he in his "absolute discretion" might determine. And during that period he had full power (a) to exercise all voting powers incident to the trusteed shares of stock; (b) to "sell, exchange, mortgage, or pledge" any of the securities under the declaration of trust "whether as part of the corpus or principal thereof or as investments or proceeds and any income therefrom, upon such terms and for such consideration" as respondent in his "absolute discretion may deem fitting"; (c) to invest "any cash or money in the trust estate or any income therefrom" by loans, secured or unsecured, by deposits in banks, or by purchase of securities or other personal property "without restriction" because of their "speculative character" or "rate of return" or any "laws pertaining to the investment of trust funds"; (d) to collect all income; (e) to compromise, etc., any claims held by him as trustee; (f) to hold any property in the trust estate in the names of "other persons or in my own name as an individual" except as otherwise provided. Extraordinary cash dividends, stock dividends, proceeds from the sale of unexercised subscription rights, or any enhancement, realized or not, in the value of the securities were to be treated as principal, not income. An exculpatory clause purported to protect him from all losses except those occasioned by his "own wilful and deliberate" breach of duties as trustee. And finally it was provided that neither the principal nor any future or accrued income should be liable for the debts of the wife; and that the wife could not transfer, encumber, or anticipate any interest in the trust or any income therefrom prior to actual payment thereof to her.

It was stipulated that while the "tax effects" of this trust were considered by respondent they were not the "sole consideration" involved in his decision to set it up, as by this and other gifts he intended to give "security and economic independence" to his wife and children. It was also stipulated that respondent's wife had substantial income of her own from other sources; that there was no restriction on her use of the trust income, all of which income was placed in her personal checking account, intermingled with her other funds, and expended by her on herself, her children and relatives; that the trust was not designed to relieve respondent from liability for family or household expenses and that after execution of the trust he paid large sums from his personal funds for such purposes.

Respondent paid a federal gift tax on this transfer. During the year 1934 all income from the trust was distributed to the wife who included it in her individual return for that year. The Commissioner, however, determined a deficiency in respondent's return for that year on the theory that income from the trust was taxable to him. The Board of Tax Appeals sustained that redetermination. 38 B. T. A. 1532. The Circuit Court of Appeals reversed. 105 F. 2d 586. We granted certiorari because of the importance to the revenue of the use of such short term trusts in the reduction of surtaxes.

Sec. 22(a) of the Revenue Act of 1934 [the predecessor of section 61] includes among "gross income" all "gains, profits, and income derived ... from professions, vocations, trades, businesses, commerce, or sales, or dealings in property, whether real or personal, growing out of the ownership or use of or interest in such property; also from interest, rent, dividends, securities, or the transaction of any business carried on for gain or profit, or gains or profits and income derived from any source whatever." The broad sweep of this language indicates the purpose of Congress to use the full measure of its taxing power within those definable categories. Cf. *Helvering v. Midland Mutual Life Insurance Co.,* 300 U. S. 216. Hence our construction of the statute should be consonant with that purpose. Technical considerations, niceties of the law of trusts or conveyances, or the legal paraphernalia which inventive genius may construct as a refuge from surtaxes should not obscure the basic issue. That issue is whether the grantor after the trust has been established may still be treated, under this statutory scheme, as the owner of the corpus. See *Blair v. Commissioner,* 300 U. S. 5, 12. In absence of more precise standards or guides supplied by statute or appropriate regulations, the answer to that question must depend on an analysis of the terms of the trust and all the circumstances attendant on its creation and operation. And where the grantor is the trustee and the beneficiaries are members of his family group, special scrutiny of the arrangement is necessary lest what is in reality but one economic unit be multiplied into two or more by devices which, though valid under state law, are not conclusive so far as §22(a) is concerned.

In this case we cannot conclude as a matter of law that respondent ceased to be the owner of the corpus after the trust was created. Rather, the short duration of the trust, the fact that the wife was the beneficiary, and the retention of control over the corpus by respondent all lead irresistibly to the conclusion that respondent continued to be the owner for purposes of §22(a).

So far as his dominion and control were concerned it seems clear that the trust did not effect any substantial change. In substance his control over the corpus was in all essential respects the same after the trust was created, as before. The wide powers which he retained included for all practical purposes most of the control which he as an individual would have. There were, we may assume, exceptions, such as his disability to make a gift of the corpus to others during the term of the trust and to make loans to himself. But this dilution in his control would seem to be insignificant and immaterial, since control over investment remained. If it be said that such control is the type of dominion exercised by any trustee, the answer is simple. We have at best a temporary reallocation of income within an intimate family group. Since the income remains in the family and since the husband retains control over the investment, he has rather complete assurance that the trust will not effect any substantial change in his economic position. It is hard to imagine that respondent felt himself the poorer after this trust had been executed or, if he did, that it had any rational foundation in fact. For as a result of the terms of the trust and the intimacy of the familial relationship respondent retained the substance of full enjoyment of all the rights which previously he had in the property. That might not be true if only strictly legal rights were considered. But when the benefits flowing to him indirectly through the wife are added to the legal rights he retained, the aggregate may be said to be a fair equivalent of what he previously had. To exclude from the aggregate those indirect benefits would be to deprive §22(a) of considerable vitality and to treat as immaterial what may be highly relevant considerations in the creation of such family trusts. For where the head of the household has income in excess of normal needs, it may well make but little difference to him (except income-tax-wise) where portions of that income are routed—so long as it stays in the family group. In those circumstances the all-important factor might be retention by him of control over the principal. With that control in his hands he would keep direct command over all that he needed to remain in substantially the same financial situation as before. Our point here is that no one fact is normally decisive but that all considerations and circumstances of the kind we have mentioned are relevant to the question of ownership and are appropriate foundations for findings on that issue. Thus, where, as in this case, the benefits directly or indirectly retained blend so imperceptibly with the normal concepts of full ownership, we cannot say that the triers of fact committed reversible error when they found that the husband was the owner of the corpus for the purposes of §22(a). To hold otherwise would be to treat the wife as a complete stranger; to let mere formalism obscure the normal consequences of family solidarity; and to force concepts of ownership to be fashioned out of legal niceties which may have little or no significance in such household arrangements.

The bundle of rights which he retained was so substantial that respondent cannot be heard to complain that he is the "victim of despotic power when for the purpose of taxation he is treated as owner altogether." See *DuPont v. Commissioner,* 289 U. S. 685, 689.

We should add that liability under §22(a) is not foreclosed by reason of the fact that Congress made specific provision in §166 [the predecessor of section 676] for revocable trusts, but failed to adopt the Treasury recommendation in 1934, *Helvering v. Wood,* [309 U. S. 344], that similar specific treatment should be accorded income from short term trusts. Such choice, while relevant to the scope of §166, *Helvering v. Wood, supra,* cannot be said to have subtracted from §22(a) what was already there. Rather, on this evidence it must be assumed that the choice was between a generalized treatment under §22(a) or specific treatment under a separate provision (such as was accorded revocable trusts under §166); not between taxing or not taxing grantors of short term trusts. In view of the broad and sweeping language of §22(a), a specific provision covering short term trusts might well do no more than to carve out of §22(a) a defined group of cases to which a rule of thumb would be applied. The failure of Congress to adopt any such rule of thumb for that type of trust must be taken to do no more than to leave to the triers of fact the initial determination of whether or not on the facts of each case the grantor remains the owner for purposes of §22(a).

In view of this result we need not examine the contention that the trust device falls within the rule of *Lucas v. Earl,* 281 U. S. 111 and *Burnet v. Leininger,* 285 U. S. 136, relating to the assignment of future income; or that respondent is liable under §166, taxing grantors on the income of revocable trusts.

The judgment of the Circuit Court of Appeals is reversed and that of the Board of Tax Appeals is affirmed.

Reversed.

MR. JUSTICE ROBERTS, dissenting:

I think the judgment should be affirmed.

The decision of the court disregards the fundamental principle that legislation is not the function of the judiciary but of Congress.

In every revenue act from that of 1916 to the one now in force a distinction has been made between income of individuals and income from property held in trust. It has been the practice to define income of individuals, and, in separate sections, under the heading "Estates and Trusts," to provide that the tax imposed upon individuals shall apply to the income of estates or of any kind of property held in trust. A trust is a separate taxable entity. The trust here in question is a true trust.

While the earlier acts were in force creators of trusts reserved power to repossess the trust corpus. It became common also to establish trusts under which, at the grantor's discretion, all or part of the income might be paid to him, and to set up trusts to pay life insurance premiums upon policies on the grantor's life. The situation was analogous to that now presented. The Treasury, instead of asking this court, under the guise of construction, to amend the act, went to Congress for new legislation. Congress provided, by §219(g)(h) of the Revenue Act of 1924 [the predecessor of sections 676 and 677], that if the grantor set up such a life insurance trust, or one under which he could direct the payment of the trust income to himself, or had the power to revest the principal in himself *during any taxable year,* the income of the trust, for the taxable year, was to be treated as his.

After the adoption of these amendments taxpayers resorted to the creation of revocable trusts with a provision that more than a year's notice of revocation should be necessary to termination. Such a trust was held not to be within the terms of §219(g) of the Revenue Act of 1924, because not revocable within the taxable year.[3]

Again, without seeking amendment in the guise of construction from this court, the Treasury applied to Congress, which met the situation by adopting §166 of the Revenue Act of 1934, which provided that, in the case of a trust under which the grantor reserved the power *at any time* to revest the corpus in himself, the income of the trust should be considered that of the grantor.

The Treasury had asked that there should also be included in that act a provision taxing to the grantor income from short term trusts. After the House Ways and Means Committee had rendered a report on the proposed bill, the Treasury, upon examination of the report, submitted a statement to the Committee containing recommendations for additional provisions; amongst others, the following: "(6) The income from short-term trusts and trusts which are revocable by the creator at the expiration of a short period after notice by him should be made taxable to the creator of the trust." Congress adopted an amendment to cover the one situation but did not accept the Treasury's recommendation as to the other.[4] The statute, as before, clearly provided that the income from a short term irrevocable trust was taxable to the trust, or the beneficiary, and not to the grantor.

The regulations under §166 of the Act of 1932 contained no suggestion that term trusts were taxable to the creator though, if the petitioner is right, they would be equally so under that act as under later ones. Thus though the Treasury realized that irrevocable short term trusts did not fall within the scope of §166, instead of going to Congress for amendment of the law it comes here with a plea for interpretation which is in effect such amendment.

* * *

---

3. *Lewis v. White,* 56 F. 2d 390; 61 F. 2d 1046; *Langley v. Commissioner,* 61 F. 2d 796; *Commissioner v. Grosvenor,* 85 F. 2d 2; *Faber v. United States,* 1 F. Supp. 859.

4. Hearings on H. R. 7835, 73d Cong., 2d Sess., p. 151; H. Rep. No. 1385, 73d Cong., 2d Sess., p. 24.

To construe either §166 or §22(a) of the statute as justifying taxation of the income to respondent in this case is, in my judgment, to write into the statute what is not there and what Congress has omitted to place there.

If judges were members of the legislature they might well vote to amend the act so as to tax such income in order to frustrate avoidance of tax but, as judges, they exercise a very different function. They ought to read the act to cover nothing more than Congress has specified. Courts ought not to stop loopholes in an act at the bequest of the Government, nor relieve from what they deem a harsh provision plainly stated, at the behest of the taxpayer. Relief in either case should be sought in another quarter.

No such dictum as that Congress has in the income tax law attempted to exercise its power to the fullest extent will justify the extension of a plain provision to an object of taxation not embraced within it. If the contrary were true, the courts might supply whatever they considered a deficiency in the sweep of a taxing act. I cannot construe the court's opinion as attempting less.

* * *

b. The Code
(i) General Principles

Internal Revenue Code:
 Section 671

Regulation:
 Section 1.671-1

Sections 671 through 678, often referred to as the "grantor trust rules" or "subpart E," operate in a two-step fashion. In the first step, sections 673 through 678, using the convention of "ownership," single out certain types of trusts, often referred to as "grantor trusts," for special tax treatment. Except under 678, only the grantor of a trust is subject to being designated as its "owner." The bulk of this chapter examines this first step, which is essentially a process of identification.

In the second step, section 671 specifies the consequences of grantor trust status: the income, deductions, and credits of a grantor trust are attributed to its "owner." In short, grantor trusts are not separate taxpayers; they are ignored for income tax purposes. Examination of this second step occurs at the end of this chapter (sec. B(3)).

Section 671 states that application of the grantor trust rules is the only permissible way to tax a grantor "solely on the grounds of his dominion and control over the trust." *See Boise Cascade Corp. v. United States,* 329 F.3d 751 (9th Cir. 2003) (in accordance with section 671, participants in employee stock ownership plan, whose dominion and control over underlying stock consisted of right to direct trustee how to vote stock and respond to tender offers, were not its owners). Nevertheless, in *Irvine K. Furman,* 45 T.C. 360 (1966), *aff'd per curiam,* 381 F.2d 22 (5th Cir. 1967), the Tax Court taxed a grantor on a trust's income after determining that

> the trust arrangement should be treated as a nullity for Federal income tax purposes. Our decision is not premised upon the retention of dominion and con-

trol over the trust by Irvine, but on the absence of economic reality. We do not believe that sections 671 through 678 of the Internal Revenue Code of 1954 preclude a decision that, in an extreme case such as this, there is such a lack of economic reality as to nullify the existence of a valid trust for Federal income tax purposes.

45 T.C. at 366. The court stated that its decision rested on the *"totality"* of eight specific factors. Two of the factors were that, in addition to retaining a reversion, the grantor had also arranged that the trust would have no income to distribute prior to termination.

Treas. Reg. §1.671-1(c) expressly states that the grantor trust rules do not preempt assignment-of-income principles.

(ii) Definitions

Internal Revenue Code:
 Section 672

Regulations:
 Sections 1.672(a)-1; 1.672(b)-1; 1.672(c)-1

Section 672 defines some of the terms used in subpart E.

Section 672(a) defines an "adverse party" as anyone "having a substantial beneficial interest in the trust which would be adversely affected by the exercise or nonexercise of the power which he possesses respecting the trust." Because trustees necessarily have powers "respecting" their trusts, they can be adverse parties. However, a trustee is not an adverse party "merely because of his interest as a trustee." Treas. Reg. §1.672(a)-1(a). Moreover, a trustee-beneficiary is not an adverse party if his powers cannot affect his beneficial interest. This is true, for example, if all the beneficial interests are fixed by the terms of the trust agreement. *See Johnson v. Commissioner,* 108 T.C. 448 (1997), *aff'd in part and rev'd in part,* 184 F.3d 786 (8th Cir. 1999); *Floyd G. Paxton,* 57 T.C. 627 (1972), *aff'd,* 520 F.2d 923 (9th Cir.), *cert denied,* 423 U.S. 1016 (1975). But if the trustee has the power to affect his own beneficial interest, he is an adverse party. Thus, if a trustee has the power to distribute all of the trust income and property to himself, he is an adverse party. *Estate of Paxton v. Commissioner,* 44 T.C.M. (CCH) 771 (1982).

The issue whether a given individual has, within the meaning of section 672(a), "a substantial beneficial interest" is often a question of fact. In *Peter B. Barker,* 25 T.C. 1230 (1956), for example, the interest involved was the right to the trust property if the grantor, then age 21, died prior to reaching age 35 and without wife or issue surviving him. The court held that such an interest was not "substantial" within the meaning of the predecessor of section 672. Mortality tables showed that the grantor stood a 97% chance of surviving to age 35. The remaindermen's chances of taking were therefore much poorer than 3%, because their interests were also contingent upon the grantor's dying without wife or issue. *Chase National Bank v. Commissioner,* 225 F.2d 621 (8th Cir. 1955), *cert. denied sub nom. Thompson v. Commissioner,* 350 U.S. 965 (1956), reached the same conclusion where the remainderman was entitled to the trust property only upon the death of a primary beneficiary prior to reaching age 35 and without surviving issue. During the first taxable year in question, one primary beneficiary was 29 and already had a child. The other was 18 and had a child the next year. Some cases, however, involve interests that are plainly insubstantial. Such was the case in *Holt v. United States,* 669 F. Supp. 751 (W.D. Va. 1987), *aff'd mem.,* 842 F.2d 1291 (4th Cir. 1988). There the interest in question was that of the grantor's parents, who stood to take the entire trust corpus if they survived the grantor, her (four) children, and all of *her children's* children and grandchildren.

A beneficiary whose only interest is in distributions that lie solely in the discretion of the trustee does not have a substantial beneficial interest. *Water Resource Control v. Commissioner,* 61 T.C.M. (CCH) 2102, 2117–18 (1991), *aff'd mem. sub nom. Whitehouse v. Commissioner,* 972 F.2d 1328 (2d Cir. 1992), *cert. denied,* 507 U.S. 960 (1993).

The term "related or subordinate party," defined in section 672(c), includes brothers and sisters of the grantor, "whether by the whole or half blood." Rev. Rul. 58-19, 1958-1 C.B. 251. However, such term does not include, as an "employee," a director of a corporation "merely because he is a director." Rev. Rul. 66-160, 1966-1 C.B. 164.

(iii) Reversions

Internal Revenue Code:
  Section 673

The Tax Reform Act of 1986 made important changes in section 673. Nevertheless, study of the former version of section. 673 is important, for several reasons. First, at least brief examination of the old rules is crucial to an understanding of the new rules and the reasons for them. Second, few of the current precedents interpret new section 673. Third, many of the trusts in the cases in this book were designed to comply with former section 673. Understanding those cases therefore requires understanding former section 673.

1. *Former Section 673.* Old section 673(a) provided that the grantor would be treated as the owner of any portion of a trust the "possession or enjoyment" of which "will or may reasonably be expected" to revert to the grantor within ten years of the creation of the trust. Section 673 thus constituted a major exception to the assignment-of-income rules. If one was willing to separate oneself from one's property for more than ten years, one could, with congressional blessing, avoid taxation on the income from that property.

a. *Reversionary interest. Crane v. Commissioner,* 368 F.2d 800 (1st Cir. 1966), inquired into the nature of the "reversionary interest" referred to in section 673(a). The grantor had retained a reversion in the principal of a nine-year trust. However, the trust agreement granted the income beneficiaries an option, exercisable at the termination of the trust, to purchase the trust's holdings, at the trust's average cost per share. Thus, so the grantor argued, he had no reversion in the appreciation element of the trust's holdings. Nonetheless, the court held that the grantor was taxable on the trust's entire income:

> At least during the period that the market value of the corpus is less than cost, the grantor has a total reversionary interest.
>
> It is true that if the market value of the corpus, at the time of the termination of the trust, exceeded cost, the beneficiaries could, although they need not, call for a distribution of the stock, returning only the original cost to the grantor. To this extent there would be a separation of the corpus, and some of it would

not revert. However, when we look at the obvious purpose of section 673(a), it must be to prevent a grantor from making a temporary transfer of assets in order to diminish, for a limited period, the receipt of taxable income therefrom. Until the termination of the trust, regardless of the possible appreciation in market value, the income was the direct product of the grantor's transfer. Even if it were to be considered at any particular moment that the grantor did not have a reversion in the part of the corpus which exceeded [cost], at the least that part of the income attributable to the portion of the corpus whose return would as of that moment be necessary to [recover its cost], should be taxable to the grantor. Since the value of the corpus of a trust composed of stock may be expected to fluctuate, elaborate calculations which we scarcely believe the statute contemplates would be required for the purpose of apportioning the income between the grantor and the beneficiaries. Moreover, even though at some moment the corpus of the trust may have appreciated, it would not follow that ultimately it might not diminish, so that the entire corpus would revert. We hold, under the circumstances, that the grantor had a sufficient reversionary interest for the statute to apply to the entire income.

368 F.2d at 802.

In Rev. Rul. 61-223, 1961-2 C.B. 125, the I.R.S. ruled that where a corporate trustee had discretion to apply trust income and principal for the "care, comfort, education and welfare" of the grantor's minor child, the grantor did not have a reversionary interest in the trust for purposes of section 673, even though trust income could have been used by the trustee to discharge the grantor's legal obligation to support the child. The I.R.S. relied upon section 677(b), which provides that a grantor of such a discretionary trust is taxable on the trust's income only to the extent such income actually is used to discharge the grantor's support obligations.

b. *Fixed term. C.O. Bibby,* 44 T.C. 638 (1965), applied former section 673(a) to a reversionary trust that was to terminate in the grantors' favor "ten years and one day from the execution hereof." No trust property was, however, delivered to the trustee until almost a year after execution of the trust agreement. Because no trust existed until delivery of the trust property, the court held that the reversion had not been delayed for at least ten years. The grantors therefore were taxable on all of the trust's income.

McGinnis v. Commissioner, 65 T.C.M. (CCH) 1870 (1993), also involved application of former section 673(a) to reversionary trusts terminating ten years and one day after creation. The grantors had, however, funded these trusts solely with assignments of rents under leases that expired prior to the trusts' termination dates. The court held that the trusts therefore failed to meet the fixed term requirement of former section 673(a). Thus, the grantors were treated as owners of the entire trusts.

In *Garvey v. Commissioner,* 51 T.C.M. (CCH) 1026 (1986), the grantor created a ten-year trust but retained the right to receive, currently, the principal portion of each annuity payment received by the trust from annuity contracts it held as its only assets. The court held that the grantor was taxable on both the principal and the income portions of such payments, because her right to share in the annuity payments constituted a reversionary interest that was to take effect within ten years. Moreover, the court held that allocation of the income portion between the grantor and the trust was unnecessary, because the grantor had retained "all the principal and principal payments." She was therefore taxable on the trust's entire income. The same result occurs if the grantor retains the current right to receive the deferred profit and principal portions of payments made under installment obligations transferred to a trust. *See Flacco v. Commissioner,* 50 T.C.M. (CCH) 632, 634 (1985).

c. *Reasonable expectations.* In *Thompson v. United States,* 209 F. Supp. 530 (E.D. Tex. 1962), *rev'd on other grounds,* 332 F.2d 657 (5th Cir. 1964), the grantor, who transferred property to a charitable trust, retained a reversion if the income from the trust ever became subject to taxation. Noting that it was extremely unlikely that Congress would ever impose an income tax on charitable trusts, the court held that the grantor's reversion could not, within the meaning of former section 673(a), "reasonably be expected to take effect in possession or enjoyment within 10 years."

d. *Death of income beneficiary.* Former section 673(c) modified the general rule of former section 673(a), so that a grantor was not treated, under section 673, as owner of any portion of a trust that was to revert to him or her only upon the death of the income beneficiary. Thus, a grantor who was content to delay his or her reversion until the death of the income beneficiary was not treated as owner of any portion of the trust under section 673, regardless of whether the life expectancy of the income beneficiary exceeded ten years. *See* Treas. Reg. §1.673(a)-1(b). But if a reversion (in the grantor's estate) was contingent upon the grantor's death, and the grantor's life expectancy was less than ten years, the grantor was treated as owner of the trust. Rev. Rul. 55-34, 1955-1 C.B. 226 (pre-1954 Code). Had the life expectancy of the grantor in Rev. Rul. 55-34 exceeded ten years, he would not have been treated as owner of the trust under section 673. Rev. Rul. 56-601, 1956-2 C.B. 458. *See also* Rev. Rul. 86-32, 1986-1 C.B. 252. A grantor whose life expectancy was less than ten years when he created a trust was, however, not treated as the trust's owner under section 673 if the reversion in his estate was postponed to the later of the grantor's death and ten years and one month after creation of the trust. Rev. Rul. 58-567, 1958-2 C.B. 365. The I.R.S. reasoned that, although the grantor was likely to die within ten years of the creation of the trust, "possession or enjoyment" of the trust property by the estate, as required by former section 673, could not occur within the ten-year period. If the reversion was payable to the grantor's estate upon the grantor's death, income from property added to the trust by the grantor after his life expectancy dropped below ten years was taxable to him rather than to the trust. Rev. Rul. 73-251, 1973-1 C.B. 324. Rev. Rul. 73-251 also set forth the I.R.S. position that, for trusts created after December 31, 1970, and before December 1, 1983, grantors' life expectancies were to be determined by reference to Table LN of former Treas. Reg. §20.2031-10(f). For trusts created after November 30, 1983, and before May 1, 1989, the appropriate table, according to the I.R.S. in Rev. Rul. 86-32, *supra,* was Table 1 of *United States Life Tables: 1969–1971,* published by the Department of Health, Education, and Welfare, Public Health Service. Under that table, the life expectancy of one 73 years old was 10.34 years, and that of one 74 years old was 9.82 years. According to the I.R.S., "[T]he age of the measuring life should be taken at the person's age at the birthday nearest to the date of the transfer." Thus, a grantor over the age of 73½ years at the time of the transfer "ha[d] a life expectancy of no more than 9.82 years as of the date of transfer."

2. *Current Section* 673. New section 673 very deliberately makes it much more expensive to side-step the assignment-of-income rules. Under new section 673(a) the income of a trust in which either the grantor or the grantor's spouse retains a reversionary interest is taxable to the grantor unless the value of the reversionary interest is less than 5% of the value of the property transferred to the trust. An exception, under new section 673(b), permits income shifting if the reversionary interest follows the death before attaining age 21 of an income beneficiary who is a lineal descendant of the grantor. As a result, retention of a meaningful reversionary interest is now inconsistent with in-

come shifting. *See generally* Westfall, *Grantors, Trusts, and Beneficiaries under the Income Tax Provisions of the Internal Revenue Code of 1986*, 40 Tax Law. 713, 716–19 (1987).

In 1988 Congress enacted section 7520, which mandated promulgation of new tables for valuing annuities, interests for life or terms of years, remainders, and reversions created after April 30, 1989. These new tables, which appear in Treas. Reg. §§ 20.2031-7(d)(6), -7(d)(7), accommodate a wide range of assumed interest rates. In addition, section 7520 calls for monthly adjustment of the applicable interest rate. Thus, the new statutory scheme responds much more quickly to changes in market interest rates than the old tables, which changed very rarely.

Prior to TRA 1986, many practitioners counselled creation of "spousal remainder trusts." Under the terms of such a trust the grantor retained no reversion. There was, however, a remainder in the grantor's spouse. Former section 673 (like current section 673) referred only to reversions retained by the grantor. Thus, section 673 supposedly did not apply. As a result, it was not necessary to delay the spouse's remainder interest even for ten years. The spousal remainder trust thus seemed to permit income shifting without regard to the ten-year requirement of former section 673. For a client with a stable marriage the spousal remainder trust seemed too good to be true. It was. In TRA 1986 Congress enacted section 672(e), which treats the grantor as holding any power or interest held by the grantor's spouse.

Problems

4-1. In 1985 G creates an *inter vivos* trust. All of the income is to be paid to G's sister, S, for 9 years. Thereafter, the trust is to terminate, and the principal is to be paid to G. Does section 673 treat G as owner of any portion of the trust?

4-2. Assume the facts of Problem 4-1, except that the trust is to terminate after 10 years and 30 days.

4-3. Assume the facts of Problem 4-1, except that the trust is to terminate upon the death of S. What if S were 99 years old when the trust was created?

4-4. This year G creates an *inter vivos* trust. All of the income is to be paid to G's sister, S, for 10 years and 30 days. Thereafter, the trust is to terminate, and the principal is to be paid to G. Does section 673 treat G as owner of any portion of the trust?

4-5. How long must the trust in Problem 4-4 endure if section 673 is not to treat G as owner of any portion of the trust? Consider Treas. Reg. § 20.2031-7(d)(6), Table B.

4-6. This year G creates an *inter vivos* trust. All of the income is to be paid to C, G's minor child, for C's life. Upon C's death, the trust is to terminate. If C dies prior to attaining age 21, the principal is to be paid to G if living, otherwise to C's estate. Does section 673 treat G as owner of any portion of the trust?

4-7. This year G creates an *inter vivos* trust. All of the income is to be paid to C, G's child, for C's life. Upon C's death, the trust is to terminate, and the principal is to be paid to G. C was 2 years of age at the time the trust was created. Does section 673 treat G as owner of any portion of the trust? Consider Treas. Reg. § 20.2031-7(d)(7), Table S.

(iv) Powers Over Beneficial Enjoyment

Internal Revenue Code:
  Section 674
All Regulations under Section 674

W. Clarke Swanson, Jr., 1950 Trust
33 T.C.M. (CCH) 296 (1974)
aff'd, 518 F.2d 59 (8th Cir. 1975)

WILES, Judge: Respondent determined deficiencies in petitioners' income taxes for the year ending December 31, 1961....

Swanco Trust Company (hereinafter referred to as petitioner) is trustee of the W. Clarke Swanson Jr. Trust, the Carol Swanson Rhoden Trust and the Gerock Hurley Swanson Trust....

On December 21, 1950, Caroline Gerock Swanson (hereinafter referred to as Caroline) transferred common stock to W. Clarke Swanson (hereinafter referred to as W. Clarke) as trustee upon oral declaration of trust to establish trusts for W. Clarke Swanson Jr., Gerock H. Swanson and Carol Ann Swanson. At the time of transfer, the stock had a fair market value of $3,000 for each trust. On various dates between January 2, 1952 and January 6, 1955, W. Clarke transferred stock which he owned to himself as trustee under the W. Clarke Swanson Jr. Trust, the Gerock H. Swanson Trust and the Carol Ann Swanson Trust in the amounts of $30,368.17, $30,893.17 and $30,368.17, respectively.

On January 3, 1955, W. Clarke codified the Swanson Trusts established by gifts from himself and Caroline. W. Clarke was named as trustee of each trust. Each trust contained a provision as follows:

> 11. The Trust instrument shall be subject to interpretation or amendment by the maker but any interpretation or amendment made shall not vest in the maker any right to property, income or corpus except as in the relationship of Trustee for the beneficiary hereof.

The trustee of each trust was given extensive powers to deal with the properties of the trust. The trusts were irrevocable.

On January 14, 1955, W. Clarke executed an interpretation of the trusts which stated that the discretion and responsibility of determining whether payments are to be made from the trusts for the maintenance of the beneficiaries during minority or majority rests wholly with the trustee. On June 14, 1955, W. Clarke resigned as trustee of the Swanson Trusts and executed an amendment appointing Cecil A. Johnson (hereinafter referred to as Johnson) as trustee and amending the successor trustee provisions.... On May 22, 1958, W. Clarke executed an interpretation stating that the trustee has the "right and absolute authority" to borrow money for the Swanson Trusts.

* * *

Swanco replaced Johnson as trustee of the Swanson Trusts on November 1, 1967.... As of the date of [W. Clarke's] death, approximately ninety-one percent of the value of the Swanson Trusts was attributable to transfers by W. Clarke and nine percent by Caroline.

* * *

Petitioner's ... contention is that ... W. Clarke must be treated as the owner of the Swanson Trusts under section 674.... Respondent contends that W. Clarke was not the owner of these trusts....

Section 674 provides that, with certain exceptions not present here, a grantor is treated as the owner of any portion of a trust in which the beneficial enjoyment of the corpus or income is subject to a power of disposition exercisable by the grantor. If the grantor can affect the beneficial enjoyment, except as prescribed in the statute, he is treated as the owner of that portion of the trust. Section 1.674(a)-1(a), Income Tax Regs.

Section 11 of each of the three trust instruments is clear on its face. Each section provides that the maker (W. Clarke) has the right to interpret or amend the trust instruments, limited only in that he could not vest any ownership in himself. Respondent apparently does not contest the validity of these trust provisions nor do we perceive any reason why W. Clarke could not retain a power to amend the trusts at least to the extent of the property which he contributed to the trusts. With this almost unlimited power to amend the trusts, W. Clarke presumably could add or change beneficiaries or alter the trust provisions so that he could have complete control over the trust property.

The provisions of section 674 are similar to the law prior to the passage of the 1954 Code. H. Rept. 1337, 83d Cong., 2d Sess., p. 63 (1954). Both parties have cited as support for their positions cases which relate to pre-1954 law. Without going into those cases in detail, we note that the weight of authority supports the position of petitioner. *Commissioner v. Buck,* 120 F. 2d 775 (C. A. 2, 1941); *Laganas v. Commissioner,* 281 F. 2d 731 (C. A. 1, 1960); and *Warren H. Corning,* 24 T. C. 907 (1955), affd. 239 F. 2d 646 (C. A. 6, 1956). Furthermore, respondent's pre-1954 regulations from which section 674 was primarily drawn provided that the beneficial enjoyment of the corpus or income of a trust is subject to a power of disposition when the grantor has the power to alter the trust instrument. Section 39.22(a)-21(d), Regs. 118.

* * *

W. Clarke retained virtually unlimited control over the administration of the trusts. He amended or executed an interpretation of the trusts on [several] occasions.... W. Clarke's retention of powers of administration over the trusts, his actual use of such powers as shown above, and his retention of the right to reappoint himself trustee of the trusts (thereby giving himself extensive powers to deal with the properties of the trust) require that he be treated as the owner of the trusts under section 674. We hold that W. Clarke would be taxed as owner of the Swanson Trusts under section 674.

* * *

W. Clarke will be considered to be the grantor only as to the portions of the trusts that are equal to the percentage of property contributed by him. A taxpayer is considered to be a grantor only with regard to the property actually contributed to the trust, *Parker v. Commissioner,* 166 F. 2d 364 (C. A. 9, 1948), and which he owns at the time of the contribution. *Curtis A. Herberts,* 10 T. C. 1053, 1062, 1063 (1948). Caroline is considered to be the grantor as to the remaining portions of the trusts.

Illustrative Material

The last paragraph of *Swanson* deals with the separate issue of what it takes to be a "grantor." That issue is present in each of the grantor trust sections. In Rev. Rul. 83-25,

1983-1 C.B. 116, a court had ordered that damages awarded as a result of a personal injury suit on behalf of a minor be held in trust for the minor's benefit. Because the trustee could use the trust income for the benefit of the minor, the I.R.S. ruled that section 677(a) required treating the minor as owner of the trust. However, the I.R.S. rationale for treating the minor as a "grantor" was sketchy at best. Stating that the minor had "received the economic benefit of the amount of damages" paid to the trustee, the I.R.S. blithely moved to the conclusion that "[a]s the owner of the damages awarded, [the minor] is considered the grantor of the trust to which the damages were transferred." Though the result may seem correct from a theoretical perspective, the minor did not, in any commonly understood way, transfer property in trust for his own benefit. To similar effect is Private Letter Ruling 9552039 (1995). In the Tax Reform Act of 1986 Congress enacted section 468B, which provides independent, non-subchapter J statutory treatment of the income of "designated settlement funds." *See also* Treas. Reg. §§ 1.468B-1, 1.468B-2 (defining, and detailing the taxation of, "qualified settlement funds"). *See also United States v. Brown,* 348 F.3d 1200 (10th Cir. 2003) (applying the regulations); *but see* Treas. Reg. § 1.468B-1(k) (permitting certain "qualified settlement funds" with only one transferor to elect treatment as grantor trusts).

In *Meek v. Commissioner,* 71 T.C.M. (CCH) 3055 (1996), *aff'd mem.,* 133 F.3d 928 (9th Cir. 1998), the taxpayers simultaneously created a trust and sold property to it, in exchange for the trustees' promissory note. Deductibility of a loss the taxpayers incurred on the sale depended on whether they were the trust's "grantors." *See* ch. 5, sec. C, *infra.* The court held that the taxpayers were "grantors," notwithstanding the fact that the trustees, on behalf of the trust, had provided the consideration for its creation. The court noted that the trustees were unrelated to both the taxpayers and the trust beneficiaries, and that the trustees "did not participate to any degree in the dispositive provisions of the trust." 71 T.C.M. (CCH) at 3058.

In Private Letter Ruling 9831005 (1998), co-guardians of an incompetent proposed to use his property to fund a revocable trust for his benefit. The I.R.S. ruled that the incompetent would be the grantor of the proposed trust. Section 671 would attribute all of the trust's income, deductions, and credits to him, despite the fact that the co-guardians would nominally create the trust.

In *Investment Research Associates, Ltd. v. Commissioner,* 78 T.C.M. (CCH) 951 (1999), *aff'd in part on this issue and rev'd in part per curiam sub nom. Estate of Kanter v. Commissioner,* 337 F.3d 833 (7th Cir. 2003), *rev'd on other grounds sub nom. Ballard v. Commissioner,* 544 U.S. 40 (2005), the Tax Court held that an individual who had provided most or all of the funding for a group of trusts was their grantor, notwithstanding the fact that the trust instrument named his mother as the grantor. On remand, the Tax Court again so held. *Estate of Kanter v. Commissioner,* 93 T.C.M. (CCH) 721, 815 (2007), *rev'd on other grounds sub nom. Ballard v. Commissioner,* 522 F.3d 1229 (11th Cir. 2008).

Treas. Reg. § 1.671-2(e) provides additional guidance in defining the term "grantor."

Estate of Hilton W. Goodwyn
35 T.C.M. (CCH) 1026 (1976)

QUEALY, Judge:

* * *

Hilton W. Goodwyn, Sr. (hereinafter variously referred to as "decedent" or "Goodwyn") died on July 27, 1962, at the age of 84 years.... He was survived by his widow, Hallie M. Goodwyn....

Petitioners Hilton W. and Hallie M. Goodwyn filed joint income tax returns for the taxable years 1956 through 1962....

The decedent lived most of his adult life in Richmond, Virginia, commencing the practice of law in that city in the early 1900's. During the course of his early practice, Goodwyn represented numerous clients in the collection of accounts and began to develop his activities in the area of real estate....

For a considerable number of years prior to his death, Goodwyn held licenses as a real estate broker and as an attorney. However, his practice as an attorney came to be confined to the investigation, inception, preparation and supervision of real estate transactions and the legal necessities incident thereto. Decedent's attentions to the accumulations of mortgage paper and contractual relationships were, of necessity, constant. At the time of his death, Goodwyn employed approximately ten persons who dealt with the public and performed bookkeeping functions for him.

[On several occasions during 1943 and 1944, under several different documents, the decedent caused to be transferred to trustees certain real properties located in or adjacent to the City of Richmond, Virginia. Various combinations of trustees were used, including the decedent and his brother, N. B. Goodwyn, and the decedent's wife, Hallie M. Goodwyn, and his brother.]

N. B. Goodwyn, brother of the decedent, died on October 23, 1951. By document dated November 2, 1951, the then brothers and sisters of the decedent joined in appointing Lloyd M. Richards, an attorney serving as the law librarian to the Supreme Court of Appeals of Virginia, as successor trustee....

As of April 1, 1956, the decedent and Hallie M. Goodwyn resigned as trustees of the trust agreements cited *supra.* Thereupon, Charles C. Russell, attorney at law, Richmond, Virginia, was appointed trustee....

From the outset until shortly before his death, the decedent exercised control over the investment and management of the trusts herein before described, making all decisions with respect to sales and purchases of property, including transfers as between the respective trusts and other Goodwyn-related entities, and determining the income, if any, to be distributed to the beneficiaries. The actual functions performed by any of the individual trustees in relation to the attention required of these trusts was minimal.

All of the records of each of the aforementioned trusts were kept in the business office of the decedent and were maintained at his discretion. Separate books of account were not set up for each of the trusts. No individual accounting statements or balance sheets were prepared for any of these trusts. However, the individual transactions for each of the various trusts as well as other entities were recorded on the books of account maintained by the decedent. The income and assets of the trusts could be determined from these records.

A common bank account was maintained in the names of Richards and Russell for all of the trusts for which they were trustees. The records of this account were also maintained at the decedent's office. As the occasion required, decedent had checks drawn on this account in payment of mortgages or other assets acquired for the trusts, to pay the expenses of administering the trust, and for distribution to the beneficiaries. Such checks were thereupon signed by the trustees. At other times, blank checks were signed by the trustees to be used by the decedent for such purposes.

The decedent determined the amount of any distributions to the beneficiaries, and that determination was accepted without question by the trustees. Up until a few years prior to the decedent's death, the beneficiaries were not aware of the existence of the trusts.

In no instance did any of the individual trustees undertake any action independently of the decedent. The decedent determined what assets were to be acquired, the means of financing those acquisitions, from whom they were to be purchased, and in most, if not all, instances, the prices to be paid for them. He performed the same functions with the sale of trust assets. The decedent also controlled the making of loans between one entity and another....

The fiduciary income tax returns for each of the beneficiaries [sic] were prepared at decedent's direction by his employees. The trustees would come to the office and sign those returns after they had been completed.

* * *

Under the terms of the deeds creating these trusts, the trustees were granted broad discretionary powers with respect to both the distribution of income to the beneficiaries and the investment and management of the corpus of the trusts. Notwithstanding the designation of Richards and Russell as trustees, it further appears that at all times from the establishment of the trusts until his last illness, with the acquiescence of the trustees, the decedent made all decisions with respect to the purchase and sale of trust assets and the investment of any proceeds and determined the amounts, if any, to be distributed to the respective beneficiaries.

There is no question that Goodwyn created legally valid trusts under state law. The provisions of these trust instruments, including those regarding the rights, duties and obligations of the trustees demonstrate the grantor's intent to relinquish the ownership of the involved assets. Although many of the beneficiaries were unaware of the existence of these trusts, such notice is not a requirement for a valid trust.[3]

Regarding the effect of the Federal income tax laws on these trusts, it is not contended here that the decedent reserved any right or power in any of the trusts whereby the income of these trusts could be attributed to the grantor. Additionally, it is clear that during the years in issue the trustees were not related or subordinate parties within the definition of 672(c) whose discretionary power to distribute or accumulate income to beneficiaries would attribute the income to the grantor. Rather, these trustees were independent trustees within the meaning of section 674(c), who may have such a discretionary power over income.

While the record indicates that the legal formalities have been complied with, it also indicates that the designated "independent" trustees, whether by agreement or otherwise, entrusted the management of the trusts' assets and the distribution of income therefrom to the sole discretion of the decedent. The decedent kept all the records, made all of the investments and decided the amount to be distributed to beneficiaries. The trustees merely acquiesced in these actions.

On the basis of these facts, the judicial decisions following the Supreme Court's decision in *Helvering v. Clifford,* 309 U. S. 331 (1940), and the later so-called *Clifford* regulations might well warrant the attribution of the income from these trusts to the decedent. However, to the extent these previous principles are not embodied in the present statutory provisions of the Code, they must be considered no longer applicable. Section 671 provides that subpart E represents the sole criterion of dominion and control under sec-

---

3. *Fleenor v. Hensley,* 121 Va. 367, 93 S. E. 582 (1917).

tion 61 (relating to the definition of gross income) and thereby also under the *Clifford* doctrine.

The Report of the Committee on Ways and Means on the Internal Revenue Code of 1954 explains clearly that this exclusivity was the intent of Congress:

> It is also provided in this section [671] that no items of a trust shall be included in computing the income or credits of the grantor (or another person) solely on the grounds of his dominion and control over the trust under the provisions of section 61.... The effect of this provision is to insure that taxability of *Clifford* type trusts shall be governed solely by this subpart. However, this provision does not affect the principles governing the taxability of income to a grantor or assignor other than by reason of his dominion and control over the trust. Thus, this subpart has no application in situations involving assignments of future income to the assignor, as in *Lucas v. Earl* (281 U. S. 111), *Harrison v. Schaffner* (312 U. S. 579), and *Helvering v. Horst* (311 U. S. 112), whether or not the assignment is to a trust; nor are the rules as to family partnerships affected by this subpart.[4]

Consequently, in order for a grantor to be held taxable pursuant to subpart E on the income of a trust which he has established, he must have one of the powers or retained interests proscribed by subpart E.

The grantor's power to control beneficial enjoyment of either the principal or the income, within the limits defined in section 674, would result in attribution of the income to the grantor. [The court quotes section 674(a).]

Although the trustees here would not be adverse parties, section 674(c) excepts the application of the general rule in certain circumstances which are applicable here.

Respondent would concede that none of the provisions of the trusts in issue would give the decedent the power proscribed by this section. It is respondent's argument, however, that although grantor does not specifically have such a power, his relationship to the trust res through its management and to the administration of these trusts generally is such that he should be deemed to be a trustee, in fact, during his life. Being considered a trustee, the trustee's power under the trust agreement to distribute or accumulate the income from these trusts would then make such income attributable to him under subpart E.

Respondent's contention in this respect is similar to that respondent raised in the *Estate of Hilton W. Goodwyn,*[T. C. Memo. 1973-153, involving the estate tax on decedent's estate]. As relevant here, respondent argued in that case that the decedent should be treated as trustee, in fact, possessing such rights and powers as to cause the inclusion of the assets thereof in his gross estate under section 2036(a)(2). That section requires the inclusion in decedent's gross estate any property for which the decedent has retained the right, either alone or in conjunction with any person, to designate the persons who shall possess or enjoy the property or the income therefrom.

We found in that case there was no basis for such inclusion. The Supreme Court has held in *United States v. Byrum*, 408 U. S. 125, 136–7 (1972), that the right, upon which the inclusion under section 2036(a)(2) is predicated, is an "ascertainable and legally enforceable power," reserved in the trust instrument or by some other means. See also *Estate of Charles Gilman*, 65 T. C. 296, 316 (1975), [*aff'd per curiam*, 547 F.2d 32 (2d Cir.

---

4. H. Rept. No. 1337, to accompany H. R. 8300 (Pub. L. No. 591), 83d Cong., 2d Sess. (1954), page a212.

1976)]. We found that Goodwyn had not retained such a right in the case of the Richards and Russell Trusts of which he was a grantor.

In this case, while a different test is applicable, the tests are similar in character. Where section 2036(a) uses the term "right," section 674 uses the term "power." The House Ways and Means Committee Report, cited supra,[6] in its explanation of this section uses the term power in the legal sense of having an enforceable authority or right to perform some action. The use of this term in this legal sense suggests that the power of a grantor upon which he will be taxed is a power reserved by instrument or contract creating an ascertainable and legally enforceable right, not merely the persuasive control which he might exercise over an independent trustee who is receptive to his wishes. Such interpretation is also, we believe, indicated by the holding in the *Byrum* case.

In this case, the trustees in question accepted the rights, duties and obligations granted them in the trust instruments. Regardless of the fact they had entrusted to the decedent the complete management and control of these trusts, this informal delegation did not discharge them from the legal responsibility they had as the trustees. As a matter of law, the trustees were liable and answerable for the decedent's acts on their behalf. See 2 Scott, Trusts 1388, 1391 (3rd ed., 1967); 3 Scott, Trusts 1794 (3rd ed., 1967).

There is nothing in the record to show that the trustees could not have undertaken exclusive control of the trust res if they had elected to do so. Whatever power Goodwyn exercised over the trust assets, administration or distribution, he did so on the trustee's behalf and not in his own right.

Because of Goodwyn's failure to have a legally enforceable right, we have already held, following *Byrum,* that the assets of these trusts were not includable in the decedent's estate under 2036(a)(2). Since a similar legal right or power is a prerequisite under section 674(a), consistency appears to require the same decision with respect to the applicability of this section. We see no other possible decision.

Section 671 precludes attributing the income to Goodwyn on any other theory of dominion and control under the definition of gross income, including the *Clifford* doctrine. We interpret this limitation to mean that if Goodwyn cannot be considered as a trustee, in fact, under the statutory provisions of subpart E, he cannot be considered as such by virtue of the judicial doctrines arising from the *Clifford* case which Congress intended to limit through the enactment of subpart E....

Illustrative Material

1. *Braun v. Commissioner,* 48 T.C.M. (CCH) 210 (1984), involved trusts under which all of the income was to be distributed annually to the grantors' children. However, the trustees had not distributed equal amounts of income to or for the benefit of each of the children. The court cited that fact for concluding, under New Jersey law, that the trustees in fact had discretion to sprinkle the income among the children on a non pro-rata basis. Because the grantors, along with a nonadverse party, served as trustees, the grantors were therefore taxable on the trusts' income under section 674(a). Similarly, in *Carson v. Commissioner,* 92 T.C. 1134 (1989), a trust agreement expressly required the trustee-grantor to distribute all of the trust income to the trust beneficiaries (her sons) annually. The agreement did not expressly authorize the trustee to make unequal distributions. Neither, however, did the agreement expressly require that the distributions

---

6. H. Rept. No. 1337, *supra,* at pages a214–216.

be equal. Relying on the fact that the trustee-grantor had, during two different taxable years, made unequal distributions, the Tax Court held that she had retained the power to make unequal distributions. Thus, she had retained a power described in section 674(a). Accordingly, she was treated as owner of all the trust income. However, in *Bennett v. Commissioner*, 79 T.C. 470 (1982), the Tax Court rejected the notion that a trustee's misadministration of a trust, by exercising "discretion" over the distribution of trust income, all of which (according to the trust agreement) was to be distributed equally among the income beneficiaries, caused the trust to be subject to a section 674 power.

2. Section 674(b)(4) provides an exception for powers to allocate principal or income among charitable beneficiaries only. Retention of such a power does not cause a grantor to be treated as owner of any portion of a trust. *See Thompson v. United States*, 209 F. Supp. 530 (E.D. Tex. 1962), *rev'd on other grounds*, 332 F.2d 657 (5th Cir. 1964); *Emerson R. Miller*, 19 T.C.M. (CCH) 1487 (1960); Rev. Rul. 79-223, 1979-2 C.B. 254.

3. For a critical overview of section 674, see Westfall, *Trust Grantors and Section 674: Adventures in Income Tax Avoidance*, 60 Colum. L. Rev. 326 (1960).

4. In *Wysong v. Commissioner*, 55 T.C.M. (CCH) 1456 (1988), taxpayers created a trust and funded it by making the trust a demand loan. The Tax Court treated the taxpayers as owners of the entire trust under section 674(a), because the loan gave them the power "to exercise complete control over the beneficial enjoyment of the corpus at any time by simply demanding it." *Kushner v. Commissioner*, 61 T.C.M. (CCH) 1716 (1991), *aff'd mem.*, 955 F.2d 41 (4th Cir. 1992), and *McGinnis v. Commissioner*, 65 T.C.M. (CCH) 1870 (1993), reached the same conclusion on similar facts.

5. For a decision that seems inconsistent with *Goodwyn*, see *Investment Research Associates, Ltd. v. Commissioner*, 78 T.C.M. (CCH) 951 (1999), *aff'd in part and rev'd in part on other grounds per curiam sub nom. Estate of Kanter v. Commissioner*, 337 F.3d 833 (7th Cir. 2003), *rev'd on other grounds sub nom. Ballard v. Commissioner*, 544 U.S. 40 (2005), in which the Tax Court held that a grantor, rather than a named trustee, "controlled" the administration of a group of trusts and was, therefore, taxable on all of their income. On remand, the Tax Court again held that the grantor was taxable on all of the trusts' income, on the grounds that he had a power to appoint trust beneficiaries, and that this was "tantamount to a power of disposition over the trust' assets." *Estate of Kanter v. Commissioner*, 93 T.C.M. (CCH) 721, 815 (2007), *rev'd on other grounds sub nom. Ballard v. Commissioner*, 522 F.3d 1229 (11th Cir. 2008).

Problems

4-8. G creates an *inter vivos* trust. The trustee is authorized to distribute such of the income to the grantor's sister, S, as the trustee, in its sole discretion, sees fit. Upon the death of S, the trustee is to distribute the trust principal and any accumulated income to S's then living issue, *per stirpes*. First National Bank is the trustee. Does section 674 treat G as owner of any portion of the trust?

4-9. Assume the facts of Problem 4-8, except that G's wife, W, is trustee. Would your answer differ if the remainder beneficiary of the trust were S's estate, rather than S's issue?

4-10. G creates an irrevocable trust, naming herself as trustee. The trustee is authorized to distribute income or principal or both to G's adult child, A, in such amounts and at such times as the trustee deems necessary for A's support, health, and education. Any accumulated income not paid to A before his death is distributable to A's estate. The trust terminates at A's death, with the remainder passing to A's descendants. Does section 674 treat G as the owner of any portion of the trust? What if accumulated income were added to principal each year and were not distributable to A's estate?

4-11. G creates an irrevocable trust, naming her brother, B, as trustee. The trustee is authorized to distribute income or principal or both to any of G's children, in such shares and amounts and at such times as the trustee deems appropriate for any purpose. At the death of the last to survive of G's children, the remaining trust assets pass to G's then living descendants. Does section 674 treat G as the owner of any portion of the trust? What if the income and principal distributions were limited to amounts that the trustee deems necessary for the support, health, and education of G's children?

(v) Administrative Powers

———————

Internal Revenue Code:
  Section 675

Regulation:
  Section 1.675-1

———————

Benson v. Commissioner
76 T.C. 1040 (1981)

FAY, *Judge*: … The only issue for decision is what part of a trust created by petitioner-husband is to be treated as being owned by him during 1974 and 1975 under section 675(3).

FINDINGS OF FACT

* * *

After earning a degree in marketing at Wartburg College, petitioner Larry Benson began working for Maytag. While in Peoria, Ill., on a special project, he became interested in opening his own business in the Peoria area. Petitioners opened a home appliance center in Peoria in January 1966.…

Petitioners initially operated their business on rented premises. In 1968 and 1969, they acquired two contiguous tracts of land in Peoria County for about $28,000. Subsequently, they erected a building and other improvements on the land at a cost of $120,624. The real estate as thus improved shall hereinafter be referred to as the "property." In March 1970, petitioners moved their appliance business from the rented premises to the "property."

On January 1, 1972, petitioners leased the "property" to Benson's Maytag, Inc., petitioner Larry Benson's wholly owned corporation. The lease, which runs until June 30, 1982, calls for a monthly rent of $1,700.

On March 31, 1972, petitioners, by quitclaim deeds, transferred the "property" to the "L. William Benson Short Term Irrevocable Trust," a trust created by petitioner Larry Benson on the same date.[2] Petitioner June Benson was named trustee of the trust. The trust

———————

2. At the time the "property" was transferred to the trust, it was subject to a mortgage executed by petitioners on Sept. 30, 1971. Petitioners remained personally liable and continued to make the mortgage payments after the transfer.

is to terminate 10 years and 10 days after the last contribution to it is made. All net trust income is to be paid annually to petitioners' four children or for their benefit with all capital gains and losses being allocated to principal.[3] When the trust terminates, all accrued but undistributed net income will be distributed to the children or to the children's appointees, while the trust principal will revert to petitioner Larry Benson.[4]

Petitioner June Benson, as trustee, has the power to invest, sell, or exchange trust property and the power to borrow money pledging trust property as security. Additionally she may as trustee, "loan trust property to any person with provision for reasonable interest and security."

Evidently the only asset ever transferred to the trust was the "property" which housed the home appliance center. Therefore, the rents paid by Benson's Maytag, Inc., were the trust's only source of income. When the "property" was transferred to the trust, its fair market value was $200,000. Its fair market value was approximately $295,000 on January 1, 1974, and approximately $325,000 on January 1, 1975.

Petitioner June Benson, as trustee, made several loans to petitioner Larry Benson. Each of those loans was unsecured, bore interest of 8 percent, and was represented by a promissory demand note. The loans were as follows:

Date of loan	Amount
May 1, 1973	$17,215
Sept. 1, 1974	5,000
Sept. 1, 1974	1,500
Nov. 1, 1974	24,000

No payments on the loans were made before January 1, 1976. The loans, including accrued interest, were paid in full on December 30, 1977. The total principal and interest amounts outstanding at the beginning of the taxable years involved herein were as follows:

	Principal	Interest	Total
Jan. 1, 1974	$17,215	$916.87	$18,131.87
Jan. 1, 1975	47,715	2,782.06	50,497.06

The trust reported the following income and deductions on its returns for 1973, 1974, and 1975:

	Income	Taxes	Depreciation	Distributions
1973	$22,150	($5,097)	($3,016)	$14,037
1974	20,400	(3,619)	—	16,781
1975	20,400	(3,724)	—	16,676

Thus, the trust reported zero taxable income for each of those 3 years.

Although distribution deductions were taken, the beneficiary children received no money or property from the trust.[8] All net trust receipts until November 1, 1974, were loaned to petitioner Larry Benson.

---

3. When the trust was created, all petitioners' children were minors, each being under 8 years of age. Thus, according to the trust terms, the children were considered "incapacitated." Their status as such gave the trustee, petitioner June Benson, the right to distribute the income either to the children, to their parents (petitioners), to their custodian, guardian, or conservator, or to anyone with whom the children resided. The trust expressly absolves the actual recipient of the distribution from responsibility for its expenditure.

4. Since the trust requires annual distribution of all net income, the only accrued income should be year-of-termination income not yet distributed to the children at the time the trust terminates.

8. The trust filed its tax returns as a simple trust each year. See sec. 651(a)(1).

In his statutory notice of deficiency, respondent determined that petitioner Larry Benson should be treated as owning the entire trust during 1974 and 1975. Thus, per section 671, respondent increased petitioners' gross income by the amount of the trust's income, $20,400, in each of those years and allowed petitioners those deductions otherwise allowable to the trust.

OPINION

The only issue for decision is what part of a trust created by petitioner-husband is to be treated as being owned by him during 1974 and 1975 as a result of loans made by the trust to him. Petitioner-husband, a trust grantor, borrowed trust funds without security and did not repay the loans before the beginning of 1974 or before the beginning of 1975, the taxable years involved herein. Thus, under section 675(3), the "portion of [the] trust in respect of which" petitioner-husband borrowed is treated as being owned by petitioner-husband. The parties disagree as to what "portion" means.

Petitioners contend that "portion" refers to the part of the trust borrowed in comparison to the entire trust. Accordingly, they maintain that the part of the trust income taxable to them is an amount which bears the same ratio to the trust's entire income as the amount of loans, including interest, outstanding at the beginning of the taxable year bears to the fair market value of the trust at the beginning of the taxable year. Respondent argues that "portion" means the entire trust whenever a grantor has the power to borrow all corpus or income and any trust property is borrowed. Alternatively, respondent contends that "portion" is a fraction arrived at by dividing the amount borrowed, including interest, by the trust's income for the year calculated without the sections 651 and 661 distribution deductions.[11] We do not adopt respondent's analysis but sustain his determination in this case for the reasons below.

Section 675 is one of a series of Internal Revenue Code sections collectively known as the grantor trust rules. See secs. 671 through 679. Sections 673 through 677 enumerate the instances in which a trust grantor is treated as owning all or part of a trust. For tax purposes, a grantor is credited with the trust income, deductions, and credits allocable to the trust "portion" he is treated as owning. Sec. 671. The purpose of those grantor trust rules is to tax a trust grantor on trust items over which he has retained substantial dominion and control, see section 1.671-2(b), Income Tax Regs., and it is with that purpose in mind that we interpret section 675(3) and "portion."

At the outset, we note that while "portion" is used throughout the Code sections comprising the grantor trust rules, its meaning varies from section to section and from case to case. Sec. 1.671-3, Income Tax. Regs.[12] "Portion's" flexible meaning is necessary to ful-

---

11. Respondent also contends that the trust is a "sham" for tax purposes. Sec. 671 provides: "No items of a trust shall be included in computing the taxable income and credits of the grantor or of any other person solely on the grounds of his dominion and control under section 61 * * * or any other provision of this title, except as specified in this subpart."
Thus, income of a trust is not attributed to the trust grantor because of the grantor's dominion and control over the trust unless one of the specific grantor trust rules, see secs. 673–677, or assignment of income principles applies. See sec. 1.671-1(c), Income Tax Regs. That rule allows taxpayers to plan their affairs knowing the tax results. Accordingly, we prefer to decide this case under the well-established grantor trust rules. See *Wesenberg v. Commissioner*, 69 T.C. 1005, 1011 (1978).

12. The regulations recognize six possible meanings of "portion": the entire trust; the trust accounting income; the trust corpus; a fraction or dollar amount of trust accounting income; a fraction or dollar amount of corpus; or specific trust property. See sec. 1.671-3(a) to (c), Income Tax Regs. See also, Schmolka, "Selected Aspects of the Grantor Trust Rules," U. Miami 9th Inst. on Estate Planning par. 1400 (1975).

fill the purpose of the grantor trust rules—taxation of a grantor only on trust items over which he has retained substantial dominion and control. See sec. 1.671-2(b), Income Tax Regs. Given a myriad of dispositive variables, "portion" must have an adaptable meaning. For example, under section 676, a trust grantor is treated as owning any trust "portion" which he can revoke. If the grantor can revoke the entire trust, then "portion" means the entire trust. However, if the grantor can revoke only the remainder interest and has no power to alter the income interest, "portion" means only the remainder interest, since the grantor has no power over the income interest and should not be taxed on it. See sec. 1.671-3(b)(2), Income Tax Regs.

In determining what "portion" of a trust should be treated as being owned by its grantor, most of the grantor trust rules focus on powers set forth in the trust instrument which evidence a grantor's dominion and control over trust property without regard to whether or not those powers are ever exercised.[13] In most cases, it is fairly simple to tell over what part of a trust a power extends; therefore, the meaning of "portion" is easily decided. For example, if a grantor has the power to distribute the entire trust to his spouse, the entire trust is treated as his even if only part of the trust is actually so distributed. See sec. 677(a)(1). On the other hand, if a grantor has the power to distribute only current income to his spouse, he is treated as owning only the current income interest in the trust. In the latter case, "portion" means only the current income interest, because that is the only trust segment over which the grantor has any power.

Section 675(3) differs from the other provisions which provide rules for determining grantor ownership of a trust, because it requires an affirmative act, borrowing, rather than a mere power, before it applies.[14] Nevertheless, the same theme underlies section 675(3) as underlies the other Code sections which treat a grantor as owning the trust. In both cases, the justification for taxation of the grantor is evidence of substantial grantor dominion and control. Thus, our proper inquiry is not what the grantor has borrowed but what the grantor's borrowing represents in terms of the grantor's dominion and control over the trust.

In order fully to understand the implications of grantor borrowing, section 675(3) must be read in conjunction with section 675(2). Section 675(2) treats a grantor as the owner of the trust anytime the grantor, a nonadverse party, or both have the power to loan income or corpus to the grantor without adequate security or without adequate interest, unless a nongrantor trustee may make such loans to any and all persons. Thus, the mere power to loan trust property to the grantor on favorable terms, vested in the grantor or a nonadverse party, evidences enough grantor dominion and control over the trust to justify taxing all the trust income to the grantor.[15] However, if a nongrantor trustee can make unsecured or no-interest loans to anyone, the grantor is seemingly on equal footing with the rest of the world, and the evidence of grantor dominion and control is less.

Section 675(2) can be avoided easily. A trust grantor can install a "friendly" trustee[16] and give that trustee a general power to make unsecured or no-interest loans to anyone.

---

13. See, e.g., secs. 674; 675(1), (2), and (4); 676; 677(a).

14. See also sec. 677(b), which applies when trust income is actually used, pursuant to a discretionary power, to support or maintain a beneficiary, other than the grantor's spouse, whom the grantor is legally obligated to support or maintain. That section clearly limits taxation of the grantor to income actually so applied.

15. Of course, if the tainted lending power extends only to a "portion" of the trust, that is, if the grantor could only lend himself corpus, then only that "portion" should be attributed to the grantor. Cf. sec. 1.671-3(b)(2), Income Tax Regs.

16. By referring to a friendly trustee, we mean one who is a related or subordinate party subservient to the grantor. See secs. 675(3) and 672(c).

In all probability, the "friendly" trustee would not make such loans to anyone except the grantor; but, nevertheless, section 675(2) would not apply. However, a grantor cannot rely on such an escape from section 675(2) if he contemplates actually borrowing from the trust. When actual borrowing occurs, section 675(3) must be considered.

As previously noted, section 675(3) treats a trust grantor as owning any "portion of a trust in respect of which" he borrows, if the loans are either unsecured or bear no interest or are made by a "friendly" trustee, unless the grantor repays the loans before the beginning of the taxable year. It might seem that section 675(3) serves to tax the grantor only on the part of the trust he actually borrows. But, such an interpretation would read 675(3) as treating the grantor as owning the "portion" he borrowed rather than owning the "portion of [the] trust in respect of which" he borrowed, which is what the statute mandates.[17] Moreover, such a reading would produce an unacceptable result. The power to make unsecured or no-interest loans to a trust grantor causes the grantor to be treated as owner of the entire trust under section 675(2). It would be incongruous if unsecured or no-interest loans actually made to the grantor caused only the part of the trust actually borrowed to be treated as the grantor's under section 675(3). That result would make avoidance of section 675(2) not only easy, but relatively harmless from the grantor's viewpoint— he could still obtain trust property in the form of favorable loans but without having to worry about being treated as owning any substantial part of the trust. Therefore, we refuse to read "portion of [the] trust in respect of which" to mean merely "portion."

Likewise, we reject petitioners' contention that "portion" refers to the amount borrowed in comparison to the entire trust. Petitioner would have us calculate a fraction arrived at by the dividing the amount borrowed by the trust corpus, and treat that fraction as the trust "portion" owned by the grantor. If such were the case, a trust grantor could borrow the entire trust income derived from the entire trust corpus but only be treated as owning a fraction of the trust, even though his borrowing evidences dominion and control over the entire trust. We find such a result patently unreasonable and unsupported by the statutory language or any other authority.[18]

On the other hand, we need not address respondent's contention that "portion" means the entire trust whenever a grantor has the power to borrow all corpus or income and any trust property is borrowed. See *Mau v. United States,* 355 F. Supp. 909 (D. Hawaii 1973). In this case, petitioner-husband borrowed all the trust income and that income was de-

---

17. In *Holdeen v. Commissioner,* T.C. Memo, 1975-29, the grantor-taxpayer established a complicated series of long-term trusts benefiting his family and various charities. His daughter served as trustee of one of the trusts and expended $80,000 from that trust for mortgage participation certificates on property the grantor-taxpayer owned which was subject to preexisting mortgages. We held that the grantor-taxpayer indirectly borrowed $80,000 from the trust which he repaid when he transferred the mortgaged property to the trust. We held further that the grantor-taxpayer was to be treated under sec. 675(3) as owner of an $80,000 "portion" of the trust during the years between the loan and the repayment.

It might seem that *Holdeen* stands for the proposition that "portion" means the amount actually borrowed. However, such does not follow from a careful reading of that case. The $80,000 borrowed in *Holdeen* was corpus and we, in effect, held that $80,000 of the corpus was the "portion of [the] trust in respect of which" the grantor-taxpayer borrowed. Furthermore, it is unclear whether any more could have been borrowed. See note 19 *infra.* In summary, *Holdeen* involved a cash loan from corpus and is thus distinguishable from most cases which involve a noncash corpus, cash loans, direct borrowing, and clearly defined borrowing perimeters. We do not find *Holdeen* necessarily inconsistent with our holding in this case.

18. Petitioners mistakenly rely on *Holdeen v. Commissioner,* T.C. Memo. 1975-29, as supporting their interpretation of sec. 675(3). See note 17 *supra.*

rived from the entire trust corpus. Thus, it is clear that petitioner-husband should be treated as owner of the entire trust. It does not matter in this case whether we reach that result via respondent's automatic entire trust rule or via calling petitioner-husband owner of the entire trust simply because he actually borrowed "in respect of" the entire trust. The same result is reached either way. It is best to wait for a case clearly presenting the problem to analyze fully respondent's "entire trust" contention.[19]

Petitioners in this case have made no showing that less than all the trust should be treated as being owned by petitioner-husband. As previously noted, he borrowed all the trust income which was in respect of all the trust corpus. His borrowings undoubtedly indicate significant dominion and control over the entire trust. Accordingly, we conclude that petitioner-husband is treated as owning the entire trust during 1974 and 1975.

Illustrative Material

1. *Bennett v. Commissioner*, 79 T.C. 470 (1982), answered, if only for one set of facts, the question left unanswered by *Benson*. In *Bennett* three trusts made unsecured loans from income to a partnership of the three grantors. The loans remained outstanding at the beginning of the taxable years in question. Because the trusts always distributed small amounts of income to their beneficiaries, it was clear the partnership had not borrowed all of the trusts' income for any given year. Yet the total amount outstanding far exceeded the trusts' income in any one year. No additional loans occurred during the taxable years in question. The Tax Court rejected the I.R.S. position that grantor borrowing of any amount caused the grantors to be treated as owners of the entire trusts. Instead, the court held that the grantors "should be taxed on that portion of the current year's trust income which the total unpaid loans at the beginning of the taxable year bear to the total trust income of prior years plus the trust income for the taxable year at issue." 79 T.C. at 485.

Such a "portion" may be appropriate on the facts of *Bennett*, but would the same portion work if, in the fiftieth year of a trust, the grantor, for the first time, borrowed 99% of the trust's current year's income? *Bennett* itself realizes this weakness and, in dictum, suggests that the grantor be treated as owner of "the portion which the current year's borrowings bear to the current year's income or on the portion which total borrowings bear to total income through the end of the taxable year, *whichever is greater.*" 79 T.C. at 485 n.26 (emphasis in original). Does either the holding or the dictum of *Bennett* find support in the Code?

---

19. Such a case would arise if, for example, a trust grantor transferred two separate income-producing stocks to a trust, but only borrowed the income derived from one of those stocks. Respondent would argue that the grantor's borrowing represents not only the grantor's control of the property he has in hand but is indicative of his ability to control all the trust property on similar terms. Just as the mere existence of a power to revoke evidences substantial dominion and control, see sec. 676, so does the mere existence of unsecured or no-interest borrowing or borrowing from a "friendly" trustee. It appears from respondent's brief in this case that, if the grantor-taxpayer could demonstrate that his borrowing does not evidence his ability to borrow the entire trust on sec. 675(3) terms, respondent would not argue that the entire trust should be treated as being owned by that grantor-taxpayer. For example, if the trust terms forbid grantor borrowing of current income, and a grantor only borrowed corpus, then he should be treated as owning only corpus, since his borrowing from corpus evidences no dominion and control over income. In other words, respondent's position would be that the grantor-taxpayer must show that all the trust could not be borrowed on the same terms that part was borrowed.

2. *Estate of Jonathan Holdeen,* 34 T.C.M. (CCH) 129, 193 (1975), distinguished in *Benson,* involved a loan, from corpus, of $80,000 to the grantor. The Tax Court held that the grantor was taxable on the income derived by the trust on $80,000. Is this rule compatible with those of *Benson* and *Bennett*? Say that a trust has corpus of $1,600,000. Assuming a 5% rate of return, the trust's annual income would be $80,000. If the trustee lends the grantor the trust's $80,000 of income, under *Benson* and *Bennett* the grantor is taxable on all $80,000 of income. But if the trustee lends the grantor $80,000 of corpus, under *Holdeen* the grantor is taxable on only $4,000 ($80,000/$1,600,000 x $80,000). Is this good tax policy? Is the grantor likely to care whether the loans come from income or corpus?

3. What if a grantor borrows both income and corpus? Which rule applies? In *Patsey v. United States,* 603 F. Supp. 60 (N.D. Cal. 1984), such loans occurred. In 1973 the grantor borrowed 60% of the trust's corpus and "nearly 100%" of its 1973 income. In 1974 his borrowings increased, to a total of 85% of the trust's corpus. But he borrowed only 90% of the trust's 1974 income. Under *Benson* and *Bennett* the grantor should have been treated as owner of something less than the trust's entire income for 1974 and 1975, ignoring, however, the massive loans of corpus. How, if at all, should the result be affected by the additional loans from corpus? The *Patsey* court, citing *Benson,* treated the grantor as owner of the trust's entire income for both 1974 and 1975 but did so on the basis that the grantor's borrowings "evidenced control and dominion over the entire trust." This is, of course, the I.R.S. position that *Benson* expressly refused to decide and that *Bennett* rejected.

For another case involving grantor borrowing, see *Investment Research Associates, Ltd. v. Commissioner,* 78 T.C.M. (CCH) 951 (1999), in which the Tax Court held that a grantor who had borrowed from his trusts was taxable on all of their income. Unfortunately, the opinion is long and complicated, the section 675 issue occupies little of the court's attention, and the court relies as well on section 674. In *Estate of Kanter v. Commissioner,* 337 F.3d 833 (7th Cir. 2003) (per curiam), the Seventh Circuit affirmed *Investment Research Associates* on the section 674 issue, studiously avoided the section 675 issue, and reversed in part. In *Ballard v. Commissioner,* 544 U.S. 40 (2005), the Supreme Court reversed *Estate of Kanter* on other grounds. On remand, the Tax Court again noted that the grantor had borrowed large amounts from his trusts but apparently rested its renewed finding of grantor status exclusively on section 674. *Estate of Kanter v. Commissioner,* 93 T.C.M. (CCH) 721, 811–16 (2007), *rev'd on other grounds sub nom. Ballard v. Commissioner,* 522 F.3d 1229 (11th Cir. 2008).

4. *Mau v. United States,* 355 F. Supp. 909 (D. Hawaii 1973), cited in *Benson,* held that section 675(3) applied to the taxable year in which the borrowing by the grantor occurred, even though the loans were made after the beginning of the taxable year. Rev. Rul. 86-82, 1986-1 C.B. 252, went one step further, ruling that repayment by the grantor before a taxable year ended did not render section 675(3) inapplicable to that year. According to the I.R.S., *Mau* stood for "the principle that section 675(3) applie[d] for any year during any part of which a loan by a trust to the grantor-trustee [was] outstanding."

5. *Bennett is* also noteworthy for its holding that the loans to the grantors' partnership constituted "indirect" borrowing for purposes of section 675(3). Another Tax Court case, *Paul Buehner,* 65 T.C. 723 (1976), however, held that loans to a corporation (of which the grantor was the overwhelmingly predominant shareholder) did not constitute such borrowing.

Rothstein v. United States
735 F.2d 704 (2d Cir. 1984)

FRIENDLY, Circuit Judge:

Harold and David M. Rothstein, as executors of the estate of Alexander Rothstein, and Reba Rothstein, his widow, appeal from a judgment of the District Court for Connecticut, which dismissed their action for a tax refund after trial before Judge Eginton and an advisory jury, 574 F.Supp. 19. Appellants urge two grounds for reversal. One involves the interpretation of §§453, 671 and 675 of the Internal Revenue Code ("IRC")....

The district court found the facts to be as follows: In 1951 decedent Alexander Rothstein ("taxpayer") and Abraham Savin formed a real estate holding company known as Industrial Developers, Inc. ("IDI"). They purchased, at a cost of $30,000 each, a parcel of land in East Hartford, Connecticut, which they conveyed to the corporation, each receiving 300 shares of IDI stock. The corporation constructed, at a cost not disclosed in the record, warehouses which were used as rental property.

On February 18, 1957, taxpayer contributed his 300 shares of IDI to an irrevocable trust he established for the benefit of his three children, Harold, David and Edna. Taxpayer's wife Reba was the trustee. Although the trust was required to distribute any dividends received on the IDI stock, which was its sole asset, to the beneficiaries at least semi-annually, no dividends were ever paid.

In October 1964, taxpayer bought Savin's 300 shares of IDI for $500,000, agreeing to pay the purchase price at a later date. On November 13, 1964, he purchased from his wife as trustee the trust's 300 shares for $320,000. Payment was made by an unsecured promissory note bearing an interest rate of 5% per annum, payable semi-annually beginning May 13, 1965. These payments were duly made. Principal payments were scheduled to be made as follows: $25,000 on or before November 13, 1969; $25,000 on or before November 13, 1970; $50,000 on or before November 13, 1971; and $50,000 on or before November 13 of each calendar year thereafter until the full sum of $320,000 had been paid.

In January 1965, taxpayer, having become owner of all of IDI's stock as a result of the transactions with Savin and the trust, dissolved IDI and had all its assets transferred to himself. He then refinanced the property, replacing an existing mortgage of less than $200,000 with a new $700,000 mortgage to Equitable Life Insurance Company and using the approximately $500,000 excess of the new mortgage over the old to discharge his debt to Savin. On February 8, 1965, he gave a second mortgage of $320,000 to his wife as trustee to secure the promissory note of that amount given in exchange for the trust's IDI shares three months before.

In their joint federal income tax return for 1965 taxpayer and his wife claimed deductions for (1) $16,000 in interest paid to the trust on the promissory note, and (2) a short-term capital loss of $33,171 on the liquidation of IDI, determined as follows:

fair market value of property received upon liquidation		$1,054,580
Less:		
IDI liabilities assumed	$267,751	
Cost of stock acquired from Savin	500,000	
Cost of stock acquired from trust	320,000	
		$1,087,751
Gain (loss) realized		($33,171)

The Commissioner, however, asserted a deficiency of $56,664 based on his disallowance of the interest deduction and his determination that taxpayer had in fact realized a substantial gain on the liquidation of IDI. As now presented by the Government, the Commissioner's theory was that, under IRC §675(3), the taxpayer was to be treated as the "owner" of the trust assets and that this crucially affected the tax consequences of the events described above. On this view, transactions involving trust assets were to be re-analyzed after substituting the taxpayer (as the "owner" of those assets) for the trust. Thus, the Commissioner disallowed the $16,000 interest deduction, since the taxpayer was not entitled to a deduction for amounts paid to himself as "owner" of the promissory note held by the trust. Similarly, in computing taxpayer's gain on the liquidation of IDI, the Commissioner reduced taxpayer's basis in the shares acquired from the trust from $320,000 to $30,000. His rationale, apparently, was that the taxpayer could not claim a full "cost" basis in stock acquired in a sale that involved nothing more than a transfer of the property from the taxpayer (as "owner" of the stock) to himself.[2]

In July 1967, taxpayer paid the asserted deficiency, together with interest of $2,470. In February 1969 Mr. and Mrs. Rothstein filed a claim for a refund in the amount of $57,942.12. After this was denied, the Rothsteins filed a protest, which the IRS held for more than five years, during which time Alexander Rothstein died. The protest was finally disallowed and Rothstein's executors and widow brought this refund suit against the United States under 28 U.S.C. §1346(a)(1).

Although both sides were entitled to a jury trial, 28 U.S.C. §2402, the case was tried by the judge with an advisory jury. After denying motions by both sides for a directed verdict, the judge put four interrogatories to the jury. The questions and answers were as follows:

1. Was the sale by the Trustee, Reba Rothstein, to the grantor, Alexander Rothstein, of 300 shares of IDI stock for $320,000 for adequate consideration?

Yes.

2. Was the trustee, Reba Rothstein, subservient to the grantor, Alexander Rothstein, when she accepted a note from Alexander Rothstein in the amount of $320,000 in exchange for the 300 shares of IDI stock from the trust?

Yes.

3. Was adequate security provided by Alexander Rothstein for the $320,000 note given by him in November, 1964 to Reba Rothstein as trustee?

No.

4. Did the note for $320,000 from Alexander Rothstein to Reba Rothstein, as trustee for the children, provide for an adequate rate of interest?

Yes.

---

2. The $30,000 basis asserted by the Commissioner seems to reflect either a carry-over of the trust's basis in the shares or perhaps, as suggested in the Government's brief, taxpayer's original basis in the shares that he transferred to the trust—the two being here identical by virtue of IRC § 1015(a). Using this reduced figure as taxpayer's basis and an appraisal that the property received was worth $950,000, the Commissioner determined that the taxpayer had realized a capital gain of approximately $152,000 on the liquidation of IDI. The Commissioner's gross adjustment—some $184,000— represents the recomputed gain plus the allegedly erroneously computed loss that appeared on taxpayer's return. After the 50% allowable deduction [under former section 1202], this yielded a net increase in taxable income of approximately $92,000, to which was added $16,000 representing the disallowance of the deduction for interest paid to the trust. The resultant deficiency was $56,664, plus interest.

The judge then made findings of fact and conclusions of law pursuant to F.R.Civ.P.52(a). He ruled that the 1964 sale of the IDI stock involved a borrowing of trust funds under the first sentence of IRC §675(3) and, in accordance with the advisory jury's answers with respect to lack of adequate security and subservience, that it did not fall within the exception created by the second sentence. Without further discussion, the judge entered judgment for the Government, presumably because he agreed with the Commissioner that, if §675(3) applied, this would entail disallowance of taxpayer's interest deduction and reduction of his basis in the shares of IDI acquired from the trust.

DISCUSSION

Taxpayer's principal argument on the merits is that his purchase, on credit, of the 300 shares of IDI did not involve a "borrowing" from the trust and therefore did not come within IRC §675(3), which applies only when the grantor "has directly or indirectly borrowed the corpus or income and has not completely repaid the loan, including any interest, before the beginning of the taxable year". The image most immediately conveyed by the statutory language is that of a grantor who has obtained an asset from the trust, whether money or otherwise, in exchange for a promise to return the same asset at some future time. Taxpayer is correct in noting that a transaction like that here in question—a sale of a trust asset on credit—involves no borrowing of the asset sold. However, the Commissioner's argument is that what was "directly or indirectly borrowed" was not the IDI stock but money in the amount of the purchase price. On the Commissioner's view, the trust's extension of credit was a "loan" within the meaning of §675(3), notwithstanding that the loan "proceeds" were immediately used to pay for the shares.

Whether an extension of credit in a sale should be deemed a "loan" for purposes of §675(3) is not easily answered on the basis of the language of the statute alone. On the one hand, Black's Law Dictionary 844 (5th ed. 1979) defines "loan" quite narrowly as the "[d]elivery by one party to and receipt by another party of [a] sum of money upon agreement, express or implied, to repay it with or without interest." This definition suggests that an extension of credit is not a loan unless there is actual delivery of loan proceeds to the obligor. A similar distinction appears to underlie the numerous decisions holding that, for purposes of a usury statute, a sale on credit is not a loan. See, e.g., *Bartholomew v. Northampton Nat'l Bank,* 584 F.2d 1288, 1295 (3 Cir.1978) (Pennsylvania law). On the other hand, it is common enough to conceive of a credit sale as involving a loan, as witness the many statutes referred to as "truth-in-lending" laws, *see, e.g.,* Consumer Credit Protection Act, 15 U.S.C. §1601 *et seq.* ("Truth in Lending Act"), although one hardly says that the purchaser has borrowed the property purchased.[3]

More important in deciding whether §675(3) should apply in the instant case is the object which the statute was intended to serve. As is well known, the purpose of IRC §§671–79 and the regulations that preceded them was to bring order out of the chaos that ha[d] been created by the decision in *Helvering v. Clifford,* 309 U.S. 331, 60 S.Ct. 554, 84 L.Ed. 788 (1940), that a grantor's continued domination of a trust might render trust income taxable to him. This led to over a hundred decisions in the courts of appeals, some holding

---

3. It could be further contended on behalf of the taxpayer that Congress dealt with the subject of purchases from a trust in §675(1) (regarding certain powers "to purchase, exchange, or otherwise deal with or dispose of the corpus or the income therefrom for less than an adequate consideration"), thus arguing for a narrower interpretation of §675(3). Against this is the fact that §675(1) applies only to powers permitting purchases for inadequate consideration, whereas §675(3) applies, irrespective of a previously existing power, where the loan is either inadequately secured or made by "a related or subordinate trustee subservient to the grantor".

Clifford to be applicable and others holding the contrary, with little difference in the facts, see 1 Surrey & Warren, Federal Income Taxation 1340 (1972 ed.). The purpose of the regulations, originally issued in 1945, amended in 1947, and codified in 1954, was "to establish a definite line separating 'Clifford trusts' where income is taxable to the grantor from trusts falling under the general trust sections [where income is taxable to the trust or its distributees]." *Id.* at 1341. The statute directs that the grantor shall be treated as "owner" of a portion of a trust not only when a reversionary interest "will or may reasonably be expected to take effect in possession or enjoyment within 10 years commencing with the date of the transfer of that portion of the trust," [former] §673(a), but in many other instances where, although the trust was expected to have a longer duration, the grantor's powers or acts were thought by the Commissioner and later by Congress to indicate that he remained in effective control.

Section 675, entitled "Administrative powers", is a subset of the many provisions dealing with the retention of substantial interests in and powers over a trust. Broadly speaking, it requires that the grantor be treated as "owner" of a trust when he could engage or has engaged in certain transactions with the trust without providing adequate consideration. In particular, §675(3) addresses those situations in which the grantor has exercised "dominion and control" over a trust by borrowing from it at less than an adequate rate of interest or without giving adequate security for his promise to repay the loan. Indeed, §675(3)'s determination to prevent a grantor's treating a trust as his private bank without paying the tax consequences is so strong that the grantor is to be treated as "owner" even if the rate of interest and the security *are* adequate, unless the loan is made by a trustee other than the grantor or "a related or subordinate trustee subservient to the grantor".

There can be no doubt that the extension of credit in the present case, made without adequate security by a subservient trustee, would fall within the scope of the statute should we deem it a "borrowing" or "loan" under §675(3). We think it is consistent with the overall purpose of Congress to do so. *First,* in view of the fact that the statute is to apply to any grantor who has "borrowed" from the trust, whether "directly *or indirectly*" (emphasis supplied), we cannot attach much weight to the distinction, mentioned above, between (1) an extension of credit in which the proceeds are actually delivered to and received by the obligor, and (2) one in which they are immediately applied to the purchase of an asset from the obligee. *Second,* we must consider the consequences of a decision that an extension of credit like this is not within the scope §675(3). A grantor wishing to obtain a loan from a trust while steering clear of the statute could always do so by arranging for the trust to purchase, for example, marketable securities with a value equal to the amount of the contemplated loan, which the grantor would then purchase from the trust in exchange for his note. The grantor could then sell the securities on the market, leaving him with cash and the trust with his note—just as if it had made him a conventional loan. The only difference would be that §675(3) would not apply, since the extension of credit in the sale did not involve actual delivery of loan proceeds to the grantor. Accepting taxpayer's argument would in effect largely annul §675(3). We therefore adopt the district court's conclusion that the extension of credit here was, at least "indirectly", a "borrowing" within the meaning of the statute.[3a]

3a. Our ruling does not rest on any conclusion that the transaction here in question was a "sham", as Chief Judge Feinberg seems to suggest. We do not question the authenticity of the sale by the trust but adhere to the not very novel proposition that the trust's extension of credit to enable Rothstein to finance the sale was a "borrowing" for purposes of §675(3).

We also note that the hypothetical in the text, which Chief Judge Feinberg would dispose of as a "sham", describes only the most egregious case. One can readily imagine situations in which the asset

While we thus agree with the Government that the taxpayer's purchase of the IDI stock in exchange for his installment note involved a "loan" under §675(3), we disagree with its contention that this requires a complete recharacterization for tax purposes of transactions involving the taxpayer and the trust. If §675(3) stood alone, we might agree that taxpayer's "ownership" of trust assets should prevent his claiming a deduction for interest paid on the note or a full cost basis in the shares acquired from the trust. However, §675 is only one of a battery of provisions, see §§673–74, 676–79, requiring that the grantor or another person be treated as the "owner" of trust assets. All of these provisions are subject to §671, in which Congress expressly stated the consequences of such "ownership":

> Where it is specified in this subpart [§§671–79] that the grantor ... shall be treated as the owner of any portion of a trust, there shall then be included in computing the taxable income and credits of the grantor ... those items of income, deductions, and credits against tax which are attributable to that portion of the trust to the extent such items would be taken into account under this chapter in computing taxable income or credits against the tax of an individual. Any remaining portion of the trust shall be subject to subparts A through D [§§641–68].

Section 671 makes it plain that it was not Congress's intention that the taxation of grantor/"owners" be governed by what might otherwise seem the sensible general principle that a taxpayer may not have meaningful dealings with himself.[4] Rather, the statute envisions (1) that the income and deductions of the grantor and the trust will be computed in the normal fashion, the trust being treated as a fully independent tax-paying entity, and (2) that the relevant "items of income, deductions, and credits against tax" that would ordinarily appear on the trust's return will instead "be included in computing the taxable income and credits of the grantor". Nowhere does §671 direct that the grantor's basis in property purchased from the trust be deemed any different from what it would otherwise be, namely, his cost in acquiring it—in this case $320,000, the amount of taxpayer's note. Nor does the statute contain anything authorizing the Commissioner to disallow an interest deduction on the ground that grantor's payments were made to the trust. Consistently with the objective of *Clifford* to prevent high-bracket taxpayers from shifting income to low-bracket trusts over which they retain or exercise excessive controls, §671 dictates that, when the grantor is regarded as "owner", the trust's income shall be attributed to him—this and nothing more.

In some instances the result of applying §671 as written will be identical with what would have obtained under the Government's approach of recharacterizing the transaction. Here, for example, application of §671 would mean that the trust's $16,000 annual interest income on the promissory note would be included in computing taxpayer's gross income, but would be offset by an equivalent deduction for the interest paid—with the same net result as under the Government's approach, where the taxpayer would be neither entitled to the deduction nor required to treat as income the payments received. But in other instances, the two approaches can yield quite different results. Here, for example, if the full amount of the note had been paid in 1965, the trust would have realized a

in question would be one already held by the trust or something other than a marketable security, but would nonetheless be an item of value for which the grantor would gladly give his unsecured note. It is unclear how such cases would be dealt with under Chief Judge Feinberg's proposal, notwithstanding that they are as much the target of §675(3) as the example in the text.

4. It should be observed that most of the provisions of §§673–79 mandate "ownership" treatment in circumstances in which there may have been no transaction between the grantor and the trust. In those instances, §671 *must* operate by imputing tax items to the grantor, not by recharacterizing his dealings with the trust.

gain in the amount of $290,000 (the excess of $320,000 over the trust's $30,000 carryover basis in the shares transferred to it in 1957, see §1015(a)). Under §671 this gain would be includable in the taxpayer's income, whereas under the Government's approach, which would "disregard" the sale for tax purposes, no one would realize taxable income unless and until the taxpayer sold the stock.

The Government's grievance apparently derives from the fact that, here, in contrast to the hypothetical where the precise application of §671 would work to its advantage in the year 1965, neither the taxpayer nor the trust had reported a capital gain on the sale of the IDI shares in 1964.[5] This, however, is simply a consequence of the provisions of §453, governing installment sales. We disagree with the district court's contention that §453 supplies little aid to the taxpayer here because it was "designed to alleviate a hardship on the *seller* by permitting an installment seller to report a proportionate share of the gain during each year in which he receives proceeds from the sale" (emphasis in original). Under §671 the income of the seller (the trust) is to be computed as in the case of an individual, and as the Government concedes in its brief "the transaction under consideration in this case may properly be characterized as an installment sale, and ... the *seller,* here the trust, may elect to recognize its income proportionately over the period of the payment schedule" (emphasis in original). It is that income, if any there be in the taxable year, which §671 directs shall be imputed to the grantor in cases where, under other sections, he is to be treated as owner of a portion of the trust. Because the trust had no reportable gain in 1965, application of §675(3) to the taxpayer should not increase his tax liability on account of the trust's sale of IDI stock. The reason why taxpayer realized no gain in the liquidation of IDI is not, as the dissent argues, that we are allowing him "to take advantage of the trust's prior election to receive a portion of its proceeds from the taxpayer/grantor on an installment basis", but that the taxpayer obtained a new basis of $320,000 as a consequence of his purchase from the trust and that this resulted in his realizing a loss on his subsequent disposition of the IDI shares. Nothing in §671 says that a grantor shall not be entitled to his usual cost basis in property purchased from a trust of which other sections direct he shall be treated as "owner"; it says only, so far as here relevant, that if his purchase results in taxable gain to the trust, he is taxable on the gain. But here the trust, having properly taken advantage of the opportunity to account for its gain on the installment basis, had no reportable income on the sale to the taxpayer that could be imputed to him under §671. The dissent simply refuses to recognize that the consequences of violating §675(3) are those and only those specified in §671. It is immaterial whether the statutory scheme envisioned by Judge Oakes would achieve better results; we are governed by the statute as it is. Congress specified the consequences of violating §675(3) and similar provisions in §671; we are not at liberty to enlarge upon it.

The judgment dismissing taxpayer's claim is reversed and the cause remanded to the district court for the entry of a judgment in favor of the taxpayer consistent with this opinion.

FEINBERG, Chief Judge (concurring and dissenting):

I feel compelled to write a separate opinion because my view of the transaction in question is entirely different from that of my colleagues. In my judgment, the crucial

---

5. The record does not show whether the trust paid capital gains tax beginning in 1969 when principal payments became taxable under the installment sale provision, IRC §453(b). Neither the taxpayer's nor the Government's counsel was able to respond to our inquiries at argument on this score. The Government's brief tells us only that "[t]he Government has not made any assertions whatever regarding the realization of gain by the seller in this case."

issue is whether IRC §675(3) applies at all to the trust's installment sale of stock to Roth-stein. This issue turns on whether that transaction is a "borrowing" within the meaning of §675(3) or a sale. Although they disagree on the consequences flowing therefrom, both Judges Friendly and Oakes agree that §675(3) applies because they apparently view the in-stallment sale as either a "borrowing" of the purchase price of the stock or an extension of credit equal to the purchase price. I disagree.

The transaction was not a sham sale. There was a mutual exchange of consideration that made both parties better off and that had genuine economic substance. For over seven years prior to the sale, the trust's asset was stock in a closely held corporation, which had paid no dividends to stockholders and for which there was apparently no market. After the sale, the trust held an asset, Rothstein's promissory note, that paid interest and that conceivably could be discounted for cash. It is significant that the advisory jury and the district judge found that the $320,000 installment note was adequate consideration for the stock. For his part, Rothstein received full title to the stock to do with whatever he pleased (which, inci-dentally, is the reason no one is arguing the stock was borrowed). This, and the coordinate purchase of Savin's stock, enabled Rothstein to liquidate the company, reorganize and re-finance it and continue the enterprise, another factor suggesting economic substance to the transaction rather than an attempt to evade the Clifford regulations. The government makes much of the fact that Rothstein did not give security for the promissory note until after the end of the taxable year. Yet Savin gave full title to his stock to Rothstein in October 1964, but was not paid until after Rothstein liquidated the company and took out a mortgage on its former assets in January 1965. Surely, that was not a loan of Savin's stock, nor do I view it as a loan of the purchase price, but simply a deferred payment date. Whatever risk Savin incurred by accepting a deferred payment date without interim security was apparently off-set in his view by the economic gain to him from the deal. The same is true for the trust.

In this case, the Commissioner seeks to recharacterize the transaction because he ap-parently does not like the favorable tax consequences for Rothstein. In a case analogous to this one and also involving the Clifford Regulations, the Ninth Circuit was presented with a sale of stock and other property to a grantor trust in return for a lifetime annuity. It refused to recharacterize the transaction as a reservation of a life estate, which would have caused the trust income to be taxable to the grantor under IRC §§677(a) and 671. *Lafargue v. C.I.R.*, 689 F.2d 845 (9th Cir.1982). The court found that the sale had genuine substance and was not a disguised conduit for distribution of the trust income. The an-nuity was fixed and was not an attempt to approximate the income production of the trust assets. The taxpayer-annuitant bore the risk of early death or appreciation of the trust assets; the trust bore the risk of late demise or depreciation of the trust assets. The court concluded that "[i]n these circumstances, Taxpayer's formal characterization of the transaction as a sale in exchange for an annuity should not be disregarded for tax purposes." Id. at 850. Similarly, because of the economic substance behind the transaction at bar, I do not believe it should be characterized as a "borrowing" within §675(3).

The sham sale analysis that I would apply in determining the applicability of §675(3) does not produce the undesirable consequences suggested by Judge Friendly's hypothet-ical case in which "[a] grantor wishing to obtain a loan from a trust while steering clear of the statute could always do so by arranging for the trust to purchase, for example, mar-ketable securities with a value equal to the amount of the contemplated loan, which the grantor would then purchase from the trust in exchange for his note." ... The hypothe-sized transaction would be patently a sham. There would be no reason for the trust to engage in such a transaction. Why would the trust give up freely marketable securities it had just purchased for a promissory note? Alternatively, if a promissory note was attractive to the trust for some reason, why wouldn't it simply give cash for the promissory note? Because of the lack of economic substance, the government would be permitted to recharacterize the two steps of the hypothetical transaction as a loan of money with which the taxpayer happened to purchase marketable securities.

The real objection that the Commissioner and Judge Oakes appear to have is to the use of the installment sale device between a grantor and trust to produce favorable tax consequences in addition to accomplishing whatever other economic objectives the parties may have. However, as long as the transaction is not a sham, the choice is one Congress has made. The taxpayer is free to structure his transactions, and specifically may choose to employ the installment sale device, to minimize his tax consequences. See *Roberts v. C.I.R.*, 643 F.2d 654 (9th Cir.1981) (installment sale of stock to grantor trust, which resold stock on open market; grantor's use of §453 to defer taxation upheld).

Having concluded that §675(3) does not apply, I have no need to consider the scope of §671. Under my approach, the appreciation of the stock is taxed to the trust as it receives installment payments. In this respect, my approach produces the same result as Judge Friendly's. However, since §671 does not come into play at all under my approach, the interest income on the installment note is also taxed to the trust and is not attributed to Rothstein. Hence he would get a corresponding deduction, which probably would not be a wash because his tax rates for the relevant years are likely to be higher than the trust's. For the purpose of the remand, my position in regard to the interest income is a minority one; both Judges Friendly and Oakes would attribute the trust's interest income to Rothstein. However, were I to view the transaction as a borrowing, as do my colleagues, I would agree with Judge Friendly's interpretation of the consequences under §671.

OAKES, Circuit Judge (dissenting):

Judge Friendly and I agree that under section 675(3), the taxpayer is to be treated as the "owner" of the trust assets because of the "dominion and control" he exercised in borrowing from a trustee who is related and subservient. His opinion also takes the position, with which I am in complete accord, that the trust's carryover basis in the stock was $30,000, i.e., the grantor's basis under section 1015(a).... Thereafter, however, we differ. In particular, we do not agree that after application of section 675(3) the grantor's basis in the IDI shares which he had transferred to the trust and "bought" back from it was $320,000, the trust's "selling price" to him. True, Judge Friendly's approach does avoid the potential danger that *nobody* would be taxed on the difference between the grantor's original basis of $30,000 (which became the trust's basis) and the sum of $320,000; it does so by providing that the grantor pay tax on that gain as if he—like the trust—had elected installment treatment under §453. But the problem with this approach is that it simply does not treat the grantor/taxpayer as if he were the "owner," which is what the statute requires. The difference is, of course, substantial. Were the taxpayer in this case, for example, truly treated as the owner of the stock, his basis would be that of the trust, *i.e.*, the "old" owner, or $30,000.

I would accordingly frame the ultimate question as follows: whether the grantor of a Clifford trust who is deemed the owner of the trust assets by virtue of section 675(3), who sells those assets in the taxable year and realizes the proceeds of such sale (directly or indirectly), can take advantage of the trust's prior election to receive a portion of its proceeds from the taxpayer/grantor on an installment basis, or whether the taxpayer must report the entire gain in the year he in fact realizes it. Thus stated, the question seems to me to answer itself. A taxpayer must report a gain when he realizes it. The taxpayer did not realize his gain on an installment basis and is therefore disentitled to benefit from an installment election on the part of the trust.

In stating the question, I use the word "portion" advisedly. Suppose that the amount the taxpayer received on liquidation (attributable to the trust's shares) was in excess of $320,000. Even under Judge Friendly's proposed result, which would permit the grantor to treat the difference between the $320,000 received and the $30,000 basis as an installment sale, the amount over and above $320,000 would surely be taxable to him as immediate, short-term capital gain.

But of course the gain on the difference between $30,000 and $320,000 is identical in kind to the gain between $320,000 and the amount ultimately received, once the benefits of the Clifford trust have been denied the taxpayer. After all, had the taxpayer never established a trust, he would have been required to report the entire difference as capital gain. He could not have elected to treat the sale on an installment basis for the simple reason that he did not receive the proceeds on an installment basis. Does it make any difference, then, that he did establish a trust which did not comply with the Clifford trust regulations, non-compliance with which triggered the statutory requirement that he be treated as the "owner" of the assets? In my view the answer has to be in the negative irrespective of the language in section 671 relied on by Judge Friendly as the sole basis for his conclusion.

I submit that the language of section 671, insofar as it includes in the grantor's taxable income "those items of income … which are attributable to that portion of the trust," simply does not bear on, indeed it has nothing whatsoever to do with, the trust's election to treat gains on an installment basis. The "item of income" attributable to the grantor under section 671 is the difference between $30,000 and $320,000. How it is to be treated on his tax return is dependent on whether *he* realized it in the taxable year or deferred it by realizing it on an installment basis and taking the installment election. The fact that the taxpayer did not realize that gain in its entirety (as turned out to be the case) simply means that he only has to report it to the extent that he did in fact realize it, not that he is entitled, as Judge Friendly's opinion would inconsistently hold, to treat the entire amount on an installment basis and to deduct the unrealizable portion in the year of his sale.

The grantor, Rothstein, was not himself an installment seller; nor is he to be deemed such by virtue of section 671. Yet under Judge Friendly's analysis, following a transaction after which Rothstein is to be treated as the owner of the assets in question, he is nevertheless allowed to take advantage of the trust's now meaningless election. Nothing in the statute, legislative history, regulations, or cases supports this anomolous [sic] result. In fact, the parties themselves did not even propose this result, which helps explain why nobody knew (or cared) on argument how the trust treated the transaction. From the trust's point of view and against any conceivable suggestion of "double taxation," I would simply point out that once the grantor is treated as the owner and the income or gain thus made attributable to him, there are no tax consequences to the trust, and any election it has made is purely moot. Judge Friendly's opinion does not, as I read it, suggest otherwise.

There is no problem with the grantor's payment of interest to the trust. Whether that payment is treated as a wash, as the Commissioner probably treated it, or whether the trust is perceived as receiving income, which is then functionally offset by allowing the grantor a deduction for interest paid to the trust, as Judge Friendly would have it, there are no tax consequences to either trust or grantor, which is as it should be, when, by virtue of the grantor's failure to comply with the Clifford trust regulations, he is treated as the owner of the assets involved.

* * *

Illustrative Material

In Rev. Rul. 85-13, 1985-1 C.B. 184, the I.R.S. announced that it would not follow *Rothstein* "insofar as it holds that a trust owned by a grantor must be regarded as a separate taxpayer capable of engaging in sales transactions with the grantor." The I.R.S. justified its position as follows:

> It is anomalous to suggest that Congress, in enacting the grantor trust provisions of the Code, intended that the existence of a trust would be ignored for purposes of attribution of income, deduction, and credit, and yet, retain its vitality as a separate entity capable of entering into a sales transaction with the grantor. The reason for attributing items of income, deduction, and credit to the grantor under section 671 is that, by exercising dominion and control over a trust, either by retaining a power over or an interest in the trust, or, as in this case, by dealing with trust property for the grantor's benefit, the grantor has treated the trust property as though it were the grantor's property. The Service position of treating the owner of an entire trust as the owner of the trust's assets is, therefore, consistent with and supported by the rationale for attributing items of income, deduction, and credit to the grantor.

This aspect of *Rothstein* is also criticized in Ascher, *When to Ignore Grantor Trusts: The Precedents, a Proposal, and a Prediction*, 41 Tax L. Rev. 253 (1986).

In *Zand v. Commissioner*, 71 T.C.M. (CCH) 1758 (1996), *aff'd on other grounds*, 143 F.3d 1393 (11th Cir. 1998), the Tax Court found section 675(3) inapplicable to certain loans from certain trusts to their grantor. Instead, the loans qualified under the statutory safe harbor: they provided for adequate interest and adequate security, and a majority of the trustees who made the loans were neither related nor subordinate to the grantor under the section 672(c) definition, though they were the grantor's lawyers.

A second aspect of *Zand* also merits attention. The I.R.S., apparently relying on an extension of Revenue Ruling 85-13, asserted grantor trust status, through non-compliance with the statutory safe harbor of section 675(3), in an effort to deny the grantor deductions for the interest on the loans. After determining that the safe harbor applied, and that section 675(3) itself therefore did not, the Tax Court continued, in dictum:

> Moreover, even if section 675(3) did apply, its effect by its terms is to tax all or a portion of the trust income to petitioner. It does not provide for the disallowance of the interest expenses claimed by him. Indeed, the net result to the grantor may be no increase in tax because the trusts' interest income taxed to the grantor may be offset by a deduction for interest on the loans.

71 T.C.M. (CCH) at 1824. This analysis is conceptually at odds with Revenue Ruling 85-13. It is also flatly contrary to Private Letter Ruling 9535026 (1995), which ruled that grantor trusts could not deduct interest they paid on indebtedness to their grantors; neither were the grantors subject to taxation on the interest their grantor trusts paid them on the indebtedness. It is also inconsistent with Proposed Reg. §1.671-2(f), announced in 1996, which states:

> For purposes of subtitle A of the Internal Revenue Code, a person that is treated as the owner of any portion of a trust under subpart E is considered to own the trust assets attributable to that portion of the trust.

An accompanying explanation states that a person treated as owner of any portion of a trust under subpart E "is considered to own the trust assets attributable to that portion of the trust *for all federal income tax purposes.*" REG-209826-96, 1996-2 C.B. 498, 503 (emphasis added).

Problems

4-12. G creates an *inter vivos* trust. All of the income is to be paid to C, G's child, for C's life. Upon C's death, the trust is to terminate, and the principal is to be paid to C's then living issue, *per stirpes*. First National Bank is trustee. Does section 675 treat G as owner of any portion of the trust?

4-13. Assume the facts of Problem 4-12, except that G retains the right to reacquire the trust property upon tendering to the trustee property of equal value.

4-14. Assume the facts of Problem 4-12, except that the trustee is authorized to make loans to the grantor without adequate interest or without adequate security. What if the trustee were authorized to make such loans to everyone?

4-15. Assume the facts of Problem 4-12. No language in the trust agreement authorizes the trustee to make loans without adequate interest or without adequate security.

a. G obtains from the trust a no-interest loan for which he gives no security. G has not repaid the loan.

b. While G's wife is trustee, G obtains from the trust a market-interest-rate loan for which he gives full security. G has not repaid the loan.

c. Assume the facts of Problem 4-15(b), except that G's partner is trustee when the loan is made.

(vi) Powers of Revocation

———————

Internal Revenue Code:
    Section 676

Regulation:
    Section 1.676(a)-1

———————

Revenue Ruling 62-148
1962-2 C.B. 153

Advice has been requested as to the person who is required to report, for Federal income tax purposes, the income from a savings account in a bank or other savings organization in the State of New York when the deposit consists of the depositor's own funds and is made in his own name "as trustee" for another person.

The taxpayer in the instant case deposited his own funds in a New York savings bank in his own name "as trustee" for his minor son. There was no other evidence as to his intention in making the deposit.

Section 676(a) of the Internal Revenue Code of 1954 provides, in part, that the grantor shall be treated as the owner of any portion of a trust where at any time the power to revest in the grantor title to such portion is exercisable by the grantor.

Section 671 of the Code provides the general rule that in cases where the grantor or another person is regarded as the owner of any portion of a trust, there shall be included in computing his taxable income and credits those items of income, deductions, and credits against the tax of the trust which are attributable to that portion of the trust to the extent that such items would be taken into account in computing the taxable income or credits against the tax of an individual.

One of the essential elements of a trust is an intention on the part of the owner of property to create a trust. A trust is created only if the settler [sic] properly manifests an intention to create a trust. Section 23, Restatement of Trusts, Second Edition.

Under New York law, [in] the absence of evidence of a different intention of the depositor, the fact that a deposit is made in a savings bank in the name of the depositor "as trustee" for another person is sufficient to show only an intention to create a revocable trust. See *In re Totten,* 179 N.Y. 112, 71 N.E. 748 (1904); also section 58 Restatement of Trusts, Second Edition. Such trusts have been variously referred to as Totten trusts, tentative trusts, pass book trusts, parole trusts, and savings bank trusts.

The depositor, in such cases, is held to have intended to reserve a power to withdraw the whole or any part of the deposit at any time during his lifetime or otherwise to revoke the trust. Thus, tentative trusts of savings bank deposits in New York are valid, although revocable; and the grantor of such a trust may revest, in himself, title to all or any portion of the trust by merely withdrawing all or any part of the account.

Accordingly, it is held that the depositor in the instant case is treated as the owner of the trust under the provisions of section 676 of the Code and is required, by section 671 of the Code, to include the income of the trust in his gross income for Federal income tax purposes.

Illustrative Material

1. For a similar result under California law, see *Heintz v. Commissioner,* 41 T.C.M. (CCH) 429 (1980).

2. *Cahill v. Commissioner,* 43 T.C.M. (CCH) 1250 (1982), cited and discussed Rev. Rul. 62-148 with approval. However, the court held that the taxpayer had proven by a preponderance of the evidence that the funds in two savings accounts registered in the name of his former wife in trust for her father had belonged not to her but to her father. The court also determined that under New York law "only where a person deposits *his own funds* as trustee for another is a 'Totten trust' created." (emphasis added) Thus, no Totten trust had existed, and Rev. Rul. 62-148 was inapplicable. As a result, the interest on the savings accounts was not taxable to the taxpayer's former wife under section 676. *Cahill* flatly rejected the I.R.S. argument that a bank account carried in one's name in trust for another necessarily constituted a Totten trust.

3. In Rev. Rul. 57-8, 1957-1 C.B. 204, the I.R.S. treated the grantor as owner of all portions of a trust under which the trustee, a nonadverse party, had discretion to pay both income and principal to or for the benefit of the grantor. The I.R.S. concluded that the trustee's power constituted a "power to revest" the trust property in the grantor under section 676(a).

4. In Rev. Rul. 66-161, 1966-1 C.B. 164, the grantor retained a reversionary interest. Under the terms of the trust agreement, capital gains were allocated to principal. Section 677(a)(2) therefore treated the grantor as owner of the principal portion of the trust. As a result, he was taxable on the trust's capital gains. In addition, the grantor retained the right to withdraw, at any time, all capital gains on which he was subject to taxation. The I.R.S. therefore ruled that he had a power to revest in himself title to the portion of the principal attributable to capital gains realized by the trust. Accordingly, section 676 treated him as owner of both the income and the principal of that

portion. As to that portion, the grantor was taxable on both capital gains and ordinary income.

5. Two grantors retained the right to terminate a trust at any time by their joint action, in which case they would share the trust property equally. The Third Circuit held that the predecessor of section 676 caused each of them to be treated as owner of one-half the trust property. The court rejected the argument that each grantor's right to succeed to all of the trust property if the other died without issue caused the grantors to be adverse parties within the meaning of the predecessor of section 676(a). *de Amodio v. Commissioner,* 299 F.2d 623 (3d Cir. 1962).

Problems

4-16. Assume the facts of Problem 4-12, except that the trust is revocable by G.

4-17. Assume the facts of Problem 4-12, except that the trust is revocable by G, but only with C's consent.

4-18. Assume the facts of Problem 4-12, except that the trust is revocable by G, but only with the trustee's consent.

(vii) Retained Income Interests

(a) In General

Internal Revenue Code:
    Section 677(a)

Regulation:
    Section 1.677(a)-1

Section 677 deals, generally, with retained income interests. It is frequently applicable, not only because the types of interests it specifies are frequently retained but also because it specifies several different kinds of retained interests.

If a grantor retains a mandatory income interest, or if a grantor creates a mandatory income interest in the grantor's spouse, section 677 treats the grantor as owner of the income portion of the trust. In such a case, in the words of section 677(a)(1), the "income ... is ... distributed to the grantor or the grantor's spouse."

Not every trust under which income "is ... distributed" to the grantor is a grantor trust, however. Section 677(a) requires that the income be distributed "without the approval or consent of any adverse party." In *Commissioner v. Makransky,* 321 F.2d 598 (3d Cir. 1963), a grantor, who was not entitled to receive income under the terms of the trust agreement, nonetheless received trust income pursuant to the agreement of all the beneficiaries. Rejecting the I.R.S. argument that the grantor should be taxed on the trust's income under section 677, the court wrote:

> [S]ection 677(a) of the 1954 Code specifies an additional situation in which trust income is taxable to the grantor, namely where trust income "is" in fact distributed to the grantor "without the approval or consent of any adverse party". In the present case, trust income was in fact distributed to the grantor, not in the

exercise of a power reserved to him in the terms of the trust or in fulfillment of an obligation to him notwithstanding the wishes of the beneficiaries, but pursuant to the request or consent of all of the adverse parties. Thus, an explicit requirement of the statute has not been met. No case has been found in which section 677(a) has been applied to an agreed distribution thus made to a grantor without supporting sanction in the terms of the trust.

A contrary result would permit tax avoidance through income-splitting for which no sanction appears in the "grantor-trust" sections. It would permit any inter vivos trust, which, in a taxable year, has earned more income than its grantor, to minimize the federal income taxes payable on the aggregate income of the grantor, the trust and beneficiaries, by paying current trust income to the grantor, with the consent of the beneficiaries. This risk would be enhanced in a case, such as this, where the grantor and the beneficiaries are the natural objects of one another's generosity.

321 F.2d at 603–04.

Makransky, however, clearly does not stand for the proposition that only grantors who retain (or create for their spouses) mandatory income interests are described in section 677(a)(1). Far from it. Retention or creation for a spouse of a discretionary income interest also causes the grantor to be treated as owner of the income portion of the trust. *See, e.g., Amabile v. Commissioner,* 51 T.C.M. (CCH) 963 (1986). In such a case, in the words of section 677(a)(1), "income ... may be ... distributed to the grantor or the grantor's spouse." Here, again, the statute limits its applicability to interests that are not subject to the discretion of an adverse party. Under section 677(a), the discretion must be that of "the grantor or a nonadverse party, or both."

In addition to being taxable on the income portion of a trust, a grantor/income beneficiary may be taxable, under section 677(a)(1), on income ordinarily allocable to principal (e.g., capital gains) if, under local law or the governing instrument, the trustee is authorized to distribute such income to the grantor/income beneficiary. *See de Amodio v. Commissioner,* 299 F.2d 623 (3d Cir. 1962) (construing predecessor of section 677). Such a situation would exist if the trustee were authorized to allocate the item in question to either income or principal, as in *de Amodio.* Or it would exist if the grantor were entitled to receive certain amounts, payable out of either income or principal, as in *Samuel v. Commissioner,* 306 F.2d 682 (1st Cir. 1962).

Duffy v. United States

487 F.2d 282 (6th Cir. 1973)
cert. denied, 416 U.S. 938 (1974)

McCREE, Circuit Judge.

The government appeals from a judgment for taxpayers in an action to recover income taxes paid upon assessment of a deficiency by the Internal Revenue Service for the calendar years 1963 to 1966.... The district court's opinion is reported at 343 F.Supp. 4 (S.D.Ohio 1972).

The taxpayers, F. Paul Duffy, a physician, and his wife, Virginia H. Duffy, purchased improved real estate in Cincinnati, Ohio on July 31, 1962, for use by Dr. Duffy in his medical practice. Shortly thereafter, on February 26, 1963, the Duffys executed a trust agreement[1] pursuant to which they conveyed this property to the Provident Bank as trustee. On the same day, the Duffys and the bank executed a five year leaseback agreement, renewable for an additional five years, in which Dr. Duffy agreed to pay an annual rent of $8,650, an amount stipulated as reasonable.

The trust agreement created four trusts, one for the benefit of each of their children: James, born on May 30, 1945; Timothy, born on November 23, 1948; Julia, born on August 7, 1951; and Eileen, born on November 8, 1956. These trusts were made irrevocable for 10 years and 30 days and amendable and revocable thereafter. The trust instrument provides that a beneficiary, while a minor, may receive, if necessary in the sole discretion of the trustee, his share of the trust principal or the income generated by it for his education, maintenance or welfare. Income not distributed for these purposes is to be accumulated by the trustee. When each child reaches his majority, his share of the accumulated and unexpended trust income is to be made part of the accumulated and unexpended trust corpus.[2] However, his share of the trust income accruing thereafter must be distributed to him. Moreover, unless the trust is revoked or amended as it may be after 10 years and 30 days, the principal and the income accumulated during the minority of each child will be distributed among the beneficiaries when the youngest becomes 25. No beneficiary has ever received any income during his minority. However, on May 30, 1966, James, the eldest Duffy child, became 21 and began receiving the income thereafter accruing to his trust.

During the tax years 1963 through 1966, taxpayers did not include in their income the taxable income received by the trust from the rental of the property to Dr. Duffy....

Pursuant to an audit of taxpayers' joint returns for the tax years 1963, 1964, 1965, and 1966, the Internal Revenue Service (IRS) concluded that ... the taxable income of the trust should have been included in taxpayers' income for these years....

The district court found that the taxable trust income for the years in question was not includable in taxpayers' income....

In this appeal the government argues that ... the district court erred in holding that the bank is an "adverse party" as defined by section 672(a) ... and that therefore the Duffys should have included in their income the taxable trust income under section 677(a)(2).... Taxpayers argue, however, that because the trust comes within the excepting clause of section 677, there is no need to consider whether the bank is an "adverse party"....

We hold that the taxable income of the trust should have been included in the taxpayers' income under section 677(a)(2)....

---

1. The trust in this case is similar to a "Clifford" trust, a designation derived from the United States Supreme Court's decision in *Helvering v. Clifford*, 309 U.S. 331, 60 S.Ct. 554, 84 L.Ed. 788 (1940). In that case, the grantor acted as trustee of a trust, created for the benefit of his wife. The present sections of the Internal Revenue Code, 26 U.S.C. §§671–78 (1967) were enacted to overcome the problems and to close the loopholes in the 1939 Code. A basic concern addressed by both the old and new trust taxation provisions is the ability of one taxable unit, for example, a family, to multiply itself into several taxable units by the creation of trusts.

2. The district court apparently misunderstood the provisions of the trust instrument. Thus, the court stated, in distinguishing *Humphrey v. C. I. R.*, 39 T.C. 199 (1962), that "[t]he clear language and intent of section 2 of the trust agreement is for the *trustee* to accumulate the income of the trust for the benefit of the *beneficiaries* and to distribute such accumulated income to the *beneficiaries* upon their reaching a certain age." *Duffy v. United States*, 343 F.Supp. 4, 8 (1972). If the trust instrument had provided that all accumulated income must be distributed to the beneficiaries, the trust income would not have been includable in the taxpayers' income.

Section 677(a)(2) … provides…. This provision is followed immediately by an "excepting" clause which [prior to amendment by the Tax Reform Act of 1986] provide[d] that

> [t]his subsection shall not apply to a power the exercise of which can only affect the beneficial enjoyment of the income for a period commencing after the expiration of a period such that the grantor would not be treated as the owner under section 673 if the power were a reversionary interest; but the grantor may be treated as the owner after the expiration of the period unless the power is relinquished.

This section is dispositive of the issues in this case: first, whether the taxpayers are exempt from the application of the general rule of the section by virtue of the excepting clause, and second, if the taxpayers do not come within the excepting clause, whether the institutional trustee is an "adverse party" within the meaning of the general rule. We hold that the taxpayers cannot avail themselves of the excepting clause and that the Provident Bank is not an adverse party.

To come within the excepting clause, taxpayers argue, they need only show that they had no power during the initial ten years of the trusts to control the beneficial enjoyment of the trust income. If during this period they could not control the disposition of trust income, they argue that the taxable trust income should be taxed to the trust, not to them. Taxpayers attempt to bolster this argument by referring to section 673 … which [prior to amendment by the Tax Reform Act of 1986] provide[d] in relevant part:

> (a) *General Rule.* — The grantor shall be treated as the owner of any portion of a trust in which he has a reversionary interest in either the corpus or the income therefrom if, as of the inception of that portion of the trust, the interest will or may reasonably be expected to take effect in possession or enjoyment within 10 years commencing with the date of the transfer of that portion of the trust.

We, however, interpret the reference to section 673 in the excepting clause to section 677 as referring not merely to the ten year period of time during which the grantor of a trust may not have an existing exercisable power to affect the distribution of trust income but also to the income received by the trust during that ten year period. Thus, we do not agree with taxpayers that a grantor of a trust is entitled to the benefits of the excepting clause of section 677 as long as he may not during the initial ten year period of the trust affect the disposition of the trust income even though after ten years and a day the grantor may cause the accumulated trust income to be distributed to himself.

Nor does the last part of the excepting clause, "but the grantor may be treated as the owner after the expiration of the [ten year] period unless the power is relinquished," compel a contrary interpretation. That part of the excepting clause provides only that subsection 677(a) does not apply to powers the exercise of which can affect the beneficial enjoyment of trust income received only after ten years. This provision was intended to insure that a power over trust income received after the initial ten year period would not itself taint the trust income received during the ten year period. It was not intended to exempt a grantor from taxation on trust income received during the ten year period if after the expiration of that period the grantor has the power to dispose of that very income. S.Rep.No. 1622, 83d Cong., 2d Sess. 371; 3 United States Code Cong. & Admin. News, pp. 4621, 5012 (1954).

Our interpretation of the excepting clause of section 677 is supported by the considered interpretation of the agencies charged with administering the tax laws. Thus, Treas.Reg.

§1.677(a)-1(e), (f) (1965) explains the excepting clause as follows.... [The court also reproduces Treas.Reg. §1.677(a)-1(g).]

Moreover, in 1957, the Internal Revenue Service issued a ruling in which it adopted the same interpretation of the excepting clause of section 677 under the following circumstances. The grantor created a trust, irrevocable for 12 years, in which an independent trustee was empowered to expend any and all of the trust principal and income for the education, maintenance and welfare of the beneficiary, the grantor's child. Any income not expended or distributed could be accumulated or invested by the trustee at his discretion. At the expiration of the trust, the trustee was required to return to the grantor any principal not expended or distributed and to the grantor or the beneficiary any accumulations of income. In that case the grantor-taxpayer also argued that the trust provisions fell within the excepting clause of section 677. However, the IRS found that because the trustee's power over current income, that is, income accruing to the trust during its 12 year life, might in fact result in the accumulation of income not for the benefit of the beneficiary but for the benefit of the grantor, the grantor was taxable for trust income received during the 12 year period. The IRS expressed its opinion in the following rule: "where the trustee has a power to withhold distribution of trust income from the beneficiary and accumulate the amount so withheld for ultimate distribution to the grantor or to his estate, the grantor will be treated as the owner of the trust under the provisions of section 677(a)(2) of the Internal Revenue Code of 1954, and the income therefrom will be taxable to him." Rev.Rul. [57-363], 1957-2 Cum.Bull. 326, 329.

This Revenue Ruling was relied upon by the court in Humphrey v. United States, 245 F.Supp. 49 (D.Kan.1965), where the court reached the result we reach here in considering the taxability of the grantor of a trust having provisions similar to the trust in this case.[4] There, the grantor-taxpayer created a trust for the benefit of his children, irrevocable for 15 years, in which the trust corpus consisted of the grantor's one-third interest in a partnership. The trustee, the grantor, his brother and his father, were authorized to invest or accumulate the earnings of the trust. The trust instrument provided that after the expiration of the trust, all trust property remaining and unexpended would at the option of the grantor revert to him. The court found that because the trustees were empowered to accumulate trust income which might, after 15 years, be distributed to the grantor, the grantor should be treated as the owner of the trust from its inception.

We believe that the Code, the regulations and rulings promulgated thereunder, and the court's decision in *Humphrey, supra,* require that when a trustee has the power to accumulate trust income during the initial ten years of the trust and this income may thereafter be received by the grantor, the grantor may not avail himself of the excepting clause of section 677.

Accordingly, the taxpayers in this case are subject to the general rule of section 677(a) unless the trustee is an adverse party within the meaning of section 672(a).... Section 672 defines an adverse party as "any person having a substantial beneficial interest in the trust which would be adversely affected by the exercise or nonexercise of the power which he possesses respecting the trust...." Section 672(a), on its face, defines an adverse party as a person having a beneficial interest in the trust, that is, a beneficiary of the trust. In this case, the Provident Bank is not a beneficiary and is not, therefore, an adverse party. This conclusion is reinforced by ... Treas.Reg. 1.672(a)-(1) (1956).

---

4. This case is substantially the same as *Humphrey v. C. I. R.,* note 2, *supra,* discussed by the district court, involving identical trusts created by one Humphrey brother in the one case, and the other Humphrey brother in the other.

We, therefore, reject taxpayers' argument that a trustee who is independent of the grantor of a trust may properly be considered an adverse party because he is required by law to act solely in the interest of the beneficiaries of the trust. Both the language of the statute requiring an adverse party to have a beneficial interest in the trust and the Treasury Department's reasonable interpretation of this definition that a trustee, *qua* trustee, is not an adverse party preclude placing such a gloss on the statute.

Therefore, because the Provident Bank, as trustee, is not an adverse party and because under the terms of the trust it may accumulate trust income during the initial ten years of the trust for possible future distribution to the grantors without the consent of the beneficiaries, we determine that the taxable trust income is properly includable in taxpayers' income.

Reversed and remanded for proceedings not inconsistent with this opinion.

Illustrative Material

1. *Adolph K. Krause*, 57 T.C. 890 (1972), *aff'd*, 497 F.2d 1109 (6th Cir. 1974), *cert. denied*, 419 U.S. 1108 (1975), reached the same conclusion on the section 677(a)(2) issue. The Tax Court held that section 677(a)(2) applied if income accumulated during the ten-year period then described in section 673 could, in the discretion of the trustee, be distributed to the grantor after expiration of the ten-year period.

2. Compare *Duffy* and *Krause* with Rev. Rul. 84-14, 1984-1 C.B. 147. In that ruling the trustee of a ten-year reversionary trust was required to "pay or apply so much of the income of the trust to or for the benefit of the [income] beneficiary, as the trustee in the trustee's sole discretion, may deem necessary or appropriate to provide for said beneficiary's health, maintenance, education and support." The I.R.S., without discussion, assumed that the grantor would be treated as owner of the trust's income only to the extent the trustee actually accumulated income. Apparently the I.R.S. reasoned that the trust's ascertainable standard made it impossible for the trustee to accumulate some portion of the income without the consent of an adverse party, i.e., the income beneficiary.

3. *Krause* is noteworthy for another reason. In *United States v. Estate of Grace*, 395 U.S. 316 (1969), the Supreme Court permitted the I.R.S., in applying section 2036, one of the estate tax "grantor trust" rules, to "uncross" reciprocal trusts. The result was that one who had not actually created a trust in which he had a life interest was treated as though he had created it, because he had created a trust in which he gave the grantor of the other trust a life interest. The Court found that the two trusts were "interrelated, and that the arrangement, to the extent of mutual value, [left] the settlors in approximately the same economic position as they would have been in had they created trusts naming themselves as life beneficiaries." 395 U.S. at 324.

Krause extended the reciprocal trust doctrine to subpart E. In *Krause*, husband and wife each created three trusts. Under each of husband's trusts the trustee was authorized, after the ten-year period then described in section 673, to pay wife accumulated income. Under each of wife's trusts the trustee was similarly authorized to pay accumulated income to husband. Because the version of section 677 then applicable described only income interests retained by *the grantor* (the current version describes income interests in either the grantor or the grantor's spouse), section 677 seemed not to apply. Under the reciprocal trust doctrine, however, husband was treated as grantor of wife's trusts, and wife was treated as grantor of husband's trusts, to the extent of mutual value. Current section 677 would treat each spouse as owner of the entire trust he or she created, unassisted by the reciprocal trust doctrine. But *Krause* nonetheless remains significant. The reciprocal trust doctrine applies to interrelated trusts regardless of whether the grantors are spouses. Section 677 does not. *See generally* Van Horn, *Reciprocal Trusts Revisited*, 19 Prac. Tax Law. 39 (2005); Hader, *Planning to Avoid the Reciprocal Trust Doctrine*, 26 Est. Plan. 358 (1999); Marty-Nelson, *Taxing Reciprocal Trusts: Charting a Doctrine's Fall from* Grace, 75 N.C. L. Rev. 1781 (1997).

4. Section 677(a)(2) "applies only where the trust indenture itself gives the grantor, or someone not having an interest adverse to his, discretionary power to divert trust income to him." *Commissioner v. Makransky,* 321 F.2d 598, 603 (3d Cir. 1963). Thus, a grantor who was not entitled to receive trust income under the terms of the trust agreement but nonetheless received it pursuant to the agreement of the beneficiaries was not described in section 677(a)(2). Presumably the same result would occur if the trustee distributed income to the grantor in violation of the terms of the trust agreement and without the consent of the beneficiaries.

Revenue Ruling 58-242
1958-1 C.B. 251

Advice has been requested concerning the Federal income ... tax treatment of an irrevocable, reversionary trust, the income of which is for the benefit of individuals other than the grantor and which terminates ten years and six months from the creation of the trust, or upon the earlier deaths of the beneficiaries.

On October 15, 1955, the taxpayer entered into a trust agreement with a bank and transferred to the trust a certain amount of cash. Under the agreement, the bank is the trustee of the trust. The income beneficiary of the trust is the taxpayer's daughter during the daughter's lifetime, but in no event is the term of the trust to extend beyond April 15, 1966. In the event of the daughter's death during the term of the trust, the income of the trust becomes payable in equal shares to any surviving children of the grantor; and, if there are no surviving children of the grantor then living, the trust income is to be paid to the grantor's husband during his lifetime, but in no event beyond April 15, 1966. On termination of the trust, the trustee is to pay over the principal of the trust to the grantor, or to the grantor's estate in the event that the grantor is not living at that time. The trust agreement is irrevocable and is not subject to modification. Neither the grantor nor her husband has retained any administrative powers over the trust or the trust property. The period of the trust is therefore for ten years and six months, or until the earlier deaths of the beneficiaries.

Section 671 of the Internal Revenue Code of 1954 provides, in part, that the grantor of a trust shall include, in computing his taxable income and credits, those items of income, deduction, and credit against tax which are attributable to or included in any portion of a trust of which he is treated as the owner under the provisions of section[s] 673 to 677, inclusive, of the Code.

[Former s]ection 673(a) of the Code provides, in part, that a grantor, in general, is treated as the owner of any portion of a trust in which he has a reversionary interest in either the corpus or income if, at the inception of the trust, the grantor's interest will or may reasonably be expected to take effect in possession or enjoyment within ten years commencing with the date of transfer of that portion of the trust. Section 1.673(a)-1(b) of the Income Tax Regulations provides, in part, that if the grantor's reversionary interest is to take effect on or after the death of an income beneficiary or upon the expiration of a specific term of years, whichever is earlier, the grantor is treated as the owner if the specific term of years is less than ten years (but not if the term is ten years or longer).

Even though the duration of the trust may be such that the grantor is not treated as the owner under section 673 of the Code, and therefore is not taxed on the "ordinary income" of the trust (*i. e.*, income for trust accounting purposes), he may nevertheless be treated as an owner under section 677(a)(2) of the Code if he has a reversionary interest in the corpus of the trust.

Section 677(a)(2) of the Code provides that if income is held or accumulated in any taxable year for future distribution to the grantor, the grantor shall be treated as an owner for that taxable year.

Under the law of the state in which the trust was created, capital gains realized by the trust must be added to the trust corpus. Since the principal of the trust is to be paid over by the trustee to the grantor on April 15, 1966, or upon the earlier deaths of the beneficiaries, any capital gains realized by the trust must be "held or accumulated for future distribution to the grantor." Under the provisions of section 677(a)(2) of the Code, the grantor is therefore considered as owner of the portion of the trust to which any capital gains are attributable.

* * *

Accordingly, it is held that the ordinary income of the irrevocable trust described herein which is distributable to individual beneficiaries other than the grantor, the principal of which reverts to the grantor or to her estate after a period of more than ten years, or upon the earlier deaths of the beneficiaries, is taxable to such beneficiaries under subpart B or subpart C of part I of subchapter J of the Code. Where applicable state law requires that capital gains realized by the trust must be added to the trust corpus, and the grantor retains no right or power other than that of reversionary interest in the corpus, the grantor must include the capital gains in the computation of her taxable income for the taxable year in which they were realized by the trust under section 677 of subpart E of part I of subchapter J of the Code.

* * *

Illustrative Material

1. Rev. Rul. 79-223, 1979-2 C.B. 254, Rev. Rul. 75-267, 1975-2 C.B. 255, and Rev. Rul. 66-161, 1966-1 C.B. 164, are to the same effect.

2. Rev. Rul. 75-267 also ruled that the estate of a grantor, to which a reversion passed upon the grantor's death, could not be treated under section 677 as owner of any portion of the trust, because "the estate [was] a taxable person separate from the grantor." Thus, upon the grantor's death the trust ceased to be a grantor trust, even as to principal.

3. In Rev. Rul. 66-313, 1966-2 C.B. 245, a grantor proposed creation of two separate trusts, each for the benefit of her three children. One of the trusts was to be funded solely with insurance policies on the grantor's life. The income payable to each child from the other trust was to be applied, pursuant to the written consent of each of the children, toward payment of the premiums on the policies held by the insurance trust.

The I.R.S ruled that the grantor would be treated under section 677(a)(3) as owner of any income so used. Clearly, the hoped-for effect of the proposed transaction was avoidance of section 677(a)(3); however, the I.R.S. articulated no reason for ignoring what seemed to be careful adherence to formalities that arguably did avoid section 677(a)(3). Such a reason might have been found in the ephemeral consent of the children to application of their shares of the one trust's income toward the payment of the insurance premiums.

In *L.B. Foster,* 8 T.C. 197 (1947), *acq.,* 1947-1 C.B. 2, a similar situation arose under a predecessor of section 677(a)(3). In *Foster,* the grantor's wife had used trust income to pay premiums on insurance policies on the grantor's life. Though the trust income technically had belonged to the wife, as beneficiary, the court detected a "plan for payment of the premiums out of trust income." The grantor therefore was taxed on all trust income so used.

4. Though section 677(a)(3) seems to apply whenever the grantor or a nonadverse party can apply trust income to the payment of premiums on an insurance policy on the life of either the grantor or the grantor's spouse, the courts have substantially limited its scope. In order for section 677(a)(3) to apply, a specified life insurance policy must actually exist. *Corning v. Commissioner,* 104 F.2d 329, 333 (6th Cir. 1939); *Genevieve F. Moore,* 39 B.T.A. 808 (1939), *acq.,* 1939-2 C.B. 25. Moreover, even when such a policy does exist, the grantor is subject to taxation on only the income actually used to pay the premiums. *Joseph Weil,* 3 T.C. 579 (1944), *acq.,* 1944 C.B. 29.

Problems

4-19. G creates an *inter vivos* trust. The trustee is authorized to distribute such of the income to the grantor's sister, S, as the trustee, in its sole discretion, sees fit. Upon the expiration of a period of years long enough to avoid the application of section 673, the trust is to terminate, and all of the trust property, including any undistributed income, is to be paid to G. First National Bank is the trustee. Does section 677 treat G as owner of any portion of the trust? What if S were trustee?

4-20. Assume the facts of Problem 4-19, except that, upon termination of the trust, G is to be paid only the trust principal; accumulated income is to be paid to S.

(b) Discharge of Obligations

————

Internal Revenue Code:
   Section 677(a), (b)
Regulations:
   Sections 1.677(a)-1(d); 1.677(b)-1

————

Victor W. Krause
56 T.C. 1242 (1971)

FEATHERSTON, *Judge:* Respondent determined a deficiency in petitioners' Federal income tax for 1964 in the amount of $91,249.05. The issue for decision is whether funds derived by trusts from dividends and loans and used, pursuant to the trust instruments, to pay the gift taxes resulting from the creation of the trusts are income taxable to petitioners.

The facts, all stipulated, show that during September of 1963, petitioner created three trusts: One for the benefit of the children of his son, Gordon C. Krause (hereinafter the Gordon trust), and one for the benefit of the children of each of his daughters, Elizabeth K. Sherwood and Ruth K. Sherwood (hereinafter the Elizabeth and Ruth trusts, respectively). To the Gordon trust, petitioner transferred 12,000 shares of common stock in Wolverine Shoe & Tanning Corp. To the Elizabeth and Ruth trusts, respectively, he transferred 8,000 shares of common stock in the same corporation. The total value of the stock was $807,000, and petitioner's basis in it was $21,700.

The Gordon trust agreement provides:

> 2. The Trustees shall promptly pay all Federal Gift Taxes and all other taxes which shall arise out of or be attributable to the transfer by this Trust Agreement of the above mentioned shares of corporate stock, and said corporate stock is transferred hereby subject to the duty and obligation of the Trustees to promptly pay all such taxes. In order to provide funds with which to pay said taxes the Trustees in their sole and absolute discretion may sell and convert to cash such portions of said corporate stock as they may deem necessary for that purpose or they may borrow sufficient funds for that purpose from such sources, including themselves or either of them, as they may deem proper, and pledge any part of the principal and income of this Trust as security for such loan, or they may obtain funds for the payment of all such taxes partly by sale of assets of said Trust and partly by loan secured by all or any part of the principal and income of this Trust, all in accordance with their sole and absolute discretion.

> 3. All income and earnings of this Trust shall be used and applied by the Trustees in such amounts and at such times as they in their sole and absolute discretion from time to time shall determine for the following purposes, namely:

> First—for the payment of all taxes and assessments and other governmental charges which may be lawfully imposed upon the principal and/or income of this Trust.

> Second—for the payment of all proper charges and expenses incurred by the Trustees and their agents and attorneys in and about the faithful administration of this Trust.

The Elizabeth and Ruth trust agreements contain basically similar provisions, differing only in that each further provides that the trustees—

> may obtain funds for the payment of all such [gift] taxes partly by sale of assets of the principal of said trust, partly from income thereof, and partly by loan secured by all or any part of the principal and/or income of this trust * * *

In April of 1964, the trustees of the three trusts pledged the stock which they had received from petitioner to Old Kent Bank & Trust Co., one of the trustees, as security for loans in the total amount of $134,500. With these funds, the trustees, on April 14, 1964, paid the joint and several gift tax liabilities of petitioner and his wife, both of whom had consented pursuant to section 2513 to having the gifts treated as made one-half by each of them. The total amount of taxes so paid was $134,331.65. During their fiscal years ending August 31, 1964, the trusts received the following amounts of dividend income:

	Sept. to Apr. 14	Apr. 15 to Aug. 31	Total
Gordon	$3,600	$4,050	$7,650
Elizabeth	2,400	2,700	5,100
Ruth	2,400	2,700	5,100
Total	$8,400	$9,450	$17,850

Beginning in September of 1964 and continuing through August of 1970, the trusts made periodic payments to Old Kent Bank & Trust Co. to discharge the loans and the interest thereon. These payments were made with dividend income received by the trusts from the stock.

The Code provides generally that the gift tax "shall be paid by the donor." Sec. 2502. When a husband and wife have consented to have a gift made by one of them treated as if made one-half by each of them, they are jointly and severally liable for the full amount of the tax liability arising from the transfer. Sec. 2513(d). The donee, under section 6324(b), is personally liable for the tax only if it is not paid when due. *Fletcher Trust Co. v. Commissioner*, 141 F. 2d 36, 39 (C.A. 7, 1944), affirming 1 T.C. 798 (1943), certiorari denied 323 U.S. 711 (1944). Thus, notwithstanding his agreements with the trustees and his wife, petitioner was liable under the Code for the payment of all the gift taxes arising from the transfers to the trusts.

Relying upon these Code provisions, respondent determined that petitioner transferred "stock in trust for several donees, reserving an income interest in the transfer for the payment of * * * [his] gift tax liability in the amount of $134,331.65; and that * * * [his] reservation of the income interest subjects * * * [him] to the provisions of section 677 of the Internal Revenue Code * * *. Accordingly, the net income of the trusts in 1964 is taxable to * * * [him] in the amount of $14,091.62." Respondent further determined that petitioner's "income interest in the trusts terminated in 1964 when the trusts paid * * * [his] gift tax liability in full; and that such payment, from funds other than trust income, constitutes a purchase in liquidation of * * * [his] income interest and results in ordinary income" in the additional amount of $120,240.03.

Section 677(a) provides.... Amplifying this provision, section 1.677(a)-1(d), Income Tax Regs., provides.... When the grantor is treated as "the owner of any portion of a trust," section 671 provides that there shall be included in the computation of his taxable income "those items of income, deductions, and credits against tax of the trust which are attributable to that portion of the trust to the extent that such items would be taken into account * * * in computing taxable income or credits against the tax of an individual."

Sections 671 and 677 are part of subpart E, part I, subchapter J, of the 1954 Code. This subpart includes revised versions of 1939 Code sections 166 and 167 and certain regulations issued under 1939 Code section 22(a), the so-called Clifford[3] and Mallinckrodt[4] regulations. The subpart "provides rules to determine when a trust's income is to be taxed to the grantor because of the grantor's substantial dominion and control of the trust property or income." S. Rept. No. 1622, to accompany H.R. 8300 (Pub. L. No. 591), 83d Cong., 2d Sess., p. 86 (1954). Section 677 corresponds with section 167 of the 1939 Code, and it deals with the grantor's retention of dominion and control over the trust income.

To the extent of the amount of the income realized by the trusts prior to the payment of the gift taxes ($8,400), respondent's position is quite clearly correct. Where a person

---

3. *Helvering v. Clifford*, 309 U.S. 331 (1940); Regs. 118, sec. 39.22(a)-21.
4. *Mallinckrodt v. Nunan*, 146 F.2d 1 (C.A. 8, 1945), affirming 2 T.C. 1128 (1943), certiorari denied 324 U.S. 871 (1945); Regs. 118, sec. 39.22(a)-22.

transfers property to a trust and, as a condition to the transfer, the trustee agrees to pay the resulting gift tax liability, the donor is taxable on any trust income which the trustee may use for that purpose. Within the meaning of section 677, he is treated as an owner of a portion of the trust because its income, in the discretion of the trustee, may be used to discharge his legal obligation. Under section 671, the donor is taxable on the income attributable to such portion of the trust—i.e., the income which may be used to discharge his legal obligation to gift tax. *Estate of Craig R. Sheaffer*, 37 T.C. 99 (1961), affd. 313 F. 2d 738 (C.A. 8, 1963), certiorari denied 375 U.S. 818 (1963); *Estate of A. E. Staley, Sr.*, 47 B.T.A. 260 (1942), affd. 136 F. 2d 368 (C.A. 5, 1943), certiorari denied 320 U.S. 786 (1943). It is of no avail to petitioner in the instant case that the proceeds of the loans rather than the trust income were used for this purpose. The controlling consideration under section 677 is the described "discretion," not the way in which that discretion is actually exercised.

Petitioner contends that the trustees of the Gordon trust were prohibited from using trust income for the payment of the gift taxes. In support of his contention, petitioner points out that paragraph 2 of the Gordon trust agreement does not specifically authorize the use of the income to pay such taxes, whereas the corresponding provisions in the Elizabeth and Ruth trust instruments do. We, however, do not attach the same significance to this difference in language as does petitioner.

Paragraph 2 of the Gordon trust agreement, quoted above, is permissive; it allows the trustee to sell part of the corpus or to borrow on the corpus to pay the gift taxes, but it does not prohibit the use of trust income for this purpose. Indeed, paragraph 3, dealing with trust income, gives the trustee wide discretion to use the trust income "for the payment of *all* taxes and assessments * * * which may be lawfully imposed upon the principal and/or income" (emphasis added) of the trust and "for the payment of all proper charges and expenses incurred by the Trustees and their agents and attorneys." Since the trust agreements required the trustees to pay the gift tax liabilities arising from the transfers in trust, such liabilities became proper charges against the principal and income of the trusts. The trustees, therefore, had the discretionary power to use the trust income to meet this charge without violating the trust agreement. In these circumstances, sections 671 and 677 require all such income received prior to the payment of the taxes to be included in petitioner's taxable income.

The income received by the trusts after April 14, 1964, when the gift taxes were paid, however, is not taxable to petitioner. As a result of the payment of the taxes, all of his obligations with respect thereto were satisfied, and, within the meaning of section 1.677(a)-1(d), *supra*, he had no further obligations to which the trust income could be applied. Thus, the payment of the gift taxes denuded petitioner of every interest in the trusts, and section 1.677(a)-1(c), Income Tax Regs., provides: "If the grantor strips himself permanently and definitively of every interest * * * he is not treated as an owner under section 677 after that divesting."[5]

---

5. The language of sec. 39.167-1(b)(5), Regs. 118, is even more explicit in stating that a grantor whose interest in a trust has been extinguished does not thereafter realize taxable income from the trust as follows:

> 5. If the grantor strips himself permanently and definitely of every * * * interest retained by him [which would cause the trust income to be taxed to him under sec. 167, I.R.C. 1939], the income of the trust realized after such divesting takes effect is not taxable to the grantor.
> * * *

The differences in the language of this regulation and the current regulation sec. 1.677(a)-1(c), quoted in the text, are only differences in form. Sec. 677 treats the grantor as the owner of a portion of the trust if income may be distributed or applied for his benefit; sec. 167, I.R.C. 1939, on the other hand,

Since petitioner, after April 14, 1964, no longer had any interest in the trusts within the meaning of section 677, none of the trust income received after that date is taxable to him. This is the rationale and holding of *Estate of Annette S. Morgan,* 37 T.C. 981 (1962), affirmed per curiam 316 F. 2d 238 (C.A. 6, 1963), certiorari denied 375 U.S. 825 (1963); *David Keith,* 45 B.T.A. 644 (1941), acq. 1942-1 C.B. 10.

Although the income which the Commissioner sought to tax in *Estate of Annette S. Morgan* and *David Keith* was actually received by the trusts in years subsequent to the ones in which the gift taxes were paid, the reasoning which those cases employ does not permit a different rule for the trust income received during the portion of the taxable year remaining after the taxes are paid. Neither represents trust income received during a period when the donor is treated as the owner of a portion of the trusts under section 677. Quite obviously if a beneficiary dies during a trust's fiscal year and after his death the trust income is to be distributed to someone else, he is not taxable on the income received by the trust during the entire year. See, e.g., *D. G. McDonald Trust,* 19 T.C. 672 (1953), acq. 1953-2 C.B. 5, affirmed sub nom. *Chase National Bank v. Commissioner,* 225 F. 2d 621 (C.A. 8, 1955). Similarly, where, as in the instant case, the grantor is divested of all interest in the trust during a taxable year, he is not taxable on the subsequently received income of the trust.[6] We hold petitioner is not taxable on the income received by the trusts between April 14, 1964, the date of the gift tax payment, and August 31, 1964, the end of the trusts' fiscal years.[7]

Contrary to respondent's contention, payment of the gift taxes with borrowed funds did not constitute a purchase or liquidation of income interests retained by petitioner. His retained interests were not limited to the right to have the trust income applied toward the payment of the gift taxes. He had the right to have the gift taxes paid out of any available funds, whether borrowed, obtained from corpus, or derived from dividends on the transferred stock. In a very real sense, his gifts in trust consisted of only the excess of the value of the stock over the amount of the gift taxes. *Richard H. Turner,* 49 T.C. 356, 363 (1968), affirmed per curiam 410 F. 2d 752 (C.A. 6, 1969); *Sarah Helen Harrison,* 17 T.C. 1350, 1357 (1952), acq. 1952-2 C.B. 2. If petitioner had transferred to the trusts, along with the stock, sufficient cash to pay the gift taxes, the use of the cash for that purpose would not have generated any taxable income. Similarly, the use of cash derived from pledging the entrusted stock did not generate any taxable income. Significantly, the pre-April 14, 1964, trust income is taxable to petitioner not because of any requirement

requires the portion of the trust income which may be used for the grantor's benefit to be included in his gross income. Both sections, however, were designed to aid in achieving the same objective— i.e., "to determine when a trust's income is to be taxed to the grantor because of the grantor's substantial dominion and control of the trust property or income," S. Rept. No. 1622, to accompany H.R. 8300 (Pub. L. No. 591), 83d Cong., 2d Sess., pp. 86, 371 (1954).

6. Trust income is, of course, computed on an annual basis, and situations may arise where the income which is taxable to the grantor can be computed only by reference to a trust's receipts and disbursements for an entire taxable year. Such a situation is not presented in this case, however, since the parties have stipulated to the amount of income received prior to Apr. 14, 1964, and petitioner has not shown that the trusts were entitled to any deductions which might be properly allocable to the income taxable to him.

7. The language on this point in *Estate of Craig R. Sheaffer,* T. C. Memo, 1966-126 ("If a taxpayer is found to be a substantial owner of a portion of a trust under the provisions of sections 671 through 678, then he is taxable on all the income of such portion during the entire taxable year in issue."), does not represent the views of this Court. This issue was present but not considered in *Estate of Craig R. Sheaffer,* 37 T.C. 99 (1961), affd. 313 F. 2d 738 (C.A. 8, 1963), certiorari denied 375 U.S. 818 (1963).

that the gift taxes be paid out of income but because the trust income, within the meaning of section 677, was subject to being used for that purpose at a time when petitioner was personally liable for the tax. When the gift taxes were paid through use, in part, of the reserved portions of the corpora, petitioner's interests in the trust terminated, but he realized no taxable income therefrom.

* * *

[The dissenting opinion of Judge Sterrett is omitted.]

Illustrative Material

1. In Rev. Rul. 57-564, 1957-2 C.B. 328, trustees similarly took out a loan in order to discharge the grantor's gift tax liability, which the trust had assumed. The I.R.S. ruled that any income of the trust "applied by the trustees in satisfying the obligation incurred to pay gift tax of the donor [was] taxable to the donor" under section 677. *Krause* guts Rev. Rul. 57-564 by allowing extinguishment of the grantor's gift tax liability to terminate grantor trust status at a time when the trustee may still be using trust income to discharge a loan taken out solely to pay that gift tax liability.

2. *Estate of Annette S. Morgan,* 37 T.C. 981 (1962), *aff'd,* 316 F.2d 238 (6th Cir.), *cert. denied,* 375 U.S. 825 (1963), reached the same conclusion as *Krause,* i.e., that the grantor was not subject, for years after her gift tax liability had been satisfied, to taxation on trust income used to repay a loan taken out by the trustees to satisfy that liability. A portion of the opinion follows:

> Section 677(a) ... clearly evidences a congressional intent that a settlor of a trust, in order to avoid tax on the income of the trust property, must receive no benefit from the income of the property without the consent of an "adverse party." Furthermore, it is clear that we should not allow the taxpayer to accomplish indirectly what Congress has prohibited. On the surface this transaction appears to be but an indirect method for diverting the income of the trust property to the decedent. It appears that income of the trust property was anticipated by obtaining the loan, the proceeds of which were given to the decedent. The loan was then repaid from the income of the trust as it was realized.
>
> Upon analysis however, this illusion disappears. Surely had the decedent sold a sufficient amount of the Morgan stock to pay the gift tax and given the remainder to the trust, she would not be subject to tax on any part of the trust income. The result would be the same if the stock had been given to the trustees and they had then sold a portion to pay the tax, at least in years after the gift tax was paid. Did the decedent then receive any monetary benefit from the method by which the trustees chose to discharge the trust obligation to pay the gift tax? Her gift tax obligation was paid when due and that is the sole benefit she would have received no matter what method had been chosen by the trustees to obtain funds for this purpose. The manner of obtaining the money was chosen independently by the trustees who were authorized to select whatever method they deemed advisable. Of course, the fact that the trustees chose to obtain money by borrowing and then repaying the loan from income means that the trust retained more corpus and less income. This, however, did not benefit the decedent because she retained no interest in the trust and could not recover the corpus. Therefore, since the decedent received no benefit from the fact that the

trustees borrowed to discharge her gift tax obligation and repaid the loan from
trust income, she cannot be held to have constructively received the income
used to repay the loan.

37 T.C. at 984–85.

3. Is it possible to avoid treatment as a grantor under section 677 if the trust agreement that governs the trust that assumes the gift tax liability contains language barring use
of trust income for the benefit of the grantor? In *Estate of Kenneth W. Davis*, 30 T.C.M.
(CCH) 1363 (1971), *aff'd per curiam*, 469 F.2d 694 (5th Cir. 1972), the trust agreement
stated: "But the Trustees shall never have or exercise any power ... to use the income arising from the trust properties, or any part thereof, for the benefit of the Trustors, or either
of them." Relying in part on this language, the court rejected a deficiency against the
grantors for the year the trust paid their gift tax liability. Additional relevant facts were
that the property on which the gift tax had been imposed generated no income in the year
involved and that the trust paid the gift tax out of other funds it had on hand prior to the
transfer.

4. For the prospective donor with a very low adjusted basis in property to be transferred by net gift, *Diedrich v. Commissioner*, 457 U.S. 191 (1982), decreased the attractiveness of the opportunity provided by *Krause* and *Morgan*. In *Diedrich* the Supreme
Court held that where a donee paid the donor's gift tax liability, which exceeded the
donor's basis in the property transferred, the donor realized income under section
61(a)(12) on the excess.

5. In *Jack Wiles*, 59 T.C. 289 (1972), *acq.*, 1973-2 C.B. 4, *aff'd mem.*, 491 F.2d 1406 (5th
Cir. 1974), trust income was used to pay off mortgage indebtedness on which the grantor
remained personally liable after transfer of the encumbered property to the trust. The
court held that the grantor was taxable on the trust's income to the extent of the indebtedness discharged. To the same effect is *Jenn v. United States*, 70-1 U.S.T.C. ¶ 9264 (S.D.
Ind. 1970).

6. Where a corporation created a trust to provide employee benefits required by the local
workmen's compensation law, the corporation was treated as owner of the trust under section 677(a) because trust income was used to discharge the corporation's legal obligations to its employees. Rev. Rul. 82-95, 1982-1 C.B. 101. To the same effect, with respect
to a trust created to pay malpractice claims against its grantor, a corporation engaged in
the practice of medicine, is *Anesthesia Service Medical Group, Inc. Employee Protective
Trust v. Commissioner*, 85 T.C. 1031 (1985), *aff'd*, 825 F.2d 241 (9th Cir. 1987). Likewise,
section 677(a) may apply when an automobile dealer uses a trust to service multi-year
vehicle service contracts. *See Johnson v. Commissioner*, 108 T.C. 448 (1997), *aff'd in part
and rev'd in part*, 184 F.3d 786 (8th Cir. 1999).

7. In Rev. Rul. 64-240, 1964-2 C.B. 172, the I.R.S. ruled that section 677 did not treat
the grantor as owner of the income of a trust required to pay its income to a charitable
organization in satisfaction of a pledge of the grantor, even though the grantor's legal
obligation was thereby discharged. The I.R.S. relied on Rev. Rul. 55-410, 1955-1 C.B.
297, which ruled that satisfaction of a charitable pledge with appreciated property did
not give rise to taxable gain. The I.R.S. therefore concluded that "a charitable pledge [was]
not a legal obligation for purposes of section 677." Is Rev. Rul. 55-410 consistent with
Rev. Rul. 83-75, discussed *supra* (ch. 3, sec. G(1)(a)), which held that a charitable lead
trust realized gain upon distribution of property in kind in satisfaction of its charitable
annuity?

Morrill v. United States

228 F. Supp. 734 (D. Me. 1964)

GIGNOUX, District Judge.

This is an action for refund of federal income taxes for the years 1959, 1960 and 1961 in the amounts of $1,736.75, $2,344.50 and $3,064.63, respectively. The only question presented is whether the amounts of the income of four trusts established by George B. Morrill, Jr., which the trustees applied to the payment of the tuition and room charges of the taxpayers' four minor children at private schools and colleges, were taxable as income to him under the provisions of Section 677(a)....

In April, 1959, Mr. Morrill established four short-term trusts, one for the benefit of each of his four minor children, and named a corporate trustee of each trust. The income of each trust was to be accumulated until the child became 21 years of age, at which time the accumulated income, and thereafter during the remaining term of the trust any current income, was to be distributed to the beneficiary. Ten years after the date of their creation, the trusts were to terminate and the corpus of each was to revert to Mr. Morrill. Each of the trusts also provided that during the minority of the beneficiary, the trustee might, in its discretion, use the trust income "for the payment of room, tuition, books and travel to and from any private school, college or other institution of learning at home or abroad."

During the tax years in question, the taxpayers' children attended Vassar College, Connecticut College, Brown University, The Holderness School and The Waynflete School. Mr. Morrill expressly assumed responsibility for the payment of the tuition, room, board and other expenses of his children at Vassar College and Connecticut College.[1] There was no express agreement between Mr. Morrill and Brown University, The Holderness School, or The Waynflete School regarding the payment of the expenses of his children at those schools. However, each school submitted its bills to Mr. Morrill. He then wrote out a personal check to the institution for that portion of the bill other than room and tuition, sent the bill with his personal check to the trustee of the appropriate trust, and requested the trustee to pay from the trust the room and tuition charges on the bill. The trustee then mailed to the institution its check in payment of the room and tuition charges, together with Mr. Morrill's check for the balance of the bill involved.

George B. Morrill, Jr. and Elizabeth H. Morrill, as husband and wife, filed joint federal income tax returns for the calendar years 1959, 1960 and 1961. They did not include in the returns any of the income of the four children's trusts. Upon audit of the returns, the Commissioner determined that the amounts of trust income which had been applied in payment of the children's tuition and room charges had been used to satisfy legal obligations of Mr. Morrill, as father of the children, and were therefore taxable as income to him under Section 677 of the 1954 Code.[2] Plaintiffs paid under protest the resulting de-

---

1. Mr. Morrill signed the following agreement with Vassar College: "In consideration of the acceptance by Vassar College of Bonnie Elizabeth Morrill I agree to be responsible for her tuition, room and board, and other incidental expenses, in accordance with the terms and conditions stated in the current catalogue." He signed the following agreement with Connecticut College: "Bills may be sent to me and I assume responsibility for their payment until further notice."

2. The Commissioner initially based his assessment on Section 677(b). The Government later shifted its ground for asserting taxability to Section 677(a). During the legal argument before the Court, counsel for the Government and for the taxpayers conceded that Section 677(b) has no application to the facts of this case. In this they were correct because Subsection (b) merely limits the tax, imposed by Subsection (a), on trust income which may be applied for the support or maintenance of a beneficiary whom the grantor is legally obligated to support or maintain, to that portion of the trust income which is so applied. Here the Government has not attempted to tax that part of the trust income which

ficiency assessments, and instituted this suit after their claims for refund were disallowed. For reasons which it will state briefly, this Court has concluded that the Commissioner was correct.

Section 671 ... provides that the income of a trust is taxable to the person specified in the Code as the owner of the trust. Section 677(a) of the Code provides.... A long line of judicial decisions applying Section 677(a) and its predecessor statutes has established that trust income which is used to satisfy a legal obligation of the grantor is, in effect, distributed to him and is, therefore, taxable to him. Douglas v. Willcuts, 296 U.S. 1, 56 S.Ct. 59, 80 L.Ed. 3 (1935) (trust income used to discharge divorced settlor's alimony obligation); Helvering v. Stokes, 296 U.S. 551, 56 S.Ct. 308, 80 L.Ed. 389 (1935) ... (trust income used to discharge settlor's legal obligation to support, educate and maintain his minor children); Helvering v. Schweitzer, 296 U.S. 551, 56 S.Ct. 304, 80 L.Ed. 389 (1935) ... (trust income used to discharge settlor's legal obligation to support, educate and maintain his minor children); Helvering v. Blumental, 296 U.S. 552, 56 S.Ct. 305, 80 L.Ed. 390 (1935) ... (trust income used to discharge settlor's debt); Helvering v. Coxey, 297 U.S. 694, 56 S.Ct. 498, 80 L.Ed. 986 (1936) ... (trust income used to discharge settlor's alimony and support obligation); Helvering v. Fitch, 309 U.S. 149, 60 S.Ct. 427, 84 L.Ed. 665 (1940) (trust income used to discharge divorced settlor's alimony obligation); Helvering v. Stuart, 317 U.S. 154, 63 S.Ct. 140, 87 L.Ed. 154 (1942) (trust income used to discharge settlor's legal obligation to support, educate and maintain his minor children).... The Treasury Regulations reflect this fundamental principle. Treas. Reg. §1.677(a)-1(d). The transaction is regarded "as being the same in substance as if the money had been paid to the taxpayer and he had transmitted it to his creditor." Douglas v. Willcuts, supra, at 296 U.S. at 9, 56 S.Ct. at 63, 80 L.Ed. 3. The income is taxable to the grantor when used to discharge his individual obligation, whether imposed by law or by contract. 6 Mertens, Federal Income Taxation §37.06 at 434 (1948); compare Douglas v. Willcuts, supra with Helvering v. Blumental, supra.

In the present case, the trust income paid to each of the schools and colleges was used to defray expenses for which Mr. Morrill was legally liable. The taxpayers concede that Mr. Morrill was personally obligated for payment of his children's expenses at Vassar College and Connecticut College, because he had expressly assumed that responsibility. It also seems very evident that Mr. Morrill had impliedly obligated himself to pay his children's bills at Brown University, The Holderness School and The Waynflete School. It is a settled principle of contract law that when one renders services to another at the request, or with the knowledge and consent, of the other, and the surrounding circumstances make it reasonable for him to believe that he will receive payment therefor from the other, and he does so believe, a promise to pay will be inferred, and there is an implied contract. 3 Corbin, Contracts, §566 (1960); Restatement, Contracts §72 (1932); Saunders v. Saunders, 90 Me. 284, 3 A. 172 (1897); Leighton v. Nash, 111 Me. 525, 90 A. 385 (1914); Gordon v. Keene, 118 Me. 269, 107 A. 849 (1919); Stinson v. Bridges, 152 Me. 306, 129 A.2d 203 (1957). The implied obligation to pay arises whether the services are rendered directly to the other person or to a third person at the request of the other. 3 Corbin, op. cit. supra, §566 at 312–14. The application of this principle to the determination of Mr. Morrill's obligations with reference to payment of the children's expenses at Brown University, The Holderness School and The Waynflete School is clear. Mr. Morrill was the parent and natural guardian of the chil-

---

was not used to pay the school and college bills in issue. Congress enacted what is now Subsection (b), 58 Stat. 51 (1944), to change the law established by the holding in *Helvering v. Stuart*, 317 U.S. 154, 63 S.Ct. 140, 87 L.Ed. 154 (1942). See 6 Mertens, Federal Income Taxation §37.21 (1948)....

dren, and insofar as the record shows, approved of their enrollment in these institutions. The record is devoid of evidence that the schools were asked, or agreed, to accept the children with the understanding that they would look only to the trusts for the payment of their room and tuition charges—in fact, there is no evidence that the schools were even aware of the existence of the trusts when they accepted the children. Nor is there any suggestion that the schools looked to the children themselves for the payment of these bills. In each instance the institutions sent their bills to Mr. Morrill. Not once did they submit their bills to the trustees or to the children. Under these circumstances, the only reasonable conclusion is that the schools believed that Mr. Morrill was to be responsible for payment of any bills incurred on behalf of his children. In this they were clearly justified, as it was reasonable for them to expect, in the absence of an express disclaimer by him of an intention to be responsible for the bills, that he would pay for his children's education.

Plaintiffs argue that Mr. Morrill at most undertook, as a party secondarily liable, to guarantee payment of the schools' bills by the children, as the primary obligors. In this view, they assert that the payments by each trustee satisfied the child's obligation and merely extinguished that of Mr. Morrill. The fallacy in this argument is that it presupposes the existence of contracts between the schools and the children. There is no indication that there were any such express contracts; nor is there any showing of circumstances from which a court could imply such contracts. Indeed, it is incredible that these institutions were looking to the children, all of whom were minors without any apparent assets of their own, for payment of these bills. The facts of the case clearly establish that Mr. Morrill, rather than his children, expressly or impliedly undertook to assume primary responsibility for the payment of the school bills here in issue, and that he, and he alone, was legally liable therefor.

The Court holds that the amounts of trust income which the trustees applied in payment of the tuition and room charges of the taxpayers' four minor children at the private schools and colleges which they attended during the tax years in question were used to satisfy express or implied contractual obligations of Mr. Morrill, the grantor of the trusts, and were therefore taxable as income to him under the provisions of Section 677(a) of the 1954 Code. In view of this disposition of the case, it is unnecessary for the Court to consider the Government's alternative contention that such income was taxable to Mr. Morrill, also under Section 677(a), on the theory that Mr. Morrill, as a parent, was under a duty imposed by Maine law to pay the school and college bills of his children....

Judgment will be entered for the defendant against the plaintiffs, with costs.

Wyche v. United States

36 A.F.T.R. 2d 75-5816 (Ct. Cl. 1974)

WOOD, Trial Judge:

In this action to recover Federal income taxes and assessed interest paid for the years 1963, 1964, 1965, 1966, and 1967, plaintiffs contend, in essence, that in taxing as income to them certain distributions of trust income of trusts created for the benefit of their three minor children ... defendant has acted erroneously and unlawfully. For reasons which follow, it is concluded that plaintiffs are entitled to recover....

The ... issue is whether or not the income from the corpus of three short-term trusts established by plaintiff for the benefit of his three children is, to the extent used to pay for private school tuition and music and dancing lessons for the children, includable in plaintiff's income for the said years. The facts relating to this issue follow.

Plaintiffs have three children, all of whom were minors throughout the period 1963–67. In 1957, 1960, and 1963, respectively, plaintiff, a successful practicing attorney in Greenville, South Carolina, established three separate trusts, each for the benefit of all of the children, and each extending for more than 10 years, with Mrs. Wyche as trustee. The corpus of each trust consisted of rental real property in Greenville.

Under each trust, the trustee was required, after collecting rentals and paying expenses, to distribute to each of the beneficiaries, in equal shares, all of the current income of each trust, at least annually, on or before April 1 following the preceding calendar year. Under the terms of each trust, the distribution of income could be made directly to the beneficiaries, or by "depositing the same in a bank or savings account in the beneficiaries' names, or by purchasing securities in the beneficiaries' names, or the expending of said sums for the education of said beneficiaries."

During each of the years in issue, a portion of the current income of the trusts (administered, at all times here relevant, as a single trust, with all receipts or disbursements processed through a bank account in the name of Mrs. Wyche as trustee) was used to pay for tuition at a private day school, and for certain music and dancing lessons, for plaintiff's children. The total amount of all such payments, for the years 1963–67, amounted to some $8,500. Plaintiff was financially able to make all such payments from his own funds.

Plaintiffs' children began to attend Christ Church Episcopal School in 1960, at which time plaintiffs' son was in the fourth grade, one daughter was in the first grade, and one daughter was in kindergarten. For two of the children plaintiff, and for one of the children Mrs. Wyche, signed an application form (essentially an information sheet) in connection with their commencement of such attendance. Thereafter, however, plaintiffs did not execute any document with or for the School.

The School had elected as a matter of policy not to enter into contractual arrangements with parents (or others) desirous of having a child attend the School. Instead, tuition charges and enrollment fees (the latter to reserve a place for a current student during the next school year) were payable in advance of school attendance. Tuition charges and enrollment fees for plaintiffs' children were paid from trust funds in advance of any due date. Thus, their accounts were never delinquent, and no bills for tuition were ever sent to plaintiffs, the trustee, or the children.

Payments to the School were made by use of a check printed "Harriet S. Wyche, Trustee." Such checks were made payable to one of plaintiffs' children, and endorsed by the child. Mrs. Wyche then either took the check, or cashed it and took the proceeds, to the School. In the latter event, Mrs. Wyche advised the School representative receiving the money (normally the Church Treasurer or a clerk in that office) that the cash payment was being made from trust funds.

During the years 1963 through 1967, free elementary and secondary public schools, primarily supported by local property taxes, were available in Greenville County, South Carolina, and plaintiffs' children might have attended such public schools at no cost to plaintiffs. Throughout at least most of that period, if not all of it, attendance of a child at any school (public, private, or parochial) was not compulsory under South Carolina law.

During the years 1963–1967, a portion of the income of the trusts was also used to pay for music and dancing lessons for one or more of plaintiffs' children. Again, there were no written contracts. Both the music teacher and the ballet teacher were informed by

Mrs. Wyche that the trusts were the source of funds for such lessons, and payments, from trust funds, were generally made in essentially the same manner as were payments to the School. On some occasions, however, a check on the trustee account was drawn in favor of the appropriate teacher.

Except for his execution of application forms for two of the children in connection with their commencement of attendance at the School, plaintiff had no contact with either the School or the music and dancing teachers. Plaintiffs' children were not required to attend private school, or to take lessons in music or dancing. One child ultimately decided to, and did, attend public school, and one or more children did not take music or dancing lessons during some of the years in suit.

Under Section 677(a) ... the grantor "shall be treated as the owner of any portion of a trust * * * whose income without the approval or consent of any adverse party is, or, in the discretion of the grantor or a nonadverse party, or both, may be * * *", distributed to the grantor. Under Section 677(b), however, trust income "shall not be considered taxable to the grantor under subsection (a) * * * merely because such income in the discretion of * * * the trustee * * * may be applied or distributed for the support or maintenance of a beneficiary whom the grantor is legally obligated to support or maintain, except to the extent that such income is so applied or distributed. * * * "

Rev. Rul. 56-484, 1956-2 Cum. Bull. 23, provides, in effect, that trust income "used in the discharge or satisfaction, in whole or in part, of a legal obligation of any person to support or maintain a minor is, to the extent so used, taxable to such person * * *. However, the amount of such income includable in the gross income of a person obligated to support or maintain a minor is *limited by the extent of his obligations under local law.*" (Emphasis supplied.)

The injection into the decisional process of the utilization of state law to determine Federal income tax consequences in a case such as this has rightfully been said to pose difficult problems in terms of tax equity and inequity. See, *e.g.,* Nitzburg, The Obligation of Support: A Proposed Federal Standard, 23 Tax L. Rev. 93 (1967); Committee on Taxation of Trust Income, Report, Trust Income Taxation and the Obligation of Support, 1 Real Property, Probate and Trust Journal 327 (1966); Note, Federal Tax Aspects of the Obligation to Support, 74 Harv. L. Rev. 1191 (1961). It is clear, however, that "local law" is here determinative.

Under South Carolina law, plaintiff had (in broad terms) a statutory obligation to provide for his children "the actual necessaries of life * * *." Section 20-303, Code of Laws of South Carolina, Annot. (1962 ed.). It is not disputed that that obligation extended (notwithstanding the absence of any state statute making school attendance compulsory throughout most if not all of the period here relevant) to education of plaintiff's minor children. See Campbell v. Campbell, 20 S.E.2d 237, 200 S.C. 67 (1942); and see Fender v. Fender, 182 S.E.2d 755, 256 S.C. 399 (1971). Plaintiff's position is, rather, that, under South Carolina law, he had no legal obligation whatever to send his children to private day school, or to provide music and dancing lessons for them, and that, accordingly, the taxing of trust income so used to plaintiff is erroneous and unlawful.

Defendant agrees that the primary issues on this phase of the matter are whether plaintiff was legally obligated under South Carolina law to send his children to private day school, or to afford them such private lessons, but contends that under South Carolina law plaintiff plainly had a legal obligation to do both. Defendant also asserts, alternatively, that plaintiff impliedly obligated himself to pay the amounts in question actually paid from trust income, and that those amounts are accordingly taxable to plaintiff under Section 677 in any event.

In Brooke v. United States, 300 F.Supp. 465 (D.C. Mont. 1969), the court, equating a court-administered guardianship with a trust for purposes of Section 677 of the Internal Revenue Code, considered whether payments by the "trustee" from "trust" income for, inter alia, private school tuition and music, swimming, and public speaking lessons for his minor children were in discharge of his legal obligations under Montana law. Under Montana law, a parent must give his child "support and education suitable to his circumstances." Plaintiff in Brooke, in the years there relevant, had income ranging from $26,000 to $30,000.

With plain cognizance of "the result that should happen as a matter of tax equality," the court nonetheless held squarely that the amounts expended for private school tuition and lessons were "not items which plaintiff was legally required to provide for the support and maintenance of the children," and, accordingly, were not includable in the parent's income. Brooke v. United States, supra, 300 F.Supp. at 466–67. That holding was unanimously affirmed on appeal. Brooke v. United States, 468 F.2d 1155 (9th Cir. 1972).

Defendant urges that the decision in Brooke reflects a narrow, minority, view of the obligation of a parent to support his minor children, and that, in other jurisdictions (indeed, defendant says, in a majority of the states), a different rule would apply. Cf. Annot., Education as element in allowance for benefit of child in decree of divorce or separation, 56 ALR2d 1207 (1957).

These arguments are wide of the mark. The determinative consideration here is South Carolina law, and upon a careful consideration of the record and the briefs and arguments of the parties, together with extensive independent research, it is concluded that, for the years here relevant, plaintiff had no legal obligation under South Carolina law to send his children to private day school or to afford them music and dancing lessons.

Defendant's reliance on Mairs v. Reynolds, 120 F.2d 857 (8th Cir. 1941) is unavailing. There, the income of a trust used to pay for tuition and education of the grantor's minor children at Yale University and other private schools was held taxable to the grantor, on the ground that under general law, and "by the public policy of the State of Minnesota in particular", such educational expenditures were in discharge of the grantor's legal obligation to support and educate his minor children. Cf. Woods, Taxability of the Income from a Trust Used to Pay the Cost of a College Education, 42 Taxes 700 (1964). That holding is, for reasons stated heretofore, inapposite here.

Defendant also asserts that, under South Carolina law, an award for child support in an action for divorce must be fair and just to the parties, and that the court making such an award should consider the father's ability to pay (here considerable), the best interests of the children, and other relevant circumstances. That broad proposition is undoubtedly sound. It is, however, unpersuasive here. Fender v. Fender, supra.

While it has been suggested on occasion that the legal obligation of support in a broken and an unbroken family situation may be less than identical,[6] that notion need not now be considered.

Defendant cites no authority whatever (and none has been found) for the proposition that during the years in question, even in a divorce action, a South Carolina court would have recognized that expenditures for private day school and music and dancing lessons were "within [a father's] legal obligations under local law."[7]

---

6. See, e.g., Federal Tax Aspects of the Obligation to Support, 74 Harv. L. Rev. 1191, 1194–95 (1961).

7. Defendant's Brief, p. 19....

Defendant alternatively contends that plaintiff had an implied contractual obligation to pay the costs of his children's tuition at private day school, and the costs of their music and dancing lessons. Relying on Morrill v. United States, 228 F.Supp. 734 (D.C. Me. 1964), defendant asserts that since the amounts here in issue were used to satisfy such an obligation, they are accordingly taxable to plaintiff under Section 677(a).

[The court summarizes *Morrill*.]

The court held that the trust income applied to payment of tuition and room charges of Mr. Morrill's children was "used to satisfy express or implied contractual obligations of Mr. Morrill," and was, therefore, taxable as income to him under Section 677(a). Morrill v. United States, supra, 228 F.Supp. at 737. Whether Mr. Morrill was under a duty imposed by Maine law so to educate his children was not reached.

Insofar as here relevant, that holding rested on a finding that the schools believed Mr. Morrill responsible for payment of bills incurred on behalf of his children, and the "settle [sic] principle of contract law that when one renders services to another at the request, or with the knowledge and consent, of the other, and the surrounding circumstances make it reasonable for him to believe that he will receive payment therefor from the other, and he does so believe, a promise to pay will be inferred, and there is an implied contract." Ibid. Thus, it was held, Mr. Morrill alone was legally liable for payment of the amounts there in issue.[8] On the facts of this cause, however, that "settled principle" is clearly inapplicable.

There being no valid basis for attribution to plaintiff of the trust income in question, plaintiffs are entitled to recover ...

Illustrative Material

1. The rationale of *Morrill* has not been widely followed by other courts. Nevertheless, the result in *Morrill*, i.e., grantor taxability for trust income used to educate the grantor's children, is perhaps more representative than the result in *Wyche*. The following excerpt from *Braun v. Commissioner*, 48 T.C.M. (CCH) 210 (1984), is typical:

> Under section 677(b), the income of a trust is taxable to the grantor to the extent that such income is applied or distributed for the support or maintenance of a beneficiary whom the grantor is legally obligated to support or maintain. Petitioners argue that under New Jersey law the petitioners had no obligation to pay college tuition and room and board expenses of an unmarried child over 18 or to pay private school expense for an unmarried child under 18. Petitioners further argue that this issue has come up in New Jersey only in controversies between divorced parents and that such cases are inapplicable to this situation. We do not agree.
>
> The recent decision of *Newburgh v. Arrigo*, 88 N. J. 529, 443 A. 2d 1031 (1982), fully reviews the obligation of parents to continue to provide educational expenses for unmarried children over the age of 18. The Supreme Court of New Jersey held that necessary education is a flexible concept that can vary in different circumstances.
>
> > In general, financially capable parents should contribute to the higher education of children who are qualified students. In appropriate circumstances,

---

8. Cf. Ziegler, Gifts to Minors — Three Variations, 24 Tax Lawyer 296, 306–7 (1971); Nitzburg, The Obligation of Support: A Proposed Federal Standard, 23 Tax L. Rev. 93, 109–10 (1967); Note, Taxation of Educational Trust Payments as Income to Settlor, 1965 Wis. L. Rev. 401.

parental responsibility includes the duty to assure children of a college and even of a postgraduate education such as law school. [*Newburgh v. Arrigo, supra* at 1038.]

In an adversarial situation, courts in New Jersey consider all relevant factors, which include 12 which were enumerated in *Newburgh v. Arrigo, supra.* It is obvious that many of these factors would have no bearing except in a controversy between divorced parents or between a child and a noncustodial parent. But the support rule is not limited to such divorced parent context. *Sakovits v. Sakovits,* 178 N. J. Super. 623, 429 A. 2d 1091, 1095 (1981). While many of these factors described by the New Jersey Supreme Court are not directly applicable to the instant facts, the import to our facts is clearly that petitioners retained the obligation to provide their children with a college education. They were both able and willing to do so, a college education was imminently [sic] reasonable in the light of the background, values and goals of the parents as well as the children, and petitioners have brought forward no facts or arguments which would militate against the recognition of this obligation on the part of these particular parents. *Newburg v. Arrigo, supra.*

   With respect to private high school education, the law of New Jersey is less clear. There is dictum in the case of *Rosenthal v. Rosenthal,* 19 N. J. Super. 521, 88 A. 2d 655 (1952), to the effect that a father is not required to provide his son with private school, college or professional training, or with any education beyond public schools, but that dictum as to college and professional education is certainly obsolete. *Khalaf v. Khalaf,* 58 N. J. 63, 275 A. 2d 132, 137 (1971), refers with approval to Annot. 56 A. L. R. 2d 1207 (1956). While that court's reference to the annotation was with respect to college expenses, the annotation also recognizes the existence of a parental obligation in similar circumstances to provide for private or boarding school education. It would be an anomaly to find a support obligation for college tuition for an emancipated child but none for private high school expense for a young child in the same family. In view of the recent New Jersey cases cited, we do not think the dictum in *Rosenthal v. Rosenthal, supra,* represents the current view of the New Jersey courts. We believe that private high school education in appropriate cases would be held by the New Jersey courts to be within the scope of parental obligation. Accordingly, we hold that the income of these two trusts, to the extent actually utilized for tuition, room and board for four of the six children of petitioners was used to discharge Dr. Braun's legal support obligations and is therefore taxable to him under section 677(b).

48 T.C.M. at 213. For a similar case, finding a parental obligation to provide private high school education under a questionable reading of California law, see *Stone v. Commissioner,* 54 T.C.M. (CCH) 462 (1987), *aff'd mem.,* 867 F.2d 613 (9th Cir. 1989).

   2. Section 677(b) describes a trust whose income may be used to support beneficiaries whom the grantor is legally obligated to support. It excepts such a trust from the general rule of section 677(a), which would automatically designate the grantor as owner of the trust's entire income, to the extent of the obligation involved. Instead, the grantor is treated as owner of the trust's income only to the extent the trust's current income is actually used to support a beneficiary whom the grantor is obligated to support. The last sentence of section 677(b) prescribes a very different rule if accumulated income or corpus is used to support such a beneficiary. In such a case, the amount so used is treated as a distribution to the grantor, deductible by the trust under

section 661 and subjecting the grantor to taxation in accordance with section 662. These two, very different branches of section 677(b) are illustrated in Rev. Rul. 74-94, 1974-1 C.B. 26.

3. In *William B.J. Tibbits*, 24 T.C.M. (CCH) 663 (1965), property originally purchased by the husband with his separate funds but owned by him and his wife in joint tenancy with right of survivorship was used to fund a trust. Later, income from the trust was used to discharge the husband's legal obligation to support his children. The I.R.S. treated the husband as grantor of the entire trust and therefore sought to tax him on all the trust income used to discharge his obligations. The court, however, treated the wife as "the true grantor in substance as well as form" of one-half of the trust. Therefore, husband was taxable on only one-half of the trust income used to discharge his obligations.

If, on the day husband creates a trust, he "gives" wife property that she immediately adds to the trust, husband surely is, and should be, treated as grantor of the entire trust. How long must wife hold the gifted property before she can become a "grantor"? In *Tibbits* the property had been purchased "some years earlier." By the same token, if a wife transfers property to her husband immediately prior to his transfer of both her and his property to a trust, the wife remains, "in substance, if not in form," a grantor of the trust, to the extent of the property she transferred to her husband. *See Balis v. Commissioner*, 63 T.C.M. (CCH) 1830 (1992), *aff'd mem.*, 987 F.2d 770 (5th Cir. 1993). In *Balis*, the transfer by the husband to the trust occurred "several days" after the transfer by the wife to the husband.

Problems

4-21. Assume the facts of Problem 4-12, except that the trustee is authorized to apply the trust's income toward C's education. What are the tax consequences of each of the following:

a. When C is 12 years old, the trustee pays for her school books?

b. When C is 12 years old, the trustee pays for her ballet lessons?

c. When C is 17 years old, the trustee pays for her tuition at the University of Texas?

d. When C is 17 years old, the trustee pays for her tuition at Princeton University?

e. When C is 22 years old, the trustee pays for her tuition at the University of Texas?

2. Others as Owners

a. Judicial Origins

Mallinckrodt v. Nunan
146 F.2d 1 (8th Cir.)
cert. denied, 324 U.S. 871 (1945)

SANBORN, Circuit Judge.

The Tax Court of the United States determined deficiencies in the income taxes due from petitioner for the calendar years 1934 to 1937, inclusive. 2 T.C. 1128. The deficiencies resulted from including in the petitioner's income for each of the years the undistributed income of an irrevocable trust created by his father in 1918. By the terms of the instrument creating the trust, this undistributed income was payable to petitioner annually upon his request, but, if not paid to him at his request, it was to be added to the corpus of the trust estate at the end of each year.

The question presented is whether the undistributed income of the trust in the years in question was taxable to petitioner or taxable to the trust.

The contention of petitioner is that by the plain language of sections 161 and 162 of the Revenue Acts of 1934 and 1936 [predecessors of sections 641(a) and (b), 661, and 662], the undistributed trust income was taxable to the trust. The respondent contends that this income was taxable to petitioner under section 162(b) of the applicable Revenue Acts [predecessor of sections 661 and 662] as income "to be distributed currently" by the fiduciaries to him as a beneficiary. Respondent also contends that the income was taxable to petitioner, under section 22(a) of these Acts [predecessor of section 61], as the owner of the income.

The factual situation out of which this controversy arises is, in substance, as follows: Edward Mallinckrodt, Sr. (who died in 1928), on April 17, 1918, executed a trust instrument, by which he transferred to St. Louis Union Trust Company and the petitioner, as trustees, property and securities under the terms and conditions stated in the instrument. At the time this trust was created, the grantor's family consisted of petitioner, petitioner's wife, and their three sons. The grantor's intention in creating the trust was primarily to provide for petitioner's children and grandchildren. Petitioner had already received a large amount of property from his father. By the terms of the trust instrument, the net income of the trust was to be devoted first to paying certain debts, obligations, and burdens growing out of a building enterprise, and, after those obligations had been paid and satisfied in full, the trustees were directed: to pay to petitioner's wife out of the annual net income of the trust $10,000 each year during her life and that of petitioner; to pay the residue of such annual trust income to petitioner during his life, upon his request; to accumulate the undistributed annual net income and, at the end of each year, to add it to the principal of the trust estate. The trust instrument conferred upon petitioner a testamentary power of appointment over the corpus of the trust estate, but provided that if he did not exercise the power, the trust should continue after his death for the benefit of his widow, his children, and the descendants of his children, and, upon certain contingencies, for the benefit of others. The trustees were empowered, upon the written request of petitioner, during his lifetime, but subject to the approval of both trustees, to "convey or pay to" him "such portions of the principal of the trust estate as it may seem wise to the Trustees to distribute to him for his benefit or that of his family; * * *." The trust was subject to termination during the lifetime of petitioner "at the discretion of the then Trustees, in case they shall decide that such earlier termination is advisable or desirable in the interest of said 'Arcade Building Enterprise', or for any other reason in the interest of the estate then held in trust or of the beneficiaries thereof." If the trust were terminated during the lifetime of petitioner, he was, by the terms of the trust instrument, to have all of the assets of the trust estate. Petitioner was authorized to appoint, by will or by written instrument, his successor as trustee, and, if no successor was named by him, the St. Louis Union Trust Company was to be the sole trustee.

The debts, obligations, and burdens of the building enterprise referred to in the trust instrument were fully paid and satisfied out of the income of the trust estate by 1933. In 1934 and thereafter, the trustees paid to petitioner's wife $10,000 each year out of the annual income of the trust. The petitioner did not request that any of the income of the trust be paid to him in 1934 and 1935. In 1936 the trustees distributed, upon petitioner's request, out of the trust income, $15,000, which was disbursed to certain educational and charitable organizations, and $4,075.82, which was transferred to a trust which petitioner had created for the benefit of his wife. Petitioner reported in his income tax return for 1936 so much of the $15,000 distribution as was taxable. He did not report in his return the taxable portion of the $4,075.82 distribution. In 1937, the trustees distributed out of trust income, upon petitioner's request, $3,109.14 by transferring that amount to the trust which he had created for his wife's benefit. The taxable portion of this distribution was not included in petitioner's income tax return for 1937. During each of the taxable years, petitioner's wife reported and paid the tax upon the $10,000 of trust income which was distributable to her and which she received from the trustees. All of the undistributed net annual income of the trust for each of the years in question was reported by the trustees as income taxable to the trust, and they paid the tax due upon it. At the end of each of the years, the trustees, as directed by the trust instrument, added the undistributed net income for that year to the corpus of the trust.

The respondent determined that the undistributed trust income for each of the years was taxable to petitioner. Petitioner had a very large taxable income. The Tax Court sustained the respondent's determination.

It seems apparent from the grantor's purpose in creating the trust, from the elaborate provisions of the trust instrument relative to the continuance of the trust beyond the lifetime of the petitioner for the benefit of others, and from other circumstances, that the powers conferred upon the petitioner and upon the trustees over the disposition of the income and corpus of the trust were not granted with the thought that they would be exercised for the sole use or benefit of petitioner. The grantor evidently conferred the powers in the belief that the petitioner and the trustees, during petitioner's lifetime, should have discretion to alter the provisions of the trust instrument relative to the disposition of the trust estate or to terminate the trust if deemed necessary or wise in the interests of the beneficiaries of the trust. It is apparent that the grantor intended that the wife and descendants of petitioner were to have a real and subsisting interest in the income and the corpus of the trust estate. It is a fair assumption that the grantor contemplated that petitioner would not, during his lifetime, seek to withdraw either income or principal from the trust estate unless he needed it or unless he believed that it could be used advantageously by him for the benefit of the family.

A majority of the judges of the Tax Court were of the opinion that, because of the powers granted to petitioner by the trust instrument, the undistributed income of the trust in each of the years in question was his income, for purposes of taxation, by virtue of the provisions of section 22(a). The basis for their opinion is indicated by the following excerpt (at pages 1136–1137 of 2 T.C.):

> "Certainly with such powers and rights in and to the trust corpus, and particularly to the income produced, there can be no question that if petitioner were the grantor he would be taxable on the income under section 22(a), Helvering v. Clifford, supra [309 U.S. 331, 60 S.Ct. 554, 84 L.Ed. 788], and petitioner makes no claim to the contrary. The fact that the powers and rights are not the retained powers and rights of a grantor but were received by petitioner as beneficiary of the trust and by grant from his father makes them no less substantial. As in the Clifford case, the rights and powers of the petitioner in and to the trust corpus and the income therefrom did not include all of the incidents of ownership, but

we think it may definitely be said that the benefits held by and belonging to petitioner, directly or indirectly, were such as to require the conclusion that he was
the owner of the income here in question, within the meaning of section 22(a),
supra. In Corliss v. Bowers, 281 U.S. 376 [50 S.Ct. 336, 74 L.Ed. 916], the Supreme
Court said:

> "'But taxation is not so much concerned with the refinements of title as it
> is with actual command over the property taxed—the actual benefit for which
> the tax is paid. * * * Still speaking with reference to taxation, if a man disposes
> of a fund in such a way that another is allowed to enjoy the income which it
> is in the power of the first to appropriate it does not matter whether the per
> mission is given *by assent or by failure to express dissent.* The income that is sub
> ject to a man's unfettered command and that he is free to enjoy at his own
> option may be taxed to him as his income, whether he sees fit to enjoy it or
> not. * * * (Italics supplied.)'

> "While in Corliss v. Bowers the Court was considering and there determined
> the validity of subsections (g) and (h) of section 219 of the Revenue Act of 1924
> [predecessors of sections 676 and 677], the thoughts there expressed are equally
> enlightening and forceful in determining the applicability of section 22(a) under
> the doctrine of Helvering v. Clifford, supra. Considerations which justified and
> sustained the enactment of [that section] may also indicate the applicability of
> section 22(a) in accomplishing the same end, namely, the taxation of income to
> the holder or recipient of the actual benefit for which the tax is paid."

Two of the judges who concurred were of the opinion that it was unnecessary to consider the effect of §22(a). They thought that the undistributed trust income was taxable
to petitioner as income "to be distributed currently" by the fiduciaries to the petitioner
as beneficiary, within the meaning of section 162(b).

Five of the judges of the Tax Court dissented. The conclusion of four of the dissenting judges is concisely stated as follows (at pages 1151, 1152 of 2 T.C.):

> "Trust No. 3660 here involved was no mere tax saving device. It was unques
> tionably a real trust set up for legitimate purposes and one which, it seems to me,
> Congress intended to tax according to the provisions of sections 161 and 162. Under
> section 161 it was the duty of the trust to include in its income tax return all
> taxable gross income and from this gross income it was entitled to take all the or
> dinary deductions granted to an individual by the statute. In addition to these
> deductions the trust was entitled to take the deductions granted by subparagraph
> (b) of section 162, * * *.

> "The trust was directed to pay annually out of the net income of the trust
> $10,000 to Elizabeth E. Mallinckrodt, wife of petitioner. This was income which
> was clearly 'to be distributed currently' to her within the meaning of (b) of sec
> tion 162 and under the terms of that subparagraph was deductible by the trust
> and taxable to the beneficiary, Elizabeth E. Mallinckrodt. Concerning this $10,000
> there is no issue in this case.

> "The remainder of the net income of the trust was not currently distrib
> utable to petitioner, Edward Mallinckrodt, Jr., but only such part of the re
> mainder of the net income of the trust, after the $10,000 distribution to Elizabeth,
> was distributable to him as he might request. The settlor of the trust directed
> that such part of the net income of the trust as might not be requested by pe
> titioner should be accumulated and should at the end of the year become a part

of the principal of the trust estate, subject to such further disposition as was in the trust indenture provided for the principal of the trust estate. Under these provisions only that part of the net income requested by petitioner was currently distributable to him and taxable to him under the provisions of section 162(b). The balance of the net income not so requested was 'income accumulated or held for future distribution under the terms of the will or trust' within the meaning of section 161(a)(1) and was taxable to the trust. The findings of fact show that 'the trustees filed income tax returns with respect to the undistributed taxable income of the trust and paid the tax shown on the returns.' In my opinion the law does not require more."

The conflicting contentions of the parties as to the applicable law are clearly reflected in the opinions of the judges of the Tax Court. 2 T.C. 1133–1138, 1150–1155. No useful purpose would be served by a further discussion.

We shall briefly state our conclusions and our reasons for them. We think that the undistributed income of the trust in suit was not income "to be distributed currently" by the fiduciaries to petitioner as beneficiary, within the meaning of section 162(b). This, for the reason that, by the terms of the trust instrument, the trustees could not distribute trust income to petitioner except upon his request, and were obliged to accumulate and to add to trust corpus all undistributed net income at the end of each year. The trustees were bound to abide by the exact terms and conditions of the trust instrument. By its terms, trust income was not distributable to petitioner unless he elected to withdraw it by requesting that it be paid to him.

We have no quarrel with the views expressed by the minority of the Tax Court relative to the applicability of section 161(a)(1).... Similar views were expressed by this Court in Clifford v. Helvering, 8 Cir., 105 F.2d 586, and by Mr. Justice Roberts in the dissenting opinion in Helvering v. Clifford, 309 U.S. 331, 338, 60 S.Ct. 554, 84 L.Ed. 788, in which case this Court was reversed.... In the absence of the construction and effect which has been accorded to section 22(a) by the Supreme Court in Helvering v. Clifford, supra, and other similar cases, one could well believe that it was the intent of Congress that a bona fide trust should be a distinct taxable entity and that its undistributable "fruits" should not be "attributed to a different tree from that on which they grew," Lucas v. Earl, 281 U.S. 111, 115, 50 S.Ct. 241, 74 L.Ed. 731, but should be taxable to the trust....

We agree with the majority of the Tax Court that implications which fairly may be drawn from the opinions of the Supreme Court in Corliss v. Bowers, 281 U.S. 376, 378, 50 S.Ct. 336, 74 L.Ed. 916, Helvering v. Clifford, 309 U.S. 331, 60 S.Ct. 554, 84 L.Ed. 788, and other cases relative to the taxability of trust income to one having command over it, justify, if they do not compel, the conclusion that the undistributed net income of the trust in suit, during the years in question, was taxable to petitioner under section 22(a). This, because the power of petitioner to receive this trust income each year, upon request, can be regarded as the equivalent of ownership of the income for purposes of taxation. In Harrison v. Schaffner, 312 U.S. 579, 580, 61 S.Ct. 759, 760, 85 L.Ed. 1055, the Supreme Court approved "the principle that the power to dispose of income is the equivalent of ownership of it and that the exercise of the power to procure its payment to another, whether to pay a debt or to make a gift, is within the reach of the statute taxing income 'derived from any source whatever.'" It seems to us, as it did to the majority of the Tax Court, that it is the possession of power over the disposition of trust income which is of significance in determining whether, under section 22(a), the income is taxable to the possessor of such power, and that logically it makes no difference whether the possessor is a grantor who retained the power or a beneficiary who acquired it from another....

Since the trust income in suit was available to petitioner upon request in each of the years involved, he had in each of those years the "realizable" economic gain necessary to make the income taxable to him. See Helvering v. Stuart, 317 U.S. 154, 168, 169, 63 S.Ct. 140, 87 L.Ed. 154; Helvering v. Clifford, supra, at pages 336, 337 of 309 U.S., 60 S.Ct. 554, 84 L.Ed. 788; Helvering v. Gordon, 8 Cir., 87 F.2d 663, 667.

The decision of the Tax Court is affirmed.

b. The Code

Internal Revenue Code:
   Section 678

Regulations:
   Sections 1.678(a)-1; 1.678(b)-1; 1.678(c)-1

Revenue Ruling 67-241
1967-2 C.B. 225

A decedent in his will gave his widow a power, exercisable solely by her, to require the trustees of the residuary trust created under his will to pay to her at her request from corpus during any calendar year an amount equal to the greater of five percent of the value of the trust corpus or $5,000. The widow's right to exercise such power was not cumulative, so that upon her failure to exercise it before the end of any calendar year, her right as to that year lapsed. The trust income was payable in equal amounts to the decedent's two sons.

Section 678(a)(1) of the Internal Revenue Code of 1954 provides a general rule that a person other than the grantor shall be treated as the owner of any portion of a trust with respect to which such person has a power exercisable solely by himself to vest the corpus or the income therefrom in himself.

Where a grantor or another person is treated under sections 673 through 678 of the Code as the owner of any portion of a trust, there are included under section 671 of the Code in computing his tax liability those items of income, deduction, and credit against tax, attributable to or included in that portion.

Section 1.671-2(d) of the Income Tax Regulations provides that items of income, deduction, and credit not attributable to or included in any portion of a trust of which the grantor or another person is treated as the owner under sections 671 through 687 [sic] of the Code are subject to the provisions of sections 641 through 668 of the Code.

Sections 661(a)(2) and 662(a)(2) of the Code treat all distributions (with certain exceptions) to beneficiaries, whether of income or principal, as deductible by the trust and taxable to the beneficiary, subject to the limitations determined by distributable net income of the trust.

Since the widow has a power exercisable solely by herself to vest a portion of the trust corpus in herself, she is treated as the owner of that portion of the trust under section 678 of the Code.

As the owner of a portion of the trust corpus, there are included in computing her tax liability those items of income, deduction, and credit against tax attributable to or included in that portion. Pursuant to the provisions of section 1.671-4 of the regulations, these items should not be reported by the trust on Form 1041, U.S. Fiduciary Income Tax Return (for estates, and trusts), but should be shown on a separate statement to be attached to that form.

The portions of trust corpus considered owned by the widow are not subject to the provisions of sections 661(a)(2) and 662(a)(2) of the Code when distributed to her.

Private Letter Ruling 8545076 (1985)

* * *

You propose to create the Trust for the exclusive benefit of the Beneficiary. The Trust Agreement provides that the Trust will terminate when the Beneficiary reaches age 30 or upon the death of the Beneficiary, whichever occurs first. When the Trust terminates, the Trustee will distribute its assets to the Beneficiary or to such persons as the Beneficiary designates by will.

You propose to fund the Trust initially with up to $10,000 in cash. You anticipate making additional contributions in future years of cash or property of varying amounts or values, probably not in excess of $10,000 each year.

You have represented that the Trust corpus will not consist substantially of insurance policies. According to the Trust Agreement, the Trustee is prohibited from: satisfying your or [your spouse's] legal obligation to support the Beneficiary; paying the life insurance premium on your life or the life of your spouse; and exercising any power other than in a fiduciary capacity. You have released any right to be named a substitute or successor trustee.

The Trust Agreement gives the Beneficiary the right to withdraw from the Trust any property you add to the Trust in an amount equal to the total value of property contributed to the trust during the year. The maximum amount that may be withdrawn each year is $10,000. The Trust Agreement requires that the Trustee give the Beneficiary written notice of his right of withdrawal when property is received from you. As the Beneficiary's natural guardian, the Trustee will receive this notice of the right to withdraw. The power to withdraw may be exercised by the Beneficiary's guardian, except that you are expressly prohibited from exercising the power on the Beneficiary's behalf. If not exercised within 30 days of written notice, the right to withdraw expires.

You have asked, first, who will be taxed on the income of the proposed Trust.

Under section 671 of the Internal Revenue Code, if a grantor or another person is treated as the owner of any portion of a trust, then there shall be included in computing the taxable income and credits of the grantor or the other person those items of income, deductions and credits against the tax of the trust that are attributable to that portion of the trust to the extent that those items would be taken into account under subtitle A, chapter 1, in computing taxable income or credits against the tax of an individual.

The Agreement discloses no provision that would cause you, the grantor, to be considered the owner of any portion of the Trust under sections 673, 674, or 676 of the Code.

None of the circumstances which cause administrative controls to be considered exercisable primarily for the benefit of the grantor under section 675 of the Code are authorized under the Agreement. Thus, whether you will be treated as the owner under section 675 will depend upon the circumstances attendant upon the operation of the Trust. This is a question of fact, the determination of which must be deferred until the federal income tax returns of the parties involved have been examined by the office of the District Director that has jurisdiction over the returns.

Section 677(b) of the Code provides that income of a trust shall not be taxable to the grantor under section 677(a) merely because such income may be applied or distributed for the support or maintenance of a beneficiary (other than the grantor's spouse) whom a grantor is legally obligated to support or maintain, except to the extent that such income is so applied or distributed.

Accordingly, the Grantor shall not be treated as the owner of a portion of the Trust under section 677 of the Code, except to the extent the current income of the Trust is applied or distributed in satisfaction of the Grantor's legal obligation to support or maintain the Beneficiary.

Section 678(a) of the Code provides, in relevant part, that a person other than the grantor shall be treated as the owner of any portion of a trust to which such person has the power exercisable solely by himself to vest the corpus or the income therefrom in himself.

Any new property transferred to the Trust by you will be an addition to the trust corpus. Since the Beneficiary has the power to vest in herself any new property, she has the power to vest in herself part of the trust corpus. Therefore, until her power is exercised, released or allowed to lapse, the Beneficiary will be treated as the owner of each item of income, deduction and credit that is attributable to any new property transferred by gift to the Trust (subject to the $10,000 per Grantor limitation contained in the Agreement). *See* section 1.678(a)-1 of the Income Tax Regulations. Accordingly, the Beneficiary will include in computing her taxable income a pro rata share of each item of income, deduction and credit of the entire Trust. *See* section 1.671-3 of the regulations for rules used in computing the pro rata share of those items.

If the Beneficiary fails to exercise the power to vest in herself any new property that is transferred by gift to the Trust, it will become a a permanent part of the trust corpus. Because the income from that portion, in the discretion of a nonadverse party without the approval or consent of any adverse party, may be distributed to the Beneficiary or accumulated for future distribution to her, the Beneficiary will be treated as the owner of that portion of the Trust under sections 671 and 677(a) of the Code.

Section 678(b) of the Code provides that section 678(a) shall not apply if the grantor of the trust is otherwise treated as the owner under provisions of subpart E of subchapter J, other than section 678. Therefore, this ruling under section 678(a) of the Code is based on the condition that the Grantor is not treated as the owner of the Trust under section 677(b) or section 675 as a result of the manner in which the Trust is operated.

* * *

Private Letter Ruling 200022035 (2000)

* * *

On D1 G created a revocable trust, Trust 1. Following G's death on D2, a marital trust and residual trust, Trust 2, were created pursuant to the provisions of Trust 1. Under the provisions of Trust 2, B, as the income beneficiary, has a lifetime power to appoint all or any part of the Trust 2 income. In addition, B has the noncumulative power to withdraw annually from the corpus of Trust 2 an amount not exceeding five thousand dollars or five percent of the market value of the net principal of Trust 2. This type of power in a trust is commonly referred to as a "five or five" power. With the exception of a partial withdrawal in Year 1, B has not exercised this five or five power.

Section 678(a) provides that a person other than the grantor shall be treated as the owner of any portion of a trust with respect to which (1) such person has a power exercisable solely by himself to vest corpus or the income therefrom in himself, or (2) such person has previously partially released or otherwise modified such a power and after the release or modification retains such control as would, within the principles of sections 671 to 677 of the Code inclusive, subject a grantor of a trust to treatment as the owner thereof.

Section 677 provides that the grantor of a trust shall be treated as the owner of any portion of the trust whose income without the approval or consent of any adverse party is distributed to the grantor.

In Rev. Rul. 67-241, 1967-2 C.B. 225, the beneficiary of a trust held a noncumulative power, exercisable solely by the beneficiary, to withdraw certain amounts of corpus annually from the trust. Rev. Rul. 67-241 concludes that, for each year that this demand power is held, under section 678(a)(1) of the Code the beneficiary is the owner of that portion of the trust which is subject to this demand power, whether or not it is exercised.

We conclude that B's five or five power is a power to vest in B part of the corpus of Trust 2. Therefore, until the power is exercised, released or allowed to lapse, B will be treated as the owner for each year of that portion of Trust 2 that is subject to the power to withdraw under section 678(a)(1).

For each year that B fails to exercise the five or five power, B will be deemed to have partially released a power to withdraw a portion of the trust corpus. B has also retained a power over the income of Trust 2 that would subject a grantor of a trust to treatment as the owner under section 677. Therefore, B will also be treated as an owner of a portion of Trust 2 corpus under section 678(a)(2).

After each succeeding year in which B fails to exercise the five or five power, B will be treated as the owner of an increasing portion of the corpus of Trust 2. The annual increase of the portion of the corpus of Trust 2 of which B is treated as the owner is the product of the amount which B could withdraw multiplied by a fraction the numerator of which is the portion of trust corpus which B is not already treated as owning and the denominator of which is the total of trust corpus from which the withdrawal could be made.

We further conclude that to the extent that B exercises the five or five power during a calendar year, such distribution shall be deemed to have been made from B's pro rata share of each asset of Trust 2 corpus that B is treated as owning.

Section 671 provides that where a grantor or other person is treated as the owner of any portion of a trust, the income, deductions, and credits against tax of the trust attributable to such portion of the trust shall be included by the grantor or other person in computing his taxable income and credits.

Section 1.671-3(a) of the Income Tax Regulations provides that a deemed owner of corpus must include his or her share of the capital gains realized by the trust if allocable to the portion of corpus which that person is deemed to own.

Section 1.671-3(a)(3) provides that if a person is treated as owning an undivided fractional share of trust corpus or an interest represented by a dollar amount, then a pro rata share of each such item of capital gain shall be allocated to that person.

We conclude that B must include, in computing B's tax liability, items of income, deductions, and credits that are attributable to that portion of the corpus of Trust 2 which B is treated as owning. Also, as the owner of an undivided fractional share of the corpus of Trust 2, B shall be allocated a pro rata share of each item of any capital gain realized by Trust 2.

* * *

Illustrative Material

Private Letter Rulings 8545076 and 200022035 illustrate that, under section 678(a)(2), powers of withdrawal may have income tax consequences in years following their lapse. *See also* Westfall, *Lapsed Powers of Withdrawal and the Income Tax,* 39 Tax L. Rev. 68 (1983).

Revenue Ruling 81-6
1981-1 C.B. 385

ISSUE

Is a minor who is a beneficiary of a trust described below treated as the owned [sic] of any portion of the trust under section 678 of the Internal Revenue Code?

FACTS

C is a minor who is a beneficiary of an irrevocable inter vivos trust created by *C's* parent, *P*, in 1979. Under the terms of the trust agreement, an independent trustee is authorized to accumulate the net income of the trust unless, in the judgment of the trustee, all or part of the current or accumulated net income should be distributed to, or for the benefit of, *C* for *C's* support, maintenance in reasonable comfort, health, and education until *C* reaches 25 years of age. Also, the trustee may distribute principal to *C* subject to the above standard.

The trust also provides that *C* has the noncumulative power in any calendar year to withdraw from principal the lesser of (1) all amount [sic] added to the trust during such year by the grantor; or (2) the sum of $3,000. *C* also has the power to withdraw the entire income of the trust until *C* reaches age 25.

Unless sooner exhausted by withdrawal or distributions, the trust is to terminate upon the death of *C* or at such time as *C* reaches age 25, and any remaining amount of trust principal and income is to be distributed to *C* or *C's* estate.

The instrument provides that trust income may be used to discharge *P's* obligation to support *C* only if *P* is unable to personally discharge that obligation.

Under applicable state law, *C*, as a minor, is legally incapable of exercising the above powers in the absence of an appointed guardian. Although no legal guardian has been appointed for *C*, there is no impediment under the trust agreement or local law to the appointment of a guardian.

LAW AND ANALYSIS

Section 678(a) of the Code provides that a person other than the grantor shall be treated as the owner of any portion of a trust with respect to which such person has a power exercisable solely by himself to vest the corpus or the income therefrom in himself. Section 678(b) provides that section 678(a) shall not apply if the grantor of the trust ... is otherwise treated as the owner under the provisions of subpart E of Part I of subchapter J, other than section 678.

The specific question presented is whether the holder of a power the exercise of which [is prohibited] by local law or by a legal or actual disability shall be treated as the owner of any portion of a trust for purposes of section 678(a) of the Code.

In *Trust No. 3 v. Commissioner*, 285 F.2d 102 (7th Cir. 1960), beneficiaries who were minors were granted a power to terminate a trust and to take possession of the trust property. The court held that the fact that no guardians had been duly appointed for the beneficiaries was immaterial in determining whether the beneficiaries became vested with a present right to use all or any part of the property of the trust upon making due demand. The court noted that the taking of such routine steps as appointing a guardian would have no bearing upon the fundamental question of the legal right of the beneficiaries to terminate the trust.

In the present case, as in *Trust No. 3*, no guardian has been appointed for the minor beneficiary of a trust with respect to which the beneficiary has a power exercisable solely by the beneficiary to vest the corpus or the income therefrom in the beneficiary. Here, C, in the absence of an appointed guardian, is legally incapable of exercising the power; however, C's inability to exercise the power because C is a minor does not affect the existence of the power. For purposes of section 678 of the Code it is the existence of a power rather than the capacity to exercise such a power that determines whether a person other than the grantor shall be treated as the owner of any part of a trust.

HOLDING

Under section 678(a) of the Code, C, a minor beneficiary of a trust, is treated as the owner of any portion of the trust with respect to which C has a power to vest the corpus or income in C, notwithstanding that no guardian has been appointed for C.

Illustrative Material

1. In Rev. Rul. 67-268, 1967-2 C.B. 226, a third party created a trust under which the trustee had discretionary power to pay income to the trustee's wife. The I.R.S. ruled that section 678(a) did not cause the trustee to be treated as the owner of the trust, because the power was "not the same as the power to vest the income in himself." The I.R.S. reasoned that the "separate identity" of the spouses could "not be disregarded even though a joint return [was] filed." Perhaps of interest is the fact that, at the time the trust was created, the couple had not yet married. The I.R.S. also ruled that the wife's status as co-trustee did not give her a power "exercisable solely by" herself to vest trust income in herself.

2. In *Mesker v. United States*, 261 F. Supp. 817 (E.D. Mo. 1966), husband had the power, exercisable solely by himself, to vest trust income in his wife. The I.R.S. argued that the power caused him to be taxable under section 678(a)(1) on the trust's income, because he could use the power to discharge his legal obligation to support his wife. (Section 678(c) was inapplicable because he did not hold the power "in the capacity of trustee or co-trustee.") The court rejected the I.R.S. argument:

Plaintiff John B. G. Mesker, individually, had no power under the terms of the trust either to *apply* the trust income for the support of his wife or to direct the trustees so to do. The only authority he had was to direct the trustees to *pay* the income, *unconditionally, to* his wife, *for her to spend as she saw fit.* The language employed by the testators, permitting plaintiff to direct the trustee to pay the income of the trusts to *his wife* does not, under any reasonable construction, empower him to apply such payment in discharge of all or any part of his obligation to furnish his wife with support consistent with his financial condition and regardless of her financial situation. Nothing in the language of the trusts evidences an intent to make a gift to the *husband,* who alone would be legally benefited if he could apply the trust income to the support of his wife in lieu of expending his own funds. The trusts contemplate only an unconditional gift to the wife at the discretion of the husband.

261 F. Supp. at 820–21.

3. *Koffman v. United States,* 300 F.2d 176 (6th Cir. 1962) (per curiam), relied on section 678 to hold a legal life tenant taxable on all the ordinary income of her husband's estate, even though she had received only a portion of it. Nine years, which the court described as "more than ample time to perform the ordinary duties of administration," had elapsed since the husband's death. *See also Brown v. United States,* 890 F.2d 1329, 1345 n.20 (5th Cir. 1989), in which the court held that, even if the taxpayer's status were that of a testamentary trust beneficiary, rather than that of an estate distributee, his extensive control over the estate property that remained undistributed nine years after the decedent's death constituted a power described in section 678. He, rather than the estate, was therefore properly taxable on its income after the time the I.R.S. determined the estate had terminated.

4. Recall *United States v. De Bonchamps,* 278 F.2d 127 (9th Cir. 1960) (ch. 1, sec. A), and the material following *De Bonchamps,* which considered use of section 678 to impose income tax liability on life tenants for gains derived from sales of assets subject to legal life estates.

Problems

4-22. G creates an irrevocable *inter vivos* trust for the benefit of her three adult children, A, B, and C. The terms of the trust authorize the trustee to pay income and principal of the trust to A, B, and C, in such amounts and in such shares as the trustee deems appropriate. The trust continues until the death of the last to survive of G's children, at which time any remaining income or principal is to be distributed to G's then living issue, *per stirpes.* G names A as sole trustee. Of what effect is section 678?

4-23. Assume the facts of Problem 4-22, except that G names both A and A's spouse as co-trustees.

3. The Consequences of Grantor Trust Status

a. Attribution of Income, Deductions, and Credits

Internal Revenue Code:
  Section 671
Regulations:
  Sections 1.671-2, -3, -4

Revenue Ruling 69-70
1969-1 C.B. 182

Advice has been requested whether the income of a foreign trust, under the circumstances described below, is taxable to the beneficiary, an individual who is a resident of the United States.

X, a nonresident alien individual, created a foreign trust for the benefit of a resident of the United States. Under the terms of the trust instrument, X reserved absolute power to dispose of the beneficial enjoyment of both the income and the corpus of the trust. The trustees were nonresident aliens, and all of the trust property had a situs outside of the United States.

When income-producing property is placed in trust, the Federal income tax liability generally shifts from the grantor to the trust and beneficiaries in accordance with subparts A through D of part 1, subchapter J, chapter 1, subtitle A of the Internal Revenue Code of 1954 (sections 641 through 669).

However, where the grantor retains dominion and control over the income and corpus of the trust, subpart E of subchapter J (sections 671 through 678), rather than subparts A through D of subchapter J, is applicable. Under section 671 of the Code, where the grantor is treated as the owner of any portion of a trust, there are included in computing the taxable income and credits of the grantor, those items of income, deductions, and credits against tax of the trust which are attributable to that portion of the trust to the extent that such items would be taken into account in computing taxable income or credits against the tax of an individual.

Since X, a nonresident alien grantor, retained the absolute power to dispose of the beneficial enjoyment of both the income and the corpus of the trust, he is treated as the owner of the trust under section 674(a) of the Code. Accordingly, an individual beneficiary who is a resident of the United States is not taxable on that portion of the income distributed to him from the foreign trust which is considered to be owned by the nonresident alien grantor under subpart E of subchapter J of the Code.

* * *

Illustrative Material

The Small Business Job Protection Act of 1996 substantially expanded section 672(f), thus overruling Revenue Ruling 69-70 with respect to many trusts with non-United States grantors. Nevertheless, Revenue Ruling 69-70 continues to illustrate the consequences of grantor trust status generally, i.e., that distributions to the beneficiary of a grantor trust are income tax free.

Glenn E. Edgar
56 T.C. 717 (1971)

FEATHERSTON, *Judge*:

* * *

[T]he trustee…, in 1962, invested the corpora in two limited partnerships.… These partnerships incurred net operating losses in 1962, 1963, and 1964, and Edgar, grantor and life income beneficiary of the trusts, deducted in his returns for those years the portion of the losses allocable to and deductible by the trusts under section 702(a). Respondent disallowed the deductions, determining that Edgar had "not established that * * * [he was] a partner of these partnerships" or that he was "otherwise entitled to deduct such an amount in the computation of taxable income." Respondent urges that the trusts, rather than Edgar, were partners, and the "loss must be charged to the capital of * * * [the trusts], which fact renders it nondistributable to * * * [Edgar]," who is entitled only to trust income.

Whether Edgar is entitled to deduct the trusts' shares of the losses depends upon the application of sections 671 and 677. [The court quotes sections 677(a)(1) and 671.]

The key language in section 671 is "those items of income, deductions, and credits * * * attributable to that portion of the trust" of which the grantor is treated as owner. This language must be read, of course, in conjunction with section 677, which says that the grantor is to be treated as the owner of "any portion of a trust" whose income may be distributed to him. Edgar argues that since he reserves all the net income from the trusts, he is to be treated as owner of the corpus and, is consequently, entitled to "deductions" for the trusts' shares of the partnership losses. We do not agree.

The crucial question is whether the partnership losses are "attributable" to Edgar's income interests within the meaning of section 671. Where a trust is divided into fractional interests of both the income and corpus, a prorata share of the "items of income, deduction, and credit" is ordinarily allocated to each interest. Sec. 1.671-3(c), Income Tax Regs. Similarly, if the portion treated as owned by the grantor consists of specific trust property, all items directly related to that property are attributable to such portion. Sec. 1.671-3(a)(2), Income Tax Regs. The more difficult problem arises where, as in the instant case, the trust is divided into income and remainder interests, with current net income being distributed to the grantor and capital gains being added to principal. Compare sec. 1.671-3(a)(1) and sec. 1.677(a)-1(g), example (1), Income Tax Regs. In such circumstances, a determination must be made as to whether each item is properly attributable to the income or the remainder portion of the trust.

We think the guiding principle in this last situation—the factual situation here presented—is stated in sec. 1.671-3(c) [second sentence], Income Tax Regs.…

The rules for computing the tax liability of a "current income beneficiary" are set forth in subparts A through D, part 1, subchapter J of the Code. Generally speaking, a trust and its beneficiaries are treated as separate and distinct taxable entities. The broad general rule is that the income of a trust is taxable to the fiduciary, and his taxable income is computed in the same manner as in the case of an individual, sec. 641(b), with specified exceptions. One exception is that a deduction is allowable for income which is distributed currently. Secs. 651 and 661. No provision is made, however, for the distribution of a trust's losses to its beneficiaries, and no provision is made for a beneficiary to deduct the losses of a trust of which he is the beneficiary. Indeed, section 642(d) specifies that "The benefit of the deduction for the net operating losses provided by section 172 shall be allowed to estates and trusts," thus indicating that they are not distributable to the beneficiaries. The last clause of section 1.671-3(c) [second sentence] — "including expenses allocable to corpus which enter into the computation of distributable net income"—does not include losses of capital incurred in the operation of a business. *Mellott v. United States,* 257 F.2d 798 (C.A. 3, 1958); *George W. Vreeland,* 16 T.C. 1041, 1049–1050 (1951); *George W. Balkwill,* 25 B.T.A. 1147 (1932), affd. 77 F.2d 569 (C.A. 6, 1935), certiorari denied 296 U.S. 609 (1935); *George M. Studebaker et al.,* 2 B.T.A. 1020 (1925).

In addition, this rule for apportioning the items of income, deductions, and credits of a trust between its ordinary income and remainder portions was previously contained in section 29.167-1(c), Regs. 111, which interpreted 1939 Code section 167. That section corresponds to section 677 of the 1954 Code. S. Rept. No. 1622, to accompany H.R. 8300 (Pub. L. No. 591), 83d Cong., 2d Sess., pp. 86, 371 (1954). Under the 1939 Code rule, expenses chargeable to corpus were not deductible by the income beneficiary. *George B. Markle, Jr.,* 17 T.C. 1593, 1599–1600 (1952).

Finally, the economic effect of losses does not fall on the current income beneficiary. Under trust law, when a trustee is empowered to continue the operation of a business, any net losses incurred by the business are allocated to corpus and are not set off against income received in later years. Revised Uniform Principal and Income Act, sec. 8(a), Uniform Principal and Income Act, sec. 7(4); Restatement, Trusts 2d, sec. 233, comment (c). Thus, the tax law accords with the economic realities.[28]

This holding is consistent with the fact that Edgar was previously allowed charitable contribution deductions for the values of the remainder interests in the trusts. A contrary holding would, in effect, allow him at least a partial double deduction—a deduction for the value of the charitable remainder interest in the corpus and a deduction for the part of the corpus consumed by such losses. We do not think sections 671 and 677 were intended to confer such largess.

* * *

---

28. Sec. 1.642(d)-1, Income Tax Regs., provides that, in computing a net operating loss, "a trust shall exclude that portion of the income and deductions attributable to the grantor or another person under sections 671 through 678." However, as discussed above, since Edgar has only an interest in the income and no interest in the corpus, his deductions are to be computed as if he were a "current income beneficiary" rather than as a grantor. In addition, contrast sec. 642(e), which provides that "An estate or trust shall be allowed the deduction for depreciation and depletion only to the extent not allowable to beneficiaries," and sec. [167(d)], which states that "In the case of property held in trust, the allowable deduction shall be apportioned between the income beneficiaries and the trustee in accordance with the pertinent provisions of the instrument creating the trust, or, in the absence of such provisions, on the basis of the trust income allocable to each." None of these special provisions applies to partnership losses of a trust.

Illustrative Material

1. Is *Edgar*'s denial of the losses to the grantor persuasive? Does section 643 exclude net operating loss deductions from the computation of distributable net income?

2. For a thoughtful analysis of *Edgar,* as well as the general problem of attributing items of income, deduction, and credit to a grantor treated as owner of the income portion only, see Schmolka, *Selected Aspects of the Grantor Trust Rules,* 9 U. Miami Inst. Est. Plan. ¶¶ 1400, 1403.2 (1975).

3. Tax-exempt income received by a trust retains its character in the hands of one treated as its owner under subpart E. Rev. Rul. 60-370, 1960-2 C.B. 203. The I.R.S. cited Treas. Reg. §1.671-2(c).

4. In Rev. Rul. 79-223, 1979-2 C.B. 254, a bank created an irrevocable trust. All of the trust's income was payable to charity. The bank retained a reversion, but the trust was not to terminate for more than ten years. Thus, under the then-applicable version of section 673, the bank was not treated as owner of the ordinary income portion of the trust. However, under section 677 the bank was treated as owner of the trust principal. The primary issue related to the charitable deduction. The I.R.S. ruled that, since the bank was not treated as owner of the trust's ordinary income, it was not entitled to the trust's charitable deduction. Instead, the trust was entitled under section 642(c) to deduct its own charitable contributions in computing such of its taxable income as was not controlled by subpart E.

On the other hand, where section 677 caused grantors to be treated as owners of all portions of a trust, each could deduct, under sections 671 and 170, his pro rata share of any contributions the trust made to charity. *Irving I. Rusoff,* 65 T.C. 459 (1975), *aff'd mem.,* 556 F.2d 559 (2d Cir. 1977). The court relied on Treas. Reg. §1.671-2(c). *See also Stussy v. Commissioner,* 73 T.C.M. (CCH) 3194 (1997).

5. Prior to enactment of section 644 by the Tax Reform Act of 1986, trusts often used taxable years ending shortly after those of their beneficiaries, in order to exploit the tax deferral potential of sections 652(c) and 662(c). In *William Scheft,* 59 T.C. 428 (1972), the grantor of several reversionary trusts was treated by section 677(a)(2) as owner of the principal of the trusts. He was therefore taxable on the trusts' capital gains. The trusts sold securities and thereby realized capital gains in 1968. However, their fiscal years did not end until March 31, 1969. The grantor argued that, in the absence of statutory language varying the rule of section 662(c), he properly included the gains in income for his taxable year ending December 31, 1969, the year in which the trusts' taxable years ended. The court rejected that argument. Citing the mandate of Treas. Reg. §1.671-2(c) to treat income as though received "directly" by the grantor, the court required inclusion of the gains in the grantor's taxable year ending December 31, 1968. The court thereby "disregarded" the separate existence of the trusts. In *Amabile v. Commissioner,* 51 T.C.M. (CCH) 963 (1986), the Tax Court extended *Scheft* to a grantor who was treated as owner of only one-half of a portion of a trust.

6. In Rev. Rul. 57-390, 1957-2 C.B. 326, an accrual-method, calendar-year taxpayer was treated under section 676 as owner of all portions of a revocable trust. The trust used the cash method of accounting and was on a fiscal year. The I.R.S. ruled that both the trust's taxable year and its method of accounting "should be disregarded," in an effort, under Treas. Reg. §1.671-3(a)(1), to tax the grantor as if the trust had "not been in existence."

Under Rev. Rul. 57-390, if subpart E treats a grantor as owner of all portions of a trust, the trust's taxable year has no significance to either itself or the grantor. Thus, in Rev.

Rul. 90-55, 1990-2 C.B. 161, the I.R.S. ruled that section 644 did not require such a trust to adopt a calendar year, notwithstanding the absence of a specific statutory exception. In the ruling, the grantor, a fiscal-year corporation, apparently wanted its fully revocable trust to adopt its own fiscal year.

7. *Return requirements.* Section 6012(a)(4) requires that Form 1041 be filed with respect to "[e]very trust having for the taxable year any taxable income, or having gross income of $600 or over." Treas. Reg. §1.671-4(a) states that "items of income, deduction, and credit attributable to any portion of a trust that, under the provisions of subpart E ... is treated as owned by the grantor or another person, are not reported by the trust on Form 1041 ... but are shown on a separate statement to be attached to that form." Rev. Rul. 75-278, 1975-2 C.B 461, nonetheless concludes that if subpart E treats a grantor as owner of a portion of a trust, the income, deductions, and credits attributable to the grantor are "taken into account" in determining whether it is necessary to file Form 1041.

If subpart E treats the grantor or another person as owner of the entire trust, Treas. Reg. §1.671-4(b), effective for tax years beginning on or after January 1, 1996, provides the trustee with various alternatives to filing Form 1041. In such a case, however, the trustee must provide various types of information detailed in the regulation to various combinations of the trust's "payors," the grantor or other owner, and the I.R.S.

8. *Termination of Grantor Trust Status.* A grantor trust loses its grantor trust status upon the death of its grantor. *See* Treas. Reg. §1.671-4(h)(2).

The terms of a trust may call for distribution of the trust property immediately upon the death of the grantor. However, the required distribution certainly will not occur immediately. In the meantime, the "trust" will continue to generate income, deductions, and credits. For discussion of the tax consequences, see Ufford, *Income Taxation of the Funded Revocable Trust after the Death of the Grantor,* 30 Tax Law. 37 (1976); Fleming, *Taxation of Income of Grantor Trusts after Death of Grantor and Before Implementation of Successor Trusts or Shares,* 63 Ill. Bar J. 78 (1974).

A grantor trust also may lose its grantor trust status upon relinquishment by the grantor of certain interests in or powers over the trust. *See* Rev. Rul. 75-307, 1975-2 C.B. 256. Thereafter, the grantor is not taxable on any of the trust's income; nor is the grantor entitled to any of its deductions or credits.

9. *Operation of the "2% haircut."* In *Bay v. Commissioner,* 76 T.C.M. (CCH) 866 (1998), the court held that a grantor who was apparently treated as owner of all portions of her grantor trust was subject to the 2% "haircut" under section 67 on deductions from the trust attributable to various expenses, such as investment advisory fees. The court explained:

> [S]ection 67(e) does not and cannot apply to grantor trusts. Because the items of income and deductions are passed through to the grantor, the adjusted gross income of a grantor trust, in effect, is not a viable notion either conceptually under the relevant statutory scheme, or for reporting purposes.... These items are treated as though received or paid by her, instead of by the trust. Sec. 1.671-2(c), Income Tax Regs.

The court also quoted and relied on Temp. Reg. §1.67-2T(b)(1).

10. In Notice 2000-44, 2000-2 C.B. 255, the I.R.S. stated that each item of capital gain or loss attributed by section 671 to a grantor is to appear on the grantor's individual Form 1040 separately, rather than as a net amount.

Problems

4-24. G creates an *inter vivos* trust. All of the income is to be paid to G during G's lifetime. Upon G's death, the trust is to terminate, and the trust principal is to be distributed to G's then living issue, *per stirpes.* This year the trust receives $10,000 in dividends and realizes a $2,000 capital gain. Its trustee receives compensation in the amount of $1,000, and G receives $9,500 of income. What are the tax consequences to G and the trust?

4-25. This year G creates an *inter vivos* trust. All of the income is to be paid to G's sister, S, for 11 years. Thereafter, the trust is to terminate, and the principal is to be paid to G. This year the trust receives $10,000 in dividends and realizes a $2,000 capital gain. Its trustee receives compensation in the amount of $1,000, and S receives $9,500 of income. What are the tax consequences to G, S, and the trust?

4-26. Assume the facts of Problem 4-25, except that the trust is to terminate after a period of years long enough to avoid application of section 673.

4-27. Assume the facts of Problem 4-26, except that the trust is revocable.

b. Collateral Consequences of Grantor Trust Status

Determining who is responsible for various items of income and who is entitled to various deductions and credits does not answer all the tax questions that relate to property held by grantor trusts. For example, the Code frequently specifies particular tax consequences upon the transfer or disposition of property by its owner. If a trust is described in subpart E, section 671 treats its grantor as the "owner" of some portion of the trust. But "ownership" in this sense is merely a statutory device. Congress clearly did not intend this "ownership" to be taken literally. So what happens if a grantor transfers property to a grantor trust in a fashion that normally would cause a particular tax consequence? Does the trust's status under subpart E change the result? The following materials represent only a sampling of the Code provisions under which the issue can arise.

(i) Dispositions of Installment Obligations

Under section 453B, if an installment obligation is "distributed," "transmitted," or "otherwise disposed of," gain or loss results to the extent of the difference between the basis of the obligation and the fair market value of the obligation at the time of disposition. Transfer of an installment obligation to a trust therefore generally results in a "disposition" for purposes of section 453B. *See* Rev. Rul. 76-530, 1976-2 C.B. 132 (transfer to trust in which grantor-transferor retained no interest). As a result, transfer of an installment obligation in trust can be an expensive proposition.

Does the fact that the transferee trust is described in subpart E matter? The answer seems to be, in general, "yes." *See* Rev. Rul. 74-613, 1974-2 C.B. 153 (transfer to revocable trust). No "disposition" occurs; instead, the grantor continues using the installment method "as if the trust were not in existence." Similarly, retransfer of installment obligations by a trust to its grantor-transferor may not be a "disposition." *See* Rev. Rul. 76-100, 1976-1 C.B. 123 (transfer from revocable trust).

Not all transfers to and from grantor trusts escape treatment as "dispositions," however. The key seems to be whether the transferor is treated as owner of the portion of the trust to which the deferred profit element of the installment obligation accrues. If a grantor retains a reversion, even if protected by section 673, he or she is nonetheless treated, under section 677, as owner of the principal portion of the trust, to which the deferred profit normally accrues. Thus, the grantor remains taxable on the obligation's deferred profit element, notwithstanding the transfer in trust. As a result, on these facts there seems to be no reason to require acceleration of the gain, and the I.R.S. has so ruled. Rev. Rul. 67-70, 1967-1 C.B. 106. In Rev. Rul. 81-98, 1981-1 C.B. 40, retention by the transferor-grantor of the current right to receive the deferred profit element of each installment payment similarly triggered section 677, causing him to be treated as owner of the principal portion of the trust. Here, too, the I.R.S. ruled that no "disposition" occurred upon the transfer to the trust. *Springer v. United States*, 69-2 U.S.T.C. ¶ 9567 (N.D. Ala. 1969), appears to be directly contrary but is poorly reasoned and written.

In contrast, in Rev. Rul. 67-167, 1967-1 C.B. 107, the I.R.S. found a "disposition" upon transfer of installment obligations to a trust, even though section 677 treated the grantor as owner of the principal portion of the trust. There, however, under the terms of the trust agreement, the entire amount of each installment payment was payable to the income beneficiary during the term of the trust. As a result, section 677 did not attribute the deferred profit element to the grantor.

In *A.W. Legg*, 57 T.C. 164 (1971), *aff'd per curiam*, 496 F.2d 1179 (9th Cir. 1974), the transferors retained what amounted to an income interest in the trust to which they transferred an installment obligation. Though they were thus treated by section 677 as the owners of the ordinary income portion of the trust, they were not treated as the owners of the trust principal, to which the deferred profit component of each installment payment presumably accrued under state law. Because the transferors would thus not otherwise be taxable on the deferred profit, the court held that the transfer constituted a "disposition."

(ii) Distribution Deduction

Estate of O'Connor
69 T.C. 165 (1977)

TANNENWALD, Judge:

* * *

The issues before us are:

(1) Whether the decedent's estate properly claimed distributions deductions in respect of amounts received by a charitable foundation on the grounds either (a) that such amounts constituted distributions to a marital trust created under decedent's last will and testament or (b) that, since the foundation succeeded to the interests in the marital trust, such amounts should be treated as distributions to a beneficiary under said last will and testament; [and]

(2) If the estate is entitled to such distributions deductions on the ground that they were made to the marital trust, whether the marital trust is entitled to distributions deductions in respect of the amounts received by such charitable foundation....

A. Lindsay O'Connor (decedent) died on May 9, 1968, a resident of Delaware County, N.Y. His last will and testament, dated December 11, 1957, was admitted to probate by decree of the Surrogate's Court, County of Delaware, N.Y., dated May 20, 1968, and letters testamentary and letters of trusteeship were issued to Dermod Ives and United States Trust Co. of New York authorizing them to act as executors and trustees under the will. A joint petition was filed herein by Dermod Ives and United States Trust Co. of New York as executors and trustees and by Olive B. Price, Robert L. and Lucille S. Bishop, and Donald F. and Edna G. Bishop, individually....

The executors filed an estate tax return on June 24, 1969. They elected a fiscal year ending October 31 for income tax reporting purposes. A short-period income tax return was filed by the estate for the period from the date of decedent's death to October 31, 1968. Thereafter, income tax returns for the estate were duly filed for the taxable years ending October 31, 1969, October 31, 1970, and October 31, 1971. The trustees elected the calendar year for income tax purposes and duly filed forms 1041 for the marital trust and for each of the other trusts for 1969, 1970, and 1971.

The dispositive provisions of the decedent's will basically provided for the division of his estate into two shares. The first share, consisting of one-half of the entire net estate, was bequeathed in trust (marital trust) for his widow, Olive B. O'Connor, who was given the income therefrom, coupled with a general testamentary power of appointment over corpus in favor of "such persons and/or corporations as she may appoint" and a power to withdraw at any time (including the year of death) any or all of the corpus by a written election to be filed with the trustees. As to the second share, the decedent made some specific pecuniary bequests and directed that the balance be divided into three equal parts, to be held in trust, with income from each part to be paid or applied for the benefit of Olive B. Price, Donald F. Bishop, and Robert L. Bishop (niece and nephews of the widow), respectively.

On May 23, 1968, the decedent's widow, Olive B. O'Connor (Mrs. O'Connor), notified the executors and trustees in writing that she elected to have all of the principal of the marital trust paid to her. By instrument, executed the same day and entitled "Gift Assignment of Interest in Estate of A. Lindsay O'Connor," Mrs. O'Connor assigned all of her right, title, and interest to the marital trust, together with any income from such property, to the A. Lindsay and Olive B. O'Connor Foundation (hereinafter the foundation). The foundation had been created by Mrs. O'Connor in 1965 and was, at all times material herein, recognized by the Internal Revenue Service as a charitable foundation within the meaning of section 501(c)(3). For the year 1968, Mrs. O'Connor filed a gift tax return in which she reported the assignment of her interest in the marital trust to the foundation; the value of such interest in both income and corpus was estimated to be $25 million.

With respect to its 3 taxable years involved herein, the parties have stipulated that "the estate made [various] distributions to the beneficiaries thereof"....

The total value of such distributions in each case exceeded the distributable net income of the estate as reflected in its income tax returns for each of its taxable years in issue. The parties further stipulated that the marital trust distributed all that it received from the estate to the foundation shortly after receipt.

The parties have further stipulated that the administration of the estate continues pending the outcome of this proceeding; that the trustees continue to administer the marital trust, receiving estate assets from time to time, and in general turning over the assets received to the foundation shortly after receipt by the trust; that a small balance of principal cash is now maintained by the trust; and that, when the controversies involved in this proceeding are finally determined and the trustees have received from the executors all property passing under the will to the marital trust (which must be distributed to the trustees, despite Mrs. O'Connor's assignment, under New York law), they will make a final judicial accounting to the Surrogate's Court and only after that accounting proceeding is completed and all assets remaining in their possession thereafter have been distributed can the administration of the trust be considered completed.

For its taxable years at issue, the estate claimed [various] distributions deductions under section 661(a)(2)....

For its taxable years in question, returns were filed for the marital trust on which the amounts distributed from the estate and passed through to the foundation in accordance with the election and assignment executed by Mrs. O'Connor were reported and deducted under section 661(a).

* * *

Respondent made [various] determinations in respect of the above-outlined distribution plan:

(1) The marital trust was not a recognizable tax entity because it was a passive trust under New York law; [and]

(2) Section 661(a) does not permit a deduction to an estate or trust for distributions to charitable entities where such distributions do not qualify for deduction under section 642(c)....

The frame of reference for issues posed by respondent's determinations can be simply stated: Who is taxable, and to what extent, on income earned and distributed by the decedent's estate during its period of administration? Resolution of the issues is not as simply divined.

The core questions with respect to the amounts received by the foundation are (a) to what extent should the marital trust be recognized for the purposes of this proceeding; (b) should section 1.663(a)-2, Income Tax Regs.,[8] be given effect; and (c) if the regulation is not given effect, should the foundation be treated as a "beneficiary" for the purposes of the distributions deduction?

Before turning to these questions, we deem it appropriate to deal with an addendum to one of petitioners' briefs in which an attempt is made to support the proposition that the distributions to the foundation qualify for the charitable deduction provided for in section 642(c). One of the critical requirements of that section is that the amount in question be paid "pursuant to the terms of the governing instrument." Petitioners seek to bring the payments to the foundation within section 642(c) by latching on to the provision in the decedent's will granting Mrs. O'Connor a general power of appointment "to such persons and/or corporations" as she sees fit. Aside from the fact that Mrs. O'Connor in form never exercised her power of appointment in favor of anyone, the mere reference to "corporations," even if coupled with decedent's knowledge of the existence of the foundation, simply does not meet the test of section 642(c), namely, that the governing instrument (in this case, decedent's will) must

---

8. That section of the regulations provides in pertinent part as follows: "Any amount paid, permanently set aside, or to be used for the charitable, etc., purposes specified in section 642(c) and which is allowable as a deduction under that section is not allowed as a deduction to an estate or trust under section 661 or treated as an amount distributed for purposes of determining the amounts includable in gross income of beneficiaries under section 662. *Amounts paid, permanently set aside, or to be used for charitable, etc., purposes are deductible by estates or trusts only as provided in section 642(c). (Emphasis added.)"*

contain some manifestation of charitable intent. See Ernest & Mary Hayward Weir Found. v. United States, 362 F.Supp. 928, 939 (S.D.N.Y. 1973), affd. per curiam 508 F.2d 894 (2d Cir. 1974). Cf. Estate of Pickard v. Commissioner, 60 T.C. 618, 622 (1973), affd. without opinion 503 F.2d 1404 (6th Cir. 1974). Accordingly, we now turn to the core questions.

We first direct our attention to the estate's claimed distributions deductions for amounts passed through the marital trust to the foundation. This issue involves an initial determination of whether the marital trust should be recognized for purposes of this proceeding.[9]

Although respondent has, by virtue of various parts of the stipulation of facts, conceded that the marital trust existed in the sense that distributions from the estate were required, by virtue of New York law, to be made to and through the trustees, he nevertheless contends that the trust was passive under section 7-1.2, New York Estates, Powers & Trusts Law, and is not recognizable for tax purposes.

We find it unnecessary to resolve the status of the marital trust for State law purposes. Even assuming arguendo that throughout the years in question a valid trust[10] existed for purposes of State law, it does not follow that it was a recognizable tax entity. Indeed, we think that by virtue of the operation of section 678 it was not.

When a grantor or other person has certain powers in respect of trust property that are tantamount to dominion and control over such property, the Code "looks through" the trust form and deems such grantor or other person to be the owner of the trust property and attributes the trust income to such person. See secs. 671, et seq. By attributing such income directly to a grantor or other person, the Code, in effect, disregards the trust entity.[12] Income is deemed, therefore, to have been received by the "owner" of the property.

The circumstances in which a person other than a grantor is considered the owner of trust property are set forth in section 678....

There can be no doubt that, prior to her election to withdraw corpus and her assignment thereof, Mrs. O'Connor's powers over the trust property were sufficiently extensive to cause her to be the owner thereof under section 678 for Federal income tax purposes.[13] By her withdrawal of corpus and her assignment, Mrs. O'Connor relinquished all powers in respect of the trust property and was no longer the owner thereof within the meaning of section 678.

---

9. There is no doubt that if the marital trust is a viable tax entity, the estate is entitled to a sec. 661(a) deduction in respect of its distributions thereto and the issue then becomes whether the trust is entitled to a distributions deduction for amounts paid to the foundation.

10. We have no doubt that a valid trust existed from the time of decedent's death until Mrs. O'-Connor's election to withdraw corpus and her assignment to the foundation. However, the only duty of the trustees thereafter was to transfer property received from the estate to the foundation. Whether this singular duty suffices to constitute an active trust is not free from doubt under New York law. See I. Glasser, "Trust, Perpetuities, Accumulations and Powers under the Estates, Powers, and Trusts Law," 33 Brooklyn L. Rev. 551, 555–556 (1967).

12. The trust is not required to report income attributed to another on its Form 1041, but should show such income on a separate statement attached thereto. Sec. 1.671-4, Income Tax Regs. To the extent that a trust does not have any taxable income and does not have gross income in excess of $600, however, it need not file a Form 1041. Sec. 6012(a)(4).

13. Indeed, petitioners acknowledge the applicability of sec. 678 to Mrs. O'Connor albeit in another context. Petitioners opine that Mrs. O'Connor was a "beneficiary" of the estate; that, by operation of that section, she was the "owner"; and that, upon her assignment, the foundation stepped into her shoes and became a "beneficiary" of the estate, thus entitling the estate to a sec. 642(c) deduction for distributions thereto.

By that assignment, however, the foundation had an immediate right to all income and corpus as it filtered into the marital trust.[14] Indeed, the nature of the foundation's rights in respect of the trust property was so extensive so as to necessarily include the somewhat lesser rights spelled out in section 678(a)(1). Thus, it is clear that, within the meaning of that section, the foundation was the "owner" of all of the trust property (both income and corpus)[15] passing from the estate to the marital trust. We recognize that the only function of section 678 is to tax income to the person having the power to vest either trust corpus or trust income in himself, but the means Congress has employed to do this (attribution of ownership) routes income from its source directly to the "owner" as though no trust exists.[16] We think it anomalous to view the estate as making distributions to the marital trust for tax purposes when the statute requires us to view the foundation as receiving distributions from the estate.[17]

As further support for the position that the marital trust was not a recognizable entity for tax purposes, we would add that it does not fall within the definition of trusts which clearly contemplates more activity on the part of a trust than the simple conduit role assumed herein. [The court quotes from Section 301.7701-4(a), Proced. & Admin. Regs.]

Even assuming the trustees took legal title under State law, it is clear that their activity in respect of the marital trust property failed to rise to the level of protection or conservation.

In sum, we think that, because of the operation of section 678, the marital trust was not a recognizable tax entity and the foundation should be treated as the owner of the trust property. Accordingly, the estate must be deemed to have made its distributions directly to the charitable foundation.

Having decided that the marital trust should not be recognized for tax purposes, we are still left with the question whether the amounts received by the foundation constitute distributions deductible by the estate.

---

14. At the time of the assignment, the marital trust was not funded. From the moment the estate passed any assets to the marital trust (the entity that the parties stipulated to be the proper estate distributee under State law), the foundation had an immediate right to the same.

15. Sec. 678 can apply to either all or part of trust property depending upon the extent of the "owner's" rights over such property. See sec. 671.

16. See generally H. Rept. 1337, to accompany H.R. 8300 (Pub. L. 591), 83d Cong., 2d Sess. A211–218 (1954). The legislative history clearly indicates an intent to disregard the trust form when ownership is attributed to a grantor or other person in that, along with ownership, all items of tax significance (income, deductions, and credits) are likewise attributed to such persons. E.g., when ownership of trust property is attributed under secs. 671, et seq., income is included in the income of the "owner" and he is allowed deductions for expenses "which he would have been entitled to if the trust had not been created." H. Rept. 1337, supra at A212 (emphasis added). See also sec. 1.671-3, Income Tax Regs.

17. If sec. 678 were construed otherwise so that a trust existed, at least insofar as the estate was concerned, the estate would get a sec. 661 deduction for amounts passed to such trust and a share of its distributable net income would be allocated to the trust. But, as between the trust and the foundation, sec. 678 would come into play to attribute all trust income to the foundation. Because of the operation of sec. 678 at this level only, the issue of whether or not the trust may claim a sec. 661 deduction for its distributions to the foundation is mooted because the trust would have no income to offset with a sec. 661 deduction.

We think it incongruous to say that, on the one hand, the trust could be allocated income from the estate and, on the other hand, the trust could not have any income.

We also note that, in the context of this case, we are dealing solely with the impact of sec. 678 insofar as other provisions of subch. J are concerned. We do not in any way imply that a similar analysis would necessarily obtain in situations where there is an interplay between sec. 678 and provisions of the Code outside of subch. J, such as are involved, for example, in the cases discussed in Judge Fay's dissenting opinion.

We turn first to the principal question on which the parties have locked horns, namely, the effect which should be given to the [last sentence] of section 1.663(a)-2 of respondent's regulations (see also n. 8 supra).

* * *

While we recognize that *Mott* [*v. United States, supra* (ch. 3, sec. F(2)),] is distinguishable from the situation existing herein in that we are concerned with distributions of income (as well as corpus) while, in that case, only a distribution of corpus was involved, we consider such factual distinction insufficient to justify not applying the test of Commissioner v. South Texas Lumber Co., supra [cited in *Mott*].[21] In so stating, we find it unnecessary to go as far as the Court of Claims did and hold that any rule, other than that embodied in respondent's regulation, would be unreasonable. Nor can we refuse to sustain the validity of respondent's regulation simply because, had we been charged with responsibility for writing the regulation, we might have constructed a different provision.[22] We go no further than to conclude that a literal interpretation of section 661(a)(2), which would permit (subject to the distributable net income ceiling) the deductibility of all amounts distributed and not otherwise expressly disallowed ... would be inconsistent with the statutory framework and overall legislative objectives of subchapter J and that, as applied to the circumstances herein, respondent's regulations should be sustained. Admittedly there are two provisions (secs. 661(a) and 642(c)) which can be said to bear on the instant case. But one (sec. 642(c)) is specific and the other (sec. 661(a)) is general. The situation, if not precisely within the ejusdem generis rule, at least falls within the principles embodied in that rule....

Casco Bank & Trust Co. v. United States, 406 F. Supp. 247 (D. Me. 1975), and Bank of America Nat. Trust & Sav. Assn. v. United States, 203 F. Supp. 152 (N.D. Cal. 1962), affd. on this issue 326 F.2d 51 (9th Cir. 1963), relied on by petitioners, which involved the status of amounts concededly constituting distributions deductions to an estate, but "trapped" as principal in the hands of the recipient trustee, are inapposite to the case at bar. The same is true of Harkness v. United States, 469 F.2d 310 (Ct. Cl. 1972), which dealt with the allocation as between beneficiaries of income that clearly qualified as distributions deductions to the estate.

Having reached the conclusion that, by virtue of section 1.663(a)-2 of respondent's regulations, the estate herein should not be allowed distributions deductions for amounts distributed to the foundation, we find it unnecessary to deal with the question whether, in any event, the foundation qualifies as a "beneficiary" of decedent's estate so as to permit the deduction of distributions to it under section 661(a). See Mott v. United States, supra at 517–518; United States v. James, 333 F.2d 748, 750 (9th Cir. 1964); duPont Testamentary Trust v. Commissioner, 66 T.C. 761, 767 (1976). Cf. Nemser v. Commissioner, 66 T.C. 780 (1976), affd. 556 F.2d 558 (2d Cir. 1977); Sletteland v. Commissioner, 43 T.C. 602 (1965); compare Cummings v. United States, an unreported case (C.D. Cal. 1969, 23 AFTR 2d 69-1322, 69-1 USTC par. 9359); Estate of McCoy v. Commissioner, 50 T.C. 562 (1968). Similarly, we find it unnecessary to deal

---

21. Even though the distributions herein included income, the consequence of invalidating respondent's regulation invites the same abuse as where no income is in fact distributed to charity. In such a case, applying sec. 661 would allocate to the charity and therefore make nontaxable an amount of income bearing no relationship to the amount of income actually distributed to the charity.

22. The opinion in *Mott v. United States,* supra, has been criticized. See M. Ferguson, J. Freeland, & R. Stephens, Federal Income Taxation of Estates and Beneficiaries 88 (1976 Supp.). See also, A. Michaelson, Income Taxation of Estates and Trusts 57 and n. 70 (1974 rev.).

with the question as to whether, assuming the foundation qualifies as a "beneficiary," deductions should be denied for amounts distributed to it because section 661(a) permits deductions only for distributions to taxable beneficiaries. See Mott v. United States, supra at 518.

Although we have determined that amounts distributed to the foundation are not deductible by the estate, we do not agree with respondent that such nondeductible distributions work an allocable reduction in the estate's claimed distributions deductions for years in which the estate made other distributions that do qualify for deduction. The operation of subchapter J permits an estate to take deductions under section 661 for all qualifying distributions up to but not exceeding the amount of its distributable net income. For its 1970 fiscal year, the estate made otherwise qualifying distributions in excess of its distributable net income and respondent does not contend to the contrary. Consequently, the amount of its distributions deduction for that year remains unaffected. The same considerations apply to the estate's 1971 fiscal year. However, in that year, the estate made qualifying distributions in an amount less than its distributable net income and it is entitled to deduct only the amount of such distributions.

* * *

[Judge Scott, in dissent, warned that to disregard the trust entity wherever section 678 treated a person as the owner of trust property would mean that the "trust entity of many marital trusts [would] be disregarded, since in many marital trusts the beneficiary has the power to vest 'the corpus or income therefrom' in herself."]

FAY, J., dissenting:

I respectfully dissent in the conclusions reached herein by the majority. Specifically, I believe the opinion to be faulty in its reasoning and holding regarding the tax status of so-called grantor trusts.

As its main contention for ignoring the trust created under the will of A. Lindsay O'-Connor, the majority makes the bold assertion that: "By attributing such income directly to a grantor or other person (via secs. 671, et seq.), the Code, in effect, disregards the trust entity." Devoid of any articulation of rationale for its holding, the logical result of the majority's opinion is that a grantor trust has no separate transactional existence under the Internal Revenue Code. I cannot agree.

Sections 673 through 678 enumerate certain situations where a grantor or other person will "be treated as the owner of any portion of a trust" over which he possesses a proscribed power or beneficial interest.[2] Reference as to the tax consequences of being so treated, however, must be made to section 671....

It is clear that the statute in its wording presupposes the existence of a valid trust. It is equally clear that the purpose of the statutory scheme of subpart E of subchapter J is merely to identify the person responsible for reporting certain income and deduction items realized by a trust. Nowhere does the statute state, much less "require," as the majority maintains,[3] that the trust not be recognized for tax purposes. Indeed, the regulations take a position to the contrary.

---

2. "Portion" could include part or all of a trust depending upon the extent of a person's rights over its income and corpus. See sec. 1.671-3, Income Tax Regs. See also L. Schmolka, "Selected Aspects of the Grantor Trust Rules," U. Miami Ninth Inst. on Est . Plan., par. 1400 (1975).

3. See text accompanying n. 17 of the majority opinion.

In discussing the concept of what is a "trust" for Federal tax purposes, section 301.7701-4(a), Proced. & Admin. Regs., in an obvious reference to a grantor trust, states....

I believe the majority in its opinion, if not expressly, has effectively invalidated this regulation altogether.

I am not proposing that a grantor trust's existence should always be recognized for tax purposes; rather, I am merely contending that an examination should be made in each case to determine if some other congressional tax policy would best be served by not regarding the trust as a separate transactional entity. If such a policy does not exist, then, absent other reasons, I would not ignore the trust....[4]

In Swanson v. Commissioner, 518 F.2d 59 (8th Cir. 1975), affg. a Memorandum Opinion of this Court, G created an irrevocable trust in which he had no beneficial interest. However, the trust instrument did permit him to amend the trust so long as such amendment did not vest in G any right to the trust's income or corpus. The trust purchased an insurance policy on G's life from a related corporation. Subsequently, G died and the trust collected approximately $914,000 compared with its total investment in the policy of about $208,000. We stated the issue as follows:

> Section 101(a) states that * * * amounts received under a life insurance policy are not includable in gross income. Section 101(a)(2)(B) provides that life insurance proceeds are includable in gross income in the case of a transfer for valuable consideration unless the transfer is to the insured * * *. The issue is whether the exception to the transfer for valuable consideration rule of section 101 is applicable to the transfer of life insurance policies to the Swanson Trusts. (T.C. Memo. 1974-61. Fn. ref. omitted.)

The taxpayer argued that because under section 674, G was treated as the "owner" of the entire trust and because he was also the insured under the policy, the proceeds received by the trust were excludable from its gross income under the general rule of section 101(a). The respondent, on the other hand, argued that the policies were transferred to the trust and not to G. In short, although G was the "owner" of the entire trust by virtue of section 674, respondent argued that the trust's existence should not be ignored for purposes of section 101.[5]

The Eighth Circuit held as follows:

> We cannot accept the government's contention that in this case Swanson, the grantor of the grantor-trusts, is not deemed the owner of the trusts for any purpose other than that of taxing trust income to him, and the trusts, therefore, retain their identity as a separate tax entity under Section 101(a) (2)(B). The provision in each trust instrument that it shall be subject to interpretation or amendment by the maker (except with respect to vesting property, income or corpus in himself as an individual) gave the grantor complete control over the insurance policies in question. Through his control over the trusts, he could exercise all of the incidents of ownership over the policies. He could, among other things, cause (1) a change in beneficiaries, (2) loans to be secured on the policies, or (3) even have the policies cancelled.

* * *

---

4. For a brief but excellent discussion of this issue, see L. Schmolka, supra n.2.

5. Because of a concession made by respondent, this Court never reached the precise issue stated in the text and dealt with by the Eighth Circuit.

The mere fact that the legislative history of Section 674 and related statutes indicates that the purpose of the legislation was to tax the income of grantor-trusts to the grantor does not require the strained construction of Section 101(a) urged by the government.

We hold that in this case, since Swanson owned and controlled the trusts, the policies were transferred to the "insured" within the meaning of Section 101(a)(2)(B) and the net proceeds are therefore excludable from gross income under Section 101(a)(1). (518 F.2d at 63–64.)

The result reached in *Swanson* seems premised on the congressional policy behind section 101 rather than on the operation of sections 671 and 674. Section 101(a)(2)(B) permits the nongratuitous transfer of a life insurance policy to an insured. Whether the transfer was made to the "insured" is a factual question, the answer to which is dependent upon the insured's relationship to the policy subsequent to the transfer. Because G had the power to control the beneficial enjoyment of the policy, his relationship to the policy was sufficient to bring into play the congressional purpose of section 101(a). Surely, it cannot be said that G's interest in the policy arose from the operation of the grantor trust rules. In other words, sections 671 and 674 will not provide the answer to whether "transfer [was made] to the insured" within the meaning of section 101(a)(2)(B). Rather, that determination is primarily one of fact.

[In *Swanson* the separate existence of the trust was ignored. But a] careful reading ... shows that the underpinning of [the] decision was not on the operation of sections 671, et seq.; rather, the crucial factor ... was the effectuation of a congressional policy expressed through another Code section when that section operated simultaneously with the grantor trust rules.[7]

---

7. In *Terriberry v. United States*, an unreported case (M.D. Fla. 1974, 34 AFTR 2d 74-6267, 74-2 USTC par. 13,002), revd. 517 F.2d 286 (5th Cir. 1975), W, decedent's wife, created a revocable grantor trust and transferred several life insurance policies on the decedent's life to the trust. Decedent, H, was named cotrustee and was specifically prohibited from exercising any incidents of ownership in his individual capacity. Subsequently, H died and the issue was whether he died possessing sufficient incidents of ownership in the policies to cause the proceeds to be includable in his estate under sec. 2042. The District Court held that because W was treated as the "owner," of the policies for all tax purposes under the grantor trust rules, H could not be said to have died possessing any incidents of ownership to cause inclusion of the proceeds in his estate. The Fifth Circuit reversed. It is interesting to note that in its reversal, the Fifth Circuit dismissed out of hand as being unpersuasive the District Court's grantor trust reasoning. That reasoning formed the foundation of the District Court's decision just as it does in the opinion of the majority herein.

[In Rev. Rul. 2007-13, 2007-1 C.B. 684, the I.R.S. conceded that when subpart E treats the insured as owner of a trust to which an insurance policy is transferred for value, the transfer-for-value rule of § 101 does not apply. The ruling involved two different fact patterns. In the first, subpart E treated each of two trusts as wholly owned by the insured. One trust, which owned the policy, transferred it for value to the other trust. As to this fact pattern, the Service concluded that, because subpart E treated the insured as owner of the policy both before and after the transfer, there was not even a transfer, for purposes of § 101. In the second fact pattern, subpart E treated the insured as owner of all portions of one of two trusts. A non-grantor trust, which owned the policy, transferred it for value to the grantor trust. As to this fact pattern, the Service concluded that, although there was a transfer, because subpart E thereafter treated the insured as owner of the policy, the transfer was to the insured, for purposes of § 101. The Service relied on authority involving subpart E, without reference to the policies of § 101, in concluding that the proceeds would continue to be excludable from gross income after the transfers. In the years preceding the ruling, there had been a number of private letter rulings to similar effect. *See, e.g.,* Private Letter Ruling 200636086 (2006); Private Letter Ruling 200228019 (2002).]

In the instant case, the decision as to whether the trust established under the will of A. Lindsay O'Connor should be recognized for Federal income tax purposes should not be made as the majority does, on the basis of an examination of section 678. The majority essentially disregards the trust for purposes of determining whether the estate should be allowed a deduction under section 661. The proper inquiry in deciding this issue should be whether there is any overriding congressional policy embodied in section 661 which would mandate our disregarding the trust in this case. Under the facts of this case, the answer to this question clearly lies in the negative.

Section 661 essentially allows a trust or estate a deduction for distributions made to its beneficiaries. The regulations under section 643 provide that "A trust created under a decedent's will is a beneficiary of the decedent's estate." Sec. 1.643(c)-1, Income Tax Regs. The mere fact that a trust is also one governed by subpart E should be of no consequence, and indeed that appears to be the position of the Service in Rev. Rul. 57-214, 1957-1 C.B. 203, which involves a trust governed, as is the case here, by the provisions of section 678. This result should follow whether the beneficiary of a trust assigns her rights under the trust to her children, her corporation, her bank, to a charity, or to whomever. In light of the fact that no congressional policy would be served by ignoring the trust for purposes of the estate's section 661 deduction, I would accordingly not disregard its existence.[8]

* * *

More specifically, in the instant case, the estate would be allowed a section 661 deduction for any distributions it made to the marital trust. Since the marital trust, by virtue of the wife's power and subsequently the foundation's power over its corpus, is a section 678 trust, its taxation would be governed by section 671. Section 671 says that where a person is treated as the "owner" of a portion, all income and expenses of the trust attributable thereto are directly reportable by that person. The statute goes on to provide that any other portion of the trust not within the reach of sections 671 through 678 will be governed by sections 641 through 669. Because the wife and subsequently the foundation are treated as the "owner" of the entire trust, sec. 1.671-3(b)(3), Income Tax Regs., there is no "portion" of the trust that is governed by sections 641 through 669 and, accordingly, we need not decide the section 642(c), 661, 662, 663(a)(2), and Mott issue.[10]

[The dissenting opinion of Judge Sterrett is omitted.]

---

8. Moreover, the Service in its ruling has not been entirely consistent in its treatment of the recognizability of a grantor trust for tax purposes. Compare Rev. Rul. 69-450, 1969-2 C.B. 168, [*revoked* by Rev. Rul. 87-61, 1987-2 C.B. 219],] and Rev. Rul. 57-214, 1957-1 C.B. 203, where the separate existence of a grantor trust is not ignored, with Rev. Rul. 73-584, 1973-2 C.B. 162, and Rev. Rul. 74-613, 1974-2 C.B. 153, where the trust's existence is apparently ignored.

10. The majority attempts to obfuscate this point in its n. 17. The footnote properly recognizes that if the marital trust exists for tax purposes then the estate would be entitled to a sec. 661 deduction for payments thereto. It also correctly points out that the foundation by virtue of secs. 671 and 678 would be responsible for reporting the income of the trust. It then goes on to make the curious statement:

"Because of the operation of section 678 at this level only, the issue of whether or not the trust may claim a section 661 deduction for its distributions to the foundation is mooted because the trust would have no income to offset with a section 661 deduction."

I cannot agree with the majority's interpretation of the operation of subpart E. The question of whether the marital trust is entitled to a sec. 661 deduction for distributions it makes to the foundation is, of course, mooted. But the reason it is mooted is not "because the trust would have no income to offset with a section 661 deduction;" rather, the reason is because the penultimate sentence in sec. 671 essentially says that where, as is the case here, an entire trust is governed by the provisions of subpart E, sec. 661 does not even apply.

The footnote goes on to make the misstatement that the trust has no income. However, sec. 671

Illustrative Material

Transfers of Life Insurance Policies. In 1975, the I.R.S. announced that it disagreed with *Swanson*, discussed *supra* in *O'Connor*. Action on Decision 38042, 1975 WL 38042. In 2007, however, the I.R.S. reversed itself. In Revenue Ruling 2007-13, 2007-1 C.B. 684, the I.R.S. considered two situations: the first in which one grantor trust transferred to another grantor trust in exchange for cash a policy insuring the life of the settlor, the second in which a non-grantor trust transferred the same policy to a grantor trust in exchange for cash. In both situations, the grantor trusts were treated as "wholly owned" by the settlor for income tax purposes. The I.R.S. ruled that, in the first situation, there was no transfer of the policy within the meaning of section 101(a)(2), because the settlor was treated as the owner of all of the assets of both trusts, including both the policy and the cash. The I.R.S. further ruled that, in the second situation, although there was a transfer within the meaning of section 101(a)(2), the transfer nevertheless qualified for the exception to the transfer for value rule under section 101(a)(2)(B), because the grantor trust transferee was treated as the same as the settlor for purposes of this rule.

(iii) Miscellaneous

Recall the controversy between *Rothstein v. United States,* 735 F.2d 704 (2d Cir. 1984), and Rev. Rul. 85-13, 1985-1 C.B. 184, *supra* (ch. 4, sec. B(1)(b)(v)), over whether a grantor takes a cost basis in property purchased from a grantor trust. For other consequences of grantor trust status, in the area of income in respect of a decedent, see *Sun First National Bank v. United States,* 221 Ct. Cl. 469, 607 F.2d 1347 (1979), *infra* (ch. 6, sec. A(4)). Concerning deductions in respect of a decedent, see Rev. Rul. 76-498, 1976-2 C.B. 199, *infra* (ch. 6, sec. B). With respect to discharge of indebtedness, see Treas. Reg. §1.1001-2(c), example 5; Rev. Rul. 77-402, 1977-2 C.B. 222; and *Madorin v. Commissioner,* 84 T.C. 667 (1985).

Ascher, *When to Ignore Grantor Trusts: The Precedents, a Proposal, and a Prediction,* 41 Tax L. Rev. 253 (1986), catalogs and attempts to correlate the relevant precedents. The author concludes that the separate existence of grantor trusts must be ignored, to effectuate the policies of subpart E, if the grantor's income tax liability is involved. However, if the grantor's income tax liability is not involved, the author concludes, along with Judge Fay, that "the answer should depend not on the fact that subpart E does or does not apply, but on whether the policies underlying the applicable Code provision require ignoring a particular trust with respect to which the grantor has retained certain powers or interests." 41 Tax L. Rev. at 302.

---

refers on its face to the "income * * * of the trust." A correct interpretation of the statute is that the trust does indeed have income. Sec. 671 merely identifies who shall report it.

Chapter 5

Manipulation of Entities: The Availability of Artificial Taxpayers under Subchapter J

A. The Proliferation of Entities

Internal Revenue Code:
  Sections 641(a), (b); 642(b); 643(f)
Regulation:
  Section 1.641(a)-0(c)

Estelle Morris Trusts

51 T.C. 20 (1968)
aff'd per curiam, 427 F.2d 1361 (9th Cir. 1970)

FEATHERSTON, *Judge*:

* * *

The issues presented for decision are: (1) Whether each of the 10 declarations of trust executed by E. S. Morris and Etty Morris on September 11, 1953, created 1 trust or 2 trusts for Federal income tax purposes; and (2) whether, depending on the resolution of issue (1), the trusts created by the 10 declarations of trust are taxable as 1 or 2 trusts as respondent contends, or as 10 or 20 trusts, as petitioner contends....

ULTIMATE FINDINGS OF FACT

On September 11, 1953, E. S. Morris and Etty Morris, by 10 written declarations of trust, created 20 separate trusts. These trusts have been separately operated and administered since their creation, and constitute separate viable entities. E. S. Morris and Etty Morris created 20 trusts rather than 2 trusts principally for tax-avoidance reasons.

OPINION

On September 11, 1953, E. S. and Etty Morris executed 10 instruments, each entitled "Declaration of Trust," designating B. R. Morris and Estelle Morris as primary beneficiaries. B. R. Morris is the son of E. S. and Etty Morris; Estelle is B. R.'s wife. Each instrument directs the trustee to accumulate the trust income for the life of the primary beneficiaries (subject to certain discretionary distributions) and, upon the death of both of them, to distribute the principal and accumulated income to trusts created for their surviving issue. The 10 instruments are identical in form except they prescribe differing periods for income accumulation and distribution, and differing termination dates. [Each is irrevocable.] Cash in amounts ranging from $500 to $1,875 was transferred to each trust by the grantors [by 10 separate checks, each of which was drawn on the personal bank account of E. S. and Etty Morris, and each was made payable to E. S. Morris, trustee, for trusts Nos. 401 through 410, respectively], and loans in amounts ranging from $1,500 to $5,625 were made to each trust by E. S. Morris. [These loans were evidenced by promissory notes signed by E. S. Morris, trustee, and payable to E. S. Morris individually.]

[On September 17, 1953, 10 separate bank accounts (one for each of the numbered trusts) were opened in the name of E. S. Morris, trustee, and the gifts and loans were deposited therein. Ten sets of printed checks were prepared, one for each account, and each bore the name of the trustee and the individual number of the respective trust.]

Each trust declaration named E. S. Morris as trustee and Etty Morris as successor trustee. E. S. Morris served as trustee until his death in December 1956. Etty served from that date until her resignation in January 1959. She was followed by Leon Kent, who served until February 1963, and Nathan Schwartz, who was trustee at the time of the trial.

The declarations of trust have always been administered separately. Treating each of the 10 declarations as two trusts, one for B. R. and one for Estelle, each trustee filed 20 separate income tax returns annually from 1953 through 1965, reporting in each return the income earned by the purported trust for which it was filed. [Separate annual financial statements have been prepared for each numbered trust by Samuel Pop & Co., certified public accountants. The trusts have not made loans to each other or otherwise commingled their assets and funds.]

Finding that the grantors created multiple trusts rather than a single trust for tax-avoidance reasons, respondent determined that the 10 purported B. R. Morris Trusts constitute a single trust for Federal income tax purposes and that the 10 purported Estelle Morris Trusts constitute a single trust for Federal income tax purposes. By amended answer, respondent asserted that all 20 purported trusts constitute a single trust for Federal income tax purposes, and alleged increased deficiencies. The statutory notices of deficiencies cover the fiscal years ending August 31, 1961 through 1965; thus, the first 8 years of tax liabilities resulting from the trusts' activities are not before us.

Petitioner contends: (1) That each declaration of trust is sufficient to create two separate trusts; (2) that the grantors did not create 20 rather than 2 trusts for tax-avoidance reasons; (3) that even if tax avoidance were the motive for creating the multiple trusts, their viability as jural entities in the years before us (1961–65) should not be affected by the settlor's motive in 1953; and (4) that tax-avoidance motive is irrelevant in the taxation of trusts. We do not fully agree with either party.

As to petitioner's first contention, respondent apparently concedes that two or more trusts may be created by one instrument in an undivided *res* by the same grantor for different beneficiaries and that such trusts would be entitled to independent recognition for tax purposes. See *U.S. Trust Co. v. Commissioner,* 296 U.S. 481 (1936). He contends, however, that these trust instruments failed to establish separate trusts for Barney R. Morris and Estelle Morris, but created a single trust having two shares.

The question is a factual one.[5] We are not concerned with the reason why the grantors desired to create two trusts by one instrument; rather, we must determine whether the language they used was sufficient to accomplish this intent. See *U.S. Trust Co. v. Commissioner, supra; McHarg v. Fitzpatrick,* 210 F. 2d 792 (C.A. 2, 1954); *Commissioner v. McIlvaine,* 78 F. 2d 787 (C.A. 7, 1935), affd. 296 U.S. 488 (1936); *State Sav. Loan & Trust Co. v. Commissioner,* 63 F. 2d 482 (C.A. 7, 1933)....

[Each declaration of trust contains the following provisions:

(A) DESIGNATION OF PROPERTY

The Trustee shall apportion the Trust Estate into two (2) equal shares, each of which shall be a separate Trust; one of which shares shall be held, managed and distributed for the benefit of BARNEY R. MORRIS, and the other of which shares shall be held, managed and distributed by the Trustee for the benefit of ESTELLE MORRIS, both of whom are hereinafter referred to as the "Primary beneficiaries."

* * *

(E) POWERS OF THE TRUSTEE

* * *

(25) Though it is the intention of the Trustors that the two shares created by the Trustors for the benefit of the Primary Beneficiaries, and all of the shares created for the benefit of the lawful issue of the Primary Beneficiaries, shall each constitute a separate Trust, nevertheless, for the sake of convenience in acquiring, holding, and managing such shares, the Trustee shall not be required to partition any property of this Trust received by him, but may hold or sell the same jointly for all shares according to their respective interests therein, and similarly, the Trustee may pool or combine the principal of all shares in making investments or re-investments, and the Trustee may hold or sell the same jointly for all shares according to their respective interest therein, assigning or apportioning to each share its interest therein, all as the Trustee, in his discretion, may determine.]

Respondent notes that the provisions in the instruments concerning administration contain singular terms such as "this trust" and "the Trust Estate." But these references are not inconsistent with the creation of separate trusts if read in the context of the whole instrument, particularly in light of the authority given the trustee to combine the assets for administrative convenience. *Kohtz Family Trust,* 5 T.C. 554, 557 (1945).

[P]aragraph (A) of each trust instrument expressly directs that the trustee "shall apportion the Trust Estate into two (2) equal shares, each of which shall be a separate Trust," one for the benefit of Barney R. Morris and one for the benefit of Estelle Morris. Paragraph (E)(25) of each instrument, while providing that "for the sake of convenience" in administration the principal and income of the two shares may be combined or pooled, expressly reaffirms the intention of the grantors that the two shares created for the primary beneficiaries shall "each constitute a separate Trust." These specific directions by the grantors, stated clearly and unequivocally, cannot be ignored.

---

5. Neither sec. 641(a) ... nor sec. 641(b) ... nor any other section of the Code gives any direct guidance as to whether income from "property held in trust" for more than one person under a single instrument is to be taxed as one trust, or as several.

We need not rely solely on the cold language of the trust instruments, however, for here the grantors, acting in their capacities as trustees, have established a basis for our interpretation by meticulously administering the several trusts as separate entities and by filing 20 separate Federal income tax returns for each year.[6] Cf. *Helfrich's Estate v. Commissioner*, 143 F. 2d 43, 46 (C.A. 7, 1944), affirming 1 T.C. 590 (1943); *Estate of Marvin L. Pardee*, 49 T.C. 140, 148 (1967). While this may have been done to avoid taxes, it by no means alters that fact that it was done. Cf. *U.S. Trust Co. v. Commissioner, supra.* We conclude, therefore, that by each "Declaration of Trust" the grantors intended to create, and in fact created, two separate trusts.

The second issue for determination is whether E. S. and Etty Morris created the multiple trusts, as respondent contends, principally, "if not solely, for tax avoidance." The burden of proof on this issue rests with petitioners. While recognizing that the burden is particularly onerous because of the lapse of time between the creation of the trusts and the attack by respondent, we are reminded nevertheless that difficulty or even impossibility of proof does not relieve petitioner of the burden. *Burnet v. Houston*, 283 U.S. 223 (1931); *Interlochen Co. v. Commissioner*, 232 F. 2d 873, 879 (C.A. 4, 1956), affirming 24 T.C. 1000 (1955); *George Ungar*, 18 T.C. 688, 689 (1952), affd. 204 F. 2d 322 (C.A. 2, 1953).

The only direct evidence offered by petitioner on this issue was the testimony of B. R. Morris, one of the primary beneficiaries, that his father was not motivated by tax avoidance in the creation of the trusts. But this testimony, uncorroborated by any evidence of what the grantors' alleged nontax motives were, must be weighed against circumstances which, we believe, require our ultimate finding that the grantors created 20 trusts rather than 2 trusts principally for tax-avoidance reasons.

* * *

The third question presented is whether the "taint" of tax avoidance has been cleansed by the passage of time, so that the motive of the grantors in 1953 did not continue to soil the trusts in the years before us. We believe that this question must be answered in the negative.

* * *

Having determined that the Morris Trusts were created primarily for tax-avoidance purposes, and that this purpose continues to "taint" the trusts' income, we must now decide the final and most difficult question presented, i.e., the legal consequences of our determinations. We must decide whether each of the several trusts for the same beneficiary should be accorded independent significance as a taxable entity, or whether, as a matter of law, all of these trusts should be consolidated for purposes of Federal income taxation.

The views of the parties on the effect of a finding of tax-avoidance purpose are widely divergent. Relying on *Gregory v. Helvering*, 293 U.S. 465 (1935); [and] *Knetsch v. United States*, 364 U.S. 361 (1960)..., respondent characterizes these trusts as shams lacking business purpose, which, apart from the anticipated tax benefit, are without substance. Petitioner contends that the tax motive in creating the trusts does not change their char-

---

6. Respondent notes that each instrument was handled as one trust insofar as purchase and administration of property was concerned. This is consistent with par. (E)(25), quoted, *supra*. However, it was still necessary to file separate tax returns pursuant to the express language of sec. (A). See sec. 1.6012-3(a)(4), Income Tax Regs.: "A trustee of two or more trusts must make a separate return for each trust, even though such trusts were created by the same grantor for the same beneficiary or beneficiaries." Cf. *Fred W. Smith*, 25 T.C. 143 (1955).

acter. He contends that in substance, as well as form, 10 separate trusts were established for each beneficiary and that, under the provisions of section 641(b), each trust should be treated as a separate taxable entity.

Proper consideration of respondent's arguments must begin with the realization that the Internal Revenue Code, by recognizing even one trust for tax purposes, sanctions to some degree income splitting and the resulting lessening of taxes. Many of the advantages of multiple trusts—including accumulation of income at a lower tax rate—may be accomplished to a lesser extent by a single trust. We are concerned here only with a quantitative extension of the advantages of a single trust, a difference in degree; and not with a qualitatively distinct phenomenon, that is, a difference in kind. See Gordon, "Multiple Trusts: The Consolidation Approach," 4 Wayne L. Rev. 25, 27 (1957).

Moreover, it must be noted that while Congress has carefully delineated certain areas in which tax-avoidance motive is the touchstone of tax liability,[10] it has enacted no such provisions in the trust area. To the contrary, since the Revenue Act of 1916, which provided for the first time that trusts would be treated as separate taxable entities, the tax laws have recognized implicitly that trusts may be used as income-splitting devices.

Furthermore, Congress has not substantially limited the tax-avoidance utility of multiple trusts despite repeated calls for legislative reform. While there is some indication that the problem of multiple trusts was considered by Congress as early as 1932,[12] the first real call for reform was contained in a message to Congress from President Roosevelt in 1937.[13] Pursuant to his request, extensive hearings were held by the Joint Committee on Tax Evasion and Avoidance. At the hearings, the Treasury Department presented in great detail evidence of the flagrant use of multiple trusts to avoid taxes.[14] Congress' only response, in effect, was to reduce the exemption for trusts from $1,000 to $100 and to state that "Further consideration and study will be given to the general problem of the proper treatment for tax purposes of multiple trusts to accumulate income."[16]

No further congressional action was forthcoming until the adoption of the 1954 Code. At that time the "five-year throw back" rule was adopted as part of subchapter J. with a

10. Sec. 269 disallows tax benefits otherwise available in the corporate area as a result of certain acquisitions, the "principal" purpose for which is tax avoidance. Sec. 306(b)(4) allows capital gains treatment on dispositions of "Section 306" stock only if the plan for such dispositions did not have tax avoidance as one of its principal purposes. Sec. 482 permits the reallocation of income among certain related entities "to prevent evasion of taxes." Sec. 532 conditions the applicability of the accumulated earnings tax on a determination that the corporation was "formed or availed of [for] the purpose of avoiding the income tax with respect to its shareholders or the shareholders of any other corporation." Sec. 1551 disallows the corporate surtax exemption or the accumulated-earnings credit, available as a result of a transfer of assets, if a "major" purpose of the transfer was to secure such exemption or credit. See also secs. 302(c), 355(a)(1)(D)(ii), and 357(b).
12. See statement of Representative Crowther, Hearings before Joint Committee on Tax Evasion and Avoidance, 75th Cong., 1st Sess., Part 2, p. 270 (1937).
13. See Message of the President of the United States, H. Doc. No. 260, 75th Cong., 1st Sess., p. 4 (1937).
14. Paul W. Bruton, an attorney in the Office of the Chief Counsel, Internal Revenue Service, summarized the Treasury's problem as follows:
    Right here I should add just what the Bureau's position has been with reference to these trusts. As I pointed out, practically all of them are created by separate trust instruments. Each trust was made entirely separate. Consequently the Bureau has felt that there was no ground on which it could assert that these trusts were not separate and distinct, and to be so treated. Hearings, *supra* fn. 12, 266.
16. H. Rept. No. 1546, 75th Cong., 1st Sess, p. 30 (1937); S. Rept. No. 1242, 75th Cong., 1st Sess., p. 32 (1937).

view to lessening the tax advantages of accumulation trusts.[17] No specific provisions were adopted concerning multiple trusts.

On November 7, 1956, the Subcommittee on Internal Revenue Taxation of the House Ways and Means Committee released a report, prepared by the Joint Committee on Internal Revenue Taxation and the Treasury Department, entitled "Substantive Unintended Benefits or Hardships," which included a list of "Problems carried over from the 1939 code." Item 16 on the list referred to multiple trusts, and contained the following statement:[18]

> With certain limited exceptions under present law trust income which is accumulated is taxable to the trust and not the ultimate beneficiaries. The trusts in these cases are subject to the regular individual income tax rates and for the most part are treated the same for tax purposes as individuals, although their "personal exemption" is limited to $100. Cases have arisen where an individual in order to avoid the effect of higher individual income-tax brackets has set up several, instead of one, accumulation trusts for gifts in trust to the same individual.

> It is suggested that solutions to this problem be examined by the subcommittee in connection with the study, now in progress, of the tax treatment of estates and trusts. The staff suggests that the subcommittee open the hearings, however, to those desiring to testify on this subject.

The matter was referred to an advisory group studying subchapter J. In May 1957, the advisory group released its first report, which it revised in November 1957, recommending a new Code section dealing with multiple trusts. The proposed section, subject to certain limitations, would have consolidated multiple trusts where the "primary beneficiaries" were "substantially the same."[19] The legislation proposed by the advisory group did not distinguish between multiple trusts created for tax reasons and multiple trusts created to satisfy non-tax motives.[20]

The advisory group recommendations were embodied in H.R. 3041, introduced on January 21, 1959, on which hearings were held by the House,[21] and objections to the proposal were made.[22] The bill did not get out of committee; instead, a substitute bill, H.R. 9662, prepared by the Ways and Means Committee and introduced on January 28, 1960,

17. Secs. 665–669. But see Kamin, Surrey, and Warren, "The Internal Revenue Code of 1954: Trusts, Estates and Beneficiaries," 54 Col. L. Rev. 1250 fn. 41 (1954), which suggests that these provisions invite the creation of multiple trusts to take advantage of the $2,000 exclusion.

18. 3 P-H. 1956 Fed. Taxes par. 28,903.

19. See Staff of Subcommittee on Internal Revenue Taxation on Subchapter J. House Committee on Ways and Means, 85th Cong., 2d Sess., Final report on Estates, Trusts, Beneficiaries and Decedents 1 (Comm. Print 1958).

20. The advisory group proposal differed significantly from that of the American Bar Association, which would have authorized the Commissioner to consolidate multiple trusts where the "principal purpose" of the trusts was "to reduce or eliminate the tax liability of such trusts." See Friedman and Wheeler, "Effective Use of Multiple Trusts," 16th Ann. N.Y.U. Tax Inst. 981 fn. 46 (1958).

21. See Hearings on Technical Amendments to Internal Revenue Code before Subcommittee of House Committee on Ways and Means, 84th Cong., 2d Sess., pp. 65, 82, 347–352, 426, 439 (1956); Hearings on General Revenue Revision before House Committee on Ways and Means, 85th Cong., 2d Sess., Part 1, pp. 576–577 (1958).

22. Norman A. Sugarman, in a paper submitted to the House Ways and Means Committee, questioned whether an attack on multiple trusts was justified without a full reconsideration of the whole area of family taxation. He recommended that if legislation were to be enacted, it should be limited to "tax avoidance" situations and accompanied by provisions for advance rulings similar to that provided by sec. 367. This proposal and the reasons supporting it are of particular interest in view of the long delay by respondent in questioning the validity of these trusts. See Sugarman, "Estates and Trusts," in Compendium of Papers on Broadening Tax Base, House Committee on Ways and Means, vol. 3,

adopted an entirely different solution to the multiple-trust problem. This bill, which passed the House, did not consolidate multiple trusts. Rather, it would have added a 10-year "throw back" rule for multiple trusts, placing the burden on the beneficiaries at the time of distribution.[23]

The multiple-trust section of H.R. 9662 received a stormy reception when presented to the Senate Finance Committee, as numerous groups objected to both the advisory group approach and the House bill approach.[24] The Senate version of H.R. 9662, reported out on June 18, 1960, rejected the House approach, and substantially reinstated the advisory group proposal.[25] The bill was passed over twice in the Senate, and was never brought to a vote during the session.[26]

Thus, we are faced with a problem that has repeatedly confronted Congress since at least 1937. The legislative history shows that Congress was fully aware of the tax-avoidance possibilities afforded by the use of multiple accumulation trusts when it adopted the exemption and credit changes in the 1937 and 1938 Acts, as well as when it wrote the 1939 and 1954 Codes. We think it significant that Congress has taken no action to restrict the use of multiple trusts. We also think that it is significant that there is a great diversity of opinion as to what measures, if any, should be taken to correct the situation. This diversity of opinion is manifested by reference to the difference in the House and Senate versions of H.R. 9662 and the testimony thereon, as well as by the numerous articles written on the subject.[28]

In these circumstances the language of the Supreme Court in *American Automobile Assn. v. United States,* 367 U.S. 687, 697 (1961), is particularly apposite:

> At the very least, this background indicates congressional recognition of the complications inherent in the problem and its seriousness to the general revenue. We must leave to the Congress the fashioning of a rule which, in any event, must have wide ramifications. The Committees of the Congress have standing com-

---

1749, 1754–1756 (Comm. Print 1959). See also Panel Discussions before House Committee on Ways and Means, 86th Cong., 1st Sess., pp. 940, 941, 946–949 (Comm. Print 1960).

23. H.R. 9662, 86th Cong., 2d Sess., sec. 113 (1960); see H. Rept. No. 1231, 86th Cong., 2d Sess., pp. 15, 64–69 (1960).

24. See Hearings before Senate Committee on Finance on H.R. 9662, 86th Cong., 2d Sess., pp. 116, 120, 143–144, 147–148, 151–152, 165–169, 175–177, 188–189, 194–198, 203–204, 208 (1960).

While the Treasury Department generally supported the "consolidation" approach of the advisory group (and of respondent in this case), it recognized that it was not enough to provide that income of multiple trusts should be consolidated, without spelling out "the method of computing the tax in connection with the consolidation of income of multiple trusts, the method of allocating the tax among the trusts, or fix [sic] the responsibility as to which trustee shall bring the several trusts together. It has been suggested that matters as basic as computation of tax, allocation of liability for tax and fixing responsibility for consolidating trust income should not be left to regulations without some statutory guidance." Statement of Jay W. Glasmann, Assistant to the Secretary of the Treasury, *id.* at 86.

The advisory group representative, testifying in support of the consolidation approach, contrasted tax liability of a single trust with that of 100 trusts. *Id.* at 124–129. Thus, again, Congress was fully advised of the tax-saving potential of multiple trusts.

25. See S. Rept. No. 1616, 86th Cong., 2d Sess., pp. 2–3, 7–10, 33–39 (1960).

26. At least one commentator has suggested that the failure of the Senate to consider the bill was in large part due to the differences in view as to the proper treatment of multiple trusts. See Surrey and Warren, Federal Income Taxation, xii (1960 ed. with 1961 Supp. Integrated).

28. See, e.g., Soter, "Federal Tax Aspects of Multiple Accumulation Trusts," 31 U. Cin. L. Rev. 351 (1962); Note, "Multiple Trusts and the Minimization of Federal Taxes," 40 Col. L. Rev. 309 (1940); Note, 24 U. Chi. L. Rev. 156 (1956); Childs, "Multiple Trusts—A Word of Warning," 107 Trusts and Estates 183 (1968). See also Surrey and Warren, *supra* at 928–929.

mittees expertly grounded in tax problems, with jurisdiction covering the whole field of taxation and facilities for studying considerations of policy as between the various taxpayers and the necessities of the general revenues. The validity of the long-established policy of the Court in deferring, where possible, to congressional procedures in the tax field is clearly indicated in this case....

We do not intend to imply that we believe congressional inaction here means complete sanction of tax avoidance through multiple accumulation trusts. Rather, we believe the lesson to be learned is that courts should be wary of broadscale incorporation of the doctrine of "tax avoidance," or "business purpose," or "sham" in an area so fraught with its own particular problems and nuances. At the very least, we are required to limit those judicially developed doctrines to the situations which they were intended to cover.

Given the foregoing legislative background, we think that the "business purpose" test of *Gregory* and the "economic reality" test of *Knetsch* ... are inapposite. [Neither] of those cases involves a history of detailed consideration by the Congress of the specific problem presented. Indeed, to have allowed the tax benefits sought in those cases would have frustrated the clearly defined legislative purposes of the controlling statutes. Moreover, we know that "business purpose" is often absent in donative dispositions of property through the device of the family trust. Cf. *Alden B. Oakes,* 44 T.C. 524, 532 (1965). Accordingly, a litmus test of "business purpose" on the part of the grantor will not suffice, and nothing in the legislative history of section 641(b), reviewed above, leads us to believe that tax motivated trusts necessarily lie outside its plain meaning. Similarly, the continuing individual economic and legal viability of the Morris Trusts preclude the application of the "economic reality" test. Cf. *Irvine K. Furman,* 45 T.C. 360, 366 (1966), affirmed per curiam 381 F. 2d 22 (C.A. 5, 1967).

After careful consideration, we are constrained to reach the conclusion that a finding of tax avoidance is simply not enough to invalidate multiple trusts. Evidence of tax avoidance does not invalidate family partnerships. *Commissioner v. Tower,* 327 U.S. 280 (1946); *Commissioner v. Culbertson,* 337 U.S. 733, 744 fn. 13 (1949). Corporations are not invalidated if the creator's aim is tax reduction, but are recognized for tax purposes if they engage in business activity. See, e.g., *Moline Properties v. Commissioner,* 319 U.S. 436 (1943).... We see no reason why the result should be different here.

Neither *Boyce v. United States,* 190 F. Supp. 950 (W.D. La. 1961), affirmed per curiam 296 F. 2d. 731 (C.A. 5, 1961), relied upon by respondent, nor *Sence v. United States,* 394 F. 2d 842 (Ct. Cl. 1968), stand [sic] for the proposition that a finding of tax avoidance will invalidate multiple trusts. In *Boyce,* the grantor executed 90 trust indentures designating his son as beneficiary and his son's father-in-law as trustee. While the District Court in *Boyce* observed that "this entire scheme is but a mockery of our tax laws" (190 F. Supp. at 957), it based its decision on the ground that the 90 trusts were a sham *because they were in fact administered as one trust.*

Similarly, in *Sence,* the Court of Claims expressly reserved the tax-avoidance question which we face here since it was able to find that the 19 trusts were in fact administered as one. As the court noted (394 F. 2d at 851–852):

> If it is permissible to create separate trusts solely for tax avoidance reasons (which as stated above, we do not decide), then it is appropriate to require a taxpayer to turn square corners—to dot his i's and cross his t's (if that metaphor is preferred)—in order to take advantage of the rule. Transactions between family members "calculated to reduce family taxes should always be subjected to special scrutiny."

Commissioner of Internal Revenue v. Tower, 327 U.S. 280, 291, 66 S.Ct. 532, 537, 90 L.Ed. 670 (1946). See also, *Helvering v. Clifford,* 309 U.S. 331, 335–337, 60 S.Ct. 554, 84 L.Ed. 788 (1940). As applied here, that principle means that the taxpayer with tax avoidance motivation must affirmatively show that he created and maintained truly separate trusts before he can claim that they should be taxed individually and not as one. In that respect plaintiffs have fallen down. * * *

Thus, the courts in *Boyce* and *Sence,* faced with multiple trusts created for tax-avoidance reasons, examined the forms used and the actions taken to see if the several trusts were in reality what they purported to be in form.

In applying this "special scrutiny" test we are aided by 13 years of operation of the Morris Trusts. We find that the trust declarations were in proper legal form to create 10 separate trusts for each beneficiary. Cash was given and loaned to each trust separately. Individual bank accounts were established for the initial receipts as well as for receipts from all subsequent transactions. An interest in specific parcels of the Johnson Ranch property was acquired by each trust. That interest was eventually sold by each trust. The proceeds were invested and reinvested by the trustee. Ten separate sets of books and records were meticulously kept and maintained. The grantors never commingled their funds with the trust funds and none of the trust administrations ever commingled their funds with any of the other trusts. There was no "blurring of the lines among the various trusts"; each trustee was at all times careful to "dot his i's and cross his t's." Cf. *Sence v. United States, supra.* In all respects they were treated as, and indeed were, separate trusts.

In reaching the conclusion that the Morris Trusts cannot be consolidated despite the motive for their creation, we find support in the fact that the Supreme Court, in a case decided less than 3 years after *Gregory v. Helvering, supra,* held that amendments to a trust instrument were effective to create three separate taxable entities despite an express finding by the Board of Tax Appeals that the purpose of the amendments was "to reduce liability for income taxes on the income of the trust." *U.S. Trust Co. v. Commissioner, supra* at 485. With the history of multiple-trust legislation as a background, and with the case law as it has developed, we cannot say that each Morris Trust is not a "trust" within the meaning of that term as Congress must be understood to have used it in section 641(b).

* * *

RAUM, *J.,* dissenting: I cannot agree that there were 20 separate trusts in this case. There was no relevant purpose other than tax avoidance for fragmenting what was essentially a single trust into a number of artificial units. Since these trusts were established by the same grantors and administered by the same trustee for the same beneficiaries, it was a matter of no consequence that there was no "commingling," a fact relied upon by the majority. Moreover, the maintenance of 10 sets of records (not 20) was but a meaningless formality, a mere "technically elegant arrangement" (*Griffiths v. Commissioner,* 308 U.S. 355, 357) without any substance, in view of the identity of grantors, trustee, and beneficiaries. In these circumstances, the difference between this case and the *Boyce* and *Sence* cases, which the majority opinion undertakes to distinguish, is the familiar difference between Tweedledum and Tweedledee. The facts of record herein establish that there was in truth and in substance but one trust, or at most two trusts (one for each of the two primary beneficiaries). Whatever may be the proper result in a multiple-trust situation generally in the light of the impressive legislative history recounted in the majority opinion, the present case involves nothing more than a pure sham. "To hold otherwise," in the words of *Gregory v. Helvering,* 293 U.S. 465, 470, would indeed be "to exalt artifice above reality and to deprive the statutory provision in question of all serious purpose."

Illustrative Material

One of the issues involved in *Estelle Morris* was whether more than one trust had been created by a single agreement. As noted by the Tax Court, this inevitably is a question of fact. Courts often suggest that the issue depends on the intention of the creator of the trust(s). *See, e.g., Commercial Bank at Winter Park v. United States,* 450 F.2d 330, 330 (5th Cir. 1971); *MacManus v. Commissioner,* 131 F.2d 670, 673 (6th Cir. 1942); *Fidelity Union Trust Co. v. Kelly,* 102 F.2d 333, 335 (3d Cir. 1939); *McGinley v. Commissioner,* 80 F.2d 692, 693 (9th Cir. 1935); *Langford Inv. Co. v. Commissioner,* 77 F.2d 468, 470 (5th Cir. 1935); *Lynchburg Trust & Savings Bank v. Commissioner,* 68 F.2d 356, 360 (4th Cir.), *cert. denied,* 292 U.S. 640 (1934); *San Diego Trust & Savings Bank v. United States,* 71-2 U.S.T.C. ¶ 9518 (S.D. Cal. 1971); *John L. Dickinson Testamentary Trust v. Commissioner,* 65 T.C.M. (CCH) 1946 (1993); *Tom R. Booth Trust,* 22 T.C.M. (CCH) 1337, 1339 (1963); *Frank C. Rand Trust,* 19 T.C.M. (CCH) 1205, 1214 (1960). If the creator intended to create only one trust, only one trust can exist for income tax purposes. Similarly, if the creator intended to create multiple trusts, then, usually, taxation as multiple trusts is available, subject to the restrictions of section 643(f).

In ferreting out the creator's intentions, the language of the governing document is highly relevant. Great, though not necessarily conclusive, significance attaches to the fact that all or many of the governing document's references to the trust(s) are in the singular. *See, e.g., M. T. Straight Trust v. Commissioner,* 245 F.2d 327 (8th Cir. 1957); *Hale v. Dominion National Bank,* 186 F.2d 374 (6th Cir.), *cert. denied,* 342 U.S. 821 (1951); *Fort Worth National Bank v. United States,* 137 F. Supp. 71 (N.D. Tex. 1956); *Tom R. Booth Trust,* 22 T.C.M. (CCH) 1337 (1963). By the same token, consistent use of the plural may be indicative of an intention to create multiple trusts. *See, e.g., Union Trust Co. of Butler v. Commissioner,* 84 F.2d 386 (3d Cir. 1936).

Details of administration of the trust(s) are also important. *See United States Trust Co. v. Commissioner,* 296 U.S. 481, 486 (1936); *Helvering v. McIlvaine,* 296 U.S. 488 (1936). In *United States Trust Co.* the Supreme Court held that multiple trusts could exist even though the trustee held the assets of several trusts *in solido.* In other words, a trustee may allocate to each of several trusts only an undivided share of property held in trust. Other actions of the trustee may, however, make it more difficult to prove the existence of multiple trusts. For example, a trustee who has, initially, filed a single income tax return may be said to have reflected the creator's intention to create only one trust. *See Huntington National Bank v. Commissioner,* 90 F.2d 876 (6th Cir. 1937). It is often difficult to overcome such an admission. *See State Sav. Loan & Trust Co. v. Commissioner,* 63 F.2d 482 (7th Cir. 1933). On the other hand, consistent trustee handling of multiple shares as separate trusts, with separate names, account numbers, ledger sheets, income tax returns, and assets, may be *additional* evidence of the creator's intention to create multiple trusts. *See Estelle Morris Trusts, supra; John L. Dickinson Testamentary Trust v. Commissioner,* 65 T.C.M. (CCH) 1946 (1993); *Frank C. Rand Trust,* 19 T.C.M. (CCH) 1205 (1960). Such trustee treatment cannot, however, justify multiple trust taxation where the creator's intention to create a single trust is evident from the governing instrument. *Tom R. Booth Trust,* 22 T.C.M. (CCH) 1337 (1963).

Judge Learned Hand, in *McHarg v. Fitzpatrick,* 210 F.2d 792 (2d Cir. 1954), inquired into the nature of the intention so frequently sought after:

All of the many decisions on the subject do, indeed, hold that the settlor's intent is decisive; but their use of the word is left somewhat uncertain. They may only mean the intent to create those limitations that the settlor in fact does create, or they may include his added belief, or his purpose, that those limitations shall be treated as one trust, or as several; and it is indubitably the case that very often they appear to regard the second factor as relevant. It can be only for that reason that they have, for instance, so often laid stress upon whether the settlor used the singular, or the plural, in speaking of the limitations he sets up. In spite of these expressions (none of them, however, having been determinative), we cannot avoid believing that the second factor should have no place in deciding the issue. Obviously, that issue is the tax actually imposed; and, whatever may be the proper differentia to determine whether there are one, or several, trusts, it would be anomalous to make any part of it the settlor's understanding of the legal effect of what he was doing—or of his purpose in doing it. It would of course be quite untrue—especially in the field of torts—to say that a man's purpose can never be a determinant of his civil liabilities; but, so far as we can recall, it is never a measure of his public duties. Income taxes are imposed upon persons because of what they receive from property held by them, or for their benefit; and it cannot be permissible to make them turn, either upon what rights the settlor supposed he had created, or what rights he may have wished to create, but did not. We do not believe that it would make the least difference in the case at bar, for example, how often, or how consistently, the testator used the singular or the plural, or that he used the word "shares" instead of "trusts" to describe the limitations set up in Paragraph Thirteenth (a). Incidentally, it is usually the pursuit of our *ignis fatuus* to try to find out whether he has meant to make one trust or more; and so it would be in the case at bar. However, we refuse to enter upon that speculation, because we hold that, even if we were to succeed, the result would be irrelevant.

Id. at 794. Judge Hand then analyzed the interests created by the governing document and found multiple trusts to exist, essentially because of their independence of each other. He explained:

Each "share," during the whole period of its existence in trust, was completely isolated from all the other "shares" in composition, in beneficiary, and in duration, as though they had all been set up by separate deeds in the testator's lifetime. Perhaps it would go too far to say that equitable limitations are to be deemed a separate trust within [the predecessor of section 641], if they retain their content for a period not determined by that of any similar concomitant limitations, without additions to them from others, or withdrawals from them to others, and without the interpolation of new beneficiaries, or the loss of any of their own beneficiaries. But it seems to us that, if these factors do all combine, as they did here; and if there are no other factors that make the limitations depend upon the course of any other set of limitations, the income of each set is to be treated as that of an individual. But, particularly, whatever may be the indicia that should settle the question, we repeat what we said at the outset: among those indicia is not the belief or desire of the settlor about what he has created. That is not for him to say; he may create what he likes, but he may not say how it shall be taxed.

210 F.2d at 795.

Judge Hand makes three distinct points. First, he argues that the creator's "belief" that the interests he or she creates "shall be treated as one trust" is irrelevant to the income tax issue. Judge Hand is clearly correct; the creator cannot obtain multiple trust tax treatment for what is, in reality, only one trust, by including in the governing document an expression of intention that it be taxed otherwise. On the other hand, Judge Hand's observation seems largely beside the point. The cases continue to search out the creator's intent. Both the cases before *McHarg* and those after look less at whether the creator intended *x* to be treated as a trust than at how many *x*'s the creator intended to create.

Second, Judge Hand sneers at judicial reliance on whether the governing document's references to the trust(s) are singular or plural. No doubt when he wrote there was over-reliance on such nuances, but that reliance has continued. In seeking the creator's intention, the document left by the creator is crucial. The language that document contains is necessarily highly relevant.

Third, Judge Hand insists on looking at the substance of the interests created. This is his most important insight. Whether a particular interest is entitled to separate income tax treatment should depend on whether it is a *separate* trust. In *McHarg* the interests were "completely isolated" and, thus, clearly did deserve multiple trust treatment. Subsequent opinions, dealing with interests that were less isolated, have struggled with where to draw the line.

In *Commercial Bank at Winter Park v. United States,* 450 F.2d 330 (5th. Cir. 1971), upon the death without issue of the primary beneficiary of one share, that share might be divided among the other shares held in trust. In addition, after-born children of the settlors were entitled to share equally in the property held in trust. Nonetheless, the Fifth Circuit held that multiple trust taxation was available. The court seems to have relied heavily on language in the controlling document specifying "separate and distinct trust funds … for each of the children of the donors." The court also relied on language directing that the assets of each fund were to be used only for the needs of its primary beneficiary. There certainly was, therefore, an important—but not complete—isolation of the separate interests. Judge Wisdom concluded that "independence and determinacy of the individual trusts was only one factor to be considered in evaluating the settlor's intention." *Id.* at 331. *Frank C. Rand Trust,* 19 T.C.M. (CCH) 1205 (1960), is to the same effect and was quoted with approval by Judge Wisdom in *Commercial Bank.*

In altogether too many instances the creator's intention, however defined, is difficult to glean from the governing document. *Robert L. Moody Trust,* 65 T.C. 932 (1976), *acq.,* 1976-2 C.B. 2, was such a case. Shortly after the birth of his first child, Mr. Moody executed a single trust agreement that was to provide for his children "living at the time of the creation of this Trust or born to the Donor at any time thereafter." After Mr. Moody's second child was born, he amended the trust agreement "to more clearly define the Estates and Trusts created." As amended, the trust agreement required the trustee

> from time to time and not less than annually [to] divide and redivide the Trust Property into equal parts or shares of such a number that one of such equal parts or shares may be held for the benefit of each child of the Donor then living and that one of such equal parts or shares may be held per stirpes for the surviving children of each child of the Donor who may have died prior thereto.

65 T.C. at 934. Similarly, the amended trust agreement divided among the other beneficiaries the share of any child who died without issue. The amended trust agreement also allowed the trustee to invade for "sums necessary for [each] beneficiary's health or education or to meet any emergency condition." Though the trustee always filed a separate

income tax return for each beneficiary's "trust," "the trustee did not maintain separate books and records in the name of each beneficiary. The investment proceeds … were not divided on the books and records into separate shares for each beneficiary. Similarly, a single bank account was maintained by the trustee…." *Id.* at 936. The Tax Court held: "While the issue is a close one, we think Moody created a separate trust for each of his children." *Id.* at 937. Noting that "[t]he issue [was] basically factual" and "depend[ed] upon the settlor's intent," the court examined not only "the instruments in their entirety" but also "the facts and circumstances surrounding the execution of the several instruments and the practical construction given the instruments by the trustees." *Id.* at 936–37. In particular, the court pointed to the various (albeit shifting) shares required by the amended trust agreement. The trust agreement's many references to "the trust," in the singular, were ignored, "since at the time the original trust indenture was executed Moody had only one child and could not be sure how many children he would eventually produce." *Id.* at 939. The court also ignored the commingling of assets: "[T]here was simply no reason to make a physical division of the trust property or to set up separate bank accounts. To divide the trust assets and maintain … separate sets of books would have been a needless expense." *Id.* at 940.

San Diego Trust & Savings Bank v. United States, 71-2 U.S.T.C. ¶ 9518 (S.D. Cal. 1971), and *Schall v. United States,* 57-2 U.S.T.C. ¶ 9894 (D. Minn. 1957), also involved documents that failed, in any definite fashion, to evidence the creator's intentions as to the number of trusts created. The former held that multiple trusts existed; the latter held that only one trust existed.

Edward L. Stephenson Trust v. Commissioner
81 T.C. 283 (1983)

NIMS, *Judge*:

* * *

[This case concerns] the recognition of multiple trusts as independent taxpaying entities. Two trusts are involved…. The respondent determined…, pursuant to section 1.641(a)-0(c), Income Tax Regs. (hereinafter referred to as the consolidation regulation or simply the regulation), that the two trusts should be consolidated into a single trust.

Petitioners maintain that the consolidation regulation is invalid and that each trust should be respected as an independent entity. They assert that they are entitled to a decision as a matter of law under *Estelle Morris Trusts v. Commissioner,* 51 T.C. 20 (1968) (Court reviewed), affd. per curiam 427 F.2d 1361 (9th Cir. 1970).

* * *

The Stephenson Trusts

By an instrument dated December 14, 1972, Edward L. Stephenson created two trusts: the Edward L. Stephenson Amanda (Amy) Stephenson Trust (hereafter referred to as the Stephenson Simple Trust), and a separate income accumulation trust (hereafter referred to as the Stephenson Accumulation Trust).

The initial corpus of the Simple Trust was 5,000 shares of Procter & Gamble Co. common stock. The Accumulation Trust corpus was composed entirely of distributions received from the Simple Trust and from its own accumulated income.

The trust instrument required the Stephenson Simple Trust to distribute all of its income currently. The trust instrument contained instructions for certain mandatory and discretionary income distributions to Edward L. Stephenson's daughter, Amy Stephenson, and to one other named individual. Income not currently distributed to the named individuals was to be distributed to the Stephenson Accumulation Trust. During the years in issue, the Simple Trust distributed nearly all of its income to the Accumulation Trust.

The trust instrument allowed the Stephenson Accumulation Trust to distribute some or all of its income to Amy Stephenson. Income not distributed to her was added to the Accumulation Trust's principal.

The trustees of both Stephenson Trusts had the power to distribute corpus in certain circumstances. Also, Amy Stephenson was vested with the power to demand and receive, at two specified times, a part of the Simple Trust's corpus. The Accumulation Trust did not contain such a provision. Further, the trust instrument provided for alternative dispositions in case the beneficiaries untimely died. The trustees of both Stephenson Trusts had broad authority to manage the trusts, but the trust instrument directed the trustees to invest primarily in high-grade equities until Amy Stephenson reached age 25.

* * *

Reporting Position and Respondent's Determination

Each trust filed a separate return for the years in issue. They reported the following amounts of taxable income and tax liability:

Trust	Year	Taxable income	Tax liability
Stephenson Simple Trust	1974	$25,349.04	$8,704.52
Stephenson Accumulation Trust	1974	4,134.03	719.49
Stephenson Simple Trust	1975	15,529.69	4,146.58
Stephenson Accumulation Trust	1975	9,060.39	1,926.91

* * *

Respondent determined under the consolidation regulation that the separate identity of the accumulation [trust] should be disregarded. Accordingly, respondent consolidated the trusts and increased the taxable income and tax liability of the simple [trust] as follows:

Trust	Year	Increase in taxable income	Increase in tax liability
Stephenson Simple Trust	1974	$4,534.03	$2,383.51
	1975	9,460.39	4,378.46

* * *

Analysis

The Treasury Department promulgated the regulation, under which respondent seeks to consolidate petitioners' trusts, in 1972. T.D. 7204, 1972-2 C.B. 352, 393....

Petitioners contend that the consolidation regulation is invalid. Petitioners argue that *Estelle Morris Trusts v. Commissioner,* 51 T.C. 20 (1968) (Court reviewed), affd. per curiam 427 F.2d 1361 (9th Cir. 1970), governs these cases because it held that tax-avoidance motive is irrelevant in determining whether multiple trusts will be recognized for tax purposes.

Respondent maintains that the regulation is valid and that he properly consolidated the multiple trusts in these cases under its authority. Alternatively, if the regulation is held to be invalid, then respondent argues that *Morris Trusts* is distinguishable from these cases and that we should examine tax-avoidance motive in deciding whether to recognize the multiple trusts as independent entities.

The Commissioner has broad authority to promulgate all needful regulations. Sec. 7805(a); *United States v. Correll,* 389 U.S. 299, 306–307 (1967). Treasury regulations "must be sustained unless unreasonable and plainly inconsistent with the revenue statutes." *Commissioner v. South Texas Lumber Co.,* 333 U.S. 496, 501 (1948). Regulations, as constructions of the Code by those charged with its administration, "should not be overruled except for weighty reasons." *Bingler v. Johnson,* 394 U.S. 741, 750 (1969); *Commissioner v. South Texas Lumber Co., supra* at 501.

Although regulations are entitled to considerable weight, "respondent may not usurp the authority of Congress by adding restrictions to a statute which are not there." *Estate of Boeshore v. Commissioner,* 78 T.C. 523, 527 (1982). See *State of Washington v. Commissioner,* 77 T.C. 656 (1981), affd. 692 F.2d 128 (D.C. Cir. 1982). A regulation is not a reasonable statutory interpretation unless it harmonizes with the plain language, origin, and purpose of the statute. *United States v. Vogel Fertilizer Co.,* 455 U.S. 16 (1982); *Durbin Paper Stock Co. v. Commissioner,* 80 T.C. 252, 257 (1983). Where the statute's provisions are unambiguous, and its directive specific, the Commissioner has no power to amend it by regulation. *Koshland v. Helvering,* 298 U.S. 441, 447 (1936); *Arrow Fastener Co. v. Commissioner,* 76 T.C. 423 (1981).[4]

To evaluate the validity of the consolidation regulation it is essential to review the following developments in the law concerning multiple trusts which preceded the regulation's 1972 promulgation: the use of multiple trusts as permanent income-splitting devices, the 1968 *Morris Trusts* case which upheld such use of multiple trusts and the 1969 Act which eliminated some, but not all, of the tax benefits associated with multiple trusts. We will review each of these developments in turn.

Multiple Trusts as Income-Splitting Devices

Generally, trusts are taxed as separate entities under subchapter J of the Internal Revenue Code. Sec. 641(b). However, trusts receive a deduction for amounts distributed or required to be distributed to the beneficiary. Secs. 651, 661. The beneficiary is taxed on amounts received from a trust during a year to the extent of the trust's distributable net income for that year. Secs. 652, 662. Subject to qualifications not relevant here, distributable net income means a trust's taxable income. Sec. 643(a) Therefore, a trust will have no tax liability, and it will exist solely as a conduit, if it distributes or is required to distribute all of its income.

A trust is taxed at its own rates on accumulated income. Sec. 641(a). Under the basic approach of subchapter J (absent application of the throwback rule discussed *infra*), the following tax consequences occur when a trust makes a distribution which includes some accumulated income: the beneficiary is taxed at his own rates up to the trust's distributable net income for the year of distribution; the beneficiary is not taxed on amounts in excess of the trust's distributable net income. Thus, the accumulated income inures to

---

4. The regulation in issue is an "interpretive" regulation issued under the general authority vested in respondent under sec. 7805 and is to be accorded less weight than "legislative" regulations issued pursuant to a specific congressional delegation of law-making authority. *Estate of Boeshore v. Commissioner,* 78 T.C. 523, 527 n. 5 (1982).

the beneficiary, tax free. This result allows a permanent income split between the trust and the beneficiary as to the accumulated income. This income split lowers the total tax collected if the trust's effective tax rate is lower than the beneficiary's effective tax rate. Multiple trusts multiply this advantage because they each offer a separate chance to have some income taxed at the lower rates of the progressive rate system.

The 1954 Code enacted the so-called "five-year throwback rule" to modify the basic approach of subchapter J and to lessen the tax advantages of accumulation trusts. See generally *Estelle Morris Trusts v. Commissioner*, 51 T.C. at 39–40. When applicable, the throwback rule taxed the beneficiary on the receipt of accumulated income as he would have been taxed had he earlier received the income in the year in which the trust received such income. Secs. 665–669.

However, limits and exceptions restricted the throwback rule's effectiveness. The throwback rule only applied to accumulated income earned by the trust during the 5 years immediately preceding the accumulation distribution. Sec. 666(a). Also, the throwback rule did not apply to the following distributions: (1) Income accumulated before the beneficiary attained the age of 21; (2) accumulated income distributed to meet the emergency needs of the beneficiary; (3) the final distribution of the trust if such final distribution was made more than 9 years after the last transfer to the trust; (4) a distribution of accumulated income not exceeding $2,000 per year; and (5) certain periodic mandatory distributions under trusts created prior to 1954. Sec. 665(b).

These limits and exceptions made it possible in certain circumstances to avoid the original throwback rule. Accordingly, accumulation trusts remained an effective way to split income, and thus to lower taxes. See, e.g., Friedman & Wheeler, "Effective Use of Multiple Trusts," 16 N.Y.U. Inst. on Fed. Tax. 967, 981–987 (1958). The 1968 *Morris Trusts* case in effect legitimatized this planning technique by recognizing each multiple trust as a separate taxpaying entity regardless of tax-avoidance motive.

The Morris Trusts Case

* * *

Tax Reform Act of 1969

Congress reconsidered the method of taxing trusts and beneficiaries in the Tax Reform Act of 1969.... The 1969 Act made changes in subchapter J for the following reasons:

> The progressive tax rate structure for individuals is avoided when a grantor creates trusts which accumulate income taxed at low rates, and the income in turn is distributed at a future date with little or no additional tax being paid by the beneficiary, even when he is in a high tax bracket. This result occurs because the trust itself is taxed on the accumulated income rather than the grantor or the beneficiary. This means that the income in question, instead of being added on top of the beneficiary's other income and taxed at his marginal tax rate, is taxed to the trust at the starting tax rate. The throwback rule theoretically prevents this result, but the 5-year limitation and the numerous exceptions seriously erode the basic principle that a beneficiary who receives income from property should pay tax on that income at his (rather than the trust's) marginal rates.
>
> *This avoidance device is compounded by the use of multiple trusts*—the creation of more than one accumulation trust by the same grantor for the same beneficiary. The splitting of the income among many taxable entities may result in still further reductions of the overall tax burden, since the accumulated

income may be taxed to each separate trust at lower rates than would be the case if only one trust were created.[1] *Although the use of multiple trusts has been attacked by the Internal Revenue Service, the courts have held that such trusts are valid in some cases.*

* * *

The committee agrees with the House that taxpayers should not be allowed to utilize accumulation trusts to allow the beneficiaries of the trust either to escape paying tax on the income or to substantially minimize their tax on the income. The committee believes that beneficiaries of these accumulation trusts should be taxed in substantially the same manner as if the income had been distributed to the beneficiaries currently as it was earned. Thus, under the House bill and the committee amendments, the beneficiaries of accumulation trusts will be placed in substantially the same tax status as beneficiaries of trusts which distribute their income currently. This approach is essentially the same treatment as has been applicable to foreign accumulation trusts created by U.S. persons since the passage of the Revenue Act of 1962. [S. Rept. 91-552, 91st Cong., 1st Sess. (1969), 1969-3 C.B. 423, 503–504. Emphasis added].

See also H. Rept. 91-413, 91st Cong., 1st Sess. (1969), 1969-3 C.B. 200, 258–259; Conf. Rept. 91-782, 91st Cong., 1st Sess. (1969), 1969-3 C.B. 644, 660.

The 1969 Act, among other changes not relevant in this case, eliminated the 5-year limitation and all exceptions to the throwback rule.... As a result, accumulation distributions were to be "treated as if they had been distributed in the preceding years in which income was accumulated, but are includable [on that basis] in income of the beneficiary for the [year of distribution]." H. Rept. 91-413, *supra,* 1969-3 C.B. at 259; S. Rept. 91-552, *supra,* 1969-3 C.B. at 505.

The Senate amended the House version of the bill to include an interest charge in the application of the throwback rule. Senate Report 91-552 explains the need for the interest charge as follows:

The committee also modified the House bill to provide an interest charge to cover the tax payments by the income beneficiaries which are deferred by the use of accumulation trusts. This interest charge is based on the additional income tax which the beneficiary would have paid if the income originally had been taxed to the beneficiary instead of the trust. *The committee believes that this interest charge is necessary because, otherwise, the deferral of the payment of the additional tax* (i.e., from the time the income is taxed to the trust until the time when the remainder of the tax is paid on the accumulation distribution by the beneficiary) *amounts, in effect, to an interest-free loan to the beneficiary by the government.* [S. Rept. 91-552, *supra,* 1969-3 C.B. at 504–505. Emphasis added.]

Nonetheless, the conference eliminated the interest charge. Conf. Rept. 91-782, *supra,* 1969-3 C.B. at 660.

The consolidation regulation was promulgated in 1972 as part of a set of regulations designed to interpret the 1969 Act. T.D. 7204, 1972-2 C.B. 352. [As discussed in the Illustrative Material, Congress repealed the throwback rule in 1997, for all practical purposes.]

---

1. The creation of multiple entities also serves to increase the number of $100 exemptions allowed to each trust as well as providing for the multiplication of exceptions to the throwback rule, especially advantageous in the case of the $2,000 exemption.

The Consolidation Regulation Is Invalid

Our review of the history of subchapter J and the restrictions on multiple trusts convinces us that the consolidation regulation is invalid because it adds restrictions not contained in the statute nor contemplated by Congress.[5] The grounds for our conclusion are: First, Congress consciously enacted clear rules in 1969 to eliminate some, but not all, of the tax benefits associated with multiple trusts. The consolidation regulation goes beyond the statute by eliminating *all* of the tax benefits of multiple trusts. Second, the consolidation regulation takes a subjective approach to the multiple trust issue. This approach conflicts with the objective approach adopted by Congress. Third, the regulation extends beyond the statute and exceeds congressional intent by purporting to overrule the *Morris Trusts* case.

We will discuss these grounds for our decision separately. Then we will consider respondent's argument that the legislative reenactment doctrine insulates the consolidation regulation from critical judicial review. Finally, we will consider respondent's argument that we should consider tax-avoidance motive, even if the regulation is invalid, because the *Morris Trusts* case is distinguishable from [this case].

Clear and Limited Rules Enacted by the 1969 Act

Congress carefully considered the tax-avoidance potential of multiple trusts in 1969. It recognized that trusts could be used to avoid the progressive tax rate structure. S. Rept. 91-552, *supra,* 1969-3 C.B. at 503–504. It also realized that "This avoidance device is compounded by the use of multiple trusts." S. Rept. 91-552, *supra,* 1969-3 C.B. at 504. Congress further acknowledged that the *Morris Trusts* case sanctioned this planning device by noting that "Although the use of multiple trusts has been attacked by the Internal Revenue Service, the courts have held that such trusts are valid in some cases." S. Rept. 91-552, *supra,* 1969-3 C.B. at 504.

Congress enacted clear rules to eliminate some, but not all, of the tax benefits associated with multiple trusts. The unlimited throwback rule eliminated the use of trusts as permanent income-splitting devices by imposing an additional tax which eliminated any advantageous tax rate differential between the trust and the beneficiary. The throwback rule accomplished this result by including in the beneficiary's tax liability for the year of distribution, a partial tax equal to the aggregate of taxes for which the beneficiary would have been liable, had the beneficiary received the accumulated income during the years in which the trust earned such income. Sec. 668(b), I.R.C. 1954, as in effect in 1970. The beneficiary was allowed a credit for taxes paid by the trust on the accumulated income. Sec. 667(b), I.R.C. 1954, as in effect in 1970. The throwback rule thus imposed an additional tax on a beneficiary in the amount by which the beneficiary's tax liability on the accumulated income, had he received it directly, exceeded the trust's tax liability on such income. Therefore, the throwback rule prevented permanent income splitting because the additional tax eliminated the tax savings which previously existed when the trust's tax rate was lower than the beneficiary's tax rate.

The throwback rule did not prevent the taxpayer-beneficiary from deferring the additional tax from the year in which the trust earned the income to the year in which the trust distributed the income to the beneficiary. This deferral allowed the trust to invest the amount of the additional tax until distribution, thus generating more money for the

---

5. We note that commentators contended that the consolidation regulation was invalid soon after it was promulgated. E.g., Newman & Kalter, "Consolidation of Multiple Trusts," 27 Tax Law Rev. 561 (1972).

beneficiary than would have been the case if the beneficiary had been taxed on the income when earned. Of course, multiple trusts multiplied the advantage of such deferral benefits.

Congress consciously decided to allow the benefit of such deferral. The Senate realized that the deferral offered by the throwback rule would mean that trusts would continue to be attractive tax-avoidance devices. S. Rept. 91-552, *supra*, 1969-3 C.B. at 504–505. As previously noted, the Senate amended the bill to include an interest charge to eliminate deferral, but the House and Senate conferees eliminated the interest charge. Conf. Rept. 91-782 (1969), 1969-3 C.B. at 660.

In addition to deferral, the 1969 Act sanctioned a multiple trust tax benefit in the newly enacted minimum tax provisions. [The minimum tax has been repealed. It was the predecessor of the alternative minimum tax. *See* I.R.C. §§ 55-59.] Section 56, I.R.C. 1954, as in effect in 1970, allowed a $30,000 exemption from minimum tax liability. Section 58(c) allowed a separate $30,000 exemption for each accumulation trust. This provision lowered the accumulation trust's effective tax rate when compared to the beneficiary's rate, thus increasing the amount deferred by operation of the throwback rule. Naturally, multiple trusts multiplied this advantage.

Congress intended that each multiple trust would be entitled to a full $30,000 exemption. When it enacted the minimum tax provisions, Congress was carefully considering the multiple trust issue, including the *Morris Trusts* holding that each trust constituted a separate taxpaying entity. Yet Congress did nothing to limit the availability of a full minimum tax exemption to each trust, although it did so in other contexts. For example, Congress restricted related corporations to one minimum tax exemption. Sec. 58(b), I.R.C. 1954, as in effect in 1970.... Also, in the multiple trust area, Congress had previously limited the availability of the basic income tax exemption for trusts in response to perceived abuses. Sec. 642(b).... These facts convince us that Congress was aware of the multiple trust issue and could have limited the minimum tax exemption available to multiple trusts had it wanted to. It did not so limit the exemption. Accordingly, we conclude that Congress intended that each multiple trust would be entitled to a full $30,000 minimum tax exemption.

In summary, a review of the 1969 Act shows that Congress deliberately eliminated some, but not all, of the tax benefits associated with multiple trusts. Congress eliminated trusts as permanent income-splitting devices, but it went no further. Congress decided that trusts could be used for deferral and that each trust was entitled to a separate minimum tax exemption. In contrast, the consolidation regulation specifically states that forming multiple trusts for the principle [sic] purpose of obtaining these deferral and minimum tax benefits is forbidden. Sec. 1.641(a)-0(c)(3), Income Tax Regs. The regulation disallows benefits allowed by the statute and thus conflicts with the plain intent of Congress. Therefore, the regulation is invalid.

Further, Congress intended that the unlimited throwback rule would be the exclusive method for dealing with multiple trusts. Congress carefully reviewed the multiple trust issue and acknowledged that *Morris Trusts* sanctioned the use of multiple trusts as planning tools. Yet Congress neither eliminated the principle that trusts are separate taxpaying entities nor did it adopt a special rule for multiple trusts, such as respondent's consolidation approach. Congress, in fact, sanctioned the use of multiple trusts to obtain certain tax benefits. These facts convince us that Congress intended the unlimited throwback rule to be the only response to the multiple trust issue. Accordingly, the consolidation regulation is invalid because it adds restrictions not contained in the carefully considered and clearly limited statutory provisions.

Subjective Approach

We are further convinced that respondent's regulation is not supported by the statute, nor could it be considered a reasonable interpretation thereof, because it takes an approach to the multiple trust problem which is completely different from the congressional approach. Congress decided to attack the multiple trust problem by retaining and refining the throwback rule, which it originally enacted in 1954. The throwback rule provides an objective approach to the trust problem. It is clear and precise, although complicated. By contrast, respondent's consolidation regulation takes a subjective approach. It focuses on factors such as tax-avoidance purpose to resolve the multiple trust issue.

Congress rejected the subjective approach to the multiple trust problem when it chose the objective approach. The subjective approach of the regulation would generate intense factual disputes concerning the grantor's motive for establishing the trust. Also, this approach would lead to uncertainty in application of the rules of subchapter J. For example, consolidation in this case would turn the Stephenson Simple Trust ... into [an accumulation trust], with concomitant changes in tax treatment. Having such results turn on subjective factors, and the uncertainty which such an approach would entail, are alien to the clear technical rules of subchapter J. If Congress intended to import such a change in the system of taxing trusts and beneficiaries, it would have said so explicitly. The legislative history contains no reference to the subjective concerns which motivate the regulation. Therefore, we conclude that the consolidation regulation is not a reasonable interpretation of the statute and is invalid.

Congressional Awareness of Morris Trusts

The fact that Congress knew of the *Morris Trusts* case but did not overrule it deserves emphasis. In *Morris Trusts,* we rejected the consolidation approach and held that multiple trusts would be respected as separate taxpaying entities. Congress was aware of this decision and concerned with its implications when it passed the 1969 Act, which to a certain extent was a response to *Morris Trusts.* However, Congress did not alter the status of trusts as separate taxpaying entities nor did it add a tax-avoidance motive provision to the statute. Instead, Congress eliminated some, but not all, of the tax benefits associated with multiple trusts. These facts convince us that Congress decided not to overrule the *Morris Trusts* holding that multiple trusts would be respected for tax purposes. Therefore, the consolidation regulation is invalid because it goes beyond the statute and exceeds congressional intent in purporting to overrule the *Morris Trusts* case.

It appears that the respondent, after losing in the courts and after failing to persuade Congress to adopt the consolidation approach, enshrined his litigating position as a regulation. We cannot now sanction a position which has already been so thoroughly repudiated.

Reenactment Doctrine

Respondent argues that Congress tacitly approved the consolidation regulation since it did not overrule the regulation when it reconsidered the multiple trust problem in 1976. We disagree. The 1976 Act shows, even more clearly than the 1969 Act, that Congress intended that multiple trusts would be respected as independent tax-paying entities.

Under the legislative reenactment doctrine, "Treasury regulations and interpretations long continued without substantial change, applying to unamended or substantially reenacted statutes, are deemed to have received congressional approval and have the effect of law." *Helvering v. Winmill,* 305 U.S. 79, 83 (1938)....

The legislative reenactment doctrine does not apply to the multiple trust consolidation regulation. The 1976 Act added a new provision to subchapter J which is fundamentally inconsistent with respondent's consolidation regulation, which, as previously noted, was promulgated in 1972....

Congress reconsidered the method of taxing trusts and beneficiaries in the Tax Reform Act of 1976....[7] Congress remained concerned about the tax-avoidance potential of multiple trusts. H. Rept. 94-658, 94th Cong., 1st Sess. (1975), 1976-3 C.B. (Vol. 2), 695, 876. To eliminate the benefits arising from the use of three or more trusts, Congress added to the Code section 667(c), the so-called Third Trust Rule....

Respondent argues that Congress knew of the regulation and desired that both the statute's Third Trust Rule and the regulation's consolidation approach be used to combat multiple trusts. We cannot agree. Nothing in the legislative history indicates that Congress took into consideration the consolidation regulation. Also, the Third Trust Rule provides a clear and detailed method which is inconsistent with the consolidation approach contained in the regulation.

The Third Trust Rule eliminates a beneficiary's credit for taxes previously paid by third and additional trusts. Sec. 665, I.R.C. 1954, as in effect in 1977. This rule strongly discourages the use of three or more trusts because it taxes accumulated income twice, once at the trust level and once at the beneficiary level. The Third Trust Rule, however, does not apply to the first two trusts or to any de minimis trusts. Thus the Third Trust Rule clearly requires that the multiple trusts which are excepted from its application must be respected as separate taxpaying entities. The fact that the Third Trust Rule specifically sanctions the separate identity of some trusts which the regulation would consolidate, clearly refutes respondent's position that Congress intended the Code amendment and the disputed regulation to be applied in pari materia.

Also, the operation of the Third Trust Rule assumes that the third and additional trusts will be respected as independent taxpaying entities. By eliminating the taxes paid credit,

---

7. Congress decided that further changes were necessary in subch. J for the following reasons:

"The progressive tax rate structure for individuals is avoided if a grantor creates a trust to accumulate income taxed at low rates, and the income in turn is distributed at a future date with little or no additional tax being paid by the beneficiary, even when he is in a high tax bracket. This result occurs because the trust itself is taxed on the accumulated income rather than the grantor or the beneficiary.

"The throwback rule (as amended by the Tax Reform Act of 1969) theoretically prevents this result by taxing beneficiaries on distributions they receive from accumulation trusts in substantially the same manner as if the income had been distributed to the beneficiaries currently as it was earned. The 1969 act made a number of significant revisions in the treatment of accumulation trusts. * * * *In the case of multiple trusts, however, the committee is concerned about the potential tax avoidance use of such trusts. As a result, the committee provided a special rule in the case of accumulation distributions received by any beneficiary from three or more trusts.* * * *

"Your committee has also reviewed other aspects of the tax treatment of accumulation trusts and provided modifications to make the rules easier to apply and be administered. For example, the committee provided an exemption for the income accumulated in a trust during the minority of a beneficiary, as was provided in the law under the throwback rule before 1969.

"[H. Rept. 94-658, 94th Cong., 1st Sess. (1975), 1976-3 C.B. (Vol. 2) 695, 876–877. Emphasis added.]"

See also S. Rept. 94-938, 94th Cong., 2d Sess. (1976), 1976-3 C.B. (Vol. 3) 49, 208–209; Staff of Joint Committee on Taxation, 94th Cong., 2d Sess., General Explanation of the Tax Reform Act of 1976, 1976-3 C.B. (Vol. 2) 1, 172–173.

the Third Trust Rule does not consolidate or otherwise eliminate the separate identity of the third and additional trusts, per se. Instead, it assumes that a taxpayer is entitled to form and use such multiple trusts as individual entities. The Third Trust Rule merely makes it expensive (and thus uneconomical) for taxpayers to form such additional trusts. It follows that the approach established by the statute recognizes that all multiple trusts are to be respected as separate taxpaying units. The regulation which consolidates multiple trusts is antithetical to this statutory scheme. Therefore, we cannot agree with respondent that Congress wanted these two approaches to coexist.

Further, the 1976 Act provided the [§ 668] interest charge for foreign accumulation trusts to eliminate the deferral benefit inuring to such trusts....

The fact that Congress did not extend the interest charge to domestic trusts is a reaffirmance of the congressional decision in 1969 to allow such deferral. Our review of the 1976 Act convinces us that the consolidation regulation, which adds restrictions not contained in the carefully considered congressional approach, is invalid.

Is Morris Trusts Distinguishable?

Respondent argues that we should review the motives for establishing the Stephenson ... trusts as a matter of common law, even if the consolidation regulation is invalid. In *Morris Trusts* we rejected respondent's argument that tax-avoidance motive invalidated multiple trusts as a matter of common law. Respondent contends that *Morris Trusts* is distinguishable and that motive should be relevant in [this case]. We disagree.

Respondent asserts that *Morris Trusts* is distinguishable from the present [case] because of differences in the type of trusts involved. In *Morris Trusts,* each of the multiple trusts was an accumulation trust, whereas the trusts in [this case] consist of one simple trust and one accumulation trust. Respondent contends that the tax benefits which inure to the pour-over trust situation were neither contemplated nor sanctioned by this Court in *Morris Trusts.*

Respondent's argument is meritless. *Morris Trusts* requires only that the grantors and trustees "dot his i's and cross his t's" in establishing and maintaining the form of separate multiple trusts.... So long as the form has been respected, *Morris Trusts* holds that each multiple trust will be treated as a separate taxpaying entity. Tax-avoidance motive is irrelevant in determining whether or not the independent identity of multiple trusts will be respected for tax purposes.... In sum, *Morris Trusts* articulates a broad principle that multiple trusts may be used as separate taxpaying entities for purposes of minimizing taxes. Accordingly, the particular structure of the trusts or the peculiar nature of the tax benefits sought by the taxpayer in actualizing his tax-avoidance motive also is irrelevant in determining whether multiple trusts should be respected as independent entities for tax purposes.

Respondent does not argue that the grantors and trustees in these cases failed to dot all the i's and cross all the t's in respecting the form of the trusts. Certainly, on the facts presented to us, each trust had its own corpus during the years in issue and their separate identities were respected by the parties. Accordingly, we reject respondent's attempt to distinguish *Morris Trusts* as meritless. The *Morris Trusts* principle applies in [this case] to require that each trust be respected as a separate entity.

Conclusion

We hold that the consolidation regulation, sec. 1.641(a)-0(c), Income Tax Regs., is invalid. On the basis of undisputed facts, we further hold that the Stephenson Simple and Accumulation Trusts ... will be recognized as separate taxpaying entities....

Illustrative Material

1. The I.R.S. finally had its way with Congress, which enacted section 643(f) (then designated as section 643(e)) in the Tax Reform Act of 1984. Given the tiny exemption under section 642(b) and the throwback rule, what is the abuse the I.R.S. and Congress had in mind? Some have suggested that Congress was or should have been concerned that taxpayers were generally ignoring the throwback rule, and that the I.R.S. had neither the will nor the skill to enforce it.

Section 643(f) is an amazingly sketchy provision, in which Congress expressly left crucial but thorny issues for the regulations to resolve. When does section 643(f) apply? Who files the return? Who pays the tax? The *General Explanation of the Revenue Provisions of the Deficit Reduction Act of 1984*, prepared by the Staff of the Joint Committee on Taxation (1984), provides some guidance:

> For purposes of these rules, a husband and wife are treated as one beneficiary or grantor. Also, trusts will not be treated as having different primary beneficiaries merely because the trusts have different contingent beneficiaries. Similarly, trusts will not be treated as having different grantors by having different persons making nominal transfers to the trusts.

> For example, Congress expects that the Treasury regulations will treat the trusts in the following example as one trust:

>> A establishes, with the principal purpose of avoidance of Federal income tax, Trust 1 for the benefit of his sister S1, his brother B1, and his brother B2; Trust 2 for the benefit of his sister S2, his brother B1, and his brother B2; Trust 3 for the benefit of his sister S1, his sister S2, and his brother B1; and Trust 4 for the benefit of his sister S1, his sister S2, and his brother B2. Under each trust instrument, the trustee is given discretion to pay any current or accumulated income to any one or more of the beneficiaries.

> Where there are substantial independent purposes, and tax avoidance is not a principal purpose for the existence of separate trusts, the trusts will not be aggregated. The following is an example of where separate trusts will not be aggregated under the Act:

>> X establishes two irrevocable trusts for the benefit of X's son and daughter. Son is the income beneficiary of the first trust and the trustee (Bank of P) is required to pay all income currently to son for life. Daughter is the remainder beneficiary. X's daughter is an income beneficiary of the second trust and the trust instrument permits the trustee (Bank of D) to accumulate or to pay income, in its discretion, to daughter for her education, support, and maintenance. The trustee also may pay income or corpus to son for his medical expenses. Daughter is the remainder beneficiary and will receive the trust corpus upon son's death.

Id. at 256. *See generally* Carter, *Section 643(e): A Vague, Subjective Way to Tax Multiple Trusts*, Tr. & Est., Jan. 1986, at 36.

Under section 1806(b) of the Tax Reform Act of 1986, section 643(f) is effective, generally, only with respect to trusts created after March 1, 1984.

In TRA 1986 Congress drastically compressed the tax brackets applicable to trusts and estates. *See* I.R.C. § 1(e). Given this change, what justification now exists for the complexity and confusion of section 643(f)?

2. The Taxpayer Relief Act of 1997 repealed the throwback rule with respect to most trusts. Effective with respect to taxable years beginning after August 5, 1997, sections 665(b) and (c) limit applicability of the throwback rule to foreign trusts, domestic trusts that were once foreign trusts, and pre-March 1, 1984, domestic trusts that section 643(f) would aggregate, if it applied.

B. "Family Trusts"

Schulz v. Commissioner
686 F.2d 490 (7th Cir. 1982)

CUMMINGS, Chief Judge.

These appeals, which were consolidated by order of this Court, are the tip of an iceberg.[1] The common issue is the appropriate treatment, for tax purposes, of so-called family or constitutional trusts. The taxpayers contend that these are bona fide trusts taxable as such. The Commissioner argues, and the Tax Court found, that they are ineffective attempts to shift the incidence of taxation by assignment of income under *Lucas v. Earl,* 281 U.S. 111, 50 S.Ct. 241, 74 L.Ed. 731, and invalid grantor trusts under Sections 671–677 of the Internal Revenue Code.... In the Schulz cases, the taxpayers appeal deficiency findings of $5,167.08 (1972), $9,645.92 (1973), and $4,630.12 (1974); the trust (curiously) appeals the decision that it is entitled to refunds of $754 (1972) and $3,446.17 (1973).[3] In the White case, the deficiencies in the individual returns amount to $293.63 (1972), $6,964.98 (1973), and $4,564.44 (1974).[4] We affirm the Tax Court decisions in all three cases.

I. The Terms of the Trusts

La Verne Schulz, a Wisconsin dairy farmer and real estate broker, created his trust in 1972. Into it he and his wife Barbara[5] conveyed all their real and personal property, including the farming and office equipment Mr. Schulz used to earn a living and Mrs. Schulz' right to receive her salary as an employee in the county courthouse. Everything from the dairy farm acreage to the real estate office's filing cabinets to the family's television set and toaster became the trust *res.* In return, the Schulzes received shares representing

---

1. As of late March 1982, our docket had seven similar cases set for appeal but stayed pending decision in the instant cases. *Horvat v. Commissioner,* decided by unpublished order, 582 F.2d 1282 (7th Cir. 1978), certiorari denied, 440 U.S. 959, 99 S.Ct. 1501, 59 L.Ed.2d 772, involved similar issues and has recently been published at the Government's request. See 671 F.2d 990. Although *Horvat* is precedent for our decision in part, we have analyzed the issues afresh since the parties could not until very recently cite or rely on that case. See Circuit Rule 35.

The Commissioner's brief also lists 32 other cases, most decided by the Tax Court in the last two years, involving the same issues....

3. 41 T.C.M. 559 (1980) (CCH) (both cases).

4. Tax Ct.Mem.Dec. ¶ 81,073 (1981) (P-H).

5. Actually Mrs. Schulz conveyed most of her interest in the jointly held property and her right to receive a salary to her husband, who in turn conveyed it to the trust. Mrs. White did substantially the same thing. Both women also conveyed some property directly to the trust. For an explanation of why they must be regarded as grantors, see Part II.C *infra,* especially notes 20–21.

100% of the beneficial interest in the trust, which they distributed to Barbara (50%), their three children (15% each), and La Verne (5%). The initial trustees were Mr. and Mrs. Schulz and Ena Lundgren, the wife of their bookkeeper; in 1976 one of the Schulzes' daughters replaced Mrs. Lundgren. The terms of the trust called for it to last for 25 years, renewable for another 25-year term with ultimate distribution to the beneficiaries or their heirs or legal representatives. Most actions could be taken by a majority of the trustees, but early termination required unanimous action. La Verne Schulz drew a salary from the trust as its consultant in running the dairy farm and real estate business he had previously conducted, and reported the salary on his individual income tax return. No distributions were made to beneficiaries. The trust paid tax on its net income *i.e.,* the accumulations to the trust minus the expenses of administration. In 1972 it had income of $9,321.49 and expenses of $4,930.57; in 1973 income of $25,461.96 and expenses of $11,448.69; the 1974 trust return is missing from the record. Included in the expenses of administration were such items as life insurance premiums on policies insuring La Verne Schulz ($660 in 1973); costs of maintaining and operating the family car; health care expenses for trustees ($680 in 1972 and 1973); gifts and charitable contributions ($1,100 in 1972 and 1973); license fees for a boat and a dog; educational expenses; and the cost of a home in Elkhorn, Wisconsin, allegedly maintained for the convenience of Schulz's employer, the Schulz family trust ($3,000 in 1972 and 1973).

Russell White set up his family trust in the same manner and in the same year. The trust *res* consisted of the White family house, stocks, life insurance policies, and assorted personal property. The trust's main asset was a contract entitling it to receive the income payable to Mr. White by his employer, Litho Productions, Inc. The beneficial interests in the trust were parceled out as follows: 20% to Mrs. White, 14% to each of the Whites' five children, 10% to the Russell White Educational Fund, and nothing to Mr. White. Mr. White did, however, receive a manager's fee, determined to be whatever amounts he needed to draw from the trust. Initially the trustees were Mr. and Mrs. White and Mrs. White's brother; the brother resigned immediately after the trust was formed and was never replaced. The duration of the trust and the powers of the trustees were the same as in the Schulz family trust—a fact that is not surprising since both trusts were drafted according to instructions contained in a pre-packaged kit. The tax returns of the White family trust show income of $26,532 and administration expenses of $21,694 for 1973; income of $22,935 and expenses of $16,493 for 1974; the 1972 return is not included in the record. Among the administration expenses listed separately on the returns are health expenses of the trustees ($2,600 in 1973 and 1974), "household expenses" ($5,400 in 1973 and 1974), home and car insurance ($2,200 in 1973 and 1974), and "automobile lease"— *i.e.,* the trust's lease of the Whites' family car ($7,850 in 1973 and 1974).

II. The Tax Consequences of the Trusts

It takes no particular acumen in tax law to know that the Schulz and White family trusts cannot be treated like ordinary trusts. The only real question is which of several established doctrines the Internal Revenue Service should use to deny their existence as taxable entities.

A. Attempted deduction of personal consumption expenses

It is fundamental to our income tax regime that personal consumption expenditures— food, clothing, travel, education, entertainment—do not generate income tax deductions unless they are somehow inextricably linked to the production of income.[8] When

---

8. "Personal consumption expenses must obviously be treated as nondeductible on the whole; if they were allowed, the individual tax base could be reduced to zero through expenditures on personal

taxpayers buy cars, travel, or take out life insurance policies, they make those expenditures out of after-tax dollars. The trust devices here are a transparent attempt to alter that state of affairs by turning all the families' expenses into expenses of trust administration. If this device worked, the Schulzes and the Whites would, unlike the rest of us, make all their consumptive expenditures with pre-tax dollars.

The Internal Revenue Service could disallow most of the administration expenses claimed in these family trust returns. But such an approach would be extremely inefficient; the Service does not have the resources to audit every return, and the chance of avoiding an audit would only encourage this form of tax evasion.

B. Anticipatory assignment of income

A broader-based attack on family trusts of the type described here is possible. Since the seminal case of *Lucas v. Earl*, 281 U.S. 111, 50 S.Ct. 241, 74 L.Ed. 731, it has been clear that income is taxed to the person who earns it, regardless of what arrangements he makes to divert the payment of it elsewhere. This is a rule of imputation that has nothing to do with, and does not affect, the validity of the particular arrangement for purposes other than computing income taxes. In the absence of such an imputation rule, taxpayers would be able to defeat the progressivity of the income tax rate structure by directing income to low-bracket recipients. That result would obviously have occurred if Mr. White's or Mr. Schulz' income had actually been distributed to their respective children and wives; but the potential deflation of the brackets exists even where — as here — there has been no distribution to the trust beneficiaries. The impact on progressivity is only postponed, owing to a special feature of trust taxation. Although the trust pays taxes on accumulated, undistributed income as if it were an individual taxpayer, when accumulated income is finally distributed to the trust beneficiaries (at the latest, when these trusts terminate), it is taxed to the beneficiary as if it had been distributed in the year it was accumulated, and the taxes previously collected from the trust are credited to the beneficiaries' tax bills. The result is that only the beneficiary is taxed ultimately and substantial tax deferral has been achieved.[12] Thus *Earl's* concern to prevent end-runs around the progressive income tax rate structure is equally implicated in these family trusts, whether there are annual distributions or only a final termination of the trust. [As discussed in the immediately preceding Illustrative Material, the throwback rule was repealed in 1997, for most practical purposes.]

Under the rationale of *Earl*, it is a distinction without a difference that Russell White was a salaried employee and La Verne Schulz was self-employed before the creation of the trusts. In either case, the income is spread so that no one is taxed at the higher marginal rates on the full amount. But Russell White's status as an employee of Litho Productions has encouraged him to make an argument that he is a "leased employee," governed by a set of tax precedents distinct from *Earl* and its progeny. In the true "leased employee" cases, an employee is under a legal duty to provide services to a corporation (or trust) and the corporation (or trust) is taxed on the income the employee's services produce. See, e.g., *Rubin v. Commissioner*, 429 F.2d 650 (2d Cir. 1970); *Laughlin v. Commissioner*, 40 B.T.A. 101 (1938), *rev'd on other grounds*, 113 F.2d 103 (9th Cir. 1940); *Fox v. Commissioner*, 37

---

living items and the notion of a tax on economic gain would have to be abandoned." M. Chirelstein, *Federal Income Taxation* ¶7.01 at 140 (2d ed. 1979). Apart from some special provisions, *id.*, not at issue here, deductions must be for ordinary and necessary business expenses (Section 162) and costs associated with investment activities (Section 212).

12. This discussion is derived from M. Chirelstein, *op. cit* (note 8 *supra*), ¶9.01 at 182. 26 U.S.C. §§ 666–667 are the statutory provisions involved.

B.T.A. 271 (1938). Here what is conspicuously missing is a legal obligation between the employee and the entity that pays the taxes: the White family trust could not make Russell White work for Litho Productions, control his activities, or determine the amount of his compensation. All the trust could do was receive whatever amounts Russell White was paid. See *Vnuk v. Commissioner,* 621 F.2d 1318, 1320–1321 and n. 5 (8th Cir. 1980) (rejecting leased-employee argument in a similar family trust context); *Johnson v. Commissioner,* [78 T.C. 882, *aff'd,* 698 F.2d 372 (9th Cir. 1982)] (assignment of professional basketball player's salary to Puerto Rican corporation ineffective for income tax purposes where corporation had no ability to force assignor to play basketball).

The taxpayers' consolidated brief seems to argue (at least for Russell White) that the conveyance of the "lifetime services" of the grantor to the trust creates the necessary legal obligation.... The short answer to that argument is that the obligation is entirely illusory. The grantor in his capacities as employee and as trustee or trust manager is on both sides of the transaction. There is no one to enforce the ostensible obligation.

C. Invalid grantor trusts

Concededly more was conveyed into both the White and Schulz family trusts than the grantors' earning abilities. A different set of rules applies to gifts (to a trust or otherwise) of income-producing property. Broadly speaking, these rules treat as gifts for income tax purposes gratuitous transfers of all the interest the donor possesses and deny that effect to attempted gifts of carved-out, partial interests.[14] To the extent, however, that the *res* of these trusts consisted of income-producing property, the trusts are invalid for tax purposes under the grantor trust provisions of the Internal Revenue Code, 26 U.S.C. §§ 671–677. These provisions are the exclusive[15] means of answering the following questions:

> How far must the grantor go in the direction of a complete surrender of his personal authority over the trust property before trust income will be treated as belonging to the beneficiaries? Put otherwise, what rights may the grantor retain without continuing to be regarded as the substantial owner of the property transferred? M. Chirelstein, *op. cit.* (note 8 *supra*), ¶ 8.04 at 175; cf. ¶ 9.01 at 183.

The application of these provisions to a family trust is painstakingly considered in *Wesenberg v. Commissioner,* 69 T.C. 1005 (1978), and we join the Eighth Circuit in *Vnuk, supra,* 621 F.2d at 1321, in adopting its analysis for our purposes.

The main thrust of the grantor trust provisions is that the trust will be ignored and the grantor treated as the appropriate taxpayer whenever the grantor has substantially unfettered powers of disposition. The hallmark of such discretion is that the grantor can act unilaterally or with the concurrence of someone who is not an "adverse party." "Ad-

---

14. See, *e.g., Helvering v. Horst,* 311 U.S. 112, 61 S.Ct. 144, 85 L.Ed. 75 (gift of annual interest coupons to son, while father retained underlying bond, is ineffective to avoid father's income tax); *Harrison v. Schaffner,* 312 U.S. 579, 61 S.Ct. 759, 85 LEd. 1055 (assignment of one year's trust income to children ineffective to avoid income tax where assignor kept right to receive income in prior and subsequent years). Contrast *Blair v. Commissioner,* 300 U.S. 5, 57 S.Ct. 330, 81 L.Ed. 465 (gift of part of trust income stream effective to shift incidence of taxes, though balance of income stream retained, where donees' and donor's interests would both last as long as the income stream did).

15. Section 671 makes clear that these provisions are meant to supplant judicial rule-making on the subject of grantor trusts. "This element of exclusivity does not * * * supersede or preempt other standing rules of income-attribution, such as those approved in the *Earl* and *Horst* cases. * * * But when the issue is of the *Clifford* variety [*Helvering v. Clifford,* 309 U.S. 331, 60 S.Ct. 554, 84 L.Ed. 788] — *i.e.,* whether the grantor's interest in the trust is so substantial as to be the equivalent of continued ownership — the specific statutory provisions are given exclusive application." M. Chirelstein, *op. cit.* (note 8, *supra*), ¶ 9.01 at 183.

verse party" is a term of art, defined in the statute as "any person having a substantial beneficial interest in the trust which would be adversely affected by the exercise or nonexercise of a power which he possesses respecting the trust," Section 672(a).

The first thing to note is that the beneficiaries, although their interests and the grantor-trustee's may diverge, are not "adverse parties" in the statutory sense because they have no "powers respecting the trust." Thus the statute does not regard the general law of fiduciary duty as an adequate guarantee that grantors will not deal with trust property as if they owned it outright. The taxpayers' contrary arguments ... must fail....

The second point is that, despite efforts to skirt the grantor trust provisions by careful draftsmanship, these trusts in substance, if not in form, violate the statute. The drafters (or more accurately the person who designed the kit these taxpayers bought and used) have labeled the husbands as sole grantors and given them little or no beneficial interest in the trust, apparently to avoid threshold problems with equivocal gifts. Then they have given the wives duties as co-trustees and substantial beneficial interests to bring them within the definition of adverse parties. The theory is that these maneuvers will prevent decisions made by husband and wife together from being unconstrained in violation of the statute.

In the case of the Schulz family trust, these strategies do not work because most actions require only two of the three trustees to agree, and one of the trustees, the bookkeeper's wife, had no beneficial interest at all in the trust and was therefore not an adverse party.[19] It was possible for any given decision to be made by one of the Schulzes and the bookkeeper trustee.

The White family trust also had a supernumerary trustee initially, Mrs. White's brother, but he resigned. For most of the period at issue in these appeals, Mr. and Mrs. White functioned as sole trustees, and Mrs. White was within the definition of adverse party. Nonetheless, the grantor trust provisions were still violated, although in a different fashion. Despite the trust document's recitation that Mr. White was the sole grantor, Mrs. White was also a grantor. Immediately before Mr. White created the trust, and by documents simultaneously executed ... Mrs. White conveyed all her interest in their jointly held property to him. That conveyance can be ignored, either on the familiar tax principle that substance predominates over form,[20] or because the parties themselves treated it as neither a sale nor a gift.[21] Mrs. White also conveyed some property directly to the trust.... Thus the statute can be applied with the focus on Mrs. White as grantor. It then becomes clear that she could make unconstrained decisions about trust property and income, because Mr. White, having no beneficial interest in the trust, was not an adverse party.

Moreover, this same argument would invalidate for income tax purposes the Schulz family trust, if it had operated without the bookkeeper's wife as spear-carrier. Mr. and Mrs. Schulz, like the Whites, owned their property jointly, and Mrs. Schulz, like Mrs. White, conveyed most of her holdings to her husband. She too conveyed some unspecified property directly to the trust. Disregarding the indirection of the main conveyance, Mrs. Schulz also is a grantor, with effective control over the trust. Her husband's 5% interest is insufficient to make him an adverse party. Consequently, the Commissioner had grounds to assess the amounts in question in the wives' joint returns.

---

19. The Schulz daughter (who did have a beneficial interest) did not succeed the bookkeeper's wife as the third trustee until 1976, a taxable year not involved in these cases....

20. See, *e.g., Redding v. Commissioner,* 630 F.2d 1169, 1175 (7th Cir. 1980); *Falkoff v. Commissioner,* 604 F.2d 1045, 1048 n. 2 (7th Cir. 1979).

21. The conveyances of both wives recite that they are made for $1.00 in cash and a trust receipt, or for $1.00 and other considerations of value.... No gift tax returns were filed by either woman....

The relationships among the parties in these trusts present exactly the sorts of potential problems the grantor trust provisions were designed to meet. Furthermore, nothing in the remaining terms of the trusts imposes any substantive limits whatever on what the trustees may do. In both trusts

> Trustees' powers shall be construed as general powers of citizens of the United States of America, to do anything any citizen may do in any state or country, subject to the restrictions herein noted. They shall continue in business, conserve the property, commercialize the resources, extend any established line of business in industry or investment, as herein specially noted, at their discretion for the benefit of This Trust, such as, viz: buy, sell or lease land for the surface or mineral rights; buy or sell mortgages, securities, bonds, notes, leases of all kinds, contracts or credits, of any form, patents, trademarks, or copyrights; buy, sell or conduct mail-order business, or branches thereof; operate stores, shops, factories, warehouses or other trading establishments or places of business of any kind; construct, buy, sell, lease or rent suitable buildings or other places of business; advertise different articles or business projects; borrow money for any business project, pledging The Trust property for the payment thereof; hypothecate assets, property, or both, of The Trust in business projects; own stock in, or entire charters of corporations, or other such properties, companies, or associations as they may deem advantageous.

> A Minute of Resolutions of The Trustees authorizing what it is they determine to do or have done shall be evidence that such an act is within their power.

In the unlikely event that these terms are not broad enough:

> The Trustees shall regard this instrument as their sufficient guide, supplemented from time to time by their resolutions (said resolution to be ratified ALWAYS by a MAJORITY of the Trustees then in office and participating in the issuing meeting) covering contingencies as they arise and are recorded in the minutes of their meetings, which are the by-laws, rules and regulations of This Trust.[22]

Lacking both procedural and substantive limits, these trusts violate Section 674(a) because there is unconstrained power to dispose of the beneficial enjoyment of trust income or corpus,[23] violate Section 676(a) because there is unconstrained power to revest title to the trust property in the grantor(s), and violate Section 677(a) because there is unconstrained power to distribute trust income (or accumulate it for further distribution) to the grantor or the grantor's spouse. The actual expenditures made document that all powers but the power to revest title to the trust were actually exercised. Since the Schulzes and the Whites retained all the indicia of ownership in the trust property, their joint personal income tax returns for 1972, 1973, and 1974 should have reflected that ownership.

III. Conclusion

Given the deeply rooted instinct not to pay more taxes than the law requires and the endless changes that can be rung in trust draftsmanship, we do not suppose that any single opinion can put a definitive end to devices like the Schulz and White family trusts. Nor do we mean to intimidate taxpayers and their attorneys in their search for the equivalent of the better mousetrap. Nonetheless, it should be clear that certain avenues of tax avoid-

---

22. Taken from the Declaration of Trust used in both the White and Schulz family trusts.

23. … Note that the beneficiaries are entitled to receive nothing until the trust terminates, and then only what the trustees have chosen to leave in the trust.

ance are closed. *Lucas v. Earl* prevents attempts to assign income away from its earner, and the "leased employee" theory is not an easy escape route from the *Earl* doctrine. And, though the analysis may differ from one case to another, the grantor trust provisions will generally defeat attempts to create trusts of family income-producing property without surrendering any of the family's rights of ownership. If taxpayers persist in ignoring these truisms, we will in the future be sympathetic to the Internal Revenue Service's assessment ... of penalties for underpayment of tax due to negligence or intentional disregard of the rules and regulations of the Internal Revenue Code....

The judgments of the Tax Court are affirmed, with costs to respondent.

Illustrative Material

1. Similarly disregarding "family trusts" or "family estates" under both assignment-of-income principles and the grantor trust rules are *Holman v. United States,* 728 F.2d 462 (10th Cir. 1984) (per curiam); *Hanson v. Commissioner,* 696 F.2d 1232 (9th Cir. 1983) (per curiam); and *Vnuk v. Commissioner,* 621 F.2d 1318 (8th Cir. 1980). In *Hillman v. Commissioner,* 687 F.2d 164 (6th Cir. 1982), and *Holman,* the Sixth and Tenth Circuits even refused to hear oral argument. The courts have thus fully embraced the position the I.R.S. took concerning such entities in Rev. Rul. 75-257, 1975-2 C.B. 251. An alternative approach, announced in Rev. Rul. 75-258, 1975-2 C.B. 503, that "family estates" were associations taxable as corporations rather than trusts, has rarely been used. In *Markosian v. Commissioner,* 73 T.C. 1235 (1980), the Tax Court provided a fourth rationale. It disregarded a family trust because "there was no economic reality or substance to the transaction which purportedly transferred everything petitioners owned, including [the husband's] future income, to the trust." For a similar case, see *Irvine K. Furman,* 45 T.C. 360 (1966), *aff'd per curiam,* 381 F.2d 22 (5th Cir. 1967). Though the lack-of-economic-reality approach is frequently mentioned in family trust cases, it is rarely applied as meticulously as it was in *Markosian* and *Furman.* Usually the cases depend primarily upon assignment-of-income principles and the grantor trust rules. For other cases disregarding trusts of this sort, as "shams," see *Zmuda v. Commissioner,* 731 F.2d 1417 (9th Cir. 1984); *Muhich v. Commissioner,* 238 F.3d 860 (7th Cir. 2001); *Lund v. Commissioner,* 40 Fed. Appx. 592, 2002-2 U.S.T.C. ¶ 50,507 (9th Cir. 2002).

2. *Holman, Hanson, Vnuk,* and *Neely v. United States,* 775 F.2d 1092 (9th Cir. 1985), all upheld the Commissioner's assessment of negligence penalties. In this connection the Ninth Circuit stated, in *Hanson,* "No reasonable person would have trusted this scheme to work." The Tax Court regularly upholds the Commissioner's assessment of negligence penalties, as, amazingly, the flood of such cases continues. *E.g., Preston v. Commissioner,* 47 T.C.M. (CCH) 417 (1983) (dealing exclusively with the negligence penalty issue); *Keefover v. Commissioner,* 65 T.C.M. (CCH) 2999 (1993); *Balis v. Commissioner,* 63 T.C.M. (CCH) 1830 (1992), *aff'd mem.,* 987 F.2d 770 (5th Cir. 1993); *Buelow v. Commissioner,* 59 T.C.M. (CCH) 502 (1990), *aff'd,* 970 F.2d 412 (7th Cir. 1992); *Keefover v. Commissioner,* 57 T.C.M. (CCH) 37 (1989), *aff'd mem.,* 923 F.2d 857 (8th Cir. 1990); *Miller v. Commissioner,* 56 T.C.M. (CCH) 728 (1988); *Sampson v. Commissioner,* 55 T.C.M. (CCH) 800 (1988); *Cheek v. Commissioner,* 53 T.C.M. (CCH) 111 (1987); *Swayze v. Commissioner,* 45 T.C.M. (CCH) 1104 (1983) (involving a family trust promoter); *Luman v. Commissioner,* 79 T.C. 846 (1982); *Vercio v. Commissioner,* 73 T.C. 1246 (1980); *Wesenberg v. Commissioner,* 69 T.C. 1005 (1978). In *Wenz v. Commissioner,* 69 T.C.M. (CCH) 2961 (1995); *Brittain v. Commissioner,* 63 T.C.M. (CCH) 3004 (1992); *McKenzie v. Commissioner,* 52 T.C.M. (CCH) 1327 (1987); *Lundry v. Commissioner,* 52 T.C.M. (CCH) 578

(1986); and *Dick H. McKenzie Family Estate v. Commissioner,* 47 T.C.M. (CCH) 834 (1984), the Tax Court upheld the Commissioner's assessment of fraud penalties in cases involving use of family trusts. In *Kooyers v. Commissioner,* 88 T.C.M. (CCH) 605 (2004), and *Buckmaster v. Commissioner,* 73 T.C.M. (CCH) 2821 (1997), the Tax Court upheld the assessment of accuracy-related penalties against taxpayers who had employed family trusts.

3. In *James E. Edwards Family Trust v. United States,* 572 F. Supp. 22 (E.D.N.M. 1983), the court granted the government's motion for summary judgment, thereby permitting the government to levy against assets registered in the name of the fiduciaries of a family trust, in satisfaction of income tax deficiencies assessed against the individuals who created the family trust. The court called the trust a "nullity and sham for tax purposes." *See also William L. Comer Family Equity Trust v. United States,* 732 F. Supp. 755 (E.D. Mich. 1990), *aff'd mem.,* 966 F.2d 1455 (6th Cir.), *cert. denied,* 506 U.S. 1023 (1992) (family trust lacked standing to challenge levies based on grantors' tax liability); *Don Gastineau Equity Trust v. United States,* 687 F. Supp. 1422 (C.D. Cal. 1987) (government liens for grantors' tax liability attached to property held by their family trust); *Schmidt Liberty Irrevocable Trust v. United States,* 88-1 U.S.T.C. ¶ 9144 (W.D. Okla. 1987) (same); *Lewis G. Allen Family Trust v. United States,* 558 F. Supp. 152 (D. Kan. 1982) (same).

4. In *United States v. Landsberger,* 534 F. Supp. 142 (D. Minn. 1981), *aff'd in part,* 692 F.2d 501 (8th Cir. 1982), the district court granted the government's motion for summary judgment and entered a permanent injunction restraining the promoter of a "scheme [that] differ[ed] little from the 'family trust' plan which has been held illegal by numerous courts" from selling and promoting such trusts. The district court also held the promoter in contempt for continuing violations of the preliminary injunction and fined him $10,000 plus $500 per day until such violations ceased. On appeal, the Eighth Circuit affirmed the order granting the permanent injunction. Though the Eighth Circuit vacated the contempt order, its opinion, describing Landsberger's "obvious contempt," left little doubt that, if the district court rewrote the contempt order, it, too, would be affirmed. In *United States v. Buttorff,* 761 F.2d 1056 (5th Cir. 1985), the Fifth Circuit affirmed issuance of a preliminary injunction against a promoter of the "Constitutional Pure Equity Trust." In *United States v. Smith,* 657 F. Supp. 646 (W.D. La. 1986), *aff'd,* 814 F.2d 1086 (5th Cir. 1987), the court granted a permanent injunction against a promoter of "The Family Preservation Trust." *See also United States v. Estate Preservation Services,* 202 F.3d 1093 (9th Cir. 2000) (affirming entry of preliminary injunction against promoters of "Asset Preservation Trusts" and "Estate Management Trusts"); *United States v. Ratfield,* 2002-2 U.S.T.C. ¶ 50,765 (S.D. Fla. 2002) (entry of preliminary injunction against promoters of "pure" or "common-law" trusts).

5. *United States v. Krall,* 835 F.2d 711 (8th Cir. 1987), affirmed the conviction, for willful filing of false income tax returns, of a taxpayer who employed a trust arrangement similar to the family trust.

6. For more on "family trusts" and the tax protester movement from which they come, see Goldstein, *"Family Estate" Trusts, "Pure" Trusts and "Constitutional" Trusts: Apocalypse Now,* 16 U. Miami Inst. on Est. Plan. ¶ 700 (1982), which includes a summary, in chart form, of fifty-eight family trust cases decided during the period April 11, 1977, through January 11, 1982.

7. Probably as a result of unanimous judicial rejection of the typical family trust arrangement, a variation has developed. The grantor does not attempt to assign his or her income directly to the trust. Instead, the grantor continues to report all income, as earned,

but claims as a deduction (presumably under section 162) a "management fee" paid to the trust. Of course, this variation works no better than the original. *Pfluger v. Commissioner*, 840 F.2d 1379 (7th Cir.), *cert. denied*, 487 U.S. 1237 (1988). *See also O'Donnell v. Commissioner*, 726 F.2d 679 (11th Cir. 1984) (per curiam).

8. From time to time, the I.R.S. issues blunt warnings against abuses involving trusts, particularly those purporting to shift compensation or business income from an individual to a trust. *See, e.g.,* Notice 2006-31, 2006-1 C.B. 751, 752 ("Frivolous Arguments to Avoid When Filing a Return or Claim for Refund); Rev. Rul. 2006-19, 2006-1 C.B. 749; I.R.S. Pub. 2193, *Should Your Financial Portfolio Include Too Good to Be True Trusts?* (rev. July 2002); Serv. Ctr. Adv. 1998-006 (March 6, 1998); Notice 97-24, 1997-1 C.B. 409.

C. Sales between Related Taxpayers

Internal Revenue Code:
    Section 267(a)(1), (b), (c), (d)
Regulation:
    Section 1.267(a)-1(c)

Joseph E. Widener Trust v. Commissioner
80 T.C. 304 (1983)

FORRESTER, *Judge*:

* * *

The question presented is whether petitioner trusts may recognize capital losses generated by various stock sales between themselves.

FINDINGS OF FACT

* * *

Petitioners Peter A. B. Widener Trust No. 5 (hereinafter PW Trust) and Joseph E. Widener Trust No. 5 (hereinafter JW Trust) timely filed their Federal income tax returns for their respective years ended January 31, 1975. The Provident National Bank of Philadelphia, Pa. (hereinafter Provident, or Provident Bank), and William P. Wood, of Philadelphia, Pa., were the trustees of the PW Trust at the time the petition in docket No. 2690-78 was filed; Provident Bank and H. Peter Somers, of Philadelphia, Pa., were the trustees of the JW Trust at the time of filing of the petition in docket No. 2689-78.

The Peter A. B. Widener Trust was created in 1915 under the Will of Peter A. B. Widener. On March 29, 1971, under a decree of the Orphans Court Division of the Court of Common Pleas for the County of Montgomery, this trust was divided into four separate trusts, one of which (the PW Trust) is the petitioner in docket No. 2690-78. Ella Widener Wetherill (hereinafter Ella) was the sole income beneficiary of the PW Trust during the taxable year in issue. By its terms, the PW Trust will terminate on December 8, 1992, and its assets will be distributed to Ella, or to her issue if she is not then living. In the event of Ella's death prior to December 8, 1992, her children will succeed her as current income beneficiaries and remaindermen. Should Ella's children also die without issue prior to December 8, 1992, then P. A. B. Widener III, if living, or his issue, or in default thereof, the issue of P. A. B. Widener, will become current income beneficiaries and remaindermen.

Joseph E. Widener created the Joseph E. Widener Trust on April 20, 1938. On April 5, 1973, under a decree of the Orphans Court Division of the Court of Common Pleas for the County of Montgomery, this trust was divided into two separate trusts, one of which (the JW Trust) is the petitioner in docket No. 2689-78. Ella was the sole income beneficiary of the JW Trust during the taxable year in issue. By its terms, the JW Trust will terminate 21 years after the death of the last to die of Ella and P. A. B. Widener III. Upon Ella's death, her income interest in the JW Trust will pass to her children. Her children or their issue will receive the principal of the JW Trust upon its termination; in the event that no issue of Ella are then alive, the trust principal will pass to the issue of P. A. B. Widener II.

Ella has two children and P. A. B. Widener III has three, all born prior to 1975.

Because Ella was in a high tax bracket prior to and during the year in issue, she preferred to receive tax-exempt income from the trusts. The trusts were aware of her desire for tax-exempt income, and both trusts acceded to it by including some tax-exempt bonds in their investment portfolios. The trustees of the JW Trust, however, placed a greater emphasis on increasing corpus than did the trustees of the PW Trust, because the former felt a fiduciary obligation to the JW Trust's future beneficiaries. On June 30, 1975, the JW Trust held a higher percentage of tax-exempt securities than did the PW Trust, but we are satisfied that this was the result of a temporary adjustment.

The terms of petitioners' trusts did not require the trustees to follow Ella's instructions concerning trust investments. Ella was not kept informed of the trusts' investments and was not consulted on any investment decisions. In particular, Ella was not consulted on the transactions in issue and was unaware of their occurrence.

On January 24, 1975, the trustees of the PW Trust and the JW Trust held a regularly scheduled meeting to discuss the portfolios of the two trusts. The relevant parts of the minutes of that meeting read as follows:

> The Trustees reviewed the capital gains position for the fiscal years ending January 31, 1975 for all three trusts. There were $285,640 of capital gains realized to date in the P.A.B. Widener * * * Trust and $124,143 gains realized to date in the Joseph E. Widener * * * Trust. In each of these accounts, stocks were held in which losses could be realized to offset these gains. After some discussion, the Trustees decided to sell certain stocks in each account in order to realize losses and minimize taxes. However, in order to preserve the consolidated position of the trusts in these holdings, which the Trustees consider to be of a good quality, it was decided that each trust would purchase the stocks being sold by the other. These transactions would all be handled in the securities markets.

* * *

Peter A. B. Widener * * * */E. W. Wetherill #65972*
  Sell
      6,000   shs. Allied Telephone Company
  Buy
      1,000   shs. A. T. Cross

2,000   shs. Sun Banks of Florida
2,000   shs. Lenox

*Joseph E. Widener * * * /E. W. Wetherill #56712*
  Sell
      1,000   shs. A. T. Cross
      2,000   shs. Sun Banks of Florida
      2,000   shs. Lenox
  Buy
      6,000   shs. Allied Telephone Company

On January 31, 1975, Provident Bank, as trustee (PW), sold 6,000 shares of Allied Telephone Co. owned by the PW Trust, and as trustee (JW) purchased those same shares for the account of the JW Trust. The price, net of commissions, was $65,157; that price was determined by choosing a price halfway between the most recent bid and asked prices for Allied Telephone Co. shares. The PW Trust's basis in these shares was $103,416.07, and the PW Trust claimed a loss of $38,259 on the transaction.

Also on January 31, 1975, Provident Bank, as trustee, sold shares owned by the JW Trust, and purchased those same shares for the account of the PW Trust, in the following amounts:

Stock	Basis	Net sales price	Loss claimed by the JW Trust
1. 1000 shares A.T. Cross Co.	$41,668.58	$24,703	$16,965.58
2. 2000 shares Sun Banks of Fla., Inc.	49,375.00	18,964	30,411.00
3. 2000 shares Lenox, Inc.	48,811.34	29,943	18,868.34
Total	139,854.92	73,610	66,244.92

The prices at which these blocks of stock changed hands were determined by the quoted price of each particular stock over the exchange on which it was listed at the time of the sale, or, in the case of the Sun Banks of Florida, Inc., shares, by choosing a price halfway between the most recent bid and asked prices.

Provident effected all of the aforementioned stock sales by placing simultaneous buy and sell orders with Institutional Networks Corp. (hereinafter Instinet). Instinet is a computerized trading service that matches, without the mediation of a broker or established securities exchange, customers wishing to sell a particular stock with customers wishing to buy that stock. Instinet's computer matched Provident's buy and sell orders for each of the aforementioned stocks, and Instinet issued confirmation slips for each transaction.

All of the shares traded in the foregoing transactions were held in the name and possession of Provident Bank's nominee, Saxon & Co., both before and after the described transactions. Provident, as trustee of petitioner trusts, made appropriate entries on its internal books to record the change in ownership of the various shares. This procedure was a common practice of Provident to effect trades between two trusts of which it was trustee.

There is no evidence in the record to suggest that either trust had an explicit or an implicit right to reacquire any of the stock sold in the transactions in issue. We find that all sales in issue brought about complete and final changes in ownership of the shares involved.

OPINION

Deductions in respect of losses from sales of property between the fiduciaries of two trusts that have the same grantor; between a fiduciary of a trust and a beneficiary of that trust; or between a fiduciary of a trust and a beneficiary of another trust, if the same person is a grantor of both trusts, shall not be allowed. Sec. 267(b)(5), (6), and (7). Losses from transactions not within the scope of section 267 may still be disallowed in certain circumstances under section 1.267(a)-1(c), Income Tax Regs....

The parties agree that section 267 does not require disallowance of the losses in issue;[5] they disagree as to whether these losses may be disallowed under section 1.267(a)-1(c), Income Tax Regs.

Petitioner points out that losses outside the scope of section 267 may be disallowed under section 1.267(a)-1(c), Income Tax Regs., only if not bona fide, and argues that since the sales between the trusts were at market prices and effected a permanent change in the legal ownership of the stocks sold, the losses in issue were bona fide.

Respondent contends that the losses in issue must be disallowed because they were not bona fide.

The transactions in issue were motivated solely by a desire to reduce current taxes; however, it is obvious that the vendee trusts each acquired the shares at reduced bases on which future gains or losses would be computed.

It is well settled that taxpayers are entitled to arrange their affairs to minimize their taxes (*Gregory v. Helvering,* 69 F.2d 809 (2d Cir. 1934), affd. 293 U.S. 465 (1935)), and we may not disallow the losses before us simply because petitioners were motivated by a desire to reduce their taxes. As we have noted, however (*Crown Cork International Corp. v. Commissioner,* 4 T.C. 19, 24 (1944)), where a transaction giving rise to a loss is motivated solely by tax avoidance, its good faith is suspect. We must therefore scrutinize the record before us with particular care to determine whether or not the transactions in issue were bona fide.

Neither section 1.267(a)-1(c), Income Tax Regs., nor the legislative history of the predecessor of Section 267 defines "good faith" or "finality" or "bona fide." Respondent has cited us to cases which, while they do not define these phrases, do, according to respondent, indicate that the transactions here in issue lacked good faith and finality and were not bona fide.

Fender v. United States, 577 F.2d 934 (5th Cir. 1978), involved losses arising out of a sale coupled with an agreement that the seller would repurchase the assets sold, at the sales price, in 90 days. On these facts, the court held that there had been no bona fide sale.

Transport Mfg. & Equipment Co. of Del. v. Commissioner, T.C. Memo. 1968-190, affd. per curiam 431 F.2d 729 (8th Cir. 1970), involved a loss arising out of a sale between two related parties at an artificially low price. We disallowed the loss on the ground that the

---

5. While respondent concedes that sec. 267 does not apply to the facts of the present case, on brief, he attempts to reintroduce sec. 267 through the back door by arguing that the relationship between petitioner trusts is very close to falling within the spirit of sec. 267(b)(5).

Sec. 267 is a carefully drafted statute that imposes an irrebuttable presumption of a lack of bona fides on taxpayers claiming losses from certain carefully defined classes of transactions, and should be narrowly construed. *Snively v. Commissioner,* 20 T.C. 136, 149 (1953)....

See also Rev. Rul. 56-222, 56-1 C.B. 155; Rev. Rul. 71-50, 1971-1 C.B. 106; Rev. Rul. 77-439, 1977-2 C.B. 85, in which respondent admits he may not go beyond the explicit language of sec. 267 to disallow various claimed deductions.

transaction out of which it arose could not reasonably have been entered into by parties acting at arm's length.

The transactions between petitioners herein were final sales with no strings attached, and the prices involved were market prices. We find no support in the aforementioned two cases for respondent's contention that the sales in issue were not bona fide.

Respondent also cites us to several cases in which losses arising out of sales at market prices, with no strings attached, were disallowed. In *Higgins v. Smith,* 308 U.S. 473 (1940), the taxpayer sold stock at a loss to his wholly owned corporation, which was, the Court found, his corporate self.[7] The Supreme Court disallowed the loss, holding that because of the taxpayer's complete control of his corporation, the purported sale did not vary control or change the flow of economic benefits and had to be dismissed from consideration.

In *Crown Cork International Corp. v. Commissioner, supra,* the taxpayer sold assets to its wholly owned subsidiary. We noted that not all transactions between parent and subsidiary corporations can be disregarded, but held that where the relationship between related corporations is such that they are in fact inseparable, any loss on sales between them must be disregarded since it does not represent a loss to the combined enterprise.

In *Wickwire v. United States,* 116 F.2d 679 (6th Cir. 1941), the two taxpayers sold jointly owned stocks to their jointly owned corporation, and simultaneously purchased other stocks from their corporation. All transfers were at market price. The court found that the sales were not made in good faith, and disallowed the taxpayer's claimed loss deductions:

> The proof sustains the government's contention, stated in its brief, that the "appellants did not intend definitely to part with their legal and beneficial ownership of the stock during the taxable year but intended to and did retain effective control so that they might make up their minds at a later date when to sell or what to do with it." [116 F.2d at 681.]

In each of the three cases just discussed, a transaction was held to be lacking in good faith or finality because one party to the transaction controlled the other party, and so retained control of the assets sold even after the purported sale. Such is not the case in the transactions here in issue.

Petitioner trusts were formed 23 years apart, by different grantors. The trust had a common trustee, but that trustee was mindful of its distinct fiduciary obligations of the two trusts. On this record, we are satisfied that neither trust controlled the other.

Respondent argues that Ella, as the income beneficiary of both trusts, controlled both trusts.[9] We agree that the fact that Ella was the income beneficiary of both trusts is material evidence on the question whether the transactions in issue varied control of the shares sold. It is not the only evidence, however.

The JW Trust investment policy emphasized growth of the corpus over the production of tax-exempt income, in deference to the interest of the future beneficiaries, in spite of the fact that Ella was the sole income beneficiary of the JW Trust during 1975; indeed, Pennsylvania law imposed upon the trustees of the JW Trust a fiduciary duty to the future beneficiaries of that trust. *In re Estate of Hamill,* 487 Pa. 592 (1980); *Thomp-*

---

7. Had present sec. 267 been in effect for the year in issue, this loss would have been disallowed by statute. Sec. 267(b)(2).

9. We note that Ella's interests in the principal of the two trusts are substantially different. She has no such interest in the trust which will terminate 21 years after the death of the survivor of herself and her brother, but the corpus of the other trust will go to her in 1992 if she is then living.

son Estate, 262 Pa. 278 (1918). This factor cuts against the conclusion that Ella controlled petitioner trusts. Ella's desire to receive tax-exempt income was respected by petitioners' trustees, at their discretion, but Ella had no voice in the specific investment decisions of either trust, and was unaware of the transactions here in issue. This also cuts against the conclusion that Ella controlled the trusts. On balance, we are persuaded that Ella, as sole income beneficiary of petitioners during the years in issue, did not control petitioners.

Respondent also argues that the transactions between the petitioners were not bona fide because they did not "change the flow of economic benefits" (*Higgins v. Smith, supra* at 476) from the stocks sold.

As we read *Higgins v. Smith, supra,* the assertion that the sale there in issue did not change the flow of economic benefits is simply a corollary of the Court's conclusion that the sale did not vary control of the assets sold.[10] On this reading, since we find that the sales before us did effect a change of control, we must conclude that those sales changed the flow of economic benefits from the stocks sold.

Our conclusion that the sales in issue changed the flow of economic benefits from the shares sold is further supported by the fact that the trusts had different contingent beneficiaries. This entails at least the possibility that future appreciation or depreciation of the shares traded by petitioners will be realized by beneficiaries other than those who would have realized such appreciation or depreciation had the sales in issue not occurred.[11]

Based on the foregoing considerations, and the entire record, we find that the sales in issue were bona fide; consequently, the deductions in respect of losses attributable to such sales will be allowed.

Illustrative Material

1. The I.R.S. has acquiesced in *Widener.* 1984-1 C.B. 2.

2. In Technical Advice Memorandum 7737025 (1977), the I.R.S. admitted that section 267 did not deny a loss realized by an estate in a sale of property to its executor. In following the language of section 267, the I.R.S. reasoned: "No artificial losses ... have occurred in this transaction. An estate, unlike a trust, partnership, or corporation, is not a flexible vehicle which is readily available for tax avoidance purposes. That is to say, one does not create an estate of his own choosing or timing." Similarly, in Rev. Rul. 56-222, 1956-1 C.B. 155, the I.R.S. ruled that section 267 did not deny a loss realized by an estate in a "bona fide sale" of property to an *inter vivos* trust created by the decedent. After amendment by the Taxpayer Relief Act of 1997, section 267 now applies to transactions between an executor of an estate and any of its beneficiaries, except for sales or exchanges in satisfaction of pecuniary bequests. I.R.C. § 267(b)(13).

---

10. This reading of *Higgins v. Smith,* 308 U.S. 473 (1940), is supported by our assertion in *Crown Cork International Corp. v. Commissioner,* 4 T.C. 19 (1944), that not all transactions between parent and subsidiary corporations can be disregarded, but only those where the two are in fact inseparable. This statement entails that a sale by a parent to a sufficiently independent subsidiary would change the flow of economic benefits even though the shareholders of the parent ultimately own both parent and subsidiary.

11. We cannot dismiss as de minimis the interest of the contingent beneficiaries, for we have held that a contingent beneficiary is a beneficiary under the intendment of sec. 267. *Hickman v. Commissioner,* T.C. Memo. 1972-208; cf. *Wyly v. Commissioner,* 662 F.2d 397 (5th Cir. 1981).

3. In *Meek v. Commissioner,* 71 T.C.M. (CCH) 3055 (1996), *aff'd mem.,* 133 F.3d 928 (9th Cir. 1998), taxpayers simultaneously created a trust and sold property to it, in exchange for the trustees' promissory note. Deductibility of a loss incurred on the sale depended, under section 267(b)(4), on whether the taxpayers were the trust's "grantors." The court held that they were, notwithstanding the fact that the trustees, on behalf of the trust, had provided the consideration for its creation. The court noted that the trustees were unrelated to both the taxpayers and the trust beneficiaries, and that the trustees "did not participate to any degree in the dispositive provisions of the trust." 71 T.C.M. (CCH) at 3058. As a result, the court denied deductibility of the loss.

Scully v. United States
840 F.2d 478 (7th Cir. 1988)

RIPPLE, Circuit Judge.

Michael J. Scully and Peter D. Scully, as trustees of nine trusts established for members of the Scully family, brought this action against the United States seeking a refund of $274,583 in income taxes paid by the trusts. The trustees argued that the trusts were entitled to the refund because the trusts had sold 980 acres of real estate at a loss of more than $500 per acre. The district court granted the government's motion for summary judgment on the ground that section 267(b)(5) ... disallowed the loss. The trustees appealed. During the pendency of that appeal, the government changed its position and concluded that section 267(b)(5) did not disallow the loss, but that section 267(b)(6) did so. Based on the government's change of position, this court remanded the case to the district court so that the trustees could file a motion seeking relief from the district court judgment.... On remand, the district court denied the trustees' motion and reaffirmed its earlier judgment. It adhered to its earlier view that section 267(b)(5) was the applicable section and that this section disallowed the trusts' claimed loss. The trustees, in accordance with the earlier ruling of this court, then filed an appeal ... that was consolidated with their earlier appeal.

We conclude that the loss was properly disallowed. However, we affirm the judgment of the district court on the ground that Code section 165 does not permit deduction of the loss, and not on the rationale relied upon by the district court.

I
Facts

A. *The Scully Tradition*

In the 1850's, William Scully, a native of Ireland, purchased 46,000 acres of land in central Illinois. Rather than farm this land himself, Mr. Scully chose to lease the land in a fashion similar to the one his family had used in Ireland for many years. Under this system, the typical lease term was only one year, but the tenants were assured that their lease would be renewed if they paid their rent promptly in cash and if they properly maintained their property. The tenants were required and encouraged to construct and maintain buildings, fences and other improvements. If the tenant wished to move or retire, he was entitled to sell his improvements to a succeeding tenant, if acceptable to Mr. Scully, as if those improvements were personal property.

Most of the 46,000 acres have remained in the Scully family ever since, and the practices instituted by William Scully are still respected. The family itself refers to the practice as the "Scully Tradition." The land is managed today by Michael and Peter Scully, the grandchildren of William, with the help of two agents, from offices in Lincoln and Dwight, Illinois. They arrange the leases, collect the rents, pay the taxes, maintain the drainage system, and ensure that the tenants abide by the leases. Many of the tenants belong to families that have leased the same land from the Scullys for three or four generations. The tenants have erected valuable improvements on the land, aggregating $10 million or more, and they rely on the Scully Tradition to safeguard their investments. Michael and Peter Scully agree that it is important that the property stay in the family.

B. *The Transaction*

In 1959 title to the land was in Thomas Scully, the son of William and the father of Michael and Peter. In that year, Thomas created two trusts (the Buying Trusts), one for the benefit of Michael's children, the other for the benefit of Peter's children. Thomas placed some of his land into those trusts. The terms of the Buying Trusts provided that the trust estate should be divided into shares of equal value for each of Michael's and Peter's children, with Michael and Peter serving as co-trustees. If Michael or Peter should have additional children, the trust estate was to be redivided so that each child would have an equal share. The Buying Trusts' dispositive provisions provided that two-thirds of the annual income from the trusts was to be paid to the children after they reached the age of 21, and one-third was to be added to corpus. The Buying Trusts were to terminate ten years after the death of the last to die of the children of Michael and Peter living in 1959. When any of the children died during the term of the Buying Trusts, that child's descendants would succeed to that interest *per stirpes*.

Thomas died in 1961. By his will, one-half of his adjusted gross estate was placed in a marital trust for the benefit of his wife Violet. She was given a general power of appointment over the assets in the marital trust "as she shall direct in her Will." If she did not exercise the power of appointment, the property in the marital trust was to be added to, and disposed of, as part of Thomas' residuary estate. Violet died on August 9, 1976. At that time, more than 7,000 acres of the Scully land was held in the marital trust. In her will, she exercised the power of appointment and directed that most of this land be divided into equal trusts for the benefit of each of Michael's and Peter's children (the Selling Trusts). Michael and Peter were named co-trustees of the Selling Trusts. All relevant provisions of the trusts were the same as for the Buying Trusts, with two exceptions. First, *all* income of the Selling Trusts, instead of two-thirds of the income, was to be distributed to the children once they reached the age of 21. Second, the Selling Trusts were to terminate ten years after the death of the last to die of Michael's and Peter's children who were living in 1961. Because three children had been born between 1959 and 1961, the termination date was therefore potentially later.

Under the terms of Violet's will, the Selling Trusts were requested to pay all taxes, expenses of administration, and other costs associated with the settlement of her estate. The trusts lacked the cash to make those payments. The Buying Trusts, on the other hand, had ample assets with which to meet the obligations. Therefore, Michael and Peter, as trustees of the Selling Trusts, sold 980 acres of land in the Selling Trusts to the Buying Trusts. The price was $1,550 per acre. This price, arrived at by means of an appraisal commissioned by Peter and Michael, had been used to fix the value of Violet's property for purposes of her estate tax return. In order to preserve the Scully Tradition, no part of the 980 acres was ever offered for sale to anyone besides the Buying Trusts.

For 1977, the year of the sale, the Selling Trusts' tax returns reported no gain or loss on the transfer of the 980 acres.[4] In 1980, however, the Internal Revenue Service (IRS) au-

---

4. Under Code § 1014, a taxpayer's basis in property acquired from a decedent normally equals the fair market value at the date of death. Hence, the Selling Trusts initially took the position that their basis in the 980 acres was $1,550 an acre, resulting in neither a gain nor a loss on the transaction.

dited Violet's estate tax return and had the property appraised. The government then concluded that Violet's estate had been undervalued. Michael and Peter compromised the dispute and agreed to revalue the land at $2,075 an acre. One month later, Michael and Peter filed administrative claims for refunds for the Selling Trusts' 1977 tax returns. Michael and Peter claimed that the trusts' basis in the 980 acres was $2,075 per acre (not $1,550 as previously reported), and that therefore the trusts sustained a loss of $525 per acre. The IRS denied the refund claim. This litigation followed.

C. *Earlier Proceedings*

In the district court, the trustees and the government filed cross-motions for summary judgment. The government argued that the Selling Trusts' claimed loss was disallowed by section 267(a)(1) and section 267(b)(5) of the Code. Section 267(a)(1) provides that no deduction is permitted for any loss resulting from the sale or exchange of property between certain related parties. Section 267(b)(5) provides that the fiduciaries of two different trusts are related parties within the meaning of section 267(a)(1) if the two trusts have a common grantor. The government contended that Thomas Scully was the grantor of both sets of trusts because Illinois law determined the "grantor" of a trust for purposes of section 267, and Illinois law treats the donor of a general power of appointment as the grantor of a trust created by the exercise of that power. The trustees argued that federal law defined "grantor," and that, under federal law, the donee of a general power of appointment was the grantor of any trust that the donee created by exercise of the power. In the alternative, the trustees argued that, even under Illinois law, the donee of a general power of appointment should be treated as the grantor of any trusts he creates.

As a second argument, the government argued that the sale lacked the bona fide, arm's length character needed to satisfy section 165 of the Code, which grants a deduction for qualifying losses sustained by a taxpayer. The government fully briefed this argument for the district court. The trustees responded to this argument, contending that the sale in this instance was made at a fair price as part of the trade or business of the Selling Trusts, and that there was no intention or motive of tax avoidance in the transaction.

The district court ruled for the government; it concluded that Illinois law, not federal law, controlled with respect to the definition of a grantor of a trust, and that under Illinois law Thomas Scully was the grantor of the Selling Trusts and of the Buying Trusts. *Scully v. United States*, 629 F.Supp. 1534 (C.D. Ill.1986). The court reasoned that Illinois applies the doctrine of "relation back," under which "'[p]roperty passing pursuant to the exercise of the power passes under the instrument creating the power, just as though the appointment were read into the original instrument.'" *Id.* at 1537 (quoting *In re Estate of Breault*, 29 Ill.2d 165, 193 N.E.2d 824 (1963)). Under this doctrine, the court noted, Thomas Scully would be treated as the grantor of any trust created by his widow's exercise of a power of appointment.[8]

The Scullys appealed that decision to this court. During the pendency of the appeal, the government changed its position; it submitted to this court that the district court had erroneously decided that state law should define the term "grantor." The government therefore moved this court to remand the case so that the district court could determine

---

8. The district court acknowledged that an exception exists to this rule when the donee of the general power of appointment treats the property subject to the power as his own for all purposes. *Id.* at 1538. However, the court noted that Violet Scully requested that the trustees pay all taxes and expenses out of the Selling Trusts' assets. This persuaded the court that she had not viewed these assets as her own. *Id.* Therefore, the district court determined that the exception was inapplicable, and that under Illinois law Thomas Scully should be deemed the grantor of the Selling Trusts.

whether the losses should have been disallowed on other grounds. Over the opposition of the trustees, this court granted the government's motion and remanded the case for further consideration by the district court.

On remand, the trustees moved the district court to reopen the judgment.... The government opposed the motion and urged the court to adhere to its prior judgment, albeit on different grounds. First, the government argued that the Selling Trusts' loss should be disallowed based on Code section 267(b)(6). That section disallows losses incurred in a transaction between "[a] fiduciary of a trust and a beneficiary of such trust."... The government conceded that the transaction here at issue was not expressly within the terms of that section, but argued that the transaction was "indirectly" within the statute. In the alternative, the government renewed its argument that the transaction was not a recognizable loss under section 165.

The trustees responded that the government's new argument under section 267(b)(6) was unavailing because the government had waived the argument by failing to present it to the district court earlier. On the merits, the trustees contended that section 267(b)(6) was inapplicable to their situation because the sale between the two sets of trusts was not a sale between a fiduciary of a trust and a beneficiary of the same trust. As to the government's section 165 argument, the trustees again contended that the Selling Trusts were engaged in a valid trade or business, and that the transaction was conducted at arm's length at a fair price.

The district court denied the trustees' motion, but not for the reasons suggested by the government.... In the court's view, neither party had presented sufficient authority to warrant a departure from the court's original decision. Therefore, the court reaffirmed its earlier decision that section 267(b)(5) prevented the Selling Trusts from recognizing any loss resulting from the transaction. In regard to the government's claim under section 267(b)(6), the court said that the government had waived this argument by failing to present it during the initial proceedings in the district court. The court added that this argument was without merit, even if it were timely. Finally, because of the court's decision that section 267(b)(5) disallowed plaintiffs' losses, the court did not address the issue of whether section 165 would also disallow the losses.

II

Discussion

This case comes to us in a rather unique posture. The government has abandoned its effort to disallow the deduction on the ground relied upon by the district court—section 267(b)(5). It now argues that the deduction can be disallowed, if at all, only on the authority of either section 267(b)(6) or section 165. Because we believe that the judgment of the district court must be affirmed on the latter of these two grounds, we shall not address the merits of the now-abandoned argument based on section 267(b)(5)....

A. *Applicability of § 267(b)(6)*

In determining whether section 267(b)(6) governs this transaction, our focus must be a narrow one. The government admits, as it must, that the sale between the Selling Trusts and the Buying Trusts was not a sale "directly" between the "fiduciary of a trust and a beneficiary of such a trust." Therefore, we must focus on whether the sale was "indirectly" between the "fiduciary of a trust and a beneficiary of such a trust."

In addressing this question, it is hardly necessary for us to define "indirectly" as it might apply to all transactions. In *McWilliams v. Commissioner*, 331 U.S. 694, 67 S.Ct. 1477, 91 L.Ed. 1570 (1947), the Supreme Court cautioned, rather explicitly, against giving the term too narrow a reading: "Congress ... could not have intended to include within the scope of § 24(b) [the predecessor to section 267] only transfers made directly or through a dummy, or to exclude transfers of securities effected through the medium of the Stock Exchange, unless it wanted to leave a loop-hole almost as large as the one it had set out to close." *Id.* at 700–01, 67 S.Ct. at 1481; *accord Miller v. Commissioner*, 510 F.2d 230, 233 (9th Cir.1975). At the same time, we must be careful that our interpretation is not one which "carries us beyond interpretation into the realm of amendment. Into that realm we are forbidden to go." *Miller*, 510 F.2d at 234.

Whatever may be the outer limits of the term "indirectly" in other contexts, we believe that, when distinctions between legal and equitable ownership are central to the inquiry, the lines drawn by Congress in the wording of this section must be respected. In section 267(b), Congress delineated with great precision those transactions involving trusts that came within the ambit of the statute. As the Tax Court noted in *Widener v. Commissioner*, 80 T.C. 304 (1983), section 267 "is a carefully drafted statute that imposes an irrebuttable presumption of a lack of bona fides on taxpayers claiming losses from certain carefully defined classes of transactions.... [W]here Congress intended to disallow losses in transactions where a trust is a party, it did so expressly." *Id.* at 309–10 n. 5. Therefore, we believe that we cannot, consistent with our duty to effectuate the intent of Congress, disregard, for purposes of interpreting section 267, the trust entities, obviously established and maintained in good faith, that undertook this transaction. Congress carefully delineated those transactions regarding trusts, their fiduciaries, and their beneficiaries that would run afoul of section 267. This transaction was not among them.

B. *Applicability of § 165*

The government submits, and the trustees do not disagree, that section 267 is not the only statutory provision by which the transaction in question must be measured.[12] The sale must also pass muster under section 165. That section permits the deduction of a loss "sustained during the taxable year...." 26 U.S.C. § 165(a). [The court quotes Treas. Reg. § 1.165-1(b).]

The government argues that the transaction between the trusts was not bona fide because there was no genuine economic loss. The transfer left the beneficiaries, the government contends, in exactly the same economic position as before. Money simply shifted "from one pocket to another." Appellee's Br. at 33. Moreover, the government argues that this transaction is a "principal target" for disallowance under section 165 because it was a sale between family members. *Id.* at 29. Thus, the government submits that a "transfer like [this], which really leaves things as they were, is not an appropriate occasion for recognizing gain or loss under the Code." *Id.* at 33. The trustees respond that they demonstrated to the district court that they had proceeded in good faith and in accordance with their fiduciary obligations in conducting the sales. Because the sale was made at a price arrived at by an independent appraisal, the trustees insist that the transaction was at arm's length and bona fide. They emphasize that the purpose of the transaction was to gener-

---

12. [The court quotes Treas. Reg. § 1.267(a)-1(c).]
The legislative history of the Revenue Act of 1937, which added the trust provisions to the predecessor of § 267, makes clear that Congress did not intend for § 267 to be the exclusive source for disallowing losses in cases involving trusts.

[I]t is not intended by this amendment to imply any legislative sanction of claiming deductions for losses on sales or exchanges in cases not covered thereby, where the transaction lacks the elements of good faith or finality, generally characterizing sales and exchanges of property.

S.Rep. No. 1242, 75th Cong., 1st Sess. (1937), *reprinted in* 1939-1 Cum. Bull. (Part 2) 703, 723.

ate cash in order to pay estate taxes, and not to avoid taxation. The trustees point out that they did not know that the transaction would generate a loss until the government reappraised the property two years after the sale. Finally, the trustees claim that they were engaged in a valid trade or business (property management), and that the farmland sold was "trade or business" property.

... The law is clear that the burden of proof is upon the trustees to establish the bona fide nature of the loss. *Burnet v. Houston*, 283 U.S. 223, 227, 51 S.Ct. 413, 415, 75 L.Ed. 991 (1931); *Fender v. United States*, 577 F.2d 934, 936 (5th Cir. 1978); *Westvaco Corp. v. United States*, 639 F.2d 700, 707, 225 Ct.Cl. 436 (1980).

... While cases interpreting section 165 vary enormously in their factual settings, the governing principle is clear:

> Losses will not be allowed which are claimed in connection with transactions which do not vary control or change the flow of economic benefits....
>
> ....
>
> ... [A taxpayer] will not be permitted to transfer assets from one pocket to another and take a loss thereby where he remains at the conclusion of the transfer the real owner of the property, either because of retention of title, command over the property, either directly or through the person who appears as the nominal vendee or transferee.

7 J. Mertens, *Law of Federal Income Taxation* § 28.26 (1980). Ever since Justice Reed's opinion in *Higgins v. Smith*, 308 U.S. 473, 60 S.Ct. 355, 84 L.Ed. 406 (1940), it has been clear that, in determining whether control has changed or the flow of economic benefits altered, the "actualities" of the situation must be assessed. *Id*. at 477, 60 S.Ct. at 358. While the existence of separate legal entities cannot be disregarded, this factor "is only one incident necessary to complete an actual sale...." *Id*. at 476, 60 S.Ct. at 357.

[W]e do not believe that the trustees have established that they can meet their burden of establishing that the claimed loss was bona fide. The trustees have offered evidence that the purpose of the transaction was to raise cash and not to avoid taxes; similarly, they have offered evidence to suggest that the sale was made at a fair price, and that the Selling Trusts were engaged in a genuine trade or business. However, they have not shown that they can establish any actual separation in the operation of the trusts, and consequently, any genuine economic loss. We have reviewed the record and can find no significant evidence of any actual separation. As the trustees admit, the purpose of the sale was to keep all the real estate in the family. The land owned by the trusts was contiguous and used a unified drainage system. There is no evidence that any of the tenants on the land are aware of the separate ownership by the trusts. The trustees of the trusts are the same. The trustees are brothers. All of the current beneficiaries of the trusts are the children of the trustees (the grandchildren of the grantors). The remainder beneficiaries of the trusts are the descendants of the beneficiaries. Most important, as the trustees admit, the purpose of the sale was to keep all the real estate in the family and to permit the trustees to operate the land in both sets of trusts as a single, integrated economic entity. This reshuffling of assets permitted the trustees to achieve this purpose. In this respect, the present case closely resembles *Northern Pac. Ry. Co. v. United States*, 378 F.2d 686, 180 Ct.Cl. 388 (1967). There the court denied a loss where a parent corporation sold stock to a subsidiary in order to preserve the voting power of a parent corporation's management. The court said:

> [A] sale of stock for the very end of preserving the voting power of the parent's management is clearly one transaction in which there is no lessening in domi-

nation and control, but an effort to maintain it intact, precisely as it was. Nor, as we have seen, was there any real alteration in the corporations' economic status. On the contrary, the design was to have everything remain as before. Despite the form of a loss-sale, that is the actuality and the substance.

Id. 378 F.2d [sic] at 692–93. *See also Crown Cork Int'l Corp. v. Commissioner*, 4 T.C. 19, 25 (1944) ("It would follow that a transfer from one to the other was no more than a shifting from one department or branch to another of the same entity, and hence that the loss is utterly lacking in finality."). We can only conclude, as did the district court, that there was, in reality, "no genuine economic loss."[15] ... Therefore, the district court's grant of summary judgment to the government must be affirmed.

Finally, we do not mean to imply by our decision that there was any bad faith on the part of the Scullys. There is no evidence to suggest that the purpose of this transaction was anything other than the obtaining of cash to pay estate taxes, and, concomitantly, the preservation of a remarkable family tradition. The taxpayer's good faith does not, however, establish the legitimacy of his loss for purposes of section 165.

Accordingly, the judgment of the district court is affirmed.

---

15. *Scully v. United States*, 629 F.Supp. 1534, 1543 (C.D. Ill.1986).
Our decision today should not be read to conflict with *Widener v. Commissioner*, 80 T.C. 304 (1983). In *Widener*, two trusts with related grantors, common trustees and a common current income beneficiary sold stock to each other to generate tax losses at the close of the year. Although the court concluded that the losses were bona fide under § 165, the court applied the same legal analysis as we do here. The cases are reconcilable because of the substantial factual distinctions between them. In *Widener*, the two trusts were created 23 years apart by different grantors (a father and his son). The trustees of one trust were the Provident National Bank and William P. Wood. The trustees of the other trust were the Provident National Bank and H. Peter Somers. Thus, both trusts had one common trustee, but that trustee was a bank, and both trusts had a trustee individual to that trust. By its terms, one of the trusts was to terminate in 1992, and its assets were to be distributed to the income beneficiary. The other trust was not to terminate until at least 21 years after the income beneficiary's death, and possibly later. Hence, the tax court [sic] noted that the income beneficiary's interest in the principal of the two trusts was "substantially different." *Id.* at 312 n. 9. The trust in which the income beneficiary had no interest in the corpus had an investment policy that emphasized growth of the corpus, in deference to the interest of the future beneficiaries. Further, the income beneficiary had no voice in any specific investment decisions, and she was unaware of the transactions at issue in the case. Thus, the court concluded that the beneficiaries did not control the trusts, and that the trustees were independent.
In the present case, unlike *Widener*, there is a complete identity of trust fiduciaries. The Selling Trusts and the Buying Trusts have identical beneficiaries, and neither set of trusts can be expected to terminate soon. The remainder interests of both sets of trusts are also held by the same individuals. The only differences between the Selling Trusts and the Buying Trusts are that: (1) the Selling Trusts might terminate later than the Buying Trusts because the Selling Trusts have three additional measuring lives, and; (2) all of the income of the Selling Trusts goes to the beneficiaries once they reach the age of 21, as opposed to the Buying Trusts, in which only ⅔ of the income goes to the beneficiaries. We do not believe that these minor differences, one of which is very contingent, alter the nature of the transaction here at issue.

Chapter 6

Income in Respect of a Decedent

A. Inclusion in Recipient's Gross Income

Internal Revenue Code:
  Sections 691(a); 1014(a), (c)

Regulations:
  Sections 1.691(a)-1, -2, -3, -4

1. Investment Income

a. Rent

Estate of Davison v. United States
155 Ct. Cl. 290, 292 F.2d 937
cert. denied, 368 U.S. 939 (1961)

JONES, *Chief Judge,* delivered the opinion of the court:

This is a suit for the refund of Federal income taxes which were paid by the estate of Helen Davison for the years 1953 and 1954. The case concerns certain cash rents which were based on the proceeds of crop production on decedent's land and certain other rents payable in crops which were attributable to leases that ran during the year 1952. On the date of decedent's death the amounts of these rents were not ascertained. Thereafter, the estate collected both rents in full and sold the crop-rents for money. The questions presented are whether the rents received in money and the rents received in crops are taxable to the estate as income in respect of a decedent.

The facts have been found by the trial commissioner without exception by either party. The decedent, Helen Davison, was on the cash receipts and disbursements method of accounting. She died on December 24, 1952, owning two parcels of real property. One parcel, 320 acres located in Coolidge, Arizona (hereafter referred to as the Coolidge tract), had been leased by the decedent to one Fred Jones for the period January 1, 1952, to January 1, 1953. The lease provided that the decedent was to be paid as rent "one-fourth of all *crops* grown" on the 320 acres.

The second parcel of land, 640 acres located in Eloy, Arizona (hereafter referred to as the Eloy tract), had been leased to one Leland Jones and one Mike Jones who later assigned the lease to the Jones Ranch Enterprises Corporation. The term of this lease was from February 1952, to January 1, 1953. It was provided in this lease that the decedent was to be paid as rent "one-half of the *net proceeds* of all crops grown" on the 640 acres. Each of the leases contained the customary provision that the tenant had the privilege of harvesting the balance of any crops that had not been harvested on the date of the expiration of the lease.

Up to the date of decedent's death, the local cotton gin company, on behalf of the lessees of the Coolidge tract and pursuant to that lease, had paid the decedent a total of $6,516.01 as her share of the seed credits and cotton sales for the period May 31, 1952, to October 20, 1952. This amount represented the proceeds from the sale of the decedent's one-fourth of 129 bales of cotton grown by the lessee.

In February 1953, subsequent to the death of the decedent, the cotton gin company, again on behalf of the lessee of the Coolidge tract, paid the decedent's estate the amount of $14,137.14, representing the sale price of decedent's final share of the crops.

The lessee of the 640-acre Eloy tract had made no payments to the decedent prior to her death. But in 1953 the corporation leasing the tract filed two interim statements of settlement for rent due to the decedent's estate. Both of these statements were rejected by the estate. On January 24, 1954, a settlement was reached between the lessee of the Eloy tract and the estate. It was agreed that the amount of rent due, pursuant to the terms of the lease agreement, was $14,429.43. Between January 27 and February 2, 1954, the estate received this sum from the lessee corporation.

Both the $14,138.14 [sic] Coolidge tract rent payment received by the estate in 1953 and the $14,429.43 Eloy tract rent payment received by the estate in 1954 were included as a part of the gross estate of the decedent in Schedule F of the Federal estate tax return filed by the estate. Neither of these two sums was reported as income to the estate. The Commissioner of Internal Revenue adjusted the estate's income tax return to show each of these amounts received as income in respect of a decedent, and notified the estate that as a result of this adjustment the estate was subject to additional income taxes in the total amount of $11,892.11 plus deficiency interest. The estate was given [an income tax deduction under section 691(c)] for the estate taxes paid as a result of the inclusion of the rent payments as part of the decedent's gross estate.

The taxpayer paid the asserted deficiency and filed timely claims for refund of income taxes for the periods 1953 and 1954 in the total amount of $13,728.28. The claims for refund were disallowed and this suit resulted.

The plaintiff maintains that the right to receive these two rental payments was part of the property of the decedent's gross estate. As such it was properly valued and taxed under the estate tax provisions. The result was that this much of decedent's property received a new basis in the hands of the estate equal to its estate tax valuation. Since the estate received in satisfaction of these claims for rent an amount which did not exceed the basis of the claims it cannot be said that the estate has received income.

The defendant maintains that the rents received by the estate in cash and in crops, which were immediately sold for its account, represent income in respect of a decedent as set forth in section 126 of the 1939 Internal Revenue Code ... and section 691 of the

1954 Internal Revenue Code.... The plaintiff is therefore entitled to a [deduction] for the estate taxes paid on the assessed value of the claims for rent, but the plaintiff is liable for ordinary income taxes on the amounts of rent actually collected.

As set forth above, we must determine whether these rents, both cash and crops, were properly taxed to the estate as income in respect of a decedent.

In order to understand the present state of the law some consideration must be given to its historical background. Prior to 1934 it was held by the courts under the then existing revenue statutes that money earned by a cash method taxpayer and accruable to him on the date of his death but which had not been received by him prior to his death could be collected by his estate without liability for income taxes. Such items were subject to death taxes but they escaped income taxes. *Nichols v. United States,* 64 Ct. Cl. 241 (1927). A taxpayer on the accrual method of accounting was required to pay income taxes both on what he received and what was accruable to him on the date of his death. This interpretation of the law produced obvious inequities between those who were on the accrual method and those who were on the cash method. In addition, sizable amounts of income which were not "accruable" as the term was then used escaped taxation. *Held v. Commissioner,* 3 B.T.A. 408 (1926).

The Congress expressed concern over this discrimination and loss of revenue. See Sen. Rep. No. 4558, 73d Cong., 2d Sess. 28 (1934). It provided in section 42 of the Revenue Act of 1934 that the last return of every decedent should include "amounts accrued up to the date of his death." 48 Stat. 680, 694. While this provision effected an equality between decedents on the cash and accrual methods of accounting, it often resulted in pyramiding into the decedent's final return large amounts of income which except for death would have been spread over a number of years and subjected to lower rates of tax. See Sen. Rep. No. 1631, 77th Cong., 2d Sess. 100 (1942). In addition, the Supreme Court in *Helvering v. Estate of Enright,* 312 U.S. 636 (1941) greatly extended the meaning of the phrase "amounts accrued up to the date of his death" beyond any accounting concept of accrual developed by the decisions to that date. Lower court decisions followed taxing to decedents various sorts of inchoate or conjectural gains with the result that the pyramiding was extended and the possibility existed that taxes requiring current cash might be exacted at death on amounts that might never be collected or collected only after many years.

An exceptional case in this period and one of importance to the present decision was *Burnett v. Commissioner,* 2 T.C. 897 (1943), were the taxpayer during his lifetime had been engaged in the cattle raising business and had kept his books on the cash method. The Commissioner sought to tax to the decedent the value of certain cattle which had been raised by the decedent but which remained unsold at the time of his death. The Commissioner theorized that the cattle represented "gross income" to the decedent which had "accrued up to the date of his death", and that the amount thereof was properly includable in decedent's income for the taxable period in which fell the date of his death. The case was governed by section 42 of the Revenue Act of 1938, 52 Stat. 447, 473, which repeated verbatim the provisions of section 42 of the Revenue Act of 1934, *supra.* The Board of Tax Appeals held for the taxpayer. It refused to extend the result of the *Enright* case and stated that in the absence of a sale or exchange there was no gross income accruable to the decedent within the meaning of section 42 merely from the ownership of property. This was so even though the property had been produced by decedent on his ranches during his lifetime.

The case was appealed, the appeal was dismissed, and the Commissioner later acquiesced in this part of the decision. 1944 Cum. Bull. 4.

Finally, however, the cumulative evidence of unfairness of section 42 prompted the Congress to eliminate this unpopular provision and to enact in the Revenue Act of 1942, 56 Stat. 798, 831, the provisions of law now effective, namely section 126 of the 1939 Code which survives now as section 691 of the 1954 Code. It was section 126 which first gave rise to the concept of income in respect of a decedent. The differences between the provisions of the 1939 and 1954 Codes are not significant in the instant case, and we shall use the 1939 Code for purposes of our discussion.

Section 126 of the 1939 Code provides in subsection (a) that the "amount of all items of gross income in respect of a decedent" which are not properly includable in the last or a prior return of a decedent shall be taxed as income in the year received to the decedent's estate or beneficiary actually receiving such amount. Any amounts so received shall be considered to have the same character in the hands of the estate or beneficiary as they would have had in the hands of the decedent if he had lived to receive such amounts. Subsection (b) makes similar provisions for certain deductions and credits, and subsection (c) permits an income tax deduction for the estate tax attributable to items taxable under subsection (a).

It is noteworthy that the statute describes how income in respect of a decedent is to be reported, but nowhere does it define precisely what is income in respect of a decedent. At least one attempt has been made to amend the law and supply the missing definition, but the measure failed of enactment. H.R. 3041, 86th Cong., 1st Sess. (1959). The courts which have been called on to construe the statute have not put forth any universal test or definition but have proceeded on a case-by-case basis to establish some dimension to the term. These cases are discussed ahead.

Simultaneously, we must also consider section 113 of the 1939 Code [predecessor of section 1014], which provides that the basis of property acquired by a decedent's estate shall be the fair market value of such property at the time of such acquisition. This means that any unrealized appreciation in property left by a decedent will escape income taxation on the amount by which the fair market value of the property at the date of decedent's death exceeds the basis of the property in the hands of the decedent. It is immediately apparent that both section 126 and section 113 cannot apply to the same property. If property gives rise to income in respect of a decedent it is not entitled to a stepped-up basis under section 113. If it is property entitled to the basis adjustment of section 113 it will not be taxed as income in respect of a decedent when it is converted into money. Treas. Reg. 111, §29.126-1 (1943), and see 26 U.S.C. (I.R.C. 1954) §1014(c).... It should be possible then to approach the problem of what is income in respect of a decedent from a different direction by determining what property is not entitled to an adjusted basis under section 113. But neither the wording of this section, the regulations nor the cases provide any significant guidelines. Indeed, section 113 has been criticized as "one of the most clearly illogical of all income tax provisions." Vickrey, *Agenda for Progressive Taxation,* 139 (1947).

We are left then only to work with section 126. Despite the vagueness of the term "income in respect of a decedent," interpretive developments of the last 15 years have established some patterns on which we may reasonably rely and against which we may trace the parties' contentions.

The plaintiff's main contention is that the scope of the present income-in-respect-of-a-decedent-provision is restricted to income which under the 1934–1942 law would have been accrued to the decedent in her last return. That is to say, only income which would properly have been accruable to the decedent on the date of her death can be designated as income in respect of a decedent when it has subsequently been collected by the estate. In the instant case, the plaintiff continues, the rents, both cash and crops, were not fully ascertainable on the date of decedent's death and were in fact in dispute until some time in 1954. Since they were not fully ascertainable they were not properly accruable to the decedent on the date of her death. Hence, as ultimately collected by the estate the rents are not income in respect of a decedent.

The defendant takes an equally steadfast position. It maintains that income in respect of a decedent is merely that money which would have been reported as income by the decedent if she had but lived to collect it herself. Undoubtedly, had the decedent collected the rents and sold the crops she would have been in receipt of income. Therefore, when her estate collected the rents after her death and sold the crops the monies received were income to the estate and taxable to the estate as income in respect of a decedent.

As fully correct statements of the law we can accept neither party's general contention. We do not agree with the defendant that all money received by the estate is to be treated as it would have been if the decedent had lived and received it. That comprehends too much, and does not adequately distinguish between income earned by the decedent and income earned entirely by the estate after decedent's death. See Rev. Rul. 57-554, 57-2 Cum. Bull. 361; Rev. Rul. 60-227, 60-1 Cum. Bull. 262. Neither can we accept the plaintiff's position that only items properly accruable to the decedent on the date of her death—in an accounting sense—are taxable to her estate as income in respect of a decedent. This comprehends too little and gives overriding significance to the indefinite term "accruable."

Certainly the Congress has been concerned with removing discrimination between cash and accrual method taxpayers, and with avoiding the unfair bunching problems which arose under prior law when all sums due to a decedent were accrued to him on the date of his death. But the Congress has also been concerned with retrieving lost revenue. Section 126 is intended to further the general purpose of the Internal Revenue Code that all income should pay a tax. We think it clear that the intent of the Congress in enacting this section continued to be, as stated by the Supreme Court in *Enright*,"to cover into income the assets of decedents, earned during their life and unreported as income." 312 U.S. at 644. The income in respect of a decedent provision represents an attempt to implement these policies in a manner which reduces the importance of death in the actual collection of the revenue. See *Commissioner v. Linde*, 213 F. 2d 1 at 5 (9th Cir. 1954).

The plaintiff's asserted position has been rejected in a series of cases which has evolved mainly in the partnership area. Money paid to the widow or to the estate of a deceased partner has been held taxable as income in respect of a decedent even though it was perfectly clear that on the date of death the deceased partner had no ascertainable claim to the money and could not properly have accrued the amounts ultimately received by his estate. In *Riegelman v. Commissioner*, 253 F. 2d 315–319 (2d Cir. 1958), the question was "whether the post-death partnership income received by Riegelman's estate constitutes 'income in respect of a decedent,' * * *." The court stated: "The payments were not gifts, nor were they attributable to anything done by Riegelman's estate. They were the fruits of the man's professional activity during his lifetime; * * *." The case of *United States v. Ellis*, 264 F. 2d 325 (2d Cir. 1959), was almost identical to *Riegelman* and the court again taxed receipts from a partnership to a deceased partner's estate as income in respect of a decedent. Similarly, in *O'Daniel's Estate v. Commissioner*, 173 F. 2d 966 (2d Cir. 1949), the court held that a bonus payment to an officer of a small corporation designated and fixed some 4 months after his death came within section 126 and "clearly represented compensation for his services and any right to receive it that was realized by his estate was acquired through him and never arose in any other way or through any other source." See also *Bausch's Estate v. Commissioner*, 186 F. 2d 313 (2d Cir. 1951).

In *Commissioner v. Linde*, 213 F. 2d 1 (9th Cir. 1954), the decedent, the owner of a vineyard, had delivered grapes to various cooperatives for conversion into wine and for the sale of the wine. The liquidation of the wine pools by the conversion of the grapes and the disposition of the wine did not occur until after the decedent's death. Even though no sales of the grapes to the cooperatives had occurred the court held that the payments which the decedent's estate received from the cooperatives after the decedent's death were realized in consequence of contracts and deals made by the decedent in his lifetime. "No act or thing taken or performed by the taxpayer [the estate] operated to procure or to give rise to this payment. Such payments had their source exclusively in the decedent's contract and arrangement with the cooperative associations." 213 F. 2d at 4. The court concluded that these payments constituted income in respect of a decedent and were taxable as such.

The situation in the instant case is much the same as in the cases cited above. These are the important considerations: the rents received by the plaintiff are directly attributable to economic activities which occurred prior to decedent's death; they would have been income to the decedent had she but lived to receive them; they were fully accruable to the decedent on the date of her death in the sense that she was fully entitled to receive them but orthodox accounting technique prevented their accrual solely because they were not ascertainable in amount; they were not attributable to any acts performed by the estate nor were they attributable to unrealized passive appreciation of property owned by the decedent at the date of her death. These diverse characteristics do not permit of easy generalization, and we cannot draw from them a rule as to what is income in respect of a decedent in all cases. It is fair to say, however, in light of the development of the statute, that each of these characteristics represents an element in the composite concept that is income in respect of a decedent.

The rent on the Eloy tract was payable in cash, albeit it was to be ascertained in amount as a percentage of the net proceeds received from the sale of crops grown on the tract. As a cash rent we find it indistinguishable from any other kind of cash rent that might have arisen, as under a residential or commercial lease. On the basis of the foregoing discussion we find that this rent, collected by the estate, is income in respect of a decedent and taxable as such.

The rent on the Coolidge tract was by the terms of the lease not only to be ascertained from the amount of crops grown on the tract but it was also to be paid in crops. While the receipt of rent in property rather than in cash would not seem to affect the income character of the payments, crop-rents have frequently received special treatment under various provisions of the revenue acts and they must now be given further consideration.

Section 61 of the 1954 Code ... specifically includes rents in the definition of gross income. The regulations repeat this directive of the Code. However, the regulations also describe the computation of farm income as follows: "Crop shares (whether or not considered rent under state law) shall be included in gross income as of the year in which the crop shares are reduced to money or its equivalent." This same rule is announced for farmers using the cash method and the accrual method of accounting. Treas. Reg. §1.61-4.... It further appears that only an actual sale of the crops is a reduction to money or its equivalent as the regulations describe. *Perry v. United States*, 58-2 USTC ¶ 9587 (D.C. Miss. 1958); *SoRelle v. Commissioner*, 22 T.C. 459 (1954). See also Rev. Rul. 56-496, 56-2 Cum. Bull. 17. The lessor who has received crop-rent has of course received an asset of value, but as a matter of administrative convenience the recognition of this value as income is deferred until the crops are reduced to money. Crops received as rent exist in the hands of the lessor as a unique kind of property which can be described, like a right to receive future income, as a potential income asset....

Now if a landlord died while in possession of certain crops which he had received as rent we believe that under present law the essential income nature of these crops would follow the crops into the landlord's estate. The crops would remain *crop-rents* in the hands of the estate and would represent a form of income in respect of a decedent. Furthermore, under section 126 these crop-rents would be considered in the hands of the estate to have the same character which they had in the hands of the decedent—the potential of producing taxable income through sale. Only when the estate finally sold the crops would income be recognized. But at that point the money derived from the sale would be taxable, and taxable as income in respect of a decedent.

* * *

In the instant case the decedent had not received the disputed crop-rents. The plaintiff can derive no benefit from this fact. The decedent's estate comprised among other things a right to collect crop-rents that had been earned prior to decedent's death. As *rents* these crops were income in respect of a decedent according to the first part of this opinion. As *crop-rents* they first became recognized as income and taxable when they were sold for the account of the estate. At that point the income-producing potential of the crops had been fully achieved and was taxable. In this manner congressional purpose is fulfilled. The privilege of not recognizing the crop-rents as income until their sale is extended from the decedent to her estate, but what is in reality earned income does not escape its intended proportionate burden of taxation.

Accordingly, the refund of income taxes here sought by the plaintiff is denied. The petition will be dismissed.

Revenue Ruling 64-289
1964-2 C.B. 173

Reconsideration has been given to Revenue Ruling 58-436, C.B. 1958-2, 366, in light of the decision of the United States Court of Claims in the case of *Estate of Helen Davison v. United States,* 292 Fed. (2d) 937 (1961), certiorari denied, 368 U.S. 939 (1961).

In Revenue Ruling 58-436 a decedent owned livestock and farm crops in various stages of growth at the time of his death. The ruling holds, in pertinent part, that livestock and farm crops (harvested or unharvested, raised by a decedent prior to his death or received from tenants as rent for farm lands, held for sale or for feeding purposes) which a decedent, who had reported his income on the cash method of accounting, owned at the time of his death, constitute items of property or inventory and not rights to, or items of, income in respect of a decedent.

* * *

Upon reconsideration, in light of the *Davison* decision, it is held that crop shares or livestock received as rent by a decedent, who had employed the cash method of accounting, prior to his death, and owned by him at the time of his death, as well as crop shares or livestock which he had a right to receive as rent at the time of his death for economic activities occurring before his death, constitute income in respect of a decedent which is required to be included in gross income, for Federal income tax purposes, in the year in which the crop shares or livestock are sold, or otherwise disposed of.

Where the decedent dies during a rent period, only the net proceeds attributable to the portion of the rent period ending with his death are income in respect of a decedent. The proceeds attributable to the portion of the rent period which runs from the day after death to the end of the rent period are ordinary income to the estate.

Where crop shares or livestock received as rent are reduced to cash and received by the lessor prior to his death, or received by the lessor in kind and sold by him before his death, the proceeds thus received are includible in gross income and reportable in the final return of the decedent. No proration is required even though the rental period does not terminate until after his death. Likewise, cash rent received by the lessor prior to his death should be reported on his final return.

Where crop shares of livestock rentals are received in kind and held by the lessor at the time of his death, and are sold later by the executor or by a beneficiary who acquires the property in kind by inheritance, the proceeds from the sale of such crop shares or livestock should be allocated between income in respect of a decedent and income under section 61 of the Code.

The amount to be allocated to income in respect of a decedent is determined by multiplying the proceeds by a fraction of which the numerator is the number of days in the part of the rental period which ends with the date of death of the lessor and the denominator is the total number of days in the rental period.

The amount to be allocated to income under section 61 of the Code is determined by multiplying the proceeds by a fraction of which the numerator is the number of days in the rental period after the date of the lessor's death and the denominator is the number of days in the total rental period.

The allocation of the proceeds from crop shares or livestock rentals, where the decedent dies during a rent period, may be illustrated by the following examples:

Example 1. — A farm owner, who used the cash receipts and disbursements method of accounting, leased land to a tenant for one-third of the crop, payable in cash when the crop share is sold at the direction of the lessor. The rental period was for 1 year beginning March 1, 1963. The lessor died June 30, 1963. He was alive 122 days of the rental period. The rental was paid in cash to the decedent's estate on October 31, 1963. 122/365 of the amount received by the estate is income in respect of a decedent. The remainder is income under section 61 of the Code.

Example 2. — On January 1, 1962, a farm owner, who employed the cash receipts and disbursements method of accounting, leased land to a tenant for 1 year for one-third of the crop (wheat and corn). The lessor died August 28, 1962. He was alive 240 days of the rental period. The lessor's share of the wheat crop was delivered to him on July 31, 1962, and was sold by him on August 5, 1962, for 12x dollars. No part of the 12x dollars is income in respect of a decedent since it should be reported on the lessor's final return. The deceased lessor's share of the corn crop was delivered on December 6, 1962, to his estate. The executor of his estate sold one-half of the corn on December 20, 1962, and sold the balance of the corn on February 10, 1963. 240/365 of the proceeds of each sale by the executor will constitute income in respect of a decedent and 125/365 of the proceeds of each sale will constitute income to the estate under section 61 of the Code.

* * *

Revenue Ruling 58-436, C.B. 1968-2, 366, is hereby modified to remove therefrom the holding that livestock and farm crops received as rent by the decedent prior to his death, and owned by him at the time of his death, do not constitute items of income in respect of a decedent.

Illustrative Material

1. To the same effect as *Davison* and Rev. Rul. 64-289 are *Estate of Davis v. United States*, 68-2 U.S.T.C. ¶ 9483 (S.D. Ill. 1968), and *Estate of Gavin v. United States*, 113 F.3d 802 (8th Cir. 1997).

2. Why is the allocation described in Rev. Rul. 64-289 not used in *Davison*?

3. *Constitutionality.* Subjecting income in respect of a decedent to income taxation in the hands of the recipient is not unconstitutional. *Richardson v. United States*, 294 F.2d 593 (6th Cir. 1961), *cert. denied*, 369 U.S. 802 (1962); *Estate of Fred Basch*, 9 T.C. 627 (1947). The fact that such income constitutes principal in the decedent's estate does not mean it has lost its status as "income" for purposes of the constitutional limitations on Congress' power to tax.

b. Interest

Revenue Ruling 58-435
1958-2 C.B. 370

Advice has been requested regarding the proper treatment, for Federal income tax purposes, to the estate of a decedent, of interest (increment in value) on Series E United States savings bonds, not finally matured, owned by the estate, if the executor thereof, making returns on the cash receipts and disbursements method, elects, under section 454(a) of the Internal Revenue Code of 1954, to treat such interest as income received when it accrues (as earned increases in their redemption values), where the bonds had been (1) purchased by the decedent with her own funds and registered in her name alone, (2) purchased by the decedent with her own funds and registered in her name and the name of her husband in the alternative as coowners, and (3) purchased by her husband with his own funds and registered in his name and her name in the alternative as coowners, and he predeceased her.

The decedent, who died in 1955, was the sole beneficiary under the will of her husband, who died in 1954. They were not domiciled in a state having community property laws. Among the assets of her estate were the above-described savings bonds. She and her husband had filed their Federal income tax returns on the cash receipts and disbursements method, as did also the executor of his estate; and neither the decedent, her husband, nor the executor of his estate had reported as income, for Federal income tax purposes, any of the interest (increment in value) on the bonds that had accrued (as earned) thereon prior to their acquisition by her estate upon her death. However, the executor of her estate, although also making Federal income tax returns for it on the cash receipts and disbursements method, reported as income, in its return for the calendar taxable year 1956, the interest (increment in value) that had accrued (as earned) on all the bonds from the dates of their purchase to the end of that year, by electing, under section 454(a) of the Code, to treat such interest as income received in that year. Immediately after the close of the year 1956, the executor of her estate, pursuant to her will, transferred the bonds to himself as trustee of a trust. He is making returns for the trust on the cash receipts and disbursements method and will report the interest (increment in value) on the bonds, accruing (as earned) after their acquisition by the trust, as income in the taxable year in which they are finally redeemed, or they finally mature, whichever is earlier, rather than report such interest annually, as it accrues (as earned), by election under section 454(a) of the Code.

Section 22(d) of the Second Liberty Bond Act, as amended by the Public Debt Act of 1941, C. B. 1941-1, 546, provides that with respect to such savings bonds, "For purposes of taxation any increment in value represented by the difference between the price paid and the redemption value received (whether at or before maturity) for savings bonds * * * shall be considered as interest." As set forth in Revenue Ruling 55-278, C. B. 1955-1, 471, at 473, "such interest (increment in value) does not accrue ratably between the dates on which the redemption values increase, but, as outlined in Revenue Ruling 54-143, C. B. 1954-1, 12, 13, the increments occur (become earned) only in specific (fixed) amounts at the end of certain periods."

Under section 454(a), of the Code, if, in the case of a taxpayer owning Series E United States savings bonds, the increase in their redemption price occurring in the taxable year does not (under the method of accounting used in computing his taxable income) constitute income to him in such year, he may elect, in his return for that year, to treat such increase as income received therein, provided he also treats as income received therein any increase in their redemption value after he acquired them that occurred prior to such year. The election shall apply to all obligations owned by him at the beginning of such year and thereafter acquired by him which were issued at a discount and are redeemable for fixed amounts increasing at stated intervals. Also, the election shall be binding on the taxpayer for all subsequent taxable years, unless upon his application the Commissioner of Internal Revenue or his delegate permits him, subject to such conditions as the Commissioner or his delegate deems necessary, to change to a different method.

I. T. 2958, C. B. XV-1, 120 (1936), holds that the interest (increment in value) on United States savings bonds of the type here involved should be reported, by taxpayers who regularly make their Federal income tax returns on the cash receipts and disbursements basis, as income for the taxable year of their redemption at or before maturity. But, if such bonds are not actually redeemed at their final maturity, the interest (increment in value) thereon is includible, on such basis, in gross income for the taxable year in which they finally matured. Section 454(c) of the Code, relating to Series E United States savings bonds held by a taxpayer at (original) maturity in which he thereafter retains his investment, provides that the increase in their redemption value (to the extent not previously includible in gross income) in excess of the amount paid for them shall be includible in gross income in the taxable year in which the continuing obligations are finally redeemed, or in the taxable year of their final maturity, whichever is earlier. Section 454(c) does not apply in the case of any taxable year for which the taxpayer's taxable income is computed under an accrual method of accounting or for which an election made by him under section 454(a) applies.

Section 691(a)(1) of the Code provides, in effect, that the amount of all items of gross income in respect of a decedent which are not properly includible for the taxable year in which falls the date of his death or a prior period (including the amount of all items of gross income in respect of a prior decedent, if the right to receive such amount was acquired by reason of the death of the prior decedent or by bequest, devise, or inheritance from the prior decedent) shall be included in the gross income, for the taxable year when received, of the taxpayer that acquires the right to receive the amount.

Section 691(c)(1) of the Code provides, in effect, that a person, estate, or trust that includes an amount in gross income under section 691(a)(1) of the Code shall be allowed, for the same taxable year, as a deduction, the portion of the Federal estate tax on the decedent's estate attributable to the inclusion therein of the net value of the right to receive such amount. The method of computing the amount of the deduction allowable under section 691(c)(1) of the Code is prescribed in paragraph (2) of section 691(c) of the Code.

Where a taxpayer purchases entirely with his own funds Series E United States savings bonds and has them registered in his name and that of another individual in the alternative as coowners, such a coownership does not constitute a tenancy by the entirety, tenancy in common, joint tenancy, or ownership similar to a joint bank account. This was pointed out in Revenue Ruling 55-278, *supra,* in connection with the determination of the proper value, for Federal gift tax purposes, with respect to the gift by a taxpayer of his coownership in such savings bonds, which he had purchased entirely with his own funds, to the other coowner. As also set forth in that ruling, the taxpayer acquired full beneficial ownership of the bonds at the time he thus purchased them; such beneficial ownership would not be extinguished during the taxpayer's lifetime until (1) he surrenders the bonds to the other coowner and gratuitously permits him to obtain redemption thereof and retain the proceeds, or (2) the bonds are reissued in the other coowner's name alone; and, in the meantime, for all practical purposes, the latter has at most only the hope or expectancy that either event (1) or (2), might occur. In fact, in many cases, the latter is not even aware that he has been named such a coowner. Therefore, it has been held that, where such savings bonds are registered in the names of two natural persons in the alternative as coowners, the interest (increment in value) earned thereon is income, for Federal income tax purposes, of the coowner whose funds were used to purchase the bonds; and, that, if the purchase price was furnished in part by each, the interest (increment in value) on the bonds is income of each in proportion to his or her respective contribution to the purchase price. See I. T. 3301, C. B. 1939-2, 75. Revenue Ruling 54-143, *supra,* consistently holds that, where such a savings bond registered in the names of two natural persons in the alternative as coowners was purchased entirely with the funds of one of the coowners, all the interest (increment in value) earned thereon is his income, even though he gratuitously permits the other coowner to redeem the bond and retain as hers the entire proceeds.

In view of the foregoing, it is held that the action of the instant executor of the estate of the deceased wife in electing to report all the interest (increment in value) on all the Series E United States savings bonds owned by such estate in the taxable year 1956, that accrued (as earned) therein and previously since they were purchased, as income received therein is proper. In other words, the interest (increment in value) that accrued (as earned) before the wife died on the bonds which she had purchased entirely with her own funds and of which she was full beneficial owner, whether registered in her name alone or in her name and the name of her husband in the alternative as coowners and also the interest (increment in value) that accrued (as earned) before she died but after her husband died on the bonds which he purchased entirely with his own funds, registered in his name and her name in the alternative as coowners and of which she became the sole (beneficial and registered) owner upon his death, is gross income in respect of the decedent (wife) under section 691(a)(1) of the Code. Compare Revenue Ruling 55-356, C. B. 1955-1, 673. The interest (increment in value) that accrued (as earned) before the husband died on the bonds which he had purchased entirely with his own funds and of which he was full beneficial owner, although registered in his name and the name of wife in the alternative as co-owners, is gross income in respect of a prior decedent, under section 691(a)(1) of the Code, and the interest (increment in value) that accrued (as earned) on all the bonds after their acquisition by the estate of the wife upon her death and before their transfer to the trust pursuant to her will is income of the estate, under the general definition of gross income for Federal income tax purposes in section 61(a) of the Code.

A trust established pursuant to the will of a decedent is a separate and distinct taxable entity from her estate, even though the same individual or trust company is executor of the estate and trustee of the trust. Therefore, the election under section 454(a) of the Code, which the instant executor of the wife's estate made to treat the interest (increment in value) accrued (as earned) on Series E United States savings bonds owned by it, as income received, is not binding on the trust, although he is its trustee. Accordingly, it is also held that the contemplated action of the trustee of the trust of reporting the interest (increment in value) accruing (as earned) on the bonds after their acquisition by the trust as income in the taxable year in which they are finally redeemed, or they finally mature, whichever is earlier, will be proper, *i.e.*, in the absence of an election under section 454(a) of the Code, by him as trustee of the trust, to treat the increases in the redemption values of the bonds occurring in each taxable year after their acquisition by the trust as income therein received.

It is further held that, under section 691(c)(1) of the Code, because of the inclusion in gross income, in the Federal income tax return of the estate of the decedent (wife) for the taxable year 1956, of (1) the interest (increment in value) on the bonds purchased by her with her own funds and registered in her name alone, from the dates of purchase to the date of her death; (2) the interest (increment in value) on the bonds purchased by her with her own funds and registered in her name and the name of her husband in the alternative as coowners, from the dates of purchase to the date of her death; (3) the interest (increment in value) on the bonds purchased by her husband with his own funds and registered in his name and her name in the alternative as coowners, from the date of his death to the date of her death; and (4) the interest (increment in value) on the latter bonds, from the dates of purchase to the date of the husband's death, since no distribution was made in 1957, therefore deductions are allowable in such income tax return of (a) the amount of the Federal estate tax on the estate of the decedent (wife) attributable to inclusion in her gross estate of the value of items (1), (2), (3) and (4); and (b) the amount of the Federal estate tax on the estate of her husband attributable to the inclusion in his gross estate of the value of item (4). The method of computing the amounts of Federal estate taxes attributable to the inclusion in his gross estate is prescribed in paragraph (2) of section 691(c) of the Code. See section 1.691(c)-2 of the Income Tax Regulations with respect to treatment of the section 691(c) deduction where an estate or trust distributes or is required to distribute income in respect of a decedent within the taxable year.

Apkin v. Commissioner

86 T.C. 692 (1986)

RAUM, *Judge*: The Commissioner determined a $6,083.85 deficiency in the 1981 income tax of petitioners, husband and wife. After concessions, the sole issue relates to the includability in petitioner's gross income of a portion of the interest accrued on Series E United States Savings Bonds upon their redemption....

Dora Apkin, the mother of petitioner Philip Apkin (hereinafter sometimes referred to as petitioner), purchased 49 Series E bonds over the years 1948 and 1953 through 1959 of an aggregate face value of $5,125, at a total cost of $3,843.75. All of the bonds were issued to "Philip Apkin or Dora Apkin as co-owners". The bonds were held by the mother until her death on May 5, 1979, when petitioner succeeded to them as sole owner. He held them until June 23, 1981, when he had them redeemed. The amount which he then received included all of the interest accrued on the bonds from the dates of their respective purchase until redemption. In their 1981 income tax return petitioners failed to report as income any of the interest thus received. In his notice of deficiency the Commissioner undertook to increase petitioners' income by the total amount of such interest. Petitioners now concede that they are accountable for that portion of the interest accrued after the decedent's death. They dispute merely the Commissioner's attributing to them the portion of the interest accrued up to the date of death.

The decedent had not reported any of the interest on the bonds that accrued during her lifetime, and in fact did not file any Federal income tax returns in the years involved since her income was not sufficient to require such filing even if the accrued interest were included in her reportable income each year. It is this circumstance upon which petitioners rely to support their position that petitioner was not chargeable with that portion of the interest received by him on redemption that was allocable to the period up to the date of his mother's death. We hold for the Commissioner.

All the accrued interest received by petitioner upon redemption is chargeable to him, including that portion accrued during the period up to the death of his mother. This result is required by section 691, I.R.C. 1954, concerning "income in respect of a decedent". [Plainly, section 691 is] applicable here unless the interest accrued up to the time of the decedent's death was properly includable in her income for the taxable period ending with the date of her death or a prior period. Rev. Rul. 64-104, 1964-1 C.B. (Part 1) 223. And it is equally plain to all of us that such interest was not includable in the decedent's gross income for any period by reason of section 454(a) of the Code....

It is clear that petitioner's mother did not make an election under section 454(a). That provision, on its face, requires that such an election be made in the taxpayer's tax return. Since petitioner's mother did not file a return in any year after the purchase of the first savings bond, she could not possibly have made the election "in the manner and in the time prescribed by Congress" as an election under section 454(a) must be made in order to be effective. Cf. Rev. Rul. 55-655, 1955-2 C.B. 253, 254. By remaining silent, she in effect made an election to have the interest included in her reportable income in the year or years of maturity (as extended) or of redemption prior thereto. Even though she was not required to file a return, there was nothing to preclude her from doing so in order to make the election and thus make sure that the interest actually received in a later year attributable to accruals in earlier years would not be taxed in such later year. Further, the fact that she was not required to file a tax return[3] in no way excused her from notifying the Commissioner of her intent to make an election. Cf. *Atlantic Veneer Corp. v. Commissioner,* 85 T.C. 1075 (1985). If it did, the election's character as one binding on the taxpayer for all subsequent years would be meaningless as a practical matter since she could then, if her

---

3. Moreover, even though the decedent did not have enough income in any one year to *require* the filing of a return, there is nothing in the record to show that had she filed a return in a later year and elected therein to include in gross income all theretofore accrued interest on the bonds, as she might have done under section 454, there might not have been sufficient taxable income to require payment of tax.

income increased sufficiently in any one year to warrant it, reverse her election without the knowledge of the IRS. Nor does it appear in this record that, as permitted by Rev. Rul. 68-145, 1968-1 C.B. 203, the decedent's executor or other representative elected under section 454 to include the previously unreported interest in decedent's gross income on a final income tax return that could have been filed, or that if such a return had been filed and election made, there would not have been at least some income tax liability.

The decedent neither redeemed the bonds nor held them to final maturity. She continued to hold them up to the time of her death in 1979; only in 1981 were they redeemed by petitioner. At her death the bonds purchased in 1948 had not yet finally matured; they had an extended maturity period of 40 years from issue so that final maturity would occur in 1988. 31 C.F.R. section 316.8(a)(2) (1985). Similarly, those bonds purchased from 1953 to 1959 would not reach final maturity until the 1990s. 31 C.F.R. section 316.8(a)(3) (1985).[4]

Petitioners place heavy reliance upon *Helvering v. Horst*, 311 U.S. 112 (1940), arguing that the interest on the decedent's bonds should be ascribed to her and not her son Philip as her successor. Although the principles of *Horst* are unassailable, they have no application here, where the specific provisions of section 691 of the Code are controlling. Indeed, any possible application of the principles of *Horst* in the case of income in respect of a decedent was specifically taken into account by Congress in 1942 when it enacted the predecessor to section 691. It at that time reversed the prevailing statutory and judicial treatment under subsection 42(a) of the Revenue Act of 1934 and *Helvering v. Enright*, 312 U.S. 636 (1941), and *Pfaff v. Commissioner*, 312 U.S. 646 (1941), of income accrued by a decedent at his death as income taxable to him in his last return. H. Rept. No. 2333, 77th Cong., 1st Sess. 48, 83–88 (1942), 1942-2 C.B. 372, 411, 435–439; S. Rept. No. 1631, 77th Cong., 2d Sess. 100–105 (1942), 1942-2 C.B. 504, 579–584. Congress then specifically considered and rejected the tax treatment that is at the very least implicit in the position that petitioners urge on us now. That legislative choice is now embodied in section 691, I.R.C. 1954, which we are bound to follow.

Illustrative Material

1. Other authorities dealing with the section 691 consequences of United States savings bond ownership are Rev. Rul. 70-467, 1970-2 C.B. 169 (all unreported increment in value through date of death is income in respect of deceased coowner who contributed entire purchase price), and Rev. Rul. 64-104, 1964-1 C.B. 223 (involving both Series E and Series H bonds). Rev. Rul. 70-467 has been declared obsolete, though apparently on grounds that are not relevant here. Rev. Rul. 95-71, 1995-2 C.B. 323.

2. *Discount bonds.* Discount bond interest that accrues after a decedent's death is not income in respect of a decedent. *Levin v. United States*, 373 F.2d 434 (1st Cir. 1967).

3. *Penalties for early withdrawal.* Despite the fact that the decedent would have suffered an interest penalty had he withdrawn funds prior to maturity, interest accrued at death on nonnegotiable savings certificates is income in respect of a decedent. Rev. Rul. 79-340, 1979-2 C.B. 320.

---

4. There is no suggestion by petitioners that the accrued interest was includable in the decedent's gross income because, by dying, she had "disposed of" the bonds within section 1.454-1(c)[(1)](i), Income Tax Regs. The matter, even if properly before us, is too outlandish for serious consideration. If there were any validity to the point, it would produce a result that would be inconsistent with what has obviously been the practice in the case of thousands of owners of E bonds who have died over a period of many years.

c. Dividends

A dividend payable to a shareholder of record as of a date that precedes his death is income in respect of a decedent if paid after such shareholder's death. M. Ferguson, J. Freeland & M. Ascher, *Federal Income Taxation of Estates, Trusts, and Beneficiaries* §3.05[C][3] (3d ed. 1998 & Supp. 2008). *See also Mabel C. Roe*, 15 T.C. 503 (1950), *acq.*, 1951-1 C.B. 3, *rev'd on other grounds*, 192 F.2d 398 (5th Cir. 1951); Rev. Rul. 64-308, 1964-2 C.B. 176.

d. Annuities

Revenue Ruling 2005-30
2005-1 C.B. 1015

ISSUE

If the owner-annuitant of a deferred annuity contract dies before the annuity starting date, and the beneficiary receives a death benefit under the annuity contract (either in a lump sum or as periodic payments), is the amount received by the beneficiary in excess of the owner-annuitant's investment in the contract includible in the beneficiary's gross income as income in respect of a decedent (IRD) within the meaning of §691 of the Internal Revenue Code?

FACTS

A purchased a deferred annuity contract providing for annuity payments to *A* beginning as of a date specified in the annuity contract. *A* named *B* as beneficiary of the contract. The contract provides that *A* may surrender the contract during *A*'s life for its account value as determined by the formula provided under the contract. The contract further provides that if *A* dies before the annuity starting date, *B* will receive a death benefit equal to the account value as determined by the formula provided under the contract. At *B*'s election, the death benefit will be paid either in a lump sum or as periodic payments consistent with the provisions of §72(s).

A dies before the annuity starting date and *B* receives the death benefit under the contract, which exceeds *A*'s investment in the contract.

LAW AND ANALYSIS

Section 72(a) provides that gross income includes any amount received as an annuity. Sections 72(b) through (d) provide rules for determining what portion of an annuity payment represents a non-taxable return of investment. Section 72(e) provides rules for amounts received under an annuity contract, but not received as an annuity (and therefore not described in §72(b) through (d)). Specifically, amounts received before the annuity starting date are generally includible in gross income to the extent allocable to the income on the annuity contract. Section 72(s) provides rules regarding the period in which an interest in an annuity contract must be distributed after the holder's death in order for the contract to qualify as an annuity contract within the meaning of §72.

Section 691(a)(1) provides that the amount of all items of gross IRD that are not properly includible in respect of the taxable period in which falls the date of the decedent's death or a prior period (including the amount of all items of gross income in respect of a prior decedent, if the right to receive the amount was acquired by reason of the death of the prior decedent or by bequest, devise, or inheritance from the prior decedent) is included in the gross income, for the taxable year when received, of: (A) the estate of the decedent, if the right to receive the amount is acquired by the decedent's estate from the decedent; (B) the person who, by reason of the death of the decedent, acquires the right to receive the amount, if the right to receive the amount is not acquired by the decedent's estate from the decedent; or (C) the person who acquires from the decedent the right to receive the amount by bequest, devise, or inheritance, if the amount is received after a distribution by the decedent's estate of the right.

Section 691(c)(1) provides that a person who includes an amount of IRD in gross income under § 691(a) is allowed as a deduction, for the same taxable year, a portion of the estate tax paid by reason of the inclusion of that IRD in the decedent's gross estate....

Section 1014(a)(1) provides that the basis of property in the hands of a person acquiring the property from a decedent or to whom the property passed from a decedent generally is the fair market value of the property at the date of the decedent's death....

Section 1014(b)(9) provides that, for purposes of § 1014(a), property acquired from the decedent by reason of death, form of ownership, or other conditions if by reason thereof the property is required to be included in determining the value of the decedent's gross estate for estate tax purposes, is considered to have been acquired from, or to have passed from, the decedent.

Section 1014(b)(9)(A) provides that § 1014(b)(9) does not apply to annuities described in § 72.

Section 1014(c) provides that § 1014 does not apply to property that constitutes a right to receive an item of IRD under § 691.

Rev. Rul. 79-335, 1979-2 C.B. 292, addresses a situation in which the owner-annuitant purchases a deferred variable annuity contract that provides that if the owner dies prior to the annuity starting date, the named beneficiary may elect to receive the present accumulated value of the contract either in the form of an annuity or a lump-sum payment. Rev. Rul. 79-335 concludes that, for purposes of § 1014, the contract is an annuity described in § 72 (as then in effect), and therefore receives no basis adjustment by reason of the owner's death because it is governed by the annuity exception of § 1014(b)(9)(A). If the beneficiary elects a lump-sum payment, the excess of the amount received over the amount of consideration paid by the decedent is includable in the beneficiary's gross income....

Although Rev. Rul. 79-335 concludes that the annuity exception in § 1014(b)(9)(A) applies to the contract described in that ruling, it does not specifically address whether amounts received by a beneficiary under a deferred annuity contract in excess of the owner-annuitant's investment in the contract would be subject to §§ 691 and 1014(c). However, had the owner-annuitant surrendered the contract and received the amounts in excess of the owner-annuitant's investment in the contract, those amounts would have been income to the owner-annuitant under § 72(e). Because those amounts would have been income to the owner-annuitant if the contract had been surrendered during life, those amounts are IRD under § 691.

Likewise, in the present case, had A surrendered the contract and received the amounts at issue, those amounts would have been income to A under § 72(e) to the extent they exceeded A's investment in the contract. Accordingly, amounts that B receives that exceed A's investment in the contract are IRD under § 691(a). As provided in Rev. Rul. 79-335, those amounts are includible in B's gross income and B does not receive a basis adjustment in the contract. However, B will be entitled to a deduction under § 691(c) if estate tax was due by reason of A's death. The result would be the same whether B receives the death benefit in a lump sum or as periodic payments.

HOLDING

If the owner-annuitant of a deferred annuity contract dies before the annuity starting date, and the beneficiary receives a death benefit under the annuity contract, the amount received by the beneficiary in a lump sum in excess of the owner-annuitant's investment in the contract is includible in the beneficiary's gross income as IRD within the meaning of §691. If the death benefit is instead received in the form of a series of periodic payments in accordance with §72(s), the amounts received are likewise includible in the beneficiary's gross income (in an amount determined under §72) as IRD within the meaning of §691.

* * *

Problem

6-1. Decedent purchased a $10,000 one-year certificate of deposit from First National Bank on January 1 of last year. The C.D. bore interest at the rate of 10% per annum, compounded annually. Decedent died on June 30 of last year. Decedent's estate collected $11,000 from First National on January 1 of this year. How much of the $11,000 is income in respect of a decedent? Who is taxed on what?

2. Sales Proceeds

Trust Company of Georgia v. Ross
262 F. Supp. 900 (N.D. Ga. 1966)
aff'd per curiam, 392 F.2d 694 (5th Cir. 1967)
cert. denied, 393 U.S. 830 (1968)

MORGAN, Chief Judge.

In these actions, which have been consolidated for trial, the plaintiffs seek the recovery of income taxes and interest paid for the year 1961 in the total amount of $1,007,376.09....

The Dinkler Hotel chain was founded in the early 1920s by Carling Dinkler, Sr., and his father.... Dinkler Hotels were operated in Atlanta, Georgia, Birmingham and Montgomery, Alabama, and Nashville, Tennessee.

* * *

On August 4, 1960, a written agreement was executed by Carling Dinkler, Sr., individually, Carling Dinkler, Sr., as Trustee for Carling Dinkler, Jr., Carling Dinkler, Jr., individually, and Dinkler Hotels Company, Inc. ("Dinklers"), with Associated Hotels Corporation, a newly formed corporation of which Robert K. Lifton, Ira J. Hechler and Howard Weingrow were the principal stockholders ("Associated"). By this agreement, the Dinklers agreed to sell and the buyers agreed to buy either the stock or assets of all the corporations making up the Dinkler Hotel chain.

* * *

The total purchase price for all of the assets and properties was stated in Paragraph 2 of said agreement as $10,946,363.00, subject to certain adjustments based upon an audit of June 30, 1960, Balance Sheets by Harris, Kerr, Forster & Company, and was to be paid in cash and by delivery of demand promissory notes, it being contemplated that the corporations involved would be forthwith liquidated so that the funds with which to pay the demand notes would be available from cash on hand in said corporations. The price at which the Dinkler-Tutwiler Corporation stock was to be sold, all of which stock was owned by Carling Dinkler, Sr., was specified in said agreement to be $3,381,933.30. Said price as stated was subject to certain adjustments provided for in said agreement, and after making such adjustments, the amount finally received by the Estate of Carling Dinkler, Sr., on February 23, 1961, for such stock was $3,539,948.00.

As provided for in Section 2 of the agreement, Associated deposited $300,000.00 and executed copies of the agreement with Frank E. Spain, as Escrow Agent, contemporaneously with the execution of said agreement. By letter dated August 31, 1960, to Frank E. Spain from Associated, the provisions of the escrow agreement were waived and the $300,000.00 was delivered to the Dinklers, and the executed copies of the agreement of August 4, 1960, were delivered to the respective parties to such agreement.

Under Section 3 of the agreement of August 4, 1960, all of the stock subject to the agreement, including the stock certificates evidencing the Dinkler-Tutwiler Corporation stock, were placed in escrow with Frank Spain, registered in the name of Carling Dinkler, Sr., with separate assignments executed by the registered holder in blank. This stock remained in the possession of Escrow Agent Mr. Spain until delivered to Associated on February 23, 1961. Section 3 of the said agreement provided in part:

> "In the event * * * that the Buyer shall default in the performance of any of its obligations under this Agreement, then the Escrow Agent shall redeliver the stock certificates and stock powers to the respective Sellers from whom they were received, and the Sellers shall retain all payments of the purchase price theretofore made as liquidated damages."

Section 17 of the August 4, 1960, agreement provided:

> *"Total Loss of Dinkler Plaza Hotel:* In the event that prior to the closing there is a total loss of the Dinkler Plaza Hotel by casualty (including fire), whether or not compensable by insurance, or condemnation, then any party on notice to the other parties may elect to cancel this Agreement within ten days of such loss in which event all obligations or [sic] the parties (except with respect to the return of amounts paid by the Buyer) shall cease and terminate."

The audit report of Harris, Kerr, Forster & Company called for by Section 2 of the August 4, 1960, agreement was received on or about November 25, 1960.

The ruling from the Treasury Department of the United States called for by Section 15 of the August 4, 1960, agreement was issued on December 2, 1960. This ruling held that Section 337 of the Internal Revenue Code of 1954 would apply to the sale of the assets of Dinkler Hotels Company, Inc., and no gain or loss would be recognized in the hands of said company if a plan of complete liquidation were adopted on the same date as the sale of such assets under the August 4, 1960, agreement.

Under the August 4, 1960, agreement, the closing was to be completed on January 3, 1961. On December 16, 1960, Mr. Spain wrote to E. M. Turlington, Sr., Vice-President of Dinkler Hotels Company, Inc., who was assisting Mr. Spain in readying all matters to complete the sale, as follows: "So for the moment I believe we have done everything needful to be done before Jan. 3". By December 16th, the legal representatives of the Dinklers and Associated were preparing the closing agenda.

By letter dated December 20, 1960, from Associated to Dinkler Hotels Company, Inc., Messrs. Carling Dinkler, Sr., and Carling Dinkler, Jr., accompanied by checks in the aggregate amount of $200,000.00, post-dated to January 3, 1961, the right of Associated to close under the August 4, 1960, agreement was extended to March 1, 1961. This postponement was provided for in the August 4th contract. Associated Hotels Corporation continued the closing date in order that Transcontinental Investing Company could obtain the permission of the Securities and Exchange Commission to make a public exchange offer, whereby Transcontinental would acquire the Dinkler properties to be acquired by Associated Hotels along with other similar properties. The initial prospectus of Transcontinental with regard to this matter was filed with the Securities and Exchange Commission in October, 1960. The Securities and Exchange Commission had not granted its approval to Transcontinental Investing Corporation by December 16, 1960, and it was unlikely that the approval would be obtained by the original closing date of January 3, 1961. The Securities and Exchange Commission granted its approval on this matter on January 27, 1961.

Carling Dinkler, Sr., died on January 30, 1961. [T]he Trust Company of Georgia duly qualified as executor of the will.

Prior to January 30, 1961, Associated Hotels Corporation had indicated to Carling Dinkler, Sr., that it did not wish to purchase any interest in the Jefferson Davis Corporation, whose stock was owned by the Dinkler-Tutwiler Corporation and others. Prior to his death, Carling Dinkler, Sr., representing the Dinklers, agreed with Associated Hotels that the Dinkler-Tutwiler Corporation would sell its stock in the Jefferson Davis Corporation, thus eliminating that stock from the August 4 contract. Subsequently, by amendment dated February 23, 1961, signed by the Estate of Carling Dinkler, Sr., and Associated, the foregoing agreement which had been reached before the death of Carling Dinkler, Sr., was memorialized.

On February 6, 1961, Mr. Spain wrote C. H. Hyams, III, a director of Dinkler Hotels Operating Company, Inc., wherein he stated as follows:

> "Fortunately all of our plans for the closing of the sale with Associated Hotels Corporation had been developed to the point where Carling's death will not effect [sic] the result. While in Atlanta I cleared with the New York attorneys on the further procedures. The recessed stockholders meeting of January 3 was to have been held on the day of the funeral. No one from outside came and the meeting was further recessed until February 22nd. You have received notice."

On or about February 1, 1961, officers of Associated advised Mr. Spain, counsel for the Dinklers, that Associated lacked $2,350,000.00 of having sufficient funds to enable Associated to close under the August 4, 1960, agreement, and asked whether the Estate of Carling Dinkler, Sr., would lend such amount to Associated. Counsel for the Dinklers, Mr. Spain, replied that he would not so advise the Executor because he did not consider it a proper loan for an executor to make. He stated that he would, and he did, introduce the officers of Associated to officers of the Commercial Department of Trust Company of Georgia. Negotiations followed in which counsel for the Dinklers did not participate. The Commercial Department of Trust Company of Georgia did lend to Robert K. Lifton, Ira J. Hechler and Howard Weingrow, the principal stockholders and officers of Associated, $2,000,000.00 on condition that the borrowers concurrently therewith loaned Associated $2,350,000.00, taking Associated's note therefor, which they then assigned to Trust Company of Georgia as security for its $2,000,000.00 loan to the stockholders and officers of Associated. The $2,000,000.00 loan was beyond the lending limits of Trust Company of Georgia, and in order to enable such loan to be made, Trust Company of Georgia, as Executor under the Will of Carling Dinkler, Sr., agreed to and did accept a $500,000.00 participation in the loan. The remainder of the purchase money was obtained from other sources.

The negotiations for the foregoing loan were conducted by Messrs. Lifton, Hechler and Weingrow with the Commercial Department of the Trust Company of Georgia, and not with the Trust Department of the latter, which was acting as Executor of the Estate of Carling Dinkler, Sr.

Mr. Augustus H. Sterne, presently President of the Trust Company of Georgia, was the principal bank officer with the Commercial Department negotiating the loan. The Dinklers had transacted its banking business with the Trust Company of Georgia for many years and the bank had found this relationship profitable. The bank was interested in keeping these accounts when Associated Hotels completed its purchase of the Dinkler properties. In late 1960, Mr. Sterne traveled to New York and spoke with Messrs. Lifton, Hechler and Weingrow to encourage them to continue doing business with Trust Company of Georgia after the sale was consummated. This desire on the part of Trust Company of Georgia to have Associated continue the business relationship it had enjoyed over the years with Dinklers, was one of the compelling reasons why the bank agreed to arrange credit of $2,000,000.00 for Messrs. Lifton, Hechler and Weingrow. Eventually, the Commercial Department of the bank obtained a participation in the $2,000,000.00 loan granted to the extent said loan exceeded its legal loan limits. The bank would have loaned the entire amount itself without any participation, but for the legal loan limit.

Thereafter, on February 23, 1961, the August 4, 1960, agreement was amended by (1) allowing Dinkler-Tutwiler Corporation to sell the stock in Jefferson Davis Corporation, which the latter owned, with the price to be paid for the Dinkler-Tutwiler stock to be correspondingly increased, (2) Associated waiving any claim it might have on life insurance policies held by Dinkler Hotels, Inc., and Dinkler-Tutwiler Corporation on Carling Dinkler, Sr., in excess of a certain figure with a resulting price adjustment, and (3) providing the purchase price would be paid in checks not exceeding $6,215,000.00, and the balance in demand notes. Item 2 of this amendment had already been agreed to by the parties by supplemental agreement dated August 4, 1960.

On the same date, the agreement as amended was consummated and the adjusted price of $3,539,948.00, representing the price of Dinkler-Tutwiler Corporation stock owned by Carling Dinkler, Sr., was paid to the Estate of Carling Dinkler, Sr.

In the fiduciary income tax return for the fiscal period ended June 30, 1961, the Executor reflected a basis for the Dinkler-Tutwiler Corporation stock of $3,539,948.00, which was the fair market value of the stock on January 30, 1961, the date of the death of Carling Dinkler, Sr. No gain was reported by the Executor on the fiduciary income tax return for the fiscal period nor by the beneficiaries of the estate ... in their respective income tax returns for their taxable years ended December 31, 1961.

The Commissioner of Internal Revenue held that the proceeds from the sale of the Dinkler-Tutwiler stock constituted income in respect of a decedent under Section 691 of the Internal Revenue Code of 1954; and further held that a long term capital gain in the amount of $3,454,863.56 was realized on the sale.

These deficiencies were paid in full by the respective parties and, after each party filed a claim for refund which was rejected, these actions, which have been consolidated for trial, were filed.

The question for determination by this Court is whether, under the facts and circumstances, any of the proceeds received by the Estate of Carling Dinkler, Sr., from the disposition of stock constitute income with respect to a decedent and thus taxable as determined by the Commissioner....

Were the proceeds from the sale of Dinkler-Tutwiler Corporation stock income to Mr. Dinkler, Sr., and taxable as such? The plaintiffs contend that no sale had occurred prior to Mr. Dinkler, Sr.'s, death, and thus the proceeds were not taxable. The Government asserts that the transaction was completed by Mr. Dinkler, Sr., prior to his death, and that all that remained was the closing and payment, and that the income was entirely generated by Mr. Dinkler, Sr.'s, activities and constitutes income in respect of the decedent, Mr. Dinkler, Sr.

Section 691 of the Internal Revenue Code of 1954 provides for taxation of income in respect of decedents. Section 691(a)(1) provides, as a general rule, that the amount of all items of gross income in respect of a decedent which are not properly includible in respect of the taxable period in which falls the date of his death or a prior period shall be included in the gross income for the taxable year when received, of (A) the estate of the decedent, if the right to receive the amount is acquired by the decedent's estate from the decedent; (B) the person who, by reason of the death of the decedent, acquires the right to receive the amount, if the right to receive the amount is not acquired by the decedent's estate from the decedent; or (C) the person who acquires from the decedent the right to receive the amount by bequest, devise, or inheritance, if the amount is received after a distribution by the decedent's estate of such right.

Section 691(a)(3) relates to the character of income, and it provides that the right, described in paragraph (1), to receive an amount shall be treated, in the hands of the estate of the decedent or any person who acquired such right by reason of the death of the decedent, or by bequest, devise, or inheritance from the decedent, as if it had been acquired by the estate or such person in the transaction by which the decedent acquired such right; and the amount includible in gross income shall be considered in the hands of the estate or such person to have the character which it would have had in the hands of the decedent if the decedent had lived and received such amount.

* * *

Section 42 of the Revenue Act of 1934, c. 277, 48 Stat. 680, required all income accrued up to the date of death, not otherwise properly includible for such period or a prior period, to be included in the income tax return of a decedent for the period in which fell the date of his death. The provision was enacted because the courts had held under prior law that income accrued before death but received by the estate was not income to the estate but a part of the corpus. Hence, prior to this provision of the Revenue Act of 1934 neither the estate nor the decedent ever paid income tax on such amounts. Similarly, in the case of capital transactions as here, no income would be payable to the estate even when the actual transfer took place after death. This resulted from the fact that the estate's basis in such assets would be their fair market value at the date of death, and hence there would be no capital gain since such value would equal the sale price.

This provision of the Revenue Act of 1934 required the inclusion of the value of services rendered, whether based on agreed compensation or on *quantum meruit,* in decedent's final return as accrued income. Helvering v. Enright's Estate, 312 U.S. 636, 61 S.Ct. 777, 85 L.Ed. 1093. In some instances, such treatment resulted in hardship as, quite frequently, amounts which would have been received over a number of years were returnable in the year of death, thus carrying the income into higher brackets due to the bunching of such income.

To alleviate such hardship, Section 126 of the Code was added to the 1939 Code by Section 134 of the Revenue Act of 1942, c. 619, 56 Stat. 798, to provide that income accruing to a decedent because of his death was not includible in his final return, but was to be treated as income and reported as income by the one receiving the right to such income. Such treatment was for the express purpose of alleviating a hardship and, at the same time, preventing certain income from escaping taxation, as above described. Eventually, Section 126 was reenacted as Section 691 of the Internal Revenue Code of 1954, without material change.

* * *

Although Congress failed to specifically define precisely what income in respect of a decedent is, this Court feels that it is clear that the intent of Congress was, as stated in Helvering v. Enright's Estate, supra, "to cover into income the assets of decedents, earned during their life and unreported as income". This section covers income from all sources, including capital gains such as in the instant case. The purpose of section 691 and its predecessor sections was to reduce the importance of death in the actual collection of the revenue.

Thus, there is no doubt that the plaintiffs acquired the right to receive the amounts from the sale of the Dinkler-Tutwiler stock from Carling Dinkler, Sr., and, under Section 691(a)(3), that right is to have the same character in the hands of the plaintiffs which it would have had in the hands of Carling Dinkler, Sr. The cases have held consistently that the criterion of taxability of income as income in respect of a decedent is whether the post-death payments are in fact due to the services performed by or economic activities of the decedent. Grill v. United States, 303 F.2d 922, 157 Ct.Cl. 804; Davison's Estate v. United States, 292 F.2d 937, 155 Ct.Cl. 290; United States v. Ellis, 2 Cir., 264 F.2d 325; Riegelman's Estate v. Commissioner of Internal Revenue, 2 Cir., 253 F.2d 315; Commissioner of Internal Revenue v. Linde, 9 Cir., 213 F.2d 1, cert. den. 348 U.S. 871, 75 S.Ct. 107, 99 L.Ed. 686; Bernard v. United States, 215 F.Supp. 256. Payments are taxable under Section 691 even though realized after the decedent's death when such payments arise from contracts, arrangements, or deals made by the decedent and would have been income to the decedent. Levin v. United States, D.C., 254 F.Supp. 640 (1966).

In the cases at hand, both the plaintiffs and the defendant strongly rely upon the case of Commissioner of Internal Revenue v. Linde, supra. In the *Linde* case, the decedent had negotiated for the disposition of his grapes and no substantial activity was required of his estate in order to produce the income, and the Court found in the *Linde* case that the payments in issue were income in respect of a decedent. There the decedent had delivered grapes to various cooperatives of which he was a member, and the latter commingled all members' grapes in a "wine pool". The grapes in such pool were crushed, processed into wine, the wine sold, expenses deducted from the wine proceeds, and each member's share of the proceeds thereafter was distributed to the member by the cooperatives. The Court held that the proceeds from the "wine pool" received after decedent's death by his beneficiary where the grapes had been delivered before death constituted income in respect of a decedent. In so holding, the Court expressly noted that it was not necessary to establish a sale by the decedent during his lifetime.

In ruling that Section 126, the predecessor section of Section 691, applied, the Court in *Linde* stated, referring to the decision in O'Daniel's Estate v. Commissioner of Internal Revenue, 2 Cir., 173 F.2d 966:

"We think that the text of section 126 as well as the history of the legislation relating to the income of a decedent demonstrate the soundness of the O'Daniel decision and that the principles there expressed must be applied in the instant case. If the decedent had lived until the day when these crop pool proceeds were paid to him the payments so received would have been ordinary income. Sec. 126 itself contains strong evidence of congressional intent to see to it that the tax upon income which would have been derived had the decedent lived should not be lost to the treasury in consequence of his death. This subparagraph (3) of section 126(a) provides that 'the amount includible in gross income under paragraph (1) * * * shall be considered in the hands of the estate or such person to have the character which it would have had in the hands of the decedent if the decedent had lived and received such amount.' The payments which the tax-payer received in 1945 were realized under and in consequence of contracts and deals made by the decedent in his lifetime. No act or thing taken or performed by the taxpayer operated to procure or to give rise to this payment. Such payments had their source exclusively in the decedent's contract and arrangement with the cooperative associations. And since in his hands had he lived and received these amounts they would have had the character of ordinary income, the quoted provision of subdivision (3) would make it appear that they have the same character, that is, ordinary income, in the hands of this taxpayer who acquired the right to receive that amount by bequest from the decedent within the meaning of subdivision (C) of subparagraph (1) of section 126(a).'"

In the cases at hand, the payment received by the estate of Carling Dinkler, Sr., on February 23, 1961, the date of the closing of the August 4, 1960, agreement, was realized as a consequence of negotiations and agreement made by Mr. Carling Dinkler, Sr., during his lifetime. It was his economic activity leading up to and including the signing of the August 4 agreement which produced the income now in dispute. There were no acts of any consequence taken or performed by the estate of Mr. Dinkler, Sr., which operated to procure or give rise to the payments involved. Such payments were the direct result of the efforts of Carling Dinkler, Sr., and nothing of substance remained to be performed after his death except the formal closing.

The evidence submitted reveals that the Dinklers had, prior to Mr. Dinkler, Sr.'s, death, accomplished all the matters needed to be performed by them to effect the closing. On the date of his death, Carling Dinkler, Sr., had only to await the date of the closing to receive the sums due under the contract of sale which he had negotiated prior to his death. The stock had been placed in escrow to await payment of the purchase price. Mr. Dinkler, Sr., was contractually bound to sell it to these particular purchasers and was not free to sell it to any other persons. The moneys eventually received by his estate at the closing were not due to any economic activity of the estate. The estate's right to the purchase price was due solely to the death of the decedent. The matters in which the estate participated and by which the closing was consummated were merely perfunctory and of no material significance.

The plaintiffs contend that (1) the August 4 agreement was an option in favor of Associated, the purchasers; (2) by the date of death, Carling Dinkler, Sr., had not made a disposition by sale or other arrangement of the stock in issue; (3) all of the conditions of the agreement had not been met by the date of Dinkler's death and performance of the management contract was rendered impossible by his death; (4) nothing was owed Carling Dinkler, Sr., at the time of his death; and (5) the sale of the stock was made pursuant to an amended agreement resulting from the efforts of the estate.

Initially, the August 4 agreement was not an option to purchase in favor of Associated. Ordinarily, where someone grants another an option to purchase, he retains control over the subject matter of the option until such time as the option is exercised and the sale is completed. In this case, the subject of the contract, namely, the stock, was placed beyond the dominion and control of Dinkler with Frank Spain, the Escrow Agent. This agreement was similar to the everyday type of agreement to sell real estate whereby the seller's only remedy, if the purchaser defaults, is to obtain the difference between the fair market value of the property at the time of the default and the contract price, for the seller is not free to dispose of the property to a third party until such default has occurred. Here, Carling Dinkler, Sr., would have had a similar remedy, except that, under the agreement, the parties agreed as to the amount of liquidated damages in advance, namely, the forfeiture of the earnest money.

The plaintiffs' second contention is that no sale or other disposition had occurred by the date of Mr. Dinkler's death. It is true that no sale of the stock had occurred; however, a significant disposition of the stock had been accomplished because months before the date of Mr. Dinkler's death, in performance of his contract, he had placed the stock in escrow, and thus beyond his control. So there had occurred, by decedent's death, a disposition similar to what had occurred in the case of Commissioner of Internal Revenue v. Linde, supra, and, as noted by the Court in *Linde*, it was not necessary that there be a sale to establish income in respect of a decedent.

It is true that all of the conditions of the contract of August 4, 1960, had not been met by the date of Mr. Dinkler's death; however, those that remained unfulfilled have no material effect on these cases, as indeed they could not have been fulfilled until the closing date by the very nature of the contract itself. Many of these conditions precedent by their very nature were required to be performed on the day of closing....

At the time of Mr. Dinkler's death, nothing was actually owed under the contract; however, he did possess a valuable right, namely, the right to the proceeds at the closing in accordance with the terms negotiated by him. It is the right to the proceeds which the estate acquired solely as a result of decedent's death, and not by virtue of any economic activity of the estate.[4]

The many diverse characteristics in the various cases dealing with this statute do not permit an easy generalization, and we cannot draw from them a rule as to what is income in respect of a decedent in all cases. It is fair to say, however, in light of the development of the statute, that each of these characteristics represents an element in the composite concept that is income in respect of a decedent.

When the facts in these cases are all viewed, it is readily apparent that the proceeds in issue were realized as a consequence of negotiations and an enforceable contract made by Mr. Dinkler, Sr., during his lifetime, and not the result of any material acts or activities by the estate. The right to the proceeds was acquired by the plaintiffs solely by virtue of the death of the decedent and not through their own efforts. Had Mr. Dinkler lived through the closing date, the proceeds would have been income to him and, consequently, they constitute income in respect of a decedent when received by the estate. Accordingly, the action of the Commissioner in taxing these proceeds as such was proper.

* * *

---

4. The participation by the estate in the loan made by the Trust Company of Georgia to Associated merely facilitated to some degree the closing of the contract negotiated by the decedent. The manner and method utilized by Associated, the purchasers, in assembling the necessary funds do not affect the rights of the parties to the contract as they existed on the date of death.

Judgment will be entered in each of these cases dismissing the complaints with prejudice and allowing the defendant his costs.

Trust Company of Georgia v. Ross
392 F.2d 694 (5th Cir. 1967)
cert. denied, 393 U.S. 830 (1968)

PER CURIAM:

The issue presented on this appeal is whether the trial court erred in holding that the gain realized on the sale of corporate stock was taxable as "income in respect of a decedent" within the meaning of §691 of the Internal Revenue Code of 1954.

The carefully considered and comprehensive opinion of the trial court is reported. Trust Company of Georgia v. Ross, N.D.Ga., 1966, 262 F.Supp. 900. It contains a sufficient factual presentation and we would adopt it in its entirety but for the test employed. The test, " * * * whether the post death payments are in fact due to the services performed by or the economic activities of the decedent", Id. at 908, is open-ended and somewhat inadequate as a precedent when considered in the scope of the statute. We do conclude, however, that the court reached the correct result and thus affirm.

The District Court was not charting a new course in employing this test. Several courts have used the same test but the *ratio decidendi* in each instance, of course, depended on the subsisting facts. For example, several of the cases related to bonus or partnership payments made after death pursuant to rights created by the decedent during his lifetime. See, e. g., Riegelman's Estate v. Commissioner of Internal Revenue, 2 Cir., 1957, 253 F.2d 315; Bernard v. United States, S.D.N.Y., 1963, 215 F.Supp. 256; United States v. Ellis, S.D.N.Y., 1957, 154 F.Supp. 32.[2] In another case the payment was made pursuant to a contract to receive payment for grapes which were delivered into a wine pool during the lifetime of the decedent. Commissioner of Internal Revenue v. Linde, 9 Cir., 1954, 213 F.2d 1. In still another case the payment was for crop rents due under contracts entered into by the decedent in his lifetime. Davison's Estate v. United States, 1961, 292 F.2d 937, 155 Ct.Cl. 290.

Although it is pertinent to inquire whether the income received after death was attributable to activities and economic efforts of the decedent in his lifetime, these activities and efforts must give rise to a right to that income. And the right is to be distinguished from the activity which creates the right. Absent such a right, no matter how great the activities or efforts, there would be no taxable income under §691....

The tortuous language of the statute is of little help in divining the proper test, but the regulation does help. The regulation, 26 CFR 1.691(a)-1 entitled "Income in respect of a decedent" provides in pertinent part:

> "(b) *General definition.* In general, the term 'income in respect of a decedent' refers to those amounts to which a decedent was *entitled* as gross income but which were not properly includible in computing his taxable income for the taxable year ending with the date of his death or for a previous taxable year under the method of accounting employed by the decedent. * * *" (Emphasis added)

---

2. In O'Daniel's Estate v. Commissioner of Internal Revenue, 2 Cir., 1949, 173 F.2d 966, a case involving a bonus payment, Judge Augustus Hand noted that the right acquired during decedent's lifetime need not be a legally enforceable one, "but merely any *right* derived through his services rendered while living. (Emphasis added.) Id. at 968.

It is implicit in the statute and in the definition that this condition or limitation has reference to the date of death of the decedent. That is, income is to be included if decedent was entitled to the income at the date of his death. The entitlement test is in accord with the right to income test discussed, supra, and is more precise than the causal connection test used by the District Court.[3]

There remains the problem of applying the right to income test to the case before us. Ordinarily, in a nonjury trial where an improper test has been applied, the accepted procedure is to remand to the trial court with the direction that the matter be reconsidered in the light of the proper test. Cf. Malat v. Riddell, 1966, 383 U.S. 569, 572, 86 S.Ct. 1030, 16 L.Ed.2d 102. Here, we conclude that the decision of the trial court, in effect, is based on the right to income test; it simply was not articulated as such.

Mr. Dinkler entered into a binding contract prior to his death. That contract required the conveyance of the property from whence the income in litigation was derived. The contract created a right to these proceeds in Mr. Dinkler at the time the contract was executed. The contract inured to and was binding upon his executor. It is true that some aspects of the transaction which the contract contemplated had to be performed by his executor but these were not of such scope as would negate the right which was his under the contract.

The contract contained a liquidated damages clause but this did not transform the contract into a mere option. See 1A Corbin on Contracts §274, pp. 608–609 (1963). The clause became effective only in the event of a default on the part of the purchaser. It did not constitute an agreement simply to permit termination of the contract in the event the seller did not wish to go forward.

Therefore, applying the entitlement or right to income test, it would appear that the disputed amount is income in respect of a decedent.

Affirmed.

Keck v. Commissioner

415 F.2d 531 (6th Cir. 1969)

McALLISTER, Senior Circuit Judge.

The Commissioner of Internal Revenue determined a deficiency in the income tax of George W. Keck and Mary Ann Keck, and also asserted transferee liability against Mary

---

3. 26 CFR 1.691(a)-2, example (5)(1) states:

"A owned and operated an apple orchard. During his lifetime, A sold and delivered 1,000 bushels of apples to X, a canning factory, but did not receive payment before his death. A also entered into negotiations to sell 3,000 bushels of apples to Y, a canning factory, but did not complete the sale before his death. After A's death, the executor received payment from X. He also completed the sale to Y and transferred to Y 1,200 bushels of apples on hand at A's death and harvested and transferred an additional 1,800 bushels. The gain from the sale of apples by A to X constitutes income in respect of a decedent when received. On the other hand, the gain from the sale of apples by the Executor to Y does not."

Note that the sale to Y was not complete. No contract had been effected. Yet negotiations had commenced and been carried on by A, the decedent, prior to his death. The sale went through after A's death. The regulations state that this is *not* income in respect of a decedent. However a contrary result could easily be reached under the broad test used by the District Court since it could well be found that the sale was a result of the negotiations by A, or a result of the "services performed by or the economic activities of the decedent" during his lifetime. What is lacking in the example, of course, is any *right* on A's part to receive the income prior to his death.

Ann Keck, as transferee of the assets of the Estate of Arthur D. Shaw, deceased. Mary Ann Keck, prior to her marriage to George W. Keck, was the widow of Mr. Shaw. The issue ... is whether certain amounts received in 1960 by Mary Ann Keck, and by the Estate, were taxable as income in respect of a decedent under the provisions of Section 691 of the Internal Revenue Code of 1954. The Tax Court decided that the amounts received by Mary Ann Keck and the Estate of Arthur D. Shaw were taxable under the provisions of the statute above mentioned, and assessed deficiencies in income, and transferee liability for income tax against Mary Ann Keck; and review of the Tax Court's decision is here sought by petitioners.

Arthur D. Shaw owned stock in three affiliated corporations as of March 1, 1956. On that date an agreement was entered into anticipating the sale of the assets of the corporation. A condition precedent to the sale was the approval of the Interstate Commerce Commission. Pending such approval and favorable ruling, the shares were placed in escrow.

On May 3, 1956, the attorneys for Mr. Shaw and other owners of the shares requested a tax ruling relative to the application of Section 337 of the Internal Revenue Code of 1954 to the proposed sale; and, by letter dated July 15, 1956, the Internal Revenue Service ruled that Section 337 would be applicable. On May 25, 1956, application was made to the Interstate Commerce Commission for approval of the proposed sale.

Mr. Shaw, the owner of the shares in question, died November 27, 1958. On May 5, 1960, the Interstate Commerce Commission approval, above mentioned, was obtained.

On July 21, 1960, pursuant to the agreement to sell the assets of the three companies by the duly constituted directors and officers, acting on behalf of the stockholders, and pursuant to the authority granted by the Interstate Commerce Commission, the three companies were liquidated, and the cash received from the sale thereof was distributed in exchange for, and in cancellation of, stock of the shares of the three companies. The Executor of the Estate of Mr. Shaw paid over to Mrs. Keck, the widow of Mr. Shaw, as above mentioned, $314,328.53 in exchange for 100 shares of one of the companies liquidated, which was acquired by her in manner as follows:

On February 8, 1960, in order to obtain funds for payment of the federal estate tax, the First National Bank of Akron, as Executor of the Estate of Arthur D. Shaw, sold 48 shares in one of the companies to petitioner, Mary Ann Keck, for $150,877.68, and distributed to her, as distribution in kind, an additional 52 shares of stock in the same company. In order to pay the Estate of Arthur D. Shaw for the 48 shares purchased, as aforesaid, Mrs. Keck borrowed $150,000 from the Executor bank, pledging the entire 100 shares of the stock of the company in her possession as security for the loan. It was this money, plus $877.68, which was paid to the Executor as the full purchase price of the 48 shares purchased.

On or before December 4, 1961, the Executor of the Estate of Mr. Shaw transferred to Mrs. Keck, as distribution of such Estate, in accordance with the will of Arthur D. Shaw, property having a value in excess of $250,000. Upon such transfer and at all times subsequent thereto, the Shaw Estate has been without any assets.

On January 27, 1965, Mrs. Keck executed an instrument for a valuable consideration to the Commissioner of Internal Revenue, in which she admitted that she was the transferee of assets received from the transferor-executor, and agreed to pay any federal income taxes finally determined as due and payable by the transferor-executor for the taxable year ended December 31, 1960, to the extent of her liability as a transferee within the meaning of Section 6901 of the Internal Revenue Code of 1954.

Petitioners, including Mary Ann Keck, the aforesaid widow of Mr. Shaw, reported distribution of stock at the liquidation sale price, and also reported that price to be its acquisition base; and thus reported no taxable income.

The chief issue is whether the amounts received upon the liquidation of the three companies in question were "income in respect of a decedent" under Section 691....

The Tax Court, by a majority of the members, held that the liquidating distributions received by Mr. Shaw's estate and by petitioner Mary Ann Keck in exchange for, and in cancellation of, the stock held by them are taxable as income in respect of a decedent within the meaning of Section 691 ... on the ground that all the significant economic activity in connection with the sale of the corporate assets had been accomplished prior to decedent's death in November 1958, and that, under these circumstances, it was immaterial that the actual consummation of the sale did not occur until after decedent's death.

Five judges of the Tax Court disagreed with the majority and, in the dissenting opinion written by Judge Featherston, declared that, in general, the term "income in respect of a decedent" in Section 691 ... applied only to "those amounts to which a decedent was entitled as gross income, but which were not properly includible" in his final return,— according to the definition contained in Section 1.691(a)-1(b) of the Income Tax Regulations; that the transaction in question, with regard to the three corporations had not "reached the point at decedent's death where it properly can be said that the decedent's stock had been converted to 'property which constitutes an item of income in respect of a decedent under Section 691.'" As was further stated in Judge Featherston's dissenting opinion:

> "The proper test for determining whether gain from the sale of property is to be treated as income in respect of a decedent is the status of the transaction at decedent's death, not who carried on the 'economic activity' which brought it to that status. Thus, as Example (4) of the Regulations explains, where, pursuant to a contract made by "A" obligating his executor to sell his stock, a sale is made, 'there is no income in respect of a decedent with respect to the appreciation in value of A's stock to the date of his death' because 'the sale of stock is consummated after A's death.' However, if "A" had in fact sold his stock prior to his death, but payment was not received until after his death, any gain from the sale would be section 691 income. Section 1.691(a)-2(b), Example (4)."

It was further pointed out by Judge Featherston that at the time of decedent's death, his stock had not been converted to an item of income "in respect of a decedent under section 691," because of the fact that the sale of the stock was subject to a number of contingencies; that it was, at that time, subject to the approval of the Interstate Commerce Commission, a condition precedent which was not met until eighteen months after decedent's death, and that such approval was neither routine or [sic] perfunctory; that, at the time of his death, neither the decedent nor the other stockholders were contractually committed to the plan to liquidate the corporations; that Owen O. Orr, the majority stockholder, for reasons of his own, might have decided not to liquidate the corporations, and that decedent's own stock was not committed to vote for the plan until May 23, 1960, when the proxies were signed and delivered.

In the prevailing opinion of the Tax Court, the case of Trust Company of Georgia v. Ross, 262 F.Supp. 900 (D.C. Ga.) was heavily relied upon, since the decision in the cited case was based on the "economic activities" test....

However, on appeal of the above case to the United States Court of Appeals for the Fifth Circuit, the "economic activities" test was rejected....

We agree with the United States Court of Appeals for the Fifth Circuit in holding that the right to income, under the provision of the statute here pertinent, is to be distinguished from the economic activities that create that right and that, absent such a right, no matter how great the activities, there is no taxable income under Section 691.

It is our conclusion that, at the date of his death, decedent Arthur D. Shaw possessed neither the right nor the power to require the corporations to liquidate and did not, prior to his death, possess the right to receive any proceeds from the contemplated liquidation. It follows that the amounts herein involved are not taxable under Section 691.

In accordance with the foregoing, there is no deficiency in income tax due from petitioner, or liability due from petitioner Mary Ann Keck, as transferee of the assets of the Estate of Arthur D. Shaw. Wherefore, the decision of the Tax Court is reversed....

Illustrative Material

In *Edward D. Rollert Residuary Trust v. Commissioner*, 752 F.2d 1128 (6th Cir. 1985), the Sixth Circuit wrote:

> In [*Keck* this] court held that "entitled", as used in the regulation, contemplated that the decedent was required to have a "right" to the income. However, [this] court failed to definitively answer whether this "right" had to be legally enforceable or whether the substantial likelihood that the decedent would receive the income would suffice.[3]

752 F.2d at 1131. *Rollert* affirmed the decision of the Tax Court, *infra* (ch. 6, sec. A(3)).

Estate of Harry B. Sidles
65 T.C. 873 (1976)
aff'd mem., 553 F.2d 102 (8th Cir. 1977)

DAWSON, *Chief Judge*:

* * *

The primary issue for our decision is whether a liquidating distribution received by the Estate of Harry B. Sidles from Bi-State Distributing Corp. constituted "income in respect of a decedent" within the meaning of section 691(a)(1)....

From January 3, 1956, until his death on June 12, 1968, the decedent owned all the outstanding common stock (500 shares) of Bi-State. At his death decedent's adjusted basis in these shares was $29,701.04.

* * *

At a special meeting held on February 28, 1968, Bi-State's board of directors adopted a plan of complete liquidation and dissolution pursuant to section 337 of the Internal Revenue Code of 1954, and section 21-2083 of the Nebraska Business Corporation Act.

---

3. While the conclusion of Judge McAllister's opinion implies that the right must be legally enforceable..., other portions of his opinion stress that the degree of certainty, at the time of his death, that the decedent would receive the income is an important consideration....

On the same day this plan of complete liquidation was approved by the decedent as Bi-State's sole shareholder.

On February 29, 1968, Bi-State filed with the Nebraska secretary of state a statement of intent to dissolve.

Bi-State owned 11,025 shares of Sidles Co. stock. On March 26, 1968, Sidles Co. made an offer to purchase these shares. The purchase agreement provided that Bi-State would receive cash of $13,429 and a 20-year, 6-percent promissory note from Sidles Co. in the face amount of $899,000. On the same day Bi-State accepted this purchase offer. Bi-State's basis in the 11,025 shares of Sidles Co. stock at the time of sale was $86,344.84.

Bi-State owned certain real and personal property at 4827 Dodge Street in Omaha, Nebr., and from November 1964 until November 1968 was actively engaged in the operation of a gift shop, Areta's, at that location. The gift shop was managed by Areta L. Kelly, decedent's mother-in-law.

After the decedent's death, Bi-State took no action to distribute any of its assets pursuant to the previously adopted plan of liquidation until November 29, 1968, when its board of directors adopted a resolution to distribute all its real and personal property to the decedent's estate. On that date a warranty deed, transferring the real property located at 4827 Dodge Street, and a bill of sale, transferring the personalty to the estate, were executed.

On November 30, 1968, Bi-State assigned all its right, title, and interest in the Sidles Co. promissory note to the estate.

As of the dates of distribution, November 29 and 30, 1968, the assets distributed in liquidation by Bi-State to the estate had a total net fair market value of $702,830.85, being the total fair market value of assets received ($731,195.88), less liabilities assumed ($28,365.03).

Articles of dissolution were executed by Bi-State on November 30, 1968, and were filed with the Nebraska secretary of state on December 17, 1968. On December 17, 1968, a certificate of dissolution was issued.

At the time Bi-State adopted its plan of liquidation and dissolution, which was by act of the corporation, section 21-2088, Nebraska Business Corporation Act, provided the procedure for the corporate revocation of voluntary dissolution proceedings.[2]

Pursuant to the provisions of section 337, Bi-State did not recognize its gain on the sale of its assets in liquidation, i.e., the gain on the sale of its Sidles Co. stock, less a $204 loss on the sale of a 1968 Buick station wagon.

---

2. This section reads in relevant part:

  By the act of the corporation, a corporation may, at any time prior to the issuance of a certificate of dissolution by the Secretary of State, revoke voluntary dissolution proceedings theretofore taken, in the following manner:

  (1) The board of directors shall adopt a resolution recommending that the voluntary dissolution proceedings be revoked, and directing that the question of such revocation be submitted to a vote at a special meeting of shareholders;

  * * *

  (3) At such meeting a vote of the shareholders entitled to vote thereat shall be taken on a resolution to revoke the voluntary dissolution proceedings, which shall require for its adoption the affirmative vote of the holders of at least two-thirds of the outstanding shares; and

  (4) Upon the adoption of such resolution a statement of revocation of voluntary dissolution proceedings shall be executed by the corporation by its president or a vice president and by its secretary or an assistant secretary....

On the decedent's Federal estate tax return, the executors included the 500 shares of Bi-State stock at a value of $702,830.85, valued as of the alternate valuation date (November 30, 1968). This valuation was accepted by respondent following an audit.

In his notice of deficiency dated June 12, 1973, respondent determined that the gain realized from the liquidation of Bi-State constituted income in respect of a decedent. The gain ($673,129.81) was calculated by subtracting the decedent's adjusted basis in his Bi-State stock ($29,701.04) from the net fair market value of the assets received by the estate as a liquidating distribution ($702,830.85)....

Respondent determined that the liquidation proceeds were income in respect of the decedent because, as of the date of his death, the decedent was entitled to and possessed the right to receive the liquidating distribution from Bi-State.

Petitioners argue that the criterion for determining whether an item constitutes "income in respect of a decedent" ... is that the decedent must be entitled to the item in the sense that he had a right to the income at the time of his death, which right had been earned during his lifetime. Petitioners further contend that neither the adoption of the plan of liquidation nor decedent's activities or economic efforts created the requisite right to income under section 691 and the regulations thereunder. They argue that the decedent had no right and was not entitled to the liquidation proceeds until the distribution had been authorized by Bi-State's board of directors.

Income in respect of a decedent is defined only in the regulations and not in the statute. An attempt to add such a definition to the Code in 1959 failed. H.R. 3041, 86th Cong., 1st Sess. (1959)....

Section 691 includes in gross income "all items of gross income in respect of a decedent which are not properly includible" in the taxable year ending with the date of his death or prior period. This reflects the same general congressional intent to tax all items which can constitutionally be considered income, but which are not exempted from taxation, as that underlying section 61 which defines gross income. However, for income to be considered "income in respect of a decedent," section 691 requires that the decedent possess a right to that income as of his date of death. This is a question of fact and each case depends upon its "subsisting facts." *Trust Co. of Georgia v. Ross,* 392 F. 2d 694, 695 (5th Cir. 1967), cert. denied 393 U.S. 830 (1968). One of the factors to be considered is whether the income received after death resulted from the decedent's activities and economic efforts during his lifetime.[5] But this right must be distinguished from the activity which created it. No matter how great the activity or effort, there can be no income in respect of a decedent under section 691 unless the decedent possessed a right to receive such income on his date of death. *Trust Co. of Georgia v. Ross, supra* at 695. Our point of inquiry must be whether the transaction had sufficiently matured as of decedent's death so as to create in him a right to receive the income when it was subsequently realized.

The facts and circumstances of this case lead us to the conclusion that the amounts received by the decedent's estate on the liquidation of Bi-State constituted income in respect of a decedent within the meaning of section 691.

On February 28, 1968, the board of directors of Bi-State Distributing Corp., consisting of Harry B. Sidles, Janice P. Sidles, and Areta L. Kelly, passed a resolution calling for

---

5. For additional factors see *Davison's Estate v. United States,* 155 Ct. Cl. 290, 292 F. 2d 937, 941–942 (1961); *Commissioner v. Linde,* 213 F. 2d 1, 4 (9th Cir. 1954); Ferguson, Freeland & Stephens, Federal Income Taxation of Estates and Beneficiaries 146–148 (1st ed. 1970).

the complete liquidation and dissolution of the corporation. The sole stockholder of Bi-State, Harry B. Sidles, approved the resolution that same day.

The liquidating distribution had its source exclusively in decedent's actions. His affirmative vote for liquidation created a right to receive that distribution, which right existed at his death. Although decedent had the power to rescind the transaction creating such a right, he had not attempted to do so before his death. Had the decedent lived to receive the liquidating distribution, it would have constituted income to him, and consequently such amounts constitute income in respect of a decedent when received by the estate.

There can be no doubt that the estate acquired the right to receive the liquidation distribution from the decedent. The estate's right to such proceeds derived solely from decedent's death and not from its own efforts. Whatever actions the estate took were of no material significance here.

Furthermore, the actions of Bi-State's board of directors which remained to be done at the time of decedent's death do not derogate decedent's right to receive the liquidating distribution. The resolution of November 29, 1968, to distribute the assets in liquidation to decedent's estate, the declaration of the liquidating dividend and the filing of articles of dissolution were mere formalities; ministerial acts necessary to complete the liquidation under State law. On the date of his death the decedent had performed enough substantive acts within his control to perfect his right to receive the liquidating distribution for purposes of section 691.[6] Cf. *Hudspeth v. United States*, 471 F. 2d 275 (8th Cir. 1972); *Kinsey v. Commissioner*, 477 F. 2d 1058 (2d Cir. 1973), affg. 58 T.C. 259 (1972).

In *Keck v. Commissioner*, 415 F. 2d 531 (6th Cir. 1969), [t]he issue ... was whether certain amounts ... were taxable as income in respect of a decedent under section 691. The deceased, Arthur D. Shaw, owned stock in three affiliated corporations as of March 1, 1956. On that date an agreement was entered into prior to the sale of the assets of the corporation. The sale, however, was contingent upon approval of the Interstate Commerce Commission. The shares of stock were placed in escrow pending such approval.

Mr. Shaw died November 27, 1958. ICC approval was not obtained until May 5, 1960. On July 21, 1960, pursuant to authority granted by the ICC, the three companies were liquidated pursuant to the agreement earlier agreed upon, and the cash received from the sale was distributed in exchange for shares of the stock of the three companies. The executor of the Estate of Mr. Shaw paid over to Mrs. Keck $314,328.53 in exchange for 100 shares of one of the companies liquidated. The [Court of Appeals] held that at the time of the decedent's death, his stock had not been converted into section 691 income in respect of a decedent. The Court of Appeals agreed with the dissenting opinion of Judge Featherston in *George W. Keck*, 49 T.C. 313 (1968), that the sale was subject to a number of contingencies which operated to prevent the cash from becoming income in respect of a decedent: (1) The sale was subject to approval of the ICC, which approval did not come until 18 months after decedent's death; (2) as of the time of decedent's death, neither decedent nor the other stockholders were contractually committed to the plan to liqui-

---

6. Although the decedent's right to the liquidating distribution at his death was an absolute and unconditional one, it should be noted that sec. 1.691(a)-1(b)(3), Income Tax Regs., provides that income to which the decedent had a "contingent claim" at the time of his death is sufficient to create income in respect of a decedent. See also Rev. Rul. 60-227, 1960-1 C.B. 262, 263.

Further, it has been held that the requisite right need not be a legally enforceable one, *O'Daniel's Estate v. Commissioner*, 173 F. 2d 966 (2d Cir. 1949), but merely free from contingencies, *Estate of Nilssen v. United States*, 322 F. Supp. 260, 264–265 (D.Minn. 1971).

date the corporation; (3) the majority stockholder (who in this case was not decedent) might have decided not to liquidate the corporation; and (4) the decedent's own stock was not committed to vote for the plan until May 23, 1960, when the proxies were signed and delivered.

The *Keck* case is clearly distinguishable on its facts. Unlike *Keck,* the decedent, as Bi-State's sole shareholder, possessed the power to compel payment of the liquidating distribution, as well as the right to that payment, when he died. His right to the liquidation distribution was not subject to the many contingencies involved in *Keck.* The transaction was not subject to the approval of any Government agency; there was no other stockholder who could vote not to liquidate the corporation. The distribution made to the Estate of Harry B. Sidles was clearly "income in respect of a decedent" within the meaning of section 691.

* * *

HALL, J., concurring in the result: I believe the liquidation gains did constitute income in respect of a decedent. However, some of the language in the Court's opinion could be construed as going farther than I would in stating the criteria for distinguishing income in respect of a decedent from mere unrealized appreciation in value of property. The issue, as properly framed by the Court's opinion, is whether at death decedent had a *right* to receive the Bi-State liquidation proceeds. Under Nebraska law, the filing of a statement of intent to dissolve without more obligates the corporation to cease doing business and distribute its assets to its shareholders. Nebraska Business Corporation Act, Neb. Rev. Stat. secs. 21-2085 and 21-2086 (1974). Should the corporate directors fail to make such a distribution, within a reasonable period the shareholders would apparently be able to sustain an action to compel such a distribution in the absence of shareholder action reversing the original dissolution resolution. At that point the shareholders are vested with a legal right to the proceeds, and the postdeath gains are income in respect of a decedent. The case is analogous to the execution of an enforceable executory contract of sale. *Trust Co. of Georgia v. Ross,* 392 F. 2d 694 (5th Cir. 1967), cert. denied 393 U.S. 830 (1968). However, I do not consider it significant that decedent, as Bi-State's sole shareholder, had the *power* to compel payment of the liquidating distribution when he died, for any sole shareholder, as a practical matter, has such power at all times. Reference to the sole shareholder's *power* proves too much. He has the effective power, for example, to cause an ordinary dividend to be declared. But when no formal directors' action declaring such a dividend has been taken, a postdeath declaration would not give rise to income in respect of a decedent, for the decedent had no *right* at death to such a distribution. What counts is whether the formal corporate actions have been taken which would give even a *minority* shareholder the legal right to compel a liquidating distribution. References to cases holding a "right" need not be a "legal" right are also inapposite here in the context of realization of gains on appreciated property. Such cases involve compensation income. Indeed, it may well be that even in the compensation cases, a *right* existed to compensation in quantum meruit, as evidenced by the very postdeath, nondonative payment which was held to be income in respect of a decedent. In any event, short of the existence of a fixed, predeath *legal* right to the proceeds of a sale or exchange, I would not consider realization of gains on the sale or exchange of property to be income in respect of a decedent.

* * *

TANNENWALD, J., dissenting [on another issue]: While the issue is not entirely free from doubt, I accept the majority conclusion that the proceeds of the liquidation are "income in respect of a decedent" within the meaning of section 691. Prior to the decedent's death, both the directors and the shareholders had not only resolved to liquidate Bi-State but had specifically provided in the respective resolutions that all of Bi-State's assets be sold, that the officers of Bi-State be "authorized *and directed* to file a Statement of Intent to Dissolve and Articles of Dissolution pursuant to the Nebraska Business Corporation Act" (emphasis supplied), and that the debts of Bi-State be paid and "the remaining assets * * * be distributed * * * as soon as practicable but in no event later than the termination of a twelve-month period." Additionally, also prior to decedent's death, the statement of intent to dissolve had been filed with the secretary of state of Nebraska. Finally, at the times the resolutions were adopted and the statement of intent to dissolve filed and at the time of his death, decedent was the sole shareholder of Bi-State. To be sure, under section 21-2088, Nebraska Business Corporation Act, Bi-State's board of directors could have revoked the dissolution proceeding after decedent's death and prior to the filing of the certificate of dissolution. But, in my opinion, this possibility is not enough to obviate the conclusion that, under the circumstances herein, decedent's right to receive the liquidation proceeds had so matured as to make him "entitled" to such proceeds and thus bring the transaction within section 691. See sec. 1.691(a)-1(b), Income Tax Regs.

* * *

In the foregoing context, I believe *Keck v. Commissioner,* 415 F. 2d 531 (6th Cir. 1969), [is] distinguishable. In [that case], the decedent ... did not have such control and the right to receive the amounts in question could have been varied or even destroyed by the action of independent third parties....[2]

FEATHERSTON, J., dissenting: I respectfully disagree with the majority's conclusion.... Section 691(a), which prescribes the general rule for the taxation of "income in respect of a decedent," refers to the "right to receive" items of gross income. Generally speaking, the term "income in respect of a decedent" applies only to "those amounts to which a decedent was entitled as gross income" but which were not properly includable in his final return. Sec. 1.691(a)-1(b), Income Tax Regs. As stated in *Trust Co. of Georgia v. Ross,* 392 F.2d 694, 695 (5th Cir. 1967), cert. denied 393 U.S. 830 (1968): "the right [to income] is to be distinguished from the activity which creates the right. Absent such a right, no matter how great the activities or efforts, there would be no taxable income under sec. 691." While the right to income need not be a legal right to *collect* a sum ascertainable on the date of death, see *Commissioner v. Linde,* 213 F.2d 1 (9th Cir. 1954), remanding 17 T.C. 584 (1951), cert. denied 348 U.S. 871 (1954); *O'Daniel's Estate v. Commissioner,* 173 F.2d 966 (2d Cir. 1949), affg. 10 T.C. 631 (1948), the right to collect the income *when realized* must have arisen prior to or at the decedent's death. The problem in the instant case, therefore, is not to weigh and assess the probabilities at decedent's death that his estate or some other beneficiary would or would not ultimately receive the proceeds of the liquidation of Bi-State, but rather to determine the *rights* of the decedent or that beneficiary as of the date of decedent's death.

This imprecise test is not easily applied to cases involving the liquidation of corporations. In my opinion, in such cases "The crucial question should be whether the re-

---

2. It is not without significance that in *George W. Keck,* 49 T.C. 313 (1968), revd. 415 F. 2d 531 (6th Cir. 1969), the dissenting judges in this Court specifically reserved the question whether they would hold to the same view if the decedent had been the controlling shareholder, which is the case herein. See 49 T.C. at 323 n. 1.

demption or liquidation has proceeded to a point beyond the control of the decedent prior to his death." Ferguson, Freeland & Stevens [sic], Federal Income Taxation of Estates and Beneficiaries 208 (1970). The issue of whether a contract for the disposition of property has created income in respect of a decedent, e.g., via sale, is analogous. In contract cases, the issue is whether, on the date of death, the transaction has proceeded to the point where the value of the property has been converted into an intangible right to receive the ultimate proceeds of the sale or other disposition. Sec. 1.691(a)-2(b), *Example 4*, Income Tax Regs. Such a conversion occurs only when the property is somehow put beyond the control of decedent prior to his death. See *Commissioner v. Linde, supra; Estate of Helen Davison*, 155 Ct. Cl. 290, 292 F.2d 937 (1961), cert. denied 368 U.S. 939 (1961); *Stephen H. Dorsey*, 49 T.C. 606, 633 (1968). In *Trust Co. of Georgia v. Ross, supra*, for example, the court, holding that the disposition of certain stock by decedent prior to his death created income in respect of a decedent, stated (392 F.2d at 696):

> [Decedent] entered into a binding contract prior to his death. That contract required the conveyance of the property from whence the income in litigation was derived. The contract created a right to these proceeds in [decedent] at the time the contract was executed. The contract inured to and was binding upon his executor. * * *

In contrast, in *Keck v. Commissioner*, 415 F.2d 531 (6th Cir. 1969), revg. 49 T.C. 313 (1968), discussed at length in the majority opinion, where a contingent or informal agreement to liquidate a corporation did not constitute a binding contract, the Court of Appeals refused to find income in respect of a decedent.

I do not think the liquidation of Bi-State, at decedent's death, had proceeded to a point beyond his control so that his stock had been converted to a mere right to receive income. It bears reiterating that decedent was *sole* shareholder of Bi-State. To the extent possible under a scheme of State regulation his control of that corporation was absolute, and his rights were in no way diluted by the presence of minority shareholders. His estate succeeded to the same quantum of control.

At any time prior to his death, decedent, the sole shareholder, could have reversed the decision to liquidate Bi-State. Neb. Rev. Stat. secs. 21-2087, 21-2088 (1974). Similarly, at any time after his death and prior to the distributions on November 29 and 30, 1968, decedent's estate, as sole shareholder, could have rescinded the resolution to liquidate and sold the stock to a third party or could have decided to keep the corporation alive so that, for example, it could continue the operation of the gift shop or the ownership of the real and personal property located at 4827 Dodge Street in Omaha. Had the estate taken either one of those steps, clearly it would not have received income in respect of a decedent. The estate received the liquidation proceeds only because it, as sole shareholder, did not revoke the liquidation resolution.

Under the *Trust Co. of Georgia* reasoning, since there was no commitment by either the decedent or his executor to permit Bi-State to be liquidated, decedent's stock at his death had not been converted to income.

* * *

The right of the decedent or his estate to rescind the liquidation resolution shows that the liquidation had not proceeded to a point beyond the control of the decedent-shareholder. His unbridled right unilaterally to reverse the liquidation decision eviscerated any claim to a "right" to the liquidation proceeds under the Nebraska statute.

* * *

Illustrative Material

In *Estate of Bickmeyer v. Commissioner,* 84 T.C. 170 (1985), the decedent owned large interests in two corporations. Prior to his death, the local county government condemned all the property of both corporations, took title to and possession of the property, and paid the corporations what it thought the property was worth. Also prior to the decedent's death, the directors and shareholders of both corporations voted to dissolve the corporations, the corporations distributed a portion of the condemnation proceeds to the decedent, and litigation for additional compensation was commenced. The Tax Court held that the additional compensation received by the decedent's estate as a result of the litigation was income in respect of a decedent. The court relied on *Sidles* and distinguished *Keck.*

Revenue Ruling 78-32
1978-1 C.B. 198

Advice has been requested whether, under the circumstances described below, the gain realized from the sale of real property is income in respect of a decedent within the meaning of section 691(a) of the Internal Revenue Code of 1954.

In June 1971, *A*, who used the cash receipts and disbursements method of accounting, acquired a tract of land for 50*x* dollars. On January 1, 1976, *A* signed a binding executory contract agreeing to sell the land to *B* for 70*x* dollars. The closing was scheduled for March 15, 1976. *A* died on February 5, 1976, after substantial fulfillment of the prerequisites to consummation of the sale. The remaining obligations to be performed were ministerial. *A*'s executor completed the sale pursuant to the contract and transferred title and possession of the land to *B* on March 15, 1976.

Section 691(a) of the Code provides, in part, that the amount of all items of gross income in respect of a decedent that are not properly includible in respect of the taxable period in which falls the date of death or a prior period shall be included in the gross income, for the taxable year when received, of: (1) the estate of the decedent, if the right to receive the amount is acquired by the decedent's estate from the decedent; (2) the person who, by reason of the death of the decedent, acquires the right to receive the amount, if the right to receive the amount is not acquired by the decedent's estate from the decedent; or (3) the person who acquires from the decedent the right to receive the amount by bequest, devise, or inheritance, if the amount is received after a distribution by the decedent's estate of such right.

Section 1.691(a)-1(b) of the Income Tax Regulations provides, in general, that the term "income in respect of a decedent" refers to those amounts to which a decedent was entitled as gross income, but which were not properly includible in computing taxable income for the taxable year ending with the date of death or for a previous taxable year under the method of accounting employed by the decedent. Specifically, section 1.691(a)-1(b)(3) of the regulations provides that the term "income in respect of a decedent" includes income to which the decedent had a contingent claim at the time of death.

Based on section 1.691(a)-1(b) of the regulations, the United States Court of Appeals for the Fifth Circuit, in *Trust Company of Georgia v. Ross,* 392 F.2d 694 (5th Cir. 1967), *cert. denied,* 393 U.S. 830, adopted the "entitlement test" for purposes of determining whether income from the disposition of property owned by a decedent is taxable as income in respect of a decedent. Under this test, such income is to be included in the gross income of the recipient under section 691 of the Code if the decedent was entitled to the income at the date of death. Applying this standard to the facts before it, the court in *Trust Company of Georgia* held that, because the decedent was entitled to the proceeds of a sale of stock under an executory contract binding at the time of death, the gain realized on the proceeds of the contract was income in respect of a decedent. See also *Keck v. Commissioner,* 415 F.2d 531 (6th Cir. 1969), *rev'g* 49 T.C. 313 (1968).

In the instant case, *A* entered into a binding contract prior to death. At the time of death, *A* had substantially fulfilled all of the substantive prerequisites to consummation of the sale and was unconditionally entitled to the proceeds of the sale at the time of death. Accordingly, the gain realized from the sale of *A*'s real property is income in respect of a decedent within the meaning of section 691(a) of the Code.

Illustrative Material

1. *Claiborne v. United States,* 648 F.2d 448 (6th Cir. 1981), found income in respect of a decedent in a situation related to, but arguably more difficult than, that in Rev. Rul. 78-32. In *Claiborne* the decedent executed an option contract to sell real property. She thereupon received $6,000, which the contract designated as the total of liquidated damages to which she would be entitled if the sale were not consummated. Prior to the decedent's death, the buyer exercised the option, entered into possession, and began site preparation. Decedent died before the closing, however. Her estate argued that the provision for liquidated damages, all of which she had received prior to her death, meant she was entitled to nothing at her death. Therefore, there was no income in respect of a decedent. The Sixth Circuit, reversing the trial court, rejected that argument, holding that, under applicable local law, by the time of the decedent's death, the buyer's actions had caused the purchase agreement to be fully enforceable. As a result, the decedent had been entitled to the sales proceeds, which, accordingly, were income in respect of a decedent.

2. In Rev. Rul. 82-1, 1982-1 C.B.26, the I.R.S. ruled that an executor could "'stand in the shoes' of the decedent" for purposes of electing under section 121 to exclude from gross income gain realized by the estate on the sale of the decedent's personal residence pursuant to a sales contract executed by the decedent. Subject to the limitations of section 121, such gain, according to Treas. Reg. §1.691(a)-1(d), was therefore not taxable to the executor. The I.R.S. stated that the executor's election was to be made on the decedent's final income tax return (Form 1040), impliedly rejecting use of the estate's income tax return (Form 1041) for that purpose, despite the fact that any gain taxed would be reportable on the latter, rather than the former. As amended by the Taxpayer Relief Act of 1997, section 121 now applies automatically, unless the taxpayer elects otherwise. The Economic Growth and Tax Relief Reconciliation Act of 2001 added section 121(d)(10), later redesignated as section 121(d)(11), which extends the exclusion to sales by a decedent's estate, individuals who acquire property from a decedent, and a decedent's qualified revocable trust, after taking into account the decedent's ownership and use. The latter changes apply, however, only with respect to decedents dying after December 31, 2009.

3. In Private Letter Ruling 9023012 (1990), the decedent entered into a real estate sales contract that, at the decedent's death, remained subject to a financing contingency. The I.R.S., citing Rev. Rul. 78-32, ruled, almost without analysis, that the sales proceeds were taxable to the executor as income in respect of a decedent. In the only justification for its ruling, the I.R.S. cited Treas. Reg. §1.691(a)-1(b)(3) for the proposition that income to which a decedent has a "contingent claim" can be income in respect of a decedent. Under

Peterson (the next principal case in this book), should not the I.R.S. have determined whether the financing contingency was "economically material?"

The Tax Court, in *Estate of Napolitano v. Commissioner*, 63 T.C.M. (CCH) 3092 (1992), took essentially that approach. There, the decedent agreed to sell certain real estate for $100,000. However, the decedent also agreed to remove all housing code violations from the property prior to closing. When he died, prior to closing, several violations remained outstanding. Thereafter, the buyer refused to close the deal without a reduction in the selling price on account of these violations. After three hours of negotiation, the buyer agreed to close the deal with a reduction in price of only $2,250. Thereupon, the sale closed. The I.R.S. argued that the sales proceeds were income in respect of the decedent taxable to the decedent's estate. The Tax Court held instead that section 691 did not apply because the acts remaining undone at decedent's death could "not be considered 'ministerial', perfunctory, routine, or insubstantial."

In Private Letter Ruling 200744001 (2007), the decedent's revocable trust entered into a real estate sales contract. Prior to the decedent's death, however, a gas pipeline was discovered beneath the property. As a result, the parties delayed the sale until they and the pipeline operating company could resolve a number of issues, including providing the company with an easement to enter the property and arranging for restitution by the company for any resulting damages. Meanwhile, the decedent died. The I.R.S. ruled that upon the eventual sale, none of the proceeds were income in respect of a decedent. The I.R.S. reasoned that "important issues needed to be addressed before the sale of the property could be closed." These issues were both "substantive" and "ministerial." Likewise, at the decedent's death, there remained "economically material contingencies that might have disrupted the sale."

Estate of Peterson v. Commissioner

667 F.2d 675 (8th Cir. 1981)

McMILLIAN, Circuit Judge.

This is an appeal from the decision of the Tax Court holding that the sale proceeds received by the estate of Charley W. Peterson from the sale of 2,398 calves did not constitute "income in respect of a decedent" under §691(a)(1).... *Estate of Peterson v. Commissioner*, 74 T.C. 630 (1980). Five of the Tax Court judges, however, concurred only in the result because the Commissioner never sought to allocate the sale proceeds between those calves which were "deliverable" and not "deliverable" on the date of the decedent's death.... For reversal the Commissioner now argues that because two-thirds of the calves were "deliverable" on the date of the decedent's death, the sale proceeds attributable to those calves should be considered "income in respect of a decedent." We affirm the decision of the Tax Court.

The facts are not disputed.... The decedent, Charley W. Peterson, was in the business of raising and selling cattle. On July 11, 1972, he entered into a "livestock sales contract" with the Max Rosenstock Co., through its agent R.E. Brickley. Under the terms of this contract, the decedent was to raise and sell to the Max Rosenstock Co. "approximately 3,300 calves" at $0.49 per pound, with the date of delivery to be designated by the decedent upon five days notice. One group of calves (the Brown County calves) was to be delivered no later than November 1, 1972; the other group (the Holt County calves) was to be delivered no later than December 15, 1972. The calves were to be from three to eleven months old and in "merchantable condition" when delivered. As provided in the contract, the Max Rosenstock Co. paid $46,500 in "earnest money" to the decedent on July 13, 1972. The risk of loss was on the decedent until delivery.

The decedent did not designate a delivery date or deliver any calves by the November 1 delivery date. The record contains no reason why the decedent did not designate a delivery date or deliver the Brown County calves on or before the November 1, 1972, delivery date specified in the contract. The decedent died on November 9, 1972. The estate (the taxpayer) assumed responsibility for the calves, designated several December delivery dates, and delivered a total of 2,929 calves, 2,398 owned by the estate and 531 owned by the decedent's sons, Willis Peterson and Charles R. Peterson. The calves were accepted by the Max Rosenstock Co. As found by the Tax Court, approximately two-thirds of the calves were in a "deliverable" condition as of the date of the decedent's death. The remaining calves were not "deliverable" on that date because they were too young.

The estate reported the sale of the calves on its fiduciary income tax return and computed the gain from the sale by subtracting the fair market value of the calves on the date of the decedent's death from the sale proceeds. The Commissioner, however, determined that the gain from the sale constituted "income in respect of a decedent" under §691(a)(1) and recomputed the estate's gain on the sale by subtracting the decedent's adjusted basis in the calves from the sale proceeds. See §§691(a)(1), 1014(a) (basis of property acquired from decedent is the fair market value at date of decedent's death), 1014(c) (§1014(a) does not apply to property which constitutes a right to receive an item of income in respect of a decedent under §691). The characterization of the sales transaction thus determines whether the estate uses the decedent's adjusted basis or a stepped-up basis (fair market value on date of death) in calculating the gain from the sale. The amount of income tax deficiency at issue is $185,384.10.

The Tax Court decided that the sale proceeds did not constitute "income in respect of a decedent" under §691(a)(1).... After noting that §691 does not itself define "income in respect of a decedent," the Tax Court reviewed the history of the section, referred to the applicable regulations, 26 C.F.R. §1.691(a)(1)-(3) (1981),[3] examined the case law,[4]

---

3. 26 C.F.R. §1.691(a)-1(b) (1981) provides....

The regulations [also] include several examples of the application of §691; the examples are slightly more illuminating than the regulations. Example (5)(1) is helpful:

A owned and operated an apple orchard. During his lifetime, A sold and delivered 1,000 bushels of apples to X, a canning factory, but did not receive payment before his death. A also entered into negotiations to sell 3,000 bushels of apples to Y. a canning factory, but did not complete the sale before his death. After A's death, the executor received payment from X. He also completed the sale to Y and transferred to Y 1,200 bushels of apples on hand at A's death and harvested and transferred an additional 1,800 bushels. The gain from the sale of apples by A to X constitutes income in respect of a decedent when received. On the other hand, the gain from the sale of apples by the executor to Y does not.

Id. §1.691(a)-2(b) (Ex. 5). The sale to X involves a "completed sale." A has sold and delivered the apples; A dies just before receiving payment. The sale to Y, however, is negotiated by A and completed by A's executor after A's death. In the view of one commentator, the wording "implies that the terms of the sale were identical to those negotiated by the decedent." 3 B. Bittker, Federal Taxation of Income, Estates and Gifts [¶ 83.1.2, at 83-7 & n.23 (1981)]. The present case involves an intermediate fact situation: A has "sold" the property in the sense that the property is the subject of a valid sales contract; however, at the time of A's death the property has not been delivered or otherwise disposed of; and after A's death the executor actually delivers the property. In other words, in the sale to Y in the example, if A had entered into a sales contract with Y and then died, leaving to A's executor the task of harvesting and transferring the apples, would the sale proceeds constitute income in respect of a decedent?

4. See *Keck v. Commissioner,* 415 F.2d 531, 533–34 (6th Cir. 1969); *Trust Co. v. Ross,* 392 F.2d 694, 695 (5th Cir. 1967) (per curiam), *cert. denied,* 393 U.S. 830, 89 S.Ct. 97, 21 L.Ed.2d 101 (1968); *Com-*

and distilled a four-factor test for determining whether sale proceeds constitute "income in respect of a decedent": (1) whether the decedent entered into a legally significant arrangement regarding the subject matter of the sale,[5] (2) whether the decedent performed the substantive (nonministerial) acts required as preconditions to the sale,[6] (3) whether there existed at the time of the decedent's death any economically material contingencies which might have disrupted the sale,[7] and (4) whether the decedent would have eventually received the sale proceeds if he or she had lived.[8] 74 T.C. at 639–41.

The Tax Court concluded that the decedent had entered into a legally significant agreement to sell the calves on the basis of the livestock sales contract. The Tax Court also found that there were no economically material contingencies which could potentially have disrupted the sale; the transaction was not contingent upon the actions or approval of third parties. *Compare Keck v. Commissioner*, 415 F.2d 531, 534 (6th Cir. 1969). Further, the decedent, if he had lived, would have received the sale proceeds; the transaction was not effective only at death. *See* note 8 *supra*. The Tax Court, however, concluded that the decedent had not performed the substantive acts required under the livestock sales contract.... At the date of the decedent's death one-third of the calves were not in "deliverable" condition; all the calves required care and feeding until actually delivered. The estate assumed responsibility for the care and feeding of all the calves until delivery (for approximately one month). The Tax Court concluded that the activities performed by the estate were not perfunctory or ministerial and that these activities were sufficient to remove the sale proceeds from the scope of §691(a)(1)....

On appeal the Commissioner does not disagree with the four-factor test developed by the Tax Court. The Commissioner argues that the Tax Court misapplied the test and that, under a proper application of the test, that portion of the sale proceeds attributable to the calves which were "deliverable" at the date of the decedent's death constitute "income in

---

missioner v. Linde, 213 F.2d 1, 4–8 (9th Cir.), *cert. denied,* 348 U.S. 871, 75 S.Ct. 107, 99 L.Ed. 686 (1954); *Estate of Sidles v. Commissioner,* 65 T.C. 873, 881 (1976), *aff'd mem.* 553 F.2d 102 (8th Cir. 1977)....

5. As noted by the Tax Court, "[t]his arrangement may take a variety of forms: an express executory contract of sale [as in *Trust Co. v. Ross, supra,* 392 F.2d 694]; an implied contract for sale [A delivers apples to Y, Y accepts the apples, A dies before Y can pay for them]; or a contractual arrangement with a cooperative marketing association [as in *Commissioner v. Linde, supra,* 213 F.2d 1 (no contract or sale, just delivery of grapes to marketing cooperative; proceeds held income in respect of a decedent when received)]." *Estate of Peterson v. Commissioner,* 74 T.C. 630, 639 (1980) (parentheticals substituted and expanded). *See also Halliday v. United States,* 655 F.2d 68, 72 (5th Cir. 1981) (the right to income need not be legally enforceable).

6. "One indicium of whether a decedent has performed the applicable substantive acts is whether he has delivered, or somehow placed, the subject matter of the sale beyond his control prior to his death." *Estate of Peterson v. Commissioner, supra,* 74 T.C. at 640. *Compare* M. Ferguson, J. Freeland & R. Stephens, Federal Income Taxation of Estates and Beneficiaries [180–84 (1970)] ("[E]ven where the property has been made the subject of a binding, executory contract of sale, if the benefits and hazards of ownership are still possessed by the decedent at his death, the property is entitled to a §1014(a) basis in the hands of his estate, and his negotiated profit will not be taxed to his estate (or to anyone) under §691 when the sale is completed after his death.") (footnote omitted), *with* Gordon, *Income in Respect of a Decedent and Sales Transactions,* 1961 Wash. U.L.Q. 30, 37 (§691 should apply to sale proceeds from sales which at the time of the decedent's death are incomplete "only as to delivery of the res and receipt of the purchase price").

7. *Cf. Keck v. Commissioner, supra,* 415 F.2d at 534 (sale of stock was contingent upon Interstate Commerce Commission approval; proceeds held not income in respect of decedent where ICC approval not granted at time of the decedent's death).

8. *See* 26 C.F.R. §1.691(a)-2(b) (Ex. 4) (buy-sell agreement effective at date of death; proceeds not income in respect of a decedent because the decedent could not have received the proceeds if he had lived).

respect of a decedent" under §691(a)(1).... This argument was not raised below by either party.[9] Ordinarily we do not consider questions of law which were not presented to the court below except in "exceptional cases or particular circumstances ... where injustice might otherwise result." *Hormel v. Helvering*, 312 U.S. 552, 557, 61 S.Ct. 719, 721, 85 L.Ed. 1037 (1941). However, in order to determine whether the Tax Court misapplied its four-factor test, we necessarily reach the Commissioner's apportionment or allocation argument. We think that the apportionment or allocation argument incorrectly empha-sizes the condition or character of the subject matter of the sale instead of the status of the transaction itself at the time of the decedent's death. For the reasons discussed below, we affirm the decision of the Tax Court.

Stated in misleadingly simple terms, whether income is considered income in respect of a decedent under §691 depends upon whether the decedent had a right to receive in-come at the time of his or her death. The focus is upon the decedent's *right or entitle-ment to income* at the time of death. [The court quotes from the Fifth Circuit's opinion in *Trust Company of Georgia* and cites cases.]

The leading commentators have proposed the following as a "tentative working defi-nition" of income in respect of a decedent:[10]

> Items of income in respect of a decedent ... are payments received toward satisfaction of a right or expectancy created almost entirely through the efforts or status of the decedent and which, except for his death and without further action on his part, the decedent would have realized as gross income. Two ob-servations should be made. First, the concept is manifestly broader than the mere accrued earnings of a cash basis decedent. Second, despite the breadth of this tentative definition, §691 does not reach the income potential in a decedent's

---

9. The taxpayer (the estate) argued that none of the sale proceeds was income in respect of a decedent; the Commissioner argued that all of the sale proceeds was income in respect of a decedent.

10. Ferguson, Freeland and Stephens identified "four salient characteristics" of income in respect of a decedent:

First, the item of income must have been taxable to the decedent had he survived to the time the income was realized. This is to say, the income must have been attributable to *his* services, *his* sales, or *his* income-producing property.

Second, although the decedent must have become "entitled" to the income by his death, his rights must not have matured sufficiently to require inclusion of the income in his final income tax return under the accounting method employed by him. This return, normally filed by the executor, is prepared on the decedent's regular method of accounting without reference to any items which might have become accruable solely because of death....

Third, what is transferred at death must be a passive right to receive income, as distin-guished from "property" entitled to a fair market value basis under §1014(a). Although the gross estate for Federal estate tax purposes includes, along with all other kinds of property rights, the value of any rights to future income, §§691 and 1014(c) force a differentiation between income rights and other assets for income tax purposes. Here, too, generalization is difficult.... Regardless of the nature of the asset, §691 applies only when the decedent performed all substantial acts within his control necessary to convert prior efforts or prop-erty into an intangible right to receive income.

Fourth, the recipient of the right to the income in question must have acquired it solely by reason of the death of the taxpayer who created it. This characteristic subjects income in respect of a decedent to two important limitations, each of which sheds further light upon the basic concept: First, §691 presupposes a gratuitous transfer from a decedent at death of a right to income. Second, the ultimate proceeds must be received solely because of the taxpayer's passive status as the decedent's transferee of the specific right.

M. Ferguson, J. Freeland & R. Stephens, Federal Income Taxation of Estates and Beneficiaries, *supra*, 146–48 (emphasis in original; footnotes omitted).

appreciated property, even if that appreciation is due to the decedent's own efforts. Further action on the decedent's part (e.g., a sale) would have been required for such appreciation to be realized as income. Within this definition
farm produce inventories grown, harvested, and processed for market, but not
delivered by the decedent before his death, even though they come very close to
representing ordinary income actually realized, are "property" rather than a bare
right to income until they are sold. Not being income in respect of a decedent,
they qualify for a new basis at death under the fair market value provision of
§1014(a).

M. Ferguson, J. Freeland & R. Stephens, Federal Income Taxation of Estates and Beneficiaries 146 (1970) (footnote omitted).

"The impact of §691 may vary according to the nature or origin of the income. Such
variation extends to questions of timing and characterization and even to the question whether
a particular receipt must be treated as income in respect of a decedent at all." *Id.* at 162.
For example, items of income attributable to the decedent's services are generally income
in respect of a decedent.[11] Characterization of items attributable to sales proceeds, as in
the present case, however, is less clear, particularly because of the operation of the basis
rules of §1014. *Id.* at 177–78.

[I]t may be difficult to determine whether the decedent's steps prior to his death
had proceeded sufficiently to treat sales proceeds received after death as income
in respect of a decedent. The test here is not quite whether the decedent "closed"
the sale or transferred title and possession of an asset before death. Rather, it is
whether his successor acquired a right to receive proceeds from an asset's disposition on the one hand, or acquired the asset itself on the other. Depending upon
the subject and the terms of a sale, death may interrupt the transaction at a number of stages which do not fall clearly on either side of this murky distinction.

Id. at 178–79.

As noted by Ferguson, Freeland and Stephens, "the definitional problem under §691(a)
is complicated by the general rule of §1014(a) according a basis equal to estate tax value
to the decedent's 'property' other than such §691(a) 'rights.'" *Id.* at 180. As illustrated by
the present case, the tax consequences of characterizing a particular item of income may
be substantial. Ferguson, Freeland and Stephens apparently do not favor characterizing
sales proceeds from sales transactions substantially "incomplete"[12] at the time of the decedent's death as income in respect of a decedent:

---

11. The decedent's personal services are the most common source of IRD [income in respect of a decedent], including payment for the decedent's final pay period, compensation
paid in installments continuing after his death, billed but uncollected fees and commissions, and accrued vacation and leave pay. Items attributable to the decedent's services but
dependent on future events can also constitute IRD, such as an insurance agent's right to
receive renewal commissions on life insurance policies sold by him, a lawyer's right to share
in contingent fees received by his firm in cases that are uncompleted at the time of his death,
and a bonus paid after an employee's death by an employer under a plan that did not vest
enforceable rights in the employees. More controversial are cases holding that allowances
paid by employers to the surviving spouse or other dependents of a faithful employee, if
not excludable from gross income as "gifts" or employee death benefits under IRC §102 or
§101(b)(1), constitute IRD....
3 B. Bittker, Federal Taxation of Income, Estates and Gifts, *supra,* ¶83.1.2, at 83-5 to -6 (footnotes
omitted). [The Small Business Job Protection Act of 1996 repealed section 101(b).]
12. Tax commentators differentiate between "executory sales contracts" and "sales," even though
such a distinction may not make much sense in contract law. *See* Note, *Sales Transactions and Income*

[W]here there is a contract of sale which would have been completed during the decedent's life but for his death, the proceeds received upon culmination of the sale by the decedent's transferee will be taxed as income in respect of a decedent if no substantial conditions remained to be performed by the decedent at his death. Thus, if the executor had only a passive or ministerial role to play in completing the sale, the proceeds should be taxed as income in respect of a decedent.

... Whenever the decedent negotiates a contract enforceable by his executor after death, the profit may properly be attributed to the decedent's bargaining and other efforts, which would seem to suggest income treatment for a part of the post-death receipts. On the other hand, the basis rules of §1014(a) suggest that, wherever the risks inherent in ownership remain with the decedent until death, adjustments to the property's basis (and hence variations in the amount of gain or loss under the contract) remain possible until actual disposition by the decedent's successor.

Id. at 183–84 (footnote omitted).

Here, the task remaining to be performed by the estate was performance of the contract. We agree with the conclusion of the Tax Court that performance of the contract, which, under the circumstances, involved care and feeding of livestock and delivery, cannot be characterized as a ministerial or minor act. However, we think that characterization of the tasks which remain after the death of the decedent should not necessarily depend upon the nature of the subject matter of the sales transaction. For example, the subject matter of the sales transaction in the present case was livestock, which obviously required care and feeding. What if the subject matter was not livestock but logs or refrigerators? It would still be the task of the decedent's transferee to deliver or otherwise dispose of the logs or refrigerators, even though that type of property does not require the care that livestock does.

We recognize that the analysis followed by the Tax Court emphasizes delivery or disposal of the subject matter of the sales transaction and, to a certain degree, discounts the significance of the sales contract. *Compare* Gordon, *Income in Respect of a Decedent and Sales Transactions,* 1961 Wash.U.L.Q. 30, 37–38 (proposing that §691 should apply to sales proceeds if the contract of sale is incomplete at death "only as to delivery of the res

---

in Respect of a Decedent,[3 Ga.L.Rev. 606, 617 (1969)] ("closed transaction"). As illustrated in the examples in the relevant regulations, *see* note 3 *supra,* delivery or actual disposition of the subject of a sales contract before death is a "completed" sale and the sale proceeds received after death is income in respect of a decedent. Actual disposition of the subject matter, in the absence of any sales contract or agreement, was sufficient to make the post-death receipt of proceeds income in respect of a decedent in *Linde, supra,* 213 F.2d at 4–8 (decedent was a member of an agricultural marketing cooperative). If the decedent neither enters into a sales contract nor delivers the property before death, the post-death disposition of the property by the executor does not produce income in respect of a decedent.

The difficult question arises where the decedent has made arrangements to dispose of the property (such as entering into a sales contract) *but* dies before delivering or otherwise disposing of the property. In *Trust Co. v. Ross,* the subject matter of the sale was the controlling interest in a hotel chain. The negotiations were completed, the contract of sale was executed, and the stock was placed in escrow before the death of the decedent. After his death, the estate made some financial arrangements and formally closed the sale. The Fifth Circuit concluded that the execution of the contract created a right to the proceeds (and thus constituted income in respect of a decedent) because the tasks left to the executor were "minor." 392 F.2d at 697. *Accord, Estate of Sidles, supra,* 65 T.C. at 880–81 (on date of death decedent had performed enough substantive acts within his control to "perfect" his right to receive liquidating distribution of corporate assets, declaration of liquidating dividend and filing of articles of dissolution characterized as "mere formalities" and "ministerial acts").

and receipt of the purchase price"). Nonetheless, this analysis is not inconsistent with *Trust Co. v. Ross, supra,* 392 F.2d at 697, where the contract of sale was executed and the stock was placed in escrow before the death of the decedent and the tasks remaining for the estate were "minor," and *Commissioner v. Linde, supra,* 213 F.2d at 4–8, where the decedent had delivered the property before death to the marketing cooperative, thus "converting" the property into a right to receive income. Moreover, "while the death of a decedent can be a fortuitous event taxwise, it is certainly hard to visualize death as a tax avoidance scheme." Note, *Sales Transactions and Income in Respect of a Decedent, supra,* 3 Ga.L.Rev. at 615. After all, the decedent in a sales case does not prearrange his death in order to shift the responsibility for delivering the subject matter of the sale transaction to his executor or to take advantage of the fair market value basis rule of §1014(a) and thus avoid the reach of §691.

Accordingly, the decision of the Tax Court is affirmed.

3. Compensation for Personal Services

Edward D. Rollert Residuary Trust v. Commissioner
80 T.C. 619 (1983)
aff'd, 752 F.2d 1128 (6th Cir. 1985)

WHITAKER, *Judge*:

* * *

The [issue is whether] rights to receive bonus payments under the General Motors bonus plan, which were attributable to an individual's employment with General Motors before his death but which were not formally awarded until several months after his death, are rights to income in respect of a decedent....

For several years prior to his death on November 27, 1969, Edward D. Rollert had been employed as an executive vice president of General Motors Corp. and had participated in the corporation's stock option plan and its bonus plan. These plans were designed to compensate corporate executives and other employees by providing cash and stock bonuses payable in installments in subsequent years. Amounts awarded under the plans were interrelated: if an employee was awarded a stock option bonus, any award under the bonus plan was reduced. All awards under the bonus plan for more than $2,000 were to be paid in cash or stock in annual installments over a 5-year period following the year of award. Bonuses under the stock option plan were in the form of contingent credits for General Motors stock. After the termination of stock options concurrently awarded to the executive, the contingent credits would entitle the executive to receive the stock. Like the bonuses under the bonus plan, the contingent credits under the stock option plan were credited in installments over a 5-year period. However, the period for applying the contingent credits started running from the date the options were terminated. Mr. Rollert's options terminated within 12 months after his death.

During the period between the award of bonus rights under either of these plans and the employee's receipt of the final installment payment attributable to such rights, the employee had to "earn out" his or her right to the award by continuing to be employed by the corporation and not committing acts inimical to the best interests of the corporation. Death relieved an employee from the duty of earning out a bonus; thus, upon an employee's death, his or her estate, or the party entitled to the right, possessed a nonforfeitable right to subsequent installments of the bonus award.

General Motors made awards to Mr. Rollert under both the bonus plan and the stock option plan for each of the years 1964 through 1968. These awards, which exceeded $300,000 for each of these years, are referred to collectively as the "lifetime bonus awards." When Mr. Rollert died on November 27, 1969, the remaining installment payments of these bonuses became nonforfeitable and payable to Mr. Rollert's estate.

* * *

On March 2, 1970, decedent was awarded a bonus under the bonus plan of 1,786 shares of General Motors common stock and $285,763 cash with respect to his almost 11-months employment with the corporation in 1969. This is referred to hereafter as the "postmortem bonus award." The parties have stipulated that decedent "had no rights to the post-mortem bonus award during his lifetime." This bonus was to be paid in five annual installments, with the first installment in March 1970, and the subsequent installments on January 10 of the next 4 years. The installments for 1970, 1971, 1972, and 1973 each consisted of $57,168 cash and 357 shares of General Motors stock. For 1974, the installment consisted of $57,090 cash and 358 shares of stock. No award was made to Mr. Rollert under the stock option plan with respect to his employment in 1969.

The procedures for awarding bonuses under the bonus plan to an executive vice president, such as Mr. Rollert, were the same as those with respect to other employees. The bonus plan stated that it was contemplated that bonuses would be awarded annually but that the committee had the right from time to time to modify or suspend the plan. Bonuses were awarded under the bonus plan in all the years 1956 through 1969, and it was the practice during this period to grant awards to all executive vice presidents.

The first step to be taken in each year in deciding whether to award bonuses under the bonus plan was for the corporation's independent public accountants to determine an amount to be set aside in a reserve to be used to pay any bonuses that might be awarded under the two plans. The amount set aside was computed under a formula based generally on the corporation's net earnings, but the corporation's bonus and salary committee (hereinafter the committee) had discretion to direct that a lesser amount be credited. For the year 1969, an initial determination of the amount available for payment of bonuses was made on October 6, 1969, approximately 1½ months prior to Mr. Rollert's death. This determination was reviewed monthly until February 2, 1970, when it was accepted as final.

The second step in awarding bonuses was the selection of eligible employees for awards under the bonus plan. To do this, the committee designated a monthly salary rate, and with a few exceptions, all employees earning in excess of that rate were considered for bonuses in that year. On November 3, 1969 (again prior to the date of death), the committee made a tentative determination of awards for all executive vice presidents, including Mr. Rollert. This determination was reviewed monthly until finalized on March 2, 1970. During the review on January 5, 1970, the committee decided to make an award on account of Mr. Rollert's service despite his death but reduced it to an amount roughly equivalent to $11/12$ of the amount originally determined. This accorded with the committee's practice of prorating awards on the basis of the amount of actual service during the year. On March 2, 1970, the award for Mr. Rollert's 1969 service was formally made. It was for the amount determined on January 5, 1970.

The provisions of the bonus plan stated that an employee would be eligible for consideration for a bonus in the year his or her employment terminated, at the discretion of the committee and under such rules as the committee might prescribe. As of the date of decedent's death, the committee had prescribed no rules dealing with the awarding of bonuses to employees who had died during the award year; but it had been the committee's practice, generally, to treat eligible employees who had at least 2-months active service in the award year the same as employees not terminating their service. Thus, the committee would deny a postmortem award to an employee with at least 2-months service in the award year only if his performance had declined to the extent that he would not have been given an award if he had lived, or if he had acted or conducted himself in a manner inimical or in any way contrary to the best interests of the corporation. None of these exceptions applied to Mr. Rollert.

Mr. Rollert did not report on his pre-death income tax returns any of the bonus awards at issue here. Nor were any of these amounts reported in Mr. Rollert's final individual income tax returns.

* * *

We are … squarely faced with the issue whether payments of the postmortem bonus award were income in respect of a decedent. Petitioner argues that Mr. Rollert had no right or entitlement to a bonus award with respect to his employment in 1969 since the bonus was not formally awarded by General Motors until March 2, 1970—over 3 months after his death. We disagree. For purposes of section 691, we believe that as of the date of his death, Mr. Rollert had a right to a bonus award for 1969, in view of General Motors' established practices in awarding bonuses and its tentative decisions to assign substantial funds to the bonus pool for 1969 and to award bonuses to all executive vice presidents.

Section 691(a) provides that gross income of an estate shall include all income in respect of a decedent, but nowhere in the Code is this phrase defined. The only definition appears in section 1.691(a)-1(b), Income Tax Regs., but this definition does little to clarify the meaning of the term. Thus, the courts have frequently been called upon to establish the dimensions of the term. *Estate of Peterson v. Commissioner*, 74 T.C. 630, 638 (1980), affd. 667 F.2d 675 (8th Cir. 1981).

In determining whether particular receipts should be treated as income in respect of a decedent, courts have focused on whether the decedent had a *right* or *entitlement* to receive income as of the date of his death. *Estate of Peterson v. Commissioner*, 667 F.2d at 679, and cases cited therein.…

Petitioner relies on several cases that have applied the "right-to-income" or "entitlement" test in determining whether post-death payments constitute income in respect of a decedent. *Estate of Peterson v. Commissioner, supra; Halliday v. United States,* 655 F.2d 68 (5th Cir. 1981); *Claiborne v. United States,* 648 F.2d 448 (6th Cir. 1981); *Keck v. Commissioner,* 415 F.2d 531 (6th Cir. 1969), revg. 49 T.C. 313 (1968); and *Trust Co. of Georgia v. Ross,* 392 F.2d 694 (5th Cir. 1967). We agree with petitioner that this test should be applied but find on the facts of this case that as of the date of his death, Mr. Rollert had a right or entitlement to a bonus for 1969.

Keck v. Commissioner, supra, and *Trust Co. of Georgia v. Ross, supra,* were the first cases to squarely reject reliance on the "economic activity" test under which the inquiry had been limited to consideration of whether the significant economic activity giving rise to income received after death had been performed prior to death. These two opinions indicated that all facts should be examined to determine whether at the date of death the decedent had the right to the post-death payments. *Trust Co. of Georgia* involved proceeds from the sale of property pursuant to a binding contract which decedent had executed prior to death. Although there were a few aspects of the transaction not completed by the date of death, the court found that these were not of such a scope as would negate the right possessed by decedent under the contract. In contrast, the *Keck* court was presented with a situation in which the occurrence of post-death contingencies would defeat the existence of a right to income. The particular fact situation before the court in the *Keck* case involved the treatment of liquidation distributions from corporations in which decedent had owned stock. Prior to decedent's death, the corporations had agreed to sell their assets in pursuance of a contemplated liquidation, but the sale was not consummated until after the decedent's death. The Court of Appeals stressed that the sale of the stock was subject to a number of contingencies, such as prior Interstate Commerce Commission approval and the continued agreement of the majority shareholder. On these facts, the court found that decedent had neither the right nor the power to require the corporations to liquidate and thus did not possess, prior to his death, the right to receive any proceeds from the contemplated liquidation.

In *Claiborne v. United States, supra,* the right-to-income or entitlement test was applied in the context of the sale of property on which the decedent had granted an option prior to her death. Because the decedent had died before the optionee paid her the purchase price, the court recognized that she was not entitled as a strict matter of law to the full purchase price as of the date of her death. However, the court found that under State law the decedent had the right in equity to specific performance of the land purchase agreement at the full purchase price because the optionee had already taken full possession of the realty prior to the decedent's death. The *Claiborne* opinion holds that the right-to-income or entitlement test is satisfied when a decedent possesses as of the date of death a legal or equitable entitlement to income. It does not state, however, that the existence of a right enforceable at law or in equity is an absolute prerequisite to finding a pre-death entitlement to income.

These three appellate opinions left considerable room for disagreement over exactly what constitutes a right or entitlement to income. However, *Halliday v. United States, supra,* and *Estate of Peterson v. Commissioner, supra,* have clarified this test.

In *Halliday,* the Fifth Circuit rejected the view that a legally enforceable right was necessary in order for income to be taxed under section 691. The court characterized the right-to-income test as simply a "more precise" definition of income in respect of a decedent, rather than as a repudiation of the line of cases that had found the existence of income in respect of a decedent in the absence of a legally enforceable right. It elaborated on the right-to-income test as follows:

> We find that for purposes of Section 691, a right to income arises where the evidence shows a substantial certainty that benefits directly related to the decedent's past economic activities will be paid to his heirs or estate upon his death, notwithstanding the absence of a legally enforceable obligation. * * * [655 F.2d at 72.]

The fact situation in *Halliday* was quite similar to that now presented to us. The *Halliday* court was asked to decide whether section 691 applied to life insurance renewal commissions received by the estate of an insurance agent after his death. The agent had no contractual right to the payment of these renewal commissions. Nevertheless, the insurance company had a longstanding policy of paying benefits at a set rate to the beneficiaries of a deceased agent, and this policy had been embodied in corporate resolutions.

On the basis of these facts, the court found that the decedent had a right, albeit not necessarily a legally enforceable one, to post-death renewal commissions, and therefore that the benefits paid to his estate by the insurance company constituted income in respect of a decedent.

The "substantial certainty" approach adopted in the *Halliday* opinion is consistent with the approach we took in *Estate of Peterson v. Commissioner, supra*. That case involved the tax treatment of sales proceeds under a contract for the sale of calves, which had been entered into by the decedent prior to his death. Based on our review of the case law and regulations, we found in *Estate of Peterson* that the following four requirements have been applied to test whether a decedent possessed the requisite right to sales proceeds at the time of death: (1) Whether the decedent entered into a legally significant arrangement regarding the subject matter of the sale; (2) whether the decedent performed the substantive acts required as preconditions to the sale; (3) whether there existed at the time of decedent's death any economically material contingencies which might have disrupted the sale; and (4) whether the decedent would have eventually received the sales proceeds if he or she had lived.[6] We found that the proceeds from the contract for the sale of the calves satisfied three of these four requirements but did not satisfy the second requirement. Substantial and essential acts that the decedent had been required to perform under the contract had not been completed as of the date of his death since one-third of the calves were too young to be deliverable as of that date and had to be raised by the estate for more than 1 month thereafter. We therefore held that the sales proceeds were not income in respect of a decedent.

We now apply to the facts of this case the right-to-income test as elaborated in *Halliday v. United States, supra*, and *Estate of Peterson v. Commissioner, supra*.

General Motors had no contractual obligation as of the date of decedent's death to pay him a bonus with respect to 1969. However, the decedent had a longstanding contractual employment relationship with General Motors, and under the terms of his employment, he was eligible to participate in the bonus plan, which was a formalized deferred compensation arrangement and under which bonuses had been paid consistently in preceding years. In this factual context, it is apparent that the bonus payments were made in relation to "a legally significant arrangement" between the decedent and General Motors. See *Estate of Peterson v. Commissioner*, 74 T.C. at 639. It is also clear that decedent's 11-months employment with General Motors in 1969 and his refraining from taking any actions that would have disqualified him from bonus eligibility for that year constituted his performance of all the substantive acts required as a precondition of his being awarded a bonus for 1969. Cf. *Estate of Peterson v. Commissioner, supra*.

When Mr. Rollert died, he had no legally enforceable right to a bonus for 1969 since the bonuses for that year had not yet been declared, and General Motors had reserved the right to modify or suspend the bonus plan. However, as a practical matter, by the date of Mr. Rollert's death, and barring some unforeseen and unpredictable change in corporate plans, bonuses would be awarded for 1969. In each of the 13 years preceding 1969, General Motors had awarded bonuses. Prior to the date of decedent's death, it was anticipated that under the net earnings formula set forth in the plan, substantial funds would be added to the bonus pool for 1969. There is no evidence to suggest the committee ever considered exercising its discretion to modify or suspend the plan in 1969 or

---

6. In *Estate of Peterson v. Commissioner*, 74 T.C. 630, 639 n.9 (1980), affd. 667 F.2d 675 (8th Cir. 1981), we cautioned that the four factors were not meant to be an ironclad formula but might change based on the type of transaction to be analyzed.

to reduce the amount added for 1969 below the amount computed under the net earnings formula. To the contrary, over 7 weeks before Mr. Rollert's death, the committee had made an initial determination of the amount available for bonuses for 1969.

It is also clear that Mr. Rollert was assured prior to his death of being one of the individuals to whom awards would be made for 1969. The committee had never denied an award to an executive vice president, and Mr. Rollert had received bonuses in excess of $300,000 for each of the 5 years preceding 1969. More importantly, over 3 weeks before Mr. Rollert's death, the committee had made a determination (albeit a tentative one) to grant bonus awards for 1969 to all executive vice presidents. The parties agree that during 1969, Mr. Rollert committed no act that would have disqualified him from receipt of an award for that year. At least implicitly, the committee recognized this fact by failing to exclude him from the executive vice president group and the possibility of forfeiture died with the decedent. Although the tentative bonus determinations were subject to monthly reviews until March 2, 1970, in point of fact, the amount formally awarded on March 2, 1970, with respect to Mr. Rollert's employment during 1969 was substantially the same as the initially determined amount, except that it was reduced by $1/12$ to reflect the fact that he performed no services for General Motors in December 1969.

The bonus plan provided the committee with discretion in determining the eligibility of employees for consideration for bonuses in the year their employment terminated, but the existence of this discretion did not significantly affect Mr. Rollert's chances of receiving a bonus for 1969. The committee had no written rules or guidelines circumscribing their discretion with respect to terminated employees. However, the committee's established practice had been to make awards to terminated employees who were otherwise qualified so long as they had at least 2-months active service in the year for which the award was being granted. *Halliday v. United States, supra* at 72, paid particular attention to the fact that the corporation had consistently followed its established policy of paying post-death benefits even absent a contractual obligation. Here, it is equally clear that under established practices, the bonus award with respect to Mr. Rollert's service in 1969 would not have been denied on the basis of his cessation of employment in that year.[7] Thus, as of the date of Mr. Rollert's death, there was no material contingency comparable to that in *Keck v. Commissioner, supra,* that might have resulted in denial of a bonus award for 1969.[8] On these facts, it is established that Mr. Rollert had a substantial certainty as of the date of his death of receiving a bonus award for 1969.

Thus, the analyses in the *Halliday* and *Estate of Peterson* opinions lead us to the conclusion that as of the date of his death, Mr. Rollert had a right or entitlement to a bonus

---

7. We note that had General Motors deviated from its established policy of treating terminated employees with at least 2-months service in the award year, in the same manner as continuing employees, and thereby denied decedent's bonus award for 1969, it may be that the estate could have sued to obtain the award. Compare *Hainline v. General Motors Corp.,* 444 F.2d 1250 (6th Cir. 1971), in which the court found that the bonus committee's discretion to allow terminated employees to receive accrued bonus awards was restricted by its past decisions, and for that reason, the committee could not arbitrarily deny the right to receive such accrued bonuses but must examine the facts of the particular case, with *Parrish v. General Motors Corp.,* 137 So. 2d 255 (Fla. App. 1962), in which the court held that General Motors had discretion under the bonus plan in granting or withholding bonus awards to its employee.

8. We note that although the Sixth Circuit did not use the term "substantial certainty" in *Keck v. Commissioner,* 415 F.2d 531 (6th Cir. 1969), revg. 49 T.C. 313 (1968), the effect of the court's stressing the contingencies affecting the sale of the stock which gave rise to the liquidation proceeds shows that it took the same practical approach as the Fifth Circuit did in *Halliday v. United States,* 655 F.2d 68 (5th Cir. 1981).

for 1969. Accordingly, the payments under the postmortem bonus award were income in respect of a decedent when received by the estate or petitioner.

* * *

Illustrative Material

1. *Bausch's Estate v. Commissioner,* 186 F.2d 313 (2d Cir. 1951); *O'Daniel's Estate v. Commissioner,* 173 F.2d 966 (2d Cir. 1949); and Rev. Rul. 65-217, 1965-2 C.B. 214, likewise involved compensation awarded after employees' deaths. All held that the payments constituted income in respect of a decedent, despite the fact that none of the employees had had legally enforceable rights to the amounts paid.

2. In *O'Daniel,* Judge Augustus N. Hand reasoned that "any right derived through [an employee's] services rendered while living" was income in respect of a decedent. In Rev. Rul. 65-217 the I.R.S. seemed to take the same position. Yet, as the efforts expended by the Tax Court in *Rollert* indicate, such a simplistic position may not be entirely accurate. Some payments arising from the employment context seem not to be income in respect of a decedent. For example, "discretionary" payments made directly to a surviving spouse by the deceased spouse's employer may not be income in respect of a decedent. Often such payments are held to be subject to taxation in the survivor's hands under only the broader authority of section 61. *See Findlay v. Commissioner,* 332 F.2d 620 (2d Cir. 1964); *Carson v. United States,* 161 Ct. Cl. 548, 317 F.2d 370 (1963). Or, if the payments can be categorized as gifts to the survivor, they may not be taxable at all, under section 102. *See, e.g., Estate of Carter v. Commissioner,* 453 F.2d 61 (2d Cir. 1971).

3. Sometimes an employer agrees with an employee to make certain payments, after the employee's death, by "pension plan" or otherwise, to someone designated by the employee (typically the employee's spouse). The employee obviously has no conventional "entitlement" to those payments. Nonetheless, it is clear that the payments are solely attributable to the services of the employee. Numerous courts have held that such payments constitute income in respect of a decedent and thus are taxable to the recipient. *Miller v. United States,* 389 F.2d 656 (5th Cir. 1968) (per curiam); *Hess v. Commissioner,* 271 F.2d 104 (3d Cir. 1959); *Estate of Nilssen v. United States,* 322 F. Supp. 260 (D. Minn. 1971); *Collins v. United States,* 318 F. Supp. 382 (C.D. Cal. 1970), *aff'd per curiam,* 448 F.2d 787 (9th Cir. 1971); *Hansberry v. All,* 68-1 U.S.T.C. ¶ 9185 (N.D. Ill. 1967); *Bernard v. United States,* 215 F. Supp. 256 (S.D.N.Y. 1963); *Estate of Machat,* 75 T.C.M. (CCH) 2194 (1998); *Ballard v. Commissioner,* 63 T.C.M. (CCH) 2748 (1992); *Estate of Arthur W. Davis,* 11 T.C.M. (CCH) 814 (1952). *See also* Rev. Rul. 73-327, 1973-2 C.B. 214. *But see Lacomble v. United States,* 177 F. Supp. 373 (N.D. Cal. 1959). The absence of an entitlement has, however, caused several courts to pause. The *Bernard* court, for example, wrote:

> It is not necessary that the decedent would have been entitled to the money had he lived. Otherwise all payments that commenced upon death would escape income tax. The critical question that must be answered is, who did the work or performed the services that gives rise to the income. If it is the decedent then such payments fall within Section 691 and are taxed to the recipient in the way that they would have been taxed to the decedent.

215 F. Supp. at 260. The *Collins* court dealt with the absence of an entitlement in a somewhat different manner:

It is submitted that where one is dealing with post-death payments attributable to the personal services of a decedent and payable upon his death, the right to receive the money has certainly matured and the decedent's entitlement to the payments is simply not relevant. If, however, decedent's entitlement is a *sine qua non* of income in respect of a decedent, I submit that such entitlement could be found under the facts of the case at bar. The decedent here bargained for these payments in return for his personal services and for his remaining employed up to the date of his death. The consideration for those payments flowed entirely from him. He could have directed the payments to any person or entity he chose. He directed that they be paid to his widow, the contract being in essence a third-party beneficiary contract. Under the circumstances, with the decedent having furnished all of the consideration and economic benefit, it would be unrealistic in the extreme to hold that the income in question is not income in respect of a decedent, because the decedent chose to have it payable to someone other than himself or his estate. In every economic sense the decedent was the person "entitled" to the income.

318 F. Supp. at 389.

4. Recall that, in order for income in respect of a decedent to exist, there must be income "not properly includible in respect of" decedent's final taxable year. One way taxpayers sometimes seek to avoid income in respect of a decedent is to argue that the income was properly reportable by the decedent. In *Estate of Fred Basch*, 9 T.C. 627 (1947), for example, the taxpayer argued that decedent's post-death bonus had been properly reportable by him. Decedent's employment contract had entitled him to a fixed percentage of his employer's profits for a year that ended prior to decedent's death. Thus, so the taxpayer argued, decedent had been in constructive receipt of the bonus at his death. The Tax Court rejected that argument. The employer's accountants had not computed the amount of the bonus until after decedent's death. Moreover, the employer had made no credit on its books in decedent's favor until after his death. Thus, according to the court, decedent had not "turned his back on income which was subject to his unfettered command." *Id.* at 630. The bonus was therefore income in respect of a decedent.

5. *Accrued employee benefits.* A lump sum payment due an employee upon separation from service but paid to a surviving spouse is includible in the surviving spouse's gross income as income in respect of a decedent. *See* Rev. Rul. 55-229, 1955-1 C.B. 75, where the payment was on account of accumulated annual leave. According to the I.R.S. it represented "salary or compensation for services rendered" by the employee. To the same effect, with respect to accrued vacation allowances, is Rev. Rul. 59-64, 1959-1 C.B. 31. Similarly, where a decedent is entitled to a bonus based on a percentage of an employer's profits, the bonus, though paid to a surviving spouse, constitutes income in respect of a decedent. Rev. Rul. 75-79, 1975-1 C.B. 184.

6. *Continuing employee benefits.* In Rev. Rul. 82-196, 1982-2 C.B. 53, the I.R.S. ruled that contributions by the decedent's employer to a health and accident plan providing for the spouses and dependents of deceased employees were not taxable to the survivors as income in respect of a decedent, because such contributions would have been excluded from the decedent's gross income under section 106. The I.R.S. relied upon Treas. Reg. §1.691(a)-1(d). The I.R.S. also ruled, using the same rationale, that taxation of the survivors on amounts received under the plan would be governed by section 105. To the same effect with respect to amounts received on account of sick pay due the decedent is Rev. Rul. 59-64, 1959-1 C.B. 31. That is, if section 105 would have allowed the decedent to exclude such amounts from gross income, they are not income in respect of a decedent.

But if section 105 would not have allowed such exclusion, the amounts are taxable to the recipients as income in respect of a decedent.

7. *Renewal Commissions.* Insurance agents often are entitled to commissions when policies they have sold are renewed. Renewal commissions received by an agent's survivors or estate are income in respect of a decedent. *E.g., Halliday v. United States,* 655 F.2d 68 (5th Cir. 1981); *Wright v. Commissioner,* 336 F.2d 121 (2d Cir. 1964) (per curiam); *Findlay v. Commissioner,* 332 F.2d 620 (2d Cir. 1964); *Latendresse v. Commissioner,* 243 F.2d 577 (7th Cir.), *cert. denied,* 355 U.S. 830 (1957); *Estate of Florence E. Carr,* 37 T.C. 1173 (1962); Rev. Rul. 59-162, 1959-1 C.B. 224. In *Latendresse* the Seventh Circuit also held that additional renewal commissions withheld by the company to offset advances it had made to the decedent constituted income in respect of a decedent. Moreover, such commissions were taxable to the decedent's widow, who was entitled to the balance of the commissions. In terming the offset commissions income in respect of a decedent the court was surely correct. But should the widow — rather than the decedent's estate — be taxed on them? *Wright* and *Findlay* each held that a widow otherwise entitled to receive commissions was not subject to taxation on commissions withheld by the company to pay foreign death taxes. Those courts reasoned that the widow had never received the withheld commissions — either in fact or constructively. Moreover, payment of the foreign death taxes discharged an obligation of the estate — not an obligation of the widow. *See also Horwitz's Estate v. Commissioner,* 181 F.2d 85 (5th Cir. 1950) (estate, rather than widow, subject to taxation on income used to discharge estate's debts).

8. *Partnership payments.* Payments representing a share of future partnership earnings, received pursuant to a partnership agreement by the successor of a deceased partner, are income in respect of a decedent, taxable as ordinary income. Rev. Rul. 68-195, 1968-1 C.B. 305. *See also* Rev. Rul. 71-507, 1971-2 C.B. 331. There are two important categories of partnership IRD. The first is payments under section 736. Under section 736(a)(1), "payments made in liquidation of the interest of ... a deceased partner" are treated as a "distributive share to the recipient of partnership income if the amount thereof is determined with regard to the income of the partnership." The same result occurs under section 736(b)(2)(A) if the payments are attributable to "unrealized receivables of the partnership." The IRD status of these payments is confirmed by sections 691(e) and 753.

The second category of partnership IRD includes rights to income held by the partnership (such as accounts receivable) that would be IRD if held by the decedent *See, e.g., Woodhall v. Commissioner,* 454 F.2d 226 (9th Cir. 1972); *Quick's Trust v. Commissioner,* 444 F.2d 90 (8th Cir. 1971) (per curiam); *United States v. Ellis,* 264 F.2d 325 (2d Cir. 1959). *Estate of Riegelman v. Commissioner,* 253 F.2d 315 (2d Cir. 1958), frequently quoted, explained:

> [Such payments] were the fruits of the man's professional activity during his lifetime; and this is so whether the payments are considered to be in the nature of additional compensation for services by him during his lifetime or are considered to be in lieu of the chose in action to which his estate would have succeeded in the absence of a specific agreement.

Id. at 319. *See also Black v. Lockhart,* 209 F.2d 308 (8th Cir.), *cert. denied,* 348 U.S. 819 (1954).

9. *Payments under corporate buy-sell agreements.* Similar to *Estate of Riegelman* is *Estate of Cartwright v. Commissioner,* 71 T.C.M. (CCH) 3200 (1996), *aff'd in part and remanded,* 183 F.3d 1034 (9th Cir. 1999). In *Cartwright,* a lawyer who owned more than 70% of the stock in his law firm died. Thereafter, pursuant to a buy-sell agreement, the firm paid his estate more than $5 million. Applying the agreement, the court held that ap-

proximately $1 million was in redemption of decedent's stock and, under Treas. Reg. § 1.691(a)-2(b), Ex. (4), was therefore not taxable as income in respect of a decedent. But the rest of the payment, which the court determined was on account of decedent's claims against the firm for "cases or work in progress," was IRD, taxable to the decedent's estate.

10. *Individual retirement accounts.* In *Bunney v. Commissioner,* 114 T.C. 259 (2000), the court held that a participant spouse was taxable on distributions from his individual retirement account to his former spouse, made in accordance with their divorce decree, even though the account consisted of community property. If *Bunney* is correct, it would appear that the share of a community-property individual retirement account that belongs to a deceased non-participating spouse cannot generate income in respect of the non-participating spouse. Likewise, it would appear that, upon the subsequent death of the participant spouse, there would be only income in respect of the participant spouse.

11. *Covenant not to compete.* In *Coleman v. Commissioner,* 87 T.C.M. (CCH) 1367 (2004), the decedent, upon selling his animal hospital to another veterinarian, agreed not to compete for ten years, in exchange for 120 monthly payments. After the decedent's death, the remaining payments were income in respect of a decedent, taxable as ordinary income, to his son. Neither was the son entitled to a step-up in basis, on account of the payments' estate tax value.

4. Miscellaneous Deferred Receipts

Sun First National Bank v. United States
221 Ct. Cl. 469, 607 F.2d 1347 (1979)

On rehearing, the opinion of the court of November 15, 1978, is withdrawn, and the following opinion is substituted:

FRIEDMAN, *Chief Judge,* delivered the opinion of the court:

This case, before us on cross-motions for summary judgment, presents a difficult question involving the federal income tax liability of a trust for capital gains it received after the death of the settlor who was the income beneficiary of the trust during her lifetime: whether the gains were "income in respect of a decedent" under section 691 of the Internal Revenue Code of 1954, so that the trust was entitled to a deduction for the estate taxes that were attributable to the gains. We answer that question affirmatively and grant the plaintiffs' motion for summary judgment.

I.

In March 1941, Jeanette Andersen established an *inter vivos* trust. The trust income was to be paid to her for life and then to her daughter. Upon the daughter's death, the corpus of the trust was to be distributed to the daughter's children. The principal asset she transferred to the trust was shares of Orlando Daily Newspapers, Inc., the publisher of two daily newspapers in Orlando, Florida, which her husband, Martin Andersen, had given her in 1936. Although the record does not show the value of the stock when Mrs. Andersen transferred it to the trust in 1941, it was valued at $11,000 in the gift tax returns filed in connection with Mr. Andersen's transfer of the stock to his wife in 1936. *Estate of Andersen v. Commissioner,* 32 T.C.M. (CCH) 1164 (1973).

Orlando Newspapers prospered, and in 1965, the trust sold its Orlando stock for more than $6,000,000. The sale price consisted of $1,557,441 in cash and 15 promissory notes payable annually from 1966 through 1980. Each of the first 14 notes was for $242,179.50, and the final note was for $1,453,077. The trustee treated the gain on the sale as income to the trust and reported it on the installment basis, pursuant to section 453 of the Code.

Because of the large increase in the value of the stock between the creation of the trust in 1941 and the sale in 1965, substantial capital gain was realized upon sale of the stock. The trustee treated this gain as income rather than as an addition to the corpus. He paid most of this income to Jeanette Andersen, as income beneficiary. In 1967, a Florida court, in reviewing an accounting Martin Andersen made upon his resignation as trustee, ruled that under Florida law this treatment of the gain was correct.[2] For federal tax purposes the trust reported the entire capital gain from the notes as income for the years 1966 through 1972, and the grantor reported amounts received as income from the trust.

Jeanette Andersen died in December 1968. In her federal estate tax return, her executrix did not include the value of the corpus of the trust. On audit, however, the Commissioner of Internal Revenue included the corpus on the ground that Jeanette Andersen's retention of a life interest in the property she had transferred to the trust made that property part of her estate under section 2036 of the Code. The Tax Court upheld that determination. *Estate of Andersen, supra.*

The trust then filed claims for refund for the years 1969 through 1972. Its theory was that Jeanette Andersen was the constructive owner of the trust property during her lifetime; and that the gain on the sale of the notes that were paid after her death was income in respect of a decedent, so that the recipient of such income (the trust) was entitled under section 691 of the Code to a deduction covering the estate tax paid on that income. The Internal Revenue Service rejected the claim for refund on the ground that the gain on the notes was not income in respect to a decedent. This suit followed.

II.

A. Section 691(a) of the Code generally provides that "income in respect of a decedent" that is not part of the decedent's taxable income in the year of his death is taxable to the recipient of such income in the year of receipt if certain specified conditions are met. Section 691(c) of the Code provides that the recipient of income in respect of a decedent is entitled to a deduction reflecting estate taxes paid by the decedent's estate on any items constituting such income.

In most cases that have arisen under these provisions the government has contended that particular items were income in respect of a decedent and therefore taxable to their recipients, and the recipients have denied that the items were in that category. The present case is the converse situation. Here the recipient (the trust) of the income (the gain on the notes) contends that the gain is income in respect of a decedent so that it may obtain a deduction for the estate taxes paid on the notes, and the government denied that the gain on the notes was income in respect of the decedent.

---

2. Under Florida law, gain on the sale of corpus was to be allocated to corpus, unless the trust instrument indicated a contrary intent on the part of the settlor. FLA. STAT. ANN. §690.04. The Florida court construed the trust instrument in this case as giving the trustee discretion to allocate between corpus and income. *Martin Andersen, as Trustee,* No. 67-1052 (Aug. 8, 1967) at 5. All the interested parties, including Jeanette Andersen, the contingent income beneficiary (her daughter), and the contingent remaindermen (her daughter's children), were represented in the proceeding.

The purpose of these statutory provisions is explained in part in our summary of their legislative history in *Estate of Davison v. United States,* 155 Ct. Cl. 290, 292 F.2d 937, *cert. denied,* 368 U.S. 939 (1961). The income-in-respect-of-a-decedent provision first appeared in the 1939 Code. Prior to 1934, neither a cash basis taxpayer nor his estate was subject to federal income taxes on income he had earned and accrued but not received prior to his death. Congressional dissatisfaction with the discrimination between accrual and cash basis taxpayers and the concomitant loss of revenue from cash basis taxpayers resulted in section 42 of the Revenue Act of 1934. This provision required the decedent to include in his final return income that otherwise would have been reported over several years, and thus subjected such income to higher marginal rates of taxation than if the decedent had lived to receive the income.[7]

Section 126 of the Internal Revenue Code of 1939, added in 1942, eliminated the inequitable pyramiding effect of the accrual-at-death income concept of the prior law by incorporating in the Code the concept of "income in respect of a decedent." Congress understood that term to include items of income that, at the time of death, the decedent had earned or accrued but not yet received. *Grill v. United States,* 157 Ct. Cl. 804, 813, 303 F.2d 922, 927 (1962); *Keck v. Commissioner,* 415 F.2d 531, 534–35(6th Cir. 1969); *Trust Co. of Georgia v. Ross,* 392 F.2d 694, 696 (5th Cir. 1967), *cert. denied,* 393 U.S. 830 (1968); *Estate of Sidles v. Commissioner,* 65 T.C. 873, 880 (1976), *aff'd mem.,* 553 F.2d 102 (8th Cir. 1977), *acq.* 1976-2 CUM. BULL. 2. The purpose of section 126 was to shift the income tax liability for income that the decedent had earned or accrued but not received before death from the decedent to the person who received payment after death.

The shifting of income tax liability to the income recipient would have resulted in a significant difference between the tax treatment of income (1) received after the decedent's death and (2) received by the decedent prior to death and passed through the estate. In the latter situation, the income subject to tax under section 2036 of the Code would be the net amount after income taxes. By shifting income tax liability to the income recipient, section 126 created the likelihood of double taxation. This would result because the gross income the decedent had accrued but not yet received would be included in the estate, and an estate tax would be levied on that amount. The recipient of that income then would pay a tax on the entire income. Thus, the gross amount of income would be subjected to both an estate tax and an income tax. In effect, an income tax would be imposed without any adjustment to reflect the estate taxes already paid upon the income.

Section 691(c) of the Code provides some relief from this double taxation and reduces the disparity in treatment between income received by the decedent and income received directly by his successor. It does this by allowing the income recipient a deduction for estate taxes paid by the estate that are attributable to income received "by reason of the death of decedent." Ferguson, *Income and Deductions in Respect of Decedents and Related Problems,* 25 TAX. L. REV. 5, 146–48 (1969).

B. This case also involves the grantor trust provisions of subpart E of subchapter J of the Code, I.R.C. §§671–78. Those provisions enumerate several circumstances in which the general rule that a trust is to be taxed as a separate entity is "departed from on the theory that to apply [the rule] would improperly permit the grantor or other person who has substantial ownership of the trust property or income to escape tax on income which

---

7. H.R. REP. NO. 2333, 77th Cong., 2d Sess. 48, 83–84, *reprinted in* 1942-2 CUM. BULL. 372, 411, 435–36; S. REP. NO. 1631, 77th Cong., 2d Sess. 100, *reprinted in* 1942-2 CUM. BULL. 504, 579–80.

should rightfully be taxed to him." 6 MERTENS §37.01; Treas. Reg. §§1.671-2(a) and (d), 1.671-3. In effect, the grantor is treated for federal income tax purposes as the owner of the trust property because he has retained a substantial beneficial interest in, or substantial control over, the property.

A grantor is treated under subpart E as the owner of the trust corpus to the extent of his retained interest in the trust. I.R.C. §671. Section 677 of the Code provides that a trust shall be treated under section 671 to the extent that the grantor has retained a right to income. The regulations further provide that in computing taxable income the grantor, not the trust, should include the portion of the trust income to which the grantor retains the right. Treas. Reg. §1.671-3(a).

The parties agree that, since Jeanette Andersen was entitled to the entire income from the trust…, the trust was a grantor trust governed by subpart E. The trust therefore should not have reported the gain reflected in the installment payments as income to the trust; it should simply have attached to the trust's income tax return an informational statement to show receipt of the income and disbursements to the grantor. Treas. Reg. §1.671-4. Similarly, in her federal income tax return Jeanette Andersen should have reported that income as received not from the trust but directly from the maker of the notes.

C. Finally, this case involves the question whether the election of the trust to report the gain on the sale of the stock in 1965 on the installment basis, as section 453 authorized, results in an immediate realization of that gain and a deferral only of its receipt and taxation until each of the notes was paid, or a deferral of both realization and receipt until payment.

If the section 453 election deferred realization of the income until actual receipt of payment, then the installment payments in question were amounts realized after termination of the grantor's interest in the trust. To the extent those payments were allocable to income, they would be directly payable to the grantor's daughter as income beneficiary at the time of realization. Thus, despite the grantor's retained interest and constructive ownership under subpart E, she would have no right to the payments in question and would not be treated as owner of the corpus which produced those payments. If, however, the section 453 election deferred only the taxation of gain, then gain on the stock sale was fully realized in 1965, when Jeanette Andersen had a right to trust income and was constructive owner of the income-producing corpus.

III.

The result in this case turns upon the answers to the following questions: (1) was the entire gain on the sale of the stock in 1965 realized at that time rather than realized *pro tanto* as each installment note was paid; (2) did the trust properly treat the entire gain on sale of the stock as allocable to income rather than to corpus, so that under the grantor trust provisions Mrs. Andersen, the income beneficiary, was viewed as the owner of that portion of the trust, the "income" of which was distributed to her; and (3) was the gain income in respect of a decedent for which the trust was taxable and entitled to a deduction for corresponding estate taxes, because the decedent was constructive owner of the corpus under subpart E? We discuss each of these questions in turn.

A. Section 453 of the Code "was enacted … to relieve taxpayers who adopted [the installment basis of reporting] from having to pay an income tax in the year of sale based on the full amount of anticipated profits when in fact they had received in cash only a small portion of the sales price." *Commissioner v. South Texas Lumber Co.,* 333 U.S. 496, 503 (1948). The provision permits a taxpayer under specified circumstances to "return as income" the amount actually received in the taxable year of receipt. The section enables a taxpayer to defer paying the tax on gain from a sale made on the installment basis until the year in which he receives payment of each installment. The section appears in subchapter E, as part of the Code generally concerned with the timing and method of accounting for income.

Generally, gain realized on a sale of assets is gross income under section 61(a) of the Code. The amount of that gain realized for federal income tax purposes includes any money "received" plus the fair market value of other property "received." I.R.C. §1001(b). Section 1001(c) of the Code states that, unless otherwise provided in the Code, the amount realized is also the amount recognized. I.R.C. §451(a) provides that a taxpayer must account for any amount "received" in the year of receipt unless the taxpayer adopts an alternative method of accounting. The installment obligations in question were received, and their value was fully ascertainable, at the time of sale. The question therefore arises whether section 453 provides an alternative accounting method, an exception to the realization rule, or an exception to the rule for recognition of gain.

The government makes what it concedes to be the novel argument that section 453 of the Code creates an exception to the general rule that income is realized when it is received, so that the gain reflected in each note was neither realized nor recognized until the particular note was paid. The plaintiffs answer that section 453 defers only the recognition of income, not its realization, until the installment obligation is paid; and that the entire gain on the sale of the stock was fully realized in the year of the sale.

We agree with the plaintiffs that section 453 defers the taxation of gain but does not defer the realization of that gain. The language of the section, its place in subchapter E, which is the part of the Code that generally governs the timing and method of accounting, and the elective and remedial nature of the provision all indicate that section 453 was not intended to alter so basic a tax concept as the date of realization of income. 2 MERTENS §15.01. The Commissioner has concurred in this view; he has stated that section 453 "provides an elective method for reporting the income from installment sales of property. That section does not postpone the date of realization of the income but serves merely to postpone the taxation thereof." Rev Rul. 60-68, 1960-1 CUM. BULL. 152.

Section 453 may be held to "postpone the taxation" of income either by deferring the recognition of gain or by providing an alternative method of accounting. We need not decide this question since, under either theory, all the gain on sale of the stock was fully realized in 1965, when Jeanette Andersen was the income beneficiary of the trust governed by section 677 of the Code.

B. The income-in-respect-of-a-decedent provision applies to installment obligations "received by a *decedent* on the sale or other disposition of property." I.R.C. §691(a)(4) (emphasis added). The next question, therefore, is whether the gain realized in 1965 was received by the trust or by Mrs. Andersen at that time. Application of the grantor trust provisions to the facts of this case leads us to conclude that the settlor, rather than the trust, received the gain at the time of sale, and that within the meaning of section 691, the trust "acquired" the remaining installment obligations from the grantor at the time of her death.

The grantor trust provisions were designed to implement and codify the decision of the Supreme Court in *Helvering v. Clifford,* 309 U.S. 331 (1940) and the regulations the Commissioner adopted after that decision. In the *Clifford* case, the Court held that where a husband had created a trust to pay the income to his wife for 5 years and had retained broad powers of control and management of the corpus and over the distribution of the income to the wife, the income from the trust was taxable to the husband. The Court stated the issue as "whether the grantor after the trust had been established may still be treated, under this statutory scheme, as the owner of the corpus." *Id.* at 334. It indicated that, in the "absence of more precise standards or guides supplied by statute or appropriate regulations, the answer to that question must depend on an analysis of the terms of the trust and all the circumstances attendant on its creation and operation." *Id.* at 334–35 (footnote omitted).

Subpart E, like the prior regulations, represents an attempt to implement the rationale of the *Clifford* decision in a manner which would provide greater certainty and predictability in administration of the Code. 6 MERTENS §37.01. Subpart E, like the regulations, defines specific circumstances in which state law and the trust form are disregarded, and the grantor is taxed because he is the real owner of the corpus or some portion thereof. *See* Treas. Reg. §§1.671-1(a) and 1.671-3; Rev. Rul. 79-84, [1979-1 CUM. BULL. 223]; Rev. Rul. 77-402, 1977-2 CUM. BULL. 222; Rev. Rul. 76-100, 1976-1 CUM. BULL. 123; Rev. Rul. 74-613, 1974-2 CUM. BULL. 153.

One of the specific circumstances in which the grantor "shall be treated as the owner of any portion of a trust" is with respect to the portion of the trust corpus whose income "may be distributed" to him in the discretion of a nonadverse party. I.R.C. §677(a). There is no claim that the trustees in this case were adverse parties. The gain on sale of the stock was income under section 61(a) of the Code. The question therefore arises whether the gain was income that the trust could properly distribute to Jeanette Andersen so that under the grantor trust provisions she would be the owner of the portion of the trust corpus which produced the gain represented by the notes.

The Florida circuit court determined that under the trust instrument Martin Andersen as trustee properly had treated the gain on the sale of the stock as income and distributed it to Jeanette.... The government correctly tells us that under *Commissioner v. Estate of Bosch,* 387 U.S. 456 (1967), the state court decision does not bind us. The government has not shown, however, that the Florida court erred. Moreover, *Estate of Bosch* indicates that, in the absence of a ruling of the highest state court, we should decide this question of Florida law as would a state court, giving proper regard to the decision of the lower Florida court. *Id.* at 465. Our analysis of the Florida law and application of that law to the Jeanette Andersen trust causes us to reach the same conclusion as did the Florida court.

As previously noted..., Florida law required that gain realized on the sale of corpus be allocated to corpus unless the trust instrument indicated a contrary intent by the settlor. The Jeanette Andersen trust stated that, "It is my intention that in the management of the Trust Estate the Trustees shall have as full and complete power, authority and discretion as they would have if they were the actual owners thereof." Paragraph 8 of the trust instrument provided that the proceeds the trust received upon certain specified dispositions of trust property (which did not include the 1965 sale of the Orlando Daily Newspapers stock) "be deemed to be principal and corpus of the Trust Estate, and not as income thereof."

A fair reading of these two provisions is that the settlor intended, as the Florida court held, that amounts the trust received under the dispositions that paragraph 8 covers were to be treated as corpus, and left it to the discretion of the trustee to decide how to treat the receipts on other dispositions of trust property. The trustee, Martin Andersen, treated the gain on sale of Orlando Daily Newspapers stock as income rather than corpus. The Florida court approved that treatment in a proceeding in which the settlor appeared and signed the consent decree approving the trustee's accounting. If this treatment of the gain on the sale of the stock was not in accord with Jeanette Andersen's intentions when she established the trust, presumably she would have made this known at the accounting proceeding. Instead, she acquiesced in and thereby approved the allocation of the gain as income rather than corpus.

This case is unlike the situation in *Estate of Bosch,* where the state court proceeding that resulted in a ruling favorable to the taxpayer's position was initiated only after the federal tax controversy had arisen. Here there is no indication or even suggestion that the 1967 Florida court accounting proceeding, which was brought to discharge Martin Andersen as trustee, was in any way motivated by the possibility that treatment of the gain as income rather than corpus might have favorable tax consequences.

C. Our rulings on the two prior issues lead us to conclude that the gain represented by the installment notes was income in respect of a decedent, on which the trust was required to pay the income tax, and that under section 691(c) of the Code the trust was entitled to deduct the portion of the estate tax that was attributable to the gain.

1. Section 691(a)(1)(B) of the Code provides that "the amount of all items of gross income in respect of a decedent" shall be included in the gross income, for the taxable year when received, of "the person who, by reason of the death of the decedent acquires the right to receive the amount...." Section 691(a)(4) provides that the gain on "an installment obligation received by a decedent on the sale or other disposition of property, the income from which was properly reportable by the decedent on the installment basis under section 453" is, "if such obligation is acquired ... by any person by reason of the death of the decedent," income in respect of the decedent for purposes of I.R.C. §691(a)(1).

As explained in point III. B, *supra,* under the grantor trust provisions Jeanette Andersen was treated as the owner of the corpus of the trust. Under I.R.C. §691(a)(4), therefore, she "received" the installment obligations when the stock was sold. The gain on that sale "was properly reportable by the decedent on the installment basis under section 453." Since under the grantor trust provisions Jeanette Andersen was viewed during her life as the owner of the installment obligations for federal tax purposes, those notes were "acquired by" the trust (which was within the statutory category of "any person") "by reason of the death of the decedent."

In other words, even though state law treated the trust as the owner of the notes, under federal tax law Jeanette Andersen was viewed as the owner during her life. The trust therefore acquired the notes from her at the time of, and because of her death. Thus, under section 691(a)(4) of the Code the gain upon the installment obligations as they matured was, for purposes of I.R.C. §691(a)(1), "considered as an item of gross income in respect of the decedent."

Under I.R.C. §691(a)(1)(B), the gain reflected in the unpaid installment notes was gross income not properly includible in the decedent's final return because of the section 453 election. The trust "acquired" the right to receive those amounts by reason of the death of the decedent. Had Jeanette Andersen lived, the trust would have distributed to her all the gain on the installment sale as the notes were paid, in accordance with the decree of the Florida court. As long as the grantor lived, the trust was merely a conduit through which the gain on the sale was distributed to Jeanette Andersen, the person entitled to that gain.

Since the trust properly included those items in its gross income, I.R.C. §691(c) entitled it to deduct the portion of the estate tax attributable to those gains.

2. The result we reach in this case furthers the basic policy of section 691(c) of the Code. That section is designed to provide relief from what many would view as the un-

fair situation of fully subjecting to income tax gain that is earned or accrued but not received by a decedent during his lifetime, where that gain has already been subjected fully to an estate tax. That is precisely the situation in this case. For under the decision of the Tax Court, the total value of the installment payments, most of which constituted gain, were included in Jeanette Andersen's taxable estate.

The effect of our decision here is to avoid the unfairness and harshness which would result if the entire gross amount of gain on the sale of Orlando Daily Newspapers stock was subjected first to the estate tax and then to the income tax without any deduction to reflect the prior estate tax levy on the same amount.[12]

The defendant's motion for summary judgment is denied, the plaintiffs' motion for summary judgment is granted, and the case is remanded to the Trial Division to determine the amount of recovery pursuant to Rule 131(c).

SKELTON, *Senior Judge,* dissenting:

* * *

The facts show that Mrs. Andersen's husband, Martin, gave the shares of stock to her in 1941. Later, marital trouble developed between them and Martin became fearful that a divorce might ensue and that his wife could remarry thus making it possible for her new husband to control the stock. Accordingly, he recommended to Mrs. Andersen on the advice of counsel that the stock be placed in an irrevocable trust with a reservation of the income to Mrs. Andersen for life and thereafter to Martin and, at his death, to their daughter. The trust was to terminate at the death of the daughter and the corpus was to be distributed to the daughter's children. If there were no children, the corpus was to be distributed to various other remaindermen. These were the purposes of the trust. An attorney drew up the trust instrument in accordance with the foregoing purposes and explained it fully to Mrs. Andersen, and "especially the fact that Jane [Mrs. Andersen] would have to part with all future control of the shares." Mrs. Andersen agreed and signed the trust instrument for the purposes stated above. Martin was named as trustee and Mrs. Andersen transferred the stock to him as the fiduciary of the Jeanette Andersen Trust in 1941.

Under the well-established law of trusts, Jeanette Andersen divested herself of ownership of the stock when she transferred it to the trust.

After the transfer of the stock to the trust, new shares of the stock were issued in the name of the trustee. It is a well-settled principle of trust law that when property is placed in trust, the legal title to the property is vested in the trustee as a fiduciary of the trust.... The vesting of legal title in the trustee as fiduciary has the effect of making the trust the owner of the property. Therefore, after the transfer, the legal title and ownership of the shares of stock were held by the Jeanette Andersen Trust. Such a trust is recognized as a taxable entity separate and apart from the grantor. See ... 26 U.S.C. §641.

It is well established that when a trust is created the trustee has only the powers and authority given to him by the settlor trust instrument, together with implied powers which are necessary to carry out the purposes of the trust. *See* BOGART [sic], LAW OF TRUSTS, §88, 4th Ed. 1963; RESTATEMENT OF TRUSTS, §186, 2d Ed. 1959.

Obviously, the Jeanette Andersen trust was a "grantor trust" governed by Subpart E of the Code (i.e., §§671–677). §677(a)(1) of the Code provides that the grantor "shall be treated

---

12. In view of our decision on this issue there is no occasion to reach plaintiffs' alternative contention that, if the gain on the installment notes were not income in respect of a decedent, the trust was entitled to a stepped-up basis for the property under I.R.C. §§1014(a) and (b)(9).

as the owner of any portion of a trust" whose income may be distributed to the grantor. Clearly, the fact that Mrs. Andersen was "treated" as the owner of the trust corpus for tax purposes did not make her the owner for the purposes of determining whether income received by the trust after her death was income in respect of a decedent.

In our prior opinion in this case, reported in 218 Ct.Cl. 339, 587 F. 2d 1073 (1978), we stated correctly:

> "That section [§677(a)(1)], however, must be read in conjunction with section 671, which limits and qualifies it. Section 671 provides that when it is specified under subpart (E) (which includes section 677) of subchapter J of the Code (which deals with the taxation of trusts) that a grantor (or other person) should be treated as the owner of trust property, the items of income, deduction and credits against a tax of the trust shall be included in computing the taxable income of the grantor or other person.

> "Section 671 is the operative provision of subpart (E); it specifies the result when a grantor is treated under subpart (E) as the owner of trust property. Section 677 is one of six subsections of subpart (E) that describe particular situations in which the grantor (or other person) is deemed to be the owner of trust property.

> "Such attribution of ownership, however, is for the purpose of shifting the tax incidence of the trust income from the trust to the grantor or other person. Under this provision Jeanette Andersen would have been liable during her life for the income the trust realized upon payment of the notes, because section 677 would have attributed the notes to her. But that section did not make her 'the owner of' the trust property for purposes of determining whether the income the trust received from such property after her death was income in respect of a decedent under section 691. Section 677 made her the owner of the property only for the purpose of shifting the trust income to her during her lifetime, as section 671 provides." *Id.* at 351–52, 587 F. 2d at 1079–1080.

Thus, §677 of the Code has a very limited application. It is used to shift trust income to the grantor for income tax purposes. It does *not transfer ownership.*

The tax law does not create legal and property interests; it merely taxes them....

Applying this principle to the case before us, it appears that Mrs. Andersen was taxable during her lifetime on the trust's income under §§671 and 677 of the Code because of her retained life estate. The Code was applied to the state-created property interest and it was taxed accordingly. Even though §677 states that she was "treated as the owner" of the trust corpus, that section does *not* make her the legal owner for all purposes because federal tax law does *not* create legal interests — it merely taxes them. The trust instrument stated that it was to be construed according to Florida law, and, therefore, the ownership of the trust corpus, as will be explained in more detail later, was vested in the trust under Florida law. As a result, Mrs. Andersen did *not* own any of the installment notes which made up the trust corpus and, consequently, the income from such notes that was unpaid and not due at the time of her death could not have been income in respect of a decedent.

* * *

[A]lthough the grantor is "treated" as the owner of the trust corpus for the taxation purposes of §§671–677 of the Code, the grantor is *not* made the legal owner of the trust corpus for other purposes by these sections of the Code.

In the instant case, the trust owned and controlled the stock from the time the trust was created in 1941 until the stock was sold in 1965, a period of 24 years, without any control or attempted control by Mrs. Andersen. The trust, and not Mrs. Andersen, sold the stock in 1965. The notes were payable to the trust and not to Mrs. Andersen. As the notes were paid, the payments were made to the trust, not to Mrs. Andersen. The trust, and not Mrs. Andersen, made the election to have the notes paid on the installment plan. The notes were always in the possession of the trust. As a matter of fact, there is no evidence that Mrs. Andersen ever claimed to be the owner of the notes. She did not dispose of them in her will. Neither did her daughter-executrix claim that the notes belonged to Mrs. Andersen's estate, as they were not listed in the estate tax returns that she filed. In her suit in the Tax Court the executrix did not claim that the notes belonged to Mrs. Andersen's estate. In fact, she stipulated in that court that they belonged to the trust. Had the notes belonged to Mrs. Andersen's estate, there would not have been any need to file the Tax Court suit.

* * *

The majority opinion states that the trust "acquired" the notes from Mrs. Andersen at her death. However, the majority fails to state how this transfer was accomplished. If Mrs. Andersen were the owner of the notes, her estate would own them at her death unless she disposed of them otherwise in her will. The facts show she left a will which named her daughter as executrix because her daughter filed the tax court suit in that capacity. The notes were not listed in the estate tax return as a part of Mrs. Andersen's property. If she owned the notes, in the absence of some testamentary transfer to the trust in accordance with Florida law, the trust could not have acquired the notes from her at her death. State law controls the transfer of property interests, *not* tax law.

The majority errs in adopting the argument of the Trustees that the notes were income and not corpus of the trust during the lifetime of Mrs. Andersen and that she owned them until her death, when somehow at the time of her death (as if by magic) the notes ceased to be income and became corpus of the trust, and by some unexplained method, which was not by a testamentary bequest or any other known or proven conveyance, the ownership of the notes was transferred from Mrs. Andersen's estate to the trust. Such an argument is pure fiction and cannot be supported by the facts or the law.

* * *

It may be that the majority became so engrossed and occupied in the herculean task of construing and interpreting the complicated tax laws involved here that they lost sight of the simple facts in the case that should control its disposition. At first, the case seemed to be very complex and difficult. Actually, it could and should be decided by several simple sentences, such as:

> "Mrs. Andersen did not own the notes at the time of her death, and, therefore, the payment of the notes after her death was not income in respect of a decedent. Consequently, the trust is not entitled to deduct the estate tax from its income taxes under §691(c) of the Code. Accordingly, the Government's motion for summary judgment should be granted."

I would deny the petition for rehearing and approve our prior decision granting the Government's Motion for Summary Judgment.

Illustrative Material

1. The Court of Claims' prior opinion in *Sun First National* is at 218 Ct. Cl. 339, 587 F.2d 1073 (1978). In result and much of its reasoning it is consistent with Judge Skelton's dissent.

2. The Installment Sales Revision Act of 1980 amended section 691(a)(4) by substituting "reportable by the decedent on the installment method under section 453" for "received

by a decedent on the sale or other disposition of property, the income from which was properly reportable by the decedent on the installment basis under section 453." By removing the requirement that the installment obligation be "received by a decedent," did not Congress make it a little easier, on a literal basis, to defend the Court of Claims' result? But is *Sun First National* based on a literal reading of the Code? What of the continuing requirement of section 691(a)(4) that the installment obligation be "acquired . . . by reason of the death of the decedent or by bequest, devise, or inheritance"? *See generally* Ascher, *When to Ignore Grantor Trusts: The Precedents, a Proposal, and a Prediction,* 41 Tax L. Rev. 253 (1986).

3. Sometimes installment obligations are cancelled (either by their own terms or by will) at the death of the obligee. In Rev. Rul. 86-72, 1986-1 C.B. 253, the I.R.S., relying on section 691(a)(5), ruled that such a cancellation caused recognition of the section 453 gain inherent in the cancelled installment obligation. That gain was taxable to the obligee's estate as income in respect of a decedent.

The Tax Court, however, in *Estate of Frane v. Commissioner,* 98 T.C. 341 (1992), *aff'd in part and rev'd in part,* 998 F.2d 567 (8th Cir. 1993), refused to follow Rev. Rul. 86-72. In *Estate of Frane,* the decedent had sold property to his children in exchange for self-cancelling installment notes ("SCINs"), under which the children's obligations ceased immediately upon the decedent's death. In a questionable opinion, from which five judges dissented, the Tax Court determined that section 453B(a) and (f) together operated to cause *the decedent himself* to realize gain in the amount of the difference between the face amount of the notes and his basis in them. Thus, such gain was reportable, not as income in respect of a decedent under section 691(a)(2) and (5), but instead on the decedent's final return. On appeal, the Eighth Circuit affirmed the portion of *Frane* holding that gain occurs upon the death of the obligee of a SCIN but reversed the portion denying the resulting gains section 691 treatment. Citing Rev. Rul. 86-72 with approval, the Eighth Circuit held that the gains were income in respect of a decedent, properly includible in the gross income of the decedent's estate, rather than by the decedent himself. *See generally* Dorocak, *Potential Penalties and Ethical Problems of a Filing Position: Not Reporting Gain on the Expiration of a SCIN after* Estate of Frane v. Commissioner, 23 U. Dayton L. Rev. 217 (1998).

4. In *Muller v. United States,* 830 F. Supp. 1259 (D. Minn. 1993), the decedent cancelled, by will, all installment obligations that remained unpaid at his death. Income in respect of a decedent did not result, however, because the decedent had elected out of the installment method during his lifetime. As a result, payment of the installment obligations would not have caused the decedent to realize income, had he lived to receive it.

5. Rev. Rul. 76-100, 1976-1 C.B. 123, held that a surviving spouse's community property interest in installment obligations owned by the surviving spouse and the deceased spouse also constituted income in respect of a decedent. To the same effect are Rev. Rul. 68-506, 1968-2 C.B. 332, with respect to the surviving spouse's community property interest in a qualified retirement plan, and *Collins v. United States,* 318 F. Supp. 382 (C.D. Cal. 1970), *aff'd per curiam,* 448 F.2d 787 (9th Cir. 1971), with respect to a surviving spouse's community property interest in a nonqualified plan. The result is to deny the surviving spouse the step-up in basis that would otherwise be available under section 1014(b)(6). *See* I.R.C. §1014(c). *Stanley v. Commissioner,* 338 F.2d 434 (9th Cir. 1964), is in accord. In *Stanley* the court held that a widow's community property share of installment obligations did not receive the section 1014 step-up in basis. Admitting that, "read literally" section 1014 allowed the step-up for the widow's share, the court construed section 1014(c) as denying the step-up, in order to avoid the disparate treatment of the dece-

dent's and the surviving spouse's community property shares that section 1014(b)(6) was designed to avoid. Though the court categorized the widow's share as "income in respect of a decedent," it did so "solely for purposes of subsection (a) of section 1014." 338 F.2d at 438. It would therefore be more accurate to say that the court merely read section 1014(c) expansively, so as to refer not only to section 691 property but also to section 1014(b)(6) property. In short, although there is authority for the proposition that the surviving spouse's share of community property income does not receive a step-up in basis at the death of the first spouse to die, it appears unnecessary (and incorrect) to refer to the surviving spouse's share as income in respect of a decedent. *See* Treas. Reg. §1.691(a)-1(b). To the same effect as *Stanley* are *Johnson v. United States,* 64-2 U.S.T.C. ¶9655 (N.D. Tex. 1964), and *Holt v. United States,* 39 Fed. Cl. 525, 97-2 U.S.T.C. ¶60,293 (1997).

<hr>

Revenue Ruling 60-227
1960-1 C.B. 262

Advice has been requested with respect to the Federal income tax treatment of certain royalty payments attributable to patent licensing contracts executed by an inventor, now deceased, under the circumstances described below.

The decedent, an inventor, had entered into nonexclusive licensing agreements with various corporations in 1957 covering the manufacture and sale of articles under a patent which he owned. In consideration thereof, the corporations agreed to pay the taxpayer specified royalties upon the sale of the articles.

The decedent died in the taxable year 1958. Under the terms of his will, the afore-mentioned patent and licensing agreements were devised to a trust. Under the terms of the trust indenture, the trustee, which was also the executor of the decedent's estate, was empowered to do all acts necessary for the proper control and management of the trust property, including the power to collect the royalty payments due or accrued under the licensing agreements at or after the decedent's death and to pay such income in regular installments to the decedent's widow.

Section 691(a) of the Internal Revenue Code of 1954 provides, in part, that the amount of all items of gross income in respect of a decedent which are now properly includible in respect of the taxable period in which falls the date of his death or a prior period shall be included in the gross income, for the taxable year when received, of either the estate of the decedent, if the right to acquire the amount is acquired by the estate from the decedent, or such person who, according to the provisions of that section, acquires the right to receive the amount.

The executor contends that the instant case is analogous to the factual situation in Revenue Ruling 57-544, C.B. 1957-2, 361, and, therefore, that the royalty payments due and accrued at the date of the inventor's death, which were paid to the executor, and the royalty payments received after his death from the licensees, on sales made by them after his death, constitute income in respect of a decedent under section 691(a) of the Code.

In Revenue Ruling 57-544, an author entered into an agreement with certain publishers in 1932 whereby he transferred to the publishers the sole right to publish his manuscript, including all revisions and future editions. The copyright was taken out in the name of the publishers. The author agreed to revise the book or cooperate with the publishers in the revision of the book whenever required. The publishers agreed to pay the author a royalty of ten percent of the retail selling price. The author died in 1952, and in that year his widow was appointed executrix of his estate.

Since the author's estate was the sole owner of all rights, title and interest arising out of the contract, and the publishers desired to publish future editions of the books, the widow, as executrix of the author's estate and a trade association entered into an agreement with the publishers in 1953 whereby they agreed to prepare and supply to the publishers later editions in accordance with the terms of the previously executed contract. The trade association agreed to provide the services of an editor whose name, together with the name of the author, would appear on the title page of the book. The publishers agreed to pay the executrix and the association specified royalties, by separate checks, based on the selling price of the book. The widow died in 1955, and, pursuant to her will, the author's daughter was receiving the royalty payments under the contract executed in 1953.

Revenue Ruling 57-544 holds that the royalty payments being received by the daughter under the contract executed by her deceased mother, as executrix of the estate of her father, constitute taxable income to her under the provisions of section 691(a). Under section 691(c) of the Code, the daughter was entitled to deduct that portion of the Federal estate tax imposed upon her mother's estate which was attributable to the inclusion in the estate of the right to receive such income.

It is the position of the Internal Revenue Service that for an item to constitute "income in respect of a decedent," within the meaning of section 691(a) of the Code, it must be an item to which a decedent was entitled in the sense that he had a right to the item, it having been earned during his lifetime, even though actual receipt thereof or determination of the amount thereof might be contingent in whole or in part.

In Revenue Ruling 57-544, the contract entered into by and between the author and the publishing company constituted a "sale" by the author of his manuscript. What the author received while he was alive was his agreed share of the proceeds of the sale of the book. Accordingly, all royalties were items to which the author had a right, as having been earned in his lifetime, and royalties due and accrued at the date of his death and royalties accrued after his death constitute income in respect of a decedent under section 691(a) of the Code. Likewise, royalty payments received under the 1953 contract, signed by the widow as executrix, constitute income in respect of a decedent since the deceased author's right to royalties, although contingent as to amount, was established upon the sale of the manuscript to the publishers. The 1953 contract, while it modified the original contract, did not alter the fact that the payments to the decedent author's successors in interest continued to be in respect of his efforts and "earned" during his lifetime.

Since the contract right at issue in Revenue Ruling 57-544 was distributed by the author's estate to the widow individually subsequent to the signing of the supplemental contract in 1953 and, in turn, was distributed to the daughter by her mother's estate, the amounts being received by the daughter were concluded to be income in respect of a decedent includible in her gross income under section 691(a) of the Code.

Based on the foregoing, it is held in the instant case that the royalty payments due and accrued at the date of the inventor's death, which were paid to the decedent's executor, constitute income in respect of a decedent under section 691(a) of the Code, includible in the gross income of the decedent's estate, since such items of income are considered as having been earned during the inventor's lifetime. Under section 691(c) of the Code, the estate is entitled to deduct that portion of the Federal estate tax imposed upon the estate which was attributable to the inclusion in such estate of the right to receive such amount.

However, those royalty payments paid after the inventor's death, and attributable to sales concluded by the licensees subsequent to the date of his death, cannot be considered as income in respect of a decedent, but are items of ordinary income includible in the gross income of the recipient, under section 61(a) of the Code, since the decedent had not sold the patent and, therefore, had not earned the payments during his lifetime. The licensees were granted only certain nonexclusive rights in the inventor's patent. There was neither a transfer of all of the substantial rights to the patent nor a transfer of an undivided interest therein. Thus, with respect to the royalty payments accrued after the date of death, Revenue Ruling 57-544 is clearly distinguishable from the instant case.

In summary, it is concluded that if a contract entered into between an inventor and a manufacturer constitutes merely a "license" to use the inventor's patent in return for the payment of royalties, and not a "sale," royalty payments due and accrued under the contract at the date of death of the inventor constitute income in respect of a decedent under section 691(a) of the Code. Where the contract constitutes a "license," royalty payments accrued after the date of death of the inventor are ordinary income includible in the gross income of the recipient under section 61 of the Code.

Illustrative Material

1. The crucial distinction between Rev. Rul. 60-227 and Rev. Rul. 57-544 appears to be that between a lease and a sale. In *Stephen H. Dorsey,* 49 T.C. 606 (1968), the court held that continuing payments made by AMF to the estates of former shareholders of Automatic Pinsetter Company pursuant to an assignment by APC to AMF of its patents for the automatic pinsetting machine used in bowling were income in respect of a decedent. The court stated:

> There was clearly a sale of the "Pinsetter" patents [by APC to AMF] in exchange for cash, stock in AMF, and a percentage of profits from [AMF's subsequent] sale or lease of automatic pinsetting machines.... This is in sharp contrast to Rev. Rul. 60-227, 1960-1 C.B. 262, ... where the decedent never *sold* the patent in question but merely granted to his licensees certain nonexclusive rights thereto.

49 T.C. at 633 (emphasis in original). In contrast, in *Grill v. United States,* 157 Ct. Cl. 804, 303 F.2d 922 (1962) (per curiam), the court held that royalties paid by Loew's to a testamentary trust as rental for *Gone with the Wind* were not income in respect of a decedent. Similarly, in Rev. Rul. 66-348, 1966-2 C.B. 433, the I.R.S. ruled that mineral royalties earned after the decedent's death were not income in respect of a decedent. This was true even with respect to royalties earned between date of death and the estate tax alternate valuation date, when the election was made. In Private Letter Ruling 9326043 (1993), an author contracted with publishers and others to exploit various literary works. The Service ruled that the contracts were "licenses," rather than "sales," of the author's copyrights. Therefore, post-death payments under the contracts were not taxable as income in respect of a decedent. To similar effect is Private Letter Ruling 9549023 (1995).

2. Amounts collected by an estate on account of litigation involving a claim for patent infringement commenced by the decedent were income in respect of a decedent includible in the gross income of the estate. Rev. Rul. 55-463, 1955-2 C.B. 277.

3. Subsequent insurance reimbursement of medical expenses incurred, paid, and deducted by the decedent on his final income tax return was income in respect of a decedent includible in the gross income of the estate. Rev. Rul. 78-292, 1978-2 C.B. 233. The I.R.S. noted that the decedent had been entitled to the reimbursement during his lifetime. Had such reimbursement been received by the decedent, it would have been includible in his gross income under Treas. Reg. §1.213-1(g)(1).

4. Accounts receivable owned by a decedent are items of income in respect of a decedent. Thus, if a decedent's estate sells receivables, it is subject to taxation on the sales proceeds to the extent the proceeds exceed the decedent's basis. *Dixon v. United States,* 96 F. Supp. 986 (E.D. Ky. 1950), *aff'd per curiam,* 192 F.2d 82 (6th Cir. 1951).

5. Treas. Reg. §1.691(a)-1(b) defines income in respect of a decedent by reference to "the method of accounting employed by the decedent." What if the decedent employed an improper accounting method? Does that method of accounting affect the identification of income in respect of a decedent? In *Poorbaugh v. United States,* 423 F.2d 157 (3d Cir. 1969), the decedent ran a business that involved sales from inventory. He thus was required to use the accrual method of accounting. *See* Treas. Reg. §1.446-1(c)(2)(i). He nonetheless used the cash receipts method. Under the accrual method, the accounts receivable due him at his death would have been includible in his final return and thus would not have been income in respect of a decedent. But under the cash receipts method, the accounts receivable were not reportable on his final return and therefore were income in respect of a decedent. The Third Circuit held that, even though the decedent's method of accounting was improper, it controlled the identification of income in respect of a decedent. The opinion emphasized the need for consistency in accounting.

6. In Private Letter Ruling 9043068 (1990), the I.R.S. ruled that the sale of artwork created by the decedent did not result in income in respect of a decedent, where the artwork had been the subject of neither negotiations nor binding contractual arrangements prior to the decedent's death. Instead, the artwork received a step-up in basis under section 1014.

7. In *Krakowski v. Commissioner,* 65 T.C.M. (CCH) 2969 (1993), the treasurer of a political candidate's campaign committee embezzled committee funds. Thereafter, the treasurer repaid a portion of these funds to the candidate's widow, who, as sole beneficiary of the candidate's estate, believed she was entitled to them. The Tax Court held that these amounts constituted income in respect of a decedent, taxable to the widow under section 691 and the claim of right doctrine in the year in which she received them.

8. In *Kitch v. Commissioner,* 104 T.C. 1 (1995), the Tax Court held that, when an estate satisfied its decedent's overdue alimony obligations to the estate of an ex-spouse, the payments were subject to taxation, as alimony, in the hands of the payee estate as income in respect of a decedent. (Pre-1985 versions of sections 71 and 682(b) applied.) Thus, the payee estate was subject to taxation on the entire amount of the payments as ordinary income, rather than as limited and characterized under section 662 by the distributable net income of the payor estate. The Tenth Circuit affirmed but seems to have applied post-1984 versions of all relevant statutes. *Kitch v. Commissioner,* 103 F.3d 104 (10th Cir. 1996).

B. Deductions in Respect of a Decedent

Internal Revenue Code:
  Section 691(b)

Regulation:
  Section 1.691(b)-1

Revenue Ruling 58-69
1958-1 C.B. 254

Advice has been requested relative to the circumstances under which an executor or administrator of an estate is entitled to deduct real estate taxes paid by the estate on real property not subject to administration.

The question as to the deductibility of real estate taxes arises in those cases where such taxes are a charge against the property at the date of death of the decedent and are paid by the executor or administrator of the estate.

Section 691(b) of the Internal Revenue Code of 1954 provides that the amount of any deduction specified in section 164 (relating to taxes) in respect of a decedent which is not properly allowable to the decedent in respect of the taxable period in which falls the date of his death, or a prior period, shall be allowed to the estate of the decedent for the taxable year in which paid, if the estate is liable to discharge the obligation.

It is well established that the allowance of a deduction for payment of taxes must be based upon liability for such taxes. If the real estate was not subject to the possession of the executor, that is, not subject to administration, then the executor is entitled to a deduction for the real estate taxes paid by the estate only to the extent that such taxes were a charge against the real estate at the date of death of the decedent.

If under the laws of the particular jurisdiction the executor is not required to pay the real estate taxes and has not taken over the property under court order, but pays the taxes, he would not be entitled to a deduction for the taxes. However, if the payment by the executor was in behalf of a beneficiary of the estate who was or would be entitled to income from the estate, then the deduction would be allowable under section 661 of the Code if the payment of the taxes was made by the executor in lieu of a direct payment to the beneficiary.

In view of the foregoing, it is held that in those jurisdictions which require the executor or administrator of the estate of a decedent to pay real estate taxes which, prior to death of the decedent, have become a charge against the real estate of the decedent, the tax so paid by the executor or administrator is allowable under the provisions of section 691(b)(1)(A) of the Code as a deduction on the fiduciary income tax return of the estate for the taxable year in which paid. On the other hand, if the executor or administrator is not required to pay the taxes, but does so, then if the payment was in behalf of a beneficiary entitled to the income from the estate a deduction would be allowable under section 661 of the Code if made in lieu of a direct payment to the beneficiary.

Illustrative Material

1. In *Greggar P. Sletteland,* 43 T.C. 602 (1965), the issue was whether a section 691(b) deduction was allowable for payment of notes endorsed by a decedent in his business. The court held that the deduction was available only for pre-death interest paid on the notes:

> It is true that section 691(b) permits an estate to deduct amounts paid by it in respect of a decedent's obligations, if the decedent had never taken a deduction and would have been able to do so if he had made payment prior to his death. However, section 691(b) is specifically limited to deductions ... authorized by Code sections ... 162, 163, 164, 212, or 611. In the instant case, [the decedent's] payment of the principal amount of his obligations on the notes would have been deductible either under section 165 (as a loss) or under [a predecessor of] section 166(f) as a bad debt; and therefore these relief provisions would not apply to the amounts paid by the estate in discharge of the principal amount of [his] obligations on the notes. [S]ection 691(b) would furnish warrant for the estate's deduction of the interest on these notes, since interest is deductible under section 163, one of the sections specifically mentioned in section 691(b).

43 T.C. at 609. Similarly, Rev. Rul. 74-175, 1974-1 C.B. 52, denied an estate deductions for decedent's capital losses under section 165 and his net operating losses under section 172.

2. In Rev. Rul. 71-422, 1971-2 C.B. 255, the decedent, an accrual-method taxpayer, had contested a proposed deficiency with respect to his federal income tax. When his estate conceded and paid the deficiency, the estate was entitled, under section 691(b), to deduct the interest it paid on the deficiency, for the period prior to the decedent's death. The I.R.S. reasoned that the decedent's liability for interest had been "contingent only" during his lifetime and therefore not deductible by him. But, as an obligation of the estate, the interest became, by analogy to Treas. Reg. §1.691(a)-1(b)(3), deductible when paid.

3. In Rev. Rul. 71-423, 1971-2 C.B. 255, an estate paid for the services of a guardian appointed to care for the person and property of the decedent prior to her death, and for the services of the guardian's lawyer. The I.R.S. ruled that the portion of such expenses that was "ordinary and necessary" and "attributable to the production or collection of income, or for the management, conservation, or maintenance of property held for the production of income" was deductible under section 691(b) by the estate, because it would have been deductible by the decedent under section 212 if paid by her. However, that portion of such expenses attributable to "the care and maintenance of the ward, and for the caring and disposing of personal property that was not held for the production of income" was not deductible.

Revenue Ruling 76-498
1976-2 C.B. 199

Advice has been requested whether, under the circumstances described below, statutory commissions paid by the estate of a decedent to the trustees of a grantor trust created by the decedent, are deductible under section 691(b) of the Internal Revenue Code of 1954, for income tax purposes, as well as under section 2053(a) for estate tax purposes.

In January 1970 the decedent, *A*, a resident of the State of New York, created a trust, the corpus of which consisted of income producing assets and certain real property not held for the production of income. Under the terms of the trust agreement, the trustees were directed to hold the properties of the trust, invest and reinvest the same, collect the income therefrom, and pay the entire net income, plus any principal as they might deem advisable, to or for the benefit of *A*. Upon *A*'s death, the trustees were directed to distribute the principal of the trust to such persons as *A* might direct or appoint by will or, in default of such appointment, to the legal representative of the decedent's estate. Thus, *A* was treated as the owner of the trust under section 677 of the Code, and under section 671 all items of income, deductions, and credits against tax of the trust were included in computing the taxable income and credits of *A* to the extent that such items would be taken into account in computing taxable income or credits against tax of an individual. *A* used the cash receipts and disbursements method of accounting.

A died on July 1, 1974, and exercised the power of appointment by will over the trust corpus, directing that the income producing assets of the trust be paid to the executors of *A*'s estate and that the real property be conveyed absolutely to *A*'s children. In addition *A* directed that all *A*'s just debts be paid out of the estate.

After *A*'s death, the trustees of the trust liquidated the income producing assets of the trust, filed their final account under the applicable provisions of New York law, and thereafter delivered the corpus of the trust to the parties entitled to it under the will.

Under New York law, Civil Practice Law and Rules section 8005 (McKinney 1975), which refers to the Surrogate's Court Procedure Act section 2309 (Mc-Kinney 1967), the trustee of a trust is entitled to: (1) annual commissions at certain statutory rates; and (2) on the settlement of the trustee's account, reasonable and necessary expenses actually paid by the trustee, in addition to a commission from principal (at the rate of one percent) for paying out all sums of money that are principal. This statutory schedule of compensation, including the paying out commission, has been interpreted by New York courts as an effort to compensate trustees for the reasonable value of all services performed during the trust period, not merely the specific acts to which the statute refers. *See Matter of Roth*, 53 Misc. 2d 1066, 281 N.Y.S. 2d 225 (1967).

The estate paid all the annual commissions due, and all the expenses and paying out commissions due at the termination of the trust. The payment of such claims was allowable under New York law.

Section 691(b) of the Code provides that the amount of any deduction specified in section 212, in respect of a decedent, that is not properly allowable to the decedent for the taxable period in which falls the date of death, or a prior period, shall be allowed to the estate of the decedent in the taxable year when paid, or, if the estate of the decedent is not liable to discharge the obligation to which the deduction relates, the deduction shall be allowed to the person who by reason of the death of the decedent or by bequest, devise, or inheritance acquires, subject to such obligation, from the decedent an interest in property of the decedent.

Section 1.691(b)-1(a) of the Income Tax Regulations provides that the expenses described in section 212 of the Code that are deductible under section 691(b) are those for which the decedent was liable but which were not properly allowable as a deduction in the decedent's last taxable years or any prior taxable year.

Section 212 of the Code provides that in the case of an individual, there shall be allowed as a deduction all the ordinary and necessary expenses paid or incurred during the taxable year for the production or collection of income, or for the management, conservation, or maintenance of property held for the production of income. Trustee's fees are deductible under section 212, if they are ordinary and necessary and paid during the taxable year. *See Trust of Bingham v. Commissioner*, 325 U.S. 365 (1945), 1945 C.B. 103.

Since *A* was treated as owner of the trust, *A* would have been treated as being liable for the commissions, if *A* had lived, to the extent that the commissions were for services rendered by the trustees prior to *A*'s death. If *A* had lived and paid the commissions and expenses *A* would have been allowed a deduction under section 212 of the Code for the commissions and expenses to the extent that they were attributable to the management of the income producing assets. Since the real property in the trust was not held for the production of income, the portion of the statutory commissions and expenses attributable to it would not have been deductible by *A*.

Accordingly, to the extent that the statutory commissions and expenses are attributable to the income producing assets of the trust and represent a fee for services rendered through July 1, 1974, the date of the decedent's death, the commissions and expenses paid by the estate to the trustee may be deducted under section 691(b) of the Code for income tax purposes. *See* Rev. Rul 71-423, 1971-2 C.B. 255. The statutory commissions and expenses paid by the estate to the trustees for services rendered after *A*'s death on July 1, 1974, are not deductible under section 691(b). An allocation of the commissions between the period before and after death is therefore necessary. Commissions that represent compensation for the services made necessary by *A*'s death cannot be deducted under section 691(b). Such services include activities in terminating the trust and making a final distribution and accounting. Under New York law the trustees are entitled to the reasonable value of such services, limited by the statutory amount. *In re Barnett's Will,* 231 N.Y.S. 2d 471 (1962).

Section 642(g) of the Code and section 1.642(g)-2 of the regulations provide, in part, that amounts allowable under section 2053 or 2054 as a deduction in computing the taxable estate of a decedent shall not be allowed as a deduction in computing the taxable income of the estate or any other person, but that this provision shall not apply with respect to deductions allowed under section 691.

Under section 2053(a)(3) of the Code, claims against the estate can be deducted from the gross estate to determine the taxable estate, to the extent that such claims are allowable by the laws of the jurisdiction under which the estate is being administered.

The portion of all the commissions and expenses that is allocable to services performed by the trustees prior to *A*'s death should be treated as a personal obligation of the decedent. Accordingly, the statutory commissions and expenses accrued prior to *A*'s death but paid by the estate are deductible for estate tax purposes under section 2053(a)(3) of the Code as claims against the estate. Also, under section 642(g), the deduction of such commissions and expenses under section 691(b) for income tax purposes (to the extent attributable to the income producing assets) is not precluded by the same deduction under section 2053 for estate tax purposes. *See* Rev. Rul. 71-422, 1971-2 C.B. 255.

Under section 2053(a)(2) of the Code, administration expenses of the estate can be deducted from the gross estate in the same manner as claims against the estate. In addition, under section 2053(b), and section 20.2053-8 of the Estate and Gift Tax Regulations, amounts representing expenses incurred in administering property not subject to claims that is included in the gross estate can be deducted, in determining the taxable estate, to the same extent such amounts would be allowable as a deduction under subsection (a) if such property were subject to claims, and such amounts are paid before the expiration of the period of limitation for assessment provided in section 6501.

Since *A* directed that the income producing assets be turned over to the estate, those assets are property subject to claims, that is, property includible in the gross estate that, under applicable state law, would bear the burden of the payment of deductions in the final adjustment and settlement of the decedent's estate. See section 20.2053-1(c) of the regulations. However, although the value of the real property is includible in *A*'s estate under section 2036 of the Code, it is not subject to claims because title passes to the designated beneficiaries as remaindermen of the trust. *See In re Rolston's Estate,* 170 Misc. 548, 10 N.Y.S. 2d 660 (1939); and *Chase National Bank of City of New York v. Central Hanover Bank & Trust Co.,* 265 App. Div. 434, 39 N.Y.S. 2d 541 (1943).

Accordingly, the statutory commissions and expenses that are allocable to services performed by the trustees after *A*'s death and that were paid by the estate are deductible by the estate under section 2053 of the Code as administration expenses. The commissions and expenses attributable to the income producing assets turned over to the estate are deductible under section 2053(a)(2), and the commissions and expenses attributable to the real property are deductible under section 2053(b) and section 20.2053-8 of the regulations. *See* Rev. Rul. 69-402, 1969-2 C.B. 176. However, since such commissions and expenses of the estate attributable to the income producing assets and to the real property are not deductible under section 691(b), their deduction by the estate under section 2053 for estate tax purposes would preclude their deduction by the estate for income tax purposes. See section 642(g).

C. Deduction of Estate Tax

Internal Revenue Code:
   Section 691(c)

Regulations:
   Sections 1.691(c)-1, -2

Revenue Ruling 67-242
1967-2 C.B. 227

The Internal Revenue Service has been requested to explain the application of section 691(c) of the Internal Revenue Code of 1954. Section 691(c) of the Code permits a person, who must include in gross income for the taxable year any amount of income in respect of a decedent, to deduct for the same taxable year that portion of the Federal estate tax on the decedent's estate which is attributable to the inclusion in the estate of the value of the right to receive such amount.

To determine the deduction allowable, it is first necessary to compute the net value of the items which are to be treated as income in respect of a decedent under the provisions of section 691(a) of the Code. This net value is the value in the gross estate of all items of income in respect of a decedent, less the claims deductible for Federal estate tax purposes which represent the deductions and credits in respect of the decedent described in section 691(b) of the Code.

The estate tax attributable to such net value is an amount equal to the excess of the estate tax over the estate tax computed without including in the gross estate such net value. The recomputation of the estate tax to arrive at the latter figure is effected by excluding from the value of the gross estate the net value of all items of income in respect of the decedent. The difference between the estate tax and the estate tax as so recomputed is the total deduction allowed under section 691(c) of the Code.

Section 1.691(c)-1(a)(2) of the Income Tax Regulations provides that in computing the estate tax without including in the gross estate the net value of the items of income in respect of the decedent, any estate tax deduction (such as the marital deduction) which may be based upon the gross estate (or adjusted gross estate) shall be recomputed so as to take into account the exclusion of such net value from the gross estate.

Where for any taxable year a taxpayer receives and is required to include in his gross income an amount of income in respect of a decedent which is less than all of the income in respect of that decedent, the taxpayer may deduct under section 691(c) of the Code an amount which bears the same ratio to the Federal estate tax attributable to inclusion in the gross estate of the net value of all items of gross income in respect of that decedent, as the value in the gross estate of the right to the income in respect of the decedent included in gross income of the taxpayer for the taxable year (or the amount included in gross income, whichever is lower), bears to the value in the gross estate of all items of gross income in respect of the decedent.

The provisions of section 691(c) of the Code and section 1.691(c)-1 of the regulations may be illustrated by the following example:

> A was an attorney engaged in the practice of law who kept his books by the use of the cash receipts and disbursements method. At the time of his death, A was entitled to fees for professional services rendered, to dividends declared before his death, but payable and paid to the record owners of the stock as of a date following his death, and to accrued bond interest, in the respective amounts of $30x$, $10x$, and $5x$ dollars, and having values in the gross estate respectively of $29x$, $10x$, and $5x$ dollars. There were deducted for estate tax purposes as claims against the estate $3x$ dollars for business expenses for which the estate was liable and $1x$ dollars for taxes accrued on certain property which the decedent owned. In all, $4x$ dollars were deducted for claims which represent amounts described in section 691(b) of the Code which are allowable as deductions to the estate for income tax purposes.

> The right to the fees for professional-services rendered, along with certain other properties totaling $171x$ dollars, was specifically bequeathed by A to his surviving spouse. During the taxable year, the right to those fees was distributed by the executor to, and they were collected by, the surviving spouse and included in her gross income. The dividends and accrued bond interest were received by the estate and properly included in its gross income. The gross estate is valued at $415x$ dollars and considering deductions of $15x$ dollars, a marital deduction of $200x$ dollars, and an exemption of $60x$ dollars [under former section 2052], the taxable estate amounts to $140x$ dollars. The Federal estate tax on this amount is $32.7x$ dollars from which is subtracted $1.2x$ dollars as a credit for State death taxes paid, leaving a net estate tax liability of $31.5x$ dollars. The deduction of the surviving spouse, as provided in section 691(c) of the Code, is computed as follows:

	Dollars
Value in the gross estate of all items of income described in sec. 691(a)(1) of the Code	44x
Less deductions in computing gross estate for claims representing deductions described in sec. 691(b) of the Code	4x
Net value of items described in sec. 691(a)(1) of the Code	40x

	40x dollars net value of items of income in respect of decedent included in gross estate (dollars)	*40x dollars net value of items of income in respect of decedent excluded from gross estate (dollars)*
Value of gross estate	415x	375x
Less:		
Deductions	15x	15x
Marital deduction	200x	
Marital deduction reduced by (29x dollars) value in gross estate of income in respect of decedent (fees for professional services rendered) included in gross income of spouse and in marital deduction		171x
Exemption	60x	60x
Taxable estate	140x	129x
Federal estate tax	31.5x	28.4x
Recomputed Federal estate tax	28.4x	
Federal estate tax attributable to net value in the gross estate of all items of income in respect of decedent	3.1x	

The section 691(c) of the Code deduction allowed the surviving spouse, in connection with the 30x dollars (professional fees) of income in respect of the decedent which she received and included in her gross income for the taxable year, is computed as follows:

	Dollars
Total Federal estate tax attributable to net value of all items of income in respect of the decedent included in the gross estate	3.1x
Value in the gross estate of all items of income in respect of the decedent	44x
Value in the gross estate of item of income (30x dollars professional fees) in respect of the decedent included in the gross income of spouse	29x
Portion of estate tax deductible by spouse	
$\left(\dfrac{29x \text{ dollars}}{44x \text{ dollars}}\right)$ of 3.1x dollars	2.05x

The deduction allowed the estate for Federal income tax purposes as provided in section 691(c) of the Code is computed as follows:

Dollars

The value in the gross estate of the items of income (10x dollars
  dividends, 5x dollars bond interest) in respect of the decedent
  received and included in the gross income of the estate   15x

Portion of estate tax deductible by the estate for Federal income
  tax purposes $\left(\dfrac{15x \text{ dollars}}{44x \text{ dollars}}\right)$ of 3.1x dollars   1.06x

Accordingly, in this example the surviving spouse is entitled to deduct 2.05x dollars and the estate is entitled to deduct 1.06x dollars.

Illustrative Material

An item of income in respect of a decedent acquired by the beneficiary of a beneficiary continues to be income in respect of a decedent in the hands of the second beneficiary. *See* Rev. Rul. 57-544, 1957-2 C.B. 361, which computed the section 691(c) deduction by reference to the estate tax attributable to the item in the estate of the first beneficiary. The I.R.S. made no mention of the estate tax attributable to such item in the estate of the person who earned it. Compare Treas. Reg. §1.691(c)-1(b). See also Priv. Ltr. Rul. 200316008 (Dec. 31, 2002).

Thomas M. Chastain
59 T.C. 461 (1972)

RAUM, *Judge*: … Pursuant to section 691(a) of the 1954 Code petitioner had reported a $632,402.84 long-term capital gain in his 1966 income tax return as income in respect of a decedent, and he had claimed a deduction of $439,856.99 under section 691(c) for estate taxes attributable to that item. Although the Commissioner treated section 691(c) as applicable, he determined, upon the basis of his computations under that section, that petitioner was not entitled to any deduction thereunder. The sole matter in dispute relates to the proper method of computing the deduction, with particular reference to the effect of a residuary charitable bequest.…

Petitioner's father, Robert Lee Chastain, died testate on June 9, 1964. Prior to his death he had conveyed certain real estate to one George Caulkins, and among his assets at the time of death were two mortgage notes receivable from Caulkins in the amounts of $641,765.32 and $152,734.68. The excess of the face amount of each note over its basis in decedent's hands was $632,402.84 and $150,506.49, respectively, and would have represented long-term capital gain to decedent if he had received payment upon the notes. The aggregate of such unrealized gains on the Caulkins notes at the time of death was $782,909.33.

Article III of decedent's will provided that the Caulkins notes should be included in a bequest to petitioner, as follows:

ARTICLE III

I give and bequeath to my son, THOMAS MALCOLM CHASTAIN, the sum of ONE MILLION ($1,000,000.00) DOLLARS, which shall include the two mortgages given me by George Caulkins for the purchase of certain lands, the stock which I own in the Atlantic National Bank of West Palm Beach, and such of the Florida Power and Light Company stock as will be required to make up the total of One Million ($1,000,000.00) Dollars. * * *

The will also made a number of other bequests and then provided for the gift of the residue to a charitable foundation, directing that "all estate taxes be paid from the residue."

The decedent's Federal estate tax return was duly filed, and the gross estate therein was valued as of the date of death.... The net estate tax payable ... was $911,346.85. That amount was computed as follows:

Gross estate		$4,513,522.29
Deductions:		
Charitable deduction in respect of the residuary bequest to the foundation	$1,476,388.30	
Others	336,953.66	
		1,813,341.96
		2,700,180.33
Exemption [former section 2052]		60,000.00
Taxable estate		2,640,180.33
Gross estate tax		1,072,495.54
Credits:		
State death taxes paid	155,615.86	
Federal gift taxes paid	5,532.83	
		161,148.69
Net estate tax payable		911,346.85

Because decedent's will had provided that estate taxes should be paid out of the residue of his estate which was otherwise bequeathed to the charitable foundation and because the amount of that bequest was allowable as a deduction in computing the taxable estate, the amounts of the estate tax liability and the charitable deduction were dependent upon one another. In the estate tax return an algebraic formula consisting of two simultaneous linear equations was used to compute these respective amounts....

At the time of decedent's death, there existed certain items of unrealized income that fell within section 691(a) and certain items of deduction that were covered by section 691(b). The section 691(a) income items were in the aggregate amount of $793,092.06 (consisting of the $782,909.33 unrealized gains on the Caulkins notes plus $10,182.73 of other unrealized income); and the section 691(b) deduction items were in the aggregate amount of $12,161.21.[2] Thus, the net value of all these items was $780,930.85 ($793,092.06 minus $12,161.21).

Petitioner received payment in full during 1966 on one of the Caulkins notes, in the amount of $641,765.32. As noted above, in his income tax return for that year, he reported $632,402.84 as a long-term capital gain, which represented the excess of the amount realized upon collection of that note over its basis in the hands of his father. That was the only item of income in respect of a decedent which petitioner received in 1966, and he claimed a deduction of $439,856.99 under section 691(c) in respect of that item. After making his own section 691(c) computation, the Commissioner determined that petitioner was not entitled to any deduction thereunder.

The parties are not in disagreement as to the general operation of section 691(c). First, a fraction is determined in which the numerator consists of the section 691(a) items of

---

2. These deduction items do not appear to have been treated as relating to the Caulkins notes.

income received by the taxpayer during the year and in which the denominator consists of the sum of all the section 691(a) items. That fraction in this case is $^{632,402.84}/_{793,092.06}$. So much is agreed to by the parties. That fraction is then to be multiplied by the amount of estate tax "attributable to the net value for estate tax purposes of all" the section 691(a) items. Both parties agree that the "net value," computed pursuant to section 691(c)(2)(B), is $780,930.85. Their disagreement relates solely to the determination of the amount of estate tax "attributable to" this net value of $780,930.85.

In his 1966 return petitioner computed the estate tax attributable to the net value of the section 691 items as $551,621.62, and, upon applying the foregoing fraction to that amount, arrived at a section 691(c) deduction in the amount of $439,856.99. The Commissioner, on the other hand, determined that no estate tax at all was attributable to the $780,930.85 net value of the section 691 items, and that therefore no deduction was available under section 691(c). Petitioner contends on brief that both parties were in error in their computations, and he now proposes a computation that results in a substantially smaller deduction than originally claimed by him. The Commissioner continues to rely upon his original position that no deduction whatever is allowable. We agree with petitioner's revised position. The heart of the controversy is the effect of the residuary charitable bequest to the foundation, which we shall consider shortly.

The statute itself sets forth the manner in which the computation in question shall be made. Section 691(c)(2)(C) provides: "The estate tax attributable to such net value shall be an amount equal to the excess of the estate tax over the estate tax computed without including in the gross estate such net value." In substance, these provisions require a recomputation of the estate tax by excluding all section 691 items, and then subtracting the recomputed tax from the actual tax. See *Nat Harrison Associates, Inc.*, 42 T.C. 601, 627, acq. 1965-2 C.B. 5. The basic dispute between the parties relates to the effect, if any, that the elimination of the section 691 items in the recomputation should have upon the residuary charitable bequest to the foundation, which in turn plays a part in the computation of the tax. The three different possibilities placed before us are as follows:

1. The computation on petitioner's return reduced the amount of the gross estate by the amount of the section 691 items, and then proceeded to recompute the residuary charitable bequest on the theory that a lower estate tax would increase the amount of that residue. The deduction of the hypothetical augmented charitable bequest in turn produced an even lower estate tax. Thus, it was assumed in that computation that the amount of the residue paid over to the foundation was $2,139,124.22, instead of the $1,476,388.30 residue that was actually paid to it. And as a result of the elimination of the section 691 items from the estate together with the increase in the amount of the charitable deduction, petitioner arrived at a recomputed "net" estate tax in the amount of $359,725.23. That amount was then subtracted from the actual net estate tax of $911,346.85, leaving $551,621.62 as the amount of estate tax claimed to be "attributable to" the net value of the section 691 items.

2. The respondent's recomputation also involves a theoretical recasting of the charitable bequest of the residue. Although he eliminated the net value ($780,930.85) of the section 691 items from the gross estate, he assumed that petitioner would still be entitled to his $1 million bequest in full. In short, he assumed that notwithstanding that the Caulkins notes were part of the $1 million bequest to petitioner, the elimination of the gain on such notes from the gross estate on the recomputation under section 691(c)(2)(C) would not diminish the $1 million bequest, and in order to achieve that result he in effect charged the entire net amount of the section 691 items ($780,930.85) against the residuary bequest. Thus, in his recomputation the respondent assumed a residuary char-

itable bequest of $695,457.45 instead of the actual residuary bequest of $1,476,388.30. By decreasing both the gross estate and the residuary charitable bequest by $780,930.85, the respondent arrived at a recomputed taxable estate identical in amount to the actual taxable estate. Accordingly, the difference between the actual tax and the recomputed tax was zero, and respondent concluded that no part of the estate tax was therefore "attributable to" the section 691 items.

3. Petitioner on brief proposes a third computation, urging that both of the foregoing computations are erroneous because they assume a residuary gift to the foundation in an amount that was not in fact made. He now contends that the correct computation requires the elimination of the section 691 items ($780,930.85) from the gross estate without otherwise changing the amount of the residuary bequest that was actually paid to the foundation. He thus recomputes an estate tax of $594,392.53 which is then subtracted from $911,346.85, leaving $316,954.32 as the "estate tax attributable to" the net value of the section 691 items. After applying the appropriate fraction to this amount, he arrives at a section 691(c) deduction in the amount of $252,736.20. We hold that this method is correct.

Both the Government's method and petitioner's original method employed in his return share a common flaw. They are both based on the assumption that the charitable deduction in respect of the residue would have been substantially different in amount upon the exclusion of the section 691 items from the decedent's estate. Thus, although the residuary charitable gift was actually in the amount of $1,476,388.30, petitioner's original computation assumed that the residue was $2,139,124.22, while the Commissioner assumed that it was $695,457.45. Both of these assumptions distort one of the primary objectives of section 691(c), which is to allocate to the net value of the section 691 items an amount which roughly approximates the portion of the estate tax that was actually imposed on such net value. In order to accomplish this result it is necessary only to subtract the section 691 items from the items on the estate tax return to which they pertain, and then to make a recomputation without assuming any further change in the facts. This is in substance the method proposed by petitioner on brief, and we think it is correct.

* * *

The fallacy in the Government's position may be perceived by assuming that instead of making a residuary bequest to the foundation that turned out to be $1,476,388.30, the decedent made a specific bequest to the foundation in precisely the same amount. Upon a recomputation under section 691(c)(2)(C), only the section 691 items would be eliminated from the bequests to which they relate, but no further alteration in any bequest would be allowed. The recomputation would then proceed in the manner proposed by petitioner on brief. Surely, no such vast difference in result as the one for which respondent contends in this case can or should turn upon the fact that the charitable bequest in the identical amount was in the form of a residuary bequest rather than a specific bequest, and nothing in the alleged purpose of the statute relied upon by the Government calls for any such difference in result. In both situations the amount of estate tax "attributable to" the net value of the section 691 items is the same, and that amount is properly computed by following the method proposed by petitioner in his brief.

The Government relies in part upon Rev. Rul. 67-242, 1967-2 C.B. 227, which in turn relies upon section 1.691(c)-1(a)(2) and example (2) in section 1.691(d)-1(e) of the Income Tax Regulations. The ruling and the regulations are concerned with the effect of the elimination of the section 691 items upon such items as the marital deduction in the recomputation under section 691(c)(2)(C). Obviously, the exclusion of the section 691 items may have an effect upon the computation of such deductions as the marital deduction, and the revenue ruling thus applies section 1.691(c)-1(a)(2) of the regulations, which provides that in the recomputation "any estate tax deduction (such as the marital deduction) which may be based upon the gross estate shall be recomputed so as to take into account the exclusion of such net value from the gross estate." That recomputation, however, assumes as fact only the elimination of the section 691 items; there is no assumption of any modification of any gift to the surviving spouse (except to the extent that a 691 item may have been part of the bequest to that spouse). It is therefore entirely proper to apply all the statutory rules (including those governing the determination of the amount of the marital deduction) in the recomputation of the tax, based on the assumption, however, that the composition and disposition of the estate are to be considered as modified only by the exclusion of the section 691 items and in no other manner. Neither the revenue ruling nor the regulations, when properly understood, call for any revision or any modification of any particular bequest apart from the elimination of the section 691 items. They certainly do not require a recomputation based upon an assumption that any particular bequest was in fact different from the one actually made, except to the extent that the excluded section 691 items were related to and thus altered the amount of such bequest. It is therefore fallacious to treat the residuary charitable bequest as comparable to the marital deduction. The marital deduction involves merely a *computation* based upon certain assumed facts. The charitable deduction, on the other hand, depends upon the amount actually bequeathed to the charitable beneficiary, and we can find no justification for applying the revenue ruling or regulations in such manner as to convert a $1,476,388.30 charitable bequest into one in the amount of $695,457.45, as was done in the Government's computation. We hold that the method proposed by petitioner is sound.

Illustrative Material

The I.R.S. has acquiesced in *Chastain*. 1978-2 C.B. 1.

Estate of Kincaid v. Commissioner
85 T.C. 25 (1985)

CLAPP, *Judge*: … [T]he only issue for our determination is the proper method of computing the deduction under section 691(c) for estate tax attributable to income in respect of a decedent where there is a formula maximum marital deduction bequest.

* * *

Mrs. Kincaid was the widow of Garvice Kincaid, who died on November 21, 1975. Mrs. Kincaid died during the pendency of these proceedings, and her estate was substituted as party petitioner. Mr. Kincaid's employment contract with Kentucky Finance Company (KFC) provided that his annual bonus payments were to continue after his death and were to be paid to Mrs. Kincaid. The value of the right to the KFC payments was includible in Mr. Kincaid's gross estate and was eligible for the marital deduction provided by section 2056(a).

Most of Mr. Kincaid's other property was bequeathed to a trust. After payment of taxes, debts, and the expenses of administering his estate, the trust property was divided into a "marital part" and a "nonmarital part." The "marital part" consisted of property equal in value to the maximum marital deduction allowable to his estate less the value of non-trust property includible in his gross estate which passed to Mrs. Kincaid and qualified for the marital deduction. The KFC payments were such nontrust property. Thus, the value of the right to the KFC payments was subtracted from the maximum marital deduction in determining the "marital part." The "marital part" passed to Mrs. Kincaid and was eligible for the marital deduction. The "nonmarital part" consisted of the remainder of the trust property. From the notice of deficiency in the estate tax for Mr. Kincaid's estate and from his estate tax return, there can be no dispute that there were other assets in his estate which would have qualified to fund "the marital part" which were not income in respect of a decedent.

Mrs. Kincaid received $153,120.41 in 1976 and $237,011.63 in 1977 pursuant to the KFC contract. She did not report all of those payments on her income tax returns for those years. The parties now agree that the payments are income in respect of a decedent (IRD) and are includible in Mrs. Kincaid's gross income under section 691(a). They disagree, however, about the amount of the deduction allowable to her under section 691(c)(1)(A) as a consequence of including the KFC payments in her gross income.

The section 691(c)(1)(A) deduction is computed by creating a fraction in which the numerator is the IRD received by Mrs. Kincaid during the year and included in her income and in which the denominator is the value of all IRD included in Mr. Kincaid's gross estate. That fraction is multiplied by the estate tax attributable to all IRD included in his gross estate. The result is the section 691(c)(1)(A) deduction. *Chastain v. Commissioner,* 59 T.C. 461, 464 (1972); *Findlay v. Commissioner,* 39 T.C. 580 (1962), affd. on this issue 332 F.2d 620 (2d Cir. 1964).

The focus of the controversy here is how to calculate the estate tax attributable to the KFC payments pursuant to section 691(c)(2)(C). This section defines the amount of estate tax attributable to the KFC payments to be the difference between the actual estate tax and the estate tax computed without including the KFC payments in the gross estate (recomputed tax). Thus, one must recompute the estate tax by excluding from the value of the gross estate the value of the KFC payments. The heart of the dispute is the effect the exclusion of the KFC payments has on the recomputed marital deduction.

Respondent, relying on Rev. Rul. 67-242, 1967-2 C.B. 227, which in turn relies on section 1.691(c)-1(a)(2), and section 1.691(d)-1(e), example (2), Income Tax Regs., contends that the proper method of recomputation is to subtract from both the gross estate and the marital deduction the KFC payments. This method produces a marital deduction less than the maximum allowed by the 50 percent of the adjusted gross estate limitation.[4] It also produces no change in the taxable estate, because the reduction in the gross estate is equalled by the reduction in the marital deduction, and therefore the estate tax remains the same. Petitioner contends that the full maximum marital deduction subject only to the 50 percent of adjusted gross estate limitation should be allowed in recomputing the estate tax. Petitioner relies on the testamentary documents which call for a maximum marital deduction bequest based on a formula and on the fact that there are sufficient non-IRD assets in the estate to fully fund this formula marital deduction.

---

4. Under section 2056(c) as in effect during the year in question, the maximum marital deduction was limited to 50 percent of the value of the adjusted gross estate.

This section was repealed by the Economic Recovery Tax Act of 1981 ... applicable to estates of decedents dying after December 31, 1981, thus allowing an unlimited marital deduction. If the unlimited marital deduction is used, there is no tax on the estate of the first spouse to die (and thus no reduction in tax in the recomputation) and no marital deduction in the estate of the last to die (because there is no surviving spouse). Thus, the dispute presented in this case would not arise.

As the following table shows, these approaches produce substantially different results:

	Actual[5] computation	Petitioner's recomputation	Respondent's recomputation
Gross estate	$1,000,000	$900,000	$900,000
Adjusted gross estate	1,000,000	900,000	900,000
Marital deduction	(500,000)	(450,000)	400,000
Exemption [former Sec. 2052]	(60,000)	(60,000)	(60,000)
Taxable estate	440,000	390,000	440,000
Estate tax	126,500	100,500	126,500
Sec. 691(c)(1)(A) deduction	—	16,000	0

The purpose behind section 691 is to provide a deduction to those required to include IRD in their gross income to offset, at least in part, the estate tax which was attributable to the inclusion of that IRD in the gross estate of a decedent. S. Rept. No. 1622, 83d Cong., 2d Sess. 87–89 (1954); H. Rept. No. 1337, 83d Cong., 2d Sess. 64–65 (1954); *Estate of Sidles v. Commissioner,* 65 T.C. 873, 883 (1976), affd. without published opinion 553 F.2d 102 (8th Cir. 1977). Although there is no guidance in the statute or the legislative history on the specific point at issue here, we conclude that petitioner's method is consistent with the purpose of the statute. The formula bequest here required that Mrs. Kincaid receive property equal in value to the maximum marital deduction out of the assets of the estate available for distribution. In the recomputation there is no IRD available in the recomputed gross estate to satisfy the marital bequest. The bequest, therefore, by its own terms, must be funded to its full extent by non-IRD property.

This method fits more logically into the scheme of the statute. The value of KFC payments was included in Mr. Kincaid's estate and taxed there. Even though the payments went to the marital share, there were other assets which could have funded the marital share to fully fund the formula maximum marital deduction bequest. The other assets which were allocated to the nonmarital share were subject to tax. The important fact is that the existence of the IRD produced additional estate tax on Mr. Kincaid's estate. The allocation of assets as between marital and nonmarital shares should be irrelevant to the discussion. Therefore, logically, it must be concluded that the surviving spouse is entitled to some deduction for the excess estate tax paid because of the inclusion of the IRD in the estate. This conclusion should be nullified by the happenstance that the IRD passed to the marital share rather than the nonmarital share.

Respondent relies on Rev. Rul. 67-242, 1967-2 C.B. 227, which in turn relies on section 1.691(c)-1(a)(2) of the Income Tax Regulations. Initially, we note that revenue rulings represent only the conclusions of respondent and do not have the force and effect of a Treasury regulation. *Helvering v. New York Trust Co.,* 292 U.S. 455 (1934). Moreover, the revenue ruling involves a specific marital bequest rather than a formula bequest. Respondent also relies on section 1.691(d)-1(e), example (2), in the regulations which assumes that the only qualifying gift to the spouse is an annuity, a portion of which constitutes the IRD. The example does not specifically address the issue of the recomputed marital deduction but rather is used to illustrate the application of section 691(d) involving a

---

5. The tax on Mr. Kincaid's estate is disputed and is pending before the Court in Docket No. 15773-79. Because the estate tax case is unresolved, we use the following assumptions to illustrate the difference between the parties' approach (1) The actual gross estate was $1 million; (2) the actual adjusted gross estate was $1 million; (3) the actual marital deduction was $500,000; (4) the right to the KFC payments was worth $100,000, and was the only item of Income in respect of a decedent in the gross estate.

joint and survivor annuity contract. Neither the revenue ruling nor the example in the regulations should control the result of this case which involves a formula maximum marital deduction bequest. Our holding is entirely consistent with section 1.691(c)-1(a)(2), Income Tax Regs., which provides:

> In computing the estate tax without including the [income in respect of a decedent] in the gross estate, any estate tax deduction (such as the marital deduction) which may be based upon the gross estate shall be recomputed so as to take into account the exclusion of the [income in respect of a decedent] from the gross estate.

Under our method, the marital deduction does not include IRD and is also limited to 50 percent of the recomputed gross estate, as required by section 2056.

Respondent also relies on dicta in *Chastain v. Commissioner, supra.* That case involved the recomputation of the tax on an estate which was distributed as follows: first, $1 million, which was paid in part out of IRD to the decedent's son; second, several other specific bequests; and third, the residue to a charitable foundation. The Court found that the correct recomputation under section 691(c)(2)(C) required the elimination of the IRD from the gross estate without otherwise changing the amount of the residuary bequest that was actually paid to the foundation. In that case, respondent relied on Rev. Rul. 67-242 and section 1.691(c)-1(a)(2) and example (2) in section 1.691(d)-1(e), Income Tax Regs., to support his argument that the residuary bequest should be recast to account for the exclusion of the IRD which passed to the son. The Court in rejecting the relevancy of the ruling and the regulations to the case at hand stated that "[the] recomputation * * * assumes as fact only the elimination of the section 691 items; there is no assumption of any modification of any gift to the surviving spouse (except to the extent that a 691 item may have been part of the bequest to that spouse)," and all statutory rules "governing the determination of the amount of the marital deduction" apply in the recomputation of the tax. 59 T.C. at 467–468. Respondent relies on this language to support his argument. However, neither the revenue ruling nor the regulations address the problem of a formula maximum marital deduction bequest. The facts in *Chastain* did not involve such a bequest, and the Court recognized that the marital deduction situation is different from the case presented before it:

> It is * * * fallacious to treat the residuary charitable bequest as comparable to the marital deduction. The marital deduction involves merely a *computation* based upon certain assumed facts. The charitable deduction, on the other hand, depends upon the amount actually bequeathed to the charitable beneficiary * * *.
> [59 T.C. at 468; emphasis in original.]

Therefore, we do not believe our holding is inconsistent with the holding in *Chastain.*

* * *

Illustrative Material

Footnote 4 of *Kincaid* points out that the Economic Recovery Tax Act of 1981 made the estate tax marital deduction quantitatively unlimited. The footnote also seems to imply that, as a result of the unlimited marital deduction, the issue in *Kincaid* is no longer relevant. Is that so? Is every married client inclined—or even well-advised—to leave everything to the survivor? *See generally* Ascher, *The Quandary of Executors Who Are Asked to Plan the Estates of the Dead: The Qualified Terminable Interest Property Election,* 63 N.C. L. Rev. 1 (1984). Could not the issue in *Kincaid* arise if the decedent left two-thirds of a large residuary estate to a surviving spouse and one-third to a child? See Priv. Ltr. Rul. 200316008 (Dec. 31, 2002) (by spousal election, wife became entitled to one-third of husband's estate, which consisted in part of income in respect of a decedent).

Estate of Cherry v. United States
133 F. Supp. 2d 949 (W.D. Ky. 2001)

SIMPSON, Chief Judge.

This case presents a dispute concerning the tax implications of the interaction between the marital deduction and income in respect of the decedent.... For the reasons set forth below, the Court will enter judgment in favor of the United States.

In December of 1968, Wendell Cherry created the plaintiff Trust by an instrument specifying that the trust would become irrevocable upon his death. In 1977, he married the plaintiff Dorothy Morton, and their union lasted until his death in mid-1991. By the terms of Mr. Cherry's 1990 will, both Mrs. Cherry and the Trust (hereinafter referred to as "Taxpayers") were beneficiaries of the Estate. The will made specific bequests and directed that the residue of the Estate would pass to the Trust, which would also bear all estate taxes.

During his lifetime, Mr. Cherry earned certain deferred benefits that were payable (and, therefore, taxable) only by virtue of his death. Although "income in respect of a decedent" ("IRD") is not statutorily defined, the parties agree that these deferred benefits, totaling $6,901,248.16, constituted "IRD" within the meaning of 26 U.S.C. Sec. 691(a). That is, these benefits were included in their entirety in the taxable estate, and would also be subject to income taxation when received by the Trust and/or by Mrs. Cherry.

Congress enacted the predecessor of Section 691(a) to correct an existing inequity between decedents using cash accounting and those using accrual methods of accounting. See, e.g., *Estate of Davison v. United States,* 292 F.2d 937, 939, 155 Ct.Cl. 290 (1961). Unfortunately, the remedy—i.e., treating all income to be received after death as being received upon death—created another species of unfairness, and Congress responded in 1942 by creating the concept of IRD, "to eliminate the neanderthal tax effect caused by the income pyramiding under the predecessor provision, while at the same time continuing the basic policy of subjecting earned income of a cash basis taxpayer to the income tax despite the fact of death." *Sun First National Bank of Orlando v. United States of America,* 587 F.2d 1073, 1083, 218 Ct.Cl. 339 (1978). Section 691 prescribes a method of deducting from income tax the amount of estate tax attributable to IRD, to avoid "imposition of both estate and income taxes on sums included in an estate as income in respect of a decedent." *United California Bank v. United States,* 439 U.S. 180, 187, 99 S. Ct. 476, 481, 58 L. Ed. 2d 444 (1978).[2]

As the parties agree that the sums constituted IRD, they also agree that a deduction from income tax was appropriate. Thus, the United States concedes that the Taxpayers are due refunds due to overpayment of income tax. The intractable dispute concerns the amount of overpayment, which turns on the manner in which the marital share is treated. 26 U.S.C. Sec. 2056 excludes from calculation of estate tax the portion of the estate that passes to a surviving spouse (with some qualifications not relevant here). The Executor qualified the Trust for this marital deduction.

---

2. While it might seem mathematically simpler and more logical to solve the double taxation problem by deducting the amount of income taxes from the estate taxes, this is impractical given that the estate might well be wound up long before the income is actually received and taxes paid thereon.

The parties broadly agree that the Section 691(c)(1)(A) deduction is to be determined by comparing the actual estate tax with the hypothetical tax on an estate which did not include the IRD. The actual estate tax was $9,561,956.74. By the terms of the will, this tax was borne in its entirety by the Trust (qualified by the executor as marital share). However, the parties disagree concerning the method of calculating the hypothetical tax. There is neither statutory nor clear case authority to guide us, and both parties rely strongly on reason and public policy, appealing ultimately to the purpose of the Section 691.

To determine the hypothetical tax, the Taxpayers propose a calculation method by which the IRD is first subtracted from the gross estate, and the estate tax is then recalculated "without adjusting the marital deduction." The Taxpayers reason that "the IRD must of necessity be allocated other than to the marital share inasmuch as the IRD has been removed from the estate entirely." ... The third step involves "an interrelated calculation" to adjust the estate taxes to take into account the interrelation of the estate taxes and the residuary marital deduction (because of the circumstance of all taxes being paid from the Trust corpus). Taxpayers argue that this method is necessary to avoid placing the Estate in a marginal tax bracket in excess of 100% on the pre-residuary bequests (of approximately $11,000,000), thus resulting in excessive tax, the evil Section 691 was designed to prevent.

The United States faults the Taxpayers' reasoning, arguing that in actuality, the proposed calculation fails to remove the IRD at the first step. This gives an inflated marital deduction, which in turn reduces the interrelated tax computation, and ultimately results in a Section 691 deduction that is actually greater than the IRD itself. The United States contends that it is illogical to suggest that the amount of estate tax resulting from the presence of the IRD could ever exceed the amount of the IRD itself, and it argues that the plaintiffs' proposal fails to serve the goals of Section 691. Even assuming that the Estate is in a marginal tax bracket exceeding 100% as to the pre-residual bequests, the government argues that this results from the choices Mr. Cherry made in drawing the will and Trust instrument, and that it is inappropriate to attempt to modify those choices by ignoring the established methods of calculating the Section 691 deduction.

The plaintiff Taxpayers contend that their approach was approved in *Chastain v. Commissioner of Internal Revenue*, 59 T.C. 461 (1972). The decedent in that case had bequeathed to the plaintiff a specific sum that included IRD; the residuary, from which the estate tax was to be paid, was left to a charitable foundation. The parties disagreed concerning the method of computing the hypothetical estate tax (i.e., excluding the IRD). The Court rejected the notion that removing the IRD would change the value of the residue (i.e., the charitable donation), stating that one of the primary objectives of the Section 691 deduction is

> to allocate to the net value of the section 691 items an amount which roughly approximates the portion of the estate tax that was actually imposed on such net value. In order to accomplish this result it is necessary only to subtract the section 691 items from the items on the estate tax return to which they pertain, and then to make a recomputation without assuming any further change in the facts.

59 T.C. at 466.

The *Chastain* court contrasted the circumstance of a charitable deduction (which depends upon the amount actually bequeathed to the charity) with the marital deduction, which "involves merely a computation based upon certain assumed facts." *Id.* The Court stated as follows:

[The] recomputation ... assumes as fact only the elimination of the section 691 items; there is no assumption of any modification of any gift to the surviving spouse (except to the extent that a 691 item may have been part of the bequest to that spouse). It is therefore entirely proper to apply all the statutory rules (including those governing the determination of the amount of the marital deduction) in the recomputation of the tax, based on the assumption, however, *that the composition and disposition of the estate are to be considered as modified only by the exclusion of the section 691 items and in no other manner.*

Id. (emphasis added).

The United States contends that the plaintiffs' reliance on *Chastain* is misplaced, in that the case actually supports the position that the IRD must be deducted from the gross estate as the first step of the hypothetical computation. The United States points to the following language in the opinion:

Obviously, the exclusion of section 691 items may have an effect upon the computation of such deductions as the marital deduction, and the revenue ruling thus applies section 1.691(c)-1(a)(2) of the regulations, which provides that in the recomputation "any estate tax deduction (such as the marital deduction) which may be based upon the gross estate shall be recomputed so as to take into account the exclusion of such net value from the gross estate."

Id. at 467.

To the extent that *Chastain* has any bearing on the instant dispute, we believe it favors the current position of the United States. We base this conclusion on *Chastain*'s insistence that the first step in the hypothetical computation is to subtract the IRD from the "items to which they pertain." In this case, the IRD is not the subject of a specific bequest (contrary to the situation in *Chastain*). Rather, the IRD is part of the residue, goes to the Trust, i.e., the marital share; if the IRD is removed from the gross estate, it must be removed from the marital share. Thus, it would appear that *Chastain* fails to support Taxpayers' argument that the IRD should be attributed to other than the marital share. At a minimum, we take from *Chastain* the counsel that in computing the hypothetical tax, the IRD should be removed from the gross estate prior to taking any other steps.

Taxpayer plaintiffs also rely on *Estate of Kincaid v. Commissioner,* 85 T.C. 25 (1985). This case arose in a legal environment that included a maximum marital share of fifty percent of the estate. The testator had included a maximum marital deduction bequest. The surviving spouse was entitled to receive IRD in the form of deferred compensation, and most of Mr. Kincaid's other property went to a trust of which Mrs. Kincaid was a beneficiary; however, the estate included sufficient assets to have funded the maximum marital share by non-IRD property. The Court rejected the suggestion that the IRD should be subtracted from both the gross estate and the marital share, and held that because there was a specific bequest requiring that Mrs. Kincaid receive property equal to the maximum marital deduction (50%), in the recomputation (in which there was no IRD available), the marital share must be funded fully by non-IRD property.

The Taxpayer plaintiffs contend that *Kincaid* stands for the proposition that a Section 691 deduction should be allowed regardless of how funds are actually allocated between marital and non-marital shares, and that the case "provides that the IRD must of necessity be allocated other than to the marital share in the second calculation, inasmuch as the IRD is, by statute, removed from the estate entirely." ... The United States, on the other hand, points to the portion of *Kincaid* that specifically acknowledged Treas. Reg. 1.691(c)-1(a)(2), which calls for the marital deduction to be recomputed to take into account the exclusion of the IRD.

Again, to the extent that *Kincaid* can be viewed as addressing a situation in which the marital share is not the subject of a specific bequest, we believe it favors the government's position. In *Kincaid,* the marital portion was the subject of a specific bequest, and specific bequests must be satisfied prior to disposition of the residue; therefore, when the IRD was removed from the estate, the specific bequest would necessarily have to be satisfied by non-IRD property. In the present case, however, the marital share is not the subject of a specific bequest; consequently, *Kincaid* provides no support for maintaining the size of the marital share as a constant once the IRD is removed from the gross estate.

Thus, while the authority is hardly overwhelming, it does appear to favor the position of the government. However, when we look specifically for the approach which will best further the purposes of Section 691, our confidence in rejecting the Taxpayers' proposal is greatly strengthened. As noted earlier, the purpose of Section 691 deduction is to diminish the tendency toward double taxation by allowing a deduction from income tax for the portion of the estate tax fairly attributable to the presence of the IRD in the estate. The logical way to accomplish this goal is first to calculate the estate tax on the entire amount (including therein the ordinary consideration of marital share), and then to begin the recomputation by removing the IRD before proceeding in the customary fashion (including therein a recomputation of the marital share). This is the government's approach. By contrast, the Taxpayers' approach (which attempts to bypass recomputation of the marital share) yields a nonsensical result, i.e., the suggestion that the amount of tax attributable to the presence of the IRD in the estate is greater than the amount of the IRD itself.

* * *

Illustrative Material

1. According to section 2001, the highest marginal estate tax rate is much less than 100%. Yet the pre-residuary bequests in *Cherry* seem to have generated an estate tax of nearly 100%. Why? Because the estate consisted in part of income in respect of a decedent? Or was there something in Mr. Cherry's will that produced a "tax-on-a-tax"?

Can you think of yet another way to improve Mr. Cherry's will? It seems to have been silent as to the allocation of an extraordinary amount of income in respect of a decedent. How might the result have differed if the will had allocated part or all of this amount to the pre-residuary bequests?

2. In Rev. Rul. 78-203, 1978-1 C.B. 199, the I.R.S. ruled that the deduction allowable under section 691(c) for the estate tax attributable to income in respect of a decedent must be claimed as an itemized deduction, rather than as an "above the line" deduction. The I.R.S. relied on section 62, which does not include the section 691(c) deduction as a deduction allowable in computing adjusted gross income.

Section 67(b)(7) excepts the section 691(c) deduction from the 2% "haircut" on miscellaneous itemized deductions.

Appendix

....

[ARTICLE] 1

DEFINITIONS AND FIDUCIARY DUTIES

SECTION 101. SHORT TITLE. This [Act] may be cited as the Uniform Principal and Income Act.

SECTION 102. DEFINITIONS. In this [Act]:

(1) "Accounting period" means a calendar year unless another 12-month period is selected by a fiduciary. The term includes a portion of a calendar year or other 12-month period that begins when an income interest begins or ends when an income interest ends.

(2) "Beneficiary" includes, in the case of a decedent's estate, an heir [, legatee,] and devisee and, in the case of a trust, an income beneficiary and a remainder beneficiary.

(3) "Fiduciary" means a personal representative or a trustee. The term includes an executor, administrator, successor personal representative, special administrator, and a person performing substantially the same function.

(4) "Income" means money or property that a fiduciary receives as current return from a principal asset. The term includes a portion of receipts from a sale, exchange, or liquidation of a principal asset, to the extent provided in [Article] 4.

(5) "Income beneficiary" means a person to whom net income of a trust is or may be payable.

(6) "Income interest" means the right of an income beneficiary to receive all or part of net income, whether the terms of the trust require it to be distributed or authorize it to be distributed in the trustee's discretion.

(7) "Mandatory income interest" means the right of an income beneficiary to receive net income that the terms of the trust require the fiduciary to distribute.

(8) "Net income" means the total receipts allocated to income during an accounting period minus the disbursements made from income during the period, plus or minus transfers under this [Act] to or from income during the period.

(9) "Person" means an individual, corporation, business trust, estate, trust, partnership, limited liability company, association, joint venture, government; governmental subdivision, agency, or instrumentality; public corporation, or any other legal or commercial entity.

(10) "Principal" means property held in trust for distribution to a remainder beneficiary when the trust terminates.

(11) "Remainder beneficiary" means a person entitled to receive principal when an income interest ends.

(12) "Terms of a trust" means the manifestation of the intent of a settlor or decedent with respect to the trust, expressed in a manner that admits of its proof in a judicial proceeding, whether by written or spoken words or by conduct.

(13) "Trustee" includes an original, additional, or successor trustee, whether or not appointed or confirmed by a court.

SECTION 103. FIDUCIARY DUTIES; GENERAL PRINCIPLES.

(a) In allocating receipts and disbursements to or between principal and income, and with respect to any matter within the scope of [Articles] 2 and 3, a fiduciary:

(1) shall administer a trust or estate in accordance with the terms of the trust or the will, even if there is a different provision in this [Act];

(2) may administer a trust or estate by the exercise of a discretionary power of administration given to the fiduciary by the terms of the trust or the will, even if the exercise of the power produces a result different from a result required or permitted by this [Act];

(3) shall administer a trust or estate in accordance with this [Act] if the terms of the trust or the will do not contain a different provision or do not give the fiduciary a discretionary power of administration; and

(4) shall add a receipt or charge a disbursement to principal to the extent that the terms of the trust and this [Act] do not provide a rule for allocating the receipt or disbursement to or between principal and income.

(b) In exercising the power to adjust under Section 104(a) or a discretionary power of administration regarding a matter within the scope of this [Act], whether granted by the terms of a trust, a will, or this [Act], a fiduciary shall administer a trust or estate impartially, based on what is fair and reasonable to all of the beneficiaries, except to the extent that the terms of the trust or the will clearly manifest an intention that the fiduciary shall or may favor one or more of the beneficiaries. A determination in accordance with this [Act] is presumed to be fair and reasonable to all of the beneficiaries.

SECTION 104. TRUSTEE'S POWER TO ADJUST.

(a) A trustee may adjust between principal and income to the extent the trustee considers necessary if the trustee invests and manages trust assets as a prudent investor, the terms of the trust describe the amount that may or must be distributed to a beneficiary by referring to the trust's income, and the trustee determines, after applying the rules in Section 103(a), that the trustee is unable to comply with Section 103(b).

(b) In deciding whether and to what extent to exercise the power conferred by subsection (a), a trustee shall consider all factors relevant to the trust and its beneficiaries, including the following factors to the extent they are relevant:

(1) the nature, purpose, and expected duration of the trust;

(2) the intent of the settlor;

(3) the identity and circumstances of the beneficiaries;

(4) the needs for liquidity, regularity of income, and preservation and appreciation of capital;

(5) the assets held in the trust; the extent to which they consist of financial assets, interests in closely held enterprises, tangible and intangible personal property, or real property; the extent to which an asset is used by a beneficiary; and whether an asset was purchased by the trustee or received from the settlor;

(6) the net amount allocated to income under the other sections of this [Act] and the increase or decrease in the value of the principal assets, which the trustee may estimate as to assets for which market values are not readily available;

(7) whether and to what extent the terms of the trust give the trustee the power to invade principal or accumulate income or prohibit the trustee from invading principal or accumulating income, and the extent to which the trustee has exercised a power from time to time to invade principal or accumulate income;

(8) the actual and anticipated effect of economic conditions on principal and income and effects of inflation and deflation; and

(9) the anticipated tax consequences of an adjustment.

(c) A trustee may not make an adjustment:

(1) that diminishes the income interest in a trust that requires all of the income to be paid at least annually to a spouse and for which an estate tax or gift tax marital deduction would be allowed, in whole or in part, if the trustee did not have the power to make the adjustment;

(2) that reduces the actuarial value of the income interest in a trust to which a person transfers property with the intent to qualify for a gift tax exclusion;

(3) that changes the amount payable to a beneficiary as a fixed annuity or a fixed fraction of the value of the trust assets;

(4) from any amount that is permanently set aside for charitable purposes under a will or the terms of a trust unless both income and principal are so set aside;

(5) if possessing or exercising the power to make an adjustment causes an individual to be treated as the owner of all or part of the trust for income tax purposes, and the individual would not be treated as the owner if the trustee did not possess the power to make an adjustment;

(6) if possessing or exercising the power to make an adjustment causes all or part of the trust assets to be included for estate tax purposes in the estate of an individual who has the power to remove a trustee or appoint a trustee, or both, and the assets would not be included in the estate of the individual if the trustee did not possess the power to make an adjustment;

(7) if the trustee is a beneficiary of the trust; or

(8) if the trustee is not a beneficiary, but the adjustment would benefit the trustee directly or indirectly.

(d) If subsection (c)(5), (6), (7), or (8) applies to a trustee and there is more than one trustee, a cotrustee to whom the provision does not apply may make the adjustment unless the exercise of the power by the remaining trustee or trustees is not permitted by the terms of the trust.

(e) A trustee may release the entire power conferred by subsection (a) or may release only the power to adjust from income to principal or the power to adjust from principal to income if the trustee is uncertain about whether possessing or exercising the power will cause a result described in subsection (c)(1) through (6) or (c)(8) or if the trustee determines that possessing or exercising the power will or may deprive the trust of a tax benefit or impose a tax burden not described in subsection (c). The release may be permanent or for a specified period, including a period measured by the life of an individual.

(f) Terms of a trust that limit the power of a trustee to make an adjustment between principal and income do not affect the application of this section unless it is clear from the terms of the trust that the terms are intended to deny the trustee the power of adjustment conferred by subsection (a).

SECTION 105. JUDICIAL CONTROL OF DISCRETIONARY POWER.

(a) The court may not order a fiduciary to change a decision to exercise or not to exercise a discretionary power conferred by this [Act] unless it determines that the decision was an abuse of the fiduciary's discretion. A fiduciary's decision is not an abuse of discretion merely because the court would have exercised the power in a different manner or would not have exercised the power.

(b) The decisions to which subsection (a) applies include:

(1) a decision under Section 104(a) as to whether and to what extent an amount should be transferred from principal to income or from income to principal.

(2) a decision regarding the factors that are relevant to the trust and its beneficiaries, the extent to which the factors are relevant, and the weight, if any, to be given to those factors, in deciding whether and to what extent to exercise the discretionary power conferred by Section 104(a).

(c) If the court determines that a fiduciary has abused the fiduciary's discretion, the court may place the income and remainder beneficiaries in the positions they would have occupied if the discretion had not been abused, according to the following rules:

(1) To the extent that the abuse of discretion has resulted in no distribution to a beneficiary or in a distribution that is too small, the court shall order the fiduciary to distribute from the trust to the beneficiary an amount that the court determines will restore the beneficiary, in whole or in part, to the beneficiary's appropriate position.

(2) To the extent that the abuse of discretion has resulted in a distribution to a beneficiary which is too large, the court shall place the beneficiaries, the trust, or both, in whole or in part, in their appropriate positions by ordering the fiduciary to withhold an amount from one or more future distributions to the beneficiary who received the distribution that was too large or ordering that beneficiary to return some or all of the distribution to the trust.

(3) To the extent that the court is unable, after applying paragraphs (1) and (2), to place the beneficiaries, the trust, or both, in the positions they would have occupied if the discretion had not been abused, the court may order the fiduciary to pay an appropriate amount from its own funds to one or more of the beneficiaries or the trust or both.

(d) Upon [petition] by the fiduciary, the court having jurisdiction over a trust or estate shall determine whether a proposed exercise or nonexercise by the fiduciary of a discretionary power conferred by this [Act] will result in an abuse of the fiduciary's discretion. If the petition describes the proposed exercise or nonexercise of the power and contains sufficient information to inform the beneficiaries of the reasons for the proposal, the facts upon which the fiduciary relies, and an explanation of how the income and remainder beneficiaries will be affected by the proposed exercise or nonexercise of the power, a beneficiary who challenges the proposed exercise or nonexercise has the burden of establishing that it will result in an abuse of discretion.

[ARTICLE] 2

DECEDENT'S ESTATE OR TERMINATING INCOME INTEREST

SECTION 201. DETERMINATION AND DISTRIBUTION OF NET INCOME. After a decedent dies, in the case of an estate, or after an income interest in a trust ends, the following rules apply:

(1) A fiduciary of an estate or of a terminating income interest shall determine the amount of net income and net principal receipts received from property specifically given to a beneficiary under the rules in [Articles] 3 through 5 which apply to trustees and the rules in paragraph (5). The fiduciary shall distribute the net income and net principal receipts to the beneficiary who is to receive the specific property.

(2) A fiduciary shall determine the remaining net income of a decedent's estate or a terminating income interest under the rules in [Articles] 3 through 5 which apply to trustees and by:

(A) including in net income all income from property used to discharge liabilities;

(B) paying from income or principal, in the fiduciary's discretion, fees of attorneys, accountants, and fiduciaries; court costs and other expenses of administration; and interest on death taxes, but the fiduciary may pay those expenses from income of property passing to a trust for which the fiduciary claims an estate tax marital or charitable deduction only to the extent that the payment of those expenses from income will not cause the reduction or loss of the deduction; and

(C) paying from principal all other disbursements made or incurred in connection with the settlement of a decedent's estate or the winding up of a terminating income interest, including debts, funeral expenses, disposition of remains, family allowances, and death taxes and related penalties that are apportioned to the estate or terminating income interest by the will, the terms of the trust, or applicable law.

(3) A fiduciary shall distribute to a beneficiary who receives a pecuniary amount outright the interest or any other amount provided by the will, the terms of the trust, or applicable law from net income determined under paragraph (2) or from principal to the extent that net income is insufficient. If a beneficiary is to receive a pecuniary amount outright from a trust after an income interest ends and no interest or other amount is provided for by the terms of the trust or applicable law, the fiduciary shall distribute the interest or other amount to which the beneficiary would be entitled under applicable law if the pecuniary amount were required to be paid under a will.

(4) A fiduciary shall distribute the net income remaining after distributions required by paragraph (3) in the manner described in Section 202 to all other beneficiaries, including a beneficiary who receives a pecuniary amount in trust, even if the beneficiary holds an unqualified power to withdraw assets from the trust or other presently exercisable general power of appointment over the trust.

(5) A fiduciary may not reduce principal or income receipts from property described in paragraph (1) because of a payment described in Section 501 or 502 to the extent that the will, the terms of the trust, or applicable law requires the fiduciary to make the payment from assets other than the property or to the extent that the fiduciary recovers or expects to recover the payment from a third party. The net income and principal receipts from the property are determined by including all of the amounts the fiduciary receives or pays with respect to the property, whether those amounts accrued or became due before, on, or after the date of a decedent's death or an income interest's terminating event, and by making a reasonable provision for amounts that the fiduciary believes the estate or terminating income interest may become obligated to pay after the property is distributed.

SECTION 202. DISTRIBUTION TO RESIDUARY AND REMAINDER BENEFICIARIES.

(a) Each beneficiary described in Section 201(4) is entitled to receive a portion of the net income equal to the beneficiary's fractional interest in undistributed principal assets, using values as of the distribution date. If a fiduciary makes more than one distribution of assets to beneficiaries to whom this section applies, each beneficiary, including one who does not receive part of the distribution, is entitled, as of each distribution date, to the net income the fiduciary has received after the date of death or terminating event or earlier distribution date but has not distributed as of the current distribution date.

(b) In determining a beneficiary's share of net income, the following rules apply:

(1) The beneficiary is entitled to receive a portion of the net income equal to the beneficiary's fractional interest in the undistributed principal assets immediately before the distribution date, including assets that later may be sold to meet principal obligations.

(2) The beneficiary's fractional interest in the undistributed principal assets must be calculated without regard to property specifically given to a beneficiary and property required to pay pecuniary amounts not in trust.

(3) The beneficiary's fractional interest in the undistributed principal assets must be calculated on the basis of the aggregate value of those assets as of the distribution date without reducing the value by any unpaid principal obligation.

(4) The distribution date for purposes of this section may be the date as of which the fiduciary calculates the value of the assets if that date is reasonably near the date on which assets are actually distributed.

(c) If a fiduciary does not distribute all of the collected but undistributed net income to each person as of a distribution date, the fiduciary shall maintain appropriate records showing the interest of each beneficiary in that net income.

(d) A fiduciary may apply the rules in this section, to the extent that the fiduciary considers it appropriate, to net gain or loss realized after the date of death or terminating event or earlier distribution date from the disposition of a principal asset if this section applies to the income from the asset.

[ARTICLE] 3

APPORTIONMENT AT BEGINNING AND END OF INCOME INTEREST

SECTION 301. WHEN RIGHT TO INCOME BEGINS AND ENDS.

(a) An income beneficiary is entitled to net income from the date on which the income interest begins. An income interest begins on the date specified in the terms of the trust or, if no date is specified, on the date an asset becomes subject to a trust or successive income interest.

(b) An asset becomes subject to a trust:

(1) on the date it is transferred to the trust in the case of an asset that is transferred to a trust during the transferor's life;

(2) on the date of a testator's death in the case of an asset that becomes subject to a trust by reason of a will, even if there is an intervening period of administration of the testator's estate; or

(3) on the date of an individual's death in the case of an asset that is transferred to a fiduciary by a third party because of the individual's death.

(c) An asset becomes subject to a successive income interest on the day after the preceding income interest ends, as determined under subsection (d), even if there is an intervening period of administration to wind up the preceding income interest.

(d) An income interest ends on the day before an income beneficiary dies or another terminating event occurs, or on the last day of a period during which there is no beneficiary to whom a trustee may distribute income.

SECTION 302. APPORTIONMENT OF RECEIPTS AND DISBURSEMENTS WHEN DECEDENT DIES OR INCOME INTEREST BEGINS.

(a) A trustee shall allocate an income receipt or disbursement other than one to which Section 201(1) applies to principal if its due date occurs before a decedent dies in the case of an estate or before an income interest begins in the case of a trust or successive income interest.

(b) A trustee shall allocate an income receipt or disbursement to income if its due date occurs on or after the date on which a decedent dies or an income interest begins and it is a periodic due date. An income receipt or disbursement must be treated as accruing from day to day if its due date is not periodic or it has no due date. The portion of the receipt or disbursement accruing before the date on which a decedent dies or an income interest begins must be allocated to principal and the balance must be allocated to income.

(c) An item of income or an obligation is due on the date the payer is required to make a payment. If a payment date is not stated, there is no due date for the purposes of this [Act]. Distributions to shareholders or other owners from an entity to which Section 401 applies are deemed to be due on the date fixed by the entity for determining who is entitled to receive the distribution or, if no date is fixed, on the declaration date for the distribution. A due date is periodic for receipts or disbursements that must be paid at regular intervals under a lease or an obligation to pay interest or if an entity customarily makes distributions at regular intervals.

SECTION 303. APPORTIONMENT WHEN INCOME INTEREST ENDS.

(a) In this section, "undistributed income" means net income received before the date on which an income interest ends. The term does not include an item of income or expense that is due or accrued or net income that has been added or is required to be added to principal under the terms of the trust.

(b) When a mandatory income interest ends, the trustee shall pay to a mandatory income beneficiary who survives that date, or the estate of a deceased mandatory income beneficiary whose death causes the interest to end, the beneficiary's share of the undistributed income that is not disposed of under the terms of the trust unless the beneficiary has an unqualified power to revoke more than five percent of the trust immediately before the income interest ends. In the latter case, the undistributed income from the portion of the trust that may be revoked must be added to principal.

(c) When a trustee's obligation to pay a fixed annuity or a fixed fraction of the value of the trust's assets ends, the trustee shall prorate the final payment if and to the extent required by applicable law to accomplish a purpose of the trust or its settlor relating to income, gift, estate, or other tax requirements.

[ARTICLE] 4

ALLOCATION OF RECEIPTS DURING ADMINISTRATION OF TRUST

[PART 1. RECEIPTS FROM ENTITIES]

SECTION 401. CHARACTER OF RECEIPTS.

(a) In this section, "entity" means a corporation, partnership, limited liability company, regulated investment company, real estate investment trust, common trust fund, or any other organization in which a trustee has an interest other than a trust or estate to which Section 402 applies, a business or activity to which Section 403 applies, or an asset-backed security to which Section 415 applies.

(b) Except as otherwise provided in this section, a trustee shall allocate to income money received from an entity.

(c) A trustee shall allocate the following receipts from an entity to principal:

(1) property other than money;

(2) money received in one distribution or a series of related distributions in exchange for part or all of a trust's interest in the entity;

(3) money received in total or partial liquidation of the entity; and

(4) money received from an entity that is a regulated investment company or a real estate investment trust if the money distributed is a capital gain dividend for federal income tax purposes.

(d) Money is received in partial liquidation:

(1) to the extent that the entity, at or near the time of a distribution, indicates that it is a distribution in partial liquidation; or

(2) if the total amount of money and property received in a distribution or series of related distributions is greater than 20 percent of the entity's gross assets, as shown by the entity's year-end financial statements immediately preceding the initial receipt.

(e) Money is not received in partial liquidation, nor may it be taken into account under subsection (d)(2), to the extent that it does not exceed the amount of income tax that a trustee or beneficiary must pay on taxable income of the entity that distributes the money.

(f) A trustee may rely upon a statement made by an entity about the source or character of a distribution if the statement is made at or near the time of distribution by the entity's board of directors or other person or group of persons authorized to exercise powers to pay money or transfer property comparable to those of a corporation's board of directors.

SECTION 402. DISTRIBUTION FROM TRUST OR ESTATE. A trustee shall allocate to income an amount received as a distribution of income from a trust or an estate in which the trust has an interest other than a purchased interest, and shall allocate to principal an amount received as a distribution of principal from such a trust or estate. If a trustee purchases an interest in a trust that is an investment entity, or a decedent or donor transfers an interest in such a trust to a trustee, Section 401 or 415 applies to a receipt from the trust.

SECTION 403. BUSINESS AND OTHER ACTIVITIES CONDUCTED BY TRUSTEE.

(a) If a trustee who conducts a business or other activity determines that it is in the best interest of all the beneficiaries to account separately for the business or activity instead of accounting for it as part of the trust's general accounting records, the trustee may maintain separate accounting records for its transactions, whether or not its assets are segregated from other trust assets.

(b) A trustee who accounts separately for a business or other activity may determine the extent to which its net cash receipts must be retained for working capital, the acquisition or replacement of fixed assets, and other reasonably foreseeable needs of the business or activity, and the extent to which the remaining net cash receipts are accounted for as principal or income in the trust's general accounting records. If a trustee sells assets of the business or other activity, other than in the ordinary course of the business or activity, the trustee shall account for the net amount received as principal in the trust's general accounting records to the extent the trustee determines that the amount received is no longer required in the conduct of the business.

(c) Activities for which a trustee may maintain separate accounting records include:

(1) retail, manufacturing, service, and other traditional business activities;

(2) farming;

(3) raising and selling livestock and other animals;

(4) management of rental properties;

(5) extraction of minerals and other natural resources;

(6) timber operations; and

(7) activities to which Section 414 applies.

[PART 2. RECEIPTS NOT NORMALLY APPORTIONED]

SECTION 404. PRINCIPAL RECEIPTS. A trustee shall allocate to principal:

(1) to the extent not allocated to income under this [Act], assets received from a transferor during the transferor's lifetime, a decedent's estate, a trust with a terminating income interest, or a payer under a contract naming the trust or its trustee as beneficiary;

(2) money or other property received from the sale, exchange, liquidation, or change in form of a principal asset, including realized profit, subject to this [article];

(3) amounts recovered from third parties to reimburse the trust because of disbursements described in Section 502(a)(7) or for other reasons to the extent not based on the loss of income;

(4) proceeds of property taken by eminent domain, but a separate award made for the loss of income with respect to an accounting period during which a current income beneficiary had a mandatory income interest is income;

(5) net income received in an accounting period during which there is no beneficiary to whom a trustee may or must distribute income; and

(6) other receipts as provided in [Part 3].

SECTION 405. RENTAL PROPERTY. To the extent that a trustee accounts for receipts from rental property pursuant to this section, the trustee shall allocate to income an amount received as rent of real or personal property, including an amount received for cancellation or renewal of a lease. An amount received as a refundable deposit, including a security deposit or a deposit that is to be applied as rent for future periods, must be added to principal and held subject to the terms of the lease and is not available for distribution to a beneficiary until the trustee's contractual obligations have been satisfied with respect to that amount.

SECTION 406. OBLIGATION TO PAY MONEY.

(a) An amount received as interest, whether determined at a fixed, variable, or floating rate, on an obligation to pay money to the trustee, including an amount received as consideration for prepaying principal, must be allocated to income without any provision for amortization of premium.

(b) A trustee shall allocate to principal an amount received from the sale, redemption, or other disposition of an obligation to pay money to the trustee more than one year after it is purchased or acquired by the trustee, including an obligation whose purchase price or value when it is acquired is less than its value at maturity. If the obligation matures within one year after it is purchased or acquired by the trustee, an amount received in excess of its purchase price or its value when acquired by the trust must be allocated to income.

(c) This section does not apply to an obligation to which Section 409, 410, 411, 412, 414, or 415 applies.

SECTION 407. INSURANCE POLICIES AND SIMILAR CONTRACTS.

(a) Except as otherwise provided in subsection (b), a trustee shall allocate to principal the proceeds of a life insurance policy or other contract in which the trust or its trustee is named as beneficiary, including a contract that insures the trust or its trustee against loss for damage to, destruction of, or loss of title to a trust asset. The trustee shall allocate dividends on an insurance policy to income if the premiums on the policy are paid from income, and to principal if the premiums are paid from principal.

(b) A trustee shall allocate to income proceeds of a contract that insures the trustee against loss of occupancy or other use by an income beneficiary, loss of income, or, subject to Section 403, loss of profits from a business.

(c) This section does not apply to a contract to which Section 409 applies.

[PART 3. RECEIPTS NORMALLY APPORTIONED]

SECTION 408. INSUBSTANTIAL ALLOCATIONS NOT REQUIRED. If a trustee determines that an allocation between principal and income required by Section 409, 410, 411, 412, or 415 is insubstantial, the trustee may allocate the entire amount to principal unless one of the circumstances described in Section 104(c) applies to the allocation. This power may be exercised by a cotrustee in the circumstances described in Section 104(d) and may be released for the reasons and in the manner described in Section 104(e). An allocation is presumed to be insubstantial if:

(1) the amount of the allocation would increase or decrease net income in an accounting period, as determined before the allocation, by less than 10 percent; or

(2) the value of the asset producing the receipt for which the allocation would be made is less than 10 percent of the total value of the trust's assets at the beginning of the accounting period.

SECTION 409. DEFERRED COMPENSATION, ANNUITIES, AND SIMILAR PAYMENTS.

(a) In this section, "payment" means a payment that a trustee may receive over a fixed number of years or during the life of one or more individuals because of services rendered or property transferred to the payer in exchange for future payments. The term includes a payment made in money or property from the payer's general assets or from a separate fund created by the payer, including a private or commercial annuity, an individual retirement account, and a pension, profit-sharing, stock-bonus, or stock-ownership plan.

(b) To the extent that a payment is characterized as interest or a dividend or a payment made in lieu of interest or a dividend, a trustee shall allocate it to income. The trustee shall allocate to principal the balance of the payment and any other payment received in the same accounting period that is not characterized as interest, a dividend, or an equivalent payment.

(c) If no part of a payment is characterized as interest, a dividend, or an equivalent payment, and all or part of the payment is required to be made, a trustee shall allocate to income 10 percent of the part that is required to be made during the accounting period and the balance to principal. If no part of a payment is required to be made or the payment received is the entire amount to which the trustee is entitled, the trustee shall allocate the entire payment to principal. For purposes of this subsection, a payment is not "required to be made" to the extent that it is made because the trustee exercises a right of withdrawal.

(d) If, to obtain an estate tax marital deduction for a trust, a trustee must allocate more of a payment to income than provided for by this section, the trustee shall allocate to income the additional amount necessary to obtain the marital deduction.

(e) This section does not apply to payments to which Section 410 applies.

SECTION 410. LIQUIDATING ASSET.

(a) In this section, "liquidating asset" means an asset whose value will diminish or terminate because the asset is expected to produce receipts for a period of limited duration. The term includes a leasehold, patent, copyright, royalty right, and right to receive payments during a period of more than one year under an arrangement that does not provide for the payment of interest on the unpaid balance. The term does not include a payment subject to Section 409, resources subject to Section 411, timber subject to Section 412, an activity subject to Section 414, an asset subject to Section 415, or any asset for which the trustee establishes a reserve for depreciation under Section 503.

(b) A trustee shall allocate to income 10 percent of the receipts from a liquidating asset and the balance to principal.

SECTION 411. MINERALS, WATER, AND OTHER NATURAL RESOURCES.

(a) To the extent that a trustee accounts for receipts from an interest in minerals or other natural resources pursuant to this section, the trustee shall allocate them as follows:

(1) If received as nominal delay rental or nominal annual rent on a lease, a receipt must be allocated to income.

(2) If received from a production payment, a receipt must be allocated to income if and to the extent that the agreement creating the production payment provides a factor for interest or its equivalent. The balance must be allocated to principal.

(3) If an amount received as a royalty, shut-in-well payment, take-or-pay payment, bonus, or delay rental is more than nominal, 90 percent must be allocated to principal and the balance to income.

(4) If an amount is received from a working interest or any other interest not provided for in paragraph (1), (2), or (3), 90 percent of the net amount received must be allocated to principal and the balance to income.

(b) An amount received on account of an interest in water that is renewable must be allocated to income. If the water is not renewable, 90 percent of the amount must be allocated to principal and the balance to income.

(c) This [Act] applies whether or not a decedent or donor was extracting minerals, water, or other natural resources before the interest became subject to the trust.

(d) If a trust owns an interest in minerals, water, or other natural resources on [the effective date of this [Act]], the trustee may allocate receipts from the interest as provided in this [Act] or in the manner used by the trustee before [the effective date of this [Act]]. If the trust acquires an interest in minerals, water, or other natural resources after [the effective date of this [Act]], the trustee shall allocate receipts from the interest as provided in this [Act].

SECTION 412. TIMBER.

(a) To the extent that a trustee accounts for receipts from the sale of timber and related products pursuant to this section, the trustee shall allocate the net receipts:

(1) to income to the extent that the amount of timber removed from the land does not exceed the rate of growth of the timber during the accounting periods in which a beneficiary has a mandatory income interest;

(2) to principal to the extent that the amount of timber removed from the land exceeds the rate of growth of the timber or the net receipts are from the sale of standing timber;

(3) to or between income and principal if the net receipts are from the lease of timberland or from a contract to cut timber from land owned by a trust, by determining the amount of timber removed from the land under the lease or contract and applying the rules in paragraphs (1) and (2); or

(4) to principal to the extent that advance payments, bonuses, and other payments are not allocated pursuant to paragraph (1), (2), or (3).

(b) In determining net receipts to be allocated pursuant to subsection (a), a trustee shall deduct and transfer to principal a reasonable amount for depletion.

(c) This [Act] applies whether or not a decedent or transferor was harvesting timber from the property before it became subject to the trust.

(d) If a trust owns an interest in timberland on [the effective date of this [Act]], the trustee may allocate net receipts from the sale of timber and related products as provided in this [Act] or in the manner used by the trustee before [the effective date of this [Act]]. If the trust acquires an interest in timberland after [the effective date of this [Act]], the trustee shall allocate net receipts from the sale of timber and related products as provided in this [Act].

SECTION 413. PROPERTY NOT PRODUCTIVE OF INCOME.

(a) If a marital deduction is allowed for all or part of a trust whose assets consist substantially of property that does not provide the spouse with sufficient income from or use of the trust assets, and if the amounts that the trustee transfers from principal to income under Section 104 and distributes to the spouse from principal pursuant to the terms of the trust are insufficient to provide the spouse with the beneficial enjoyment required to obtain the marital deduction, the spouse may require the trustee to make property productive of income, convert property within a reasonable time, or exercise the power conferred by Section 104(a). The trustee may decide which action or combination of actions to take.

(b) In cases not governed by subsection (a), proceeds from the sale or other disposition of an asset are principal without regard to the amount of income the asset produces during any accounting period.

SECTION 414. DERIVATIVES AND OPTIONS.

(a) In this section, "derivative" means a contract or financial instrument or a combination of contracts and financial instruments which gives a trust the right or obligation to participate in some or all changes in the price of a tangible or intangible asset or group of assets, or changes in a rate, an index of prices or rates, or other market indicator for an asset or a group of assets.

(b) To the extent that a trustee does not account under Section 403 for transactions in derivatives, the trustee shall allocate to principal receipts from and disbursements made in connection with those transactions.

(c) If a trustee grants an option to buy property from the trust, whether or not the trust owns the property when the option is granted, grants an option that permits another person to sell property to the trust, or acquires an option to buy property for the trust or an option to sell an asset owned by the trust, and the trustee or other owner of the asset is required to deliver the asset if the option is exercised, an amount received for granting the option must be allocated to principal. An amount paid to acquire the option must be paid from principal. A gain or loss realized upon the exercise of an option, including an option granted to a settlor of the trust for services rendered, must be allocated to principal.

SECTION 415. ASSET-BACKED SECURITIES.

(a) In this section, "asset-backed security" means an asset whose value is based upon the right it gives the owner to receive distributions from the proceeds of financial assets that provide collateral for the security. The term includes an asset that gives the owner the right to receive from the collateral financial assets only the interest or other current return or only the proceeds other than interest or current return. The term does not include an asset to which Section 401 or 409 applies.

(b) If a trust receives a payment from interest or other current return and from other proceeds of the collateral financial assets, the trustee shall allocate to income the portion of the payment which the payer identifies as being from interest or other current return and shall allocate the balance of the payment to principal.

(c) If a trust receives one or more payments in exchange for the trust's entire interest in an asset-backed security in one accounting period, the trustee shall allocate the payments to principal. If a payment is one of a series of payments that will result in the liquidation of the trust's interest in the security over more than one accounting period, the trustee shall allocate 10 percent of the payment to income and the balance to principal.

[ARTICLE] 5

ALLOCATION OF DISBURSEMENTS DURING ADMINISTRATION OF TRUST

SECTION 501. DISBURSEMENTS FROM INCOME. A trustee shall make the following disbursements from income to the extent that they are not disbursements to which Section 201(2)(B) or (C) applies:

(1) one-half of the regular compensation of the trustee and of any person providing investment advisory or custodial services to the trustee;

(2) one-half of all expenses for accountings, judicial proceedings, or other matters that involve both the income and remainder interests;

(3) all of the other ordinary expenses incurred in connection with the administration, management, or preservation of trust property and the distribution of income, including interest, ordinary repairs, regularly recurring taxes assessed against principal, and expenses of a proceeding or other matter that concerns primarily the income interest; and

(4) recurring premiums on insurance covering the loss of a principal asset or the loss of income from or use of the asset.

SECTION 502. DISBURSEMENTS FROM PRINCIPAL.

(a) A trustee shall make the following disbursements from principal:

(1) the remaining one-half of the disbursements described in Section 501(1) and (2);

(2) all of the trustee's compensation calculated on principal as a fee for acceptance, distribution, or termination, and disbursements made to prepare property for sale;

(3) payments on the principal of a trust debt;

(4) expenses of a proceeding that concerns primarily principal, including a proceeding to construe the trust or to protect the trust or its property;

(5) premiums paid on a policy of insurance not described in Section 501(4) of which the trust is the owner and beneficiary;

(6) estate, inheritance, and other transfer taxes, including penalties, apportioned to the trust; and

(7) disbursements related to environmental matters, including reclamation, assessing environmental conditions, remedying and removing environmental contamination, monitoring remedial activities and the release of substances, preventing future releases of substances, collecting amounts from persons liable or potentially liable for the costs of those activities, penalties imposed under environmental laws or regulations and other payments made to comply with those laws or regulations, statutory or common law claims by third parties, and defending claims based on environmental matters.

(b) If a principal asset is encumbered with an obligation that requires income from that asset to be paid directly to the creditor, the trustee shall transfer from principal to income an amount equal to the income paid to the creditor in reduction of the principal balance of the obligation.

SECTION 503. TRANSFERS FROM INCOME TO PRINCIPAL FOR DEPRECIATION.

(a) In this section, "depreciation" means a reduction in value due to wear, tear, decay, corrosion, or gradual obsolescence of a fixed asset having a useful life of more than one year.

(b) A trustee may transfer to principal a reasonable amount of the net cash receipts from a principal asset that is subject to depreciation, but may not transfer any amount for depreciation:

(1) of that portion of real property used or available for use by a beneficiary as a residence or of tangible personal property held or made available for the personal use or enjoyment of a beneficiary;

(2) during the administration of a decedent's estate; or

(3) under this section if the trustee is accounting under Section 403 for the business or activity in which the asset is used.

(c) An amount transferred to principal need not be held as a separate fund.

SECTION 504. TRANSFERS FROM INCOME TO REIMBURSE PRINCIPAL.

(a) If a trustee makes or expects to make a principal disbursement described in this section, the trustee may transfer an appropriate amount from income to principal in one or more accounting periods to reimburse principal or to provide a reserve for future principal disbursements.

(b) Principal disbursements to which subsection (a) applies include the following, but only to the extent that the trustee has not been and does not expect to be reimbursed by a third party:

(1) an amount chargeable to income but paid from principal because it is unusually large, including extraordinary repairs;

(2) a capital improvement to a principal asset, whether in the form of changes to an existing asset or the construction of a new asset, including special assessments;

(3) disbursements made to prepare property for rental, including tenant allowances, leasehold improvements, and broker's commissions;

(4) periodic payments on an obligation secured by a principal asset to the extent that the amount transferred from income to principal for depreciation is less than the periodic payments; and

(5) disbursements described in Section 502(a)(7).

(c) If the asset whose ownership gives rise to the disbursements becomes subject to a successive income interest after an income interest ends, a trustee may continue to transfer amounts from income to principal as provided in subsection (a).

SECTION 505. INCOME TAXES.

(a) A tax required to be paid by a trustee based on receipts allocated to income must be paid from income.

(b) A tax required to be paid by a trustee based on receipts allocated to principal must be paid from principal, even if the tax is called an income tax by the taxing authority.

(c) A tax required to be paid by a trustee on the trust's share of an entity's taxable income must be paid proportionately:

(1) from income to the extent that receipts from the entity are allocated to income; and

(2) from principal to the extent that:

(A) receipts from the entity are allocated to principal; and

(B) the trust's share of the entity's taxable income exceeds the total receipts described in paragraphs (1) and (2)(A).

(d) For purposes of this section, receipts allocated to principal or income must be reduced by the amount distributed to a beneficiary from principal or income for which the trust receives a deduction in calculating the tax.

SECTION 506. ADJUSTMENTS BETWEEN PRINCIPAL AND INCOME BECAUSE OF TAXES.

(a) A fiduciary may make adjustments between principal and income to offset the shifting of economic interests or tax benefits between income beneficiaries and remainder beneficiaries which arise from:

(1) elections and decisions, other than those described in subsection (b), that the fiduciary makes from time to time regarding tax matters;

(2) an income tax or any other tax that is imposed upon the fiduciary or a beneficiary as a result of a transaction involving or a distribution from the estate or trust; or

(3) the ownership by an estate or trust of an interest in an entity whose taxable income, whether or not distributed, is includable in the taxable income of the estate, trust, or a beneficiary.

(b) If the amount of an estate tax marital deduction or charitable contribution deduction is reduced because a fiduciary deducts an amount paid from principal for income tax purposes instead of deducting it for estate tax purposes, and as a result estate taxes paid from principal are increased and income taxes paid by an estate, trust, or beneficiary are decreased, each estate, trust, or beneficiary that benefits from the decrease in income tax shall reimburse the principal from which the increase in estate tax is paid. The total reimbursement must equal the increase in the estate tax to the extent that the principal used to pay the increase would have qualified for a marital deduction or charitable contribution deduction but for the payment. The proportionate share of the reimbursement for each estate, trust, or beneficiary whose income taxes are reduced must be the same as its proportionate share of the total decrease in income tax. An estate or trust shall reimburse principal from income.

[ARTICLE] 6

MISCELLANEOUS PROVISIONS

SECTION 601. UNIFORMITY OF APPLICATION AND CONSTRUCTION. In applying and construing this Uniform Act, consideration must be given to the need to promote uniformity of the law with respect to its subject matter among States that enact it.

SECTION 602. SEVERABILITY CLAUSE. If any provision of this [Act] or its application to any person or circumstance is held invalid, the invalidity does not affect other provisions or applications of this [Act] which can be given effect without the invalid provision or application, and to this end the provisions of this [Act] are severable.

SECTION 603. REPEAL. The following acts and parts of acts are repealed:

(1) ....

(2) ....

(3) ....

SECTION 604. EFFECTIVE DATE. This [Act] takes effect on ....

SECTION 605. APPLICATION OF [ACT] TO EXISTING TRUSTS AND ESTATES. This [Act] applies to every trust or decedent's estate existing on [the effective date of this [Act]] except as otherwise expressly provided in the will or terms of the trust or in this [Act].

Index